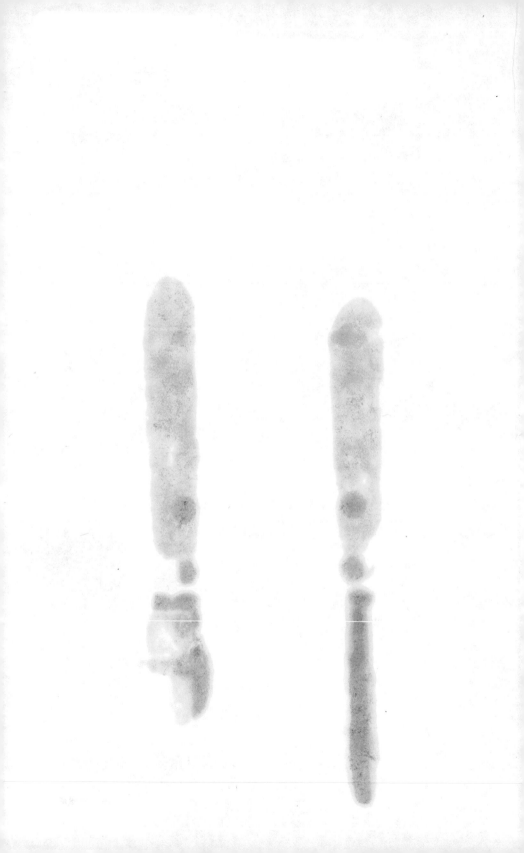

THE PHILOSOPHY OF
ERNST CASSIRER

THE LIBRARY OF LIVING PHILOSOPHERS

Paul Arthur Schilpp, *Editor*

Already Published:

Ernst Camin

THE PHILOSOPHY
OF
ERNST CASSIRER

EDITED BY

PAUL ARTHUR SCHILPP

OPEN COURT PUBLISHING COMPANY
LA SALLE, ILLINOIS 61301

THE PHILOSOPHY OF ERNST CASSIRER

Printed in the United States of America

Open Court Publishing Company, LaSalle, Illinois 61301

ISBN: 0-87548-131-0

Library of Congress Catalog Card Number: 72-83947

10/26/76

GENERAL INTRODUCTION *
TO
"THE LIBRARY OF LIVING PHILOSOPHERS"

ACCORDING to the late F. C. S. Schiller, the greatest obstacle
to fruitful discussion in philosophy is "the curious etiquette
which apparently taboos the asking of questions about a philosopher's meaning while he is alive." The "interminable controversies which fill the histories of philosophy," he goes on to say, "could
have been ended at once by asking the living philosophers a few
searching questions."

The confident optimism of this last remark undoubtedly goes
too far. Living thinkers have often been asked "a few searching
questions," but their answers have not stopped "interminable controversies" about their real meaning. It is none the less true that
there would be far greater clarity of understanding than is now
often the case, if more such searching questions had been directed
to great thinkers while they were still alive.

This, at any rate, is the basic thought behind the present undertaking. The volumes of *The Library of Living Philosophers* can in
no sense take the place of the major writings of great and original
thinkers. Students who would know the philosophies of such men
as John Dewey, George Santayana, Alfred North Whitehead, Benedetto Croce, G. E. Moore, Bertrand Russell, Ernst Cassirer, Karl
Jaspers, *et al.*, will still need to read the writings of these men.
There is no substitute for first-hand contact with the original
thought of the philosopher himself. Least of all does this *Library*
pretend to be such a substitute. The *Library* in fact will spare
neither effort nor expense in offering to the student the best possible guide to the published writings of a given thinker. We shall
attempt to meet this aim by providing at the end of each volume in
our series a complete bibliography of the published work of the
philosopher in question. Nor should one overlook the fact that the
essays in each volume cannot but finally lead to this same goal.
The interpretative and critical discussions of the various phases of

* This *General Introduction*, setting forth the underlying conception of this
Library, is purposely reprinted in each volume (with only very minor changes).

a greater thinker's work and, most of all, the reply of the thinker himself, are bound to lead the reader to the works of the philosopher himself.

At the same time, there is no denying the fact that different experts find different ideas in the writings of the same philosopher. This is as true of the appreciative interpreter and grateful disciple as it is of the critical opponent. Nor can it be denied that such differences of reading and of interpretation on the part of other experts often leave the neophyte aghast before the whole maze of widely varying and even opposing interpretations. Who is right and whose interpretation shall he accept? When the doctors disagree among themselves, what is the poor student to do? If, finally, in desperation, he decides that all of the interpreters are probably wrong and that the only thing for him to do is to go back to the original writings of the philosopher himself and then make his own decision—uninfluenced (as if this were possible) by the interpretation of any one else—the result is not that he has actually come to the meaning of the original philosopher himself, but rather that he has set up one more interpretation, which may differ to a greater or lesser degree from the interpretations already existing. It is clear that in this direction lies chaos, just the kind of chaos which Schiller has so graphically and inimitably described.[1]

It is curious that until now no way of escaping this difficulty has been seriously considered. It has not occurred to students of philosophy that one effective way of meeting the problem at least partially is to put these varying interpretations and critiques before the philosopher while he is still alive and to ask him to act at one and the same time as both defendant and judge. If the world's great living philosophers can be induced to co-operate in an enterprise whereby their own work can, at least to some extent, be saved from becoming merely "dessicated lecture-fodder," which on the one hand "provides innocuous sustenance for ruminant professors," and, on the other hand, gives an opportunity to such ruminants and their understudies to "speculate safely, endlessly, and fruitlessly, about what a philosopher must have meant" (Schiller), they will have taken a long step toward making their intentions clearly comprehensible.

With this in mind, _The Library of Living Philosophers_ expects to publish at more or less regular intervals a volume on each of the greater among the world's living philosophers. In each case it will

[1] In his essay on "Must Philosophers Disagree?" in the volume by the same title (Macmillan, London, 1934), from which the above quotations were taken.

be the purpose of the editor of *The Library* to bring together in the volume the interpretations and criticisms of a wide range of that particular thinker's scholarly contemporaries, each of whom will be given a free hand to discuss the specific phase of the thinker's work which has been assigned to him. All contributed essays will finally be submitted to the philosopher with whose work and thought they are concerned, for his careful perusal and reply. And, although it would be expecting too much to imagine that the philosopher's reply will be able to stop all differences of interpretation and of critique, this should at least serve the purpose of stopping certain of the grosser and more general kinds of misinterpretations. If no further gain than this were to come from the present and projected volumes of this *Library*, it would seem to be fully justified.

In carrying out this principal purpose of the *Library*, the editor announces that (in so far as humanly possible) each volume will conform to the following pattern:

First, a series of expository and critical articles written by the leading exponents and opponents of the philosopher's thought;
Second, the reply to the critics and commentators by the philosopher himself;
Third, an intellectual autobiography of the thinker whenever this can be secured; in any case an authoritative and authorized biography; and
Fourth, a bibliography of the writings of the philosopher to provide a ready instrument to give access to his writings and thought.

The editor has deemed it desirable to secure the services of an Advisory Board of philosophers to aid him in the selection of the subjects of future volumes. The names of the six prominent American philosophers who have consented to serve appear below. To each of them the editor expresses his sincere gratitude.

Future volumes in this series will appear in as rapid succession as is feasible in view of the scholarly nature of this *Library*.

P. A. S.
Editor

PREFACE TO THE THIRD PRINTING

IN MY Preface to the first edition (August 3, 1948) I reported the unhappy fact that at that time not only were most of Cassirer's works out of print and practically unavailable even in their original German editions, but that very little of his work had yet appeared in English translation. Fortunately, I can now record that both of those lacunae have, in the meantime, been largely filled. English-speaking students of Cassirer can now find most of his works available in good English translations. The appearance of our own *Cassirer*-volume in 1948 may have some influence in this regard. The philosophical world cannot afford to be oblivious of Cassirer's contributions.

The present edition is already the third printing of our *Cassirer*-volume, and the first one to be done by Open Court. Inasmuch as there have been no changes (or even corrections) in this edition, it is only a reprinting (not a new edition). It affords the editor, however, a most welcome opportunity to express his gratitude publicly to the Carus family in La Salle, Illinois, who, as the owners and publishers of the Open Court Publishing Company, are doing all in their power to keep the volumes of our LIBRARY OF LIVING PHILOSOPHERS permanently in print. When it is remembered that this series is, after all, a scholarly enterprise, no individual volume of which is ever in danger of appearing on any best sellers list, such dedication to scholarship, which does not count financial success, certainly deserves much more than mere casual mentioning. I am sure that the philosophical world joins the editor in this sincere expression of gratitude and appreciation.

PAUL ARTHUR SCHILPP

DEPARTMENT OF PHILOSOPHY
SOUTHERN ILLINOIS UNIVERSITY
MAY 1, 1973

ADVISORY BOARD

TABLE OF CONTENTS

PREFACE

AS SOON as it had become clear that there was a real place
in philosophic literature for the type of book which it is
the aim of this *Library* to present, it was also quite evident that
such a series would not be complete without a volume on *The
Philosophy of Ernst Cassirer*. If there could ever have been any
doubt on this point, it existed merely among such provincial
philosophical scholars as had not become personally acquainted,
let alone familiar, with the writings and work of this prodigious
and acute contemporary thinker. Anyone at all aware of Cassirer's philosophical contributions, and of the ever growing influence of his thought upon younger thinkers, knew quite well
that Cassirer's philosophy would *have to be* treated in this
Library. It was not at all surprising, therefore, that the editor
found a ready response among scholars everywhere to his invitation to contribute to a projected Cassirer volume. The present
co-operative effort, accordingly, had been largely planned long
before Professor Cassirer left the hospitable shores of Sweden
to come to the United States in 1942.

At the time, therefore, that the tragic news of Professor
Cassirer's unexpected death, on April 13, 1945, reached the
editor, many of the essays now appearing in this volume were
already in the editor's hands and many others had been in the
process of being written by their authors for some time past.

Nevertheless, this tragic blow—among its manifold unhappy
consequences—seemed to place a volume on the philosophy of
Ernst Cassirer in the *Library of Living Philosophers* forever
beyond the pale of possibility. For, with Cassirer *dead*, how
could a volume on his philosophy appear in such a series? This,
at any rate, was the first reaction of the editor to the unbelievable news of Cassirer's passing. And it was in this spirit,
therefore, that letters went out almost immediately, notifying

all contributors to the present book that, with the death of Cassirer, the original project of a volume on his philosophy—if not actually completely abandoned—would at least have to be changed so radically as no longer to fit into the framework of the *Library*.

The storm of protest and the almost unanimity of objection which greeted this announcement forced, in the first place, a careful reconsideration of the hasty decision, and very quickly indeed, a complete reversal. Many of the contributors complained that the editor was conceiving of the word "living" in the title of the series far too literally or at least too narrowly. That, despite the fact that we would now never be able to present to the philosophical world either Cassirer's own autobiography or his formal "Reply" to his critics, it was perhaps all the more necessary that the philosophical world should have an opportunity to see and view this great contemporary thinker's ideas from the varied points of view made possible precisely in the kind of book which the volumes in this series have been.

Although it is true that the editor yielded to this almost universal pressure and even more to the force and decisiveness of this argument, the yielding certainly did not take place in the least reluctantly. Of course it is true that he greatly regrets the anomaly of having a volume appear in a series dealing with "living" philosophers, when the philosopher with whose thought the volume is concerned is no longer among the—physically—living. But, on the other hand, he would not be truthful, where he to claim that he feels that the present volume has—for these reasons—no legitimate place within the bounds of this particular series. After all, the volume on *The Philosophy of Alfred North Whitehead* (Vol. III of this *Library*) also had no formal "Reply" to the expository and critical articles in the book from the pen of Whitehead—and yet seemed to fill a real philosophical need just the same. And, in the case of the Whitehead volume, this problem was—in a sense at least—even more serious than it would appear to be in the present instance. For, when the Whitehead volume appeared in print, Professor Whitehead himself was still very much alive—even though he had just gone through a terrible siege of double pneumonia at the age of eighty. If, in Whitehead's case, we were prevented from carrying out the fundamental idea of this series by the commanding imperative of very serious illness, in the case of Cassirer we found ourselves stopped—at the point of "The Philosopher's Reply"—by the finality of death itself. But, though death might prevent us from giving our readers the very careful and minute formal "Reply," which the editor knows Cassirer had planned to write for the present volume, even that tragic fatality was not able to stop the continued strong influence which Cassirer's thought is having upon serious reflection in the contemporary world. Nor should it be allowed to stop the present volume. For better or for worse, therefore, the volume now is done—or, more accurately speaking, is done as much as it *could* be done once Cassirer himself was no longer with us. And, frankly, though the reviewers almost inevitably will pick on the anomaly of the appearance of this book under the title of this series, after reading the material which has gone into the making of this book, the editor himself does not at all feel apologetic for its publication. For this volume will best fulfill its real function in philosophical literature if—like its predecessors in this series—it will send the reader of *The Philosophy of Ernst Cassirer* to the books and other writings of Cassirer himself, where he may learn by experience why he would have been the loser, if he had never made the detailed acquaintance of this acute philosophical mind and of the great and profound contributions which that mind has made to the thinking and knowing of man.

There is one temptation—in the writing of this Preface—to which the editor dare not yield. It is all too tempting to discuss Cassirer the philosopher; but this is done by twenty-three contemporary philosophers who have contributed to this volume and most of whom are far better qualified for this task than is the editor. It is even *more tempting* to trespass upon the good taste of editorial prerogatives by discussing here Cassirer the man, the gentleman, the personal friend. But to this temptation also the editor must turn a deaf ear, since others, who have known him much longer and far more intimately, have discussed this aspect within the covers of this book. I shall merely say that I consider the personal acquaintance and contacts with Ernst Cassirer to be among the greatest experiences and privileges of my life. In the judgment of this writer, it is not too much to say of Cassirer: *Ecce Homo!* It is profoundly sad to contemplate his leaving us in the midst of his great creative and productive career, with dozens of tasks which he had set himself unfinished and others barely begun.

The editor's debt of gratitude to each of the contributors to this volume is so self-evident that a mere mention of this fact should suffice. But, in view of the fact that many of them have had to wait four years, or even longer, to see the arduous work of their mind finally in print, the editor's debt, in this instance, is even greater than usual. The reasons which have delayed the appearance of this volume time and again are, however, far too numerous to bear repetition here. Suffice it to record the editor's sincere regrets and abject apologies for a situation which has caused him much agony and ever increasing embarrassment, but over much of which he had little (if any) control.

Special words of gratitude and appreciation need, however, to be penned for the never failing helpfulness and encouragement—through all these three and one-half years since her illustrious husband's death—given by the widow of Ernst Cassirer, Mrs. Toni Cassirer. When at times the obstacles seemed almost insurmountable, it was Mrs. Cassirer's everlasting faith which kept the project going. Here truly is a woman who knew— and still knows—her husband's greatness and who never failed to understand the significance of what he was trying to do with his life and thought.

Death did not spare the *contributors* to this volume either. Two of these are no longer with us. First, Kurt Lewin, whose essay for the present volume had been mailed to the editor on January 3rd, 1947, passed away very suddenly only five weeks later, namely on February 11th, 1947. Thirteen months later, in March 1948, the news of F. Saxl's death reached us. The latter's contribution to this volume were remarks he delivered on the occasion of the Memorial Services held for Cassirer at Columbia University. Little did he realize that, by the time his remarks would appear in print, he himself would have joined those for whom it is altogether fitting to hold memorial services. Of Kurt Lewin, Alexander M. Dashkin, writing in *Jewish Education* (for Feb.-March issue, 1947), had the following to say: "Kurt Lewin was one of the very few men in our midst who had the right to be called a genius. He was an inventive, comprehensive mind, a warm large personality, with an indefatigable capacity for resourceful work." The editor is proud to be able to present, in this volume, what was undoubtedly one of the last pieces of such creative work from the pen of Kurt Lewin.

These lines are being written on the very eve of the editor's departure for five months' sojourn in Europe, including a semester's lecturing in one of Germany's newly re-opened universities. This means that the burden of proofreading and seeing this volume through the press will largely have to fall upon other shoulders. In the editor's absence he counts himself exceedingly fortunate in having been able to secure the able assistance of his present colleague, old friend and former student, Professor Robert W. Browning, of the department of philosophy at Northwestern University. Upon Dr. Browning and such additional aids as he is able to marshal,—such, for example, as that of Dr. David Bidney of the Viking Fund, New York City, who has already kindly offered his good services because of his deep interest in this project and his knowledge of the editor's temporary absence—, the detailed technical work of seeing this volume to final fruition will largely devolve. To them the editor, as well as the contributors and readers, owe a deep and great debt of gratitude, especially in view of the fact that all such service on a project like this—unsupported as it is by endowments or by any university press—can only be a labor of love. The same goes for Professor Robert S. Hartman, of the Department of Philosophy of Ohio State University, another one of the editor's former students, who again was kind enough to undertake the laborious task of preparing the index and of seeing it through the press. A brief look at the index will convince even the casual observer of the immensity of this task and of the consequent obligation under which the editor feels himself to Dr. Hartman.

In conclusion the reader's attention must be called to the deplorable fact that the main works by Cassirer have been out of print for some time and are simply not to be had anywhere. This situation should certainly be remedied as soon as at all possible. New German editions of Cassirer's works are sorely needed. But, if Cassirer is ever truly to come into his own in the English speaking world, it is high time that some enterprising university press in this country should soon supply the philosophical reading public with authorized translations into English of at least most of Cassirer's major works. Certainly some well-to-do reader of the present volume could do far worse than offer his financial aid to· such an enterprising university press for the purpose of at least partial subsidies for such publication.

P. A. S.

DEPARTMENT OF PHILOSOPHY
NORTHWESTERN UNIVERSITY
EVANSTON, ILLINOIS

August 3, 1948

ACKNOWLEDGMENTS

Grateful acknowledgement is made to the Yale University Press, to the Open Court Publishing Company, to Harper and Brothers, and to the Princeton University Press, for their kind permission to quote at length from the works of Ernst Cassirer, without requiring a detailed enumeration. Exact title, name of publisher, and place and date of publication of each of Cassirer's works are enumerated in the Bibliography to this volume, found on pages 885 to 909.

We also wish to express our appreciation to the editors and publishers of the numerous philosophical and literary journals quoted, and to the publishers of all other books used by our contributors, for the privilege of utilizing source materials therein found relevant to the discussion of *The Philosophy of Ernst Cassirer*.

A

Dimitry Gawronsky

ERNST CASSIRER: HIS LIFE AND HIS WORK

A Biography

ERNST CASSIRER: HIS LIFE AND HIS WORK

ERNST CASSIRER was born in Breslau on July 28, 1874. He was the fourth child of a rich Jewish tradesman; a brother and two sisters preceded Ernst. His brother died in infancy, before Ernst was born, and his mother therefore bestowed upon the second boy, the impassioned love she had felt for her lost son and in memory of this tragic loss and the ordeal she underwent she called her second son Ernst. To the last days of her life, Ernst was her most cherished child, although two other sons and three daughters came after him.

As a boy, Ernst was exceptionally cheerful and buoyant, yet easy to handle. In his games he displayed an inexhaustible imagination; he was full of new tricks and pranks, and nothing in his nature seemed to reveal that his life would be devoted to quiet and concentrated contemplation. He was endowed with a great courage and, as a boy of ten, it was nothing to him to swim the broad Oder River across and back. The most outstanding feature of the boy was his keen sense of fair play and justice. Althought the most beloved child of the family, he never tolerated the slightest discrimination against his brothers and sisters, never accepted any favors, refused anything which was not also given to the others.

Ernst was an impassioned music lover and never missed an opportunity to attend a concert or an opera. In his early classes at the "Gymnasium" he was just an average pupil, much more likely to be at the bottom than at the head of his class. He kept so busy playing with his brothers and friends that there was little time left for study.

But a change was not far off. Ernst's maternal grandfather, although a self-taught person, was an exceptionally cultured man of wide intellectual scope and truly philosophical mind. He lived not far from Breslau, and every summer Ernst paid a visit to his grandfather. There, in conversations with his grand-father, whom he dearly loved, and in the latter's vast library, awoke and grew Ernst's interest in the problems of the intellectual life. All his life Cassirer was convinced that he inherited his philosophical vein of thought from his grandfather. At the age of twelve he had already thoroughly read many literary and historical works. Shakespeare, whose work he found in his father's library, especially appealed to him and Ernst read and reread all of Shakespeare's plays several times; only *Hamlet* was missing from his father's library, and Ernst was quite unaware of the existence of this play. Then, on his thirteenth birthday, he received a book containing Shakespeare's complete works and he was most amazed and thrilled to "discover" *Hamlet*.

At this early age—and for the remainder of his life—Cassirer acquired the capacity for concentrated and persistent work. His entire behavior began to change slowly. Now there was only little time left for play, and in his class he became admittedly the best pupil. In higher classes Cassirer's teachers were often amazed at the depth of his knowledge and maturity of his judgment, and when he completed his studies at the "Gymnasium" his graduation certificate contained the highest marks.

Without losing any time, Cassirer entered the University of Berlin. He was then eighteen years of age and the major subject he had selected for a study was jurisprudence. He made this choice more upon the insistence of his father, who was largely interested in the field of law, than of his own free will. Soon he gave up this line of study and began to concentrate upon German philosophy and literature. In addition he listened eagerly to lectures on history and art. And yet all these studies somehow did not give Cassirer complete satisfaction; something was lacking in them; he missed in them a certain degree of depth in understanding and failed to find any solution of fundamental problems. It was undoubtedly this sense of dissatisfaction which caused Cassirer to change universities several times; he went from Berlin to Leipzig, from there to Heidelberg, and then back to Berlin. In the meantime he further enlarged the scope of his studies and found himself becoming more and more interested in philosophy. Thus it happened that in the summer of 1894 he decided to take a course on Kant's philosophy given by Georg Simmel, then a young and brilliant Privatdozent at the University of Berlin.

This was a time when strong idealistic tendencies seemed to win a decisive victory over mysticism, which for many centuries had dominated German spiritual culture. Already in the first half of the thirteenth century Meister Eckhart, one of the greatest of the German mystics, had impressively revealed the very core of his creed in the following words: "Man, yes, I stood with God before time and the world were created; yes, I was included in the eternal Godhead even before it became God. Together with me God has created and is still and always creating. Only through me He became God." This conception, born out of titanic pride, infinite egotistic power, and ecstasy of passion, for five long centuries and virtually unopposed had dominated German spiritual culture; it never remained a movement of intellectuals only, or of any other small group of people; in fact, all the great folk movements in Germany during those five centuries were movements of outspoken mysticism.

In the eighteenth century, however, tendencies of a very different nature came to the fore within German culture. Leibniz and Wolf, Lessing and Goethe, Schiller and Kant created in Germany a bright atmosphere of genuine humanism; idealistic tendencies, intermingled with radical rationalism, became most potent in Germany's intellectual life. Yet, this triumph of reason and of humanism was only shortlived; with the beginning of the nineteenth century a huge wave of mysticism again arose in Germany, breaking through all ramparts of measure and reason and overflowing the spiritual culture of Germany. Then again, in the last third of the nineteenth century Otto Liebmann and Hermann Cohen initiated a philosophical movement which harked back to Kant and to the idealistic tendencies of the eighteenth century. Several philosophical "schools" soon arose in Germany, all quite similar in this basic tendency and diverging from each other in only more or less important details. When Ernst Cassirer began his academic studies, this neo-Kantianism dominated many of the German universities to an almost exclusive degree. Hans Vaihinger for a score of years kept in his desk the completed volume of his *Philosophy of As If*, a fictional and pragmatistic conception of knowledge, and wrote his commentary on Kant in which he embarked upon an orthodox interpretation of Kant's texts, word by word and sentence by sentence. And Simmel, the future leading "philosopher of life," wrote and lectured on Kant's philosophy.

For some weeks Cassirer regularly attended Simmel's lectures. Once, when lecturing on Kant, Simmel dropped the following remark: "Undoubtedly the best books on Kant are written by Hermann Cohen; but I must confess that I do not understand them."

Immediately after the lecture, Cassirer went to his bookshop and ordered Cohen's books; and no sooner had he begun studying them than his decision was made—to go to Marburg and there to study philosophy under Cohen's guidance. However, Cassirer did not want to go to Cohen at once. The young student studied Kant's and Cohen's works thoroughly, as well as those of several other philosophers essential for the understanding of Kant, such as Plato, Descartes, and Leibniz. In addition he devoted a large part of his time to the study of mathematics, mechanics, and biology—sciences which were indispensable for an understanding of Cohen's interpretation of Kant.

When, in the spring of 1896, Cassirer finally arrived in Marburg to hear Cohen for the first time, he knew a great deal about Kant's and Cohen's philosophies. There was something very peculiar about Cohen's appearance: he was stout and short, with an incredibly huge head towering over his broad shoulders. He had an almost abnormally high forehead. His eyes flashed, fascinated, and penetrated, despite the dark glasses which he always wore. In his lectures and seminars, and even in his private conversations, one could not help experiencing the presence of a great mind and the heart of a prophet, filled to overflowing with an ecstatic belief in the value of truth and the power of goodness. No matter what problem Cohen discussed—a mathematical, epistemological or ethical one—he always spoke with a deep, intense passion, which was usually controlled perfectly by the measured flow of his slow and powerful language—until the passion broke through in a few words or short sentences. Then Cohen would shout with mighty voice at his listeners, emphasizing the importance of his words with an energetic movement of his hands.

However interesting Cohen's lectures were, his seminars were even more stimulating. He was truly a spiritual "midwife" in the Socratic sense. Always using the method of the Socratic dialogue, he had a great pedagogical ability to let the students themselves find the answers to questions discussed. His patience and his personal interest in the intellectual development of every single one of the students was inexhaustible. At the same time he was keenly concerned with their general welfare, and whenever his help was needed, he always gave it to his utmost.

In the first seminar hour which Cassirer attended he volunteered to answer a rather difficult philosophical question asked by Cohen. A conversation arose between them, and within a few minutes Cohen was quite aware of the type of student that sat before him. Later on this first meeting with Cassirer belonged to Cohen's most pleasant reminiscences, and he enjoyed telling it frequently and in great detail; how a new student, whom he had never seen before, very youthful in appearance, a little shy but determined, raised his hand and in a firm voice gave a quite correct and complete answer to his question. "I felt at once," said Cohen, "that this man had nothing to learn from me." At that time Cohen was surrounded by quite a few disciples, and some of them already had studied philosophy with him for years; but from the first moment Cassirer towered above them all. He was quite at home in all the most intricate problems of Kantian and Cohenian ways of thinking.

It was a firmly established custom in Marburg that after every seminar Cohen's disciples, often five or six at a time, accompanied him to the threshold of his house. But Cassirer, who in every seminar distinguished himself by the scope of his knowledge and by the brilliancy of his philosophical mind, at first did not approach Cohen or his students. For years already Cassirer had been entirely absorbed in his studies and had little time to spare for social intercourse; he did not enjoy any type of discussion with his friends, probably because his own intensive thinking furthered his intellectual progress even more. He became almost unsociable. In this mood he came to Marburg; he was always most polite and friendly to everybody, but kept so obviously aloof that Cohen's disciples nicknamed him "the Olympian." Most amazed of all was Cohen himself; he took a great liking to Cassirer and keenly felt the latter's outstanding philosophical talent; but he wondered at his strange behavior. Finally Cohen developed a peculiar suspicion. There was one group of people whom Cohen could not tolerate: the converted Jews; he never even shook hands with them. Cohen evidently thought that Cassirer was also converted and was avoiding any personal contact with his teacher because he was aware of Cohen's attitude towards such people. When Cassirer finally heard of this surmise, he at once called on Cohen, and this was the beginning of an intimate friendship between them which lasted to the end of Cohen's days.

Now Cassirer became the acknowledged leader in the circle of Cohen's disciples. He lived in a house which for decades was a sort of headquarters for Cohen's students, and with several of these students Cassirer came into close personal contact. It was, however, still quite impossible to entice Cassirer to go to a party or to spend an evening in a cafe, which was the almost obligatory pastime of the German students; but he took a fancy to studying with some of his new friends. Thus he read Dante and Galileo with an Italian disciple of Cohen; he studied intricate Greek texts with a classical philologist, and for hours he discussed difficult mathematical problems with a mathematician. And the most interesting part of it was that all these people, although they were experts in their respective fields, willingly acknowledged Cassirer's superiority and received from him a great deal more than they were able to give him in return. Soon all students of Cohen knew that, whenever they needed a helping hand, they could turn to Cassirer, and this very busy man who treasured every minute of his time was always ready to spend hours explaining difficult problems to anybody who approached him.

By the end of Cassirer's first semester in Marburg not only all the University, but all the town as well, knew of the prodigy. Cassirer became quite popular, but he did not enjoy popularity at all; he sincerely hated any kind of notoriety in connection with his person.

Undoubtedly the credit for Cassirer's stupendous knowledge must be attributed to a large degree to his exceptional memory. Cohen told us several times that as a young student Cassirer was able to quote by heart whole pages of almost all the classical poets and philosophers. And, in a sorrowful voice, Cohen never forgot to add: "Even all modern poets, like Nietzsche and Stefan George, he could quote you by heart for hours!" This prodigious memory served Cassirer faithfully to the end of his days and made him capable of finding with the greatest of ease any quotations he needed in all those countless books he had read during his life time. Yet Cassirer's memory was not just a passive capacity, a sort of storage for acquired knowledge—it was rather an *er-innern* in Goethe's sense, a process of repeated and creative mental absorption, combined with a keen ability to see all essential elements of a problem and its organic relation to other problems. Cassirer's sharp and most active intellect constantly used the rich material of his memory, incessantly reviewing and reshaping it under different aspects, thus keeping it vividly present in his mind.

When Cassirer came to Cohen, the latter's philosophy was in a state of transition. Cohen worked at that time on his own system of philosophy, which he began publishing a few years later. Cohen's chief goal at that time was to free Kant's philosophy from inner contradiction and to emphasize more strongly its fundamental methods and ideas. In his "critique of reason" Kant tried to measure the real power of the human intellect and the part it played in the cognition of the external world. The result Kant reached was the following: the human intellect not only classifies and combines our sensations and perceptions, but does much more besides; it forms them from the outset and makes them possible, so that even the simplest sensation exists in the human mind owing to the analytical and synthetical power of the human intellect which carries in itself visible marks of this power. We are very much mistaken when we think that, for instance, a "white ceiling" or a "brown floor" are just simple sensations; quite the contrary is true: "white," "ceiling," "brown," "floor" presuppose already whole systems of concepts, continuous application of analytical and synthetical functions of our intellect. Any sensory intuition, Kant taught in the central chapter of his *Critique of Pure Reason*, in the "Transcendental Deduction of the Pure Concept of Reason," is only possible as a product of the creative activity of the fundamental functions of our intellect; yet in the chapters preceding and following this one Kant insisted upon the necessity of accepting the sensory intuition as the very source of the creative synthetic power of our intellect. Furthermore, having showed the indispensability of reason for the true understanding of nature, for the creation of natural science as a thoroughly consistent system of knowledge, Kant still did not part with his conception of the "thing-in-itself," according to which all our knowledge has nothing to do with the world of ultimate reality, but can only deal with the sphere of humanly (*i.e.*, sensorily) conditioned appearances.

Thus Kant decisively broke with the naïve and shallow belief of the German Enlightenment in the miraculous power of the intellect, with its tendency to solve with the help of trite and schematic reasonings all mysteries of the cosmos; he put the greatest stress upon the necessity of clear insight into the basic limitations which characterize the creative work of human reason. Yet all these limitations Kant accepted only for the realm of theoretical knowledge, not for the field of ethical activity; in this latter sphere Kant was convinced that the knowledge of good as well as its materialization depend exclusively on the human intellect, that all emotions and feelings —such as friendship, sympathy, love—insofar as they are instrumental in the realization of good, only obscure and debase the purity of moral principles.

Cohen tried to rectify these inconsistencies. To him "sensation" was only a problem which could be consciously put and solved by the methods of the human intellect: this bright yellow stain in the skies is in reality the centre of a whole planetary system which reveals in its substance and movements a miraculous chain of natural laws. This knowledge is genuine and is directed towards the true object, behind which no "thing-in-itself" is hidden. Yet, our knowledge is deficient and is able to progress slowly and painfully; only as a result of the infinite progress of science can a true knowledge of the object be won. And only the completely explored object, reached at the infinitely remote limit of our knowledge, is the real "thing-in-itself."

Thus, Cohen's philosophy decisively preached the predominant rôle of the intellect in the realm of knowledge and did away with some of the basic limitations of intellectual power which were accepted by Kant. Yet, it was quite different in the realm of volition; there Cohen was much less rationalistic than Kant and was convinced that it was the intensity of our emotions and feelings on which depended the energy of our volition; they supplied the "motor power" for our actions.

Hence came Cohen's preference for mathematics and natural science; there the work of our intellect could be observed and studied in its unadulterated form. And, since the intellect was to Cohen the backbone of the human mind, he strongly insisted upon the necessity of starting philosophical studies with epistemology. Cassirer knew this already from Cohen's books and eagerly studied mathematics and natural science before he went to Marburg. Now he devoted almost all of his time to these disciplines and to the problems of knowledge.

During the first semester Cohen already began asking Cassirer which subject he would like to choose for his doctor's thesis. After some hesitation Cassirer decided to write on Leibniz. Many reasons determined this choice. First of all there was the great versatility of Leibniz's prolific genius and his fundamental achievement in the fields of logic, mathematics, and natural science, in which at that time Cassirer was primarily interested. Next, the exceptional difficulty of the task also challenged Cassirer; Leibniz had set forth his philosophy not in book form mainly, but piecemeal, in his vast correspondence; and the system of his philosophy consequently had to be reconstructed out of these dispersed elements. In addition, the slowly developing recognition of Leibniz's great importance for the development of modern philosophy caused the Berlin Academy to make Leibniz the subject for a prize competition, and Cassirer decided to participate in this competition.

In less than two years Cassirer had completed his sizable work on Leibniz. The first part of it, dealing with Descartes' theory of knowledge, was accepted by the Marburg philosophical faculty as a doctor's dissertation and obtained the highest possible mark in form of the very seldom conferred "opus eximum." Cassirer was at once admitted to the oral examination, during which he once more kept his teachers breathless by the immensity of his knowledge and brilliancy of his understanding, and was awarded the doctor's degree "summa cum laude." The entire book on Leibniz Cassirer presented to the Berlin Academy. There he was not quite so fortunate: the Academy decided not to give the first prize to anyone; Cassirer's book obtained the second prize, followed by a long and most flattering commendation, where his great erudition, philosophical talent and brilliancy of presentation were highly praised, but the prevalence of rational and systematic tendencies, along with the primary concentration upon the epistemological problems were given as reasons for the withholding of the first prize from him. Some 130 years before the Berlin Academy had made a similar grave mistake, which world opinion had to correct in subsequent years, by withholding the first prize from Immanuel Kant. Did not that famous Academy commit a similar error in Cassirer's case?

Upon receiving his Doctorate from Marburg University, Cassirer went back to the home of his parents, who meanwhile had moved to Berlin. There he at once began working on a new problem, which grew out of his research on Leibniz—he decided to give a comprehensive picture of the development of epistemology in the philosophy and science of modern times. He continued to live in seclusion, devoting all his time to his studies. Yet, his aloofness never was a matter of unsociability: it was his vivid awareness of the greatness of the task he had embarked upon, combined with the all-devouring interest in his work, which forced him to spare to the limit his time and energy.

It was on the occasion of a close relative's wedding in Berlin, in 1901, that Cassirer met his first cousin from Vienna. He had previously seen her only once, eight years earlier, when she was a child of nine. All artistic traits of Cassirer's nature, his love and deep understanding of music, his fine feeling for genuine beauty had in no way suffered from his assiduous scientific researches and philosophical meditations; they always added a great deal to the irresistible charm of his personality and were immediately and deeply felt by the young girl. This first meeting determined their whole future. They fell in love with each other and married a year later in Vienna.

This was indeed an exceptionally happy and harmonious union. Their mutual understanding was perfect, and Cassirer's wife always succeeded, thanks to her remarkable understanding and insight, in creating for her husband, even during the most stormy periods of their life, appropriate conditions for his continuous work.

Immediately after the wedding the young couple went to Munich, where they lived for more than a year. It was during this year that their first son, Heinz, was born (he is now member of the philosophical faculty at the University of Glasgow, Scotland). In 1903 Cassirer returned with his family to Berlin, where he began writing his history of epistemology. Cohen constantly pressed upon him and urged him to embark upon an academic career, yet Cassirer showed little desire to go to some small university town and live there for years in its atmosphere of gossip and latent anti-Semitism. He much preferred to stay in Berlin, where most of his and his wife's relatives lived and where the treasure of the State and University libraries were at his disposal. His work developed rapidly, and as early as 1904 the two volumes of his *Erkenntnisproblem* ("Problem of Knowledge") were finished. It was one of Cohen's most cherished stories how once, while visiting Cassirer in Berlin in 1904, he had asked Cassirer how his work was progressing. "Without saying a word," Cohen would relate, "Cassirer led me into his study, opened a drawer of his desk, and there it was, a voluminous, completely finished manuscript of his new work."

In 1906 the first volume of the *Erkenntnisproblem* ("Problem of Knowledge") was published, followed by the second one in 1908. The outstanding qualities of this work were rapidly recognized by students of philosophy all over the world; it appeared in several editions and slowly became one of the standard works on the history of human thought. Cassirer's original intention had been to give a broad picture of modern European thought as it led to, and culminated in, the philosophy of Kant. This he did in the first two volumes of his *Erkenntnisproblem.* Fifteen years later he added one more volume, in which he set forth the development of epistemology in post-Kantian philosophy; and shortly before he came to America (in the summer of 1941) he finished the—as yet unpublished—fourth volume, where he has given a broad picture of the evolution of epistemology up to our own days.*

The more one studies this work of Cassirer, the more one admires the intellectual scope of the man who was able to write it. Immense was the number of books Cassirer had to study and familiarize himself with in the interest of this work. And yet, this is the least spectacular part of it. Really amazing is Cassirer's ability to penetrate scores of individual systems of thought, reconstruct them in all their peculiarities, accentuate all that is original and fruitful in them, and reveal all their weaknesses and inconsistencies. Cassirer had an incredibly fine mind for the slightest nuances of thought, for the minutest differences and similarities, for all that was of fundamental or of secondary importance; with steady grasp he picked up the development through all its stages and ramifications; and, in showing how the *same* concept acquired a *different* meaning, according to the diverse philosophical systems in which it was applied as a constructive element, Cassirer laid the first foundation for the ideas which he later developed as his theory of "symbolic forms." Scores of Italian and German, French and English philosophers, almost or completely fallen into oblivion, came back in Cassirer's book to new life and historical impor-

---

* EDITOR'S NOTE: This (fourth) volume of Cassirer's *Erkenntnisproblem* is now being translated into English under the direction of Professor Charles W. Hendel and will in due time be published by the Yale University Press.

tance as organic links in the development of ideas or as connections between well known philosophical systems; thus making the continuity of philosophical thought more consistent and
true. He was the first to introduce into the history of philosophy
such names as Kepler, Galileo, Huygens, Newton, and Euler,
by giving a detailed analysis of their philosophical conceptions,
scientific methods and achievements, and by proving their
fundamental importance for the theory of knowledge. Kant's
own assertion that he tried to introduce Newton's method into
philosophy now became quite clear in Cassirer's representation
of Newton's and Kant's systems of thought. Yet Cassirer's
greatest achievement in this work consisted in the creation of a
broad general background by connecting the evolution of
knowledge with the totality of spiritual culture: mythos and
religion, psychology and metaphysics, ethics and aesthetics—
Cassirer drew all these problems into his deliberations as soon as
he found some links missing in the development of their
epistemology.

Most noteworthy is also the style and the whole manner of
presentation in this work. The most intricate philosophical problems are treated in a quite clear and simple way; one gets the
impression that the author deeply felt his responsibility to truth
and to the reader; in every sentence he sincerely tried to help
the reader to advance on the thorny path of truth. Cassirer's
style makes any subject he discusses almost transparent, and
his argumentation glides along like a broad and mighty stream,
with great convincing power.

The great success of his *Erkenntnisproblem*, which became
obvious immediately after the appearance of the first volume,
caused Cassirer to yield to Cohen's ardent desire and to embark
finally upon an academic career. Yet, there was one condition
attached to it—he was ready to become Privatdozent only in the
University of Berlin, since he still did not want to leave the
city. He knew how difficult this undertaking was, first, because
he was a Jew, and secondly, because he was Cohen's disciple and
considered himself a member of the Marburg school, which
at that time was one of the most renowned—and hated—
"schools" in Germany. In his quiet manner Cassirer said to

Cohen: "In this way I do not risk anything. I need not go anywhere and waste my time. And if they do not want me—it is all
right with me."

At that time philosophy was by no means brilliantly represented at the University of Berlin. The famous Dilthey was
already retired and only occasionally gave a few lectures for a
selected group of students. Simmel was still there, but owing
to his Jewish lineage and notwithstanding the importance of
his books (especially his voluminous *Soziologie,* which became
a standard work of pre-Hitlerite German science) and the
brilliant success of his lectures, he was an assistant professor and
virtually without any influence. The leading rôles were played
by Stumpf and Riehl, both quite serious scholars, but without
any real importance (the following untranslatable pun was then
very popular with the students at the University of Berlin:
"Philosophie wird in Berlin mit Stumpf und Riehl aus-
gerottet"). Stumpf was bitterly opposed to any form of idealistic philosophy; Riehl tried to interpret Kant in a realistic sense
and was an outspoken antagonist of the Marburg "school." Yet
it was precisely these two men that Cassirer had to deal with
when he decided to become Privatdozent of the University of
Berlin.

According to the regulations valid at that time in the University of Berlin a candidate for "Privatdozentur" had to present a scientific study—in the form of a book or manuscript—
and then, if his study had been accepted, he was invited to a so-
called colloquium, where he had to give a trial lecture and to
answer questions or critical comments on views expressed by
him. Cassirer sent in his *Erkenntnisproblem,* which was at once
accepted. A few weeks later he was invited to the colloquium,
and as subject for his trial lecture he had chosen the *"Ding an
sich,"* one of the most intricate concepts of Kant's philosophy. In
his *Erkenntnisproblem* Cassirer had given a very interesting
interpretation of this notion: he showed that the *"Ding an
sich,"* being within Kant's philosophy always a limit of a
maximum or minimum value, radically changed its meaning
according to the particular group or system of concepts with
reference to which in any given case it played the rôle of the

limit. Thus, the *"Ding an sich"* has one meaning in the "Transcendentale Aesthetik" (Part I of *Kritik der reinen Vernunft*), and an essentially different meaning in the "Deduction der reinen Verstandesbegriffe" (Part II of the same work), and it is, therefore, fruitless to define this notion without taking into consideration the peculiar nature of the specific ideas with which it is connected in any special case.

Here again we can vividly feel the future originator of the theory of "symbolic forms." Yet, Stumpf and Riehl were, of course, not satisfied at all, and they both, especially the latter, violently attacked Cassirer's theory. "You deny the existence of real things surrounding us," said Riehl. "Look at that oven there in the corner: to me it is a real thing, which gives us heat and can burn our skin; but to you it is just a mental image, a fiction!" Time and again Cassirer tried to explain the true meaning of the Kantian criticism, that human reason creates our *knowledge* of things, but *not* the things themselves; yet without avail. When the colloquium was over, both Stumpf and Riehl pleaded against admitting Cassirer as Privatdozent. But Dilthey, who was also present at the colloquium, decisively took Cassirer's side and finished his plea with these words: "I would not like to be a man of whom posterity will say that he rejected Cassirer." This was sufficient to turn the tide: without further discussion the faculty gave Cassirer the *venia legendi*.

In subsequent years the writer of this biography came to Berlin many times and frequently had the opportunity of attending Cassirer's lectures. Thus he was able to observe Cassirer's rapidly growing popularity; he saw how the original attendance of a few students grew to several dozens, then to many scores. This was an outstanding success; for at that time Cassirer's lectures were not obligatory for anyone, and his classroom was, therefore, crowded only because the students felt that what they got from him was true and substantial knowledge. Besides, his delivery was most attractive, his speech was very vivid and fluent, exact and eloquent at the same time. Especially popular were Cassirer's seminars; there, in close personal contact with his students, he displayed all the charm and benevolence of his nature, he analyzed with endless patience and sympathetic understanding any expressed opinion and, if necessary, cautiously corrected it or interpreted it in the most fruitful possible way. He was a true *paidagogos* in the Platonic sense, deeply convinced that the teacher is largely to blame for the insufficiencies of his pupil.

However, when circumstances demanded it, Cassirer could show that he was a real master of fencing. Once—it was in Berlin, in 1910—our common friend persuaded us to attend a lecture of a disciple of Avenarius. The lecture was quite confused and Cassirer was quite irritated by the lack of knowledge and understanding shown by the speaker. During the discussion, Cassirer took the floor and in the short space of less than half an hour he not merely revealed his amazingly deep and exact knowledge of Avenarius, but he uncovered so brilliantly all the inconsistencies of the main speaker that the entire lecture seemed literally to dissolve into thin air before our very eyes. When he finished, the audience cheered and laughed and went home without even listening to the lecturer's attempted stammering rejoinder. Much more important, however, was another occasion where Cassirer displayed his qualifications as a brilliant polemicist. It was when Leonard Nelson, the founder of the so-called New-Friesian "school," violently attacked Hermann Cohen. Here again it was the unfairness of the criticism, the lack of understanding or any desire for true understanding which induced Cassirer to answer Nelson. A polemic developed which could have become very interesting, if the opponents had been equal in intellectual stature. As things were, Cassirer towered above his antagonist to such a degree that all the time they fought on different levels: Nelson tried to ridicule single sentences, taken out of Cohen's books, especially of his *Logik der reinen Erkenntnis*, which is a profound and creative work but a hard nut to crack; whereas Cassirer was mainly interested in the very roots of the dissension and tried to show, by analyzing the original Kant-Fries relationship, the dangers of an exaggerated psychologism for epistemology.

The first great systematic work of Cassirer appeared in 1910, his *Substanzbegriff und Funktionsbegriff*. Despite the originality of the basic conception and whole structure of this work—

or, maybe just because of this—, it was several years before the importance of this work was duly recognized by the scientific world and by the philosophically interested public. Then, however, it became the first work of Cassirer to be translated into several foreign languages, including English and Russian. As the title of the book indicates, it is devoted to the problem of concepts. (Although in the title of the authorized English translation, viz., *Substance and Function*, this fact is almost lost sight of.) For more than two thousand years the science of logic was based upon Aristotle's doctrine of concepts, which says that generalization is always the result of abstraction: from a group of similar things,—for instance, round, oval, square, rectangular tables—the attributes common to them all are abstracted and summarized in a general concept, "table." This theory, Cassirer argues, has one decisive weakness: whence and how do we get those groups of similar things that we allegedly use as the basis for our abstractions? How does it happen that from one perception, say that of a round table, we proceed to other perceptions which are *similar* to the first one and not to the perceptions of, for instance, "auto," "star," "water," in which case we would not obtain a group of similar things? Is it not obvious that we use the first perception as a kind of criterion with the help of which we are able to decide what belongs to our group of similar things and what not? Thus Aristotle's abstraction becomes only possible as the result of a selection, of the coördinated activity of the human reason, which is the first and fundamental step toward general notions. "What lends the theory of abstraction support is merely the circumstance that it does not presuppose the contents, out of which the concept is to develop, as *disconnected particularities*, but that it tacitly thinks them in the form of an ordered manifold from the first. The concept, however, is not deduced thereby, but presupposed; for, when we ascribe to a manifold an order and connection of elements, we have already presupposed the concept, if not in its complete form, yet in its fundamental function."[1]

Thus Aristotle's theory of concept, based upon the abstraction

[1] Ernst Cassirer, *Substance and Function*. Chicago—London, 1923, p. 17.

of common elements from a group of similar things, is nothing else than an obvious *circulus viciosus*. Yet this is not all. The theory of abstraction shows also another decisive weakness: in order to form a concept only such attributes are retained which are common to all elements of a given group, whereas all particularities are not included in a general concept—they are just thrown aside and fade away. And the more general a concept is, the less attributes it contains, the more particularities disappear in the process of abstraction. Yet, "the genuine concept does not disregard the peculiarities and particularities which it holds under it, but seeks to show the *necessity* of the occurrence and connection of just these particularities. . . . Here the more universal concept shows itself also the more rich in content."[2] Scientific concepts are all of this kind; they are general ideas, but their true function consists of expressing the rule from which a number of concrete particular forms can be derived.

In his *Substance and Function* Cassirer also undertook the difficult task of showing what particular kinds of concepts underly the different realms of the exact and natural sciences, what is the logical essence of such categories as number, space, time, energy, and so forth. Cassirer was particularly interested in the problem of how the structure of concepts changes its character when we pass from one field of science to another; for instance, from mathematics to physics, or from physics to biology, etc. In carrying out this plan, he made, for the first time in the history of human thought, the very important and successful attempt to give a systematic analysis of concepts which underly the science of chemistry. The last part of the book is devoted to the theory of knowledge proper, to the concepts and methods by which human reason transforms sensory impressions into the systems of objective science.

The members of the Marburg school were very proud of this new performance of Cassirer. Yet, the opposition came this time from a quarter from which it had been least expected—from Hermann Cohen himself. Already while reading the proofs, Cohen obtained the impression, that—as he expressed it later in a letter to Cassirer—"our unity was jeopardized." Especially

[2] *Ibid.*, pp. 19-20.

one long paragraph in Cassirer's book seemed to Cohen to be quite inconsistent with the teachings of the Marburg school, and, although all of Cohen's closest disciples were convinced that Cohen was mistaken, Cassirer, who invariably held Cohen in deepest respect, at once decided to reshape the whole page, despite the fact that he did not agree with Cohen and that his book was already in the final stages of printing. Upon reading the finished book, Cohen wrote to Cassirer: "I congratulate you and all members of our philosophical community on your new and great achievement. If I shall not be able to write the second part of my *Logic*, no harm will be done to our common cause, since my project is to a large degree fulfilled in your book."[3] But the criticism comes after that: "Yet, after my first reading of your book I still cannot discard as wrong what I told you in Marburg: you put the center of gravity upon the concept of relation and you believe that you have accomplished with the help of this concept the idealization of all materiality. The expression even escaped you, that the concept of relation is a category; yet it is a category only insofar as it is function, and function unavoidably demands the infinitesimal element in which alone the root of the ideal reality can be found."

The controversy goes back to Cohen's daring attempt to establish the infinitesimal numbers as an absolute element, to put this absolute element before the whole number and to derive the latter from the former. There can be little doubt, logically as well as mathematically, that this is an impossible undertaking; the value of a number depends always on its relation to other numbers in which it may be contemplated: five is only five in relation to one, yet it is an infinite number in relation to an infinitesimal one, and an infinitesimal number in relation to an infinite one. Cassirer's "function," as contrasted with "substance," meant just that: it is impossible to ascribe an absolute value to a mathematical element, since this value is determined by different relations to which it may belong.

Cassirer's theory of concept proved its great fruitfulness for the whole field of theoretical knowledge; it freed the principles and methods of human reason from the shadow of absoluteness

---

[3] From Cohen's letter to Cassirer of August 24, 1910.

and disclosed their functional nature as flexible instruments of human knowledge. And just as the functional concept contains a direction, a certain point of view which serves as a basis of measurement for the similarity of single elements and arranges them in groups and series according to their affinity, so "the ideal connections spoken of by logic and mathematics are the permanent lines of direction, by which experience is orientated in its scientific shaping. The function of these connections is their permanent and indestructible value, and is verified as identical through all changes in the accidental material of experience."[4]

The publication of this important work brought about no change in Cassirer's academic career; he was still Privatdozent in Berlin, and not one single German university invited him, even as an assistant professor. Every time a chair in philosophy became free, Cassirer was invariably listed by the respective faculty as a candidate, but, oddly enough, his name was always put in the second place. Cassirer himself was quite content with his limited academic activities in the University of Berlin; he not only never complained, but he did not even seem to feel the unfairness of the situation. He enjoyed his life and work in Berlin, his great success as teacher and scholar, even though officially it remained unrecognized.

Harvard University was the first to invite him, in 1914, for two years as visiting professor. However, personal reasons prevented Cassirer at that time from accepting this invitation. The same year he was awarded the Kuno Fischer Gold Medal by the Heidelberg Academy. Upon Cassirer's special request he was given a bronze medal instead, and the difference in monetary value—3,000 R.M.—was sent to the Red Cross.

Although Cassirer was highly absorbed by his research work and academic activities, he still found time to organize and direct a new edition of Kant's works. For this edition he wrote an extensive biographical and philosophical introduction to Kant's system. In this introduction he gives a very clear—both popular and truly scientific—picture of the evolution of Kant's central ideas and makes several important contributions to the understanding of Kant's philosophy. Perhaps the most important

[4] *Op. cit.*, p. 323.

of these contributions is Cassirer's analysis of the fundamental ideas of Kant's *Kritik der Urteilskraft* and his explanation of why Kant based his theory of judgment upon two seemingly so different roots as the philosophy of art, on the one hand, and biology, on the other.

Thus far all of Cassirer's publications had been devoted to the problem of knowledge. Although he was vitally interested in all the problems of art, ethics, and religion, and assiduously worked on them, he somehow did not feel ready to write down the results of his research; and meanwhile he was busy with the preparations for the third volume of his *Erkenntnisproblem*. The outbreak of the First World War changed his plans. He was drafted for Civil Service, and his work consisted of the reading of foreign newspapers. Thus he was able to contemplate the war from different points of view and to obtain a truer picture of events; he knew already in the early stages of the war that Germany was doomed. Besides, his whole nature was absolutely contrary to the imperialistic megalomania of Prussian militarism. Yet he was a philosopher, not a politician, and he found his own way of expressing his attitude toward the ultimate spiritual values around which the struggle raged: he published his book *Freiheit und Form*.

All truly humanitarian and idealistic tendencies of German culture, everything which proclaimed the dignity and freedom of individuals and of nations—Lessing and Schiller, Kant and Goethe—was convincingly and eloquently expounded by Cassirer in this book, providing a magnificent picture of man's struggle for his spiritual liberation, showing Lessing's cosmopolitanism and sublime tolerance, Schiller's keen sensitiveness and passion for freedom, Kant's radical conception of natural right, and Goethe's redemption of the individual as milestones of this eternal process.

Cassirer showed in this book that his feeling for all forms of poetry was just as deep and incisive as his understanding of science. His interpretation of Goethe's lyrics, his analysis of Goethe's poetical work in the different stages of its development belong to the best that has ever been written on this subject. Cassirer's strong artistic vein enabled him to grasp the inner core of Goethe's symbols, to provide those symbols with profound and most surprising interpretation. "Mahomed," "Pandora"—to mention only two examples—in Cassirer's masterly exposition appeared suddenly in a new light and their unfathomable wisdom and beauty became visible to anyone. No less penetrating was his analysis of Goethe's achievements in the fields of aesthetics, morals, and religion. Cassirer always felt keenly that great poets and belletrists were, in their innermost, endeavoring to find a solution to the eternal problems of being and life, akin to the search of the great philosophers; they only expressed their thoughts and beliefs in the form of concrete symbols and images, and not in the form of abstract reasoning. Goethe's titanic personality, the originality, depth and versatility of his creative power irresistibly attracted Cassirer all his life, and in a long series of special articles he followed up his study of Goethe. Brilliant was the way in which he revealed the deepest ideological roots of Goethe's polemic attitude towards Newton, or described Goethe's conception of history, or compared the spiritual worlds of Goethe and Plato. All who knew Cassirer personally admitted that his face reminded them of Goethe; yet their mental similarity was even more striking—it was the same wide scope of spiritual interests, the same tendency to regard every event in the light of endless historical perspectives, to transform every single fact into an element of an infinite system. It was undoubtedly this affinity of mental tendencies which accounted for Cassirer's unique understanding of Goethe—

> Wär nicht das Auge sonnenhaft,
> Die Sonne Könnt' es nie erblicken. . . .

World War I brought a deep spiritual crisis in Europe. One belief especially had been shattered to its very foundation: the idea that human reason was a decisive power in the social life of man. When, at the beginning of the twentieth century, Georges Sorel advanced his theory that not reason but social myth was the driving power of human history, that the actions of human societies were determined not by objective truth and cool deliberation but by peculiar images, mostly born out of hatred, revulsion, contempt, and filled with strong impulses and emotions, images, which have nothing to do with truth and often represent the greatest possible falsehood—the scholars only laughed at him and paid no attention at all to his "queer" ideas. Yet, the progress of the war and the subsequent years which saw the birth of several totalitarian ideologies and their victorious march to power in the largest countries of Europe, ruined and disarrayed by the war, clearly showed the extent of truth contained in Sorel's social theories. The stormy pace of historical events demanded a new approach to the problems of reality, different ways and means for its understanding. This was the background for Cassirer's theory of symbolic forms— his great contribution to the understanding of the most vital problems of our time and of history.

When the author of this article again met Cassirer, shortly after the termination of World War I, Cassirer was already quite absorbed in his new work. Cassirer once told how in 1917, just as he entered a street car to ride home, the conception of the symbolic forms flashed upon him; a few minutes later, when he reached his home, the whole plan of his new voluminous work was ready in his mind, in essentially the form in which it was carried out in the course of the subsequent ten years. Suddenly the onesidedness of the Kant-Cohen theory of knowledge became quite clear to Cassirer. It is not true that only the human reason opens the door which leads to the understanding of reality, it is rather the whole of the human mind, with all its functions and impulses, all its potencies of imagination, feeling, volition, and logical thinking which builds the bridge between man's soul and reality, which determines and moulds our conception of reality. "The true concept of reality cannot be pressed into a plain and abstract form of being, it rather contains the whole manifold and wealth of spiritual life. . . . In this sense any new 'symbolic form'—not only the concept and system of knowledge, but also the intuitive world of art or myth or language, represents—according to a saying of Goethe's—a revelation directed from the inside toward the outside, a 'synthesis of world and mind,' which alone makes certain for us the genuine unity of both."[5] The whole world of reality can be grasped

[5] Ernst Cassirer, *Philosophie der symbolischen Formen*. Vol. I, p. 46.

only with the help of certain mental images, symbolic forms, and the task of philosophy consists in the understanding of those mental and psychical functions which determine the structure of these symbolic forms. A queer image of primitive totemism may be vastly different from the modern conception of four-dimentional space, yet they both show a definite regularity of inward structure, they both can be reduced to some fundamental functions of the human mind. Even the spiritual world of lunatics reveals to an attentive analysis some definite regularities which find their expression in queer but still understandable symbolic forms and their study proved to be helpful for the diagnosis and treatment of certain mental diseases.

The whole of human culture is reflected in our mind in an endless row of symbolic forms, and Cassirer now embarked upon the titanic task of first trying to analyze the structure of these forms in general, and, secondly, to show what special kind of symbolic forms underlie the different realms of human life —religion, art, science, social activities. For many years the external conditions of his life were greatly favorable to this immense task: during World War I two new universities were founded in Germany, one in Hamburg and the other in Frankfurt, both quite progressive and democratic, and the first thing they both did was to offer Cassirer a full professorship in philosophy. Cassirer decided to accept the offer of the University of Hamburg because it showed an exceptionally great eagerness for securing his services. He never regretted his choice—in Hamburg he found everything he could desire: a large and most interested audience for his lectures, and the famous private "Warburg Library" with a rich collection of materials which Cassirer needed for his researches into symbolic forms. Many times Cassirer expressed his positive amazement at the fact that the selection of the materials and the whole inward structure of this library suggested the idea that its founder must have more or less anticipated his theory of symbolic forms as a system of fundamental functions of the human mind underlying all basic tendencies of human culture and explaining the particular nature of any one of them.

In the years 1923-1929 the three volumes of his *Philosophie der symbolischen Formen* were composed and published. Based upon vast historical and systematical material, the work gives a penetrating analysis of Cassirer's general theory of symbolic forms and of its application to the problems of language, of myths, and of knowledge. Almost incredible is the wealth of concrete facts and original ideas by means of which Cassirer shows the fruitfulness of his theory. Almost the entire world's literature on language and myths, almost all the realms of human science had been closely explored by him and the particular kinds of symbolic forms in those different realms shown in bold and broad relief. Yet, even this immense job did not take all of Cassirer's time and energy. During the same years, while working out and writing down his *Philosophie der symbolischen Formen,* he finished the third volume of his *Erkenntnisproblem,* he wrote a book on Einstein's theory of relativity and published literally scores of philosophical and literary articles. Besides, he eagerly performed his duties as academic teacher, gave weekly several lectures and seminars, and was most accessible to any student who desired his help on philosophical problems.

Despite this immense amount of intellectual work which Cassirer performed day after day, there was nothing of the ivory tower pedant in him; he spent almost every evening in the circle of his family and of his friends, and he showed a lively interest in all world-events. It was amazing to what a degree he was able to keep abreast of so many things which had no relation whatsoever to his scientific work—he was a thorough connoisseur of classical music, and in the classical operas he knew not only every single melody, but also every word of the text, often even in several different languages. He knew a great deal about many fields of sport and was able to discuss some intricate problems of passiance or skat. He was even interested—in the most impersonal manner—in stock exchange prices and tried to understand what was hidden behind their seemingly grotesque and unpredictable movements. Yet, there was only one game which he really cherished: chess. Only on rare occasions did he have the time and opportunity to play a game of chess or to analyze the game of an outstanding master; but when he did take the time for such it absorbed him to such a degree that as long as he busied himself with chess he did not hear or see anything that was going on around him.

This great versatility proved to be a real blessing to Cassirer when, in 1930, he was elected rector of the University of Hamburg. Now he had to represent the University at the various academic functions and to make speeches on literally every type of subject—one day he spoke on the development of modern traffic, another day on the breeding of hogs, then again on the importance of athletic sports. And the most amazing part of it was that the scope of his understanding and the wealth of his knowledge were so vast that whatever subject he touched upon he was able to illuminate its different aspects and to show its true place in the whole of cultural life.

Fourteen most prolific years of his life Cassirer spent in Hamburg; into this period fell also two large research works on the history of philosophy, one concerning the time of the Reformation, the other dealing with the development of Platonism in England. This latter work, published in 1932, was the last one he ever published in Germany. Meanwhile heavy storm clouds darkened the skies over Germany, the Hitler movement was on the verge of its first decisive victory, ready to take over the Reich government. Already years before Cassirer had recognized the great danger of this movement; he never listened to the speeches of Hitler or his henchmen, he never read their books and pamphlets; yet he seemed to know with uncanny foresight what Nazism was about to do to Germany and to the rest of the world. When their notorious slogan: "Right is what serves our Fuehrer" first came up, and Cassirer heard of it, he said: "This is the end of Germany." Cassirer, therefore, did not wait to be dismissed by the Nazis— he tendered his resignation immediately after Hitler became Chancellor of the German Reich. He knew that there would be nothing for him to do in the "new" Germany, and he decided to emigrate. Within a very few weeks he was offered three professorships in three different countries—one in Sweden (Upsala University), one in England (Oxford University), and one in the U.S.A. (New School for Social Research in New York). Cassirer went first to Oxford, where he lectured for two years (1933-35). When he arrived in England, he was only able to *read* English, but he could not *speak* a word of it. Yet, three months later he was already lecturing in English. Meanwhile he had received another offer, this time from the University of Goeteborg (Sweden). He decided to accept it, but only on one condition: that he would be given a personal chair, in order that no Swedish professor would have to lose his job. This condition was readily accepted, and, in September, 1935, Cassirer went to Goeteborg.

He stayed in Sweden for almost six years; and those years again were very fruitful years for him. In 1937 he published his book on *Determinismus und Indeterminismus in der modernen Physik*. Cassirer himself regarded this book as one of his most important achievements. His capacity to penetrate into all the details of the most intricate problems of modern physics, as shown by this book, is truly amazing. Cassirer had been prompted to embark upon this difficult task by a prolonged and somewhat confused discussion which had arisen among several leading physicists and which had touched upon the fundamental problems of epistemology, especially upon the principle of causality. The structure of the atom, the peculiar manner in which an electric particle jumps, as it were, from one predestined trajectory to another, the difficulties in recognizing and characterizing individual elements, and the necessity of applying statistical methods to the solution of quantum-theoretical problems convinced many physicists not only of the impossibility of going on exclusively with the methods of the so-called classical mechanics but even induced some of them to discard the principle of causality altogether and to introduce the concept of purpose into the interpretation of purely material phenomena. In order to analyze this problem, Cassirer gave a vast and detailed picture of the development of the basic concepts of mechanics and physics in modern times; he showed the historical continuity of thought, which led to the conception of the quantum theory, and convincingly demonstrated that it was not the principle of causality which was to blame for the difficulties with which this theory had to struggle, but the fact that the system of symbols used in it was too narrow: modern physics "is confronted with the necessity of applying different types of symbols, of schematic 'explanation,' to one and the same occurrence."[6]

This idea, in which Cassirer saw a consistent method of interpretation of the fundamental results of atomic physics, is one of the basic principles of his philosophy of symbolic forms. He once expressed it in a simple, yet truly classical, manner with the aid of the following concrete example: "We begin with a certain perceptual experience: with a drawing which we see before us. We may turn our attention, first of all, to the purely sensory 'impression' which we comprehend as a simple combination of lines." Now we change our approach to this geometrical figure, we apply to it another set of symbolic forms, and "the spatial image becomes an aesthetic one: I comprehend in it the character of a certain *ornament*, with which there is connected in my mind a certain artistic *sense* and *significance*. . . . And once again the form of my contemplation may change, insofar as that which at first appeared to me as a pure ornament now reveals itself as the bearer of a mystic-religious significance."[7] Thus the same thing, in this particular case a geometrical figure, appears, when treated from different points of view, as the bearer of a very different significance, as a concept with different meanings.

No sooner had Cassirer finished his epistemological interpretation of the quantum theory than he began working on the fourth volume of the *Erkenntnisproblem*. In this volume, which is now awaiting publication, Cassirer is giving us an integral analysis of the development of epistemological and logical problems for the period of the last hundred years— from the middle of the nineteenth century to practically our own day. This volume also contains a critical analysis of all important movements in the realm of contemporary philosophy.

---

[6] *Determinismus*, p. 265.

[7] From "Das Symbolproblem und seine Stellung im System der Philosophie" in the *Zeitschrift für Aesthetik und Allgemeine Kunstwissenschaft*, Vol. 21, pp. 194-195. Both of the above quotations come from this article; the translation is by the present writer.

There were two more books Cassirer published during the six years he lived in Sweden, both of them very typical of his almost incredible versatility and mental adaptability. For, despite his advanced age, he mastered the Swedish language perfectly and so thoroughly imbued himself with Swedish art, philosophy, literature, and history that he was able to make a very important contribution to the development of Swedish philosophy with his book on *Hägerström*. Cassirer's second book is devoted to Descartes and his relation to the Swedish queen Christine; here he discusses one of the most difficult problems of Swedish history: why did Queen Christine resign her throne? Cassirer attempts his solution of this problem by spreading new light upon Descartes, on his influence upon Christine, and by giving a broad picture of the spiritual life of Europe in the seventeenth century.

When Cassirer left Germany he arranged everything for the emigration of his daughter and two sons. One son and the daughter joined him almost immediately in England. But it took all of five years before his second son could join him in Goeteborg. This was a great sorrow of the emigration years— he was never able to live together with all his children and grandchildren, whom he loved so dearly; there was always a separation from one or the other.

In the summer of 1941 Cassirer accepted the invitation of Yale University and came to the United States as a visiting professor. His original intention was to remain here two years only and then to return to Sweden, where he had, in the meantime, become a citizen. However, the outbreak of World War II upset his plans. At the end of two years he was unable to return to Sweden and willingly agreed, therefore, to prolong his contract with Yale University for another year. During this period Cassirer received an invitation to teach at Columbia University and in the summer of 1944, he left New Haven and went to New York.

His arrival in America opened a new page in Cassirer's life. Here again one has to admire his great adaptability. This time it was not the English language, which he knew quite well by now, nor was it American philosophy the development of which he had studied closely for decades. In *Substance and Function* one already finds numerous references to American scholars and philosophers. But the methods of academic teaching in America are quite different from those of Europe. The co-operation between students and professors is much closer and more informal here than in Europe. Cassirer not only adapted himself willingly and easily to these different ways of teaching —he sincerely liked and greatly appreciated them. He often said that to work together with a group of eager students who recognized no other authority than truth itself and kept questioning their teachers until they were entirely and thoroughly satisfied was to him a new and most fruitful experience.

During the last twelve years of his life Cassirer devoted increasingly more time to research in the fields of the social sciences. He felt that now the time had come for him to apply his philosophy of symbolic forms to this realm of human culture which had always strongly attracted him, but which he had never yet discussed systematically in his books. There had been good reasons for this delay. The social sciences cannot easily free themselves from the influence of deeply rooted subjective tendencies in the form of national and class ideologies, religious and racial prejudices, economic interests, etc. Cassirer undertook to explore in the first instance those aspects of human culture where the attitude of (at least relative) objectivity could more easily prevail. But the victorious advance of the totalitarian ideology in some of the largest countries of Europe finally urged him on to take a stand against these destructive forces which—as was so obvious to him—threatened to engulf the whole world. In 1941 he wrote, therefore, his first more comprehensive study in the field of the social sciences. Even this, however, dealt, in the main, with the epistemological side of the problem, with the characteristics of the particular methods and principles upon which this branch of human knowledge is based.

His *Essay on Man*, published in 1944, and written by him in English, contains a comprehensive and integral exposition of his philosophy of symbolic forms and their application to different realms of human culture. In this book Cassirer not only summarizes his more than half-a-century long researches on languages and science, myth and religion, but he also shows, for the first time, at some length the decisive rôle the symbolic forms play in the realms of art and historical science. At the same time Cassirer also published several important articles on various subjects. In one of them he gave a quite original analysis of the Bible and showed why the Nazis had chosen the Jews as their ideological enemy Number One—while the Nazis based their power upon historical and social myths, the Jews have always shown little inclination for mythical thought.

Meanwhile he also persistently worked on what he now considered to be his main task, namely, an undertaking of the driving forces of human history, especially those forces which made possible the appalling growth of totalitarianism in our time. In 1944 he finally put into finished form a voluminous manuscript which offers his solution to this problem. This book —which was to be Cassirer's last—is entitled *The Myth of the State*, and was written in English. Even if this were the only book ever written by him, it would still secure a considerable name for him as a scientist and philosopher for many generations to come. This book begins with an exhaustive analysis of mythical thought, uncovering the intellectual, emotional, and volitional roots upon which the myth thrives in the social life of man. Then it gives a broad and general delineation, quite original in nature, of the development of political theory from the days of the early Greek philosophy to the very threshold of our own time, and uncovers, step by step, the technique—not always clever, but always treacherous and persistent—of the modern political myth which led human culture to the brink of complete destruction. The result of this penetrating and illuminating investigation into the myth of the state is found, in concentrated form, in Cassirer's following words:

"In the Babylonian mythology we find a legend that described the creation of the world. We are told that Marduk, the highest God, before he could begin his work, had to fight a dreadful combat. He had to vanquish and subjugate the serpent Tiamat and the other dragons of darkness. He slew Tiamat and bound the dragons. Out of the limbs of the monster Tiamat he formed the world and gave to it its shape and its order. .... The world of human culture may be described in the words of this Babylonian legend. It could not arise before the darkness of myth was fought and overcome. But the mythical monsters were not entirely destroyed. They were used for the creation of a new universe—and they still survive in this universe. The powers of myth were thus checked and subdued by superior forces. As long as these forces—intellectual, ethical, artistic forces—are in full strength, myth is tamed and subdued. But once they begin to lose their strength chaos arises again. Mythical thought then begins to rise anew and to pervade the whole of man's cultural and social life."*

Despite his advancing age, Cassirer kept on working continuously, persistently, almost as much as he had worked in his youth, and, in fact, throughout his life. How often did he sit, writing at his desk, till late into the night, and the next morning the first rays of the rising sun found him again busy with his work. On April 13 (1945), the day of his death, Cassirer got up very early and spent the whole morning at his desk writing; then he went to Columbia University, never to return to his home.

Ernst Cassirer belongs to the great tradition of classical philosophy. Goethe, trying to define the essence of classicism, once said: "Classicism is sanity, romanticism is illness," and Novalis, one of the greatest among the romanticists, unwittingly provided the key to this judgment by his assertion that the essence of romanticism consists in the transformation of a single event or individual fact into an absolute and general principle of the whole. To Novalis and Schlegel everything was the emotion of love, even mathematics or a death sentence; to Fichte and Schopenhauer everything was volition, just as to Hegel everything was Objective Mind or to Schelling intellectual intuition: in each case one principle, one function, one special power dominates and determines the whole. Classicism, on the contrary, always recognizes several principles as quite independent

* EDITOR'S NOTE: Apparently Mr. Gawronsky, in making this quotation, had access to a manuscript version of the book; cf. pp. 297-98 of the published work, New Haven (1946).

of each other, although closely connected and organically related and capable only in their organic interrelatedness of creating and forming the spiritual world of man. This was the very core of Cassirer's philosophical conviction. Throughout the multifarious realms of human culture he demonstrated the originality and independence of their respective symbolic forms and at the same time showed the closest connection to exist among all these forms, thus uniting them into one organic and harmonic whole. So great, moreover, was the scope of Cassirer's mental gifts, so inexhaustible his energy, so faithful his memory, so deep, swift, and versatile his power of comprehension, his mind so original and imaginative, that he was able to undertake a unique voyage around the entire spiritual world of man and to discover, on his journey, innumerable treasures of human thought.

Cassirer liked to tell the following story: once he met the great mathematician Hilbert, the "Euclid of our time," and asked him about one of the latter's disciples. Hilbert answered: "He is all right. You know, for a mathematician he did not have enough imagination. But he has become a poet and now he is doing fine." Cassirer always heartily laughed, when he told this story, and he had good reason for doing so, but a reason, of which he was never aware:—*he* had enough imagination to become a true scholar and philosopher. His mental associations were amazingly rich, colorful, and always quite exact. He possessed in high degree the gift which Goethe called "imagination for the truth of reality" or "exact sensory imagination." However keen and daring his thinking was—it always remained measured, objective, realistic.

Truly original and prolific thinkers are usually very modest. Goethe wrote in the introduction to his absolutely new and revolutionary conception of botany that, in this work, he had not said anything which any man of common sense could not easily discover for himself. Kant frankly expressed his regret that he was not as gifted as Mendelssohn. And we all know how absolutely modest is Einstein. Thus, modesty was also one of Cassirer's most outstanding traits. He never claimed that this or that idea or conception had first been discovered or formulated by him. On the contrary, he was always in the habit of quoting numerous authorities both of the past and in the present who expressed similar ideas; and he always pointed out that really important ideas usually appear as the result of the close co-operation of many human minds. Goethe's assertion that only mankind as a whole is able to find the truth was part of Cassirer's very nature and made him largely oblivious to the uniqueness of many of his own deepest insights and significant contributions.

It was this trait of Cassirer's mental attitude which made him so tolerant in all spiritual things and so appreciative of all earnest and sincere striving. His deep conviction that truth is immensely beyond the insight of any one individual mind never permitted him to discard any opinion without thorough investigation. And, just because he found so much truth in other thinkers, he never attempted to found a philosophical school of his own. And it was precisely his great love of truth which made deliberate falsehood and evil all the more loathsome to him. Throughout his life, therefore, he did not stop fighting against falsehood and evil in his own quiet but determined manner.

Cassirer was a deeply religious man. He cared little for differing rites, rituals, confessions, or denominations; these only split mankind into so many groups and often turn them against each other. Yet the very core of any true religion, the cosmic feeling, a love as wide as the universe and as intense as the light of the sun, was always vivid in his heart. It was this feeling which urged Cassirer incessantly to explore all material and spiritual things, which filled his heart with deep sympathy for everything good in the world, which strengthened his will to fight for this good. And it was this feeling which was the source of his charming humour—the Infinite All was always present in his mind, it never permitted him to take either himself or his surroundings too seriously, and he was, therefore, able to joke for hours in the most spirited and sympathetic manner.

To the very end of his life Cassirer retained his youthful spirit, his vivid interest in all the aspects of life around him and his readiness to be helpful to other people. It is difficult to imagine a kinder and more sympathetic person, a man with such an absolute devotion to the good. Symbolic of his whole nature, therefore, was the way of his passing: on the street he was met by one of his students, who addressed a question to him. Cassirer turned to answer, smiled kindly at the young man, and suddenly fell dead into his arms.

DIMITRY GAWRONSKY

NEW YORK CITY

B

FOUR ADDRESSES

Delivered at Memorial Services, held under the Auspices
of the
Department of Philosophy
of
Columbia University
Brander Matthews Theater, Columbia University
June 1, 1945

IN MEMORIAM: ERNST CASSIRER

This is the locust season of our days
When the ripe meadows of the mind are bare,
This is the month of the never-born maize
Upon whose golden meats we shall not fare.
This is the week of the stunted stalk
And fruit that is dust on the bones of rock,
This is the day of the hungry hawk
And the songbirds dead by the fallen flock.
This is the noon of our derelict plain,
The sun-parched hour of most desolate pain.

Yet there is a valley where sweet grain grows
In strong-rooted stands, in tall splendid rows.
Here toiled in the meadows a man wise and serene,
And the meadows bore fruit and the meadows are green.

EDWARD MURRAY CASE

2

ERNST CASSIRER

WITH the passing of Ernst Cassirer one of the great philosophical interpreters of human civilization has been taken from us. The last true scion of the classic tradition of German idealism has been laid to rest. While we are wondering whether the Germans will ever be able to produce a new moral and intellectual order by returning to the liberal humanism of their own past, which they renounced so violently in recent decades, this meeting is a demonstration of our confident faith in these ideas as a precious part of our own culture.

Soon after the classic school of German philosophy had been deprived of its great creative leaders with the deaths of Hegel and Schelling, German philosophy lost its dominant position to the new natural and historical sciences. Simultaneously German philosophy began to retreat from an active participation in the discussion of the fundamental political issues of the age. The programs of the political parties were little affected by the humane philosophy of the early part of the century.

In the last third of the century, however, a renascence of philosophical thought took place, which is usually called the rise of neo-Kantianism. But though a great deal of the new philosophical discussion centered around a fresh study and appreciation of Kant, the new philosophical movement did not aim at the enthronement of the Königsberg philosopher as the patron saint of a new scholasticism but had much broader and deeper objectives. It sprang from the moral and intellectual dissatisfaction with the then fashionable ideas which seemed incapable of overcoming the growing materialism and naturalism. Many went even so far as to consider these philosophies the logical outcome of modern scientific research. In contrast, the new generation of German philosophers asserted that the progress of the individual natural and historical sciences stemmed very largely from the discoveries of classic philosophy and that research would lose its direction and meaning without a critical awareness of its basic methods. However, philosophy was not only to act as a guide to the various academic departments but was to gain fresh vigor from them.

Ernst Cassirer began his studies when the new philosophical movement had already gained influence in German universities. Lotze was probably the chief bridge-builder between the classic idealism and the neo-idealism which then found its leaders in Dilthey and in the neo-Kantian schools of Marburg and the South-West, represented by Cohen and Natorp and by Windelband and Rickert. But it should not be forgotten that the sciences and arts took an active part in producing the new philosophy. German mathematics and physics from Helmholtz to Planck and Einstein were deeply conscious of their philosophical roots and not all the historians got lost in contemporary national politics. Harnack and his school of ecclesiastical history, the school of the history of religion from which Troeltsch made his way into philosophy, and Meinecke's work in the history of ideas are only a few examples of the manner in which historians helped to buttress the new philosophical movement.

Ernst Cassirer took his place among the best scholars of this group, and while he remained always grateful for being the member of a group of common spirit and purpose, he soon began to chart a course of his own in accordance with his personal gifts. In his early studies Cassirer concentrated on achieving a fuller understanding of the much-praised and little-known Leibniz, the real founder of the German philosophical tradition. Leibniz was the father of the theory of knowledge which, in contrast to almost the whole philosophy of the 18th century, Kant included, saw in the study of nature and of history two manifestations of the one human quest for knowledge. He did not consider the humanities a lower, or less mature, form of academic achievement. Both were branches of *Wissenschaft*, science, i.e., both were producing scientific truth though by different methods. Throughout his life Cassirer remained a student of Leibniz by keeping abreast both of the progress of the natural sciences and of the liberal arts.

However, Cassirer believed that his basic approach to philosophy was Kantian in origin. Kant had maintained that the way to a transcendental order could be gained only through an analysis of the forms and methods of human thought, and he had demonstrated the power of his new critical idealism in the philosophical study of the natural sciences, ethics, and finally aesthetics. The neo-Kantians and particularly Cassirer went farther. Their epistemology included the methodology of history and moreover of all forms of creative civilization, finally encompassing even the expressions of pre-scientific human thought and imagination as revealed in language and mythology.

This is the key to the truly universal scope of Cassirer's studies. In addition to Leibniz and Kant, it was the spirit of Goethe which gave life to Cassirer's thought,

> Wer nicht von 3000 Jahren
> Sich weiss Rechenschaft zu geben
> Bleibt im Grunde unerfahren
> Muss von Tag zu Tage leben.[1]

In Cassirer's personality and work Goethe's program of education became a living reality again. The totality of Western civilization was to be reconstructed and made a part of the consciousness of the modern individual and of present-day civilization. The study of the processes and creations of civilization would lift the individual to a position from which he could see farther than "from day to day" and could begin to grasp the ideal forms and categories of the human mind.

In this version of idealistic philosophy philosophical studies became in large sections identical with historical research. In general, Cassirer confined his historical interest to the history of human thinking and avoided the discussion of the social and political forces. However, he was not satisfied with the old-

---

[1] Tr.: He who cannot account for 3000 years is basically inexperienced and therefore can only exist from day to day.

fashioned type of history of philosophy which dealt chiefly
with the doctrines of the leading philosophers, and linked them
together by a loose chain of abstract speculation. Thus, between
a social and political interpretation of historical civilization on
one side and a history of mere ideas on the other his history of
human thought held its own place. His work ranged from the
tedious editing of small texts and discoveries to his monumental edition of Kant. Beyond the editing it proceeded to the
analytical and interpretative monographs and articles covering
ancient science and the philosophy of practically all ages of
Western civilization. Even those historians who care little about
philosophy cannot by-pass the new historical vistas which he
opened particularly on the Renaissance and the European
Enlightenment.

But as closely as his historical and philosophical studies were
intertwined, the unity of his many interests is to be found in
the philosophical conviction that man can participate in a
higher order of life only through the realization of the perennial forms of human thought. He drew these philosophical conclusions most clearly in his great *Erkenntnistheorie* and in his
Philosophie der symbolischen Formen. Cassirer's writings mirror far more than do those of most of his German colleagues
his unusual gift as a teacher. He had a unique facility for clear
and logical exposition, and all the products of his pen display
his extraordinary sense of balance and aesthetic form. His capacity to project himself into the psychological and mental
environment of a past age or of an individual thinker of the
past did not make him forget the individual needs of a present-
day audience or student. His understanding of human nature
made him take his listeners or pupils as seriously as the
philosophical and historical subjects he tried to expound to
them. These qualities explain his success as a teacher in Germany, in Sweden, and in America.

Cassirer gave up his professorship in Hamburg when the
Hitlerites came to power in Germany. This was natural, considering that he was one of the chief exponents of that liberal
tradition of German thought which the Nazis tried to destroy
by all means. But, being at the same time a Jew, he had to

take refuge in foreign countries. No German was as deeply steeped in the German cultural tradition and very few had contributed so much to its growth within his generation as Ernst Cassirer. Many other German scholars who found themselves in a similar situation preferred to cut all their ties with their Jewish origin. Prior to Hitler not very many Germans would have criticized anyone for doing just that; on the contrary, many would have applauded such an attitude. Actually, Cassirer's unwillingness to abandon his Jewish faith proved a handicap in his earlier academic career, but he was too honest to dissimulate his heritage. He was also conscious that a great deal of his moral integrity and intellectual strength had come to him through his Jewish culture. Nor did this make him feel suspicious or bitter. There was little of Heinrich Heine in him, but much more of Felix Mendelssohn, to whom he can be compared in many respects. As Mendelssohn helped to discover for the Germans some of the greatest treasures of their cultural past, and at the same time contributed by his own creative work to the continuation of their classic tradition, so did Cassirer in the philosophic field.

Yet Cassirer's life and work do not belong to Germany alone. The philosophical revival of the last third of the nineteenth century was not merely a German event. It had its parallels and found its students in many lands, e.g., in the Italy of Benedetto Croce and to a lesser, though considerable, degree in modern French philosophy or in the Spain of Ortega y Gassett, from where it recently has spread far over Latin America. Among his German contemporaries, Cassirer was probably the one most conscious of the international significance of philosophy. Certainly he was the one German philosopher of distinction who had least indulged in construing the Kantian and post-Kantian German philosophy as a complete refutation of the philosophy of Western European Enlightenment. While German philosophers and historians were prone to describe the Kantian philosophy as a separation of the superior German from Western-European civilization, Cassirer was always mindful of the fact that Kant had his roots in the Western European Enlightenment, or for that matter, that it was impossible to think of Goethe without Shaftesbury and Spinoza. These were some of the reasons which made him approach Western-European thought with the same warmth of understanding which he showed in his German studies. He deserved the respect and affection of the philosophers of other countries which they showed him so often. Never did scholars of so many lands coöperate in expressing their admiration for a colleague of theirs as happened in the symposium on *History and Philosophy*, which the Oxford Press presented to him at his 60th birthday.

His knowledge of other civilizations, his truly cosmopolitan outlook, and the friendships which he acquired among his American colleagues and students, made the years of his exile not only bearable, but fruitful. Others of his age never again came into their own after being separated from the world in which they had spent the major part of their life. No doubt the events cast a tragic shadow over the last years of his career, but they did not change his fundamental beliefs, nor even his joy in research and teaching. The core of his personality was unaffected. He was unassuming and undemanding. His greatest satisfaction lay in giving others knowledge and wisdom.

HAJO HOLBORN

YALE UNIVERSITY

3

ERNST CASSIRER

IT MUST have been in 1920 that I first met Ernst Cassirer. Although the war had been lost by Germany, the air was full of hope. The collapse of material power had produced a strong and favourable reaction in the intellectual field, and one of the symptoms of this was the foundation, in Hamburg—now more anti-militaristic than ever—of a new university. High hopes were entertained for the new institution, which was to be of good standing and to form an intellectual centre for the Hansa city. Of particular importance was the chair of philosophy, for which Cassirer had been chosen. The new university elected a man whose international reputation at that time was far greater than the recognition which the older seats of learning had bestowed on him. He lent a peculiar dignity to the young arts faculty, and an ever-growing number of students came to his courses, eager for the truth and for learning, after the many deceptions of the war years.

On a day memorable in the annals of the Warburg Institute, Cassirer came to see the library collected by Professor Warburg over a period of about thirty years. Warburg's nerves had broken down in 1920 under the strain of the post-war events, and he had been sent to Switzerland for recovery. Being in charge of the library, I showed Cassirer around. He was a gracious visitor, who listened attentively as I explained to him Warburg's intentions in placing books on philosophy next to books on astrology, magic, and folklore, and in linking the sections on art with those on literature, religion, and philosophy. The study of philosophy was for Warburg inseparable from that of the so-called primitive mind: neither could be isolated from the study of imagery in religion, literature, and art. These

47

ideas had found expression in the unorthodox arrangement of
the books on the shelves.

Cassirer understood at once. Yet, when he was ready to
leave, he said, in the kind and clear manner so typical of him:
"This library is dangerous. I shall either have to avoid it altogether or imprison myself here for years. The philosophical
problems involved are close to my own, but the concrete historical material which Warburg has collected is overwhelming."
Thus he left me bewildered. In one hour this man had understood more of the essential ideas embodied in that library than
anybody I had met before. Why, then, did he seem to hesitate?
I expected that, if anyone, he would help me with the difficult
task of continuing the library without its founder. But it seems
that the workings of his mind would not allow him—or, at
least, not *yet* allow him—to be drawn into the dangerous chan-
nels of Warburg's creation. Only much later did I understand
that the reason was not narrowness, but self-restraint. Those
who knew Cassirer will realize that the decision to keep aloof
from certain problems at a certain moment was dictated by
the austere logic of his own method.

But, after an interval of waiting, the situation changed
radically; and, from that moment on, for ten years, I never
appealed in vain to Cassirer for collaboration. He had begun
writing the first volume of his *Philosophie der symbolischen
Formen* and, in developing his systematic ideas, he studied the
voluminous concrete material prepared by ethnologists and
historians. Warburg had collected the very material which
Cassirer needed. More than that: looking back now it seems
miraculous that Warburg had collected it for thirty years with
a view to the very problems which Cassirer was then beginning
to investigate. In the 1890's (inspired by Friedrich Theodor
Vischer), Warburg had set out to study symbolic expression
in art. His experience in studying the rites and arts of the
New Mexico Zunis had taught him that the study of symbolic
expression in art could not be isolated from that of religion,
magic, language, and science. (In a number of still unpublished
writings, Warburg had, on the one hand, tried to formulate
a practical theory of the symbol in the history of civilization;

while, on the other hand, he had built up a library containing the concrete materials for these studies, beginning with books and articles on the general problem of symbolic expression and arranging all the historical sections with a view to this problem.) At the time of Cassirer's first visit, *Die Philosophie der symbolischen Formen* was just taking shape in Cassirer's mind. It came as a shock to him, therefore, to see that a man whom he hardly knew had covered the same ground, not in writings, but in a complicated library system, which an attentive and speculative visitor could spontaneously grasp. That was the reason why, at our first meeting, Cassirer immediately felt that the alternative confronting him was either to ignore the Institute or else to submit to its spell.

When the time was ripe for him, Cassirer became our most assiduous reader. And the first book ever published by the Institute was from Cassirer's pen. It dealt with the problem on which Warburg had started, namely to establish the categories of primitive thought in the primitive cultures proper, as well as in modern primitivism, as for example in astrology.

Warburg was a man of a very imaginative and emotional type, in whom historical imagination, nourished by concrete historical experience, always struggled against an ardent desire for philosophical simplification. Yet he had created a tool which a master, whose greatest gifts were in the line of systematization, could use, and who, just at this moment, was eager to find the concrete material on which to build his system. Cassirer found it laid out in the library of a man who was still alive, but who was living in darkness behind doors which seemed never again to open for him.

Years went by. The first volume of Cassirer's *magnum opus* appeared, while we published some corollaries to it and some lectures. One day Cassirer went to Switzerland to pay a visit to Warburg. It was a meeting of which both Cassirer and Warburg often spoke in later years. The patient had prepared himself for this day for weeks and months previously. Cassirer came, full of sympathy and with the apprehension and awe that mental illness inspires. In the years of anguish and isolation Warburg's thought, which had never been arrested by the illness, had centred around Kepler. Warburg had come to the conclusion, although separated from all books, that modern thought was born when Kepler broke the traditional supremacy of the circle, as the ideal form in cosmological thought, and replaced it by the ellipse. Cassirer, who never took notes but possessed a memory of almost unlimited capacity, at once came to Warburg's aid, giving chapter and verse for this idea by quoting from Kepler. It was, probably, Warburg's first ray of light in those dark years. He learnt through Cassirer that he had not wandered in a pathless wilderness, but that his scientific thought at least was sane. Cassirer's memory was always miraculous; but it had never worked as miraculous a cure as it did on that day.

In later years, when Warburg was back in Hamburg, a warm friendship sprang up between the two men. Warburg admired the clarity of thought and form in the philosopher; and Cassirer was impressed by the man who grasped life and history with such passion and who had gone through mental experiences which gave every utterance of his about art or religion, about philosophy and literature, a deep and wise ring.

The character of Cassirer's scholarship, however, was such that, though enriched and extended, its intrinsic direction was never changed by his co-operation with Warburg. A reader familiar with Cassirer's work, but unfamiliar with these personal details, would never divine the intimate relationship which existed between the two men, so much did all the writings of those years appear as the necessary continuation of Cassirer's earlier work. When Warburg died in 1929, it was Cassirer who spoke at his grave: a commemoration of the strange and fruitful meeting of two thinkers of almost diametrically opposed character and tendency. Yet they had one great goal in common: to understand the nature and history of the symbolic expression of the human mind.

If the Warburg Institute has grown into a stable institution, we owe much of its success to Cassirer's advice and help. If Warburg were alive, he would testify how greatly he admired Cassirer. But above all, he would express his deep gratitude to the man who, better than any psychiatrist, had helped him to find the way back into the world. Even those of you who knew Cassirer could hardly imagine the immense impression that his clear and calm personality made on a mind cut off from the world and striving hard to reach the port of health by exerting his powers of reason. Cassirer, Olympian and aloof, was yet the most humane and learned doctor of the soul. Higher praise could hardly be given to any man.

F. SAXL

THE WARBURG INSTITUTE
UNIVERSITY OF LONDON
LONDON, ENGLAND

4

A STUDENT'S *NACHRUF*

Friends of Ernst Cassirer:

I SHOULD like you to know something of what the students in the Department of Philosophy at Columbia felt for Ernst Cassirer. By recounting to you the substance of my own experience and my own feelings I shall be summing up the experience and the feelings of all of us here who were the students of Ernst Cassirer. For, my relations with Ernst Cassirer were surely typical and most representative.

As a mere apprentice to that trade in which Ernst Cassirer was a revered guild-master, I am aware that language is a fragile bridge to understanding, and one that is too easily collapsible. Thus, if someone were to ask me: "How well did you know Ernst Cassirer?," I should feel the need of beginning my answer by making a certain verbal distinction. In terms reminiscent of one of the great problems with which Professor Cassirer came boldly to grips, I should have to reply: "Just what do you mean by the word 'know'?"

If by your question you mean to inquire whether I enjoyed a personal friendship with my teacher, whether our acquaintance was an intimate one, then regretfully I should have to answer that in this sense I did *not* "know" Ernst Cassirer. The time was too short, the days were too few for this.

But if your meaning is: "Did I have an understanding of the kind of man that Ernst Cassirer was?," then I should answer, and every one of his students would answer with me: "I did, and I do."

Ernst Cassirer was an exile, a Jew, who wrote: "In our life, in the life of a modern Jew, there is no room left for any joy or complacency. All this has gone forever. No Jew whatsoever can and will ever overcome the terrible ordeal of these last years." And yet Ernst Cassirer was a man whose presence bespoke serenity as surely as do the green leaves bespeak the springtime. This sereneness of countenance and mind was noted by all. But it was not the serenity which is unconscious of the storm; it was, rather, a kind of winged serenity which surveyed, which comprehended, and yet which nobly overrode the storm. And so, having seen this, we knew that Ernst Cassirer was a good man. For only the good are serene.

We were impressed by the depth and variety of his knowledge. The depth we were prepared for, but the variety amazed us. I recall that, after I had seen *An Essay On Man,* I asked two members of the department whether Professor Cassirer were really at home in all the varied fields surveyed by this book. They assured me that, in truth, he was. And I am ashamed to confess that I was dismayed at this confirmation; for it seemed to me that I, a beginner in philosophy, could never hope myself to be the master of such a manifold of learning. But this dismay was supplanted soon by a spirit of emulation; and the kind of scholarship which was Ernst Cassirer's became for me something to strive for, a goal which I might not attain, but a goal which was truly clear, for I had seen it defined in the being of a living man.

In the lecture hall we were particularly impressed by the profound and appropriate allusions made to every field of knowledge. In the seminar room we learned to wait for the brilliant interjection, the almost casual sentence which put a philosopher or a problem in a new and more illuminating light. In short, we came to realize, all of us, in time, that as a man of learning and wisdom, as a scholar, Ernst Cassirer was unique.

He was an ardent man. I understood this on the day of the last class he taught. I was on my way to class that day, when in the distance I was glad to see Professor Cassirer walking in the same direction. I quickened my pace in order to catch up with him. When I came closer I saw that, as he walked, he was reading a book, which absorption accounted for the slowness of his step. As I watched him, he paused to concentrate on what he was reading, and, in that moment, I perceived that Ernst Cassirer, at the age of seventy, was more ardently interested in the contents of that book than most young men have ever been interested in the contents of any book. And so I did not disturb Professor Cassirer, and I am glad now that I did not, for the discreet man does not intrude upon a lover.

Thus, being serene and good, being learned and wise and ardent, being all these things, Ernst Cassirer was a *great* man.

And so we, the students of philosophy at Columbia esteem it to have been a great privilege and a great honor in our lives that, in this great university of the New World, we were the last students of the lineal descendant of Immanuel Kant, that we were the last students of the last flowering of German philosophy. And I do not speak from paper or from notes or in words formulated coldly and with deliberation, but I speak from the heart when I say: *We loved Ernst Cassirer.*

EDWARD MURRAY CASE

COLUMBIA UNIVERSITY

5

ERNST CASSIRER

WE ARE gathered together in a memorial to Ernst Cassirer. We meet here to convey to each other, in some poor words, what he meant to us as man and philosopher. It will take more, of course, than we have to give in this meeting to reveal what significance his work has and will continue to have for many others besides ourselves; and, fortunately, there is to be a volume of studies of his philosophy, where this further and more adequate appraisal may have place. But we can, at this moment, do something good for ourselves and for the memory of our friend, if we simply speak of the things that promptly stand out in our consciousness now rather than strain at the impossible task of offering a comprehensive picture of the whole man and his work. These first thoughts that come in the dawning realization of our loss have a very personal character. Each one of us has his own individual feelings and appreciations. We are sharing these together in this hour and making the man we have known even more real for each other as we here tell how we best remember him.

Four years ago, almost to the day, Ernst Cassirer came to this country, accompanied by his wife, without whom we who have but known him these few years cannot think of him. They came here direct from Sweden, on the last ship permitted to go out, in May, 1941. They made themselves at home in America, where they already had some dear ones waiting for their arrival. I believe that we can say that Ernst Cassirer was happy here, both in New Haven, where he first came to live, and then in New York.

Let me speak to you after his own fashion. It was always his way, when telling of some other thinker or philosopher,

55

first to quote something that was completely characteristic of the man. He often quoted at greater length, some people felt, than he needed to do. I recall a publisher saying this in criticism of one of his manuscripts. "We want more Cassirer," he complained, "and less of what other people have thought." But what other people had learned and thought was too important to Ernst Cassirer to be made so little of. He always knew that many artists of the mind had searched for and shaped the truths or the problems for inquiry with which he himself was concerned and he believed it a duty to give *their* "authority," in this fine and original sense of the term, before he ventured to present his own contribution to the matter. This was his style of life and thought. It expressed both his generous regard for other thinkers and his modest estimate of his own place alongside them in the halls of philosophy.

I have in my hands a precious document and memento written in his own hand. Last year at this time he was saying farewell to his friends at Yale. He spoke at the Philosophical Club meeting where all of us assembled to express to him our appreciation of the three good years we had been privileged to have together in our study of philosophy. This is what he said to us on that occasion:

Looking back on my long academic life I must regard it as a long Odyssey. It was a sort of pilgrimage that led me from one university to the other, from one country to the other, and, at the end, from one hemisphere to the other. This Odyssey was rich in experiences—in human and intellectual adventures. What was most delightful and gratifying in this long academic journey was the fact that it became also, more and more, a sentimental journey. For at any new place I was lucky enough to find new friends. I found colleagues who were ready to help me in my work, and I found students who were interested in my philosophical views.

When I came to this country I cherished the hope that the same would happen here. And this hope was not disappointed. But, on the other hand, I found something more and something better—something that passed all my expectations. I was not only supposed to give my own lectures and hold my own courses. I was invited to have a share in the work of my colleagues. During my first year I had the pleasure and the great privilege to be invited to a seminar on the philosophy of history . . .; in my second year I could participate in a seminar on the philosophy of science . . .; in my third year we had a conjoint seminar on the theory of knowledge. . . . That was, indeed, a new experience to me—and a very suggestive and stimulating one. I look back on these conjoint seminars with real pleasure and gratitude. I am sure I have learned very much from them.

Of course, it was in a sense a rather bold enterprise, the bringing together of so many philosophers. As a rule philosophers seem not to be very fond of such a close coöperation. They are apt to disagree in their views, in their interests, in their very definition of what philosophy is and means. And the task that had to be solved here was so much the more doubtful and risky since three different generations were expected to have a share in a common work. To the struggle between philosophers there was added the struggle between the generations. In many of our modern systems of education we are told that it is hopeless to reconcile the views of men belonging to different generations. We are told that there is a deep and insurmountable gap between the generations; that every new generation must feel in its own way, think its own thoughts and speak its own language. I regard this as a misleading and dangerous dogma—and as a dogma that throughout my life I found constantly contradicted by my own personal experience. The older I grow, so much the more I become interested in the work and the thoughts of the younger men. And I always found that they readily answered to my interest. To my great satisfaction I had the same experience here. . . .

Of course the younger people criticized me sometimes rather severely. They could not always agree with me; they thought perhaps that they had outgrown, a long time ago, some of the philosophic ideas and ideals that were still very dear to me. But, after all, they listened to me and they tolerated my very old-fashioned philosophy. They could see my point—as well as I could see theirs.

This ended his "brief report," as he then called it, on his life amongst us, though he had even other things to express, more personal, on that occasion. But what he said in these words just quoted belongs to no particular group of colleagues and students or university. It was as much his message to Columbia this year as it was to Yale then. It was his report on his American sojourn. And while it reports our academic life as he really saw it, it has greater truth still as a revelation of himself.

That friendship of which he told, the eager interest in ideas, the tolerance of mind . . . "they could see my point as well as

I could see theirs." All this happened because of him. It was his doing. "I was lucky enough to find new friends." Lucky? Oh no, he was himself the architect of these rewarding personal and academic relations which we all so much enjoyed. He was the philosopher who brings to birth the philosophic spirit and way of life in those who lived and worked with him.

"The older I grow," he had said, "the more I become interested in the thoughts of the younger men." Very few men of seventy will even *think* of saying that, and there are fewer still who, if they were to say it, would ever be believed. We know that he said this, however, in all sincerity and without the shadow of a boast. He spoke with transparent honesty when he acknowledged such an intellectual benefit for himself in his association with youth and with the younger scholars. It was a confession made in fine simplicity by one who was a genuine teacher of men.

He rejoiced, as you saw, at the idea especially of keeping three generations in touch with each other in common work, the young, the middle-aged and the old. He was well aware of the risk involved in such an enterprise in education. We realize from his own words, too, that he felt the severity of the youthful criticism directed at his particular philosophic beliefs and ideas; but we saw him, too, meeting the criticism with reason and patience and generosity, and it was, in fact, by so doing that he *brought* several generations so happily together in adventures of learning. Here is another classic trait of the philosopher. We all remember Socrates at the same age and doing the same things.

No man of his high caliber could live through these last twenty-five years without giving profound thought to the whole plight of humanity in all the nations of the world. He knew what adversity meant close at home. His knowledge of vast periods of history brought multitudes of other instances that could weigh down the spirit with a heavy burden. He was sensitive to the pain and the hopelessness that many have to suffer and must continue to suffer. Yet his vision kept in view the dignity and continuity of man's long struggle forward to a life that befits humanity. Thus he succeeded in attaining serenity himself. Yet he was never aloof and abstracted, for he gave thought and individual sympathy for the small personal trials of everyone whom he knew. It was good for one's soul to be with him. And no one who knew him at all could miss that *cheerfulness* which was a sort of spiritual radiance that warmed and brightened our fellowship. This is the thing, I believe, we should bear in mind now, as we go on to recall all the other things that Ernst Cassirer has meant to us.

CHARLES W. HENDEL

DEPARTMENT OF PHILOSOPHY
YALE UNIVERSITY

C

Hendrik J. Pos

RECOLLECTIONS OF ERNST CASSIRER

RECOLLECTIONS OF ERNST CASSIRER*

HONORED by the invitation to contribute to the Cassirer volume, I should like to carry out this assignment by saying something about Cassirer, the man, as well as about his philosophical significance. I had the privilege of studying Cassirer's works even before I first heard his lectures in Hamburg during the summer semester of 1928. I then met him in the Spring of 1929 at the Second University Congress in Davos; and since 1934 I have been in closer personal relationship with him, which led to my spending a month with him in Göteberg in the summer of 1936, for the purpose of co-operating on a task which, due to unforeseen circumstances, was never brought to completion. The last word I ever had from him was a postcard, dated May 1940, expressing his concern over how I had fared since the invasion. Shortly thereafter I was interned, and when the war was over the news of his death reached me.

When I was a young student, Ernest Cassirer's works on the history of the theory of knowledge, *Substance and Function,* as well as on Einstein's theory, opened up to me the whole world of scientific thought, which was far removed from a student of classical philology. This study became determinative for my philosophical development, insofar as I learned from it the nature of natural science in contrast to cultural (social) science, and how the former has gradually created its own correct path for itself, a path which leads form Galileo through Newton to Einstein and the moderns. If, as a young admirer of the Greeks, one is inclined to take all of Plato's and Aristotle's speculative thought for immutable truth, then nothing is more instructive than to take cognizance of the inexorable course pursued by

* Translated by Dr. Robert W. Bretall.

63

science since the Renaissance. To this end Cassirer's *Erkenntnis-problem* is an excellent guide. Endowed with a wonderfully flexible style, he knows how to transpose himself into every point of view, to present it *con amore*, and at the same time to trace the great lineage which leads from speculative ontology and abstract verbalism to the rational empiricism of modern natural science. It is most gratifying that the three volumes which carry the treatment up to Hegel, are very soon, through the interest of Professor Hendel of Yale, to be completed with the fourth volume, which Cassirer had left in manuscript. In this major work of its kind Cassirer exhibited an unexcelled mastery, command, and disposition of his material, and in addition, a luminous facility of presentation, which remains unique in German philosophy. It is a history of recent philosophy from the standpoint of the progress of the natural sciences. It may be that here and there in the quotations there is some room for improvement: the whole [work] is the expression of an idea, which emerges clearly from the development of the natural sciences in modern times, the idea, namely, of the transition from metaphysical speculation to rational understanding. Here it is shown how, by a gradual process of trial and error, and under the decisive influence of scientific savants, the intellectual and technical mastery over nature has come about; and how, in this process, the basic viewpoints have altered. One cannot claim that any old philosophical position fits into this development equally well: ontologism sees itself compelled to separate the empirical development of science from the philosophical determination of fundamental principles, in order thus to keep the changes of empirical science far away from the philosophical enterprise. Cassirer demonstrated at what cost the *a prioristic* and established results of philosophy are purchased by this method. He also showed how the historical development has shoved aside this dualism, which amounts to a doctrine of the twofold nature of truth, and how Kant's method of the analysis of basic principles—an analysis which proceeds from the very fact of existing science—does justice to the progress of science without robbing philosophy of her own task. Further, he showed how the application of Kant's analysis to natural science today makes it necessary to go beyond the content of Kant's doctrine. Of this the Relativity theory is the classical demonstration, insofar as it modifies the intuition of space and time, which Kant still was able to lay down as the foundation of physics. This [theory] makes it clear that the advance of knowledge consists not only in the material of new experience being incorporated into the fixed categories, but also in the fact that the basic assumptions themselves must be revised from time to time, in order to bring new facts into non-contradictory connection with old. Philosophically considered, Cassirer taught how to extend the idea of the process under which the Marburg school subsumed "knowledge," to include the basic categories themselves and their determination—thereby going beyond Kant and his orthodox adherents. This was the only way of safeguarding Kantianism against the reproach of dogmatism, and of preventing it from being left behind by the advance of science, as had happened in the case of ontological speculation. Through his "scientism" Cassirer's philosophy has achieved an international reputation which puts him close beside the kindred figure of Léon Brunschvicg. At Davos I was present at conversations during which the two thinkers made the discovery of their spiritual affinity.

Cassirer was so many-sided, that his total work was far from exhausted by his writings in the field of epistemology. To others it may be left to come to closer terms with the abiding merit of his studies in the history of epistemology, in theory of relativity, and in the problem of causality in recent physics. I turn now to his philosophy of culture, set down in the first two volumes of the *Philosophie der symbolischen Formen*. In 1923 appeared the volume on language, and in 1925 that on mythical thought. The first is a phenomenology of the formation of our worldview in terms of a philosophy of language; whereas the second volume lays bare the driving force which conditioned the creation of a religion. Cassirer was the first to apply the basic ideas of neo-Kantianism concerning spirit and its creative energy to the pre-scientific world-view. Here, too, he was guided by that historical sense which distinguishes his treatment of the problem of knowledge. With the aid of an intensive study of the struc-

tures of primitive languages—for which the Warburg Institute
in Hamburg provided him with the materials—he sought to
construct a line of development leading from the most elementary categories of the world to the more objective ones, and
finally to the cognitive results of the sciences. The primitive
languages, taken as witnesses to a very remote stage of the human grasp of the universe, offered him valuable supporting
evidence for his notion of the gradually advancing "symbolical"
formation of the world-picture, which in the interest of objectivity and of comprehensive unification, gets farther and
farther away from the original, primitive intuitions. He showed
in a convincing manner how an originally strong, vital, and
qualitatively conditioned world-view gives way gradually to an
objective and more universal one, this transition attesting itself
in the transformations of language as it proceeds from a sensory,
qualitative stage to a symbolical-abstract mode of expression.
Thus it becomes clear how the requirements of science make it
necessary to introduce symbols which in precision and fruitfulness surpass those of language.

One may perhaps harbor some doubt as to whether the current linguistic structure of a society is, indeed, always so faithful
an expression of its manner of thought and feeling—whether
now and then, let us say, the external structure may not be inadequate to the thought-content. No damage is thereby done
to the methodological principle of Cassirer's theory of language,
and it is to be gratefully acknowledged that through him the
researches instigated by Wilhelm von Humboldt and by Wundt
have been fruitfully continued and have received their philosophical foundation. The basic idea which sustains both the
theory of language and the theory of knowledge is the fact
that, by introducing symbols, the human consciousness succeeds
in ordering and governing the welter of sensations. The categories expressed in languages pave the way for that *logical*
order for which the sciences are striving.

Cassirer's philosophy of culture is a philosophy of the *logos*,
not in the narrow sense of "ratio" or of the intellect in the purely
theoretical sense, but rather in the sense of that spiritual, form-
inducing energy which appears in science, society, and art. As a

critic Cassirer was as ill disposed to metaphysics as toward that irrationalism which stirred mightily in Germany between the two world wars. His Kantian rationalism was bound to come into conflict with the intuitionism of the waxing phenomenology, and especially with the ontological and "philosophy of life" stamp which Heidegger imparted to it. The Kant interpretations presented by Cassirer and Heidegger, together with the ensuing discussions, constituted the focal point of the International Davos University course in 1929.

The two standpoints could be mutually clarified, but they could not be brought any closer together. Cassirer [on his part] emphasized the spiritual law, the form, by means of which man liberates himselfs from his immediacy and his anxiety. This is the way in which the finite mind participates in the infinite. Whereas Heidegger expounded his book on *Kant and the Problem of Metaphysics*, which had just been published. He expressed the opinion that Kant's central problem was not at all that of scientific knowledge, but rather the problem of the metaphysical comprehension of being. Kant's philosophy he declared to be a philosophy of finite man, whose access to the Infinite is denied, but whose orientation toward the transcendent confirms his very finitude. The difference was clear. Heidegger persisted in the *terminus a quo*, in the situation at the point of departure, which for him is the dominating factor in all philosophizing. Cassirer [on the other hand] aimed at the *terminus ad quem*, at liberation through the spiritual form, in science, practical activity, and art. The contrast was not theoretical, but human. Here stood, on the one side, the representative of the best in the universalistic traditions of German culture, a man for whom Idealism was the victorious power which is called to mold and spiritualize human life. This man, the heir of Kant, stood there tall, powerful, and serene. His effect upon his audience lay in his mastery of exposition, in the Apollonian element. From the beginning he had within him the liberal culture of Central Europe, the product of a long tradition. In both spiritual lineaments and external appearance, this man belonged to the epoch of Kant, of Goethe, and of Kleist, to each of whom he had dedicated some of his literary efforts. And over against

him stood an altogether different type of man, who struggled
with Cassirer over the deepest intentions of Kant's writings. This
man too had a gigantic intellect. As a man, however, he was
completely different. Of *petit bourgeois* descent from southwest
Germany, he had never lost his accent. In him this was readily
forgiven, being taken as a mark of firm-rootedness and peasant
genuineness. There was, however, much more that was of interest in this man. In his youth he was destined for the priesthood,
and was to receive his seminary education at Constance. He ran
away, however, and became a renegade. At home as almost no
one else in Aristotle and the scholastics, in Kant and Hegel, he
constructed for himself a philosophy which, on the side of
method, came close to the phenomenology of his teacher, Husserl. In point of content, however, this philosophy was of course
entirely his own: there lay feelings at the base of it which
were concealed by the gigantic intellectual superstructure. But
when one listened to his lectures, listened to this gloomy, somewhat whining and apprehensive tone of voice, then there flowed
forth the feelings which this man harbored or at least which he
knew how to awaken. These were feelings of loneliness, of op-
pression, and of frustration, such as one has in anxious dreams,
but now present in a clear and wakeful state of mind.

The bearer of this mood-philosophy had the ear of Germany's
academic youth, not on account of his prodigious knowledge of
the history of philosophy, but rather because he translated feelings which in that youth found a soil already prepared. This
man came to be regarded as the great hope. His searching book
on Kant had succeeded in showing those dark, melancholy feelings as determinative even for the philosophy of the famous
sage of Königsberg. Man is a finite being and cannot escape his
finitude—this, the book taught, was to have been the deepest
meanings of Kant's thought. This carried conviction, from the
very first, for the youth of a land where the feeling of frustration had for ten years now been alive in a sense other than the
merely metaphysical one. The little man with the sinister wilful
speech, who was at home with these morose feelings, who loved
to say that philosophy is no fun, the despiser of Goethe—[this
man] over against the representative of Enlightenment, basking

in spiritual fortune, for whom the philosopher's life was joy and inspiration, and who in Goethe paid homage to the universal man.

The whole discussion was the intuitive representation of this profound cleavage between the two men. The one abrupt, negative, his attitude one of protest; the other kindly, gracious, accommodating, always concerned to give his partner more honor than he deserved. The two men reached an agreement on the meaning of Kant's Schematism, which represents the original intermingling of sense and understanding. This, however, left the main questions undecided: each one viewed Kant from the standpoint of his own humanity, with the difference, however, that the one admitted that metaphysical expressions are not lacking in the text, whereas the other would in no wise grant that the main concern of the *Critique of Pure Reason* was aimed at grounding the scientific knowledge of nature philosophically. Long went the discussions back and forth, until finally they terminated. The conclusion was not without human symbolism; the magnanimous man offered his hand to his opponent: but it was not accepted.

The Davos conversations were symbolical of the tragic decline toward which German philosophy was hastening. Whoever at that time still did not grasp what was going on, could get a glimpse of it four years later, when fate divided the two Kant interpreters as irreconcilably as had their manners of thought: for Ernst Cassirer there no longer was any room in Germany. He emigrated to Oxford. In the same year his opponent in the Davos discussions was appointed rector of the University of Freiburg, and in his inaugural address professed himself unreservedly for National Socialism. Germany's spiritual collapse had taken place, and Heidegger placed his philosophy at the service of the self-destruction of the German intelligentsia.

When Ernst Cassirer was forced to leave the University of Hamburg in 1933, he stood at the peak of his international reputation. It was primarily because of him and Husserl that German philosophy, at that time, flourished before the world. For the regime, quite naturally, this was no reason whatsoever for making an exception in his case. On the contrary, international recognition was then taken as a proof of unreliability, especially if on top of this one was a non-Aryan. Cassirer loved the free-thinking Hamburg, whose newly founded university he had co-operatively helped to build ever since 1919. The leave-taking must have been painful, perhaps even more so than the cutting injustice perpetrated by his dismissal. So magnificent a person was he, however, that no word of bitterness was ever heard from him about the injustice done. With Olympian serenity he departed. A man who for many years had lived in Cassirer's shadow became his successor, and expressed his pleasure at the course of events. Cassirer rapidly made friends in Oxford. He learned English and delivered lectures. It was not easy to gain a genuine understanding for neo-Kantianism. It was during his stay in England that Cassirer celebrated his sixtieth birthday. The co-operative volume, *Philosophy and History*, which was presented to him on this occasion (Oxford, Clarendon Press, 1936) is a living testimonial to the diversity of influence and of inspiration which radiated from him upon philosophers and historians of culture in all countries. The twenty-two essays had been edited by Cassirer's student Klibansky and the Oxford Kantian scholar and historian of philosophy, H. J. Paton. The contributions came from England, France, Holland, Germany, Switzerland, Italy, Spain, and America. In the preface the editors wrote: "It is our hope that this book may bear witness to that enduring spiritual bond which unites scholars of different countries and different traditions." The name of Cassirer actually symbolized a universalism and internationalism which recognizes every member of mankind for its spiritual contribution to the whole culture pattern, on the presupposition that through such mutual recognition, the unity of mankind will be honored and promoted.

The further course of Cassirer's life was to bear still further testimony to this universalism. In 1935 he emigrated to Sweden, where his former student Jacobson vacated for him the chair in philosophy at the University, while he himself accepted the appointment as Governor of the Province of Bohnslau. Here too Cassirer made devoted friends and enthusiastic students. And here in the summer of 1936 I had the privilege of being allowed to carry on a series of conversations with him in a subject for which we had conceived the plan of a co-operative volume during his stay in Amsterdam: the influence of the Greek language on philosophy. Was Greek from the very first a language well adapted to philosophical thought? Or did the thinkers rather take the instrument at hand in its natural state and adapt it to their particular needs of expression? How far does the unconscious influence of the inner linguistic form of Greek extend to the construction of metaphysical concepts? These and similar questions we discussed intensively; during which process Cassirer unfolded his masterly gift of intellectual sympathy and dialectical skill. After these preparatory conversations we promised each other to work them out during the next summer. It never got that far. Since 1936 I have remained in correspondence with Cassirer, but have never seen him again. A very promising participation in a Hegel conference at Amersfoort had to be declined by him for reasons of health. In Sweden too Cassirer did fruitful work. His stay in the North furnished him the occasion for taking up his Cartesian studies once more and for engaging in documentary research on Descartes' life in Stockholm. The fruits of these years were many an article in the philosophical journal *Theoria*, edited by Ake Petzäll, a book on the development of the concept of causality, and the book on Descartes.

In May, 1941, Cassirer came to America with the last ship which was permitted to make the crossing. Of his work at Yale, until 1944, and at Columbia until his death on April 13, 1945, Professor Charles Hendel has given a beautiful account in the *Journal of Philosophy and Phenomenological Research* (Sept., 1945, 156-159). The quotation there reproduced really constitutes the autobiography of Ernst Cassirer. A great man looks back upon the Odyssey of his life, in the course of which he has had to wander from land to land and from continent to continent. He did it modestly, cheerfully, and magnificently. Subjectively considered, this man's gratitude to others is perfectly sincere; whereas taken objectively, it is not without irony, since it was not he but the others who had cause to be grateful. But that is the way Ernst Cassirer was; he sought no glory, and yet he gained it; he esteemed others higher than himself, but actually was their superior. This was the secret of the inspiring and uplifting effect which emanated from his presence. There was nothing in him of professorial vainglory, and yet he was a teacher beyond compare. He did not hesitate to cite the writings of a man who had lived for many years in his shadow and who was openly jealous of him. And I can still hear him speaking, in Davos, to a very young instructor: "You and I have the same philosophical interests, and I am very glad of this." This was his self-giving virtue, the *générosité* of the Descartes he so greatly admired. One scarcely knows what to marvel at most, this man's gigantic intellect, his consummate form of expression, or his chivalrous humanity.

His philosophy reveals his character through its capacity for transposing itself sympathetically into various and sundry philosophical viewpoints, without thereby losing the distinctive lines of his own thinking. To the editor of this book I have to express my gratitude for the opportunity of bearing witness, by a short and fleeting sketch, to my grateful admiration for a man to whom German philosophy owes more than to any other of its current representatives—(viz.,) that in the time of its shame and its decline, it has been able to maintain its age-old renown in the eyes of the world.

HENDRIK J. POS

PHILOSOPHICAL FACULTY
UNIVERSITY OF AMSTERDAM

I

Carl H. Hamburg

CASSIRER'S CONCEPTION OF PHILOSOPHY

CASSIRER'S CONCEPTION OF PHILOSOPHY

IF IT IS the mark of a great thinker that death cannot interrupt the continuity of his intellectual influence, and if, furthermore, an ever growing demand for his published thought may be taken as one way of measuring his greatness, the late Ernst Cassirer must well be accorded this rare title. Within three years after an untimely death cut short his teaching career at Columbia University, there have rolled off the presses several printings of his *Essay on Man* (first published in 1944), *Language and Myth* (translated in 1946 and already out of print) and *Myth of the State* (fourth printing since 1946), all of which have simultaneously been translated into Spanish and some of which will soon appear in French, German, and Dutch. In addition, we may expect in the not too distant future English editions of *Determinism and Indeterminism in Modern Physics*,[1] the fourth volume of his famous *Erkenntnisproblem*,[2] the *Philosophy of the Enlightenment*,[3] and possibly, the *Logic of the Humanities*,[4] Spanish translations of *Kant's Life and Work*,[5] and the *Philosophy of Symbolic Forms*[6] as well as posthumous publication in German of

[1] *Determinismus und Indeterminismus in der modernen Physik;* Historische und systematische Studien zum Kausalproblem. (Goeteborgs Hoegskolas Arsskrift. Vol. XLII; 1936); ix, 265 pp.

[2] To be published sometime in 1948, this volume will deal with physical, biological and historical methods. (Approx. 500 pp.)

[3] *Die Philosophie der Aufklaerung.* (Tuebingen, Mohr, 1932); 491 pp.

[4] *Zur Logik der Kulturwissenschaften;* Fuenf Studien. (Der Gegenstand der Kulturwissenschaft; Ding- und Ausdruckswahrnehmung; Naturbegriffe und Kulturbegriffe; Formproblem und Kausalproblem; Die "Tragoedie der Kultur".) (Goeteborgs Hoegskolas Arsskrift; Vol. XLVII; 1942); 139 pp.

[5] *Kant's Leben und Lehre.* Vol. XI of E. Cassirer's edition of *Kant's Schriften* (Berlin, Bruno Cassirer, 1918); viii, 448 pp.

[6] *Philosophie der symbolischen Formen* (see *Bibliography* in this Vol.)

his *Kleinere Schriften*[1] and the collection of essays into a *Goethe*-book.

Now, if these publishing announcements may be taken to reflect a considerable preoccupation with the work of Cassirer, such interest is certainly not properly taken cognizance of in our teaching curricula. It is doubtful whether in any of the many courses, offered on the subject of "Contemporary Philosophy" in American colleges and universities, more than summary— if any—mention is made of the philosophy of Cassirer. In the case of this thinker, we seem to be facing the rather familiar paradox that a lively 'interest' in his philosophy goes hand in hand with just as lively an ignorance concerning what his philosophy is about. Although there is undoubtedly more than one reason for this circumstance, a decisive one, I believe, must be seen in the fact that, whereas Cassirer achieved early fame with his historical works, his philosophy proper was not developed before the publication of his *Philosophie der symbolischen Formen*, the latest volume of which appeared in 1929, at a time when in Germany phenomenology and the *"lebensphilosophischen"* precursors of existentialist philosophies had all but eclipsed the classicism of Cassirer's theme and style.

Cassirer's philosophy proper has, accordingly, neither received the attention that a German intelligentsia gave to lesser intellectual events in the anxious pre-Hitler years nor has an English-speaking audience had the opportunity to satisfy—by a closer study of a translated version of the *Philosophie der symbolischen Formen*—the interest in his thought which such books as *An Essay on Man* and *Language and Myth* have already provoked. Although it is to be hoped that arrangements for an English translation of Cassirer's *magnum opus* will soon be made, in the meantime there may be some value in sketching somewhat broadly what may be termed his 'conception of philosophy.' To this purpose we shall examine Cassirer's symbolic-form concept, upon the proper understanding of which hinges both his conception of what philosophy has been and what it must be, if it is to give full and impartial attention to the

[1] Containing a number of previously published essays, most of which are out of print by now.

phenomena of the "natural" as well as of the "cultural" sciences, to both the *Natur- und Kulturwissenschaften.*

THE SYMBOLIC—FORM CONCEPT

a. *Terminological distinctions*

The term "symbolic form" is employed by Cassirer in at least three distinct, though related, senses:

(1) It covers what is more frequently referred to as the "symbolic relation," the "symbol-concept," the "symbolic function," or, simply, the "symbolic" (*das Symbolische*).

(2) It denotes the variety of *cultural forms* which—as myth, art, religion, language, and science—exemplify the realms of application for the symbol-concept.

(3) It is applied to space, time, cause, number, etc. which— as the most pervasive *symbol-relations*—are said to constitute, with characteristic modifications, such domains of objectivity as listed under (2).

In correspondence with this division, we shall in the sequel deal first with the "symbol-concept." Indication will be given of both the "cultural" import attributed to it by Cassirer and the essentially Kantian epistemological provisions within which it is developed. We shall attempt an adequate definition of this concept and consider both objections and a possible defense for its maintenance. We shall examine, secondly, how a philosophy thus oriented may be conceived as a transition from a critique of *reason* to a critique of *culture.* As such, it would suggest a widening of the scope of philosophic concern by putting the "transcendental question" beyond science to other types of institutionalized activities which, such as art, language, science, etc., actually define the meaning of the term "culture." And, thirdly, we shall view Cassirer's inquiry into symbolic forms as a study of the basic (intuitional and categorial) forms of synthesis (space, time, cause, number, etc.) and their characteristically different functioning in a greater variety of contexts than was considered by Kant. If presented thus, one could clarify just what type of metaphysics would be both possible and profitable within Cassirer's philosophy of symbolic forms.

b. *The Symbol-Concept. Epistemological considerations*

As the most universal concept to be formulated within Cassirer's philosophy, the symbol-concept is to cover "the totality of all phenomena which—in whatever form—exhibit 'sense in the senses' (*Sinnerfuellung im Sinnlichen*) and in which something 'sensuous' (*ein Sinnliches*) is *represented* as a particular embodiment of a 'sense' (*Bedeutung*, meaning)."[8] Here a definition of the symbol-concept is given by way of the two terms of the "sensuous" on one hand and the "sense" (meaning) on the other, and a relation between the two, which is most frequently referred to as "one representing the other." The extremely general character of this pronouncement must be noted. Cassirer's claim exceeds by far what has ordinarily been admitted about the "symbolical character" of knowledge. Although not all philosophers would subscribe to the idea that *all* knowledge is of a mediate type, it could perhaps be said that *to the extent* that knowledge is taken to be mediate, it may also be said to be "symbolical" by virtue of its dependence upon (sets or systems of) signs which determine the discursive (linguistic or mathematical) medium within which it is attained. Whereas the history of ideas discloses a varying emphasis put by different thinkers upon sometimes one, sometimes another of the (symbolic) media to be trusted for the grand tour to the "really real," it also appears to substantiate Cassirer's general formula, according to which all knowledge—as mediate—is defined as implying (besides an interpretant, mind, *Geist*) both: the given-ness of perceptual *signs* (sensuous vehicles, *ein Sinnliches*) and something *signified* (meaning, *Sinn*). But, although Cassirer's above quoted symbol-definition would indeed be wide enough to cover such area of considerable agreement with respect to the symbolically mediate character of knowledge, note that it formulates no restrictions with respect to cognitive discourse. The "representative" relation which is asserted to hold between the senses and the sense (meaning) is, in other words, not taken to be exhaustively defined by

---

[8] *Philosophie der symbolischen Formen*, Vol. III, 109. To be abbreviated henceforth as: *PSF*.

grammatical, logical, or mathematical syntax-types, which determine the conventional forms of discourse within which knowledge is held to be mediated. Instead, it is to cover "the whole range of all phenomena within which there is sense in the senses," i.e., in all contexts in which (e.g., on the expressive and intuitional levels) experience is had as of "characters" (persons) and "things" in space and time. The issue, therefore, of a confrontation by "signs" of "facts," which would be germane to all those views which consider essentially the discursive dimension of symbol-situations, cannot even come up for a philosophy according to which "facts" cannot be evidence for (or against) "symbols," simply because their very "factuality" is not considered meaningful outside of some determinate symbolic context. The objection, therefore, raised by many philosophers against scholasticism, to the effect that the latter replaced the consideration of facts by that of symbols (names), need not invalidate Cassirer's position for which

there is no factuality . . . as an absolute . . . immutable datum; but what we call a fact is always theoretically oriented in some way, seen in regard to some . . . context and implicitly determined thereby. Theoretical elements do not somehow become added to a 'merely factual,' but they enter into the definition of the factual itself.[9]

Once the "facts," the state of affairs, the objects, which are designated by conventional signs, are realized as themselves partaking of expressive (qualitative) and perceptive (intuitional) "symbolisms" of their own, the question of the application of symbols to facts is replaced by the question concerning the "checking" of one symbol-context by another, considered more reliable or more easily institutable.

In this connection, a brief consideration of the issue of confirmation may be to the point. In Carnap's version

the scientist describes his own observations concerning a certain planet in a report O_1. Further, he takes into consideration a theory T, concerning the movements of planets (also laws assumed for the justifiable application of his instruments. C.H.). From O_1 and T the astronomer

_____

[9] *PSF*, Vol. III, 475. See also: *Substance and Function*, 143.

deduces a prediction; he calculates the apparent position of the planet for the next night. At that time, he will make a new observation and formulate it in a report O_2. Then he will compare the prediction P with O_2 and thereby find it either confirmed or not.[10]

A theoretical symbolism, in other words, is confirmed when the phenomena, which the symbolism predicts, are observed. Concededly, however, there is a hypothetical reference to context not only in the theory to be confirmed but also in the observations which do the confirming. "All observation involves more or less explicitly the element of hypothesis."[11] On the view proposed by Cassirer, to say that a theory (in combination with statements regarding initial conditions) is confirmed by "observation" would not require recognition of and recourse to any non-symbolic factuality, disclosed to the senses free from all elements of interpretation; but it would, instead, be equivalent to saying that hypothetically constructed contexts (theories regarding the orbit of a planet) would be confirmable if from it certain data can be deduced (its position at a certain time) such that, by appropriate co-ordination of a perceptual context, what are defined as light-rays in one context, will be interpreted as the determinate color and shape of a "thing" (planet) in another. Furthermore: we have an "interpretant" with his attendant "perspectives," a sign-signified relation on both the theoretical and the observational levels. To hold that the former stands in need of confirmation by the latter—and not vice versa—, to maintain that "the scientific criterion of objectivity rests upon the possibility of occurrence of predicted perceptions to a society of observers" (ibid., 5), is fully intelligible within the provisions of Cassirer's view which cannot except observation from a symbolic interpretation. Whether as observation of pointer-readings or of "things," the "confirmatory" character of observation does not depend upon its confrontation by non-symbolic facts of symbolic theories, but rather upon the easily (almost immediately) institutable and shareable nature of the perceptual context in which we have "facts" and to

[10] Rudolf Carnap, Foundations of Logic and Mathematics, 1.
[11] Victor Lenzen: Procedures of Empirical Science, 4.

which all other contexts can be co-ordinated in varying degrees of explicitness.

We suggest, therefore, that whereas the import of symbolic media for the *intelligibility* of reality is certainly not a new discovery and has been realized by philosophers from Plato to Dewey, the thesis that a symbolic relation obtains for any possible (culturally encounterable) context in which we perceive or observe a "world," expresses what is most distinctive in Cassirer's conception of philosophy.

A comparable extension of the philosophical concern beyond the cognitive to other types of signifying and modes of sign-usages has been advocated more recently by positivistic thinkers, who are intent upon establishing a more secure foundation for the discipline of semiotics. Unfortunately, Cassirer himself nowhere explicitly differentiates his own type of inquiry from the kind of sign-analyses carried on by, e.g., Carnap and Morris.[12] We shall, therefore, briefly consider both areas of agreement and points of divergence characteristic of the two schools of thought before proceeding to examine the epistemological orientation within which Cassirer's own philosophy of symbolic forms is developed.

Note that Cassirer could well agree with a view according to which "the most effective characterization of a sign is the following: S is a sign of D for I to the degree that I takes account of D by virtue of the presence of S,"[13] where I stands for the interpretant of a sign, D for what is designated, and S for the vehicle (mark, sound, or gesture) by means of which D is designated to I. Yet, although the proposal to understand sign-processes as "mediated-taking-accounts of" is also implied in Cassirer's conception of the matter, there would be a characteristic shift of terms. Where Morris, e.g., has his "interpretant," Cassirer would speak in terms of *"Bewusstsein"* or *"Geist:"* "the meaning of spirit (*Geist*) can be disclosed only in its expression; the ideal form (what is designated) comes to

---

[12] Rudolf Carnap; *Foundations of Logic and Mathematics*, 1939. Charles W. Morris, *Foundations of the Theory of Signs*, 1938; and *Language, Signs and Behavior*, 1946.

[13] Charles W. Morris, *Foundations of the Theory of Signs*, 4.

be known only in and with the system of sensible signs by means of which it is expressed."[14] Likewise, the distinction between the sign-vehicle (S) and the designation of the sign (D) by Cassirer is put in terms of a correlation alternatively called "the sign and the signified," "the particular and the general," "the sensuous and its sense" (*das Sinnliche und sein Sinn*). There is agreement, then, on this basic point: for anything to be a sign does not denote a property characterizing a special class of objects, but—speaking in the material mode—it indicates that it participates in the sign-process as a whole within which it "stands" to somebody for something, or—in the formal mode —that it can be defined only in terms of a three-term relation of the form "I-S-D," where "I" designates the "taking-account-of," "S" the mediators of the "taking-account-of," and "D" what is taken account of. In Cassirer's language: "The act of the conceptual determination of what is designated (*eines Inhalts*) goes hand in hand with the act of its fixation by some characteristic sign. Thus, all truly concise and exacting thought is secured in the '*Symbolik*' and '*Semiotik*' which support it."[15]

For a correct understanding of Cassirer's position all depends here upon the interpretation we put upon this metaphor of "the sign and the signified going hand in hand." For Morris, manifestly, the relationship suggested is one interchangeably alluded to as one of signs "indicating," "announcing," or "suggesting" the presence of whatever they denote, designate, or signify. For Cassirer, on the other hand, Husserl's dictum in the matter holds: "*Das Bedeuten ist nicht eine Art des Zeichen-Seins im Sinne der Anzeige.*" (To signify is not a way of being a sign in the sense of being an indication.)[16] The indicative function of signs, upon the broad basis of which Morris attempts to sketch the foundations of a semiotic, is accordingly of just the kind that Cassirer would have to consider as inadequate for an understanding of the symbolic function properly speaking. In the formulation of this distinction by Susanne Langer: "The fundamental difference between signs and symbols is this difference

---

[14] *PSF*, Vol. I, 18.
[15] *PSF*, Vol. I, 18.
[16] Edmund Husserl, *Logische Untersuchungen*, Vol. II, 23.

of association, and consequently of their use by the third party to the meaning function, the subject: signs *announce* their objects to him, whereas symbols lead him to *conceive* their objects."[17] Against this establishment of a "fundamental" difference, Morris has advanced the objection that too much is made of what essentially seems to amount to a mere difference of degree.

A symbol is on the whole a less reliable sign than is a sign (that is a signal) . . . (the latter) being more closely connected with external relations in the environment is more quickly subject to correction by the environment. . . . But, since signals too have varying degrees of reliability, the difference remains one of degree.[18]

Now, regardless of whether or not one agrees with Morris that environmental correction in the case of signals is in all contexts more reliable than purely symbolic procedures such as provided, e.g., by derivations or calculations, one need not argue that, once the behavioristic approach is taken with regard to both signs and symbols, they may indeed be considered as comparable—and not fundamentally distinct—means through which behavior may be informed in different degrees of reliability. To take signs as related to dispositions of behavior is to be primarily interested in the modes in which they come to inform, incite, appraise, or direct action. To emphasize signs in their symbolic use is to inquire not so much into what they "announce," "appraise," etc., but into their "meaning," the "domain of objectivity" they appear to condition. An inquiry into the symbolic function of signs, as Cassirer puts it,

is not concerned with what we see in a certain perspective, but (with) the perspective itself . . . [so that] the special symbolic forms are not imitations, but *organs* of reality, since it is solely by their agency that anything real becomes an object for intellectual apprehension and as such is made visible to us. The question as to what reality is apart from these forms, and what are its independent attributes, becomes irrelevant here.[19]

Cassirer insists, in other words, that the truly symbolic (the

---

[17] Susanne K. Langer, *Philosophy in a New Key*, 61.
[18] Charles W. Morris, *Signs, Language and Behavior*, 50.
[19] *Language and Myth*, translated by S. Langer, 8.

properly "significative") meaning of sign-functions cannot be looked for in the indicative office performed by them, but refers to their rôle as "organs of reality" as which they are said to "bring about" (condition) what is meant by an "object" in the various universes of discourse, intuition, and expression.

In accordance with three senses in which the symbolic-form concept is used (see above), to say that "the symbolic forms are . . . organs of reality" would be equivalent to the following three expressions of the thesis:

(1) No meaning can be assigned to any object outside the cultural (mythical, artistic, common-sensical, scientific) contexts in which it is apprehended, understood, or known.

(2) No meaning can be assigned to any object except in reference to the pervasive symbolic-relation types of space, time, cause and number which "constitute" objectivity in all domains, with the modifications characteristic of the media listed under (1).

(3) No meaning can be assigned to any object without, in whatever form, assuming a representative relationship—expressed in the symbol-concept—which, abstractable from any context, would be said to hold between given "sensuous" moments, on the one hand, and a (in principle) non-senuous "sense" moment, on the other.

How, we must ask now, is both the pervasiveness and the objectifying office of the symbolic-form concept to be demonstrated? Keeping Cassirer's Kantian orientation in mind, it will follow that his inquiry into the objectifying pervasiveness of symbols cannot properly be expected to point to or to discover facts or activities hitherto unknown or inaccessible to either the sciences or such other culturally extant types of experience-accounting as religion, myths, the arts. Kant, it will be remembered, set out to clarify his "misunderstood" *Kritik* by demonstrating in the *Prolegomena* that neither mathematics nor the physical sciences would be "possible" unless the pure forms of intuition and certain categorial determinations were presupposed as valid for all experience. Analogously, Cassirer maintains that the symbol-concept must be taken as just as pervasive as are, in fact, the sciences, arts, myths, and languages of common sense, all of which may be conceived as employing symbols in their respective experience-accountings. To say, furthermore, that symbols "objectify" would, on this interpretation, mean nothing else than that these various domains themselves, in their symbolic evaluation of the perceptive data to which they apply, furnish the only contexts within which one can meaningfully speak of any kind of "objectivity." There is, in other words, no point in producing examples to illustrate what exactly Cassirer means when he credits symbols with "bringing about" rather than merely "indicating" objects, simply because all sciences, arts, myths, etc. would have to be taken as illustrating this general contention. We must distinguish here two aspects of this contention: (1) That all the above-listed "domains of objectivity" do indeed presuppose the employment of symbols, and (2) That there is no objectivity outside the contexts established by these various domains.

As regards the latter aspect, its acceptance follows from Cassirer's endorsement of what he took to be Kant's transcendental method. Could Kant prove the adequacy of this method by the use he made of it with respect to "experience as science?" The answer may be in the affirmative, if one keeps in mind the state of the mathematical and physical disciplines with which he was familiar. As a contemporary writer has put it: "In relation to his information Kant's intuition of Euclid's axioms is unobjectionable. . . . Without the aid of Einstein's conception of a curved physical space, we should not conclude that Kant is altogether wrong."[20] The answer may be in the negative, if one considers that Kant presented his "forms" of intuition and understanding as immutable human faculties, and took them to be as *final* as Aristotelian logic, Euclidean geometry, and Newtonian physics were thought to be *necessary*. But, whatever be one's evaluation of Kant's position, this much of it is never questioned by Cassirer, namely that the determinateness with which we experience the "objective" world is never passively received *ab extra*, but that it is, in principle, analyzable as "conditioned" by acts of synthesizing the manifold given in per-

[20] Andrew P. Ushenko, *Power and Events*, xv.

ception. What Kant had maintained was that there can be no objectivity in the physical sense without assumption of the synthesizing forms laid down by the Transcendental Analytic. This point is generalized by Cassirer to include other than physical domains, to be accounted for by types of synthesis other than those listed in the first *Kritik*. That aspect of Cassirer's general contention, then, according to which there can be no objectivity outside the contexts established by the sciences, arts, myths, etc., instead of being explicitly demonstrated, constitutes his basic philosophical commitment to Kant's viewpoint.

Regarding the other aspect of his thesis, viz., that all the contexts within which such objectivity is encountered, are to be taken as sign-systems, in so far as all of them imply specific evaluations of the "same" sensory data, on what evidence are we to accept it? Or better: what sort of evidence is possible for this contention within the commitment to Kant's position as indicated? With respect to Kant's inquiry it is maintained by Cassirer that he aimed to develop the epistemological consequences from the facts of the sciences with which he was familiar. It was their actual employment of "judgments" both related to experience (synthetic) and yet necessary (*a priori*) which seemed to Kant to demand a revision of both the empiricist and the rationalist pronouncements with respect to the character of human knowledge. In the stage at which he analyzed it, it could be said that his analysis was adequate for science as he knew it. Kant, in other words, was not concerned with adducing evidence that there are synthetic judgments *a priori*—the evidence for their actual employment being taken to issue from an impartial examination of the sciences themselves. It was but their "possibility" that Kant felt had to be accounted for by making those necessary presuppositions about human cognition through mediation of which science—as a result of the activation of that cognition—would become intelligible. Consequently, these presuppositions, the forms of intuition and understanding, are not the evidence from which the synthetic *a priori* judgments of the scientist are thought to be derivable, but the sciences themselves are taken as the evidence that justifies and postulates the epistemological characterization of the "mind" with which the first *Kritik* is concerned.

This brief reminder serves to explain Cassirer's analogous conviction that his theory of the symbolically-mediate character of reality, far from standing in need of ingenious philosophical demonstrations, merely formulates, on a level of highest generality, a semiotic function which, in various modifications, is assumed as a matter of fact by all who, within the legitimate contexts of their respective branches of investigation, inquire into the nature of physical, artistic, religious, and perceptual "objects." A re-examination of this evidence in the light of more recent developments in the mathematical, physical, psychological, linguistic, religious and anthropological researches considered by Cassirer, would be both surpassing the competency of one inquirer and not be to the immediate purpose.

For the remainder of this section, it will be our chief concern to elucidate how the symbol-concept must be understood in order to warrant the universal use and significance which Cassirer attributes to it. Before proceeding to this task, however, note that—rightfully or not—Cassirer did take for granted its actual employment, not just in the analysis of the various disciplines, but in the very construction of the domains to which these analyses refer. In support of this contention, we point to the following:

(1) Early in the first volume of the *Philosophie der symbolischen Formen,* where Cassirer prepares for the introduction of the symbolic-form concept, he raises the question ". . . whether there is indeed for the manifold directions of the spirit . . . a mediating function, and whether, if so, this function has any typical characteristics by means of which it can be known and described."[21] Yet, although it is a foregone conclusion that such a "mediating function" must be ascribed to the symbol-concept, Cassirer, instead of presenting specific arguments for this core idea, immediately goes on to say: "We go back for an answer to this question to the symbol-concept as Heinrich Herz has postulated and characterized it from the point of view of physical knowledge." *(ibid.)* As soon as the

[21] *PSF*, Vol. I, 16.

question is raised, in other words, whether there is a function both more general and flexible than, e.g., the concepts of "spirit" and "reason," elaborated by traditional philosophy, the answer, in the form of the proposed symbol-concept, is not argued for at all but is presented as being actually effective and recognized as such by Herz with respect to physical science, and such other thinkers as Hilbert (mathematical logic), Humboldt (comparative linguistics), Helmholtz (physiological optics), and Herder (religion and poetry).

(2) In 1936, the Swedish philosopher Konrad Marc-Wogau had commented upon certain difficulties he found inherent in Cassirer's various versions of the symbol-concept. In a rejoinder to these objections, Cassirer makes this very characteristic statement: "In his criticism, Marc-Wogau seems to have overlooked this one point, namely that the reflections to which he objects, are in no way founded upon purely *speculative* considerations but that they are *actually* related to specific, concrete problems and to concrete *matters of fact*."[22] It is significant that, here again, where the "logic of the symbol-concept" has been challenged, Cassirer makes no attempt to take up his critic's suggestions on the same analytical level on which they were made, but, instead, goes on to cite a variety of instances (drawn from psychology, linguistics, mathematics, and physics) for which outstanding representatives have emphasized the symbolical character of their respective subject-matters.

Strange as this attitude may appear to those who would expect an original philosophy to develop and reason from its own axioms, it is only consistent in the light of the above-mentioned transcendental orientation in which Cassirer read and accepted Kant. The thesis, accordingly, that the mind (*Bewusstsein, Geist*) is symbolically active in the construction of all its universes of perception and discourse is not suggested as a discovery to be made by or to be grounded upon specifically philosophical arguments. Instead of presupposing insights different from and requiring cognitive powers or techniques superior to those accessible to empirical science, the thesis is developed as

---

[22] *Theoria;* (Tidskrift for Filosofi och Psykologi.) II, 158.

issuing from an impartial reading of the scientific evidence in all branches of investigation.

Certain difficulties about such a position could perhaps be felt from the outset. It may be questioned, for instance, whether scientific situations could be encountered at any time which would give univocal testimony to the symbolically-mediate character of both their methods and their subject-matters. One may also wonder whether the scientific crown-witnesses (on whom Cassirer relies so heavily), when reflecting upon the symbolic nature of their domains, do so *qua* scientists, or whether, when so reflecting, they must be considered philosophical rather than scientific spokesmen for their disciplines. Finally, a philosophy resting its case squarely on the evidence of not just one (especially reliable) science, but of all the sciences —including all religious and imaginative sense-making as within the province of what Cassirer calls *"Kulturwissenschaften"*—seems dangerously committed to generalize upon enterprises notorious for their proneness to scrap both their own theories and attendant philosophical explanations of their theories.

Considerations of this type need not be fatal, however, to a philosophy thus far considered. A philosophical reading of the evidence of the sciences will indeed not face "univocal situations." Nor will such situations be encountered within any other inquiry. The cognitive enterprise, whether in the form of large philosophical generalizations, or of the more readily controlled scientific generalizations, is admittedly guided by hypotheses and thus does imply decisions with respect to the data that are considered relevant for their respective generalizations. The further contention that the methodological *testimony* of the scientists cannot be credited with the same respectability as his methodological *effectiveness* also need not be damaging to a philosophy whose center of gravity is determined by the scientist's findings. Any philosophy, one could say, which is proposed as a critique and mediation of symbolisms, must obviously do justice to the most reliably constructed symbol-systems of the sciences and, in doing that, it can hardly afford to disregard the statements on method merely because they come from somebody who employs them successfully. At any rate, an adequate interpretation of the scientific symbolisms always requires attention to both the factual and the (methodo-) logical subject-matters, and there does not seem to be any *prima facie* evidence why the method-conscious scientist is to be trusted less in this connection than the science-versed philosopher. The objection, finally, that any philosophy whose ambition it is to bring into conformity its account of "reality" with the latest results of the sciences is doomed to "eternalize" highly contingent validity-claims, need likewise not endanger the position taken by Cassirer. It would be the alternative to the self-corrective character of the evidence trusted by him that would be fatal to any philosophy. The ambition to make final pronouncements, to issue once-and-for-all "truths," is certainly not germane to a thought-system which, by Kantian orientation, is not straining to lay hold upon a final reality-structure, but which is advanced frankly as an attempt to discharge the "culture-mission" of mediating the reality-accounts offered by the various cultural disciplines.

We must conclude therefore: the thesis that all contexts (in which we—objectively—have a world, structure, domain of reality) may be analyzed as differently oriented symbolic evaluations of the perceptive data, is offered as evidenced by all the inquiries made of these contexts. As such, the thesis is suggested as a generalization upon the pervasive features of the artistic, religious, and scientific domains, guided by Kant's transcendental hypothesis that the pervasive features of all experience cannot be prior to and independent of the synthesizing activities of a symbol-minded consciousness which has and reflects upon them.

What Cassirer never tires of attributing to Kant is the latter's *"Revolution der Denkart,"* by which philosophers were freed from having to attain a reality more profound (or more immediate) than the only one given in experience, either as encountered or as reflected upon by the only valid methods of scientific synthesizing. Instead of undertaking—in the fashion of ontological metaphysics—to determine fixed traits of being, the transcendental method would bid us to examine the types of judgments which logically condition whatever may validly be asserted as "objective." The "objectivity," however, with which the first *Kritik* furnishes us, actually turns out to be an exclusively "physical" one. The transcendental method, as used in the *Kritik*, has not provided us—Cassirer thinks—with the clue for "*Objektivität überhaupt*" but specifically with just one type of objectivity, viz., the one that may be formulated within the system of principles constitutive of Newtonian physics.[23]

In brief: what Cassirer accepts of Kant is the transcendental method which, instead of revealing immutable structures of Being, inquires into the culturally given "fact" of science and, "being concerned not with objects but with our mode of knowing objects,"[24] makes for a more flexible analysis of experience by allowing for different types of "objectivity," comprehended as corresponding to different "modes of knowing." In Cassirer's version: "The decisive question is always whether we attempt to understand function in terms of structure or vice versa. . . . The basic principle of all critical thinking—the principle of the primacy of the function before the object—assumes a new form in each discipline and requires a new foundation."[25] Cassirer's position implies both an acceptance of Kant's methodological strictures and a demand for a wider application of the "critical method." More specifically: Kant's method was to limit the philosopher's concern to an elucidation of the mode of knowing governing "reality" as scientifically accessible. It was, in consequence, to deny him the right of engaging in ontological pursuits, i.e., to discover or construct "realities," offered as "metaphysical," apprehension of which would involve an employment of cognitive powers superior to those certified by the first *Kritik* as "constitutive" of (or regulative for) experience, i.e., of science as the only legitimate inquiry through which the permanent structure of this experience may be known.

[23] We are concerned here merely with Kant's attempt to formulate his "*Grundsätze*" in conformity with Newtonian physics, not with the success of this attempt. On this point, see A. Pap: *The Apriori in Physical Theory*, Pt. II. King's Crown Press, 1946.

[24] Immanuel Kant, *Kritik der reinen Vernunft*, "Einleitung," Par. VII.

[25] *PSF*, Vol. I, 10.

If then the philosopher—*qua cognitor*, not *qua* moralizer—
was to be restricted to an examination of the source, scope and
validity of the "mode of knowing" that makes possible experience as science, or if, in Cassirer's extended version, he is to be
restricted to an examination of all the various modes of knowing
and comprehending that make possible experience, however
structured (as science, or myth, art, religion, or common sense),
the issue of highest philosophical universality will logically arise
as one of attempting to reduce the variety of such distinguishable modes to so many comparable instances of one fundamental
function. And such a function would at once have to be general
enough to characterize all modes of knowing and comprehending through which experience is realized as structured, and yet
permit of all the differentiations that specifically modify the
various cultural media for which it must account. Now, it is
Cassirer's contention that, historically, philosophy both aimed
and fell short of elaborating principles of such high generality
that would, on the one hand, be valid for all domains and, on
the other, be susceptible of modifications characteristic of the
specific differences distinguishing these domains. Before turning
to a closer examination of the symbol-concept which, Cassirer
believes, satisfies the requirements of such a universal yet
modifiable function, it is significant to note here that Cassirer
conceives of his own efforts as within the general direction of
what philosophers, with varying degrees of awareness and success, have always striven for. In this connection, Cassirer has
spoken of both the "culture-mission" of philosophy and the
"antinomies of the culture-concept." By the latter, reference is
made to the characteristic conflicts that arise as the various
cultural media of religion, art, language, and science tend to set
off their special domains by claiming superiority of insight for
their respective perspectives. Thus, although the first cosmological and physical scientists everywhere started out from the
distinctions and discriminations made by common sense and
reflected by language, they soon opposed to this basic fund of
accumulated knowledge specifically new principles of division,
a new "*logos*" from the vantage-point of which all non-scientific

knowledge appeared as a mere distortion of "the truth." Similarly, while both art and religion in their early stages developed closely together, if not at times in actual interpenetration, further development of these two cultural media resulted in either of them claiming superior vision and closer approximation to the "really real" as over against the other. Instead of contenting themselves with the specific insights which they afford, the various cultural disciplines tend—Cassirer points out —to impose the characteristic form of their interpretation upon the totality of being, and it is from this tendency towards the "absolute," inherent in each one of them, that there issue the conflicts that Cassirer considers "antinominal" within the culture-concept. Yet, although it is in intellectual conflicts of this type that one would expect philosophy, as a reflection on the highest level of universality, to mediate among the various claims, the different "dogmatic systems of metaphysics satisfy this expectation and demand only imperfectly; they themselves are immersed in this struggle and do not stand above it."[26] Upon analysis, it is suggested, most philosophical systems turn out to be merely so many hypostatizations of a particular logical, ethical, esthetical, or religious orientation.

We have briefly adduced these considerations because it is against their background that one can understand the importance Cassirer attributes to his own "philosophy of symbolic forms," which is presented as having a chance of succeeding where all former "systems" could only fail; not in the sense, to be sure, that it holds the key to all the problems that have or will come up, but in the sense, nevertheless, that with the symbol-concept it puts at the philosopher's disposal an intellectual instrument of greatest universality and modifiability. As such, it is commended as impartially comprehending all "domains of reality" as of a determinable, symbolically-mediate type for which philosophical analysis may indicate their specific modalities of sign-functioning, instead of super-imposing one privileged modality of meaning (logical, esthetic, ethical, etc.) with respect to which all other "visions" are reduced to mere

[26] *PSF*, Vol. I, 13.

approximations and appearances (at best), or illusions (at worst).

c. *Exposition of the Symbol-Concept*

We have considered so far the epistemological setting within which Cassirer's thesis is developed. We have listed what, we believe, represent three essentially distinct senses in which the symbolic-form concept is employed, and we have contrasted it from both the usually agreed upon view, according to which knowledge-as-mediate is indeed taken as "symbolical," and from the more current behavioristic position, according to which the pervasive character of sign-situations is interpretable as involving objects which—as signs—indicate the presence (or the conditions for the realization of the presence) of other objects-as-signified. We have then attempted to render meaningful Cassirer's contradistinction from this position by stressing that his concern is with symbols, taken not as "indications" but as "organs of reality." Interpreting "organs of reality" in a sense termed "transcendental" by Kant, we could say that Cassirer's type of inquiry constitutes a most erudite attempt to provide evidence for the thesis that no empirical "reality" (objectivity, structure) can be meaningfully referred to except under the implicit presupposition of the symbolic (constitutive) "forms" of space, time, cause, number, etc. and the symbolic (cultural) "forms" of myth, common sense (language), art, and science, which furnish the contexts (*Sinnzusammenhänge*) within which alone "reality" is both encounterable and accountable.

We must now examine more closely exactly what is asserted when it is said of the constitutive and cultural "forms" which condition "reality," however accounted, that they are "symbolical." For this purpose, let us go back to the already stated definition of the symbol-concept, according to which "it is to cover the totality of all those phenomena which exhibit in whatever form 'sense in the senses' (*Sinnerfüllung im Sinnlichen*) and all contexts in which something 'sensuous'—by being what it is (*in der Art seines Da-Seins und So-Seins*)—is represented as a particular embodiment as a manifestation and incarnation of a meaning."[27] According to this passage, the symbol-concept

[27] *PSF*, Vol. III, 109.

would apply to all contexts in which a "sensuous" moment may be distinguished from a "sense" moment, with the proviso that a relation holds with respect to these two terms which is most frequently referred to as "one representing the other." For Cassirer (as for most other philosophers) the term "senses" covers all perceptual cues which—such as colors, sounds, etc.—suffice to act as vehicles for any and all meaning, where "meaning" covers all the embodiments to which the senses are amenable as related to an interpreter of these cues, i.e., to the full complexity of perspectives which the term "interpreter" (*Geist, Bewusstsein*) suggests. To realize yet more distinctly what both the "senses" and the "sense" (meaning) connote in this definition, we must attempt further to clarify the relation that is supposed to hold between the two terms, if they are to function symbolically. This relation, we suggest, is taken by Cassirer both in a *polar* and a *correlative* sense.

(1) The polarity of "sense" and "senses."

Stressing the polarity of this relation, Cassirer states succinctly that "the symbolic function is composed of moments which are different in principle. No genuine meaning (*Sinn*) as such is simple, but it is one and double—and this polarity, which is intrinsic to it, does not tear it asunder and destroy it, but instead represents its proper function."[28]

This function, we may say, establishes a relation between the "senses"—as signs—and the "sense"—as signified by them—in such a way that these two terms must be conceived as polar, opposite and (potentially, if not actually) distinguishable from each other. This polar distinction of the two symbol-moments, as maintained by Cassirer, can be read from a variety of pronouncements made by him apropos the three modal forms, termed respectively: the expression-function (*Ausdrucksfunktion*); the intuition-function (*Anschauungsfunktion*) and the and the conceptual-function (*reine Bedeutungsfunktion*). Space forbids even a selective reproduction of the illustrative material offered by Cassirer. The gist of the matter will be intelligible, however, if the following points are kept in mind.

[28] *PSF*, Vol. III, 110.

a. If the representative relation between the senses and their sense is of an expressive type (of which myth, art, and the realization of "persons" are taken as instances), "reality" is had as a universe of "characters," with all events in it having physiognomic traits and all manifestation of sense through the senses being restricted to what is expressible in terms of man's emotive, affective (evaluational) system. Where the "world," in other words, is taken in its primary expression-values, all of its phenomena manifest a specific character which belongs to them in an immediate and spontaneous fashion. Cassirer's description of these "expression-phenomena" as "being inherently sombre or cheerful, exciting or appeasing, frightening or reassuring"[29] parallels Dewey's account, e.g., according to which "empirically, things are poignant, tragic, settled, disturbed . . . are such immediately and in their own right and behalf . . . any quality is at once initial and terminal."[30] It would therefore be a misreading of what Cassirer terms the *"reine Ausdrucksphaenomene,"* if they were taken to issue from secondary acts of interpretation, as products of an act of "empathy." The basic error of such an "explanation" would consist in the fact that it reverses the order of what is phenomenally given. This interpretation "must kill the character of perception, it must reduce it to a mere complex of sensory data of impression in order to then revive the dead matter of impression by an act of empathy."[31] What is overlooked in the empathy-theories is that, in order to get at the sensory data (the hot and cold, the hard and soft, the colors, sounds, etc.), we must already disregard and abstract from the expressive *"Urphaenomene"* in which a "world" is had prior to the working out of the various representative schemes and conceptual frameworks to which it subsequently submits. What typifies an expression-phenomenon, we conclude, is that, whereas it possesses specific (immediate, non-derivative) meanings not realized—on the *perceptual level*—as distinct from the sensuous vehicles with which they go "hand in hand," it must still be recognized as an instance of a symbolic function,

---

[29] *PSF*, Vol. III, 85.
[30] *Experience and Nature*, 96.
[31] *PSF*, Vol. III, 85.

in so far as subsequent analysis, on the *level of reflection,* will make what Cassirer considers a "polar distinction" between its two constitutive moments which, as the sign (senses) and the signified (sense) define that function.

b. The polarity between these two moments is encountered in a more developed form in the intuitive mode of the symbolic function, for which a perception is not merely taken as a qualitative presence (*Praesenz*) but as a cue for the representation of something else.

The construction of our perceptive world begins with such acts of dividing up the ever-flowing series of sensuous phenomena. In the midst of this steady flux of phenomena there are retained certain determinate (perceptive) units which, from now on, serve as fixed centers of orientation. The particular phenomenon could not have any characteristic meaning except if thus referred to those centers. All further progress of objective knowledge, all clarification and determination of our perceptive world depends upon this ever progressing development.[32]

The passage from the expression-mode to the intuition-mode of "making sense in the senses" is described by Cassirer as a development in which progressively an organization of the sensory flux is brought about by singling out certain data, realized as comparatively constant, significant or relevant for action, by operating, in brief, a division of the perceptually given into "presentative" and "representative" moments.[33] Now, the selective and organizing office of sensory perception has been noted by both scientists and philosophers for some time. If a symbolic interpretation is put upon whatever evidence exists for this fact, it is because such "selectivity" entails a distinction of the constant from the variable, of the necessary from the contingent, of the general from the particular, distinctions, in brief, which, for Cassirer, "imply the very source of all objectification."[34] And it is to language that we are referred as both the outstanding *agency* which establishes the basic objectifying distinctions and the *medium* which reflects the "foci of atten-

---

[32] *PSF,* Vol. III, 165.

[33] This, of course, is a metaphorical, not a genetic account. A "flux" prior to any and all "organization" is a contrary-to-fact abstraction.

[34] *PSF,* Vol. III, 180.

tion," the "perspectives" which condition whatever discrimination is exercised when some (rather than other) perceptions are taken to "represent" the quasi-permanent units as which, on the intuition-mode, we have the world as organized in spatio-temporal "things-with-properties." Skipping at this point further consideration of the evidence adduced by Cassirer for this view,[35] what matters for the present purpose is that the intuition-mode of symbolic representation is conceived as involving, besides the sensory data, an "original mode of sight" (*eine eigene Weise der Sicht*) and that both these moments are said to stand in a polar relationship to each other in so far as the "sight," the "perspective," as something posited (*ein Setzungs-modus*), is not reducible to or constructible from the sensory data which it "sees." Cassirer argues in this connection against both rationalist and empiricist epistemologies which, regardless how differently they provide answers to the question of the "relation of our perceptions to an object," take the same basic course in explaining this relation either in terms of "associations" and "reproductions" or in terms of judgments and "unconscious inferences." "What is overlooked in either approach is the circumstance that all psychological or logical processes to which one has recourse come rather too late. . . . No associative connection of them can explain that original *Setzungsmodus*, according to which an impression (taken representatively) stands for something 'objective'."[36] The intuition-mode of the symbol function is proposed therefore as both an original and ultimate mode of *sight* which, although inseparable from the sensory impressions which it *sees*, must be distinguished from them as sharply as the dimensions of "meaning" (sense) from the dimension of "signs" (senses).

c. The polar relation between the sensuous- and the sense-moments is even more readily realized in Cassirer's discussion of the theoretical mode of the symbol function. Within this

[35] In his *Die Sprache und der Aufbau der Gegenstandswelt*, Jena, 1932 (see *Bibliography* for translations). Also in the *Philosophie der symbolischen Formen*, *Language and Myth*, and "The Concept of Group and the Theory of Perception," (*Journal of Philosophy and Phenomenological Research*, Vol. V, 1944, 1-35.)
[36] PSF, Vol. III, 148.

dimension, also referred to as the "level of cognition," there obtains, as within the expression- and the intuition-modes, an organization and determination of sensory data, with this difference, however, that now "the moments which condition the order and structure of the perceptual world are grasped as such and recognized in their specific significance. The relations which, on the former levels, were established implicitly (*in der Form blosser Mitgegebenheit*) are now explicated."[37]

This "explication," proceeding by way of an abstractive isolation of the relations which, while applicable to perception, are, in principle, of a non-perceptual character, is evidenced, "writ large" so to speak, in the constructive schemata, the conventional systems of conventional signs by mediation of which scientific knowledge is attained. A considerably detailed demonstration of this thesis was given by Cassirer long before the development of his philosophy of symbolic forms. His contention that all scientific concept-formation is definable as an ever more precise application of relational thinking was first presented in his influential *Substanzbegriff und Funktionsbegriff* (1910) and reasserted in the concluding sections of his "Phaenomenologie der Erkenntnis" (*PSF*, Vol. III.) where recent developments (until 1929) of the mathematical and physical sciences are considered in confirmation of this thesis. What is established by the scientific concept is referred to variously as a "function," a "principle," a "law of a series," a "rule" or "form," where all these terms are employed with the same connotation which his early work had given them, i.e., as expressing relations between (terms designating) phenomena. "To 'comprehend conceptually' and to 'establish relations' turn out—upon closer logical and epistemological analysis—to be always correlative notions."[38] Instead of defining the concept as extensively determining a class, having members, it is maintained that theoretical concepts

always contain reference to an exact serial principle that enables us to connect the manifold of intuition in a definite way, and to run through it

[37] *PSF*, Vol. III, 330.
[38] *PSF*, Vol. III, 346.

according to a prescribed law. . . . (Thus) no insuperable gap can arise between the 'universal' and the 'particular,' because the universal itself has no other meaning and purpose than to represent and to render possible the connection and order of the particular. If we regard the particular as a serial member and the universal as a serial principle, it is at once clear that the two moments, without going over into each other and in any way being confused, still refer throughout in their function to each other.[39]

The symbolic function, implied in the theoretical mode, becomes comparable to both the expression- and intuition-modes in that here too we are bidden to distinguish between the "principle of the series" and the "manifold" ordered into the members of the series.

Let us put this polarity into the language of symbolic logic. If we are to define the meaning of a concept not extensionally (by specification of the members that are subsumed) but in terms of a propositional function $p(x)$, we are clearly designating two distinguishable moments.

The general *form* of the functions designated by the letter 'ϕ' is to be sharply contrasted with the *values* of the variable 'x' which may enter this function as 'true' values. The function determines the relation of these values, but it is not itself one of them: the 'ϕ' of '$\phi(x)$' is not homogenous to the x_1, x_2, x_3, etc. [Both the function and the values of the variables belong to an entirely different conceptual type *(Denktypus)*.][40]

And this formulation only throws into relief the distinctness of the two moments which, as the principle (form) of the series and its members (material) are held to define all theoretical (conceptual) symbolisms. The distinctive trait of theoretical concept-formation must, accordingly, be sought in the elaboration of distinctive "points of view" which, as "principles" or "forms" determine the selection of the perceptually given manifold into specifically ordered series. In this connection, Cassirer argues against certain empiricist doctrines which regard the "similarity" of the intuitively apprehended phenomena as a

[39] *Substance and Function* (Swabey tr.), 223f.
[40] *PSF*, Vol. III, 349-350.

self-evident psychological fact, fit to account for the serial relations established by concepts. But, as he points out,

the similarity of certain elements can only be spoken of significantly when a certain point of view has been established from which the elements can be designated as like or unlike. The difference between these contents, on the one hand, and the conceptual species by which we unify them, on the other, is an *irreducible fact;* it is categorial and belongs to the form of consciousness.[41]

It designates, as we have seen, the polar contrast between the members of a series and the form of the series.

(2) The correlativity of "sense" and "senses."

Above, we have considered a number of passages indicative of Cassirer's conviction that on all levels on which we, symbolically, have a world,—be it as organized in qualitative expression-characters, be it as "broken" into spatio-temporally ordered "things-with-properties," be it in the relational order-systems of the sciences,—we are always in a position to make a *"distinctio rationis"* between the "sight" (*die Sicht;* the form of a manifold) and the sensory data that are variously determinable within these different sights. We have treated of this conviction as implying an interpretation of polarity between the two moments of the symbol function. We must now qualify this characterization by pointing out that, in another sense (to be specified), both moments are taken as correlative to a degree that makes it inconceivable to refer to or define either moment except under implicit presupposition of the other. If, in agreement with Cassirer's actual usage, we call the perceptive manifold the "matter" of the symbolic function and the sense-perspective (*Sinn-Perspektive*) its "form," we are bidden to think of these terms as correlative in such a way that it is not only impossible—in any actual context—to separate one from the other, but also to assign any meaning to either term without implication of the meaning of the other.

Our problem here makes contact with the metaphysical controversy about universals. From what has been said so far about

[41] *Substance and Function,* 25.

the relation between the "form" and "matter" of a series, there can be no doubt that Cassirer could not, without qualifications, have subscribed to either the realist or the nominalist position. Partial agreement is indicated with St. Thomas,[42] whom he credits with having maintained a "strict correlation, a mutual relationship between the general and the particular."[43] What attracts him in this version is the fact that it is free from the various space- and time-metaphorical separations that have traditionally been assumed to characterize the universal as being before or after, within or outside the particular. Cassirer's insistence that no meaning can be given to the universal "form" independently of a "matter" for which it is valid, is reasserted in a number of ways, such as, e.g., the "sight" determining the "how"-character of "what" is seen, or the "principle of a series" exhausting its meaning in the order it establishes among the members of the series, or the "p" of a propositional function not being definable independently of the variables for which it holds.[44]

Now, it has been suggested that Cassirer's thought here is not free from contradiction on the grounds that the two moments by which he aims to define the symbol-concept cannot both: (a) belong to two entirely different dimensions and (b) yet be tied together in such close correlation that the definition of one could not be given except in terms of the other. These objections were voiced by the Swedish philosopher Marc-Wogau.[45] It is to these objections that we must now give some attention, before considering Cassirer's defense in the sequel.

d. *The Symbol-Concept. Objections and Defense*

Marc-Wogau writes:

A closer examination seems to me to lead to the result that the positive meaning of Cassirer's "symbolic relation" is of a dialectical character; the symbolic relation, as conceived by Cassirer, covers both the idea of an opposition between the sensuously given (the sign) on the one hand,

---

[42] "Universalia non sunt res subsistentes, sed habent esse solum in singularibus." *Contra Gentiles*, Lib. I, 165.

[43] *PSF*, Vol. III, 351.

[44] On this point, see also B. Russell, *Principles of Mathematics*, 85.

[45] In: *Theoria* (Tidskrift for Filosofi och Psykologi, 1936), 279-332.

and the *"Sinnerfuellung"* (the signified) on the other, and also the idea of an identity between the two. The first idea is clearly asserted by Cassirer, the second issues as a consequence from certain of his definitions and assertions.[46]

Now, the second idea concerns the correlativity of the two symbol-moments which, according to Marc-Wogau, entails their identity as a consequence. Let us follow his reasoning:

'Sign' and 'Signified' . . . are to be mutually conditioned by each other in their determinate character. One moment has meaning only in relation to the other. But that implies that the thought about the one term involves the thought about the other. If the one term is being thought of, the other is *thereby* being thought of too. The two moments of the relation would, in consequence, coincide. If A and B are to be connected in such a way that A can be determined only with reference to B and B can be determined only in reference to A, it becomes impossible to distinguish A and B: they coincide *(zusammenfallen)*.[47]

With respect to another characterizatioin of the symbol by Cassirer, according to which it is said to be "immanence" and "transcendence" in one: in so far as it expresses a meaning—non-intuitive in principle—in an intuitive form,"[48] Marc-Wogau remarks:

In this definition, two moments are distinguished which are related in a specific way. When Cassirer characterizes this relation by saying that "the symbol is not 'the one or the other,' but that it represents the 'one in the other' and 'the other in the one,' " the question seems to crop up how, under such circumstances, a possible distinction between the 'one' and the 'other' could even be made. By this definition is there not posited an identity between the two moments of the symbolic relation which would conflict with the insistence upon their polarity?[49]

In Cassirer's rejoinder to these objections,[50] at least two different lines of argumentation may be distinguished. For one, considerations are adduced, designed to render questionable

---

[46] *Theoria*, (1936), 291.
[47] *Theoria*, (1936), 292.
[48] *PSF*, Vol. III, 447.
[49] *Theoria*, (1936), 331.
[50] In *Theoria*, (1938), 145-175.

Marc-Wogau's belief that there are logical grounds on which the maintained correlativity of the two symbol-moments could be refuted. Furthermore, illustrations from empirical sciences are reproduced for the purpose of supporting his contention that the two symbol-moments (although correlative) cannot only still be distinguished, but purporting to show that and how such isolation of the two moments has been accomplished. In this connection, Cassirer quotes extensively from contemporary research into color and acoustical phenomena which are presented by him as documenting as a *fact* what Marc-Wogau had denied as a *possibility*.

(1) The logical issue.

Marc-Wogau's objection that, if two terms of a relation are thought of as "mutually determined," they will, of necessity, also be identical, is countered by Cassirer's reference to the actual employment of "implicit definitions" in modern mathematical logic. Now, implicit definitions may be defined as "denoting anything whatsoever provided that what they denote conforms to the stated relations between themselves,"[51] where the stating of the relations is presumably to be given within the axiom-system selected. With the discovery of non-Euclidean geometries, Cassirer remarks, it became increasingly clear to those concerned with their logical foundation, that their elements—the points, lines, angles, etc.—could not be defined anymore in the explicit way in which Euclid could take them as intuitively evident. "Neither the basic elements, nor the basic relations could have been defined, if by a definition one understands the indication of the '*genus proximum*' and of the '*differentia specifica*'."[52] A way out, Cassirer suggests, was opened by Pasch's investigations[53] which were continued and brought to a systematic conclusion with Hilbert's *Grundlagen der Geometrie*.[54] Hilbert's analyses, of considerable influence upon the development of mathematical logic, may be summarized by saying that, for him, the geometrical elements and relations are

---

[51] Cohen and Nagel, *An Introduction to Logic and Scientific Method*, 135.
[52] *Theoria*, 169.
[53] See *Substance and Function*, 101.
[54] *Ibid.*, 93.

not to be taken as independent entities, intuitively grasped, for which explicit definitions could be given, but as terms whose meaning is specified by the relations which are axiomatically prescribed for them. "The axioms which they satisfy determine and exhaust their essence."[55] Basic geometrical concepts are, accordingly, held to be only implicitly definable, i.e., within a logical system; and it is gratuitous to ask for a determination of their meaning independently of this system. It follows, of course, that, if in Hilbert's geometry the signification of points, lines, the relations of "between-ness," "outside," etc., cannot be formulated except in relation to a selected axiom-group, a variety of other elements and relations, if they satisfy the formal conditions of the same axioms, must be considered as equivalent to it. Against the very possibility of structural isomorphisms, of different (though logically justifiable) interpretations of the same basic calculus, the objection could perhaps be raised that they merely prove the impossibility of arriving at completely determined elements by means of implicit definitions. This apparent limitation, however, also marks the very strength of mathematical, deductive thought, as was stated by Cassirer distinctly in his *Substance and Function*:

Two different types of assertions, of which the one deals with straight lines and planes, the other with cycles and spheres . . . are regarded as equivalent to each other in so far as they provide for the same conceptual dependencies. . . . The points with which Euclidean geometry deals can be changed into spheres and circles, into inverse point-pairs of a hyperbolic or elliptical group of spheres . . . without any change being produced in the deductive relations of the individual propositions . . . evolved for these points. . . . Mathematics recognizes (in these points) no other 'being' than that belonging to them by participation in this form. For it is only this 'being' that enters into proof and into the processes of inference and is thus accessible to the full certainty that mathematics gives to its subject-matter.[56]

The relevance of these considerations for the problem at hand may perhaps be put thus: Marc-Wogau's contention that, if the terms of a relation are mutually determined, they there-

---

[55] *Theoria*, 169.
[56] *Substance and Function* (Swabey tr.), 93.

by must also be identical, is refutable, if we maintain the justifiability of implicit definitions, respectively of the different mathematical (logical) calculi which they make possible. And vice versa: Marc-Wogau's charge, if taken seriously, would not only refute the "logic" of the symbol-concept (with its two distinct, yet correlative moments, its "sensuous" representation of the "non-sensuous"), but it would also have to refute the "logic" of all those disciplines that could not constitute their respective syntax-forms except by employment of implicit definitions. In consequence, Cassirer is convinced that, if the scientist can proceed effectively with elements the meaning of which is indefinable outside the axiom-system within which they occur, the philosopher neither may (nor need) hope for more secure foundations regarding the symbol-concept. Marc-Wogau's charge of a contradiction inherent in this concept is thus countered by Cassirer's reference to scientific syntax whose elements are not considered identical merely because their definition implies mutual determination.

(2) The empirical issue.

Regardless, however, whether correlativity of the relational terms implies their "identity" or not, is there any other than just formal evidence for the "fact" that, notwithstanding such correlativity, a distinction between the symbol-moments is not only *logically* permissible but also *actually* achievable? Before examining the empirical evidence adduced in answer to this question, it will be worth while to consider the issue here raised in its full generality.

The symbol-concept, we suggested above, was to result from Kant's epistemology, in so far as it was to cover all the "synthesizing acts" which variously condition the many expressive, perceptual, and conceptual forms in which we have the respective worlds of myth, art, common sense, and science. Instead of departing from a taken-for-granted opposition between a statically conceived "self" and a just as statically conceived "world," the philosophy of symbolic forms was proposed

to examine the presuppositions upon which that opposition depends and to state the conditions that are to be satisfied if it is to come about. It finds that these conditions are not uniform, that there are rather different dimensions of apprehending, comprehending and knowing the phenomena and that, relative to this difference, the relationship between 'self' and 'world' is capable of characteristically different interpretations. . . . True, all these forms aim at objectification on the level of perception (*zielen auf gegenständliche Anschauung hin*), but the perceived objects change with the type and direction of such objectification. The philosophy of symbolic forms, accordingly, does not intend to establish a special dogmatic theory regarding the essence and properties of these 'objects,' but it aims, instead, to comprehend these types of objectification which characterize art as well as religion and science.[57]

It follows that, if no objectivity is held to be encounterable except *within* the symbolic forms of myth and religion, of art, common sense, and science, there also can be no chance to break out of the "charmed circle" of these forms. If it is only under the pervasive presupposition of these forms that we can apprehend, comprehend and know all the objects, however structured, how then will it be possible even to conceive of a polar concept which, such as the "sensuous manifold," is claimed to be distinguishable from the formal moment of the symbol-relation? What answer, in other words, can be given to Marc-Wogau's charge that, to be consistent, Cassirer cannot hope even to make a "*distinctio rationis*" between the perceptual "matter" and the significant "form" of the symbol-concept? As mentioned earlier, it is typical of Cassirer's procedure that the resolution of this problem is not left to logical or specifically "philosophical" considerations as have conventionally been devoted to the "form-matter" issue. The latter is to be evaluated, instead, in the light of empirical evidence. Let us be clear once more for just exactly what this empirical reference is to provide evidence. What is under discussion concerns the question whether the "material" moment of the symbol-concept (to which we have variously referred as the "sensuous manifold," the "sensory- or perceptual data")—although indeterminable outside any given context ("perspective," "sight," "principle" or "form of a series")—can nevertheless be distinguished, i.e., conceived as different in principle from the sense-perspectives within which it becomes manifest.

For evidence of the fact that this problem has been realized

[57] *Theoria* (1938), 151.

by scientists, Cassirer quotes these remarks from Karl Buehler:

No theory of perception should forget that already the most simple qualities, such as 'red' and 'warm' usually do not function for themselves but as signs for something else, i.e., as signs of properties of perceived things and events. The matter looks different only in the *comparatively problematic borderline-case where one seeks to determine the 'Ansich' of these qualities in perception.*[58]

But it is, of course, exactly this "borderline-case," i.e., whether conditions for the isolation of the "Ansich" of perceptual data can be instituted or not (and how such isolation is to be interpreted), that is at issue. The question, in other words, is whether perceptual data can be stripped of their various representative functions, and the relevance of having recourse to empirical investigations would concern the technical possibility of operating such a reductive stripping of these data. For evidence of the empirical feasibility of that reduction, Cassirer mentions the German physiologists Helmholtz, Hering and Katz. Katz, e.g.,[59] had initiated a procedure involving, a.o., the observation of colors through a punctured screen (*Lochschirm*). "It turned out that hereby (the colors) change their phenomenal character and that there takes place a reduction of the color-impression to . . . the dimension of plane- (*Flaechen-*) colors."[60] Hering performs similar reductions by means of a vision-tube (*eine irgendwie fixierte Roehre*), whereas Helmholtz, more ingeniously, gets along without any instruments and achieves comparable effects by "looking from upside down, from under one's legs or under one's arms." Thus, Hering:

Place yourself near the window, holding in your hands a piece of white and a piece of grey paper closely together. Now, turn the grey paper towards the window, the white one away from it, so that the retinal image of the grey paper will be more strongly illuminated than the white one; but even though one will notice the change in light-intensity, the now "lighter" but really grey paper will still appear as grey, while the now "darker" but really white paper will be seen as white. If now both papers are looked at through a tube, one will soon

---

[58] *Die Krise der Psychologie* (1927), 97.
[59] In his *Der Aufbau der Farbwelt*, (2nd edition 1930).
[60] *Grundzüge einer Lehre vom Lichtsinn*. Paragraph 4.

see both papers (if held so that one will not shade the other) on one and the same level, and now the grey paper will be seen as the lighter one, the white one as the darker one, corresponding to the difference in the two light-intensities.[60]

And Helmholtz:

We know that green plains appear—at a certain distance—in somewhat different color-tones; we get used to abstract from this change and we learn to identify the different 'green' of distant lawns and trees with the corresponding 'green' of these objects, seen at close range. . . . But as soon as we put ourselves into unusual circumstances, when we look, e.g., from under our legs or arms, the landscape appears to us as a flat picture. . . . Colors thereby lose their connection to close or distant objects and now face us purely in their qualitative differences.[61]

Similar reductions with respect to other than color-phenomena are also referred to by Cassirer in this connection.[62]

Now it seems that, if examples of the above-mentioned type are taken as evidence for the fact that the severing of sensory data from representative contexts is not only possible but actually (technically) achievable, Cassirer would both be proving too much (with respect to what can be maintained within his own strictures) and not enough (with respect to what he presumes to prove). For one, to suggest that Helmholtz's, Hering's, and Katz's investigations succeeded in "*de facto*" isolating the "pure color-phenomena" from their representative office, would be to maintain more than Cassirer could allow for, after taking pains to point out that the sensuous moment can never actually be encountered independently of the sense (context-) moment. To maintain such "isolation" would certainly not be compatible with his contention that "there is nothing in consciousness without thereby also positing . . . something other and a series of such 'others.' For each singular content of consciousness obtains its very determination from consciousness as a whole which, in some form, is always simultaneously represented and co-posited by it."[63] Nor could, or need, the alluded empirical

---

[61] *Handbuch der Physiologischen Optik*, (1896), 607.
[62] For *haptical* phenomena: Katz, *Der Aufbau der Tastwelt* (1925), 255. For *odor* phenomena: Henning, *Der Geruch* (1924), 275, 278.
[63] *PSF*, Vol. I, 32.

illustration prove that this is *not* the case. What they may be taken to support is not the view that color-values can be stripped of their representative function, but only that—by an appropriate shift from a normal perception perspective to a controlled two-dimensional perspective—different interpretations hold with respect to color-phenomena. The latter have, in effect, not "really" been stripped of their representative office, but they now "represent" plane instead of surface colors.

That the above is a preferable way of stating the matter is suggested by an earlier pronouncement:

(After) the complete reduction of the color-impressions, they do not represent . . . a particular thing . . . (but) appear as members of a series of light-experiences (*Lichterlebnisse*). But even these '*Lichter-lebnisse*' betray a certain structure in so far as they are sharply contrasted with each other, and in that they are organized in that contrast. Not only do they have different degrees of coherence so that one color appears separated from the other by a larger or smaller distance (wherefrom issues a determinate principle of their serialization), but there are assumed in this series certain privileged points around which the various elements can be organized. *Even when reduced* to a mere light-impression, the individual color-nuance is not just 'present' as such but it also is representative. The individual 'red,' given here and now, is given as 'a' red, as a member of a species which it represents. . . . Without this (co-ordination to a series), the impression would not even be determinable as 'this one,' as τοδε τι in the Aristotelian sense.[64]

We must conclude, therefore, that it becomes impossible on Cassirer's own view to conceive of the sensory moment of the symbol-concept as isolable from any serial context. Thus, whereas, under specifically controlled conditions, color-, sound-, and other sensory data may cease to function representatively for esthetic qualities, thing-surfaces and shapes, or for conventional language-signs, their reduction will still not go beyond the physical and physiological contexts within which they are identifiable as of a determinate wave-length, intensity, pitch, etc. Marc-Wogau's charge that the "material" moment of the symbol-concept is not distinguishable from its sense-moment would, accordingly, hold if and only if the symbol-concept

[64] *PSF*, Vol. III, 157.

allowed of application in one and not more than one sense-context. To be sure, within any one perspective, the "whatness" of a phenomenon is never determinable in separation from its "how-ness," from the respective "sight" in which it is seen. With a variety of symbolic contexts, however, there is also given the possibility of their contrast and of distinguishing them as differently oriented "modes of sight," of which it can be said that they are "of" sensory data in the sense that a reduction to the physico-descriptive dimension can be performed for all of them. When Cassirer insists, therefore, that "there is always a world of optical, acoustical and haptical phenomena in which and by means of which all 'sense,' all apprehending, comprehending, intuiting and conceiving alone is manifest,"[65] then the conceivability of these sensory phenomena, as distinct from the "sense" they manifest, must be interpreted to mean that a physical context (acoustics, optics, etc.) can be co-ordinated to all other contexts in which the senses represent different types of (expressive, intuitional, theoretical) sense.

The "material" moment of the symbol-concept, we could say, as reference of and relevance for the sense-endowing "formal" moment, may not be separately encountered or isolable *within one context*, but it is nevertheless distinguishable *as one context*. To speak of it as "material," would seem to be justified, if one considers the term to stand—in the Aristotelian sense—for what is taken as that of which manifold determinations are possible. What the term also suggests is that we are dealing here with what—as matter—in space and time, is accessible to physical determination. In this sense, the material moment refers not just to one among other contexts, but to the most reliably controlled and pervasive one to which all other contexts may indeed be "reduced."

In support of our belief that this interpretation of the "independent variability" of the two symbol-moments is adequate with respect to what Cassirer aims to maintain, let us turn, in conclusion, to an illustration adduced by him on various occasions:[66] Cassirer bids us to think of a black line-drawing, a

[65] *Theoria* (1939), 153.
[66] E.g in: *Zeitschrift für Aesthetik*, 1927, (Vol. XXI), 195. *PSF*, Vol. III, 231. *Theoria* (1938), 154.

"Linienzug," distinguished as a simple "perception experience." Yet, while I still follow the various lines of the drawing in their visual relations, their light and dark, their contrast from the background, their up-and-down movements, the lines become, so to speak, alive. The spatial form (*das Gebilde*) becomes an aesthetic form: I grasp in it the character of a certain *ornament* . . . I can remain absorbed in the pure contemplation of this ornament, but I can also apprehend in and through it something else: it represents to me an expressive segment of an artistic language, in which I recognize the language of a certain time, the *style* of an historical period. Again the 'mode of sight' may change, in so far as, what was manifest as an ornament, is now disclosed to me as a vehicle of a *mythico-religious significance,* as a magical . . . sign. By a further shift in perspective, the lines function as a sensuous vehicle for a purely *conceptual structure-context.* . . . To the mathematician, they become the intuitive representation of a specific *functional connection.* . . . Where, in the aesthetic sight, one may see them perhaps as Hogarth beauty-lines, they picture to the mathematician a certain *trigonometric function,* viz., the picture of a sin-curve, whereas the mathematical physicist may perhaps see in this curve the *law of some natural process,* such as, e.g., the law for a periodic oscillation.

All depends here upon what is taken to remain "identical" in all these modes of sight. When we say that it is the *"Linienzug"* which figures as the material moment in all contexts, in what sense can we say that it is the "same" one, since we know that it is seen as so many different things from context to context? Cassirer's rather metaphorical pronouncements in this connection can be clarified in the light of our interpretation. In the passage quoted above, he speaks of the simple (*schlichte*) "perception experience" in which the line-drawing is phenomenally given *before* it "comes to life," i.e., enters into the various perspectives mentioned. But clearly, if experienceable at all, this "simple perception experience" must itself be taken as a mode of sight and not as a moment prior and common to all other sights. This formulation is particularly unhappy in the light of other passages where Cassirer generalizes upon the illustration given above by remarking that

the material moment is *no psychological datum,* but rather a liminal notion (*Grenzbegriff*). . . . What we call the 'matter' of perception is not a certain sum-total of impressions, a concrete substratum at the basis of artistic, mythical or theoretical representation. It is rather a *line towards which the various formal modes converge.* (*Eine Linie . . . in der sich die verschiedenen Weisen der Formung schneiden.*)[67]

This space-metaphorical version of the issue would be amenable to the interpretation suggested in so far as the "matter of perception" *qua* "convergence of the various formal modes" could well be taken as the "reductibility" of all contexts to the physico-physiological one from which Cassirer's actual evidence is concededly derived. (Helmholtz, Hering, Katz, Buehler, etc.)

SYMBOL-CONCEPT AND PHILOSOPHY OF SYMBOLIC FORMS

We conclude from the preceding discussion that a consistent meaning may be assigned to Cassirer's theory of the symbol-concept. The extreme generality of this concept is manifest when expressed as a propositional function. We could say that the property (of a "sensuous" representing "sense") limits in no way whatsoever the scope of the particulars which may enter the argument as true values. A symbolic relation, in other words, must hold for all facts, because, as indicated above, no facts are held to be statable without reference to some context; and no context can fall outside the symbol formula, because, as a context (*Sinnzusammenhang*), it must establish some exemplification of a representative relationship. Now, this "representation of sense through the senses" can take three distinct modal forms: (1) If the referent of the senses is the affective-emotive system of man, the senses are said to make "expressive sense." (2) If the referent of the senses is the volitional-teleological system of man, the senses make "common"-(thing-perceptual) sense. (3) If the referent of the senses is a system of theoretical order-signs, the senses make conceptual, i.e., scientific sense.

It is to each of these "modi" of the symbolic relation that there correspond the various cultural media. Thus:

---

[67] *Theoria* (1938), 155-156. ED. NOTE: Cf. *infra* 330 f.

(1) The *expression-modus* is taken to be exemplified in the domains of myth, art, and (the substrata of) language, in all of which media we deal with what Cassirer terms *"Ausdrucks-Charaktere"* and what are variously referred to by other contemporary philosophers, in related connotations, as "tertiary qualities," "essences," "prehensions," "significant forms," etc.

(2) The *common sense* or empirical-intuitional-(*empirische Anschaulichkeit*)-modus is taken to be exemplified in the "natural world-view" which is both constituted and reflected, Cassirer holds, by the "world of language."

(3) The *conceptual* (theoretical) modus is taken to be exemplified by the order-systems in which we have the "world of science."

The philosophy of symbolic forms is, accordingly, a philosophy of the cultural forms from which alone we can read the various modalities within which symbolic functioning occurs and of which the symbol-concept furnishes the most general formulation.

From these cultural exemplifications of the "modi" of the symbol-concept we must distinguish the "qualities" of the most pervasive symbol-relations which, such as space, time, cause, number, etc., are "constitutive" (in the Kantian sense) of any and all objectivity. "The form of the simultaneous constitutes a quality distinct from the form of succession."[68] But since each "quality" is never manifest but in one of the three specified modal forms,

we may conceive certain spatial forms (e.g. certain lines) as an artistic ornament in one case, as a geometrical draft in another . . . so that, in consequence, the quality of a relation can never adequately be given except in reference to the total system from which it is abstracted. If, e.g., we designate the temporal, spatial, casual, etc., relations as R_1, R_2, R_3 . . ., there belongs to each of these a special 'index of modality' μ_1, μ_2, μ_3 . . . which indicates the context within which they are to be taken.[69]

It follows that Cassirer could not consider as adequate any

[68] *PSF*, Vol. I, 29.
[69] *PSF*, Vol. I, 31.

philosophical analysis of space, time, cause, number, etc., unless, besides mathematical and physical spaces, it also attempted to account for the expressive and intuitional spaces of common sense, art, myth, and religion.

In the light of the above, it will now be clear in which sense Cassirer's theory of symbolic forms could be presented both as a "philosophy of culture" and a "metaphysics of experience." There can be little doubt that Cassirer himself preferred to think of his work as providing "Prolegomena" for a philosophy of culture. In this form, the *Philosophie der symbolischen Formen* is actually developed, starting, as it does, from a philosophy of language (Volume I, 1923) and moving on to a philosophy of myth (Volume II, 1925) and to a philosophy of (perceptual and conceptual) knowledge (Volume III, 1929).[70]

All that would seem to be required, however, in order to formulate Cassirer's various analyses of language, myth, and the sciences as a "metaphysics of experience," would be to bring together the many penetrating examinations of "expressive space" (in the volumes on *Language and Myth*), of the "empirical space" of common sense (in the volumes on *Language* and *Phenomenology of Knowledge*), of mathematical and physical spaces (in the volumes on *Phenomenology of Knowledge* and *Substance and Function*), and to arrange them within a single scheme of exposition, doing the same for the other "categories." The result would be at least as universal a treatment of the pervasive (symbolic) traits of "Being" as is expected of a metaphysical treatise.

To develop Cassirer's philosophy of symbolic forms as a "metaphysics of experience" may appear bold, if not outright paradoxical, in view of both Cassirer's frequent polemics against "metaphysical speculations" in his early writings and in consideration of the pronounced anti-metaphysical tenor of the entire neo-Kantian movement of which Cassirer was one of the most brilliant exponents. A closer examination of some of the relevant passages, however, will back our contention that the issue is essentially a terminological one. It concerns not so much

---

[70] In accordance with the then ongoing Hegel-Renaissance, Cassirer preferred the title: *"Phaenomenologie der Erkenntnis."*

the possibility (or legitimacy) of metaphysics as a significant philosophical enterprise as rather the questionability of what the term "metaphysics" has connoted so far. Take, e.g., this passage from *Substance and Function*:

When empirical science examines its own procedure, it has to recognize that there is in the (metaphysical) struggles a false and technical separation of ways of knowing that are both alike indispensable to its very existence. The motive peculiar to all metaphysics of knowledge is here revealed. What appears and acts in the process of knowledge as an inseparable unity of conditions is hypostatized on the metaphysical view into a conflict of things.[71]

Now compare this passage with another one, written almost thirty years later:

The history of metaphysics is by no means a history of meaningless concepts or empty words . . . it establishes a new basis of vision and from it gains a new perspective for knowing the real.[72]

What appears on the surface as a complete shift from a *rejection* to an *acceptance* of metaphysical thinking must be recognized, however, as a mere shift in emphasis with respect to an essentially identical point of view. To be sure, Cassirer's statements in *Substance and Function* are not as positive with regard to metaphysics as the point he makes in the study on *Hägerström*, where he asserts that "the genuine, the truly metaphysical thoughts have never been empty thoughts, have never been thoughts without concepts" (*ibid.*). Yet, in this same context he goes on to warn us—exactly as he did in his earlier work—that

the difficulties, dangers and antinomies of metaphysics arise from the fact that its 'intuitions' themselves are not expressed in terms of their true methodological character. None (of the great metaphysical insights) is considered as giving insight into only a portion, but all are claimed to generally span the whole of reality. . . . The subsequent contest, resulting from such (partial) claims becomes at once a dialectical conflict. (*Ibid.*)

---

[71] *Substance and Function* (Swabey tr.), 237.

[72] *Axel Hägerström; Eine Studie zur Schwedischen Philosophie der Gegenwart*, Ch. I.

Cassirer's position is thus a consistent one. He does not side with the positivistic contention that metaphysics is not only "false," but also "meaningless." Instead, he distinguishes the genuine character of the *problems* with which the great metaphysicians have dealt, from the still imperfect modes in which their *findings* have been presented. The metaphysical *objective* is taken to be legitimate, whereas the metaphysical *results* cannot be accepted without qualification, simply because metaphysicians have offered "partial truths" as "universal" ones and because, in focussing upon one aspect of symbolization (viz. the mathematical, religious, aesthetic, or moral one), they have lost sight of the equal validity of such other aspects as also must be accounted for as legitimate paths to what—in any perspective —may be referred to as the "real."

Now, since this denial of a privileged status for any one form of representation is exactly what Cassirer has claimed for his philosophy of symbolic forms, there does not seem to be any reason why—within his own pronouncements—his work may not indeed be considered as a kind of metaphysics, oriented around the central notion of the symbol-concept, which characterizes all aspects (contexts; *Sinnzusammenhänge*) of the "real," pervading as a common theme, the polyphony of all cultural forms in which reality is perceived, understood, and known. Now, if emphasis is put upon the most universal relational forms (space, time, cause, number, etc.) which reappear in characteristic modifications in all of these forms, we would be offered a metaphysics of (cultural) experience. If, on the other hand, our exposition proceeds by way of separate analyses of language, myth, religion, the mathematical and physical sciences, the character of Cassirer's work would be more obviously one of a philosophy of culture. Regardless, however, which form of presentation is chosen, each will center around the idea of the symbol-concept.

Cassirer himself, when offered an opportunity to present (in abbreviated form) his thoughts to an English-speaking audience, subtitled his *Essay on Man* "An Introduction to a Philosophy of Human Culture." Here, the emphasis is on the cultural realities, the languages and rituals, the art-masterpieces and scientific procedures. To comprehend them philosophically requires to realize them as so many symbolic manifestations of different types of synthesizing activities.

The content of the culture-concept cannot be separated from the basic forms and directions of significant (*geistigen*) production; their 'being' is understandable only as a 'doing.' It is only because there is a specific direction of our aesthetic imagination and intuition that we have a realm of aesthetic objects—and the same goes for all our other energies by virtue of which there is built up for us the structure of a specific domain of objectivity.[73]

An analysis of culture could, correspondingly, proceed along both "material" and "formal" lines. It could either undertake a descriptive classification of the products of the various cultural activities, or it could seek "behind" this great diversity of manifestations the characteristic types of intuiting, imagining, and conceiving, i.e., the "doings," in terms of which the "works" become intelligible. It is only in focussing on the "doings" that, according to Cassirer, we may hope to find a common denominator. "We seek not a unity of *effects*, but a unity of *action*; not a unity of products, but a unity of the creative process."[74] But this "unity of the creative process"—as is obvious by now—can be nothing else than the unity and universality of the symbolic function, expressed in the symbol-concept.

The "culture-concept" must, accordingly, eclipse the "nature-concept" which, in *Substance and Function*, still stands for the regulative idea of "lawfulness" *per se*. It does so by reason of the circumstance that, whatever the "nature-concept" connotes at various historical periods, it is intelligible only as a function of what the cultural media of art, religion, and science take it to mean. Whereas "culture" creates, in an uninterrupted flow, ever new linguistic, artistic, religious, and scientific symbols, both "philosophy and science must break up these symbolic languages into their elements. . . . (We must learn) to interpret symbols in order to decipher the meaning-content they

[73] *PSF*, Vol. I, 11.
[74] *Essay on Man*, 70.

enclose, to make visible again the life from which they originally came forth."[75]

Measured against this considerable task, what we have in
the three volumes of the *Philosophie der symbolischen Formen*
can hardly be expected to provide a full answer. Doubtless, a
more detailed examination of the various cultural phenomena
than offered so far would be required to make good the implied
promise. Cassirer himself was aware of the tentative character of his attempts in what he thought was the right direction.

The 'Philosophy of Symbolic Forms' cannot and does not try to be a
philosophical system in the traditional sense of this word. All it attempted
to furnish were the 'Prolegomena' to a future philosophy of culture.
. . . Only from a continued collaboration between philosophy and the
special disciplines of the 'Humanities' (*Geisteswissenschaften*) may one
hope for a solution of this task.[76]

CARL H. HAMBURG

TULANE UNIVERSITY

[75] *Logik der Kulturwissenschaften,* 94f.
[76] *Theoria* (1938), 173.

2

William Curtis Swabey

CASSIRER AND METAPHYSICS

2

CASSIRER AND METAPHYSICS

ERNST CASSIRER is known to students of epistemology and metaphysics as a learned, lucid, and skillful representative of the neo-Kantian or "critical idealistic" point of view; no one can deny the competence with which he reviews "the problem of knowledge in the science and philosophy of the modern age," expounding, quoting, and criticizing innumerable authors, himself always firmly anchored in the critical idealism of the Marburg School. In what follows I undertake, with all becoming diffidence, to make explicit certain difficulties which I find, not so much in Cassirer's writings as such, but in the point of view of idealism itself. The learned material which Cassirer presents, the information concerning mathematics and physics from Galileo and Cusanus down to Einstein and the quantum theory, is after all susceptible of more than one interpretation; just as scripture supports various systems of theology, so science does not oblige a philosopher to embrace either idealism or realism. Cassirer's assemblage of historical material, which he so eloquently and persuasively interprets in the light of Kantianism, could be interpreted in the light of realism, were there a sufficiently learned and skillful realistic philosopher who was willing to undertake the task. Naturally, in such a wide-spread application of the historico-critical method, Cassirer has had to leave behind most of the scholastic architectonic, which Kant offered to the world as never to be changed; the modern disciple merely retains a "point of view," which is, as a matter of fact, extremely difficult to reduce to a few definite assertions. The Kantian "thing-in-itself" has disappeared and with it that vestige of realism, which was always in the back of Kant's mind: the *a priori* has become fluid and indefinite. The old opposition to metaphysics, on the one hand, and to empiricism, on the other, remains. Emphasis is placed on relations, especially upon those involved in serial order.

The comments which follow will be made in the name of metaphysics. By metaphysics I understand a theory of being in general, a science which would deal with the fundamental types of being and reality. It would take its stand on the inescapable ontological claims of all our thought and speech. I do not, however, understand by metaphysics a discipline which would deal primarily with those problems which Kant dealt with under the caption Transcendental Dialectic; it may be true that a degree of agnosticism is indeed the proper attitude with regard to the dogmas of the metaphysics of religion; metaphysics, as I understand it, is not to be understood as primarily the science of the meta-empirical (and consequently the unverifiable), but rather as that science which clarifies the fundamental ontological claims of our thought. It is my opinion that metaphysics, in this sense, is led to a standpoint of dualistic realism, a standpoint which is perhaps not final, but which is at any rate the only natural way of thinking. The dualism of Descartes and Locke, although encumbered with many dubious assertions in each case, still seems to me the philosophy which is most clearly suggested by our common ways of talking; it is perhaps in the end the only intelligible system, or, if it too conceals some insoluble problems, it is the least unintelligible system. By dualistic realism I mean a system which posits a world of bodies and minds in continual interaction. Bodies are self-existent entities with spatial attributes; minds are non-spatial beings which continually interact with bodies and furthermore know them both by perception and in other more elaborate and indirect ways. Dualistic realism seems to the idealist utterly unworthy of philosophy; for him, it is commonplace, if not downright vulgar; he would prefer to leave behind mere things and delve into the mysteries of symbolism and the super-sensuous regions. The realist, although sharing to some extent the aspirations of the idealist, nevertheless puts common sense clarity and intelligibility first, in his list of philosophic values, and views mathematics as a dubious guide with regard to problems of being and real existence. The idealist of the type of Cassirer does not regard natural science as concerned with a self-existent nature. On the contrary, nature is the product of a synthesis of sensations and the history of science is a process in which thought perpetually re-creates its object.

The attitude of the criticist is one of reflection; he deals not with things, but with thought about things; he lives in a world of second intentions. Thus, such a philosopher as Cassirer does not offer us a theory of bodies and minds, or of universals, essences, relations and individuals in general; he speaks rather as a scholar writing in a well-stocked library; nature is for him something known only indirectly, primarily through the books of scientists; it is an object postulated and described by a series of authorities. Ultimately it exists only in their minds; it undergoes, in the advance of science, modifications making for greater extensiveness and unity. Cassirer, it is true, has come to recognize points of view other than that of science; namely, the standpoints of language and myth. Nevertheless the world exists, for the critical idealist, primarily as an object of consciousness. In the end, I presume, it will be found to exist only in the minds of historians; they, in turn, will exist only in each other's minds. Being is everlastingly dependent upon being known. My thesis is that the attitude of critical idealism cannot consistently be maintained; thought always claims to know an independent reality (or at least being); and a consistent philosophy can only be reached by following out the ontological claims of our unsophisticated thinking.

The sub-title of Cassirer's *Substanzbegriff und Funktionsbegriff* is: *Untersuchungen über die Grundfragen der Erkenntniskritik.* The phrase *Erkenntniskritik*, or "critique of knowledge," is worthy of our attention. How can knowledge be criticized? If knowledge is knowledge it knows its objects as they are. The knowledge which can be destroyed by criticism is not true knowledge; it is mere seeming knowledge and nothing can replace such false knowledge save true knowledge. Critique of knowledge must mean a criticism of certain sciences as they actually exist, in which it is shown that they use convenient fictions and are thus not literally true. Still this is a criticism of historically existing sciences and not of knowledge as such. How can one criticize the sciences without in some way *knowing?* One would, otherwise, have no way of being aware of the shortcomings of the disciplines he was attempting to criticize.

It is characteristic of the critical standpoint which Cassirer consistently occupies that metaphysics is regarded as obsolete. As Cassirer uses the word, metaphysics is merely a name for certain bad habits of thought inherited from a crude and unenlightened past. In this Cassirer is in agreement with the pragmatists and positivists. But philosophers are not to be left without any employment at all; they may study "critique of knowledge." They may pore over the treatises of mathematicians and physicists and note the methods used and the fundamental trends. Yet it cannot be said that Cassirer, in the chapters he has devoted to mathematics, physics, and chemistry, writes merely as an historian of science. An account of these sciences, taken merely as offered in the works of scientists, would generally be in realistic terms; such an account, made into philosophy, would be what is called materialism or mechanism. But Cassirer is an idealist; he thinks of the sciences as dealing with "experience." What a strange object is experience! It is neither a body nor a set of bodies, neither a mind nor a set of minds. From the standpoint of dualism experience is the result of the interaction of mind and body; our bodies are affected by external things in various ways and our brains, parts of our bodies, affect, according to certain laws of psychophysical correspondence, our minds; the result is what we call experience. Experience is not as such the object of knowledge; it is better to say that we know material things and minds (including our own) by means of experience. To make "experience" the all-inclusive object is itself a form of metaphysics; it inescapably commits us to idealism. Or, if we suppose that the intention is merely to deny the ontological validity which science naturally claims for its assertions, still such denial implies that philosophy possesses, at least in general terms, a knowledge of what is, of being. The traditional name of the branch of philosophy which deals with the fundamental types of being is metaphysics. My contention is that every philosophy, even that sort which makes a point of repudiating metaphysics, involves some theory, however obscure, of the nature of being as such. The criticist himself deals with metaphysical problems, but in an indirect and inconsistent fashion.

If we start from the world as given to us in daily life and common language, we easily distinguish between bodies and minds. We find a world of bodies characterized by size, shape, and state of motion or rest, having a continuous existence in contrast to the coming and going of our perception, and displaying regularity of behavior. But there are also minds which have sensations, thoughts, and feelings; by means of these sensations and thoughts we somehow know bodies and are in continual interaction with them; now it is true that, if we regard knowledge as a matter of being affected from without, we are likely to conclude that we know only our own sensations. But the causal theory of sensation itself presupposes knowledge of an external world. This world, by acting upon our organisms, engenders an awareness of sense-qualities. The idealist abandons the external material world on the basis of facts drawn from that world itself; the realist feels that the path of true philosophy consists in following the fundamental ontological assumptions. As an historian, Cassirer postulates a common sense world in which such persons as Leibniz, Newton and Kant really existed as psycho-physical beings. And yet, like Kant, Cassirer is an idealist. Locke had laid the foundations of a dualistic outlook; but, by thinking of the immediate object or idea as "in the mind," he prepared the way for Berkeley, Hume, and Kant. The world of bodies lost its absoluteness and substantiality. Physical nature came to be replaced by experience taken substantively. But what definite conception can we form of experience? We know that neither Kant nor his modern disciple would plead guilty to any simple form of Berkeleyanism (such as that recently outlined by Professor

Stace),[1] which would reduce the world to spirits and their sense-data, following one another according to inexplicable laws.

Cassirer's discussions of logic, mathematics, physics, and chemistry, emphasize the importance of judgment in discovering relations. In general he is antagonistic to any purely empirical account of mathematical or scientific conceptions. The great object of science is relations, especially those giving rise to serial orders. Relations, he holds, are not given to the senses, but are evidence of the comparative and postulational activity of the mind. But it is precisely here that difficulties appear. Kant sharply distinguishes between what "comes in from without" and the mind's own contribution. From the standpoint of realism, however, it is obvious that the mind cannot produce relations between things which are not already related; thus, if two things are correctly judged to be similar or different, it must be because they are already similar or different, etc. Kant thought of the mind as "receiving" the "raw material of sense" from "outside;" but this is all built upon a dubious metaphor. Let me indicate how, as I suppose, the matter would stand from the standpoint of psycho-physical dualism. We postulate a brain as well as a mind; the latter is really merely a series of thoughts. When the brain is stimulated in certain ways sensa appear or occur; they occur, however, in relation to other sensa which are either actually present or belong to the recent or remote past; we experience sensa as simultaneous or successive, similar or different. When the brain is stimulated probably a considerable area is affected; old "traces" and habits are reactivated and the mind finds itself perceiving a real thing in a world of material things. In all this there is no more occasion to think of relations as creatures of pure consciousness or of a transcendental mind than there is to think of the sensa themselves in such a way. What we know is merely that perception of things occurs; the categorial interpretation as well as the data are the psychic accompaniments of brain-processes. Thus the brain or the laws of psycho-physical correspondence may take the place of the transcendental ego and its supernatural spontaneity. But, at the same time, we must maintain

[1] Stace, W. T., *The Nature of the World* (Princeton University Press, 1940).

also our essential doctrine that such perception, even though occurring under such psycho-physical laws, is still perception, a revelation of what is.[2] A psychological theory, whether it comes under such transcendental psychology as Kant gives us or such physiological psychology as has just been suggested, nevertheless merely tells us under what conditions we come to know a part of the real world. But the idealist thinks of "synthetic activity" as creating a second world within the mind, which in turn soon becomes the one real world.

In the first chapter of *Substance and Function* Cassirer reviews the theories of ancient and modern logicians concerning the concept; the general trend of his discussion may be described by saying that he finds the traditional class-concept to be in process of being supplanted by a new form of concept, which is that of serial order. Modern mathematical science no longer views nature as made up of *things* or substances; it is primarily concerned with relations, and these relations give rise to series of points, numbers, instants, etc. Hence Cassirer holds that the form of the concept which is fruitful for modern mathematical science is no longer the generic concept which merely expresses what a number of pre-existent entities have in common, but rather the "principle of serial order," which, once assumed, "generates" the individuals which conform to it. Against this view, I would suggest the following objections. Cassirer is mistaken if he imagines that such "principles" can ever take the place of class-concepts. For a serial order presupposes a group of entities which are ordered, whether real or unreal, such as points, numbers, colors, temperatures, etc. We can only refer to these elements by means of concepts in the traditional sense. Furthermore, a principle of serial order is not a concept at all; it is a proposition. Thus, of a row of soldiers, I may be able to say that each man is taller than the one before him. This is a mere description of given individuals, but it is expressed in a proposition. In mathematics I may grandly postulate a series of unreal entities, such that each one is related to the preceding one in a certain way; still here too

[2] *Cf.* Sellars, R. W., *The Philosophy of Physical Realism* (New York, Macmillan, 1932), 70.

the principle of serial order is not what is commonly called a concept. Or, consider such relations as similarity, equality, greater than, etc. How are relations in any sense rivals of class-concepts? Relations are relations, concepts are concepts, but of course there are concepts of relations and relations of concepts. Here I shall venture a definition. Concepts are universals connected with words as their meanings; universals are potentially recurrent features of either real or unreal entities. They are capable of appearing more than once (*cf.* blue, square, *etc.*), while individuals are unique beings which occur once and once only. Individual things may be unreal, e.g., points, instants, geometrically perfect bodies, etc.; but all such things have, with reference to concepts, what is called their essence, which consists of those properties which entitle them to belong to a given class. Thus an individual man may be considered merely as a man and must have those properties which warrant us in so considering him. These properties are said to constitute the essence of man. The concept of man has these properties as its connotation. When we take these points into account, it becomes highly doubtful whether there is any justification for replacing the class-concept by a "principle of serial order."

Everything to which we can refer has its concept, points, instants, numbers, relations, as well as the types of plant and animal. Thus, if we speak of circles or triangles or of numbers, of variables, or of series, we do so by means of words, which have the traditional type of class-concept as their meanings. It is true that all members of a class are similar to each other in certain respects; nevertheless similarity alone does not define a class (since the members of *all* classes are similar to other members of their respective classes) unless we tell wherein the members are similar, and this can be done only by mentioning the feature that all the members of the class have in common. This common element may be either determinate or determinable. Thus color is a determinable feature and can occur in actuality only when rendered perfectly specific, namely, as this nuance of this particular color. When the common element is determinable it demands supplementation; nevertheless, we cannot deny that all the things named by a generic term have something in common; this is a universal and may belong to the essence of those individuals. This doctrine, however, implies nothing which would minimize the importance of relations. Still, it is true that the relations of a thing do not make it what it is, that is, do not belong to its essence. Thus a lamp or a shoe is what it is by virtue of its definitive properties, without regard to when or where it is, by whom manufactured or to what use it is put. It should be remarked, however, that nothing has an essence save with reference to some defining concept. Thus, if a lamp is no longer regarded as a lamp but as a piece of metal it is said to have a different essence. Furthermore, nothing can lose its essence without being annihilated; if the lamp is thrown into a furnace and melted, it ceases to exist as a lamp. The properties of water as water do not change when water is frozen or vaporized or made to stand upright in a glass tumbler; its nature includes the facts that it will evaporate when heated, solidify when chilled, stand upright when enclosed in a glass, etc. Thus the essence of a substance is not affected by its relations to other things; if we consider water solely as a liquid, then we know from experience that it continues to exist as a liquid only as long as a certain range of temperatures persists; if these temperatures pass beyond certain limits, liquid water is annihilated. Thus, whether a thing exists or not depends on its relations, but its essence is not so dependent. There is, therefore, a good meaning in the old doctrine that relations are all extra-essential, the only exceptions being found in those cases in which things are named by the relations in which they stand; husband, captain, servant, etc. The chief point which I wish to make is that the logic of the concept and essence applies to all things, including points, instants, numbers, propositions, and relations; it can by no means be replaced by "functional relations" or "principles of serial order." Thus, beings may stand in serial relations, but they must have their essence prior to and apart from their relations; this is because we are dealing, in our statements about essence, merely with entities as such. Numbers, points, instants and the rest must be entities before they can stand in relations to each other.

Cassirer is in general an advocate of a "logical" theory of number; but he rejects the emphasis upon the correspondence of classes characteristic of Frege and Russell. His fundamental aim is to vindicate the priority of serial order as a basis for mathematical science. His theory is therefore the opposite of that which defines number in terms of equivalent classes. Two groups are said, according to Russell, "to belong to the same number" when there is a relation of possible co-ordination between the members of the two groups. Cassirer's opinion that the definition of number as a class of classes by no means corresponds to the meanings of the names of numbers in daily life seems to be sound. "The 'how many' of the elements, in the ordinary sense, can be changed by no logical transformation into a bare assertion concerning 'just as many'."[3] Cassirer himself advocates an ordinal theory of numbers according to which "the individual number never means anything by itself alone" and "a fixed value is only ascribed to it by its position in a total system."[4] According to the "cardinal" theory, to which Cassirer is opposed, "the members (of the number series) are determined as the common properties of certain classes before anything whatever has been established as to their relation of sequence. Yet in truth it is precisely in the element here at first excluded that the peculiar numerical character is rooted."[5] This is Cassirer's statement of his view. The philosophy of number is a matter concerning which a non-mathematician may well be cautious. Perhaps I shall not be wrong, if I call attention to a principle which is rather generally accepted, namely, that we gain insight into the meaning of even the most general propositions only by analysis of particular illustrative cases. In application to the problem of number it is difficult to see how mathematicians or anyone else can understand anything whatever save with reference to relations which are actually given in sensuous experience. I can well believe that

[3] Cassirer, Ernst, *Substance and Function*, (Swabey tr., Open Court Publishing Company, Chicago, 1923), 48. Since most of my quotations from Cassirer's writings will be from this particular volume, I shall hereafter abbreviate it: *SF*.

[4] *Ibid.*

[5] *Ibid.*

in the case of ordinary calculation blind symbol-manipulation takes the place of "intuitive" understanding, and there is no reason why it should not; mathematics is, on the whole, a technique for dealing with relations far too complex for us to understand. Nevertheless, the basis of mathematics must be in the relation of small numbers which can easily be grasped. The relations of small numbers may be illustrated by sense-data and those of the larger numbers understood by analogy with the smaller ones. Taking its start from simple sensuous experiences the mind conceives and postulates an infinite system of numbers; number is given to sensuous experience as the form-quality of a group of entities. Three-ness is a quality of each and every group of three, etc. Now it is true that numbers form a series, a series stretching to infinity. My point, with regard to Cassirer's theory of number, is that the "principle" or "form" of the series cannot be understood save by reference to its individual members, which must be given before "the principle of the series" can be understood. If we say that a given number can only be understood in its relations to all other numbers, it follows that no number can be understood; for the series of numbers can never be given as a whole. If, therefore, to understand "3" it were necessary to understand all the numbers, the task would be an impossible one. But knowing what 1, 2, and 3, etc., are, as patterns or form-qualities, with reference to small groups, we see that they are capable of being arranged in a series such that each number is equal to the preceding number plus one. But, if I did not know what numbers were and had no notions of addition, equality, etc., I could form no idea of such a series or its principles. The elementary number-equations seem to be related to a fact of experience, namely, that the same group can always be taken in different ways. Thus six apples can be taken by the mind as one group, or, in various ways, as two or three groups: the fact that these transformations are always possible is so easily verified that it is natural to suppose that the laws of arithmetic are *a priori*. They may, however, be regarded as well-established generalizations based on easy and oft-repeated mental experiments.

It is quite true that such numbers as zero, fractions, and those which are labelled negative, irrational, and imaginary are not "funded qualities" of given groups; they require a more involved derivation. Fundamentally, however, the point must be insisted upon that these are not numbers in the original sense of the word; they are rather fictions or quasi-numbers, which could never be understood did we not have definite concepts of the small integers. ½ represents a division which cannot be carried out; the symbol is meaningful only because we are ready to substitute for the abstract concept of pure unity the concept of distance or area or material object. In the same way, to understand −2 we go beyond the notion of number to that of a series having direction. According to Dedekind, irrational numbers are "cuts," or divisions in the number-series. "The 'cuts' may be said to be numbers," says Cassirer, "since they form among themselves a strictly ordered manifold in which the relative position of the elements is determined according to a conceptual rule."[6] But there is here a point which calls for comment. Words may change their meanings, but meanings themselves do not change. A new concept of number is only a new meaning attached to an old word. The point I would make is that, whereas irrational numbers may be in some sense as good as other numbers, i.e., they may conform to certain laws, still they are not numbers in the original sense of the word. Unless we start with what Frege scornfully referred to as "pebbles and gingerbread nuts," i.e., with that conception of number, of "how many," which the child applies to his fingers and toes, we cannot understand the new extended sense of the word in which $\sqrt{2}$ may be said to be a number. The technical kinds of number are not numbers in the primary sense of the word, and they can only be defined in terms of experience in roundabout ways, as, for example, imaginary completions of processes, which cannot in fact be completed. A number is a quality of a finite group; an infinite number is, on the face of it, something inconceivable, or even self-contradictory. Cassirer would say that we grasp an infinite series when we know the law by which it is generated. I would say,

[6] *SF*, 61.

however, that we know that law only in terms of the relations of small whole numbers; these relations seem to me to be simply given in the same elementary way in which the sense-qualities are given; there seems no point in speaking, as Kant did, of a dual origination of sense-qualities "coming in from the outside" and relations having the more noble characteristic of having been generated in the mind. From the standpoint of physiological psychology, both qualities and relations originate within the mind on the occasion of the activation of the brain; from the standpoint of realistic epistemology, relations hold between material things, whether or not these relations are known by any mind.

A question of prime importance for the understanding of Cassirer's position is concerned with the meaning to be attached to the phrase *a priori*. I presume that the meaning which most philosophers would give to the term would be simply the *intuitively certain*. Thus the multiplication table and the axioms of Euclid are commonly regarded as at least legitimate examples of what was formerly regarded as *a priori*. The *a priori* in this sense cannot change; it is capable of becoming intuitively certain to all who understand the meaning of the propositions. Man may be mistaken as to what is self-evident; but the rule holds that "once self-evident, always self-evident." If a principle is at a later time discovered not to be self-evident, this implies that the earlier thinkers were mistaken in regarding the principle as self-evident. Thus, if the "axioms" of geometry are not, in the light of modern thought, self-evident, they were not so in the days of Kant, either, although he falsely thought that they were. The *a priori* then admits of no variation. Kant claimed this sort of truth not only for the axioms of Euclidean geometry but for his whole transcendental system as well. Modern mathematical science, however, no longer recognizes the unique authority of Euclidean geometry; it recognizes other systems which it offers impartially to physics; this science chooses, for certain purposes, a non-Euclidean system; indeed, no one has given a more lucid account of this whole development than Cassirer himself in his essay, *Einstein's Theory of Relativity*. How, then, can one still defend the *a priori*? The answer is, only by changing the meaning of the term and ascribing this new meaning to Kant as his "deeper meaning." And if this is done it becomes a real question whether rationalism differs significantly from empiricism. Cassirer emphasizes the "active," "synthetic," and "relating" functions of the mind as opposed to the passive receptivity of sense-perception. The mind exercises its intellectual functions and in this consists its *a priori* character. Yet it may be questioned whether this doctrine has a clear meaning. The mind can only distinguish that which is already different; it can rightly regard as similar only that which is already similar, etc. If we assume, as dualistic realism does, a world of independently existent things, these things must have numerical, spatial, and causal relations. The mind cannot create these relations. Or, if we retreat to a Berkeleyan world of bodiless spirits, there will still be relations of one sort or another between these spirits. Our minds are active in shifting their attention from one object to another and, furthermore, in speaking and in writing; using words, we "create worlds," "weave relations," "split asunder," and "recombine what we have separated," etc. In the use of words, therefore, we are no doubt creative; but it is difficult to see how our "judgmental activity" can actually either affect or create things or relations.

However, let us return to the subject of space. Cassirer, in *Substance and Function,* quotes with approval the view of Wellstein that Kant's intuitive theory of mathematics was a "residuum of sensualism still attached to the Kantian idealism."[7] The new mathematics, Cassirer believes, brings out the logical rather than the empirical character of pure mathematics. Now this opinion seems to be widespread if not universal among students of modern mathematics. We may sum up the matter by saying that, in so far as mathematics is a logically necessary system of deductions, it is certain but not true; in so far as it is true, it is not certain *a priori*. It was only Kant's extraordinary invention of an *a priori sensibility* which was compatible with the supposed character of Euclidean geometry, namely, that it was both *a priori* and true of real things. It is interesting to recall

[7] *SF,* 106.

here the view of geometry which Hume propounds in his *Treatise of Human Nature*. He tells us that in geometry "we ought not to look for the utmost precision and exactness. None of its proofs extend so far. It takes the dimensions and proportions of figures justly; but roughly, and with some liberty."[8] For Hume the only possible criteria of existential truth were sense-data, and sense-data are often compatible with several geometrical propositions. Modern geometry may well be, as Cassirer says, a purely logical system dealing with postulated relations in an abstract manifold; this, however, is not the elementary geometry of the older thinkers; with regard to *that* (elementary) system events seem to have shown that Hume, who was no great admirer of mathematics, was more nearly correct than Kant, who earnestly sought to eternalize the mathematical science of his time by giving it a transcendental foundation.

Metaphysics deals with problems of an entirely different order. It deals with the nature of being and of real existence, if the two are to be distinguished, with the difference between mind and matter, universal and individual, etc., but without taking anything from the special sciences. But for Cassirer metaphysics is merely a name for certain unfortunate intellectual tendencies, which disappear in the light of critical philosophy. Let us see what he has to say in the chapter entitled "The Problem of Reality" in *Substance and Function*. The fundamental vice of metaphysics is, in general, that it sets up, as an opposition of things *(Widerstreit der Dinge)* what in the process of knowledge is an inseparable unity of conditions. Thus persistence and change, unity and plurality, thought and being are falsely opposed to each other in the metaphysical approach.[9] "If once things and the mind become conceptually separated they fall into separate spatial spheres, into an inner and an outer world, between which there is no intelligible causal connection." (271) But this is a very cavalier way of speaking. It refers to metaphysics in a broad condemnatory way without distinguish-

---

[8] Hume, *Treatise of Human Nature*, Book I, Part 2, Section 4. (Selby-Bigge ed., p. 45).

[9] *SF*, 237.

ing the actual doctrines held by metaphysicians. It is not clear that metaphysicians must fall into the fallacies named. Mind and body may be entirely distinct from each other in essence and yet in constant interaction. If mind is essentially non-spatial, it cannot be spatially separated from bodies, since only what is in space can be spatially remote from anything else. Furthermore, the essential distinction of mind and body does not imply that mind cannot know body.

If we consult immediate experience, which is free from re-flection, says Cassirer, we find that it is wholly without the distinction between the objective and the subjective. (272) For such experience there is only one level of being which con-tains all content within itself. The intellectual experiment which Cassirer proposes is a difficult one; just what are we to subtract to reach "immediate experience?" Still, without chal-lenging the proposition laid down, we may point out that most of us are familiar with two distinctions, namely, that between the objective and the subjective and that between the mental and the physical. Thus, another person's mind is objective, in the sense of really existent, although wholly mental in charac-ter. The same is true of our own minds. On the other hand, an hallucinatory dragon may be physical in nature and yet unreal, which is, I suppose, what Cassirer means by subjective. Even if we grant that the supposed "immediate experience" does not contain the opposition between the subjective and the objective, it might contain the opposition between the mental and the physical. If we were conscious of any distinctions at all (and otherwise how could we be conscious or how could there be experience?) we might note the difference between sense-data and the thought which plays over them and calls, as Cassirer says, some of them subjective and others objective. In fact, if our words referring to the mind have a *bona fide* meaning, there must be an immediate experience by the mind of the mind itself, an original form of self-knowledge, an awareness of awareness. At a later stage, our primitive awareness of sense-data becomes a perception of things and our awareness of the activity of thought becomes an explicit knowledge of the mind by itself.

But let us return to the contemplation of the one plane of immediate experience; at this stage all seems objective, and hence there is no occasion for the "false metaphysical problem" as to how we pass from the subjective to the objective. But, says Cassirer, at the first appearance of reflection a division sets in, according to which, data are not simply accepted but are distinguished in their value. Unique and fleeting observations, he says, are forced into the background while typical experiences which recur under similar conditions are emphasized. Cassirer is here attempting a hypothetical reconstruction of the process by which our belief in an external world arises. The mind sorts out its impressions and there emerges a consciousness of objective things.

Along with the loose associative connections of perceptions united only under particular circumstances (as, for example, under definite physiological conditions) there are found fixed connections, which are valid for a whole field of objects and belong to this field independently of the differences given in the particular place and time of observation. We find connections which hold their ground through all further experimental testing and through apparently contrary instances and remain steadfast in the flux of experience while others dissolve and perish. It is the former that we call "objective" in a pregnant sense, while we designate the latter by the term "subjective."[10]

Now none can doubt that in the pursuit of empirical knowledge, it is important to separate trivial and accidental connections from those which are universal and are said to be "essential" and "necessary." But how is this connected with the distinction between the subjective and the objective? It is a fact, let us say, that on Friday the 13th I lost my purse, and it is also a fact that water is essential to life. The first is no more subjective than the second. If, however, I permitted myself to generalize from the former occurrence, I would propound a false superstitious law of bad luck. Such a generalization would indeed be false and would be founded on inadequate observation. A law of this type might be called "subjective;" but the occurrences which cause some men to accept it as true are as

[10] *SF*, 273.

objective as any other occurrences. It seems that Cassirer is seeking to reduce the distinction between the subjective and the objective to that between particular events and universal laws. But the former are as objective as the latter. He says:

We finally call objective, those elements of experience which persist through all change in the here and now and on which rests the unchangeable character of experience, while we ascribe to the sphere of subjectivity all that belongs to this change itself and that only expresses a determination of the particular unique here and now.[11]

But this sentence is obscure, particularly with reference to the phrase "elements of experience;" it might mean that colors, sounds, tactile qualities, and the like are objective, for they are recurrent elements in all experience; we gather from the context, however, that this would be far from what he means. He has in mind *laws* or *connections*, but laws or connections are merely propositions supposed to be true descriptions of the way in which events occur; and what occurs universally is no more objective (really existent) than what occurs once and once only.

However, perhaps we can make clear what Cassirer means if we refer to the classic instance of the wine which was sweet to Socrates when well, but bitter to Socrates when ill. Should we say that the wine is objectively sweet because it is normally tasted as sweet by Socrates and others; while it is tasted as bitter only by Socrates when he is ill? This would be a way of permitting the feelings of the majority to function as the criterion of objectivity; although this is an attractive and popular answer to the question, it seems scarcely well founded; unless, perchance, we choose to define objectivity with reference to the majority. There is another way of dealing with this problem which commences by asking us to define our terms. Let us say that those features of bodies are objective which belong to them without reference to observers. Sweetness is merely an effect produced by bodies acting on our psycho-physical organisms and belongs to the wine no more than does the bitterness, save in the sense that the wine has the power to produce a certain sensation in the minds of most people. It is merely *con-*

---

[11] *SF*, 273.

venient to name the wine according to the more common response. But this convenience does not constitute objectivity in the sense of real existence, apart from all onlookers.

Cassirer himself goes on to mention the Democritean distinction between the primary and secondary qualities of bodies. For him it is an illustration of the "transformation of objectivity into subjectivity." "The seen color, the heard tone, remains something 'real;' only this reality does not subsist in isolation and for itself, but results from the interaction of the physical stimulus and the appropriate organ of sensation."[12] Similar considerations apply to the illusions of the senses. The distinction between the subjective and the objective is thus, for Cassirer, not a fixed line of demarcation but a moving and relative barrier, such that the same content of experience can be called subjective and objective, according as it is conceived relative to different logical frames of reference.

Sensuous perception, as opposed to the hallucination and the dream, signifies the real type of the objective; while measured by the schema of exact physics, sense perception can become a phenomenon that no longer expresses an independent property of things but only a subjective condition of the observer.[13]

Such a view commits us to a boundless relativism in which no definite distinction can be drawn between the mental and the physical. The mental is identified with the subjective and unreal. *Erkenntniskritik* thus seems to involve an attitude of intellectual nihilism, in which both mind and nature disappear in a bottomless abyss of relativity.

The standpoint of dualistic realism, on the other hand, even if not capable of proof, is not self-refuting. At an early stage men, and probably animals too, become conscious of the thing-world of which they themselves are parts; they find themselves continually interacting with these things. When we consider the way in which sensations originate it becomes probable that colors and tones belong to external things only in the sense that they are produced by them. The seen color may be considered either

[12] *SF*, 274.
[13] *SF*, 275.

as a predicate of external things or in its own right; when taken in its own right, it becomes what some call a sense-datum and others as essence. In any case, the seen color is not mental in the sense of belonging to the inner essence of mind as consciousness or knower; on the other hand, it does not belong to nature as an interacting system of bodies. Taken merely as objects by themselves colors, sounds, odors, and the like belong to the non-existent, to the realm of *being,* which is so much broader than the realm of existence. Thus the change which took place with regard to the secondary qualities need not be described as one in which what was previously thought to be physical comes to be thought of as mental; it may be described as a change in which what was previously thought to be an intrinsic property comes to be regarded as a mere relative predicate.

Cassirer's approach to the problem of knowledge is that of a reflective historian of philosophy and science; he thus seems to avoid any definite metaphysical position of his own; nevertheless, it seems fair to say that a definite ontological platform is involved in so far as we may speak of Cassirer as an idealist. This position is one of phenomenalism. The things which we postulate in daily life are posited to explain, as Hume put it, the constancy and coherence of our perceptions. The senses alone do not show us a world of nature, but our minds have a natural tendency to postulate as much uniformity as they can; sense-perception gives us a fragmentary, incomplete order which we make perfect by the assumption that things exist before and after our actual perceptions. Science carries the process further. The "things" which it posits are "metaphorical expressions of permanent connections of phenomena according to law and thus expressions of the constancy and continuity of experience itself."[14] In comment upon this position, which Cassirer maintains in agreement with the views of Hume and Kant, it may be remarked that an account of how we come by a belief need not involve the notion that that belief is itself false. To explain, as John Stuart Mill did, the origin of our belief in an external world does not imply that no external world exists. In fact, we may say that such an explanation starts with an assumption of the validity of that belief in so far as there is talk

[14] *SF,* 276.

of "sensations" or "perceptions" which are *intermittent*, a notion which is significant only in contrast to continuously existent things. Does the mind "construct" things? Why should we not say that, on the occasion of the occurrence of sensations, the mind comes to *know* of things as continuously existent entities which interact with each other and with the mind itself?

But let us seek to discover the proper formulation of Cassirer's idealism. Metaphysical realism, he says, postulates an absolute gap between the immanent and the transcendent, and declares that there is no logical inference by which we can pass from the former to the latter. The realist, he says, finds it necessary to leap the gap by insisting on the transcendent reference of knowledge. Cassirer denies, however, that such considerations invalidate his own form of critical idealism.

Critical idealism, [he writes,] is distinguished from the realism here advocated, not by denying the intellectual postulate at the basis of these deductions of the concept of objective being, but, conversely, by the fact that it grasps this intellectual postulate more sharply and demands it for every phase of knowledge, even the most primitive. Without logical principles which go beyond the content of given impressions there is as little a consciousness of the ego as there is a consciousness of the object. . . . No content can be known and experienced as "subjective" without being contrasted with another content which appears as objective.[15]

The essential thought here is that the subjective and the objective are correlative and that consciousness is not immediately given to itself as such. This doctrine is no doubt derived from the position taken by Kant in his "Refutation of Idealism" in the *Critique of Pure Reason*, namely, that knowledge of the subject is secondary and is dependent upon knowledge of the object "with regard to its determinations in time." But why cannot the realist welcome considerations of this sort? There is a directness of reference in the mind's knowledge of external things as well as in its knowledge of itself; no doubt the two forms of knowledge develop *pari passu* and cannot exist apart from each other. Still, if there is *knowledge* of things, those things must exist apart from knowledge and prior to it. In a

[15] *SF*, 295.

word, *being* must antedate *being known;* we cannot suppose that things known exist only in our knowledge of them; for, "creative knowledge" is not knowledge at all in the human sense of the word. The thought that being depends on being known brings us to most surprising results. For then the knower would also derive his being from being known either to himself or to another. It is impossible, however, for a thing to depend on itself, and not plausible to suppose that one knower derives his being from being known by another and so on *ad infinitum.* Surely in the end we must reach a type of being which is self-existent.

We have just seen that Cassirer holds that there is no consciousness of the ego nor of material things without "logical principles" which "go beyond the content of given impressions." However, this position seems open to question. A man may think of whatever he likes, gods, devils, angels, or atoms. There is, in such thinking, a certain directness; we contemplate our object, whatever it may be, without, however, necessarily affirming its existence. A man may, therefore, consider his own mind, which he does whenever he speaks of it. Where are the "logical principles" said to be involved? No doubt it is true that the self, however it may be defined, is not among given impressions or sense-data. Still, I can *mean* myself just as I can *mean* the table. All objects of thought are given as objects; although we are not thereby entitled to regard them as real. The real existence of the self is postulated to explain certain facts just as that of the table is postulated to explain certain others; no doubt this "explanation" does presuppose certain logical principles. Nevertheless, has Cassirer shown that the assertions of the "metaphysical realist," namely, that there are minds and that these minds know things external to themselves, are false?

"If we determine the object, not as an absolute substance beyond all knowledge, but as the object shaped in progressing experience, we find that there is no epistemological gap to be laboriously spanned by some authoritative decree of thought, by a 'trans-subjective command'."[16] Naturally the object is not

[16] *SF*, 297.

"beyond all knowledge," since by definition it is the *object of knowledge*. How can an object be "shaped in progressing experience?" Do scientists re-make the world? Does Cassirer mean to deny that the thing known is distinct from the knowing mind and existentially independent of that mind? Cassirer himself goes on to say:

This object may be called transcendent from the standpoint of a psychological individual; from the standpoint of logic and its supreme principles, nevertheless, it is to be characterized as purely "immanent." It remains strictly within the sphere which those principles determine and limit, especially the universal principles of mathematical and scientific knowledge. This simple thought alone constitutes the kernel of "critical idealism."[17]

Here then we have a statement offered as the essence of critical idealism and well worthy of our attention. Cassirer grants that the object is transcendent from the standpoint of the psychological individual. Does he mean that the object is not transcendent with reference to the "mind" taken in some other sense? Apparently he does, for he goes on to say that the object is immanent "from the standpoint of logic and its supreme principles." However, we may well ask whether there is anything to which logic does *not* apply. In asserting that the object is immanent in this sense, have we not a meaningless statement, since there is no transcendent realm with regard to which the immanent is a limited sphere? In a word, in so far as Cassirer's idealism merely asserts (if we may cite such laws as noncontradiction and excluded middle as "supreme principles of logic") that "what is" is self-consistent and determinate, we can hardly deny that the doctrine is not in conflict with dualistic realism. Such idealism would be merely a re-affirmation of logic and mathematics and not a recognizable epistemological assertion. If Cassirer's idealism contradicts realism at any point it must be because he regards the principles of logic and mathematics as inherent in the mind, just as Kant did. Cassirer goes on to assert "the objective validity of certain axioms and norms of scientific knowledge." "*Die Wahrheit des Gegenstands—dies allein ist die Meinung—hängt an der Wahrheit dieser Axiome und besitzt keinen anderen und festeren Grund.*"[18] But how can an object be true? An object is real or unreal; only a proposition is capable of truth. The fact that certain logical laws are universally presupposed in other propositions does not imply that being is dependent upon being known and is therefore not incompatible with dualistic realism. The assertion of the involvement of logical principles in more particular judgments implies a conflict with realism only if logical truths are supposed to represent the necessary thoughts of a universal consciousness; all things may then be said to be within this universal mind. But this universal mind seems to be merely a postulated correlative of universal truths. Cassirer says nothing about a universal mind, and thus seems to leave the conception of idealism indefinite. He does, however, conceive of the mind as perpetually engaged in a constructive activity. We are left with a protean "thought" which postulates, on the one hand, bodies, and on the other, selves. The thesis which we seek to defend in this criticism is that such "construction" is merely metaphorical. The mind may range through the realm of being, the world of thinkables, in an exploratory fashion, merely considering hypotheses; but, in all this it creates nothing; it merely discovers pre-existent possibilities. When it posits some one of these thinkable objects as really existent it likewise produces nothing; it merely makes an assertion which may be either true or false. But such idealism as that of Kant and Cassirer would lose much of its attractiveness were it deprived of the picturesque and poetic notion of mind, the supreme magician, endlessly producing and destroying worlds.

The concept of thing, according to Cassirer, is merely a supreme ordering concept of experience. At first we believe that we know things directly; but reflection destroys this naïve confidence. The impression of the object comes to be separated from the object itself, which becomes an unknowable and elusive thing-in-itself. But from the standpoint of critical idealism, Cassirer says, the concept of an object or thing is merely

---

[18] *Substanzbegriff und Funktionsbegriff* (original German edition, 1910), 395.

an instrument of knowledge; this amounts to saying that objects are merely fictions, useful in stating propositions regarded as true. Helmholtz took the position that "Each property or quality of a thing is in reality nothing but its capacity to produce certain effects on other things." On this Cassirer makes the following comment:

We do not grasp the relations of absolute things from their interaction, but we concentrate our knowledge of empirical connections into judgments, to which we ascribe objective validity. Therefore the relative properties do not signify in a negative sense that residuum of things that we are able to grasp, but they are the first and positive ground of the concept of reality.[19]

We see then that, for Cassirer, the great objects of knowledge are *relations*. Thing-concepts are merely means for stating relations. Now, undoubtedly this view is an attractive one; yet it contains certain difficulties. How can there be relations without *relata?* The weight of a body can perhaps be defined in terms of its power of influencing other bodies, and the sense-qualities are explained as mere powers, possessed by bodies, of producing sensations. Nevertheless, size, shape, and relative position cannot be taken from bodies without annihilating them. Relativism of this extreme sort constitutes a species of nihilism which forces us to admit that we can form no conception of the real whatsoever. Or, if we are left with *truths,* what are these truths *about?* If realism is to be defended, it must be because not all the properties of bodies are relative. Thus the numerical expression of size varies with the unit of measurement, but *size is what is measured;* it is not the result of measurement. So, too, although a body appears differently when viewed from different angles, we need not deny that bodies possess determinate shapes. The difficulty which I feel here is concerned with the question whether such a complete relativism can really be intelligibly stated. At any rate, Cassirer and other idealists must continue to use language which implies the existence of the world of material things. Who are the knowers who "use the thing-concept to organize their experiences?" Are they men?

[19] *SF*, 306.

And what is experience? From the standpoint of dualism, experience involves the interaction of minds and things; it is primarily a matter of minds being affected by things. Experience is itself not a *thing* made up of parts, and it is not the primary object of knowledge; "we" do not "deal with" experience, but rather we have experience of things and thus learn their ways. The making of an object out of experience is, of course, the irremovable mark of Kantian idealism.

The realist believes that physical things are more than mere ordering concepts. It is true that physical things, whether those dealt with by common sense or those postulated by physical science, are not "given to sense," if we are to understand thereby a wholly passive process. We must distinguish between sensing and perceiving; the latter involves the use of "thing-concepts." In postulating public and continuously existent things we necessarily go beyond the sensations of the moment. The very concept of really existent things, in contrast to things which are merely thinkable, implies at least some degree of lawfulness of behavior, in other words, some sort of interaction and causality. Cassirer seems to say the same thing but with a different emphasis; he seems to think that what we must postulate is a creation of our own minds, enjoying no absolute being. We may, however, appeal to the parallel case of the religious man who feels that he must postulate a God; he nevertheless postulates this God as an eternal and indestructible being. Must we not postulate nature as (very likely) an everlasting system of things in perpetual interaction: some of their interactions constitute the occasions for the occurrence of minds who know them and interact with them in various ways? But for Cassirer there is no self-existent nature of which we have real but imperfect knowledge; hypothesis replaces hypothesis, and "reality" is defined by the law of sequence, by which world-system overcomes world-system; for him, there is progress towards comprehensiveness and consistency, but no progressive revelation of a reality which is there, whether known or not.

WILLIAM CURTIS SWABEY

DEPARTMENT OF PHILOSOPHY
NEW YORK UNIVERSITY

3

I. K. Stephens

CASSIRER'S DOCTRINE OF THE *A PRIORI*

3

CASSIRER'S DOCTRINE OF THE *A PRIORI*

I

WHEN Locke cleared the philosophical stage of its "props" in the form of innate ideas, he offered, as a substitute for this particular traditional basis of certainty, our immediate perception of the agreement or disagreement of our ideas. Whatever ground this theory might have supplied as a basis for empirical certainty, however, was shattered by Hume when he called attention to the fact that "relations of ideas" differ in principle from "relations of matters of fact." He admitted that there are necessary relations between our ideas, but denied that there are any such relations between "matters of fact." Since, for Hume, knowledge must be based upon ideas, and certainty must be based upon necessary connections, the only field in which the mind can possibly attain certainty is in the field of the "relations of ideas." Since relations of matters of fact lack this character of necessity, our knowledge pertaining to this field of experience is deprived of all logical grounds for a claim to certainty.

The problem which Hume raises here is simply that concerning the objective validity of the conceptual order of the mind. If one desires to defend a claim to certainty in knowledge pertaining to "matters of fact," it is incumbent upon him to show how the mind can impose its concepts upon "matters of fact," upon the "given in experience," in such a manner as to guarantee that conceptual necessity will govern the given. He must show how the relation between the ideas of the mind and matters of fact can be so interpreted as to furnish a solid ground on the basis of which the necessity which admittedly holds for relations of ideas can be guaranteed to hold in the mind's conceptual dealings with matters of fact. This is essentially the problem of the *a priori;* and every significant doctrine of the *a priori* which has been formulated in philosophy since Hume raised the problem has been designed as a basis for its solution.

Now this bit of skeptical infection, which Hume injected into the thought stream of modern science and philosophy, first took effective hold in the mind of Kant. After a long period of intellectual insomnia and after many mental contortions and gyrations, Kant finally came out of the attack with a new Copernican Revolution in philosophy and with a brand-new conception of the *a priori,* which he regarded as a sound basis for the defense of the citadel of empirical certainty against Hume's skepticism. Subsequent developments in the fields of science, mathematics, and logic have, however, shaken the Kantian foundation and torn gaping holes in his defenses. As these defenses have disintegrated, under the bombardment of the guns of recent developments in science, mathematics, and logic, however, a long line of "successors to Kant" have appeared on the scene to render valiant service in attempts to secure the foundations and to repair the breaches, through some sort of modification, or reformulation, or regrounding of the Kantian *a priori.* It should be pointed out, however, that in spite of all these gallant efforts, Hume's denial of certainty in the realm of empirical knowledge still stands.

II

In that long line of "critical philosophers" who claim a philosophical lineage from Kant, possibly no one is more worthy of the distinction than is Cassirer. His penetrating and thorough analysis of Kant's system of philosophy, his precise understanding of just what Kant was attempting to do, and his profound and extensive knowledge of the recent developments in science, mathematics and logic, revealed to him many of the fundamental weaknesses in Kant's position; but, despite these facts, he still seems to me to find more of permanent value in Kant's system of philosophy than do most of those who claim to "stem from Kant." His doctrine of the *a priori,* however, is not simply

Kant's doctrine reformulated with its elaborate *architectonic* omitted; nor is it Kant's doctrine revised and brought up-to-date in the light of recent developments in science, mathematics, and logic. Kant's doctrine of the *a priori* and the ingenuity with which Kant applied it in his attempt to solve Hume's problem seem to be to Cassirer—as they have been to many other Kantians—a source of inspiration and a useful guide in the formulation of his own doctrine of the *a priori*. As he himself puts it, he sees in Kant "not an end, but an ever new and fruitful beginning for the criticism of knowledge."[1]

With Kant, and with most Kantians, Cassirer is in fundamental agreement on at least two points with respect to the *a priori;* (i) that the *a priori* is of the mind, and (ii) that all certainty is based on logical necessity and that logical necessity is grounded in the *a priori*. Also like Kant and most Kantians, Cassirer conceives the major task of philosophy to be the critical analysis of knowledge and the explication of the *a priori;* to the accomplishment of this task he devotes his entire ponderous system of philosophy. Nowhere in his voluminous writings, so far as I have been able to determine, has Cassirer set forth, in any sort of definite and summary statement, his doctrine of the *a priori*. It pervades every phase of his philosophy and appears on almost every page of his philosophical writings; but it is a difficult and hazardous task to analyze it out of his system and to pin it down in a definite statement which will do justice to its total meaning and value. This difficulty is further increased by two other factors. (i) His doctrine of the *a priori* seems to have gone through at least two phases of development, and the detailed results of these two different phases of its formulation are significantly different. (ii) In each of these two formulations his doctrine of the *a priori* is so inextricably bound up with some other special aspect of his philosophical theory that it is extremely difficult to isolate it and evaluate it, without going thoroughly into these intimately associated theories.

The first phase of its development, set forth in his *Substanzbegriff und Funktionsbegriff* (1910), is formulated on the

---

[1] *Das Erkenntnisproblem*, Vol. I (1922), 14.

basis of a very thorough critical analysis of the physical sciences and of mathematics, and is thoroughly dominated by what seems to me to be a tremendously exaggerated regard for the position and the value of mathematics and the mathematical concept in the theory of knowledge. Throughout this whole work, as Gerard Heymans remarks, "Cassirer looks steadfastly towards mathematics and insists that what is valid for this is valid also for all the other sciences."[2] Here his doctrine of the *a priori* is intricately bound up with his "mathematical theory of the concept" and reflects a powerful influence from the mathematical interest. Since another essay in this volume deals with Cassirer's "theory of the mathematical concept,"[*] I shall omit its discussion here and shall confine my discussion to those more basic aspects of this earlier formulation which seem to carry over into the later formulation.

This second formulation, which is contained primarily in Cassirer's *Philosophie der symbolischen Formen,* is based on a critical analysis of the whole of culture and is, in a definite sense, a modification and extension of the earlier formulation to constitute a basis for a "general theory of meaning." Here Cassirer has relinquished, to some extent, his former emphasis upon the place and value of mathematics and the mathematical concept. And, though he still insists that "for such a theory of meaning, mathematics and mathematical natural science will always constitute a weighty and indispensable paradigm," he admits that "it in no wise exhausts its content."[3] In this second formulation, however, his doctrine of the *a priori* has found a new "love" in the form of his elaborate doctrine of "signs." Since any attempt to extricate it from its many "entangling alliances" with this theory would lead far beyond the intended scope of this paper, I shall feel justified here in avoiding also any discussion of this aspect of his doctrine, except in so far as it seems necessary in order to do justice to his doctrine of the *a priori.*

Cassirer agrees with Kant that the correct approach to the

---

[2] "Zur Cassirerschen Reform der Begriffslehre," *Kant-Studien,* Vol. 33 (1928), 109-128.

[*] EDITOR'S NOTE: Cf. Professor Harold R. Smart's essay *infra* on this subject.

[3] "Zur Theorie des Begriffs," *Kant-Studien.* Vol. 33 (1928), 130.

discovery of the *a priori* is through the method of a critical analysis of knowledge. He emphasizes, over and over, the futility of the attempts on the part of previous "metaphysical philosophers" to deduce the "fundamental forms of the mind" from some "original fundamental principle." The original difficulty in such an attempt always consists in the fact that such philosophers can determine neither the correct "beginning point" nor the correct "end point." If they were granted these two points, "they might succeed in connecting them through the constant application of one and the same methodological principle in a synthetic-deductive process." But since they have neither "point," they are much in the same position as Kant's speculative "dove," which succeeded in generating a tremendous amount of action, but was unable to produce any forward motion. As Cassirer correctly asserts, such philosophers have always started out from "some definite metaphysically hypostatized logical, or aesthetic, or religious principle," and the results obtained from the process have never been worth the efforts spent.

Granted, however, that the critical analysis of knowledge is the only method that will lead to the discovery of the genuinely *a priori* elements of knowledge, the question naturally arises, How is one to recognize it, when he comes upon it in the analysis? Unless one has some distinguishing criterion in terms of which to recognize the *a priori* when he finds it, he would still be in the same position as the "metaphysical philosopher" who had no "end point." Cassirer's answer to this question, in the first formulation of his doctrine of the *a priori*, would seem to run as follows: Since the *a priori* is an "element of form," which is necessarily involved in every creative act of mind, and since all knowledge is the product of such creative activity, a critical analysis of knowledge will reveal the *a priori* as that "element of form" which is always present in every creative act of mind and which remains *invariant* through all the changing and shifting contents of experience. It is to the end of discovering just such a set of "invariant elements of form" that he devotes that searching and exhaustive critical analysis of science and mathematics set forth in his *Substanzbegriff und Funktionsbegriff*.

One of the most obvious aspects of science, says Cassirer, is that it is a going concern, "a historically self-developing fact." Kant's failure to recognize this fact becomes, according to Cassirer, one of the chief sources of weakness in Kant's system. Kant developed and formulated his doctrine of the *a priori* under an undue predilection for Newtonian Mechanics, which he seemed to regard as an example *par exellence* of pure Reason, and as definitely finished. Scientific knowledge, however, is never static; it is in constant process of development; and the one definite end toward which it seems ever to be directed is the discovery of certain *permanent elements* in the flux of experience, "that can be used as *constants* of theoretical construction." Of such nature are the concepts of science: hypotheses, laws of nature, scientific principles, and the like. In the history of this process, however, we are met with a constant changing and shifting of just such seemingly constant elements. What seems to be secure on one level of development is found inadequate on the next level. One particular system of concepts follows another in constant succession; hypotheses formulated on one level yield their place to other hypotheses on the higher level; scientific principles, which seem to be secure and firmly established on one level of development, are supplanted by other principles on the next level of development; and even "the categories under which we consider the historical process must themselves be regarded as mutable and susceptible to change." But no system of concepts, no single hypothesis or system of hypotheses, no scientific principle, and no category which gives way to a successor is ever entirely annihilated. In each case of substitution the earlier form is taken up into the new form which must contain the answers to all the questions raised under the previous form. This one feature, Cassirer claims, guarantees the logical continuity from stage to stage; establishes a logical connection between the earlier and the latter; and "points to a common forum of judgment to which both are subjected."[4]

This "common forum of judgment," at the bar of which

' *Substance and Function*, 268.

every concept, hypothesis, principle, and category must justify its relative claim to truth, consists in a set of logically prior "supreme principles of experience in general," which must always be present and effective as an "ultimate constant standard of measurement" in terms of which these relative claims may be measured and established.

Since we never compare the system of hypotheses in itself with the naked facts in themselves, but always can only oppose one hypothetical system of principles to another more inclusive, more radical system, we need for this progressive comparison an ultimate constant standard of measurement of supreme principles of experience in general. Thought demands the identity of this logical standard of measurement amid all the changes of what is measured.[5]

Now, according to Cassirer, the critical analysis of knowledge ends in just such a set of ultimate logical principles, a set of "fundamental relations, upon which the content of all experience rests," and beyond which thought can not go, for "only in them is thought itself and an object of thought possible."[6]

They are the "universally valid formal functions (*Functionsform*) of rational and empirical knowledge" and constitute

a fixed system of conditions, and only relative to this system do all assertions concerning the object as well as those concerning the ego, concerning object and subject, gain an intelligible meaning. There is no objectivity outside the frame of number and magnitude, permanence and change, causality and reciprocal action; all these determinations are only the ultimate invariants of experience itself and therefore of all reality which can be established in it and by it.[7]

These forms, then, constitute the genuine *a priori* elements of knowledge, for they are "those ultimate logical invariants which lie at the foundation of every determination of a connection in general according to natural law" and "only such ultimate logical invariants can be called *a priori*."[8] To this list of ultimate invariants, Cassirer adds "the categories of space and time, magnitude, and the functional dependency of magni-

---

[5] *Ibid.*
[6] *Substanzbegriff und Funktionsbegriff.* (1910), 410.
[7] *Ibid.*, 411.
[8] *Ibid.*, 357.

tudes, etc.," since they, too, are "established as such elements of form, which cannot be lacking in any empirical judgment or system of judgments."[9] This group of "logical invariants" constitutes that system of "unchanging elements demanded by all scientific thought" and "fulfill a requirement clearly urged by inductive procedure itself."[10] They also seem to constitute the basic structural form of the mind, and the basic principles of that "transcendental logic" upon which alone a truly universal logic can be developed. For Cassirer insists that "a truly universal logic can be constructed only upon a 'transcendental' logic, i.e., a logic of thought-objects." Such a logic, he insists, is in diametrical opposition to the formal logic, which, as Kant defined it, has as its chief excellence the fact that it "abstracts from all experience of objects and their differences."[11] In this traditional formal logic, the concept is a mere "form emptied of all its objective content and meaning;" whereas, in his "truly universal logic," concepts are "concrete universals" which not only "embrace" but "comprehend" the particular subordinated to them.

Now when Cassirer defines the *a priori* as "those ultimate logical invariants which lie at the foundation of every determination of a connection in general according to natural law," he designates this as "a strictly limited meaning of the *a priori*." It seems that a more comprehensive meaning of the term would include all those concepts, categories, and interpretive principles which are implicitly contained in this set of "ultimate forms," all arranged in a logical structure of superordination and subordination. The task of science is to discover these concepts, categories, etc.; and the procedure by which it accomplishes this task is the constant comparison of these various concepts, hypotheses, etc., with this "constant standard of measurement of supreme principles of experience in general." And the method followed here, says Cassirer, "shows the same 'rational' structure as was found in mathematics."[12] Induction and deduc-

---

[9] *Substance and Function*, 269.

[10] *Ibid.*, 268.

[11] "Zur Theorie des Begriffs," *Kant-Studien*. Vol. 33 (1928), 131.

[12] *Substance and Function*, 269.

tion do not differ in their goal, but only in the means of reaching their goal.

"The tendency to something unchanging, to something permanent in the coming and going of sensuous phenomena, is thus characteristic of inductive thought no less than of mathematical thought."[13] Genuine theoretically guided induction is never satisfied, says Cassirer, short of the establishment of a connection in the given "which can be . . . clearly surveyed according to the principle of its construction."[14] All thought is a process of objectifying. Its function and purpose, both in induction and in deduction, is to establish unity in the flux of sensory experience. This can be done only on the basis of those transcendental forms which constitute the structural unity of the mind. In so far, then, as induction, through its method of continually testing its conceptual devices by constant reference to that body of "ultimate invariants" is able to develop concepts, hypotheses, etc., which stem logically from this system of invariant principles, and to apply them in its conceptual dealings with "matters of fact," it can gain knowledge of empirical objects which possesses the same degree of necessity and certainty as does knowledge of the objects of mathematics. For "we do not know 'objects' as if they were already independently determined and given *as objects,*—but we know *objectively,* by producing certain limitations and by fixating certain permanent elements and connections within the uniform flow of experience."[15] The superiority of the mathematical concept over the ordinary generic concept, its "greater value for knowledge," its "superior objective meaning and validity," seems to be due to its closer logical affinity for this set of "supreme principles."

In the first formulation of his doctrine of the *a priori,* Cassirer's attempt to solve Hume's problem seems to have turned out to be much the same as the attempt made by Kant, namely, to show how, at least in the realm of mathematics and the exact sciences, synthetic propositions *a priori* are possible. He seems to have become conscious later, however, that he had

[13] *Ibid.,* 249.
[14] *Ibid.,* 253.
[15] *Ibid.,* 303.

committed the same fallacy of which he accused Kant, i.e., he had confined his critical analysis within too narrow limits. For, if the *a priori* is the "necessary condition for all meaningful experience," and its function is to guarantee the unity of all knowledge, then it must be present and effective wherever there is meaningful experience and a claim to knowledge. The world of mathematics and the exact sciences is not the beginning, but the end of this "objectifying process," and its roots reach down into earlier levels of "fashioning." Thus these *a priori* forms, which come to clearest expression on the level of scientific knowledge, must apply no less, *mutatis mutandis*, to all the fundamental functions of mind on all the lower levels of culture and in all its special "phases." Thus, for Cassirer, in the second attempt to formulate his doctrine of the *a priori*,

The Critique of Reason becomes, therefore, the Critique of Culture. It seeks to show how all the content of culture, in so far as it is more than a mere single content, in so far as it is grounded in a formal principle, presupposes an original act of the mind. Herein the fundamental thesis of Idealism finds its essential and complete verification. So long as philosophical consideration has reference simply to the analysis of purely formal knowledge and is limited to that task, just so long the force of the naïve realistic world view cannot be broken.[16]

An initial clue to Cassirer's position here is revealed in his statement of the demand made upon critical philosophy. The demand is

. . . to include the various methodological tendencies of knowledge, in all their recognized originality and independence, in a system in which the individual members, in exactly their necessary variety, are reciprocally conditioned and required. The postulate of a kind of pure functional unity now enters in the place of the postulate of the unity of the substrate and the unity of origin, by which the ancient concept of being was essentially governed. From this there arises a new task for the philosophical criticism of knowledge. It must follow as a whole and survey as a whole the course which the special sciences have traveled individually. It must put the question, whether the intellectual symbols under which the special disciplines consider and describe reality are to be thought as

[16] *Philosophie der symbolischen Formen.* Vol. I (1923), 11.

a simple juxtaposition or whether they can be understood as *different expressions of one and the same basic mental function*. And if this latter presupposition should be verified, then there arises the further task of setting up the universal conditions of this function and of clarifying the principle by which it is governed.[17]

In the light of this statement, it would seem that Cassirer's first fundamental assumption is that knowledge, which philosophy is to subject to critical analysis, is necessarily a unity; and, furthermore, that this unity must be assured and explained in terms of certain "basic mental functions" and a "rule" which "governs the concrete multiplicity and variety of these knowledge functions," integrating the totality of their products into an organic whole. These "basic mental functions" for which all the varieties of intellectual symbols are to be regarded as different expressions, together with the "rule" which governs these functions, seem now to constitute, for Cassirer, the fundamental *a priori* elements of knowledge. The categories, which Kant considered as the "original concepts of the understanding," as its basic *a priori* forms and the necessary conditions for the possibility of experience, are here relegated to a subordinate level in the structure of the *a priori*. Kant's error, both as to the number and nature of these categories, says Cassirer, was due to the fact that he did not know at that time what the subsequent developments in "critical and idealistic logic" have made completely clear on that point, namely, that

the forms of judgment mean only unified and living motives of thought, which pervade all the diversity of its special forms and are constantly engaged in the creation and formulation of ever new categories. The richer and more plastic these variations prove to be, the more do they testify to the individuality and to the originality of the logical function out of which they arise.[18]

In the light of these considerations, critical analysis must, according to Cassirer, be extended to the whole of culture, to all its different "phases" or "provinces," Art, Language, Myth,

---

[17] *Ibid.*, 8-9. *Italics* are mine.
[18] *Das Erkenntnisproblem*. Vol. I (1922), 18.

Religion, and Science, and to all the different levels of its development. For,

It is proper not only for Science, but for Language, for Art, and for Religion, that they supply the building materials, from which is constructed for us not only the world of the "real," but also the world of the "mental," the world of the "ego." We cannot insert them in the given world as simple creations, but *must conceive them as functions,* by means of which every specific fashioning of Being and every special division and differentiation of the same is carried out.[19]

Each of these special "provinces" is determined by a special "point of view" which the mind "freely takes" with respect to the given in experience. This special point of view determines a special function which governs the mind's dealings with the given, in that special province. It determines the formulation of the categories and the concepts by means of which the mind interprets and expresses the real from that specific "point of view." In each of these special provinces, therefore, we get a manifestation of "one side of the real." And in all these provinces, taken together as a unity, we get a complete picture of the totality of the real. True, the pictures of the real presented from these different "points of view" are very dissimilar. But this is just what we should expect. For,

Since the means utilized by these functions in the performance of these acts are different, and since the standards and the criteria which each separate one presupposes and applies are different, the result is different. The scientific conception of truth and of reality is different from that of Religion or of Art—thus it is indeed a special and incomparable fundamental relation which is, not so much indicated, as rather established in them between the "inner" and the "outer," between the Being of the ego and of the world.[20]

The results obtained in each of these provinces must, therefore, be measured and evaluated in terms of its own standards and not in terms of the standards and demands of any other. And only in such manner of dealing with them can the question

[19] *Philosophie der symbolischen Formen.* Vol. I (1923), 24.
[20] *Ibid.*

be raised "whether and how all these different forms of world-comprehension and I-comprehension can be unified—if they do not indeed portray one and the same self-existing 'thing', they at least perfect (*ergänzen*) a totality, a unified system of mental performance (*Tuns*)."[21]

Now if, under these conditions, the unity of knowledge, which it is the specific function of the *a priori* to guarantee, seems to fall apart into several separate provinces of knowledge, each with its own *a priori* forms, its special categories, standards and criteria, which apply only within its own special field of "construction," Cassirer informs us that it is just as much the function of the *a priori* to preserve this diversity as it is to guarantee the unity of knowledge. This "unity in diversity'" he says, is an essential demand of consciousness. In spite of this essential diversity, there is still a "unity of meaning" which binds all these provinces together into a "unity of systems" without destroying the separate and distinctive meaning and value of any system. This, he insists, is just what an analysis of culture reveals.

For every one of these "connections of meaning" (*Bedeutungszusammenhänge*), Language as well as scientific knowledge, Art as well as Myth, possesses its own constitutive principle which impresses all the special fashionings in it as if with its seal. . . . It belongs to the essence of consciousness itself, that no content can be posited in it without, positing, at the same time, through this simple act of positing, a complex of other contents with it.[22]

Myth, Art, Language, and Science are, in this sense, impressions to Being (*Prägungen zum Sein*): They are not simple portrayals of a present reality, but they exhibit the great lines of direction of mental movement, of the ideal process, in which the real as *one and many* is constituted for us—as a multiplicity of configurations, which are still, ultimately, *held together through a unity of meaning.*[23]

One ground on which Cassirer rejects the single system of the structure of the mind, which speculative philosophers of

[21] *Ibid.*
[22] *Ibid.*, 31.
[23] *Ibid.*, 43. *Italics* mine.

the past have attempted to deduce from a "single original
principle" and to arrange in a unique progressive series, is the
fact that such a system is inadequate for the explanation of this
diversity. Explained in terms of such a system, the diversity
gets swallowed up in the unity of the system. Instead of such a
system, says Cassirer, critical philosophy demands, and the
analysis of culture reveals, a complex system in which

> Every form is, so to speak, assigned a special plane within which it
> operates and in which it unfolds, with complete independence, its own
> specific individuality—but just in the totality of these ideal modes of
> operation appear, at the same time, definite analogies, definite typical
> modes of relating, which can be singled out and described.[24]

Now as a means of explaining how all these various levels
and phases of culture are integrated into a logically unified
system of systems, Cassirer appeals to that set of "fundamental
relations upon which the content of all experience rests." These
logical *invariants*, he claims, permeate all the forms which
determine all the fashionings of experience on all the different
levels and in all the different phases of culture. From the
lowest level of "Expression" in terms of mythical concepts,
through the level of "Representation" in terms of the concepts
of language, to the highest level of "pure Meaning" comprehended in terms of the "concepts of natural law," he traces the
development of culture. In doing so, he offers an incredible
array of evidence in support of his claim that the same "motive
of construction" and the same basic "structural form of the
mind" persist through all these different levels of development. Although he admits that, in the advancement from stage
to stage in the process of development, certain changes and
"transformations," certain "characteristic metamorphoses"
occur, he still insists that these "supreme principles" remain
fundamentally the same, though appearing, on each successive
level, under a "new form and covering." With every transition
from a lower to a higher level of culture, there occurs a "transformation" in the "point of view" which the mind takes. This

[24] *Ibid.*, 29.

transformation gives rise to new demands and requires new "norms" in terms of which to meet them. As the development proceeds, there is a constant "shifting of mental meaning" and "out of every one of these shiftings there arises a new 'total meaning' of reality."[25]

Even on the mythical level of culture, says Cassirer, we find exhibited, in all its various "fashionings," a certain definite "mental tendency," a "fixed direction of thought," which the mind follows in all its expressions of experience on this level. This fixed direction of thought he attributes to the "form of the mythical consciousness," which is "nothing more than the unity of the mental principles by which all its constructions, in all their variety and in all their vast empirical richness, are ultimately governed."[26] Also on this level of "Expression," there is a "unity of point of view" under the dominance of which man's "mytho-religious intuition" shapes all the conceptual devices by means of which he carries out the organization of society as well as the organization of the world. And although this "point of view" may be more definitely determined in each particular society by the living conditions under which that society exists and develops, we can clearly detect, as a common element in all of them, certain "general and pervading motives of construction."[27]

The mental principles which the mind employs in carrying out these constructions are, Cassirer claims, the general categories which constitute the fundamental forms of the social consciousness on this level of cultural development. They reveal, he says, "the lawfulness of consciousness," the unity of a "structural form of the mind," and are just as genuinely *a priori* as are the fundamental forms of "knowledge" exhibited on the various successive higher levels of cultural development. They are, in fact, the logical ancestors of those forms; for all those forms of culture, Art, Law, Science, and all the rest, had their genesis in this mythical consciousness. Not one of them had, in

---

[25] *Philosophie der symbolischen Formen.* Vol. III (1929), 523.

[26] *Philosophie der symbolischen Formen.* Vol. II (1925), 16.

[27] *Ibid.,* 220.

the beginning, anything like a distinct and clearly defined form. They can all be traced back to a primitive stage in which they all existed together in the immediate and undifferentiated unity of mythical consciousness. And out of this undifferentiated state, all those fundamental forms of knowledge, space, time, number, continuity, property, and the rest, have been developed.

They are the most general forms of perception, which constitute the unity of consciousness as such, and, therefore, just as well that of mythical consciousness as that of pure knowledge. In this respect it can be said that each of these forms must have run through a previous mythical stage before receiving its definite logical form and impress.[28]

It is obvious that the world picture presented on the level of Myth is quite different from that presented on the scientific level. This difference, Cassirer claims, is not to be explained on the assumption that these world-pictures are constructed on the basis of a difference in the "nature" or the "quality" of the categories used, but on the basis of a difference in the "modality" of the categories. Space, time, number, causality, and all the rest of the basic forms of consciousness are present and effective on the mythical level just as they are on all the higher levels of culture, but with a difference in "modality." By the "quality" of a relation he means "the special manner of connecting, by means of which it creates a series in the whole of consciousness," such as is exemplified in the form of "together" as compared with "successive," the "simultaneous" as contrasted with "successive connection." By the "modality" of a relation, however, he means its "meaning for the whole" (Sinnganzen). This character of a relation "possesses its own nature, its own self-contained formal law. Thus, for example, that universal relation which we call time represents equally an element of theoretical scientific knowledge, and also an essential moment for definite structures of aesthetic consciousness."[29] Although it may seem that these two senses in which the concept

[28] Ibid., 78.
[29] Philosophie der symbolischen Formen, Vol. I (1923), 29.

time is used, namely, as the uniform measure of all change and as the rhythmical measure of music, have nothing in common except the name; nevertheless, says Cassirer,

> This unity of naming contains in itself a unity of meaning, at least in so far as there is posited in both that universal and abstract quality which we designate by the expression "succession." But it is obviously a special "manner," indeed a unique "mode" of succession which rules in the consciousness of natural law, as the law of the temporal form of events, and that which rules in the comprehension of the rhythmical measure of a tone structure.[30]

Now the transition from a lower to a higher level in the development of culture is always the result of a "transformation" or a "permutation" in the "modality" of those various fundamental forms "within which alone thought and its world are possible." This "permutation" in the "meaning for the whole" seems to arise out of a new "point of view" with respect to experience. And experience interpreted from this new point of view gives a new world-picture. In order to express the new relations and meanings which emerge with this transformation in the modality of those fundamental relational forms, the mind is under necessity of creating a new set of concepts. Even the old concepts that are retained on the new level take on an entirely different meaning from that which they express with respect to the lower level. For instance, the concept of "truth" and the concept of "reality" have a meaning for science which is entirely different from that which they express on the level of myth. It is the function of the concepts utilized on each level of culture, however, to express with objective validity the relations and meanings which are characteristic of that particular level, i.e., those relations and meanings logically determined by the specific formal modalities operative on that particular level. The function of thought on all the different levels of culture is to "objectify;" and this is done in each case by "producing certain limitations and fixating certain permanent elements and connections within the uniform flow of experi-

[30] *Ibid.*

ence." This task is performed by means of the concepts used. Thus the concepts used on any particular level of culture express the meanings and fixate the relations peculiar to that particular level with a sufficient degree of logical necessity to guarantee their objective validity. But since the concepts utilized by the mind on the different levels are different, and express different meanings and relations, the world-picture presented on the different levels will be different. All these different world-pictures, however, present different views of the one total reality. And all these different processes of objectifying contribute to one and the same ultimate end, namely, the reduction of the world of mere impressions to a logically integrated objective world.

The different creations of mental culture, Language, Scientific Knowledge, Myth, Art, and Religion, in all their inner variety, become, therefore, members of one great problem of connection—manifold tendencies, all of which are related to the one goal of transforming the passive world of mere impressions . . . into a world of pure mental expression.[31]

The problem posed by Hume, however, was not the problem of developing in the mind a system of ideas with their necessary connections, but the problem of finding a logical basis on which to guarantee that these necessary connections of ideas must hold in the mind's dealings with matters of fact. In his first formulation of his doctrine of the *a priori*, Cassirer seems to attempt to solve this problem, at least in part, by an implicit denial that any such problem exists. He seems to think that the problem arose for Hume because he, like Kant in the first part of his *Critique of Pure Reason*, was assuming an untenable dualism between a *"mundus sensibilis"* and a *"mundus intelligibilis."* In the second formulation, however, he seems to realize more fully that there is some necessity of explaining how and why there must be a necessary harmony between the conceptual order of the mind and the "uniform flow of experience." Here the "symbol" becomes the mediating device which seems to turn the trick. Symbols, he seems to think, are created by "a pure

[31] *Ibid.*, 12.

activity of the mind" and are specifically and peculiarly designed by the mind to perform this feat. "All those symbols appear from the beginning with a definite claim to objective value. They all transcend the circle of the mere phenomena of consciousness and claim, in opposition to them, to represent a universal validity."[32] In fact, their "structure" represents the "essential kernel of the objective, of the real." Every symbolic structure, furthermore, possesses a characteristic "double nature." On the one side, it is essentially bound to the sensuous; but "its subjection to the sensuous contains in itself at the same time a freedom from the sensuous," an essential connection with the mental, with the conceptual order of the mind.

"In every linguistic 'sign', in every mythical or artistic 'image' appears a mental content which, in and for itself, transcends the sensuous, *permuted into the form of the sensuous,* the visible, the audible, the tastable."[33]

Cassirer attributes to Pierre Duhem the credit for being the first to show that only within the structure of a definite symbolic world is it possible to approach the world of physical reality. It was his claim that what first appears to us as a purely factual manifold, as a factual variety of sense impressions, gains physical meaning and value only when it is portrayed in the province of numbers. This portrayal, however, is wrongly interpreted, says Cassirer, if we think it simply consists in "substituting for the individual contents given in experience contents of another kind and coinage. To every special class of experience, is co-ordinated a special substrate which is the complete expression of its genuine, its essential 'reality'."[34]

Now it is Cassirer's claim that the function of mind in all its objectifying processes is to establish harmony between opposites. This harmony, however, is essentially different from the mere matter of agreement, and requires a genuine synthetic act of the mind. It seems to be the function of the symbol to mediate this synthesis and the function of the concept to "fix" the connections established in the synthesis. For the first work of the con-

---

[32] *Ibid.*, 21.

[33] *Ibid.*, 41.

[34] *Philosophie der symbolischen Formen.* Vol. III (1929), 478.

cept, he asserts, is "to grasp, as such, the moments upon which rests the organization and order of perceptual reality and to recognize them in their specific meaning. The connections which are posited implicitly in perceptual existence in the form of mere 'given-withness' (*Mitgegebenheit*) are developed from it...."[35] Furthermore, "The logical concept does nothing more than fix the lawful order which already lies in the phenomena themselves; it follows consciously the rule set up, which experience follows unconsciously."[36] It is the mind itself, guided by the logical demands of its "supreme logical functions" which "sets up" the rule which the concept follows consciously and experience follows unconsciously. Thus those functions seem to determine both the conceptual order of the mind and also the "uniform flow of experience," and do it in such a fashion that there must be complete harmony between these two "opposites." The mind's task is to make a synthesis of the two and it accomplishes this feat by means of the concept. For,

Such a "synthesis of opposites" lies concealed in every genuine physical concept and in every physical judgment. For we are always concerned with referring two different forms of the manifold to one another and, in a certain measure, penetrating them with one another. We always proceed from a mere empirical, a "given" plurality; but the goal of the theoretical construction of the concept is directed at changing it into a rationally surveyable, into a "constructive" plurality.[37]

On the lower levels of culture, these concepts and symbols are so completely immersed in the sensuous that it is difficult to detect in them any connection with those "fundamental functions" of the mind which they express. As the process of objectifying advances from the lower to the higher levels, however, the mind gradually succeeds in extricating them from their subjection to and their contamination with the sensuous and in creating concepts and symbols which reveal more and more the genuine nature of those functions. On the lower levels, we see those forms only "as if through a glass darkly," only in their distorted "modalities;" but when the highest level is

[35] *Ibid.*, 330.
[36] *Ibid.*, 333.
[37] *Ibid.*, 480.

reached, the level of pure mathematics and the pure mathematical natural sciences, where they have "put off the corruptible and put on incorruption," we shall "see them face to face" and recognize them for what they genuinely are, "pure meanings." This is the ultimate end towards which the whole creative process is directed, the "one far-off divine event to which the whole creation moves." For this is the realm in which

the bond between "concept" and "reality" is severed with complete consciousness. Above "reality," as the reality of phenomena, is raised a new realm: The realm of pure meaning; and in it henceforth is grounded all certainty and all constancy, all final truth of knowledge. On the other hand, the world of "ideas," of "meanings," although it renounces all "similarity" with the empirical sensuous world, it cannot dispense with its relation to it.[38]

III

This is, admittedly, an inadequate and in some respects, no doubt, an erroneous exposition of Cassirer's doctrine of the *a priori*. It has omitted many aspects of his doctrine which, if taken into consideration, might effect a "transformation" in the "modality" of those aspects that are considered here. My first reaction to the whole delineation of his doctrine of the *a priori* is simply to regard it as an extremely thorough, meticulously painstaking attempt on the part of another brilliant philosopher to elaborate and defend a theory of the *a priori* which is, from the beginning, palpably indefensible. A careful analysis of his doctrine, however, reveals many points which, if taken in isolation from the rest of his system or if given a slightly different interpretation from that which his whole system demands, would appear perfectly sound and thoroughly defensible. This slight difference in interpretation is, however, to use Whitehead's expression, "just that slight difference which makes all the difference in the world."

To his claim that the *a priori* is of the mind and is the basis of all necessity and of all certainty in knowledge, I readily agree. But I contend that his conception of the essential nature of the *a priori* is untenable, both in the light of logic and from

[38] *Ibid.,* 527.

the standpoint of what is revealed in a critical analysis of knowledge. Furthermore, such a conception of the *a priori* is inadequate as a basis for explaining and guaranteeing that type of necessity which grounds the only type of certainty which the mind can have with respect to matters of fact. An analysis of knowledge does not reveal any set of *invariant* principles which are necessarily common to all thinking minds and which, by some inherent logical power which they possess, are operative in any of the mind's categories and concepts in such a fashion as to force their character of logical necessity upon the given in experience. The *a priori* character of any concept or category of the mind is not derived from any logical connection which it may have with any fundamental set of "basic functions;" but from the definitive attitude of the mind which gives rise to this conceptual order and determines the characteristics which the given *must* exhibit, *if* it is to be classified under the category or the concept determined by that definitive attitude. The only certainty the mind can have with respect to any sensory datum yet to be given rests upon the mind's certainty with respect to the meaning of its own concepts and categories. This meaning is established and determined by the mind itself, by virtue of the definitive attitudes which it takes, and can be strictly and consistently adhered to regardless of what may be given in experience. This definitive attitude determines the criteria which any given datum must satisfy if it is to be interpreted under the concept or under the category which embodies and expresses these criteria. Failing to satisfy these criteria, the given datum is excluded from such classification and interpretation. For every classification which the mind makes is an implicit interpretation. But every interpretation is an implicit prediction with respect to some subsequent datum of experience. The interpretation of any set of sensory data under any definite concept or category implicitly asserts that such a set of data will be followed by certain other definitely specifiable data, namely, those which are implicitly demanded by the definitive criteria which constitute the essential meaning of the concept or the category under which the original data were classified. The only necessity which the mind can impose on the given, therefore, is the necessity which the given is under of conforming to certain definitive criteria of the mind or else being excluded from classification and interpretation under the specific concept or category which those definitive criteria establish. The mind can know, then, prior to the experiencing of any particular datum of experience, the character which that particular datum *must* exhibit if it is to be classified under any definite concept or category. The mind knows this because the mind itself, by its own definitive attitudes, determines those criteria to which the datum must conform, *or else*, and can make them hold regardless of what the given datum may or may not do. Thus all the necessity which the mind is capable of imposing on the given, through the use of its "conceptual order," is derived (i) from the character of its own legislative acts which determine the essential meaning of its conceptual devices and, (ii) from the alternative which the mind has of excluding from classification under any concept or category any given element of experience which does not conform to the criteria which are established by those legislative acts for the concept or the category in question. Such necessity, therefore, does not rest upon some logical connection which these concepts and categories have with some "fixed system of conditions," relative to which alone any assertion concerning anything whatsoever can have any meaning. This contention of Cassirer reflects the powerful influence of his undue predilection for mathematics, and also his misconception of the genuine nature of mathematics itself.

There is a definite sense in which the *a priori* principles of knowledge may be considered as the "formal structure of the mind," but not the sense in which Cassirer uses the expression. Those initial principles and criteria of interpretation which formulate the mind's definitive attitudes constitute the formal conceptual structure with which the mind meets and interprets the given in experience. It is in this way that the mind organizes and systematizes the chaotic flux of the given into a predictable and intelligible world. This conceptual "structure of the mind," however, is neither an inherent structure of all thinking minds; nor is it by any means *invariant*. Even those most fundamental categories of the mind, those which formulate the mind's definitive attitudes that determine the different types of the real, are not invariant, at least not in the sense that they must remain the same regardless of any change in the complexity of the given which the mind must encounter; or regardless of any possible change in the dominant interests and purposes of society. In fact, it seems to be carrying the defense of a claim to the point of absurdity to insist that those "rational functions" which Cassirer designates as "the ultimate invariants of experience itself" have remained invariant throughout the history of culture. Furthermore, if the character of invariance be designated as the criterion of the *a priori*, I doubt that any single "element of form," not even excepting such forms as Space, Time, Number and Magnitude, Permanence and Change, Causality and Reciprocal Interaction would qualify as *a priori;* for these fundamental forms have certainly undergone rather remarkable change in the process of man's cultural development from the primitive level to its present state. Cassirer does, of course, allow for certain "shiftings of intellectual accent" and certain "modal transformations" in the process; but I doubt whether the difference between the primitive man's vague sense of time and of space and the modern scientist's conception of a fused space-time can be explained in terms of such "shiftings" and "transformations;" or whether man's hazy anthropomorphic conception of a mythical causal agent could be reconciled in this way with the purely formal definition of cause as it is used today by the theoretical scientist. If the change be explained in terms of a refinement in definition, it can be said in reply that a relation *is* what it is by definition, and any refinement in definition means a change in the nature of the relation. Even those forms are creations of the mind; and what the mind has created it can change when the demand arises. And the demand for such a change is, usually, not merely a logical demand, but a practical one, a demand created by the appearance of some new type of the "given" for the proper interpretation of which the previous forms have proven inadequate.

The relative permanence of these forms and also their *a priori* character I would readily grant; but I would deny that they are invariant and also that invariance is the criterion for the determination of the *a priori* character of any form. It may be that, to paraphrase Wordsworth, "Each hath had elsewhere its origin and commeth from far" and that each does come "trailing clouds of glory." Such clouds of glory may be marks of their ancient origin; but neither the clouds of glory nor its ancient origin is a mark of its *a priori* character. In the case of these forms, as in the case of all other forms and "functional relations of rational and empirical knowledge," whatever character of the *a priori* they may possess is due to a definitive and legislative act of the mind itself. Whatever degree of permanence or invariance they may show is explicable, I think, on the grounds of their practical value as instruments for handling the given, and not on the grounds that they satisfy some "ideal logical demand." Furthermore, if invariance and antiquity of origin be sure marks of the *a priori*, then I see no grounds on which to exclude the category of substance, against which Cassirer so vigorously inveighs throughout his entire system; for certainly this category has as ancient and as honorable a history as can be claimed for any of those "functional relations" to which he attributes the *a priori* character.

It is true, as Cassirer claims, that Culture, in all its different forms and on all its different levels, is a creation of the mind. It includes all those devices, both mental and physical, which the mind has created for the purpose of handling the given in experience and of reducing that given to an ordered and intelligible world. It seems to be the characteristic function of the mind to create just such conceptual tools and to use them to this definite end. The "original motive" which lies behind this "constructive activity," however, is not a "will to logic," but a "will to live," a will to satisfy certain vital and emotional interests of the organism. And it is the "will to live" rather than a "will to logic" which tends to determine those definitive attitudes of the mind and, thus, the nature and meaning of its categories and concepts. Cassirer, it seems, would insist that

> There's a Logic that shapes our concepts,
> Rough-hew them how we will.

I would insist on substituting for "logic" certain vital and emotional interests of the organism. For the thinking organism, confronted with the chaotic welter of experience, is confronted likewise with a practical necessity of doing something about it. Otherwise I doubt that any tendency to think would ever have arisen. The ability to think is, I take it, an evolutionary product, and has developed in the human species as a result of its survival value. The tendency to regard man as primarily a "thinking being" rather than as an "acting being" has led to many misinterpretations of the function of mind. Mind's function is not that of "harmonizing thought and Being," but rather that of adjusting the organism to the chaotic flux of experience in ways that will preserve and promote certain vital and emotional interests which the organism has. This function it performs by taking certain definitive attitudes towards the given in experience and in formulating these attitudes into definite categories and concepts which will serve as efficient guides to the organism in its processes of adjustment. Thinking is only one means of solving these problems of adjustment; and most beings, who have the ability to think, generally use it only when more primitive means prove inadequate. The human mind itself is only man's ability to create and to use conceptual devices as a means to that end. Such conceptual devices are created by the mind, usually, just to serve that end. They may be changed or even discarded when they prove inadequate to serve this purpose or when the mind hits upon other devices which serve the purpose better. The standard against which the mind is constantly checking its categories, concepts, hypotheses, etc., is not a set of invariant logical functions, but usually the practical results derived from their application to the flux of experience and the consonance of those results with experience itself.

Cassirer admits that "No number . . . 'is' anything other than it is made in certain conceptual definitions." This is true, of course; but the same can be truly said of all the concepts and categories which the mind uses. The superior value which number and all other mathematical concepts have for deductive purposes rests upon the exactness and precision with which they may be defined. Again, the relations in terms of which mathematical concepts are defined are quantitative relations and, therefore, susceptible to more definite and precise expression and analysis than are those with which ordinary classificatory concepts are defined. The very essence of number is simply a definite position in a purely logical series. Number is not a "concrete universal," but a purely abstract universal, a purely logical entity, the quintessence of abstraction. The relata themselves are creations of the mind and, for that reason, the mind is able to force them to conform to relations established by its concepts. The given sensory data of experience, however, are not created by the mind and cannot be forced to conform to those relations. They either do, or they do not. If they do not, the mind has the alternative of excluding them from classification under the concept which established those relations. Upon this ability of the mind to formulate concepts by definition, and to reject from classification and interpretation under those concepts any datum which does not conform to the criteria which their definitions establish rests the *a priori* character of all concepts, mathematical as well as the ordinary generic concepts.

Mathematics is, in its entirety, a creation of the mind and is the most efficient tool for handling certain types of the given—those types in which the quantitative aspects are more important than are the qualitative aspects—that the mind has ever created. Mathematics, however, demands nothing more than that, if a certain relation holds among a certain set of entities, be they abstract or be they concrete entities, then certain other sets of relations *must also hold* among those same entities. But those certain other sets of relations which must hold are implications of the definition which established the meaning of the original relation. If three points in a plane are arranged in the form of a right triangle—these are all pure abstractions—, then the square on the hypotenuse must be equal to the sum of the squares on the other two sides. The certainty of the statement contained in the "then" clause of this theorem is assured by the implications of the definition of a right triangle. The relations stated in the "then" clause can be known to hold *a priori*, necessarily, only on the ground that the mind is in position to exclude from the class of right triangles all triangles which do not conform to the criteria specifically stated or implied in the definition of a right triangle. If we substitute for these abstract entities certain concrete entities, a triangular plot of ground for the plane and fence posts for the abstract points, we know that the same relations must hold among these entities also. If we measure accurately the distances between the posts along the shorter sides of the triangle and, upon these measurements, calculate accurately the length of the supposed hypotenuse and, then, upon these calculations, buy the wire to fence the piece of ground, we may come out several rods short. Such a disappointing and inconvenient result does not constitute an empirical demonstration of the falsity of the Euclidean theorem, but demonstrates the falsity of the original assumption that the posts were related in the form of a right triangle. It is just this character of mathematical concepts which makes them so useful as means of discovering relations among concrete entities which would likely never be discovered otherwise. But the certainty obtained in this way is of the same type, and rests upon the same basis, as that gained through the mind's application of any of its concepts to the concrete data of experience. For all certainty in empirical knowledge rests upon the mind's ability to formulate definitions of concepts and to make those definitions hold with respect to the given by rejecting all cases which do not conform to the demands established in those definitions. The application of mathematical concepts in the interpretation of the given can, therefore, like the application of any other type of concepts, never be more than hypothetical. And the certainty derived from their application is of the same type as that derived from the application of other types of concepts. Also the *a priori* character of mathematical concepts is of the same nature as that of any other type of concepts. Whatever superiority they may have over the ordinary classificatory concept is due to properties which they possess other than their *a priori* character.

The *a priori* is not some inherent character of logical necessity or "logical priority to the possibility of experience" possessed by any relation or group of relations. Those initial principles and definitive criteria which have the character of *a priori* necessity and certainty possess it by virtue of the definitive attitude which the mind takes toward them and the alternative which the mind has of excluding from classification under them any given case which fails to conform to the definitive attitude formulated in them. The chemist, for instance, may know with absolute certainty the truth of the chemical formula $HCl + NaOH \rightarrow NaCl + H_2O$; but only on the grounds that in the case of any experiment in which these results fail to follow, the chemicals used were either not HCl or not NaOH or were neither HCl nor NaOH. In such a case he may demand either a re-labeling or a re-filling of the containers from which the chemicals were obtained. On this same basis, one may assert with absolute certainty that all crows are black. This statement may be accepted as a mere hypothetical principle, susceptible to verification or refutation by future experience, or it may be taken as a definitive principle and, in that case, it would not be susceptible to refutation at all. It would be an *a priori* principle. The difference between the two cases is simply a difference in the attitude which the mind takes with respect to the principle. It is just such a definitive attitude of the mind that establishes the *a priori* character of any principle, not excepting space, time, number, magnitude, permanence, change, causality, reciprocal interaction, or any other relation.

The assertion that this particular set of "universal functions," or any other particular set of relations or presuppositions "form a fixed system; and only relative to this system do assertions concerning the object, as well as concerning the subject, gain any intelligible meaning" is an assertion which is not only unwarranted but definitely untenable in the light of recent developments in logic and mathematics. These developments have definitely shown that various sets of postulates may serve as a logical basis from which the same deductive system may be derived. They have also definitely shown that deductive systems are purely analytical and tautological and that there are no synthetic propositions *a priori*. As Reichenbach has correctly said, "The evolution of science in the last century may be regarded as a continuous process of distintegration of the Kantian synthetic *a priori*."[39] In the light of the combined results of the developments in science, mathematics, and logic during the last

[39] Hans Reichenbach, "Logistic Empiricism in Germany," *Journal of Philosophy*, vol. 33 (1936), 145.

century, it would be difficult, at least, to justify the claim that
any one set of postulates is the only one relative to which experience would be possible; or that any one set of presuppositions is the only one in terms of which valid judgments concerning the object or the subject of knowledge can have any
meaning. It must be admitted that *some set* of logically prior
principles is necessary for the possibility of any knowledge of
anything at all. But this logical priority is not the inherent
birthright of any particular set of principles. If there has ever
been any justification for the Rationalist's claim that any certain
set of "first principles" is logically indispensable for the explanation of the experienced world of particulars, and that such
logical priority is a guarantee for the truth of those principles,
the grounds for that justification have been definitely eliminated by the revelations of modern logic and mathematics relative to the nature of deductive systems.

It is true, of course, that all knowledge is purely relational
and that man's whole categorial and conceptual scheme is a
purely relational scheme. It is also true that such a relational
scheme has meaning only within a more or less definitely fixed
set of "reference objects" which constitute a general "frame of
reference" somewhat analogous to a set of co-ordinate axes,
the points of the compass, meridians of longitudes and parallels
of latitude, etc. Those relations which Cassirer designates as the
"fixed system" of "supreme principles" may be regarded, in the
main, as just such a system of reference objects, and as constituting such a "frame of reference." But such reference objects
are neither true nor false, neither right nor wrong. They are
only methodological devices which render possible the achievement of some desired end. They may be convenient or inconvenient, adequate or inadequate, for the accomplishment of this
end. And although some such set of "reference objects" is necessary for the accomplishment of this end, no particular set is
necessarily invariant. Nor is any particular set of such relations
indispensable.

It is true, of course, that no given datum of experience ever
comes with its meaning attached, so that it may be read off by
the mind in some sort of *intellectuelle Anschauung* or some

Wordsworthian state of "wise passiveness." Each given datum receives meaning only through some interpretive construction being put upon it. And interpretation always involves the application of some set of distinguishing and definitive criteria and interpretive principles, some set of "reference objects," in terms of which interpretation gives meaning to the given datum of experience. Some such set of "elements of form" must, therefore, be logically prior to any knowledge at all. Such elements are creations of the mind and are *a priori*. Even the most primitive judgment involves the implicit application of such elements to the object of the judgment. This certainly does not imply, however, that any particular set of such *a priori* elements can be legitimately singled out and designated as the only set in terms of which even a meaningful experience is possible.

If one desires, therefore, to seek for the *a priori* either in the intellectual creations of the childhood of the individual or in those of the childhood of the race, he will likely find it there. For the *a priori* always serves as a means for the conceptual handling of "matters of fact," and wherever man is engaged in this sort of enterprise he will be using it. It is also true that any adequate conception of the *a priori* must be one that is applicable anywhere, on any level and in any phase of human experience where the work of an interpretive mind is recognizable. On this ground, there is certainly justification for Cassirer's insistence that certain *a priori* "elements of form" may be found on every level and in every phase of human experience. But I see no justification for his extension of the Critique of Reason into a Critique of Culture for the purpose of discovering the nature of the *a priori*. If his purpose was to show that the *a priori* consists of a set of *invariant* principles, then it seems to me that his monumental efforts have turned out to be a case of "Love's Labor's Lost."

I. K. STEPHENS

DEPARTMENT OF PHILOSOPHY
SOUTHERN METHODIST UNIVERSITY

4

Felix Kaufmann

CASSIRER'S THEORY OF SCIENTIFIC KNOWLEDGE

4

CASSIRER'S THEORY OF SCIENTIFIC KNOWLEDGE

I

FUTURE writers of textbooks on the history of philosophy will have little difficulty in assigning Ernst Cassirer a place within their neat schemes of philosophical doctrines. He will be classified as a neo-Kantian, and, more specifically, as an outstanding member of the Marburg school of neo-Kantians, alongside of Hermann Cohen and Paul Natorp. Cassirer himself frequently professed his close affiliation with this group of thinkers[1] and was profoundly influenced by Cohen's interpretation of Kant's philosophy.

It is one of Cohen's lasting accomplishments to have shown that Kant's intuitionistic theory of mathematics, as exhibited in some of the arguments in his Transcendental Aesthetics, represents only a transitory, pre-critical, stage in his philosophical development, which led to the *transcendental method* in the strict sense. This can be seen from Kant's diary, as well as from a comparison of the first edition of the *Critique of Pure Reason*, with the *Prolegomena* and with the second edition of the *Critique*. Cohen submits that this trend in Kant's thought represents genuine philosophical progress, the full implications of which were grasped neither by Kant himself nor by the idealistic schools which emerged after him. Accordingly, he assigns the task to his own generation of philosophers of understanding Kant better than he understood himself,[2] just as Kant had demanded that we understand Plato better than he understood

---

[1] See e.g., Cassirer's Preface to *Determinismus und Indeterminismus in der modernen Physik*, viii.

[2] See Preface to the 1st ed. of Hermann Cohen's *Logik der Reinen Erkenntnis*, xi, xii.

himself. A substantial part of Cassirer's life-work is an execution of this program. It will, therefore, be appropriate to start our analysis of his theory of knowledge with a brief outline of his interpretation of Kant's epistemological doctrine.

II

In a famous passage of the preface to the second edition of the *Critique of Pure Reason* Kant has drawn an analogy between his work and the work of Copernicus.

The experiment . . . ought to be made, whether we should not succeed better with the problems of metaphysic, by assuming that the objects must conform to our mode of cognition, for this would better agree with the demanded possibility of *a priori* knowledge of them, which is to settle something about objects, before they are given us. We have here the same case as with the first thought of Copernicus who, not being able to get on in the explanation of the movements of the heavenly bodies, as long as he assumed that all the stars turned round the spectator, tried, whether he could not succeed better, by assuming the spectator to be turning round, and the stars to be at rest. (F. Max Müller translation [1896:1922], 693.)

This analogy suggested the facile interpretation of Kant's philosophy, of his "Copernican Revolution," as a subjectivistic, anthropocentric doctrine. But more penetrating students of Kant—as were the members of the Marburg school—realized that this interpretation is apt to conceal the core of Kant's transcendental method. They realized that his approach was far more "revolutionary." He did not try to offer a new solution to the time-honored problem of the *origin* of knowledge by proposing a transformation which makes the subject the initial system, the "center of the universe." Kant rather disposed of the whole problem in its traditional formulation by refuting all attempts toward explaining pre-scientific and scientific experience in terms of the dogmatic assumption of things-in-themselves. This point is emphasized by Cassirer time and again, perhaps most forcefully in his analysis of Kant's philosophy in the eighth book of the *Erkenntnisproblem*.

Kantian philosophy is not primarily concerned with the ego, nor with its relations to external objects, but with the principles and the logical structure of experience. Neither "internal" nor "external" objects exist in- and for- themselves; they are given under the conditions of experience. Accordingly, we have to develop the norms and rules of experience before we make statements about the nature of things. Hitherto things and the ego had to be projected on a metaphysical background, to be derived from a common substantial origin in order to be grasped in their context; but now the question takes a new turn. What is now sought is the fundamental logical form of experience as such, which must apply to "internal" as well as "external" experience. Knowledge with respect to objects cannot be entirely different from knowledge with respect to our ego; both kinds of knowledge should be united by an all-embracing principle. In this principle we have the genuine, true unity of "origin," and we need only go back to this unity to dispose of the "absolute contrasts" presupposed by traditional ontology. These observations amount to a clear delineation of Kant's method; judgments about things rather than things are its theme. A problem of logic is posed, but this logical problem is exclusively related to and aimed at that peculiar and specific form of judgment by which we claim to know empirical objects.[3]

Kant's transcendental method starts from the fact of (scientific) experience and seeks to determine how this fact is possible. In other words, he clarifies the meaning of "objective experience." In making explicit the elements of experience and the different types and levels of synthesis involved, we arrive at synthetic propositions *a priori*. These propositions are *a priori for* experience inasmuch as they contain constitutive principles of experience, but they are *not independent of* experience in the sense of being valid beyond the realm of (possible) experience. The time-honored ontological principles are found to be pseudo-principles and the related ontological problems to be pseudo-problems, as soon as it is recognized that the "transcendent use" of the categories implied in their formulations is illegitimate. Yet this "extermination" of ontological principles does not amount to their complete annihilation; they are reinterpreted as regulative principles of scientific inquiry.

The unity of empirical knowledge is not "given" (*gegeben*) but "set as a task" (*aufgegeben*); in other words, it is not preestablished by things-in-themselves, but conceived as an ideal,

[3] *Erkenntnisproblem*, Vol. II, 662 f. Cf. also Vol. III, 3 ff.

a guiding principle, for scientific inquiry. Critical philosophy seeks to grasp the nature of this unity by analyzing it into its elements and determining the place of each element within the whole, in teleological terms, by determining its function in the constitution of the whole.

III

In referring to *this* meaning of the term "function" in Cassirer's philosophy, we are led to another strong influence in shaping his thought, the influence of Hegel. Broadly speaking —and making allowance for the unavoidable inaccuracy of such a formula—we may say that Cassirer used a somewhat modified Kantian method in promoting a goal set by Hegel. Although he is well aware of the basic defects of Hegel's metaphysical system,[4] he accepts as leitmotif of his own analysis Hegel's principle that truth as the "whole" is not given all at once but must be progressively unfolded by thought in its movement. The unity of knowledge must be discovered in the progress of knowledge from its primary and primitive stages to "pure" knowledge; it reveals itself in the form of this process. None of the phases of this process must be disregarded if we are to grasp the form of the process.[5]

Accordingly, Cassirer sets himself the task of determining what particular type of unity is sought and (temporarily) found in the different domains and at the different stages of human thought, and he seeks to disclose how the transition from one stage to another is necessitated by the inner dialetic of the movement of thought.

In his first systematic work, *Substanzbegriff und Funktionsbegriff*, Cassirer was guided by the idea that the structure and basic principles of knowledge could be most clearly discerned in mathematics and mathematical physics, where knowledge had reached its highest level. His chief aim was to corroborate his thesis that the progressive emancipation of thought from the so-called data of immediate experience manifests itself in the development of these sciences. This process of emancipation,

[4] See *Erkenntnisproblem*, Vol. III, 362-377.
[5] See e.g., Preface to Vol. III of *Philosophie der symbolischen Formen*, vi fl.

which can never be completed, is most conspicuous in the replacement of the thing-concept by the concept of law. Even the thing-concept is an intellectual construct of a highly complex structure, yet it shows a close affinity to the (allegedly) pure data of immediate perceptual experience. As long as it is made not only the starting-point but also the pivot of philosophical analysis, a certain kind of interpretation of mental activity in general and of the formation of scientific concepts in particular is suggested, an interpretation which has, indeed, prevailed in philosophical thought from the very outset. According to this view the activity of the mind consists exclusively in determining and isolating common qualitative elements within the vast variety of existing things, uniting them into classes, and repeating this procedure as long as possible. By comparing and distinguishing actually present objects of thought—mathematical objects as well as empirical objects—we arrive at an ever more embracing hierarchy of beings. The proposed interpretation seems to be in harmony with common sense and to save us from a dualism between percept and concept. The universals are taken to be *"in re,"* to be part of the perceptible world.

However, this traditional view does not bear closer examination. In the first place, it fails to account for the fact that scientific (and even pre-scientific) concepts are not random aggregates of qualities, but are established with a purpose. We do not—as Lotze remarked—form a class of reddish, juicy, edible things, under which cherries and meat might be subsumed; and the reason why we don't do it is that we consider such a notion quite irrelevant for theoretical as well as practical ends. Reference to it is not supposed to be productive of any new results. Thus we are led to the conclusion that qualitative similarity is not the only basis in all instances for the formation of concepts. Realizing that this process involves judgments concerning the relevance of a concept for the promotion of given ends, we can no longer maintain that the mental activity involved is confined to the recognition of qualitative similarities or differences and to selections on this basis.

But this is only half the story. It might still be suggested that such a similarity is a *necessary* condition for the formation of concepts. But even this view is untenable. What is required is rather a *relation* in terms of which the variety of (actually or potentially) given objects may be ordered. Such a relation does not dispose of the qualities of the individual objects concerned—if it did, it would not be of any aid in investigating specific objects—; but it replaces fixed qualities by general rules which enable us to grasp *uno actu* a total series of possible, qualitative determinations. This is of decisive theoretical and practical import. As inquiry proceeds, thing-concepts are gradually replaced by relation-concepts, and a hierarchy of laws, stating invariant relations in terms of mathematical functions, occupies the place formerly held by a hierarchy of intrinsic qualities. The transition from Aristotle's physics to Galileo's and Newton's physics is marked by this change in the conceptual framework of science.

Cassirer insists that there are guiding principles in arranging perceptual material, even on the pre-scientific level, principles which cannot be considered as inherent in the material; but this autonomy of form, this spontaneity of the mind, becomes ever more conspicuous and extensive as science advances. The totality of experience as it represents itself on any given stage of knowledge is not a mere aggregate of data of perception; it has a complex and intricate structure which constitutes its unity.

But this coherence of the body of knowledge established at a given time does not exhaust what we mean by "unity of science." There is, moreover, a "dynamic unity" of scientific procedure. The dynamic unity becomes manifest in the very process of the reconstruction of scientific systems. Even if we change most general principles—like those of Newton's mechanics—, which we avoid as long as less incisive changes in the theory can restore its agreement with the results of observation, we do not alter the fundamental form of experience, nor break the continuity of inquiry. This is seen when we consider that the new system is supposed to yield solutions of problems that emerged within the frame of the old system, but could not be solved there. It would indeed be impossible to demonstrate the advantage of the new system, unless there were invariant standards of comparability. These standards are the fundamental invariants of experience; to make them explicit is the main objective of critical (transcendental) philosophy, which, accordingly, may be regarded as the general theory of the invariants of experience.

If we say that knowledge of these "logical invariants" is knowledge *a priori*, this should not be taken to mean that it is prior (in time) to experience. It only means that these "logical invariants" are implicitly presupposed in any valid statement about facts. That is why the notion of space, but not that of color, is considered *a priori* in Kant's theory of knowledge; space is indeed an invariant for every physical construction; color is not.

IV

When Cassirer laid down these views in *Substance and Function* and supported them by a thorough analysis of mathematical and physical terms, as they emerged in the historical development of these sciences, Einstein's Special Theory of Relativity had only recently been developed and the General Theory had not yet been formulated. Cassirer's analysis of physical concepts in this work is therefore confined to classical physics in the strict sense. But soon after the General Theory of Relativity had been well established, Cassirer extended his analysis to both the Special and the General Theory.[6]

The geometry underlying Einstein's General Theory of Relativity is Riemannian geometry, which is a "Non-Euclidean" geometry. The Euclidean parallel postulate is replaced in it by the postulate that no "straight line" (geodesic) can be drawn through a given "point" which is "parallel" to a given "straight line." Still Euclidean geometry remains applicable in the "limiting case" of weak gravitational fields, like that of the earth, where the "curvature of space," determined by the strength of the gravitational field, comes close to zero. (Euclidean space is then interpreted as the space of zero-curvature.) The establishment of Einstein's theory had been considered by empiricist philosophers as a death-blow to Kant's doctrine.

[6] Cf. *Einstein's Theory of Relativity*. (The authorized English translation of this work from the pen of Cassirer is printed as a "Supplement"—pp. 347-456— in the Swabeys' English rendition of *Substance and Function*; Open Court, 1923.)

They claimed that his whole system breaks down with the collapse of one of its chief pillars, the aprioricity of Euclidean geometry. Is this claim well founded?

Even when Gauss, Lobachevski, Bolyai, and Riemann first constructed systems of non-Euclidean geometries without, however, applying them to physical science, it had been maintained that such systems are in conflict with Kant's philosophy. Yet this view was certainly wrong. What had been demonstrated by the non-Euclidean geometries—provided it could be shown that they were free from contradictions—was only that the Euclidean postulate is not an analytical consequence of the other postulates; but Kant had never maintained that a system of geometry different from Euclidean geometry is self-contradictory. Rather he had, in distinguishing the synthetic *a priori* from the analytical *a priori*, precluded such a view.

Kant did maintain that Euclidean geometry is *a priori* for physics; and this statement cannot be squared with Einstein's General Theory of Relativity. But it is another question whether this fact—and the fact that space and time cannot be isolated in Einstein's theory so that they apparently lose their physical objectivity—undermines the roots of Kant's doctrine. Cassirer submits that either of these facts leaves the fundamentals of critical philosophy untouched. In support of this view he offers a penetrating analysis of the meaning of "physical objectivity," which he prefaces by a declaration of the *partial* independence of the epistemologist from the scientist. The epistemologist is bound to accept scientifically established facts and laws, and these delimit indeed his universe of discourse; but he is not bound to accept the scientist's interpretation of these facts and laws in general philosophical terms, such as the term "objectivity." The main reason why the epistemologist is not bound to accept the scientist's interpretation is that analysis made by the former reaches beyond that of the scientist.

Each answer, which physics imparts concerning the character and the peculiar nature of its fundamental concepts, assumes inevitably for epistemology the form of a question. When, for example, Einstein gives as the essential result of his theory that by it "the last remainder of physical objectivity" is taken from space and time . . ., this answer of the physicist contains for the epistemologist the precise formulation of his real problem. What are we to understand by the physical objectivity, which is here denied to the concepts of space and time? To the physicist physical objectivity may appear as a fixed and sure starting-point and as an entirely definite standard of comparison; epistemology must ask that its meaning . . . be exactly defined.[7]

We arrive at such a definition by clarifying the function of the notion of objectivity in physical inquiry. Similar considerations apply to Kant's doctrine that Euclidean geometry is the one *a priori* true geometry.

We are no longer concerned with what space "is" and with whether any definite character, whether Euclidean, Lobatschefskian or Riemannian, is to be ascribed to it, but rather with what use is to be made of the different systems of geometrical presuppositions in the interpretation of the phenomena of nature and their dependencies according to law.[8]

We could say that Euclidean space was indeed *a priori* for Newtonian physics, since Euclidean geometry is presupposed in it, whereas, by this very token, Riemannian space is *a priori* for the General Theory of Relativity. This interpretation seems to be in harmony with Einstein's view, lucidly expressed in his lecture on *Geometrie und Erfahrung*.[9]

Kant, on the other hand, held undoubtedly that Euclidean geometry would have to underly physical science at any stage of its development, and this view was mistaken. But to concede this is not to admit that Einstein's General Theory has refuted the fundamentals of Kant's transcendental method. This method can be upheld after it has been freed from some time-bound limitations.

Commenting upon Cassirer's argument I would suggest that aprioricity in a more incisive sense could be claimed for some topological properties of space. Hermann Weyl has made the point (in his remarkable *Philosophie der Mathematik und Naturwissenschaft* [München, 1927], 97) that the number four of the dimensions of the space-time continuum is *a priori*

---

[7] *Einstein's Theory of Relativity*, (Swabey tr.) 356.
[8] *Ibid.*, 439.
[9] Berlin, (1921.)

in Kant's sense. This would imply, it seems to me, that the four-dimensionality of space-time is implicitly presupposed in perceptual experience—perceptual experiences being located in four-dimensional space-time—so that it could never be refuted by perceptual experience. This interpretation is in harmony with Kant's general conception of synthetic *a priori* as pertaining to the form of experience; and it is, moreover, supported by modern psychological analysis of the structure of perception.

V

When Einstein's Special and General Theories had been firmly established, they were first regarded as a revolution in physics, rendering the fundamental notions and principles of classical physics obsolete. But Einstein himself has always stressed the continuity of the process of inquiry leading to this theory; and nowadays his theory is considered the perfection of classical physics rather than its destruction. But the second great event in twentieth century physics, the emergence of quantum physics, is taken to be more truly revolutionary, and to impose on us a revision not only of fundamental physical notions, but also of philosophical categories, particularly of the category of causality. Here, then, seems to exist an even deeper cleavage between the Kantian theory for which Newton's *magnum opus* represented the *"fact of science,"* and a theory of knowledge which is in conformity with modern physics.

But even in this case we are cautioned by Cassirer against assuming that the transcendental method has been rendered obsolete by recent developments in physics. He discusses quantum physics in his *Determinismus und Indeterminismus in der modernen Physik,*[10] a work which offers perhaps the most accomplished elaboration of his theory of science. It is essential for the transcendental method, Cassirer points out, that it deals not directly with things but rather with our empirical knowledge of things, more precisely with the form of experience. Kant agrees with Hume's critique of the notion of causality

[10] *Determinismus und Indeterminismus in der modernen Physik.* (Sub-title: Historische und systematische Studien zum Kausalproblem.) Göteburg (1936).

inasmuch as it established that there is no innate, self-evident idea of causality, no subjective necessity rooted in our mental organization which compels us to acknowledge a rigid causal nexus among phenomena. But Kant's epistemological analysis does not stop at this point, as did Hume's. Whereas he admits that the principle of causality does not enable us to state any specific physical law, he vindicates this principle as a "postulate," as a "regulative principle" of science. It is a statement of the resolution not to give up the search for causes and to strive toward an ever more comprehensive system of knowledge, a resolution which is basic for scientific inquiry.

Cassirer is, of course, fully aware of the fact that Kant had not been quite consistent in the development of this idea, that he had, in the "Analogies of Experience," offered a "deduction" of the principle of causality. But this, Cassirer declares, is one more point where we have to understand Kant better than he understood himself, if we are to be true Kantians. We have to follow him only so long as he does not part with his own professed principles, the principles of the transcendental method.

The preceding remarks should not create the impression that *Determinism and Indeterminism in Modern Physics* is primarily concerned with a defense of Kant's transcendental method. This is by no means the case. The object of this book is rather a reconsideration of the structure of physical science in the light of the development of quantum physics. One of Cassirer's most important points is the distinction between three types of statements in physics, viz., a) statements of the results of measurements (*Massaussagen*), b) laws, c) principles. This distinction was suggested by Russell's theory of types which had been established for the purpose of precluding the emergence of antinomies in logic and Cantorian set theory. The theory of types is governed by the so-called Vicious Circle Principle: "Whatever includes all of a collection must not be one of the collection," which "enables us to avoid the vicious circles involved in the assumption of illegitimate totalities."[11] Cassirer's hierarchy of types of physical statements is

[11] Whitehead-Russell, *Principia Mathematica*, Vol. I, 40.

meant to preclude similar predicaments in the analysis of empirical science.

Concerning (a): Statements of the results of measurement are attained by transposing reports of sensory experiences into determinations in terms of numerical relations. These "statements of the first order" are singular propositions. They relate to definite space-time points.

Concerning (b): Realization that physical laws are a distinct type of physical statements implies rejection of the sensationalists' view—most vigorously defended by J. S. Mill—that a physical law is but an aggregate of particular truths, and that "all inference is from particulars to particulars." This view has always been one of the chief targets of Cassirer's criticism. Time and again he has pointed out that it is not in accordance with actual scientific procedure and that the great scientists of the modern age, from Galileo on, were fully aware of the heterogeneity of fact-statements and laws. A law is a hypothetical judgment of the form: "If x then y;" it does not connect single magnitudes with definite space-time points; rather it refers to classes of magnitudes, classes which have an infinite number of elements and are thus inexhaustible by simple enumeration.[12]

Concerning (c): The distinction between fact-statements and laws had been widely recognized before; but the difference between laws and principles had remained almost unnoticed. Whereas facts are brought into a definite order by laws, the laws themselves are integrated into a higher unity by principles, such as the principle of the conservation of energy or the principle of least action (which is the most general of all physical principles).

The three types of statements may be differentiated in a formal way by calling them, respectively, "individual," "general," and "universal."

In defending the tripartition against the tendencies (represented by Mill) toward levelling down these distinctions, Cassirer makes an interesting remark which indicates his attitude

[12] *Determinismus . . .*, 51 ff.

toward "dogmatic empiricism." "The defect of dogmatic empiricism," he points out,

does not consist in its attempt to link all knowledge to experience and to recognize nothing but experience as a criterion of truth, but rather in its failure to go far enough in the *analysis* of experience, in its stopping short of a clarified notion of it. It is not infrequently a vague assumption of continuity that leads to this attitude; empiricism refrains from strictly separating the various stages of knowledge in order to be able to develop them from each other. But this development is deceptive, if one seeks to understand it as a mere reproduction of similarity. Somewhere in the process of knowledge we must acknowledge a genuine *"mutation"* which leads to something new and independent.[13]

The failure of dogmatic empiricism to give a proper account of the practice of physical inquiry becomes most obvious in an analysis of statistical laws which latter have gained an ever higher significance since Gibbs' and Boltzmann's foundation of statistical mechanics. Boltzmann's kinetical theory of gases interprets the physical properties of a gas, such as its density, its pressure, its specific heat, as resultants of the movements of its molecules; but it does not attempt to determine the movements of each single molecule. Some hypothetical assumptions concerning statistical averages, for instance average velocity, are made, and the behavior of the gas is explained in terms of these hypotheses. It is clear that such a procedure cannot be interpreted as an inference from particulars to particulars, as Mill and his disciples would have it.

There is one more methodological conclusion which we may draw from Boltzmann's theory, a conclusion which provides a cue to the philosophical interpretation of quantum physics, namely that physics does not attempt to answer every "Why-question"[14] which may possibly be asked, and that its success is largely due to this self-restraint, and to a selection of problems in accordance with certain regulative principles of inquiry.

Having realized this, we shall no longer maintain that Heisenberg's principle of indeterminacy, which occupies a central

[13] *Ibid.*, 68f.
[14] *Ibid.*, 132.

place in quantum physics, means a complete break with the
fundamental ideas of classical physics. Heisenberg's principle
states that the precision in determining simultaneously two
"conjugate magnitudes," such as the position and the velocity of
an electron, is limited by *Planck's* constant h. In the older (uncritical) view, which interpreted electrons as "material points,"
pre-established thing-like entities, this principle seemed to involve sceptical resignation, the acknowledgment that the finite
human mind cannot trespass certain boundaries. Critical analysis,
however, reveals that the traditional formulation of these
"insoluble problems" is inadequate, and that the pertinent
arguments of the sceptics lose their point as soon as we formulate the problems adequately. We have to dispose of the idea
that a material point is a pre-established entity, existing independently of the relations into which it may enter, and to
realize that "material point" is defined in terms of the system
of these relations. Cassirer points out that there is no basic
difference in this respect between the notion of a "material"
physical point and the notion of an "ideal" mathematical point.
In the so-called axioms of geometry, a mathematical point is
"implicitly defined" in terms of a system of formal relations.
"Material point," on the other hand, is implicitly defined in
terms of a system of relations which we call a physical theory.
Hence "material" points are intellectual constructs, as are
"ideal" geometrical points; and the demand that "absolute"
locations should be assigned to them is as illegitimate as would
be the corresponding demand for geometrical points.

VI

We have already mentioned that Cassirer's analysis of physical theories is performed with the purpose of corroborating his
thesis that the decisive stages in the advancement of science are
marked by a progressive emancipation from "naïve" realism,
which starts from a conception of things-in-themselves and
interprets knowledge as a conformity of our thoughts with those
pre-established "objects." Each new stage in scientific progress
is characterized by a specific type of "objectification," by the
creation of new scientific objects, represented in the symbols
of the language of science. All of Cassirer's elaborate and en-

lightening interpretations of scientific theories are but so many variations of this central theme. The same is true of his analysis of mathematical concepts.

A substantial part of *Substance and Function* is devoted to this analysis. Russell's *Principles of Mathematics* had, at the time, been published only a few years before, and Whitehead-Russell's *Principia Mathematica* had not yet appeared. The number of mathematicians and philosophers engaged in working on problems of the "foundations of mathematics" was still small. This situation changed rapidly during the following two decades. *Principia Mathematica* demonstrated what can be achieved in the way of a unification of logic and mathematics; Hilbert took the final step in the "formalization" of mathematics, and Brouwer advanced his criticism of the application of the principle of excluded middle, a criticism which seemed to affect not only Cantor's set theory, but large sections of classical mathematics. Spirited controversies between logicists (Russell), formalists (Hilbert), and intuitionists (Brouwer) ensued and attracted wide attention; and it was generally assumed that basic philosophical issues were at stake. However, there were only a small number of philosophers who were prepared to face the difficulties in studying the rather "technical" books and papers in the field.

Cassirer was one of those few. In chapter IV of Part III of the third volume of his *Philosophie der symbolischen Formen* (1929) he offers a well-considered interpretation of some of the major pertinent problems, an accomplishment which deserved more attention than it has actually received. Philosophers should be grateful to him for his placing these problems in their proper historical setting. And they should, moreover, find some of his critical remarks apt and incisive. I, for one, have no doubt that he is right in rejecting 1) Russell's reduction of the number concept to the class concept, 2) Brouwer's (and Becker's) interpretation of the rôle of time in mathematics, and 3) Hilbert's philosophical interpretation of his formalization of mathematics, according to which the visible marks as such would be the object of mathematics.[15] Each of these points

---

[15] The present writer came to similar conclusions, in a book, *Das Unendliche in*

is of major philosophical significance. Russell's way of relating the class concept to the number concept is closely linked with his sensationalist and nominalist view concerning universals. Brouwer's emphasis on the time factor in mathematics (and his demand for actual construction in mathematics) raises the basic issue of the meaning of possibility (which is indeed the problem of universals seen from another angle). And Hilbert's interpretation of his formalization involves the same problem.

Cassirer never tires of stressing that we have to interpret "reality" and "experience" in terms of "possibility", though there is no "realm of possibilities" beyond experience. He analyzes mathematical systems, for instance those of different types of geometry, in order to make it clear that they do not contain any assertions about "real" things or facts, but deal with pure possibilities. These possibilities cannot be derived from sense perception. "Experience as such does not contain in itself a principle for the production of such possibilities, its rôle is confined to a selection among them in the application to given concrete cases. Its real accomplishment consists in determination rather than in constitution."[16] "One could say, using a metaphor taken from the language of chemistry, that sense experience has essentially a 'catalytic' function in the development of the theories of the natural sciences."[17] Sense experience is indispensable for the process of forming exact concepts, but it is no longer contained as an independent ingredient in the product emerging from this process, in the scientific concept. And the process of establishing scientific concepts, which is a process of objectification, has its own immanent principle of development. Each subsequent (higher) stage of development terminates the earlier stage, but it assimilates rather than exterminates that earlier stage.[18] A striking example is the progress from Newton's system to Einstein's Special Theory and General Theory of Relativity.

---

der Mathematik und seine Ausschaltung, which appeared shortly after the publication of Cassirer's work.

[16] Philosophie der symbolischen Formen, Vol. III, 487.

[17] Ibid., 485.

[18] Hegel expresses this view by using the word "aufgehoben," which may mean cancelled (abrogated) or "preserved."

VII

Each stage of objectification is represented by a specific system of linguistic symbols. But this fact must not be interpreted as a creation of concepts (meanings) by words, as radical nominalists would have it. The meaning is the nuclear point, the true πρότερον φύσει. However we should not regard the word as a mere appendix to the concept, it is rather one of the most important means for the actualization of the concept, for its separation from the "immediately given." Hence linguistic signs are indispensable in the process of objectification, and it is proper to approach the theory of knowledge from the angle of an analysis of scientific language. But in doing this we should bear in mind that the theory of knowledge is not the whole of philosophy, and that the activity of the scientist is not the only nor the first attempt of man to transform a chaos of immediate experiences into a cosmos. The symbolism of scientific language is therefore not the only symbolism a study of which is required for an understanding of the nature of man, who should be defined as an *animal symbolicum* rather than as an *animal rationale*.[19]

It is the task of systematic philosophy . . . to grasp the *whole system* of symbolic forms, the application of which produces for us the concept of an ordered reality, and by virtue of which subject and object, ego and world are separated and opposed to each other in definite form, and it must refer each individual in this totality to its fixed place. If we assume this problem solved, then the rights would be assured, and the limits fixed, of each of the particular forms of the concept and of knowledge as well as of the general forms of the theoretical, ethical, aesthetic and religious understanding of the world. Each particular form would be "relativized" with regard to the others, but since this "relativization" is throughout reciprocal and since no single form but only the systematic totality can serve as the expression of "truth" and "reality," the limit that results appears as a thoroughly immanent limit, as one that is removed as soon as we again relate the individual to the system of the whole.[20]

The three volumes of Cassirer's *Philosophie der symbolischen*

[19] *An Essay on Man* (1944), 26.
[20] *Einstein's Theory of Relativity*, (Swabey translation), 447.

Formen (summarized in his *Essay on Man*) represent a remarkable contribution towards this goal. The chief critical outcome of this approach is a refutation of sensationalism as well as of dogmatic realism. Cassirer realized that such a refutation, in order to be fully convincing, must start at the level of sense-perception.

We shall conclude our brief outline of Cassirer's epistemology by referring to his important study "The Concept of Group and the Theory of Perception,"[21] which suggests a mathematical interpretation of some of the results of Gestalt psychology, and contains a devastating criticism of the traditional sensationalist theory of perception, according to which perception is merely a bundle of sense-impressions.

This doctrine, Cassirer points out, has been definitely shattered by physiological and psychological research initiated by Helmholtz's and Hering's investigations. There is first of all the established fact of perceptual constancy involving both color constancy and constancy of spatial shape and size. A sheet of paper which appears white in ordinary daylight is recognized as white in very dim light as well; a piece of velvet which looks black to us under a cloudy sky looks also black to us in full sunshine; a piece of paper which looks blue to us in daylight looks blue also in the reddish-yellow light of a gasflame. Considering that every change of illumination is accompanied by a modification in the stimulation of the retina, we realize that these facts cannot be squared with the sensationalist's theory of perception, which claims that the stimuli are simply "copied" in perception. We have to admit, on the basis of this evidence, that the stimuli are transformed in a certain direction.

Experiments concerning perceptions of shape and size lead to similar conclusions.

When an object is moved away from our eyes, the images on the retinae become smaller and smaller. Nonetheless, within certain distances, the perceptual size of the object is constant. Variations of shape, which result from the fact that a figure is turned out of the frontal-parallel position,

---

[21] This article appeared first in French in the *Journal de Psychologie* (1938), 368-414. It was recently translated into English by Dr. A. Gurwitch and published in *Philosophy and Phenomenological Research*, Vol. V (1944-45), 1-35.

are also "counterbalanced" by the eye to a high degree, so that we perceive the figure in its "true" shape. *What is meant by this "truth"*— a kind of truth which seems to contradict the objective facts, the real conditions of physical stimulation? In raising this question, psychological inquiry comes close to the fundamental epistemological problems of the theory of perception, even though it may try to confine itself strictly to empirical observation.[22]

The theory of knowledge has to take account of the fact that "we do not merely *'re-act'* to the stimulus, but in a certain sense act *'against'* it," and thereby accomplish a "transformation." This fact gives rise to the question whether the group concept, the nuclear concept in the mathematical theory of transformations, can offer a clue for an interpretation of the phenomena of perception.

Group theory, which has developed in the last hundred years into one of the most important mathematical disciplines, has also substantially contributed to a deeper understanding of the nature of mathematics, and particularly of geometry. A group (as defined by Lie and Klein) is a system of unique operations A, B, C, . . . so that from the combination of any two operations A and B there results an operation C which also belongs to the totality: $A \cdot B = C$. The system must contain the Identity Element which, when combined with any other element, leaves this other element unchanged. Furthermore, there must be an inverse operation S^{-1} established for any given operation S, such that S^{-1} cancels out (reverses) S; and finally, the associative law $A(BC) = (AB)C$ must hold. Now it has been definitely established in F. Klein's famous "Erlanger Program of 1872" that the geometrical properties of any figures are completely describable in terms of group theory. Our familiar metrical Euclidean geometry is a member of a family of geometries, each of which investigates the invariant properties of a particular group. The groups may be classified in an order of increasing generality. We arrive from metrical geometry successively at affinitive geometry, projective geometry, and topology (*analysis situs*) by considering movements with re-

[22] *Ibid.*, 10.

spect to ever wider "principal groups of transformations." With every extension of the "principal group" some distinctions which could be made in a geometry corresponding to the narrower principal group disappear. Thus the distinction between circles and ellipses disappears in affinitive geometry; all kinds of conic sections (circles, ellipses, hyperbolae, parabolae) become indistinguishable in projective geometry, and as we come to topology we can no longer differentiate between any figures that may be derived from each other by continuous reversibly unique distortions.

Helmholtz was the first to attempt an application of group theory to an investigation of the phenomena of perception. But this approach could not stand up under experimental tests. Since that time the psychology of perception has made great strides, particularly through the work of the Gestalt psychologists (Wertheimer, Köhler, Koffka, Katz, and many others) who followed a trend of thought suggested by Ehrenfels. Gestalt psychologists have performed systematic studies of invariances of perceptual experiences with respect to certain kinds of variations in the stimuli. It is characteristic of phenomenal forms (*phaenomenale Gestalten*) that their specific properties remain unchanged when the absolute data upon which they rest undergo certain modifications. Thus a melody is not substantially altered when all of its notes are subjected to the same relative displacement; an optical spatial figure remains approximately the same when it is presented in a different place or on a different scale, but in the same proportions.[23]

These phenomena, Cassirer submits, are closely related to group theory.

What we find in both cases are invariances with respect to variations undergone by the primitive elements out of which a form is constructed. The peculiar kind of "identity" that is attributed to apparently altogether heterogeneous figures in virtue of their being transformable into one another by means of certain operations defining a group, is thus seen to exist also in the domain of perception. This identity permits us not only to single out elements, but also to grasp "structures" in perception. To

[23] W. Köhler, *Die physischen Gestalten in Ruhe und im stationären Zustand*, (1920), 37, quoted by Cassirer in *Ibid.*, 25.

the mathematical concept of "transformability" there corresponds, in the domain of perception, the concept of "transposability."[24]

However, we must not interpret this correspondence as an identity. There is no complete invariance of phenomena of perception with respect to such variations as mentioned above. Gestalt psychologists have fully recognized that we should speak of more or less effective tendencies toward invariance, the degree of effectiveness depending on various factors of which we have to take account in describing a perceptual field. Wertheimer has, accordingly, introduced the concept of "Gestalt dispositions," by which he understands tendencies toward "laws of organization" of the perceptual material.

It could not escape Cassirer's attention that these results of modern psychology square well with Plato's conception of the relation between perception and thought. Moreover, he emphasized that they vindicate some basic ideas of Kant's concerning the function of imagination which Kant had laid down in the *Critique of Pure Reason* (chapter on Schematism) and in the *Critique of Judgment*. But the most obvious philosophical conclusions to be drawn from these psychological results is the untenability of the sensationalist's interpretation of perception as a process of mere reproduction. Considering that this interpretation is at the very heart of the sensationalist doctrine, it is difficult to understand how this doctrine should be able to continue to have any influence after its lifeline has been cut.

VIII

Brief and fragmentary as our presentation of Cassirer's contributions to the theory of knowledge had to be, it has, I hope, brought into sharp focus the guiding principles of his analysis of cognition. This should enable us to determine in a broad way the relation of his teachings to other contemporary philosophical doctrines.

Although he is inclined to stress points of agreement rather than points of disagreement, and generously acknowledges merits even where he disapproves, Cassirer makes it unmistakably clear that he is strongly opposed to uncritical realism and

[24] *Ibid.*, 25.

sensationalism. Moreover, he rejects all varieties of transempirical metaphysics; philosophy is, to him, as it was to Kant, analysis of experience. He combats "atomism" wherever he finds it and endorses a coherence theory of truth which bears some resemblance to Hegel's pertinent views; but he would not accept the chief tenets of the doctrines of Bradley and other neo-Hegelians, who claim that the real subject of a judgment is the Absolute, and that our particular judgments are inconsistent.

Can it then be said that Cassirer is a "positivist" who disposes of metaphysical sentences as meaningless pseudo-statements? We should hardly expect a historian of philosophy, who has taken so much pains in interpreting the teachings of the great "metaphysicians" of the past, to endorse this view without qualifications. Although he concedes that metaphysical sentences are not meaningful at face value, he insists that they can be transformed into meaningful sentences by interpreting ontological principles as regulative principles of cognition. "What metaphysics ascribes as a *property* to things in themselves now proves to be a necessary element in the process of objectification."[25] This way of dealing with metaphysical doctrines had been established in Kant's "Transcendental Dialectics," and the philosophers of the Marburg school have consistently followed this clue. It would be a good thing for the more uncompromising anti-metaphysicians to give this Kantian and neo-Kantian approach a second thought. Desirable as it is to get rid of pseudo-problems, we should, in disposing of them, be careful lest we pour out the baby with the bath.

Cassirer took issue with this cavalier way of treating metaphysical doctrines in one of his later works.[26] There he quotes with approval a statement made half a century ago by the great physicist Heinrich Hertz, which was aimed at the anti-metaphysicians among his fellow-scientists. "No consideration which makes any impression on our mind can be disposed of by labeling it as 'metaphysical;' every thinking mind has needs

---

[25] *Substance and Function.* 303f.
[26] *Axel Hägerström: Eine Studie zur schwedischen Philosophie der Gegenwart* (1939).

which the natural scientist is wont to call 'metaphysical'."

Heinrich Hertz was anything but a metaphysician; his great work, *Die Prinzipien der Mechanik*, from which the sentence quoted above is taken, has indeed more definitely disposed of the "metaphysical" concept of force than any preceding treatise on physics. But he realized that the attempts of scientists towards making their fundamental notions clear frequently stop short of the level of clarity that can be reached if clarification of meaning is made the primary objective of inquiry. That's where the philosopher steps in, but in doing this he has to be constantly on his guard against hasty interpretations of scientific findings which seem to lend support to his specific doctrine. It is shown by the record that scientists who become philosophers in their leisure hours are hardly less exposed to this danger than professional philosophers, though in a slightly different form. Whereas their accounts of the work accomplished in their own field are usually accurate, they are prone to exaggerate the range of applicability of their methods to other domains of inquiry and, consequently, to underrate the significance of other methods. But we should gratefully acknowledge the fact that a number of prominent scientists—like Helmholtz, Mach, and Poincaré—who discussed the "foundations" of their sciences, have offered most valuable aid to philosophers in their attempts to grasp thoroughly the methods of science. Ernst Cassirer used this help to the best advantage.

There is one more point to be made in this context. The fact that the process of clarification is carried farther by philosophers than by scientists, *qua* scientists, may be stressed by saying that philosophical analysis penetrates deeper than scientific analysis. Understood in this sense, the statement is legitimate. But it should not be taken to imply that the "realm" of scientific knowledge is strictly separated from the "deeper realm" of philosophical knowledge, and that the scientist *qua* scientist and the philosopher *qua* philosopher have to refrain from crossing the borderlines. This view, which may be historically linked to the medieval doctrine of the twofold truth, has been defended —more or less explicitly—by prominent contemporary philosophers and scientists, such as Whitehead, Eddington, and Jeans, but it is certainly not endorsed by Cassirer. He holds that the scientist can—in principle—never go too far in the process of clarification of his terms and methods, and that the philosophers can never come too close to the scientist's work.

Cassirer's "scientific attitude" and his familiarity with modern mathematics and physics represents no minor link between his teaching and the doctrine of logical positivism, which has so emphatically stressed this attitude and so thoroughly analyzed the principles of mathematics and natural science.[27] This affinity became even greater as logical positivism gradually freed itself from vestiges of sensationalism, which were largely due to the influence of Mach and Russell. But there are important doctrinal differences which should not be overlooked. The logical positivists are radical anti-metaphysicians in the sense described above. They regard ontological statements as altogether meaningless and seek to eliminate them by a logical analysis of language; whereas Cassirer transforms them into regulative principles of inquiry. Another point of difference is Cassirer's rejection of "physicalism," (radical behaviorism), which has for some time prevailed among logical positivists. But it should be noted that the leading philosopher of the group, Rudolf Carnap, has, in the last decade, modified his physicalism to an extent which comes close to its complete abandonment.[28]

There is, moreover, the issue of the universals which divides the two doctrines. Cassirer is clearly opposed to nominalism, whereas the logical positivists are among the staunchest nominalists in contemporary philosophy. Cassirer's "conceptualistic" view is well expressed in the following sentence:[29]

That the general birch-tree "exists" can only mean that what is to be

[27] Philipp Frank, one of the leading members of this group, is basically in agreement with Cassirer's interpretation of quantum physics and considers his philosophical work as a whole as a (highly welcome) symptom of a "disintegrating process inside of school philosophy." See his discussion of Cassirer's *Determinismus und Indeterminismus in der modernen Physik* in his volume, *Between Physics and Philosophy* (Cambridge, 1941), 191-210.

[28] I have discussed this change in Carnap's view in Ch. XI of my *Methodology of the Social Sciences*, New York, (1944).

[29] *Axel Hägerström*, 51.

stated by it is not a mere name, not simply a *flatus vocis;* the statement is meant to refer to *relations* of the real. We express by the notion "general birch-tree" merely the fact that there are *judgments* which do not refer to this or that—here and now given—birch-tree, but claim to apply to "all" birch-trees. I can uphold this logical participation, this μέτεξις of the particular in the general, without transforming it into an ontological statement in which two fundamental forms of reality are posited.

In the paper mentioned above, Philipp Frank quotes Jacques Maritain as saying "that the aim of the Vienna circle and of the whole movement of logical empiricism was to 'disontologize science'."[30] We might say with equal right that one of the aims of Cassirer's theory of knowledge is to disontologize philosophy without destroying it.

IX

The relation of Cassirer's philosophy to pragmatism in general, and to Dewey's instrumentalism in particular, might, at first glance, seem to be more remote than its relation to logical positivism, and to imply a larger number of conflicting tenets. But this cannot be unreservedly maintained. The neo-Kantianism of the Marburg school is, indeed, in some important respects closer to pragmatism than to logical positivism. We shall confine ourselves to a brief comparison between Cassirer's and Dewey's theories of knowledge and make the point that some striking differences between their doctrines are less fundamental than one might suppose them to be. Dewey's philosophy, it might be suggested, is through and through naturalistic; Cassirer's philosophy, on the other hand, is through and through idealistic. We are thus confronted with two diametrically opposed philosophical approaches.

But such an interpretation is all too facile, and cannot bear closer examination. We should be aided in a more thorough appraisal of the relation between the two philosophies by considering their historical settings. Dewey, as well as Cassirer, was profoundly influenced (though in a different way) by Kantian and Hegelian teachings; and both were also under the impact

[30] *Between Physics and Philosophy,* 195.

of the naturalist-empiricist reaction to these teachings. Each
of the two men was too penetrating a thinker to ignore the
strong points in either of the conflicting philosophical trends.
It is, of course, undeniable that Dewey broke determinedly
away from the Hegelian tradition and rejected in unambiguous
terms Kant's apriorism and dualism (as he saw them); whereas
Cassirer considers himself as a faithful, though not orthodox,
follower of Kant, and to some extent, even of Hegel. Quite
a number of doctrinal differences, which should by no means
be minimized, can be historically interpreted in terms of this
split. But we have to ask whether the split goes to the roots,
whether it leads to opposite theoretical or practical conclusions.

We might look for a clue to an answer to this question by
considering the manner in which our two philosophers deal
with the notions of "development" and "progress." When Cassirer uses these terms, we are reminded of Aristotle's entelechy
and self-perfection, of Leibniz' monads, and of Hegel's dialectical movement of the objective mind. When Dewey uses
these terms, one is under the spell of Darwin's *Origin of
Species*. We know that the effect of this shift in meaning from
spiritual development to biological evolution can be tremendous. It is apt to lend support to a transvaluation of traditional
values and to the irrationalism of a Nietzsche, Pareto, Sorel.
But we know as well that Dewey is most vigorously opposed to
these irrationalist tendencies, and shall therefore not conclude
that an irreconcilable conflict between the two doctrines is
proved by a pragmatic test. Since we cannot thoroughly understand diversities unless we are able to grasp the underlying
identities, we shall start by referring to the common features
of the two doctrines.

First of all, they are close to each other in the professed aim
of their theories of knowledge, which is to clarify the basic
principles of scientific inquiry. Consequently, they are opposed
to any interpretation of philosophy, according to which philosophy could and should "legislate" to science. Moreover, they
agree that one should rather define "(factual) truth" in terms
of knowledge, as outcome of inquiry, than knowledge in terms
of "truth." Both philosophers reject the correspondence theories

of truth as proposed by realists and by sensationalists, e.g., Bertrand Russell. They endorse a coherence theory of truth, where "coherence" is not understood as mere consistency of the body of established knowledge, but interpreted in terms of the principles of empirical procedure. Linked with this point is the conception of inquiry as a process which is guided by a set of "postulates." Kant's regulative principles as interpreted by the Marburg school, are not very different in function from Peirce's and Dewey's leading principles—though the latter are more flexible—and the resemblance between Cassirer's and Dewey's reinterpretations of traditional epistemological controversies in terms of such methodological principles is sometimes striking.

These considerations should suffice for a rejection of the view that Cassirer's decidedly idealistic approach is diametrically opposed to Dewey's decidedly naturalistic approach. As a matter of fact, we need not go very far in the study of Dewey's work to discover that his naturalism is heavens apart from those crude types of naturalism which would "reduce" human activity to behavior of inanimate bodies. I do not see why Cassirer should have had to take issue with a naturalism which is characterized as follows:

The term "naturalistic" has many meanings. As it is here employed it means, on one side, that there is no breach of continuity between operations of inquiry and biological operations and physical operations. "Continuity," on the other side, means that rational operations *grow out* of organic activities, without being identical with that from which they emerge.[31]

Nor was he bound to have any substantial objections to Dewey's outline of the "cultural matrix of inquiry" in the third chapter of the *Logic* (and in earlier works), which might well have led to the definition of man as a symbol-making animal, as suggested by Cassirer.

Yet there are indeed incisive differences between the two doctrines which have direct bearing upon methodological issues. We shall briefly examine two of them. The first relates

[31] Dewey, *Logic: The Theory of Inquiry*, 18f.

to the problem of the nature of meanings. While Dewey is not an extreme nominalist, he is much closer to nominalism than Cassirer, even though Cassirer is as little a conceptual realist as was Kant.[32] Dewey treats comprehension of meaning and sensation on an almost equal footing. Immediate experience of both types is taken to be preliminary; it indicates a problem, but it cannot by itself establish knowledge. Only in its proper setting within the context of empirical inquiry is such experience conducive to knowledge. Cassirer would endorse this view as far as sensation is concerned. This tenet is indeed as essential in his philosophy as it is in Dewey's. But he would not accept the view that comprehension of meaning is in a similar sense controlled by empirical inquiry as is sensation. He would, moreover, insist upon a sharp differentiation between *verités de raison* and *verités de fait*, and, accordingly, upon the autonomy of pure logic and pure mathematics.

Although I am in agreement with Cassirer on this issue, I think that in another respect Dewey's theory of inquiry is superior to Cassirer's; namely, in its analysis of scientific testing. One might be tempted to emphasize this point by declaring that Cassirer's interpretation of science is static, whereas Dewey's approach is dynamic. These terms are indeed suggestive of an important difference between the two approaches, but they should not mislead us into conceiving of Cassirer as an orthodox disciple of Parmenides. He realizes as well as any pragmatist that scientific inquiry is a potentially endless self-correcting process; but (like the classical economist) he focuses his attention upon states of equilibrium, where the material of available perceptual experience is "absorbed" by theoretical systems. Dewey, on the other hand, concentrates upon the processes that emerge from (particular) states of disequilibrium—indeterminate situations—and lead to the attainment of new equilibria (determinate situations). And he deals more thoroughly with the conditions of "warranted assertability," with the criteria for the distinction between warranted and unwarranted assertions.

The analysis of warranted assertability is intimately con-

[32] See *supra*, 189 f., 208 f.

nected with the problem of determining the relation between propositional meaning and the criteria of verification of propositions (the so-called truth-conditions). Cassirer's discussion, in his *Erkenntnisproblem*, of Kant's criticism of the ontological argument gives some hints as to where he stands on this issue; but I do not think that it suffices for a full understanding of his position. This problem is as actual in contemporary theory of knowledge as was the problem of the relation between essence and existence in Greek and medieval philosophy; and I would even submit that it is a "modern" version of this time-honored metaphysical issue. As such it is closely linked with the perennial problems of matter and form, which are a leitmotif throughout Cassirer's work.

It would be a rewarding task to compare Cassirer's general treatment of these problems with their treatment in Husserl's phenomenology. But in making such an attempt I should have to overstep the boundaries of space allotted to me and the limits of my assignment, and I am too well aware of Heraclitus' warning to venture this. I shall therefore confine myself to the remark that Husserl's approach to the problems of matter and form[33] is rather different from Cassirer's approach, which is more in line with the classical interpretation of matter as both a challenge and an obstacle to the 'forming' activity of the mind.

In the General Introduction to *The Library of Living Philosophers*, the editor resumes F. C. S. Schiller's question: "Must philosophers disagree?" When one studies Ernst Cassirer's work, which sheds a flood of light on different philosophical aspects with a view towards synthesizing them, one feels that disagreement among philosophers need not persist unabated.

FELIX KAUFMANN

GRADUATE FACULTY
NEW SCHOOL FOR SOCIAL RESEARCH

[33] In the 5th and 6th of his *Logische Untersuchungen*, in the *Ideen*, in *Formale und transcendentale Logik*, and in *Erfahrung und Urteil*.

5

Dimitry Gawronsky

CASSIRER'S CONTRIBUTION TO THE EPISTEMOLOGY OF PHYSICS

CASSIRER'S CONTRIBUTION TO THE EPISTEMOLOGY OF PHYSICS

NO OTHER epistemological problem has caused philosophers and scientists as great a headache as the application of mathematics to the cognition of real things. Mathematics and material things seem to belong to two quite different worlds —mathematical concepts, relations, and laws reveal such an absolute precision and necessity, two qualities, these latter, which do not exist in the same form in the world of reality. The geometrical straight line, for instance, is physically a quite impossible concept: first, because this line consists exclusively of one dimension and, not having any thickness, could not be represented by any really existing thing; and, secondly, it is conceived as a form which has absolutely no curbs or bends, and this, again, is a physical impossibility. One could argue that the concept of straight line is given us—even if not in a perfect, then at least in an approximative form—by real things, for instance by a straight slender stick. Yet, this argument is hardly sound; first of all, this slender stick is not just a gift of nature, but had been manufactured by man who was guided in this job by his idea of a straight line; and, secondly, even if by some miracle such a rod could be found in nature, even then it could be transformed into an exact mathematical concept only through an infinite process of attenuation and straightening, whereby the straight line itself, as the limit of this infinite process, would always be present in our mind as a directing and controlling prototype.

The more obvious it becomes that mathematical concepts and real things belong to two different spheres, the more difficult grows the question: how is it possible that even the subtlest and most complicated mathematical relations and laws find their successful application to the world of reality? Only two directly opposite philosophical tendencies—naïve empiricism and absolute idealism—avoid with ease this epistemological difficulty; but they both do it at the cost of even greater difficulties. Empiricism locates the source of mathematical notions and conceptions in the sphere of real things, without being able to explain satisfactorily their absolute validity and necessity, the infinite character of their methods of construction and calculation. And absolute idealism does exactly the opposite: in its mystical belief in the infinite power of human reason, it regards all real things as derived in all their qualities and functions from this reason; it disregards the simple fact that reason may be largely instrumental in the understanding of the universe. At the same time, the conception that reason "creates" the universe is overbearing and ridiculously false.

Plato's idealism reveals its close connection with Orphism in its conception of the Idea as a prototype of which real things endeavor to partake; and it discloses the same exaggerated belief in the power of the human mind in its ethical teaching of virtue as the knowledge of good. Yet the revival of Platonism in modern times struck deep roots in the realm of exact knowledge and influenced decisively the founders of exact science: Copernicus, Kepler, and Galileo. The problem of knowledge ceased to be the concern of pure philosophy only—the great men of science felt keenly the desire to elucidate this problem and to understand the very nature—the principles, the methods, the attainable goals—of the creative work they were doing.

Exact science, this rewriting of nature in mathematical letters, became now a crucial test of man's successful mental conquest of nature, and this fact induced Ernst Cassirer to devote a large part of his research to this field of human knowledge: "only in exact science—in its progress which, despite all vacillation, is continuous—does the harmonious concept of knowledge obtain its true *accomplishment* and verification; everywhere else this concept still remains only a demand."[1]

To this problem—the contribution of exact science to epis-

[1] Ernst Cassirer, *Das Erkenntnisproblem in der Philosophie und Wissenschaft der neueren Zeit.* Vol. I., p. 11.

temology—Cassirer devoted constant and assiduous study throughout his entire life. He first approached the problem from the historical point of view—he showed how slowly and painfully the scientific notion of nature detached itself from purely mystical and metaphysical conceptions. Even Copernicus, who methodically controlled and reversed immediate sensory impressions by mathematical reasoning and proceeded upon the principle *"Mathemata mathematicis scribuntur,"* introduced aesthetic motives into his demonstrations and regarded, for instance, our sun as the center of the entire universe, since no other place would be more suitable to its dignity and majestic brilliancy.

It was Leonardo da Vinci who freed exact science from all arbitrary elements and waged a systematic battle against all attempts to introduce spiritual causes into the explanation of physical phenomena. (Only mathematics, every concept and law of which is permeated by the spirit of absolute necessity, is able to provide us with an adequate basis upon which to build our knowledge of nature.) Kepler already had gone so far as not only to recognize clearly both sense impressions and intellectual concepts as fundamental sources of our knowledge of nature, but also to emphasize their thorough and organic interrelation. According to him, perception incites and controls our reasoning and is a genuine and reliable beginning of our knowledge; but all this only because it contains—though in a hidden and obscure form—elements of intellectual concepts and mathematical relations.

All these basic tendencies were decisively deepened and enlarged by Galileo. He, too, recognized sense impressions as a fundamental source of our knowledge; yet for him these impressions did not remain in the realm of individual perceptions —rather they acquired the form of organically unified experience, founded upon and formed by mathematical concepts and laws of absolute necessity. Truth is what is organically connected with the whole of experience, what belongs to this whole as a consistent part of it; and the knowledge of any single fact is only possible by way of studying its relations to the totality of known and established facts.

The second generation of great scientists—Huyghens, Boyle, and Newton—showed much less interest in general epistemological problems and tried primarily to purify and clarify their experimental methods. They tried to avoid all general concepts and theories and they went so far in this direction that —as Goethe put it—"they expressed the clear intention to observe natural phenomena as well as their own experiments separately, placing them side by side and without making any attempt to connect them somehow artificially with one another." Yet, continued Goethe, they put a firm trust in mathematics and stood in awe before the usefulness of its application to physics and thus, "while they tried to be on their guard with ideality, they admitted and kept the highest ideality." Those great scientists—and especially the greatest of them, Newton—developed their mathematical methods to an amazing degree, methods which enabled them meticulously to control their experiments and to deduce from them exact and fundamental knowledge. Newton's purely mathematical and seemingly quite abstract concepts of "absolute" space and time, of force and movement, soon became the very foundation of all physical science. The basic epistemological problem—the application of ideal concepts to reality—attained, through Newton's procedure, such a degree of precision that it soon became the focal point of an impassioned and prolonged controversy in which Clarke, Leibniz, and Euler played the leading part, and which so decisively influenced the young Kant that not only did Newton's system become the very object of his theoretical philosophy, but Kant even tried to introduce Newton's methods into philosophy.

In the first two volumes of his *Erkenntnisproblem in der Philosophie und Wissenschaft der neueren Zeit* Cassirer described and analyzed, step by step, the historical development of the struggle of human thought with this basic epistemological question; the same question lies at the core of his extended work, *Substanzbegriff und Funktionsbegriff*. In this book, however, Cassirer's approach to the problem is different—here he seeks the solution by a subtle analysis and systematic reconstruction of the whole complex of epistemological principles and methods. His first step is to show that a logical concept is never a simple summing up of qualities common to a certain group of similar things; before this summing up can take place the human mind must have the ability to establish in its consciousness such a grouping of similar things. This is done by a special mental process of identification which establishes a criterion. This process of identification, using any one particular as an instance which satisfies the conditions set forth by the criterion, collects a group of similar particulars, related to one another, and bound together by the criterion common to them all. The material of our perceptions can be formed and ordered in many different ways according to the criterion which is used in any single case; every given criterion forms a special series of perceptions in which a certain relation among the single elements of this series prevails. This relation can be determined by the degree of similarity or difference among the successive terms of the given series, but it also can be determined by number or size, by dimensions of space or time.

This structure of concept as a succession of terms connected with one another by a certain criterion Cassirer named "functional" concept. Mathematical concepts are all of this kind— what an integral number is can be understood only if this number is regarded as a term within an infinite series where the relation of any two contiguous terms is that of n to n $+1$; negative, fractional, irrational and even transcendent numbers can be defined only as terms of infinite series whose structure is determined by certain rules, according to which all terms of these series are connected with one another and derived from one another. This holds true of all fields of mathematical science —geometry and algebra, the infinitesimal calculus, quantum theory, and so forth. As Georg Cantor once said, mathematics is a free science, free in the sense that its concepts are neither derived from nor limited by the world of real things. Infinity is the very soul of mathematical concepts; and the law which determines the relation between single terms spreads endlessly in all directions and forms a perfectly harmonious system whose every term is bound by infinite relations to all other terms of the same system.

The concepts of mechanics reveal the same nature, the same inward structure as the mathematical concepts. Take as examples the concepts of velocity as uniform and rectilinear motion, of uniform acceleration, of continuous space and of mass reduced to a point—they all represent ideal constructions and criteria determining an infinite succession of forms, which can be derived from one another according to a constant rule. Yet, all these sharply and exactly formed ideal concepts not only help and further our knowledge of real things, but they actually constitute the very foundation of this knowledge. In order to understand this paradox one must ask himself the following question: what exactly is it to which we apply these ideal notions? Is it sensations, perceptions, or objects of the external world? The philosophy of critical idealism, whose basic tendencies Cassirer faithfully espoused and strongly developed throughout his life, gives the following answer: the primary stuff of our consciousness consists of disconnected, fluctuating, chaotic sensations, into which the human mind slowly and steadily brings regularity and order by connecting (and binding) dispersed sensations and forming them into objects. It would be quite wrong to think that there exist two sharply separated realms—the realm of sensations and the realm of objects—and that the true goal of our knowledge consists in an unequivocal connection of sensations with the corresponding objects. The truth is that in the given form these two separated realms do not exist at all and that the actual process of our knowledge consists in something quite different. Take the simplest sensation, and you will find present in it already a considerable amount of objective elements. Modern psychology teaches us that an infant of six months, not yet able to distinguish separate sensations from one another, is, none the less, already able to comprehend the expressions of his mother's face correctly, and consequently feels whether his mother is pleased with him or not. On the other hand, take any object, even a highly complex and well known one, and you will always find that some subjective impressions doggedly stick to it. What really and truly is going on in our consciousness is not a grasping at objects but a continuous process of objectification—the raw material of our sensations is gradually and systematically being worked over by the concepts and methods of our mind, is being formed and objectified; what we name "objects" are in reality nothing else but more or less advanced stages of this infinite process of objectification. A completely finished object, one freed of all elements of uncertainty and subjectivity, can be given only as the ultimate result of the development of science, it is the infinite and final goal of human knowledge. And, conversely, our sensations are always, to a greater or smaller degree, imbued with elements of objectivity—an absolutely pure sensation is only thinkable as the ultimate result of an endless process of subjectification.

These considerations open the way toward the solution of our epistemological problem: the profuse and fruitful application of the ideal concepts of mathematics and mechanics to the world of real things. Now we can see just what made this problem so difficult: the primary separation into two different and independent worlds—the world of ideal concepts and the world of real things—is nothing more than a wrong presumption. Take, for instance, such a "real thing" as matter which surrounds us everywhere in such impressive quantities. Greek science first thought that matter was continuous substance; then it surmised that matter was of atomic structure. And now we know that matter is nothing but condensed energy and that this energy has—miraculously enough—an atomic structure! Our knowledge of the atomic bomb—no matter how real and potent its destructive power may be—is still only one, and by no means the final, stage within the infinite process of objectification; and our ideal concepts of mathematics and mechanics are the driving forces, which mold and regulate this process, which transform our sensations into more and more advanced stages of objectification. The intellect and its ideal concepts from the outset perform an organic and absolutely necessary function within this process—no knowledge of real things would be possible without them.

Guided by this conviction, Cassirer, in his book, *Substanzbegriff und Funktionsbegriff*, unfolded step by step the systematic work of objectification performed by natural science and showed the basic importance of some very complicated branches of mathematics, including the quantum theory. However, strangely enough, not once in this book did he mention the theory of relativity, although Einstein's first fundamental publication concerning this subject had appeared five years earlier and had aroused a truly sensational interest. In 1921, two years after Einstein's concept of the curvature of light (when it passes through a field of gravitation) was brilliantly proved by astronomical observations, Cassirer published a booklet on the theory of relativity. Yet even in 1910 Einstein's theory was already very much talked of, and that not merely in scientific circles, but everywhere and by everyone. Thus, there must have been some reasons for Cassirer's silence on relativity at that time, which should prove to be of great interest, if it could be discovered what "precisely" the reasons were.

In his first publication on the theory of relativity, the famous "Elektrodynamik bewegter Systeme," (1905), Einstein, for the first time in the history of human thought, put the following question in so many words: We all know Newton's definition of "absolute, true, and mathematical time;" but in what way can this concept be applied to the world of real occurrences? Suppose, for some special purpose, we have to synchronize three watches—one in New York, another in San Francisco, and the third halfway between them, say in Norfolk, Nebraska. The only correct way to do that would be to send, let us say at 12:00 P.M. sharp, a light signal from Norfolk to the two other cities, and when this signal would arrive in each of the two cities, the time on their watches should be put at 12:00 P.M. plus one hundredth of a second, since it would take the light signal that much time to reach those cities. This procedure seems to be quite correct and even matter-of-course; yet Einstein proved that it was incorrect, since it did not allow for the rotation of the earth. In our example the light signal would reach New York earlier than San Francisco, since New York would, so to speak, move to meet this signal, whereas San Francisco would, as it were, run away from it. Thus, concluded Einstein, time, within a given system, depends on whether this system is moving or not and—if it is—on the velocity of its movement.

In a second example Einstein showed that there is only one way to measure the length of a moving object, namely, to use light signals and synchronized watches; but, inasmuch as synchronization of watches depends upon the movement of a given system, the length of an object must also depend on this movement.

These two examples given by Einstein were so surprisingly novel, so impressive, so convincingly true that the attention of the scientific world was immediately focused on him. However, this was only the beginning; he also discovered other most ingenious and important physical laws, as, for instance, the exact correlation between electric and magnetic fields, and, in particular, the relation between mass and energy: $E = mc^2$; this formula was made so popular by the atomic bomb that one can now find it even in newspaper advertisements. The great authority of Einstein as a true genius of natural science was, thus, firmly and indisputably established.

And yet: an objective study of the whole complex of Einstein's theories shows clearly that there is also another side to them and that Einstein's case at certain points repeats a phenomenon which is sometimes met in the history of natural science, namely, that a well recognized authority advances a theory which is obviously inconsistent and later may even be proved wrong. Yet such a theory may nevertheless be immediately accepted and, supported as it is by the weighty name of its famous originator, it is likely to become a part of accepted science. The most striking example of this kind is provided by the physics of Aristotle: as late as in the seventeenth century the official doctrine in physics accepted Aristotle's thesis that the velocity of a falling object is proportional to its weight; viz., ten bricks tied together fall ten times faster to the earth than a single brick; or that a stone dropped on a moving ship from the top of a mast falls not to the base of this mast but into the water, an experiment Aristotle *allegedly* performed many times. So great was Aristotle's authority that the physicians among his followers implicitly believed his assertion that the heart is the center of the nervous system. Galileo tells us that at one time a human body was dissected in the presence of a large group of Aristotelians and the dissection incontrovertibly proved that it is the brain which is the center of the nervous system. Thereupon the spokesman of the Aristotelians declared: "You gave us such clear and evident proof, that, were it not asserted by Aristotle that the nerve-center lies in the heart, we would be forced to the admission that you are right." Yet, Aristotle is not the only great authority of whom this sort of thing is true. Other instances could easily be cited. But this is not the place for such—however interesting—stories.

Something akin to it we find in some elements of Einstein's theory of relativity. Having proved that the necessity of using light signals for the measurement of time and space in moving systems is bound to influence the results of this measurement, Einstein, without reason or explanation, stops following up this absolutely correct and revolutionary idea and supersedes it by another explanation which is quite wrong: in a moving system the time and the length of objects change because the movement of a system influences the motion of watch mechanisms by slowing them down and influences the length of material objects by physically contracting them. This sounds so incredible that we must quote Einstein himself. "A balanced watch placed on the equator moves by a very small amount slower than an exactly identical watch would move under otherwise quite identical conditions except that it is placed at the pole."[2] In this quotation Einstein does not speak of the watch in general, but rather he stresses that it has to be a balanced watch. Why? Because, according to Einstein and his most famous followers, like, for instance, Max von Laue, only the balance wheel (this regulating gear of a watch), is slowed down by the velocity of the moving system to which this watch belongs. At once the question arises: And how about other kinds of timepieces which work without coiling spring and balance wheel, for instance, clepsydra or hourglass? Einstein did not think of them; yet he did think of the pendulum-clock, and therefore added the following words: a balance-watch "in

[2] Einstein's "Elektrodynamik bewegter Systeme," reprinted in the *Fortschritte der mathematischen Wissenschaften*, No. 2, p. 38. (Translation by the present writer.)

opposition to a balance-clock which represents—from the point of view of physics—the same system as the terrestrial globe; this case has to be excluded." If what Einstein says here is true, then there is nothing easier than to avoid all complications by simply using pendulum-clocks exclusively, never the balance-watches; then the theory of relativity would not be a novel and revolutionary conception of time and space, but merely a question of using incorrect or correct technical instruments. Yet Einstein's attempt to make his theory dependent on the kind of timepieces used is just as strange and contains just as much truth as, for instance, the assertion that the validity of non-Euclidean geometry depends on the type of glasses a mathematician wears.

Einstein's so-called special theory of relativity, the only one to which we are here referring, did not introduce any new mathematical formula; it was rather an attempt to give a new interpretation to the Lorentz-transformation, and the fallacy of Einstein's interpretation could not in any way invalidate the importance and fruitfulness of the Lorentz-transformation. Yet this fallacy of interpretation is the source of all the paradoxes and inconsistencies of Einstein's theory. Take, for instance, the so-called—and very famous at that—"paradox of the watch" which Einstein later expressed in the following drastic form:

If we could put a living organism into a box and compel it to perform the same regular movements as a balance-watch does, then it would be possible to achieve that this organism would return to its starting place after as long a flight as you like and would not show any changes whatsoever, whereas quite similar organisms which all this time stayed quietly in their place would be superseded by several consecutive generations. The long time which this journey lasted was for the moving organism not more than one single moment, provided only that it moved approximately with the velocity of light. This is an inevitable consequence of our fundamental principles imposed upon us by experimental knowledge.[3]

In reading these words one involuntarily thinks of what

[3] Einstein, "Die Relativitätstheorie." *Vierteljahrsschrift der naturforschenden Gesellschaft*, Zürich, Vol. 56, p. 12. (Translation by the present writer.)

Aristotle said after asserting that a stone, dropped on a moving ship from the top of the mast, falls into the water: "This experiment I performed several times." First of all, Einstein's allegation completely contradicts Einstein's own "fundamental principle" of relativity. According to this principle, movement is always relative to some other system, and there is no way of ascertaining which of these two systems really moves and which is in the state of immobility, or which part of this relative movement is performed by either of these systems. Yet Einstein's example of a moving organism brings back the idea of absolute movement: the surviving organism was really in a state of motion, whereas the extinct generations were in a state of immobility. Furthermore, the assertion that time slows down under the influence of movement is quite wrong. If one follows up Einstein's brilliant example of the synchronization of three watches in three different cities, one finds the following phenomenon: so long as a watch recedes from the observer, the time on this watch appears to him as retarded; but the moment this watch begins approaching the observer, the time on it appears as accelerated in the same degree, and as an ultimate result there is absolutely no loss or gain of time.[4]

Truth is always simple, understandable, impressive. This is the case with all elements of Einstein's theory which are verifiably correct. Only those elements of Einstein's theory are difficult which are basically wrong. The famous originator of the quantum theory, Max Planck, once said of the theory of relativity: "It is hardly necessary to emphasize that this novel conception of time puts the highest demands upon the power of imagination of a physicist and upon his ability of abstraction. Its boldness surpasses everything which previously had been accomplished in the speculative philosophy of nature and even in philosophical epistemology; compared to it, non-Euclidean geometry is mere child's play."[5] It certainly was not Einstein's intention to enrich the "speculative philosophy of nature" with

[4] See my booklet, *"Der physikalische Gehalt der speziellen Relativitätstheorie,"* Stuttgart, Engelhorns.

[5] Max Planck, *Acht Vorlesungen über theoretische Physik,* 1910, p. 117. (Translation by the present writer.)

his theory; he is a great physicist, and some parts of his theory will probably live forever in the science of men; but the incorrect parts of his theory belong nowhere, not even to speculative philosophy.

It is most interesting to observe in what manner Cassirer, in his booklet, *Zur Einstein'schen Relativitätstheorie,* deals with the theory of relativity, this amazing combination of profound truths and striking inconsistencies. Cassirer knew Einstein personally and, as he tells in the preface to his booklet, showed the manuscript to Einstein before having it printed. In the whole booklet one does not find one single word of criticism or doubt; at the same time, only those elements of Einstein's theory are discussed which are undoubtedly fruitful and true. Cassirer regards the theory of relativity as one link in the long chain of scientific and philosophical development, as an important constituent in the whole structure of epistemology. He starts with the general problem of measuring and shows that it is the first step to the objectification of our sensations, their transformation into elements of scientific experience. Our methods of measuring are always based upon some principles and axioms. One of these axioms always was that units of time, length, mass, are quite independent of whether they are applied in a moving or a motionless system. Einstein showed the incorrectness of this axiom by proving that these units themselves depend on the velocity of a given system. Cassirer does not at all discuss the question: What is the cause of this change? He does not even *mention* Einstein's explanation according to which even uniform and rectilinear motion physically affects the mechanism of a watch, an explanation which, by the way, directly contradicts Galileo's and Newton's principle of inertia.

In order to explain the crisis into which science was thrown by the negative result of Michelson's experiment, let me use the following imaginary example: an observer on a highway sees an automobile moving with the velocity of a hundred miles per hour; at the same time he sees a plane flying in the same direction with the velocity of three hundred miles per hour; the observer does not doubt for a moment that—if the passengers of the car compared their velocity with the velocity of the plane—they would find a difference of two hundred miles. How greatly amazed one would be, if he were told that in relation to him the plane still flies at the velocity of three hundred miles! Einstein's method of solving this difficulty was the following: he showed on the examples of synchronization of watches and measuring of length within a moving system that both operations could be performed only with the help of light signals; and then he said (not literally, to be sure): You see, our units of time and length are not at all as matter-of-course as we used to think of them; they are rather uncertain, they change along with the velocity of a given system, and, since this is the case, why should we not presuppose that the changes these units undergo are just big enough to explain the fact that our plane flies relatively both to the highway and to the speeding car with the same velocity of three hundred miles?

One can hardly regard this as a solution to our problem, inasmuch as the problem itself is simply transformed into a supposition. At the same time Einstein's analysis of the problem of synchronization contains all the elements of the correct solution. Yet, amazingly enough, he did not follow up the novel and most promising road he had himself discovered. But this method—to transform the problem into a supposition—Einstein used once more, when he replaced Newton's law of gravitation with a slightly different law of a very complicated mathematical structure. Newton derived his law of gravitation from Kepler's third law of planetary motion; this was a simple and most convincing demonstration of Newton's law. Einstein's procedure was different; he tried to construct a mathematical formula which had to satisfy the following conditions: to contain Newton's formula as first approximation and to produce the amount of the perihelion movement of the planet Mercury; it was an *ad hoc* formula, a transformation of a problem into a supposition.

Cassirer does not criticize or reject this procedure; he gives a quite adequate description of it and introduces his own analysis with the following spirited words of Goethe: "The highest art in science and life consists in transforming a problem into a postulate; one gets through this way." But Cassirer does not dwell on this subject; whereas Einstein's conception of matter as condensed energy, this daring and practically most important of his theories, is discussed at great length. Cassirer shows that the entire history of physics had been dominated by a peculiar dualism in the apprehension of nature. Democritus introduced the concepts of the atom and of empty space as the only sources of physical reality. In the subsequent centuries this dualism transformed itself into the acceptance of pure form concepts (like space and time), on the one hand, and of substance concepts (like matter), on the other. Descartes was the first to attempt a unification of these two concept groups; by levelling any distinction between them he dissolved, as it were, the substance of a physical object into a system of purely geometrical relations. Yet Cartesian physics proved to be ineffectual, and Newton refuted Descartes' physical theories and went back to the old dualism of space as a kind of a vessel and of matter as substance contained in it. Faraday was the first to bring about a new conception of matter, by advancing the theory that matter consists of lines of force, that it is nothing but a spot within a field of force. This theory stirred up a strong development of the so-called "field-physics," which did not accept the existence of matter and space as two separate factors, but regarded matter as an "offspring of field." Einstein's theory of relativity represents the last link within this development; it does not accept space, time, matter, and force as independent factors, but regards the physical world as a four-dimensional multiplicity. Along with this new conception of the world another historical development has been brought to its conclusion. Leibniz already had completely dissolved matter into force, yet he retained a distinction between two kinds of forces, "active" and "passive" forces. Einstein's theory brings about the ultimate fusion between the two fundamental principles of modern physics—the principle of the conservation of mass and the principle of the conservation of energy. The qualitative difference between matter and energy disappears entirely.

This method is typical of Cassirer's treatment of Einstein's theory—the historical continuity of scientific thought appears clearly and convincingly in Cassirer's argumentation. The prin-

ciples of physics introduced by Galileo and further developed
by Newton are only confirmed and enlarged in the theory of
relativity. And since Cassirer, with his keen sense of consistency and exactness of scientific truth, concentrated his attention only on those elements of Einstein's theory which are
correct and fruitful, Cassirer acquitted himself of this task most
brilliantly. He does not mention with even one single word
Einstein's assertion that uniform and rectilinear movement
influences a watch mechanism and slows it down, or that this
movement keeps a living organism indefinitely alive, or that
there is a basic difference between a balance-watch and pendulum-clock. Only one of Einstein's assertions is casually mentioned by Cassirer, despite the fact that it definitely belongs
to the group of erroneous elements within Einstein's theory.
I am referring to Einstein's assertion (repeated several times
by himself, and many thousands of times by his followers) that
Euclidean geometry loses its validity within a system which is
in a state of motion, even of uniform and rectilinear motion.
Take, for instance, the ratio of the circumference of a circle to
its diameter (pi); it changes its value within such a moving
system, it becomes smaller, according to Einstein. Why? The
reason, says Einstein, is quite simple. If you have a rotating
disk, then, since all moving objects become shorter in the direction of their movement, the circumference of this disk will
be smaller than the circumference of the same disk in the state
of immobility, and the corresponding ratio will drop below pi.
This whole argument is entirely wrong; and the fact that so
many earnest scientists willingly accepted it is very strange
indeed. This is such a striking example of mass-suggestion (not
to say gullibility) in the field of "exact" (!) science that it is
worth while to dwell a bit more upon this subject.

In order to prove that moving objects become shorter in the
direction of their movement, Einstein invented a very ingenious
example which, when adapted to American geography, might
take the following form: suppose that an immensely long airship of approximately 3000 miles in length is flying in west-
east direction over American territory, with one end over San
Francisco and the other end over New York, just at the moment

when we are trying to find out the precise length of this airship. There is only one way to do that, namely, to notice, at precisely the same moment, both ends of the airship, one in San Francisco and the other in New York, and then figure out the distance between these markings. For this purpose we must have perfectly synchronized watches placed in both cities. Yet this is impossible, as we have already seen—the watch in San Francisco will be slower than the watch in New York; therefore we shall be marking the rear end of the airship later than the front end, and the airship will consequently appear to us to be shortened. Very well. But now suppose that two airships move simultaneously, but in opposite directions—is it not absolutely clear that in this case the second ship will appear longer in exact proportion as the first ship will appear shorter? Thus, if you take a rotating disk, you will have to admit by the same reasoning that, since the two halves of its circumference always move in opposite direction, one half shortens in exactly the same proportion in which the other half lengthens; the effect of rotation is neutralized, pi remains absolutely unchanged, and there is no reason whatsoever to dethrone Euclidean geometry on this illusory ground.

During the last years of his stay in Germany Cassirer devoted increasingly more time to the study of the quantum theory, and when, in the spring of 1933, he decided to leave Germany, he went to Switzerland and there he wrote the first draft of his *Determinismus und Indeterminismus in der modernen Physik.* This book was his last major contribution to epistemology and to the philosophy of natural science. The subsequent years of his life, with their frequent peregrinations and changes of place of activity, deprived him to some degree of the steady tranquillity which was so favorable to his assiduous work. Besides, the new social phenomenon which suddenly appeared on the stage of history and at once began threatening the future of mankind—totalitarianism based upon and supported by the fanaticism of deceived masses—moved Cassirer to transfer the center of gravity of his studies to the problems of social science.

Quantum theory and the theory of relativity are the two outstanding achievements of theoretical physics in the last half-

century. Yet, how different was their ultimate fate! Max Planck
was compelled to advance his incredible and almost incomprehensible conception that energy has a discontinuous structure
and consists of elementary quanta, of which all other amounts of
energy are multiples, since otherwise it was impossible to explain the peculiar and quite "unclassical" manner in which
energy is radiated by a black body. From the outset it was
obvious that here a perfectly new and truly revolutionary
principle was being introduced into physics. Yet Planck tried
by every means to retain the continuity of scientific thought and
was only willing to admit the quite "inevitable deviation from
the laws of electrodynamics in the smallest possible degree.
Therefore, as far as it concerns the influence of a radiation field
upon an oscillator, we go hand in hand with the classical
theory."[6] Which means that Planck, although accepting energy
quanta for the radiation, still retained the point of view of
classical physics upon the absorption of energy by an oscillator.
From the very beginning Planck based his theory strictly upon
experience and experiment, and his hypothesis, despite its
breath-taking character, advanced therefore from one great
triumph to another, never meeting with any serious opposition.

The road of the theory of relativity was quite different. Einstein made a great discovery by recognizing the decisive rôle
the light signals play in the measuring of time and space; this
discovery was in perfect harmony with the Galileo-Newtonian
mechanics; it was a correct and most important materialization
of their general concepts of time and space. Yet, instead of continuing this line of development, he made a quite inconsistent
and "anti-classical" supposition to the effect that uniform and
rectilinear motion influence the mechanism of a balance-watch.
This was a violent and quite unwarranted break with classical
mechanics. And the paradoxes involved in the suppositions of
a living organism surviving in a fraction of a second several
consecutive generations of its kind, or of a rotating disk invali-
dating Euclidean geometry, helped to create such an unsound

[6] Max Planck, *Vorlesungen über die Theorie der Wärmestrahlung*, 3rd Ed. p.
148. Quotation taken from Cassirer's book, p. 136 (Translation by the present
writer).

sensation around this theory that it slowly became even a political issue—the reactionaries were against it because of Einstein's Jewish lineage, and the communists were for it because of the "revolutionary spirit" of this theory. A line of cleavage in the field of science which is nothing short of scandalous. But now back to Cassirer's book, *Determinismus und Indeterminismus*.

Cassirer's first step consists in the analyzing of the factual procedure of physics, of the concrete way in which it achieves its knowledge of nature. He distinguishes three different forms of assertion within the physical sciences, three basically different stages on the way towards the objectification of our "world of sense" into the "world of physics." The first form of physical assertions Cassirer calls "judgments concerning measurement"—the data of our perceptions are gradually transformed, with the aid of concepts of measurement and of number, into more and more objectified assertions. The sensibility of our organs of perception is superseded by the sensibility of our physical instruments. In this way the material of our knowledge has increased tremendously and the horizon of reality has been widened in all directions. This enriched material of our experience becomes the basis for the next step, for its unification and systematization with the help of natural laws; Cassirer called this stage of objectification "assertions about laws." These laws combine smaller or larger groups of facts into one single formula. Yet our science does not stop here; it is not satisfied with unification of innumerable facts through a limited system of laws; it constantly explores the possibility of unifying these laws, of connecting them with one another and sometimes deriving them from one another. This endeavor characterizes the third stage of objectification which Cassirer calls "assertions of principles." Thus, D'Alembert's "principle of virtual displacement" made possible the unification of statics and dynamics under one and the same system of mechanical laws; and the principle of conservation of energy builds bridges connecting all branches of physics.

Yet human thought does not confine itself to these three stages of physical knowledge—it belongs to the very essence of the human mind to continue the search for ever more and more general laws and principles, and it finds such in the systems of mathematical, logical, and epistemological concepts. The law of causation belongs to the system of epistemological concepts; it does not contain any assertion about this or that special occurrence in nature; it only asserts the thorough and consistent uniformity of all natural events and of nature as a whole. Every single law of nature may some day turn out to be incorrect, even the sunrise in the morning; yet, even if this event should occur, one thing will be absolutely certain: there will be some cause for that event. Without this law of causation no natural laws, and, therefore, no human knowledge is possible.

The law of causation was always regarded as the main pillar of the classical physics. But when the development of the quantum theory convincingly revealed its fundamental difference from the classical physics, there appeared a tendency within this theory to break even with causality and to replace the classical determinism with a modernized form of indeterminism. This attack upon the law of causation has been launched by some physicists mainly from the following point of view: the first point of view is based upon a statistical interpretation of quantum theory—it operates only with immense numbers of elementary particles of electricity and denies the possibility of a precise description of the conditions of single elements within a given system; only laws of probability can be applied to such systems, only statistical results can be obtained by these laws— there remains, therefore, no place for causation within these systems. It is with ease that Cassirer uncovers the fallacy of this point of view. Statistical results, he points out, very often have the character of strict necessity; the only condition being that they must not be arbitrary or incoherent, but based upon laws. The kinetic theory of gases is the best example of how statistical methods and laws of probability lead to strict uniformity and, therefore, to a complete vindication of the law of causation.

The second point of view which has led to the denial of causality is more radical, even if not so well founded. This attack is led by the well-known physicist and Nobel prize-winner Heisenberg and is based upon his principle of "uncertainty" or "indeterminacy." All elements of physical observation and experiment are given to us, says Heisenberg, not in the form of absolutely exact knowledge, not as Kantian transcendent "things-in-themselves"—rather they are the results of our instruments of measurement and depend strictly on the delicacy of these instruments. But this quite matter-of-course fact leads us within the quantum theory to the following peculiar paradox: suppose that an observer has the task of determining exactly the position and the velocity of an electron; in order to do that he must irradiate this electron and put it under a microscope; the experiment shows that the shorter the waves of light are which we use for this irradiation the more exactly can the position of this electron be determined; but at the same time the electron, as a result of the "Compton-effect," changes its velocity, and this change is the greater the shorter are the waves of the irradiating light. Thus, concludes Heisenberg, it is quite impossible simultaneously to perform an exact measurement of both the position and the velocity of an electron, since the more exact one measurement is the more uncertain the other one becomes. Heisenberg's conclusion is: "Thus quantum mechanics has definitely established the worthlessness of the law of causation."

It is almost incredible how many serious scientists have been influenced by this conception of Heisenberg's. A new wave of mass-suggestion was on the verge of submerging a large number of physicists—people who by the very virtue of their profession should be fairly rational. Cassirer's attempt to combat this contemporary aberration in science was quite timely, therefore. His method of demonstrating the erroneousness of Heisenberg's deduction was as simple as it was convincing. He showed that Heisenberg, in order to demonstrate his "principle of indeterminacy," at every step applied the very same law of causation which he tried to disprove with the help of these "uncertainty relations." Take, for example, the "Compton-effect," upon which Heisenberg's demonstration rests; the impact between light quanta and electrons makes an application of the law of causation and yields experimental results strictly in accordance with this law.

Cassirer died less than four months before the first explosion of the atomic bomb proved to the entire civilized world the great danger which lies in the mere development of exact science: it releases forces too powerful to be controlled; it makes man so powerful that the very existence of mankind appears to be endangered. This dark prospect reminds us of the philosophical thesis Cassirer defended and developed all his life—that scientific progress is only beneficial for man in so far as it is supported and guided by equally as vigorous progress of man's ethical, spiritual, cultural, and social life.

DIMITRY GAWRONSKY

NEW YORK CITY

6

Harold R. Smart

CASSIRER'S THEORY OF MATHEMATICAL CONCEPTS

6

CASSIRER'S THEORY OF MATHEMATICAL CONCEPTS

IN AN important article in *Kantstudien* (XII, 1907), entitled "Kant und die moderne Mathematik," Cassirer makes an assertion which throws much light on his theory of mathematical concepts. He declares that "it cannot be denied that 'Logistik' [i.e., symbolic or mathematical logic] has revivified formal logic, and . . . nourished it anew with the life blood of science." And this development, he continues, is of great significance with respect to Kantian doctrines. Although it is certainly true that symbolic logic "can never supplant or replace 'transcendental' logic," it is equally certain that formal logic as thus rejuvenated "offers more pregnant suggestions and affords more trustworthy 'guiding threads' than Kant possessed in the traditional logic of his time."

This statement clearly foreshadows one of the principal tasks Cassirer set himself early in his career, which he has attempted to carry through by means of his profound and critical study of the history of mathematics in its relations both with philosophy and with the other sciences, from the earliest times down to the immediate present. That it is a truly formidable undertaking thus to seek to preserve and reinterpret the transcendental logic of Kant in such a way as finally to bring it into good and fruitful accord with recent tendencies in formal symbolic logic and mathematics, will readily be admitted. Indeed, it is not going too far to say that most authorities would at the very outset declare that purpose to be one which could not possibly be realized; so far apart are Kantian doctrines—at least as usually presented—and those of most contemporary logicians and mathematicians, that, like oil and water, they simply cannot be made to mix.

Did not Kant firmly declare that concepts without percepts are empty; was it not his settled doctrine that mathematical judgments are synthetic *a priori;* did he not maintain, at least in the "transcendental aesthetic," that mathematics is possible as a science only because space and time are pure forms of intuition or pure intuitions; was it not in particular his thesis that mathematical inference proceeds by means of 'constructions' which must be either directly intuitable in actual space, or clearly imaginable? Taking these and kindred doctrines into account, is it not the consensus of authoritative commentators that Kant deceived himself both in underestimating the revolutionary character of his contributions to logic, and in cherishing the belief that the validity of the main tenets of *formal* logic was unimpaired thereby? And finally, do not contemporary symbolic logicians and mathematicians, with one unanimous voice, sharply oppose every one of those typical Kantian doctrines and assertions?

Initially improbable though success in such a venture might seem, however, Cassirer does not shrink from facing courageously all of the tremendous difficulties it involves; and whatever may be one's final judgment in the matter, all hands will readily agree that, quite apart from his success or failure in this particular regard, his own positive doctrines stand forth as of intrinsic worth on their own account. It soon becomes clear, indeed, to Cassirer's readers, that one has to do with no slavish disciple of any of the traditional lines of thought. The historical and critical studies so assiduously pursued are by no means ends in themselves, but serve rather as most carefully selected source material for constructive philosophical undertakings of the most significant and original sort. Such being the case, it is to be expected that the materials supplied in this way will be handled with the greatest freedom and boldness, and that, as finally presented, Cassirer's doctrines will frequently diverge more or less widely from their anterior sources of inspiration.

Take, for example, the concept of number—the concept which Cassirer significantly declares to be not merely basic to the special science of mathematics but "the first and truest expression of rational method in general."[1] Although critics frequently charge Kant with basing this concept upon the pure intuition of time, this is true, so Cassirer avers, only in so far as time appears as "the type of ordered sequence" as such. In Kant's own words,

the pure image . . . of all objects of the senses in general is time. But the pure *schema* of quantity, in so far as it is a concept of the understanding, is number, a representation which combines the successive addition of one to one (homogeneous). Thus number is nothing but the unity of the synthesis of the manifold of a homogeneous intuition in general—a unity due to the fact that I generate time itself in the apprehension of the intuition.[2]

As Cassirer sees it, however, further development of this doctrine has followed two very different directions, the one emphasizing the active 'understanding' and the process of creative synthesis, the other stressing the passive 'sensibility' and irrational intuition.

The latter alternative is that adopted, for example, by most varieties of empiricism, and by intuitionism, and it naturally conforms best to the traditional formal logic of the generic concept—i.e., the logic which regards the concept as a common element abstracted from a class of particulars.[3] Against all three of these lines of thought—empiricism, intuitionism, and the subject-predicate logic—Cassirer brings to bear a devastating criticism, supported by profuse historical evidence. These historical and epistemological studies demonstrate convincingly that in terms of no one, nor of any combination of the three, can Kant's question as to the 'possibility' of the science of pure mathematics be answered at all satisfactorily.

There remains, then, for further consideration, what Cassirer regards as the only other genuine alternative, namely the postulation of the creative synthesis of the pure understanding

---

[1] *Substance and Function*, Eng. transl., 26.

[2] Translation quoted from N. Kemp Smith's *Commentary to Kant's Critique of Pure Reason*, 2nd ed., 129. Cassirer makes a similar gloss on Kant's notion of space with reference to geometry.

[3] *Philosophie der symbolischen Formen*, Ch. III, 402f.

as the absolutely essential epistemological and logical *prius,* upon which the possibility of number in particular and of mathematics in general must depend. In Kantian language, the synthetic activity of knowing is a process of generating relations —i.e., to know is to relate; and to relate, so Cassirer continues, is to introduce order into a 'manifold' or series; and serial order, in this precise sense of the word, finds its first and fundamental expression in the series of ordinal numbers. Logical or critical idealism maintains, in short, that there is nothing more ultimate for thought than thinking itself, and thinking consists essentially in the positing of relations (*das Beziehungssetzen*).

From this point of view, Cassirer declares, "number appears not merely as a *production* of pure thought, but actually as its prototype and *origin* . . . as the primary and original act of thought," which all further scientific and logical thinking presupposes.[4] In this pregnant sense of the word, number is, indeed, the "schema" of serial order in general, the "ideal axis," so to speak, about which thought organizes its world. Pythagoreanism erred only in its too enthusiastic identification of number with the whole truth, with the entire system of ideal relations constitutive of reality. Only "after we have conceived the plan of this system in a general logical theory of relations," whereby the members of a series may be variously ordered—for example, "according to equality and inequality, number and magnitude, spatial and temporal relations, . . . causal dependence," and the like—can we ascribe to the several sciences their true epistemological import as so many progressively successful applications of this logical theory to the data of experience.[5]

In further elucidation and development of this thesis— which is perhaps more accurately and directly anticipated by the Cartesian-Leibnizian theory of a *mathesis universalis* than it is by the Kantian transcendental logic—Cassirer refers, on the one hand, to the so-called calculus of relations as recently worked out by the symbolic logicians, and, on the other hand, to the relevant stages in the origination and subsequent history

[4] *Ibid.*
[5] Cf. *Substance and Function*, Ch. I.

of such basic mathematical concepts as those of number and space.

The main purpose of the critical study of the history of mathematics is to illustrate and confirm the special thesis that ordinal number is logically prior to cardinal number, and, more generally, that mathematics may be defined, in Leibnizian fashion, as the science of order. Cassirer's readers do not need to be told how impressive in both amount and quality is the historical evidence he adduces in support of these tenets, nor how great is the skill with which he marshalls his interpretative expositions to the same end.

As Cassirer is no doubt well aware, however, other authorities, among them some as critical of mere empiricism as he himself is, differ sharply with this interpretation of the same historical data, and at least two other plausible alternatives have been ably presented, namely the exactly opposite thesis that cardinal number is logically prior to ordinals, and the perhaps even more inviting thesis that cardinal and ordinal are strictly complementary aspects of number, neither of which can claim priority over the other. Thus it seems rather unwise to place too much confidence in any one interpretation, unless indeed weighty evidence of another sort can be marshalled in support of one of the three, which cannot be matched in favor of either or both of the others.

And of what sort can such evidence be? Not of any epistemological variety, it would seem; for to ground an historical interpretation on an epistemological theory, and then to claim that the interpretation confirms the theory, is hardly justifiable at the bar of logic. As for the logical evidence, Cassirer himself concedes that order "does not exhaust the whole content of the concept of number."[6] A "new aspect," he declares, "appears as soon as number, which has hitherto been deduced as a purely logical *sequence* of intellectual constructs, is understood and applied as an expression of *plurality*."

But when—the question almost asks itself—is it not so understood and applied? Certainly many unbiassed witnesses are prepared to answer, in no uncertain voice, that it functions

---

[6] *Substance and Function,* 41.

in this sense from the very beginning. Nay, testimony on this point is well-nigh universal to the effect that 'in the beginning' was simple counting, a process resting directly on the concept of cardinal number. And, as far as contemporary logic is concerned, an able expositor of the doctrines of *Principia Mathematica* explains, in terms exactly matching those used by Cassirer, but having a precisely opposite import, that "two important concepts" essential to the formation of the series of ordinal numbers, namely '0' and 'successor,' "introduce a new idea not used in the definition of cardinal number, namely the idea that the cardinal numbers form a discrete series of next successors beginning with 0."[7]

These comments are not offered, however, as by any means indicating a complete refutation of Cassirer's doctrines, but rather merely to reveal the diversity of views prevailing on this matter. Epistemological theories apart, it is tacitly admitted by all hands that cardinal and ordinal actually function, mathematically, as complementary to each other. In any event, Cassirer relies more heavily upon the aforementioned calculus of relations, than he does upon the historical evidence, in direct and positive support of his theory of the formation of mathematical concepts. For it is by means of this calculus, so he avers, that number can indeed be "deduced as a purely logical sequence of intellectual constructs." More specifically, in the classification of relations into transitive, intransitive, symmetrical, asymmetrical, and so on, Cassirer sees, ready to hand as it were, the perfect instrumentality whereby "the more exact definition of what we are to understand as the order of a given whole" is to be attained. Prior to this development the basic thesis of critical idealism, namely that thinking consists in the positing or generating of relations, appeared as a bare epistemological postulate, illustrated, and even, if you please, in a sense confirmed by the history of scientific thought, but all the while lacking its fundamental logical articulation, its systematic exposition and confirmation. In particular, to Bertrand Russell and his colleagues Cassirer gratefully attributes the epochal dis-

---

[7] Eaton, *General Logic*, 468.

covery "that it is always some transitive and asymmetrical relation that is necessary to imprint on the members of a whole a determinate order."[8]

From this point of view, numbers—ordinal numbers, that is —stand forth as "a system of ideal objects whose whole content is exhausted in their mutual relations." In such a system, Cassirer maintains, the 'what' of the elements is disregarded, and merely the 'how' of a certain progressive connection is taken into account. Here, in short, is

a general procedure which is of decisive significance for the whole formation of mathematical concepts. For whenever a *system of conditions* is given that can be realized in different contents, then we can hold to the form of the system itself as *invariant*, undisturbed by the difference of contents, and develop its laws deductively.[9]

This state of affairs is as clearly evident in geometry as it is in the science of number. Mathematical space may be defined, in Leibnizian terminology, as an "order of coexistence." Geometricians may still talk of points, straight lines, and planes; but in the course of time these familiar objects have become divested of all intuitive content, and all connection between these elements is developed deductively from purely conceptual definitions. The relation expressed by the word 'between,' for example, though seemingly possessing an irreducible sensuous connotation, has nevertheless been freed from this narrow restriction, and is now determined, mathematically, solely by means of definite logical prescriptions, which alone endow it with the meaning it possesses in the deductive procedure of mathematics. In other words, according to Cassirer, it is always and everywhere "the relational structure as such," rather than any absolute properties of the elements entering into the structure, which constitutes the real 'object' of mathematical investigation. The particular elements entering into any deductive complex of relations,

are not viewed according to what they are in and for themselves, but

---

[8] *Substance and Function*, 38.
[9] *Ibid.* 40.

simply as examples of a certain universal form of order and connection; mathematics . . . recognizes in them no other 'being' than that belonging to them by participation in this form. For it is only this being that enters into proof, into the process of inference, and is thus accessible to the full certainty, that mathematics gives its objects.[10]

Thus the fundamental work of the science does not consist, for example, in comparing, dividing, and compounding specific given magnitudes, but rather "in isolating the generating relations themselves, upon which all possible determination of magnitude rests, and in determining the mutual connection of these relations." Although it may be true, psychologically speaking, that the meaning of a relation can only be grasped by means of some given terms which thus serve as its material basis, still (Cassirer insists) the logical import of the relation is wholly independent of any such origin, and is the resultant of a purely rational and deductive procedure. To put the point in terminology long since familiar to British and American philosophers, Cassirer apparently concurs in the doctrine that relations are prior to, and independent of, or 'external' to their terms.

On the logical plane, therefore, it seems that Cassirer simply appropriates for his own purposes and construes in his own fashion that special portion of formal symbolic logic having to do with relations, in abstraction from other branches of the subject,—towards which, indeed, he manifests, on occasion, considerable opposition. With respect to this state of affairs the following points naturally suggest themselves for discussion.

The first of these points, put in the form of a question, is: What becomes of Kant's doctrine of the categories, in the light of the significance Cassirer attaches to the calculus of relations? Partly by explicit statement, partly by plain implication, the answer is that that doctrine is completely nullified. For, as a little reflection will suffice to show, it is quite impossible to reconcile the basic thesis of Kant's transcendental logic that the categories are functional forms of relationship immanent in scientific knowledge as embodied in synthetic judgments, with

[10] *Op. cit.*, 92f.

the thesis advanced by Cassirer that the "generating relations" productive of "serial order" are logically prior to, and independent of their terms, and purely ideal in nature. This is, in short, entirely to abandon the Kantian conception of the *a priori*, and to revert, instead, to that of Leibniz.

Now it would be a natural though a serious error to assume that this point concerns only students of Kant and Leibniz, and that it is without intrinsic importance for anyone who is simply trying to understand contemporary mathematics. For to follow Cassirer in this respect is definitely to play into the hands of those formalists who see in mathematics not a genuine science among others, but a mere extension and elaboration of formal logic—is to rededicate oneself to that very abstract rationalism which Kant did so much to overthrow. In fact, it almost seems as if preoccupation with the sins and omissions of a one-sided empiricism had induced Cassirer, against his own better judgment, to adopt the opposite extreme, even in the face of Kant's convincing demonstration that such a one-sided rationalism is just as untenable.

This interpretation of Cassirer's position gains further confirmation by a closer examination of his attitude of acceptance towards the calculus of relations. In view of his just and penetrating criticism of other parts and aspects of the doctrines of the symbolic logicians (to be touched upon later in this essay), his exemption of this particular calculus from the force of those criticisms can only be explained as due to certain inherently formalistic tendencies in his own thought. That is to say, it is not, in the last analysis, with abstract formalism in logic and mathematics as such, but rather merely with certain specific features and portions of that formalism, that Cassirer finds himself in disagreement. Otherwise he would readily perceive, for example, that, since the calculus of relations is in many essential respects strictly analogous to the calculus of classes—a fact to which attention is explicitly called by the highest authorities— the charge of circularity which he so acutely brings against this latter calculus also applies, *mutatis mutandis*, to the former. If the derivation of cardinal numbers from classes be condemned as circular reasoning, then, for strictly analogous reasons, the derivation of ordinal numbers from relations must be circular also; and if, on the contrary, the latter can be successfully defended against such a charge, then, again for strictly analogous reasons, so can the former.[11] Since, however, Cassirer simply contents himself with laying down the general thesis, and nowhere undertakes such an explicit derivation on his own account, it is impossible to justify this contention further by a critical study of details.

What still further complicates matters here, and beclouds the specific issue in question, is the fact that Cassirer envisages the issue as one ultimately involving a conflict between "the logic of the generic (or class) concept" and "the logic of the relational concept." As he sees it, "if the attempt to derive the concept of number from that of a class were successful, the traditional form of logic would gain a new source of confirmation. The ordering of individuals into the hierarchy of species would be, now as before, the true goal of all knowledge. . . ."[12]

But surely this antithesis between the two species of concepts is not as definitive as the preceding statement implies. As good a historian of science as Cassirer does not need to be told of the inherently important, if largely subsidiary, rôle which classification as a matter of fact does play, even in such an abstract science as mathematics. Granting that "the ordering of individuals into the hierarchy of species" is not the "true goal" of any science, still it is quite impossible to deny that classification does represent a most useful and perfectly legitimate scientific procedure, or that it is explicitly recognized as such by scientists and logicians. If 'to relate,' in the widest possible sense of the word, be taken to mean what Kant meant by it, namely, not merely to establish order in a series, but, more generally, 'to organize into a system,' then may not a class be construed as a rudimentary kind of a system, and may not classification itself be looked upon as a kind of relating? For that matter, no small part of the business of the very calculus of relations itself consists in classifying relations into a hierarchy, and determining

[11] See, on this whole question, the illuminating discussion, in Ch. V, of Lewis and Langford's *Symbolic Logic.*

[12] *Substance and Function,* 53.

the differentiæ of the various species and sub-species of relations. Thus little indeed would be left of the calculus, if the 'logic of the generic concept' were to be rejected as entirely unsound.

In view of such considerations, Cassirer will find many supporters for his strictures on the logic of the generic concept who will yet not feel inclined to follow him all the way in denying to it any epistemological value whatsoever and thus leaving the logic of the relational concept in sole possession of the field. But for students of Kant there is a still more fundamental consideration which may appropriately be emphasized here.

From a strictly Kantian point of view, as Norman Kemp Smith well points out,[13] generic and relational concepts, as here defined, both refer to a distinction, not in the form, but in the specific content of knowledge. Just as a generic concept (or universal) expresses a common quality or qualities to be ascribed to each distinguishable element of a nexus of complex contents, so a relational concept (or universal) expresses relationships specified as holding amongst the elements severally. A category, on the other hand, is not a content of any sort, or any aspect of a content, but a general form of organization, a "function of unity," whereby contents are related in the judgment. No superficial verbal similarity turning upon the common use of the term 'relation' should be allowed to conceal the fact that Kant and the symbolic logicians are concerned with two vastly different matters, nor that their basic logical doctrines are fundamentally opposed in principle. The problems Kant wrestled with in his transcendental logic are in large part simply ignored by the symbolic logicians, or handed over to epistemology; whereas what the symbolic logicians regard as basic logical problems could scarcely have appeared in that light to Kant.

Precisely in this connection, however, a fundamental epistemological antithesis or antinomy appears between the doctrines of orthodox symbolic logicians and Cassirer's critical idealism. For precisely at this point certain other Kantian influences make themselves most strongly felt and give rise both to a criticism of epistemological theories of the Russellian type, as well as to the

[13] *Commentary to Kant's Critique of Pure Reason,* 38, 178.

application and development of an epistemology on Leibnizian and Kantian lines. Not only does Cassirer call attention to the circularity inevitably involved in the attempt to derive cardinal number from the concept of a class,[14] but he also stoutly insists —quite in the spirit of Kant, and in complete opposition to more fashionable contemporary tenets—on the synthetic character of mathematical propositions or judgments. In the article already drawn upon, "Kant und die moderne Mathematik," Cassirer explains that by synthetic he means, (a) not reducible to that species of subject-predicate propositions, in which the predicate merely explicates the meaning of the subject term; (b) not deducible from the mere formal laws of thought; and (c) the functional relationship in which mathematical propositions stand to empirical phenomena, and, lacking which, mathematical concepts would be nothing better than hollow fictions.

Since points (a) and (b) are now conceded by everyone, their mere mention seems sufficient here; but point (c) is a different matter. After the most elaborate epistemological *tour de force* by which Russell and his collaborators seek to convince themselves and others that, although their absolutely basic "atomic propositions" admittedly stem directly from sense experience, nevertheless the world of logic and mathematics, as such, in its unsullied purity, is a transcendent realm, they can only account it a "lucky accident," which might just as well have been otherwise, that the propositions of logic and mathematics apply to the realm of physical phenomena. In other words, the two realms having been severed so completely by those thinkers, Cassirer points out that it is actually an epistemological and logical impossibility to establish any real connection between them. As Cassirer sees it, on the other hand, the objectivity of scientific knowledge of phenomena is guaranteed precisely by virtue of the "synthetic unity of the concept"—to use an appropriate Kantian phrase—whose sole function is to introduce order into the ideal 'manifolds' of mathematics, and, through them, in turn, into the experiential manifolds of the spatio-temporal world of physics.

[14] *Substance and Function*, Ch. II, sec. iii; see also Smart, *The Philosophical Presuppositions of Mathematical Logic*, Ch. VI.

Thus, to take a simple example, Cassirer maintains that thought follows a straight, undeviating path, in proceeding from the logical calculus of relations, to such a special type of generating relation as is compactly symbolized by the general algebraic equation of the second degree, from which, in turn, every species of conic section—circle, ellipse, parabola, etc.— may be deductively derived. And this same mathematical concept of the conic section it is which alone enables the natural scientist to introduce order or synthetic unity into the manifold of astronomical phenomena, thus making possible knowledge of those phenomena which is at once objective and systematic. Only in this wise, so Cassirer declares in a pregnant passage,

only when we clearly understand that the same basic syntheses upon which logic and mathematics depend, also control the formation of experiential knowledge, thereby for the first time making it possible to speak of the ordering of phenomena according to scientific laws and thus to ascribe objective meaning to these phenomena, is the true justification of those principles attained.[15]

Nor is this by any means the end of the matter. Not only are single concepts and judgments thus synthetic, but the whole process of deduction, characteristic of mathematical inference, is itself progressive, productive of new knowledge. In this respect also Cassirer opposes the essentially static ideal of logic and mathematics fostered by the symbolic logicians, in their thesis that the propositions of these sciences are analytic or tautological, and also in their complementary doctrine that deduction is a mere re-arranging of the elements of discourse in accordance with fixed rules of procedure. Epistemologically speaking, this doctrine becomes the thesis that thought merely 'discovers' relationships eternally 'there,' subsisting in that transcendent realm which reveals itself to a critical inspection to be nothing but the naïve hypostatization of certain logical and mathematical concepts, and their consequent deprivation of any objective meaning or truth.

Now according to Cassirer this ideal of mathematical knowledge is not only self-contradictory; it directly conflicts with the

[15] "Kant und die moderne Mathematik," *Kantstudien*, vol. XII, 45 (1907).

plainest possible evidence, namely, the progressive character which the long history of that science reveals as its most outstanding feature. Every important advance in mathematics, from the earliest times down to the immediate present, involves both an extension and a deepening or enrichment of fundamental concepts, and their progressive liberation from what have conclusively shown themselves to be extraneous sensuous connotations. "Just as the field of rational numbers is broadened by gradual steps of thought into the continuous totality of real numbers, so, by a series of intellectual transformations, does the space of sense pass into the infinite, continuous, homogeneous and conceptual space of geometry . . ."[16]—illustrative examples which could be repeated *ad nauseam* in confirmation of this view of the continuing 'creative advance' of mathematical thought.

Hence arises for Cassirer a question which the symbolic logicians, in their blindness, blandly ignore, namely how is this creative advance possible; how, in epistemological terms, can it be justified to reason, and how, more precisely, is it to be described?

In the case of the physical sciences answers to such questions are comparatively easy to come by, the only difficult logical problem being that of the closer determination of the nature of induction. But in common with many, perhaps most contemporary logicians, Cassirer denies a rôle to induction in the mathematical sciences. True, he apparently does not share the vulgar prejudice or presupposition dominating the thinking of so many authorities on this matter, namely, that there is some necessary connection between induction and specific experimental techniques confined to certain natural sciences, so that it is dogmatically and arbitrarily settled beforehand that where there *is* no experimentation of the sort in question, neither *can* there be any induction. Rather Cassirer excludes induction (and analogy!) from mathematical inference, on the ground that, whereas the former "proceeds from the particular to the universal . . . [and] attempts to unite hypothetically into a whole a plurality of individual facts observed as particulars without

[16] *Substance and Function*, p. 106.

necessary connection," the latter proceeds always from "the law of connection," which serves as "the original basis by virtue of which the individual case can be determined in its meaning." In other words, "the conditions of the whole system are pre-determined, and all specialization can only be reached by adding a new factor as a limiting determination while maintaining these conditions."[17] In sum, mathematical inference always "proceeds from the properties of the connection to those of the objects connected, from the serial principle to the members of the series," and never in the reverse order.

One minor but nevertheless interesting point included in the preceding general statement may appropriately be mentioned here before proceeding to a more detailed study of this conception of mathematical inference. The symbolic logicians never tire of proclaiming it as an ideal of their procedure that "all of pure mathematics" can (or should) be shown to follow deductively from a certain set of primitives—primitive or undefined ideas, primitive propositions or postulates, and the like. Nothing not explicitly included or provided for in this foundational nexus is to be permitted entry into the subsequent unfoldment or 'development' of the series of logico-mathematical propositions. Otherwise the purely analytical or tautological nature of those propositions might easily become infected with a 'synthetic' impurity! Cassirer, on the other hand, realistically points to the actual practice of mathematicians, and shows conclusively that their practice never conforms to any such extraneously imposed ideal. In fact, quite the contrary is the case. Only by and in so far as modifications and specifications *not* explicitly provided for or foreseen in the formulation of the foundational nexus, but deliberately introduced at certain stages as new facts or limiting determinations, as the deduction proceeds, can the special cases or conclusions, in which the procedure characteristically issues, be derived. To employ the same simple example utilized earlier in this exposition: from the general equation of the second degree, the equations of such conics as the ellipse, the parabola, etc., could never be derived simply by the analytical 'development' of that equation. On the contrary, such

[17] *Ibid.* 81, 82.

special cases can be derived from the general equation only by introducing limitations not explicitly contemplated in the formulation of that equation, and not *formally* connected with it in any way. In this sense they are added from without, somewhat as the minor premise is added to the major premise in the traditional syllogism; the only restrictions on this typical deductive procedure being such as are prescribed by the basic laws of thought themselves.

This is not, however, the major factor in mathematical deduction. It will be recalled that one main epistemological thesis of Cassirer's critical idealism is that the creative, synthetic activity of thought displays itself in the positing or generating of relations; and, as was indicated above, it is in terms of this thesis that he construes all scientific reasoning. Thus the problem of the 'possibility' of mathematics, as one progressive science among others, may be more definitely characterized as the problem of determining the rationale, the logical 'go,' so to speak, of that process in the special field in question.

At this point the Kantian doctrine that mathematical reasoning proceeds by means of the 'construction' of its objects, either in intuition or imagination, reveals its positive significance for Cassirer. Not that he views the reference to intuition or imagination as the important factor in that conception; for what mathematician does not realize that such limitations on his creative activity have long since been transcended; and does not Cassirer himself, on every appropriate occasion, proclaim the liberation of mathematics from reliance on sensuous or perceptual guides as one of the greatest intellectual triumphs of recent times? Rather what on this view is of permanent worth in the Kantian doctrine is the emphasis upon construction as a typical mode of procedure; only the construction must be understood in a purely ideal sense, and as carried out by pure thought, independently of experience. And here again, as so frequently happens, Cassirer turns to Leibniz, rather than to Kant, for further insight, for more positive guidance, in developing his own ideas. To put it very briefly, it is by means of what Leibniz called real, causal, or genetic definitions, that, according to Cassirer, the ideal constructions characteristic of mathematical deduction are carried through. Such definitions, which Cassirer regards as perhaps the most striking exemplification of the productivity of thought, serve in effect as rules or laws for the construction of specific mathematical objects, or complexes of such objects. For the traditional definition of a circle, for example, in terms of genus, species, and differentia, Leibniz would substitute a definition revealing its "mode of generation," and similarly for the definition of parallel lines and of all such mathematical constructs.

No doubt these and the other specimens Leibniz offers of this type of definition are rather too elementary, too empirical, to be wholly convincing as samples of purely ideal constructions; but Cassirer maintains that the principle involved can easily be generalized in such a way as to bring out its full significance.[18] At all events, in presenting his proposed new type of definition, Cassirer points out that Leibniz envisaged it as an instrumentality for combatting two erroneous tendencies prevalent in the logical theories of his time, tendencies, which, as Cassirer maintains, still confuse fundamental issues in contemporary logic.

The first of these tendencies is nominalism—the Hobbesian doctrine that all definitions are merely nominal. It needs no citing of names to confirm the fact that this doctrine is enthusiastically fostered by many logicians of the present time. And nominalism in this respect inevitably leads on to the sweeping conclusion that mathematics in its entirety is nothing but a symbolic technique, a manipulation of conventional symbols, which as such is devoid of objective import, and in respect to which it is nonsense to talk of truth. The "freedom" of mathematics is hereby purchased at the heavy expense of its renunciation of all claims to yielding knowledge of the real world. Consistency in the formulation and application of conventional rules of an empty symbolism is all that remains.

The second erroneous tendency is in a sense antithetical to the preceding, in that it hypostatizes ideas, endows them with a

[18] See the article, "Kant und die moderne Mathematik," and also *Leibniz' System in seinen wissenschaftlichen Grundlagen,* 108 ff., and *Philosophie der symbolischen Formen,* Pt. III, Ch. IV.

quasi-ontological status, and attributes to them 'being' in a transcendent realm quite apart from human experience. On this view, the sole test of the reality of an idea is its abstract possibility of being thought in complete abstraction from any question as to its actual realization in experience, its epistemological functioning. Adoption of this doctrine commits one to the 'copy' theory of truth, reduces thought to the rôle of a passive spectator, and sets up an impassable barrier, a dualism, between the world of ideas and the factual world—between truths of reason and truths of matter of fact. Finally it should be emphasized that neither of these tendencies has anything to do with the actual science of mathematics as such, but is instead the product, pure and simple, of abstract, gratuitously *a priori* theorizing.

Thus, according to Leibniz's distinguished commentator and disciple, these two equally untenable lines of thought, far from providing a satisfactory foundation for the formation of mathematical concepts, succeed only in setting up an empty scaffolding of formal consistency and abstract possibility. Through the instrumentality of the causal or genetic definition, on the other hand, thought can produce out of its own creative, synthetic resources, all that is so conspicuously lacking in the rejected doctrines—such at least is Cassirer's profound conviction. To define the circle—to revert to this simple example—as a plain curve, so constituted that it encloses a maximum area within a given perimeter, is merely a matter of words, which leaves it doubtful whether there actually be such a curve; and, even in case this question can be answered affirmatively, it still remains open to doubt whether the prescribed condition be fulfilled by just the one sort of curve. Such doubts can be stilled if and only if a fully determinate "mode of generation" can be specified, and if the desired characteristics can be shown to be actually produced by this mode of generation by a rigorous deductive proof. In this wise, according to Cassirer, the definition may truly be said to generate the object in question out of its constituent elements. And what is true in this simple case holds true (so Cassirer maintains) of mathematics generally. Always and everywhere the necessary and sufficient prerequisite to the formation of mathematical concepts, and to the ascription to them of definite contents, shows itself to be the same. What Cassirer calls a genetic definition may on occasion (he points out) find more detailed embodiment in a set of axioms or postulates, especially where not a specific object but a whole branch of mathematics—multi-dimensional geometry, the theory of groups—is in question. But in any case, the creative synthesis, involving one or more elementary structural elements, and producing out of these elements, by means of the generating relations embodied in the definitional nexus, the whole contextual content of the field in question, is what characterizes the differentia of mathematical inference as such.

Now it can hardly be denied that Cassirer's criticisms of fashionable tendencies in contemporary logic—such as the nominalistic theory of definitions, the thesis that mathematical propositions are analytical or tautological, and the static concepion of deduction—are well-founded and that his own contrasting views on these matters are much nearer the truth. His basic contention, moreover, that mathematics is a progressive science, sharing with the other sciences the common search for, and attainment of objective knowledge, is one of those truisms which too many contemporaries, in their over-zealous preoccupation with symbolic techniques as such, have seemingly lost from view. The question remains, however, whether, on the basis of Cassirer's own theory of the formation of mathematical concepts, the 'possibility' of mathematics, in the sense just described, can be fully accounted for. As already pointed out, in spite of his opposition to abstract formalism in certain important respects, Cassirer nevertheless concurs with such a line of thought in other equally decisive respects. He concurs, for example, in holding that mathematics is nothing but a prolongation of formal logic, differing only in the somewhat more restricted range of its assertions; and also in the widely prevalent view that mathematical inference, unlike inference in other fields, is purely deductive in character. And these two doctrines imply the strictly *a priori* character of the propositions in both logic and mathematics, in the anti-Kantian, rationalistic sense of that word.

Nevertheless a close study of such a work as *Substance and*

Function will reveal highly significant evidence pointing in another direction. So sincere is the author's desire to let the historical record speak for itself, uncolored by his personal predilections, that he actually succeeds, to a remarkable degree, in allowing that record to bear witness directly opposed to all of those formalistic tenets. Both arithmetic and geometry, he is at pains to emphasize, developed from humble beginnings in common sense experience, and both numerical and spatial concepts were for long encumbered with all sorts of sensuous connotations. In mathematics, quite as in the other sciences, more general principles had to wait upon the acquisition and analysis of particular facts; and the more general principles, in turn, led to the discovery of other particular facts, which, again in turn, led to the formation of still more general principles—such is the plain historical record, as faithfully presented by Cassirer himself, there for all who have eyes to read. Yet in every other science this doubly reciprocal relationship between particulars and universals is held to exemplify and to depend upon the cooperative procedures of induction and deduction; and no one more persuasively than Cassirer himself insists upon the inseparability of these two aspects of scientific inference—in every other science except mathematics!

Why the exception? Why refuse to designate by the same name a procedure so obviously the same in every significant respect; why refuse the name of induction to a procedure in mathematics which would undoubtedly be called by that name, if pursued in any other department of human knowledge? Or why, save for some extraordinarily compelling reason, adhere to or postulate a theory of mathematical inference which not only runs counter to the whole history of that special science, but renders impossible a consistent logical theory of scientific inference in general? This is surely a question definitely demanding an answer; a question that only stares one the more fully in the face the more persistently it is ignored by the vast majority of logicians. Every logician construes reasoning by analogy as an essential and characteristic instrument of inductive generalization; histories of mathematics are full of examples of reasoning by analogy; yet the obvious conclusion is not drawn. New mathematical theories are evolved to embrace and systematize under a set of common principles various particular theorems and topics hitherto regarded as unrelated or independent—so Cassirer, like every other historian, repeatedly points out. Precisely the same result attained in any other science would be held up as a typical product of inductive reasoning; yet in the special case of mathematics no one seems to be willing to conceive that it could possibly call for a modification of the hallowed doctrine that mathematical inference is purely deductive. Could any more conspicuous example of Bacon's "Idols of the Tribe" easily be found? And—observe well!—it is, in the last analysis, precisely and solely because of the uncritical acceptance of this doctrine that certain puzzling (not to say insoluble) epistemological problems with regard to the nature and import of mathematical knowledge rise up to plague so many contemporary logicians.

It would be grossly unfair, of course, to criticize Cassirer alone in this connection; the point is, rather, that by his clear presentation of the historical evidence he supplies all the requisite material to overthrow that prevalent but one-sided theory of mathematical inference, which is actually merely the consequence of unjustified epistemological presuppositions, and which so blindly ignores such abundant and conclusive evidence to the contrary.

What these presuppositions are, and that they are indeed unjustified, it will not, perhaps, be too difficult to discover, once attention is turned in their direction. At bottom, it will be found, there is little save verbal terminology, and sometimes scarcely even that, to distinguish Cassirer's critical idealism from lines of thought he vigorously opposes, so far as this important matter is concerned.

Who, for example, is the author of the assertion that "the mathematician need not concern himself with the particular being or intrinsic nature of his points, lines, and planes, . . . ;" on the contrary, a 'point' merely "has to be something that satisfies our axioms?" Not Cassirer, though (as noted above) he says the same thing in other words, but Bertrand Russell.[19] And who

[19] *Introduction to Mathematical Philosophy*, 59.

declares that in mathematics "a field of free and universal activity is disclosed, in which thought transcends all limits of the 'given'," in that "the objects which we consider . . . have only an ideal being?" Not Bertrand Russell, but Cassirer.[20] True, according to Russell thought merely *discovers* the subsisting essences of this ideal, trans-empirical realm; whereas according to Cassirer thought actively *creates* those universals, thus generating its own world out of its own internal resources. Nevertheless both thinkers emphasize equally the complete "liberation" of thought from all experientially imposed limitations.[21]

The fact that Cassirer presents such a telling criticism of Russellian epistemology, in this regard, cannot be allowed to obscure the complementary fact that precisely analogous objections may be urged against his own epistemology. Surely 'discovery' is no more a pure metaphor, as applied to the rôle of thought in knowledge, than is 'creation.'[22] In plain language, the relation of mathematics to logic is equally close, and the separation of mathematical concepts from experience is equally complete, whichever metaphor may be used to characterize the actual functioning of thought. On no other grounds can it be explained why Cassirer explicitly recognizes that he as well as Russell has to show how mathematical concepts, originally construed as non-experiential and purely logical in origin, can yet be 'applied' so directly and effectively to the solution of empirical problems. To insist upon the inseparability of mathematics and formal logic is *ipso facto* to cut mathematics off from all essential connection with experience; and to insist, with Cassirer, that nevertheless mathematical knowledge is as objective as all other scientific knowledge, because, forsooth, all truth is literally created by thinking, is *ipso facto* to reduce scientific truth as such to formal consistency within a closed

---

[20] *Substance and Function*, 112.

[21] The hostile critic would be tempted to express the same idea in rather different terms, to the effect that the "liberation" in question actually amounts to a confinement of thought within the four walls of an *a priori* formalism.

[22] Cf. the present writer's *The Philosophical Presuppositions of Mathematical Logic* Chs. III—VI, on this point, and also for a remarkable similarity between the views of Josiah Royce and Cassirer on such matters.

circle of ideas—the whole world, in Schopenhauerian language, *is my idea*—and objectivity (as Russell has somewhere justly observed) must be construed, in the last analysis, as merely a species of subjectivity.

There is, however, here as in other contexts, another tendency, or another phase of Cassirer's thought, which sharply conflicts with such abstract rationalism. For above everything else he insists on the essential continuity of scientific thought in general, and of mathematical thought in particular. And, although carrying on a persistent warfare against all species of empiricism and positivism, he at the same time emphatically maintains that it is the prime function of scientific laws and general mathematical formulas alike to render the 'particulars' —particular scientific facts, or specific mathematical truths— intelligible, by incorporating them in a concrete systematic nexus. Apart from such a nexus, he insists, neither particulars nor universals have any meaning. Even in the case of mathematics, he seems to argue, the construction of concepts does not take place in complete abstraction from perceptually given and intuitively apprehended data, though it does of course involve, from the very beginning, an attempt to free those concepts more and more, not from their roots in experience as such, but rather simply from irrelevant, transitory, and *merely* sensuous connotations.[23] The historical accuracy of this contention cannot be denied, and neither can its epistemological significance be overemphasized.

The point is that in mathematics, just as in all other sciences, new concepts and new theories are evolved in the process of seeking a solution to some hitherto recalcitrant problem inherited from an earlier stage in the development of the science. These new concepts and theories usually represent the end product of a long and arduous labor of preparation, of trial and error; and their significance is measured, not merely by reference to the particular problem or problems they solve, but also in terms of the enrichment of meaning they bestow upon previously accepted concepts and theories. As Cassirer so well says,

[23] *Philosophie der symbolischen Formen*, III, 452ff., esp. 468f.

the unity and self-sufficiency of the mathematical method depends upon the fact that the creative, generative procedure to which the science owes its origin, never comes to an end at any given point, but displays itself in ever new forms, and in this wise maintains itself forever as one and the same, as an indestructible totality.[24]

What is of decisive significance here is that within the science of mathematics itself (quite as in every other science) there is, on such a view, what may be called an immanent logic, which carries the science forward on its own momentum. The history of mathematics in its entirety is nothing less than a standing repudiation of any and all attempts to 'deduce' its fundamental concepts and theories from any fixed and arbitrary set of formal postulates and definitions. For that matter logical principles, as such, differ absolutely, both in nature and function, from the premises or other foundations of any given science—such at least is one lesson plainly taught by the transcendental logic of Kant. And on the other hand, the only logic mathematics (or any other science) needs or uses, in the course of its own progressive development, resides in those logical principles *according to which*, but not *from which*, mathematical reasoning proceeds. In the very nature of the case, the foundations of no science are properly to be described as logical; for the good and sufficient reason that it is their proper function to define or determine (and this means progressively to redefine), not the method, but the general nature of the content, the subject-matter, of the science in question. If it be true, as everyone acknowledges it to be, that the elementary content of mathematics was supplied by, or taken from crude experience, then it is equally true and undeniable that the whole history of the science must logically be regarded as an account of the precise way in which that first crude material has been (as Cassirer is fond of repeating) elaborated, refined, enriched in meaning, and increased in extent. It cannot be too strongly emphasized that an enormous burden of proof rests upon the shoulders of anyone trying to maintain any other thesis—proof which would not only have to disregard all the historical evidence, but run directly counter to it.

[24] *Op. cit.*, 469.

Thus it is only as an inevitable consequence of the quixotic endeavor to base mathematics on formal logic, that the self-stultifying thesis that the science has absolutely no content can be understood, and that the insoluble problem of the 'application' of mathematical concepts rises up to plague both scientists and philosophers. On the view clearly implicit in Cassirer's emphasis on the continuity and progressive character of mathematical knowledge, on the other hand, no such artificial problems can arise, for the good and sufficient reason that on that view mathematics has never entirely lost contact with experience.

What, then, it may be asked, is the true import of the dictum proclaimed by Cassirer himself, along with so many other authorities, that no other meaning is to be ascribed to any mathematical concept (even to such as seem most empirical, such as the solids of geometry), than that contained in and prescribed by the basic postulates and definitions? Does not this fundamental methodological principle render any reference to experience logically inoperative and purely incidental? No matter what the whole previous history of mathematics says or implies, who can deny that such is the state of affairs at the present time?

But surely the answers to these questions are not far to seek. The phrase 'no other meaning than that prescribed by the basic postulates' means just what it says; and it does not say that no meaning whatsoever is to be ascribed to such basic concepts and propositions. For that matter, precisely the same assertion, *mutatis mutandis*, may be made concerning the basic concepts and definitions of any science—biology, for example—; for precisely herein lies the only justification for calling them 'basic.' That such an assertion lends itself to misinterpretation to the effect that 'no other meaning' means 'no meaning at all' has, however, unfortunately revealed itself to be the case. It is true, of course, that the only experience immediately and directly relevant to mathematics at any given stage is the highly abstract experience represented, in the main, by what the next preceding stage of the science has made of space, number, and the like; just as, in physics, the only directly relevant experience is what the next preceding stage of that science has made of space-time, the constitution of the atom, and the like. No developed science ever falls back upon the crude experience of the 'plain man,' for the purpose of verifying or testing its concepts and theories; comparatively rarely does it do so, indeed, even in the most elementary laboratory work of the undergraduate. In all cases the experience really in question is that which both insures the continuity of scientific knowledge and provides the material essential for further progress. It goes without saying that experience, in such contexts, is restricted to what is relevant to the science in question; and, just as the mathematician abstracts from all or most of the *physical* properties, attributes, and relations of things, so the physicist abstracts from all of the properties, attributes, and relations of things, other than such as logically come within his purview as a physicist.[25] But just as physics yields genuine knowledge of the real world only because it does not abstract from *all* properties, attributes, and relations, precisely the same is true, *mutatis mutandis*, of mathematics— a fact which disposes of all those problems concerning the application of mathematics to experience, as neither the theories of Russell nor even those of Cassirer himself are able to do. Moreover, it is only because, and to the extent that this is so, as Kant plainly intimated, that its 'possibility' as a science can be understood. What Cassirer says so well of mathematical symbols, namely that they are neither meaningless signs, as some would argue, no mundane instrumentalities for communication with a transcendent realm of hypostatized ideas, as others suggest, but are rather explicative of meanings immanent in mathematical thought, is directly to the point in this connection. And for this very reason, if for no others, a calculus of relations, conceived as a branch of formal symbolic logic, is just as impotent, and for strictly analogous reasons, as the so-called subject-predicate logic, with respect to the generation of the synthetic concepts and judgments of mathematics.

In the light of the preceding discussion it would seem that much the same observation applies to Cassirer's theory of math-

[25] See the present writer's article entitled "Cassirer versus Russell," in *Philosophy of Science*, Vol. X., no. 3 (July, 1943), 174.

ematical concepts, with respect to its relation to contemporary symbolic logic, that commentators apply to Kant's transcendental logic, with respect to its relation to traditional formal logic. That is to say, it is rather in spite of misleading associations and entanglements with abstract formalism than because of any positive guidance accruing from such a source, that Cassirer, like Kant before him, has accomplished so much of solid and enduring worth.

HAROLD R. SMART

SAGE SCHOOL OF PHILOSOPHY
CORNELL UNIVERSITY

7

Kurt Lewin

CASSIRER'S PHILOSOPHY OF SCIENCE AND THE SOCIAL SCIENCES

7

CASSIRER'S PHILOSOPHY OF SCIENCE AND THE SOCIAL SCIENCES

THE following remarks[1] on the relation between Cassirer's views on the development of science and the recent history of psychology are the expression of a person who has always felt the deep gratitude of a student to his teacher.

During the period from 1910, when, as a graduate student, I listened to the lectures of the then *"Privatdocent"* Cassirer, to 1946, psychology has undergone a series of major changes related to basic issues of Behaviorism, Gestalt psychology, Psychoanalysis, Field Theory and the present problem of an integrated social science. The experiment has reached out from "psycho-physics" into any number of areas including motivation, personality, and social psychology. The mathematical problems of representing psychological fields and treating data statistically have proceeded step by step to new levels. Techniques of interviewing, observation, and other forms of fact-finding have grown into a rich and well-established methodology. The scientific infant of 1910, which had hardly cut his cord to mother philosophy and was looking with astonished eyes and an uneasy heart to the grown-up sciences, not knowing whether he should try to copy them or whether he ought to follow his own line—this scientific infant has perhaps not yet fully developed into maturity, but has certainly reached a stage of strength and progress which makes the psychologies of 1910 and 1946 rather different entities. Still, throughout this period, scarcely a year passed when I did not have specific reason to

[1] Some sections of this paper are also published in Lewin, Kurt, "Problems of Group Dynamics and the Integration of the Social Sciences: I. Social Equilibria." *Human Relations* (1947) Vol. I.

acknowledge the help which Cassirer's views on the nature of science and research offered.

The value of Cassirer's philosophy for psychology lies, I feel, less in his treatment of specific problems of psychology—although his contribution in this field and particularly his recent contributions are of great interest—than in his analysis of the methodology and concept-formation of the natural sciences.

To me these decades of rapid scientific growth of psychology and of the social sciences in general have provided test after test for the correctness of most of the ideas on science and scientific development expressed in his *Substanzbegriff und Funktionsbegriff*. Since the primitive discussions of the psychologists of 1910 about whether or not psychology ought to try to include not only qualitative but also quantitative data, and Cassirer's general discussions of the problem of quality and quantity—up to the present problems of research in personality, such as the treatment of biographical data, and Cassirer's discussion of the interdependence of "historical" and "systematic" problems—, I have felt with increasing strength the power and productivity of his basic approach to science.

It is not easy to point in Cassirer's work to a specific concept or any specific statement which provides a striking new insight and solves a previously insoluble problem. Still, as "participant observer" of the recent history of psychology, I may be permitted to state that Cassirer's approach seems to me a most illuminating and constructive help for making those decisions about methods and about the direction of the next step, upon which it depends whether a concrete piece of research will be a substantial contribution to a living science or a well polished container of nothing.

1. THEORY OF SCIENCE AND EMPIRICAL RESEARCH

The relation between logic and theory of science on the one hand and the progress of empirical science on the other is not a simple one and is not easily transformed into a mutually productive state of affairs.

Since Kant philosophers have tried more or less successfully to avoid telling the empirical scientist what he "ought" to do or

not to do. They have learned, with a few exceptions, to regard
science as an object they should study rather than rule. This
laudable and necessary removal of philosophy from the authori-
tarian place of the boss or the judge over science has led to a
tendency of eliminating all "practical" relations between philosophy and the empirical sciences, including the perhaps possible and fruitful position of philosophy as a consultant to
science. As the scientist tries to progress into the eternal frontier
of the unknown, he faces highly complex and intricate problems
of methods, concepts, and theory formation. It would seem
natural that he should turn to the philosophical study of the
nature of science for information and help on the methodological and conceptual aspects of the pressing problems he is
trying to solve.

There are certain lines along which such help might be forthcoming and certain dangers involved in the all around co-
operation of scientists and philosophers on the theory and practice of such an "applied theory of science." To start with the
latter: as a rule, the philosopher can hardly be expected to have
the detailed knowledge of an active research worker in a specific
branch of an empirical science. As a rule, therefore, he should
not be expected to make direct contributions to empirical
theories. The tragi-comic happening of half a decade ago, when
a certain group of philosophers tried to revive good old classical
behaviorism just after it had fulfilled its usefulness for psychology and was happily dying, should be a warning against
such inappropriate overstepping of boundaries. On the other
hand, such danger should not minimize the essential advantages
which a closer coöperation between the philosopher and the
scientist should offer to both.

As far as I can see, there are two main lines along which
valuable and more than accidental help for the empirical and
particularly the social sciences may emerge from a closer relation to philosophy. One has to do with mathematical logic, the
other with comparative theory of science.

The development of mathematical logic has proceeded considerably beyond what Cassirer had to offer. Mathematical logic
seems to provide a fruitful possibility of assistance for specific

problems of measurement for basic mathematical questions regarding qualitative and quantitative data, for general mathematical problems of representing social and psychological fields, and so on. The insight provided by mathematical logic could probably have avoided some of the past headaches and should be of considerable potential assistance to the social scientist in the coming period of the quantitative measurement of social forces.

Mathematical logic has, however, not been of much avail and, in my judgment, is not likely to be of much avail for guiding the psychologist or social scientist through certain other major methodological perplexities.

The logician is accustomed to deal with problems of correct conclusions or other aspects of science and concepts which are "timeless," which hold as much for the physics of Copernicus as for modern physics. These problems are doubtless of great interest to the research-worker. They make up, however, only a small section of the problems of scientific strategy which are the concern of the daily struggle of progressing into the unknown. The main problems, which the scientist has to face and for which he has to find a solution, are inevitably bound to the particular state of development of his science, even if they are problems of method rather than content.

It is unrealistic and unproductive for an empirical scientist to approach problems of scientific method and procedure in a way which does not take cognizance of the basic fact that, to be effective, scientific methods have to be adjusted to the specific state of affairs at a given time. This holds for the techniques of fact-finding, for the process of conceptualization and theorizing, in short, for more or less all aspects of research. Research is the art of taking the next step. Methods and concepts, which may represent a revolutionary progress today, may be outmoded tomorrow. Can the philosopher gain insight into the development of science in a way useful for these vital time-bound aspects of scientific labor?

The logician may be inclined to place these problems outside the realm of a theory of science. He may be inclined to view them not as philosophical problems but as questions which should be dealt with by historians. Doubtless the researcher is deeply influenced by the culture in which he lives and by its technical and economic facilities. Not these problems of cultural history, however, are in question when the social psychologist has to make up his mind whether or not "experiments with groups" are scientifically meaningful, or what procedure he may follow for developing better concepts of personality, of leadership, or of other aspects of group life. Not historical, but conceptual and methodological problems are to be answered, questions about what is scientifically right or wrong, adequate or inadequate; although this correctness may be specific to a special developmental stage of a science and may not hold for a previous or a later stage. In other words, the term "scientific development" refers to levels of scientific maturity, to levels of concepts and theories in the sense of philosophy rather than of human history or psychology.

It is this approach to science as emerging systems of theorems and concepts to which Cassirer has contributed so much. Whenever Cassirer discusses science, he seems to perceive both the permanent characteristics of scientific systems and procedures and the specific conceptual form.

Philosophy of science can come to an insight into the nature of science only by studying science. It is, therefore, in permanent danger of making the science of the past a prototype for all science and of making past methodology the standard by which to measure what scientific methods "ought" to be used or not to be used. Cassirer has in most cases successfully avoided this danger by looking at the scientific mehods of the past in the way in which the research-worker at that time would perceive them. He discloses the basic character of science as the eternal attempt to go beyond what is regarded scientifically accessible at any specific time. To proceed beyond the limitations of a given level of knowledge the researcher, as a rule, has to break down methodological taboos which condemn as "unscientific" or "illogical" the very methods or concepts which later on prove to be basic for the next major progress. Cassirer has shown how this step by step revolution of what is "scientifically permissible" dominates the development of mathematics, physics, and chemistry throughout their history.

A second reason why I feel Cassirer's approach is so valuable to the social scientist is his comparative procedure. Although Cassirer has not fully developed what might be called a systematic *comparative theory of the sciences*, he took important steps in this direction. His treatment of mathematics, physics, and chemistry, of historical and systematic disciplines is essentially of a comparative nature. Cassirer shows an unusual ability to blend the analysis of general characteristics of scientific methodology with the analysis of a specific branch of science. It is this ability to reveal the general rule in an example, without destroying the specific characteristics of a particular discipline at a given stage of development, which makes the comparative treatment of some branches of mathematics and of the natural sciences so illuminating for research in the social sciences. This comparative approach opens the way to a perception of similarities between different sciences and between apparently unrelated questions within the same science.

We shall discuss here only one type of problem as an example of the structural similarities between the conceptual problems of the present social sciences and problems of mathematics and the physical sciences at certain stages of development, namely that of "existence."

2. The Problem of "Existence" in an Empirical Science

Arguments about "existence" may seem metaphysical in nature and may therefore not be expected to be raised in empirical sciences. Actually, however, opinions about existence or non-existence are quite common in the empirical sciences and have greatly influenced scientific development in both a positive and a negative way. Labelling something as "non-existing" is equivalent to declaring it "out of bounds" for the scientist. Attributing "existence" to an item automatically makes it a duty of the scientist to consider this item as an object of research; it includes the necessity of considering its properties as "facts," which cannot be neglected in the total system of theories; finally, it implies that the terms by which one refers to the item are accepted as scientific "concepts" (rather than regarded as "mere words").

The problem of "existence" is, therefore, one of the most illuminating examples for the way in which facts, concepts, and methods are closely interdependent aspects of an empirical science. To demonstrate the way in which this interdependence is functioning in every phase of science is the central theme of this aspect of Cassirer's philosophy.

Cassirer follows the steps by which mathematics is gradually transformed. Geometry and the theory of numbers, for instance, changes from a study of separate forms or entities, which are to be described and analysed one by one—with the objective of finding "permanent properties"—into a discipline which deals with problems of interrelations and transformations.[2]

Geometry, as the theory of invariants, treats certain unchangeable relations; but this unchangeableness cannot be defined unless we understand, as its conceptual background, certain fundamental changes relative to which they hold. The unchanging geometrical properties are not such in and for themselves, but only in relation to a system of possible transformations that we implicitly assume. Constancy and change thus appear as thoroughly correlative moments, definable only through each other.[3]

In physics an equivalent change occurs on the basis of an increasingly close interdependence of fact finding and theory.

It has been shown, in opposition to the traditional logical doctrine, that the course of the mathematical construction of concepts is defined by the procedures of the *construction of series*. We have not been concerned with separating out the common element from a plurality of similar impressions but with establishing a principle by which their diversity should appear. The unity of the concept has not been found in a fixed group of properties, but in the rule, which represents the mere diversity as a sequence of elements according to law.[4]

In truth, no physicist experiments and measures with the particular instrument that he has sensibly before his eyes; but he substitutes for it an ideal instrument in thought, from which all accidental defects, such as necessarily belong to the particular instrument, are excluded. For example, if we measure the intensity of an electric current by a tangent-compass, then the observations, which we make first with a concrete

[2] *Substance and Function* (Swabey tr.), 68.
[3] *Ibid.*, 90; wording changed by K. Lewin, in line with German original.
[4] *Ibid.*, 148.

apparatus, must be related and carried over to a general geometrical model, before they are physically applicable. We substitute for a copper wire of a definite strength a strictly geometrical circle without breadth; in place of the steel of the magnetic needle, which has a certain magnitude and form, we substitute an infinitely small, horizontal magnetic axis, which can be moved without friction around a vertical axis; and it is the totality of these transformations, which permits us to carry the observed deflection of the magnetic needle into the general theoretical formula of the strength of the current, and thus to determine the value of the latter. The corrections, which we make and must necessarily make with the use of every physical instrument, are themselves a work of mathematical theory; to exclude these latter, is to deprive the observation itself of its meaning and value.[5]

Until relatively recently psychology, sociology, and anthropology were dominated by a methodology which regarded science as a process of "collecting facts." This methodology showed all the earmarks of early Greek mathematics and pre-Galilean physics. During the last ten years the hostility to theorizing has greatly diminished. It has been replaced by a relatively wide-spread recognition of the necessity for developing better concepts and higher levels of theory.

This change has its corollary in certain changes regarding what is considered "existing." Beliefs regarding "existence" in social science have changed in regard to the degree to which "full reality" is attributed to psychological and social phenomena, and in regard to the reality of their "deeper," dynamic properties.

At the beginning of this century, for instance, the experimental psychology of "will and emotion" had to fight for recognition against a prevalent attitude which placed volition, emotion, and sentiments in the "poetic realm" of beautiful words, a realm to which nothing corresponds which could be regarded as "existing" in the sense in which the scientist uses the term. Although every psychologist had to deal with these facts realistically in his private life, they were banned from the realm of "facts" in the scientific sense. Emotions were declared

[5] *Ibid.*, 144.

to be something too "fluid" and "intangible" to be pinned down by scientific analysis or by experimental procedures. Such a methodological argument does not deny existence to the phenomenon, but it has the effect of keeping the topic outside the realm of empirical science.

Like social taboos, a scientific taboo is kept up not so much by a rational argument as by a common attitude among scientists: any member of the scientific guild who does not strictly adhere to the taboo is looked upon as queer; he is suspected of not adhering to the scientific standards of critical thinking.

3. THE REALITY OF SOCIAL PHENOMENA

Before the invention of the atom bomb the average physical scientist was hardly ready to concede to social phenomena the same degree of "reality" as to a physical object. Hiroshima and Nagasaki seem to have caused many physical scientists to change their minds. This change was hardly based on philosophical considerations. The bomb has driven home with dramatic intensity the degree to which social happenings are both the result of and the conditions for the occurrence of physical events. The period during which the natural scientist thought of the social scientist as someone interested in dreams and words (rather than as an investigator of facts which are not less real than physical facts and which can be studied no less objectively) has gradually been coming to an end.

The social scientists themselves, of course, have had a stronger belief in the "reality" of the entities they were studying. Still this belief was frequently limited to the specific narrow section with which they happened to be familiar. The economist, for instance, finds it a bit difficult to concede to psychological, to anthropological, or to legal data that degree of reality which he gives to prices and other economic data. Some psychologists still view with suspicion the reality of those cultural facts with which the anthropologist is concerned. They tend to regard only individuals as real and they are not inclined to consider a "group atmosphere" as something which is as real and measurable as, let us say, a physical field of gravity. Concepts like that of "leadership" retained a halo of mysticism even after it had been demonstrated that it is quite possible to measure and not only to "judge" leadership performance.

The denial of existence of a group or of certain aspects of group life is based on arguments which grant existence only to units of certain size, or which concern methodologic-technical problems, or conceptual problems.

4. REALITY AND SIZE

Cassirer[6] discusses how, periodically throughout the history of physics, vivid discussions have occurred about the reality of the atom, the electron, or whatever else was considered at that time to be the smallest particle of physical material. In the social sciences it has usually been not the part but the whole whose existence has been doubted.

Logically, there is no reason for distinguishing between the reality of a molecule, an atom, or an ion, or more generally between the reality of a whole or its parts. There is no more magic behind the fact that groups have properties of their own, which are different from the properties of their subgroups or their individuals members, than behind the fact that molecules have properties, which are different from the properties of the atoms or ions of which they are composed.

In the social as in the physical field the structural properties of a dynamic whole are different from the structural properties of their subparts. Both sets of properties have to be investigated. When one and when the other is most important, depends upon the question to be answered. But there is no difference of reality between them.

If this basic statement is accepted, the problem of existence of a group loses its metaphysical flavor. Instead we face a series of empirical problems. They are equivalent to the chemical question of whether a given aggregate is a mixture of different types of atoms, or whether these atoms have formed molecules of a certain type. The answer to such a question has to be given in chemistry, as in the social sciences, on the basis of an

[6] Ibid., 151-170.

empirical probing into certain testable properties of the case in hand.

For instance, it may be wrong to state that the blond women living in a town "exist as a group" in the sense of being a dynamic whole that is characterized by a close interdependence of their members. They are merely a number of individuals who are "classified under one concept" according to the similarity of one of their properties. If, however, the blond members of a workshop are made an "artificial minority" and are discriminated against by their colleagues, they may well become a group with specific structural properties.

Structural properties are characterized by *relations* between parts rather than by the parts or elements themselves. Cassirer emphasizes that, throughout the history of mathematics and physics, from Anaxagoras and Aristotle to Bacon, Boscovich, Boltzman and the present day, problems of constancy of relations rather than of constancy of elements have gained importance and have gradually changed the picture of what is considered essential.

The meaning of the mathematical concept cannot be comprehended, as long as we seek any sort of presentational correlate for it in the given; the meaning only appears when we recognize the concept as the expression of a *pure relation*, upon which rests the unity and continuous connection of the members of a manifold. The function of the physical concept also is first evident in this interpretation. The more it disclaims every independent perceptible content and everything pictorial, the more clearly its logical and systematic function is shown. . . . All that the "thing" of the popular view of the world loses in properties, it gains in relations; for it no longer remains isolated and dependent on itself alone, but is connected inseparably by logical threads with the totality of experience. Each particular concept is, as it were, one of these threads, on which we string real experiences and connect them with future possible experiences. The objects of physics: matter and force, atom and ether, can no longer be misunderstood as so many new realities for investigation, and realities whose inner essence is to be penetrated—when once they are recognized as instruments produced by thought for the purpose of comprehending the confusion of phenomena as an ordered and measurable whole.[7]

[7] *Ibid.*, 166.

5. REALITY, METHODS, AND EXPERIENCE

If recognition of the existence of an entity depends upon this entity's showing properties or constancies of its own, the judgment about what is real or unreal should be affected by changes in the possibility of demonstrating social properties.

The social sciences have considerably improved their techniques for reliably recording the structure of small or large groups and of registering the various aspects of group life. Sociometric techniques, group observation, interview techniques, and others are enabling the social scientist more and more to gather reliable data on the structural properties of groups, on the relations between groups or subgroups, and on the relation between a group and the life of its individual members.

The taboo against believing in the existence of a social entity is probably most effectively broken by handling this entity experimentally. As long as the scientist merely describes a leadership form, he is open to the criticism that the categories used reflect merely his "subjective views" and do not correspond to the "real" properties of the phenomena under consideration. If the scientist experiments with leadership and varies its form, he relies on an "operational definition" which links the concept of a leadership form to concrete procedures of creating such a leadership form or to the procedures for testing its existence. The "reality" of that to which the concept refers is established by "doing with" rather than "looking at," and this reality is independent of certain "subjective" elements of classification. The progress of physics from Archimedes to Einstein shows consecutive steps, by which the "practical" aspect of the experimental procedure has modified and sometimes revolutionized the scientific concepts regarding the physical world by changing the beliefs of the scientists about what is and what is not real.

To vary a social phenomenon experimentally the experimenter has to take hold of all essential factors, even if he is not yet able to analyze them satisfactorily. A major omission or misjudgment on this point makes the experiment fail. In social research the experimenter has to take into consideration such factors as the personality of individual members, the group structure, ideology and cultural values, and economic factors. Group experimentation is a form of social management. To be successful it, like social management, has to take into account all of the various factors that happen to be important for the case in hand. Experimentation with groups will therefore lead to a natural integration of the social sciences, and it will force the social scientist to recognize as reality the totality of factors which determine group life.

6. Social Reality and Concepts

It seems that the social scientist has a better chance of accomplishing such a realistic integration than the social practitioner. For thousands of years kings, priests, politicians, educators, producers, fathers and mothers—in fact, all individuals—have been trying day by day to influence smaller or larger groups. One might assume that this would have led to accumulated wisdom of a well integrated nature. Unfortunately nothing is farther from the truth. We know that our average diplomat thinks in very one-sided terms, perhaps those of law, or economics, or military strategy. We know that the average manufacturer holds highly distorted views about what makes a work-team tick. We know that no one can answer today even such relatively simple questions as what determines the productivity of a committee meeting.

Several factors have come together to prevent practical experience from leading to clear insight. Certainly, the man of affairs is convinced of the reality of group life, but he is usually opposed to a conceptual analysis. He prefers to think in terms of "intuition" and "intangibles." The able practitioner frequently insists that it is impossible to formulate simple, clear rules about how to reach a social objective. He insists that different actions have to be taken according to the various situations, that plans have to be highly flexible and sensitive to the changing scene.

If one tries to transform these sentiments into scientific language, they amount to the following statements. a) Social events depend on the social field as a whole, rather than on a few selected items. This is the basic insight behind the field theoretical method which has been successful in physics, which has steadily grown in psychology and, in my opinion, is bound to be equally fundamental for the study of social fields, simply because it expresses certain basic general characteristics of interdependence. b) The denial of "simple rules" is partly identical with the following important principle of scientific analysis. Science tries to link certain observable (phenotypical) data with other observable data. It is crucial for all problems of interdependence, however, that—for reasons which we do not need to discuss here—it is, as a rule, impracticable to link one set of phenotypical data *directly* to other phenotypical data. Instead, it is necessary to insert "intervening variables."[8] To use a more common language: the practitioner as well as the scientist views the observable data as mere "symptoms." They are "surface" indications of some "deeper-lying" facts. He has learned to "read" the symptoms, like a physicist reads his instruments. The equations which express physical laws refer to such deeper-lying dynamic entities as pressure, energy, or temperature rather than to the directly observable symptoms such as the movements of the pointer of an instrument.

The underlying methodological principle is but one expression of the nature of the relation between concepts, scientific facts and scientific fact finding. In the words of Cassirer,

Strictly speaking, the experiment never concerns the real case, as it lies before us here and now in all the wealth of its particular determinations, but the experiment rather concerns an ideal case, which we substitute for it. The real beginnings of scientific induction furnish the classical example of this. Galileo did not discover the law of falling bodies by collecting arbitrary observations of sensuously real bodies, but by defining hypothetically the concept of uniform acceleration and taking it as a conceptual measure of the facts. This concept provides for the given time-values a series of space-values, such as proceed according to a fixed rule, that can be grasped once for all. Henceforth we must attempt to advance to the actual process of reality by a progressive consideration of the complex determinations, that were originally excluded: as, for example, the variation of acceleration according to the distance from the centre of the earth, retardation by the resistance of the air, etc.[9]

[8] Tolman, E. C., "The Determiners of Behavior at a Choice Point," *Psychological Review*, (1938), Vol. 45, 1-41.

[9] *Substance and Function* (Engl. tr.), 254.

If we consider the factors involved in the measurement of motion, . . . it is evident that the physical definition of motion cannot be established without substituting the geometrical body for the sensuous body, without substituting the "intelligible" continuous extension of the mathematician for sensuous extension. Before we can speak of motion and its exact measurement in the strict sense, we must go from the contents of perception to their conceptual limits. . . . It is no less a pure conceptual construction, when we ascribe a determinate velocity to a non-uniformly moving body at each point of its path; such a construction presupposes for its explanation nothing less than the whole logical theory of infinitesimal analysis. But even where we seem to stand closer to direct sensation, where we seem guided by no other interest than to arrange its differences as presented us, into a fixed scale, even here theoretical elements are requisite and clearly appear. It is a long way from the immediate sensation of heat to the exact concept of temperature.[10]

The dynamics of social events provides no exception to this general characteristic of dynamics. If it were possible to link a directly observable group behavior, B, with another behavior, B^1,—$B = F$ (B^1) where F means a simple function—then simple rules of procedure for the social practitioner would be possible. When the practitioner denies that such rules can be more than poor approximations he seems to imply that the function, F, is complicated. I am inclined to interpret his statement actually to mean that in group life, too, "appearance" should be distinguished from the "underlying facts," that similarity of appearance may go together with dissimilarity of the essential properties and *vice versa*, and that laws can be formulated only in regard to these underlying dynamic entities— $k = F$ (n,m) where k,n,m refer not to behavioral symptoms but to intervening variables.[11]

For the social scientist this means that he should give up thinking about such items as group structure, group tension, or social forces as nothing more than a popular metaphor or analogy, which should be eliminated from science as much as possible. Although there is no need for social science to copy the specific concepts of the physical sciences, the social scientist should be clear that he, too, needs intervening variables and

[10] *Ibid.*, 142.
[11] Cf. Lewin, Kurt, *A Dynamic Theory of Personality* (tr. by D. Adams and K. Zener), New York: McGraw-Hill (1935).

that these dynamic facts rather than the symptoms and appearances are the important points of reference for him and the social practitioner alike.

7. MATHEMATIZATION AND INTEGRATION OF THE SOCIAL SCIENCES

The relation between theory formation, fact finding and mathematization, which Cassirer has described in regard to the physical sciences, has come much to the fore in the psychology of the last decade. Different psychological trends have led from different sides and with partly different objectives to a strong emphasis on mathematization. This need springs partly from a desire of a more exact scientific representation of the results of tests or other fact findings and has led to an elaborate development of statistical procedures. In part the emphasis on mathematization springs from the desire of a deeper theoretical insight.[12] Both geometrical and algebraic concepts are employed to this end.

Mathematical economics since Pareto (1909) is another example of the development of a social science which shows many of the characteristics discussed by Cassirer.

One of the most striking illustrations of the function of theorems, concepts, and methods in the development of science is their rôle in the integration of the social sciences which is just beginning to take place. It may be appropriate to mention this problem and to refer briefly to considerations I have presented elsewhere.[13]

Many aspects of social life can be viewed as quasi-stationary processes. They can be regarded as states of quasi-stationary equilibrium in the precise meaning of a constellation of forces the structure of which can be well defined. The scientific treat-

[12] Hull, C. L., *Principles of Behavior*, New York: Appleton Century (1943); Köhler, W., *The Place of Value in a World of Facts*. New York: Liveright (1938); Lewin, Kurt, "The Conceptual Representation and the Measurement of Psychological Forces," *Contributions to Psychological Theory*, Vol. I, No. 4, Duke University Press (1938); Lewin, Kurt, "Constructs in Psychology and Psychological Ecology," *Studies in Topological and Vector Psychology*, III, University of Iowa.

[13] Lewin, Kurt, "Problems of Group Dynamics and the Integration of the Social Sciences: I. Social Equilibria," *Human Relations* (1947), Vol. I.

ment of social forces presupposes analytic devices which are adequate to the nature of social processes and which are technically fitted to serve as a bridge to a mathematical treatment. The basic means to this end is the representation of social situations as "social fields."

This technical analysis makes it possible to formulate in a more exact way problems of planned social changes and of resistance to change. It permits general statements concerning some aspects of the problem of selecting specific objectives in bringing about change, concerning different methods of bringing about the same amount of change, and concerning differences in the secondary effects of these methods. The analytic tools used are equally applicable to cultural, economic, sociological, and psychological aspects of group life. They fit a great variety of processes, such as production levels of a factory, a work-team and an individual worker; changes of abilities of an individual and of capacities of a country; group standards with and without cultural value; activities of one group and the interaction between groups, between individuals, and between individuals and groups. The analysis concedes equal reality to all aspects of group life and to social units of all sizes. The application depends upon the structural properties of the process and of the total situation in which it takes place.

How is it possible, one may ask, to bring together under one heading and procedure such diversified data? Does that not necessarily mean losing in concreteness what one might gain in scientific generality?

In the same way as the natural sciences, the social sciences have to face the problem of how to get hold conceptually of the disturbing qualitative richness of psychological and cultural events, how to find "general" laws without giving up reaching the individual case. Cassirer describes how the mathematical constructive procedure solves this problem by changing, as it were, the very meaning of equality and scientific abstraction. Speaking of equalities of mathematical sets he says, "This similarity, however, means nothing more than that they are connected by a definite rule, such as permits us to proceed from one manifold to another by continued identical application of the same fundamental relation;"[14] "The genuine concept does not disregard the peculiarities and particularities which it holds under it, but seeks to show the *necessity* of the occurrence and connection of just these particularities."[15]

The individual case is not excluded from consideration, but is fixed and retained as a perfectly determinate step in a general process of change. It is evident anew that the characteristic feature of the concept is not the "universality" of a presentation, but the universal validity of a principle of serial order. We do not isolate any abstract part whatever from the manifold before us, but we create for its members a definite relation by thinking of them as bound together by an inclusive law. And the further we proceed in this and the more firmly this connection according to laws is established, so much the clearer does the unambiguous determination of the particular stand forth.[16]

The consideration of quasi-stationary equilibria is based on analytic concepts which, within the realm of the social sciences, have emerged first in psychology. The concepts of a psychological force, of tension, of conflicts as equilibria of forces, of force fields and of inducing fields, have slowly widened their range of application from the realm of individual psychology into the realm of processes and events which had been the domain of sociology and cultural anthropology. It seems that the treatment of economic equilibria by mathematical economics, although having a different origin, is fully compatible with this development.

The fusion of the social sciences will make accessible to economics the vast advantages which the experimental procedure offers for testing theories and for developing new insight. The combination of experimental and mathematical procedures which Cassirer describes has been the main vehicle for the integration of the study of light, of electricity, and of the other branches of physical science. The same combination seems to be destined to make the integration of the social sciences a reality.

KURT LEWIN

MASSACHUSETTS INSTITUTE OF TECHNOLOGY

[14] *Substance and Function* (Engl. tr.), 31.
[15] *Ibid.*, 19.
[16] *Ibid.*, 20.

8

Robert S. Hartman

CASSIRER'S PHILOSOPHY OF SYMBOLIC FORMS

CASSIRER'S PHILOSOPHY OF SYMBOLIC FORMS

I DWELT on the birth of the ego out of the mythical collective. . . . [The] ego detaches itself from the collective in the same way that certain figures of Rodin wrest themselves out of the stone and awaken from it." Thus, in a speech at the Library of Congress,[1] Thomas Mann described his creation of the Joseph figures. In a similar way Cassirer could have described—and did describe[2]—the birth of modern self-consciousness from the matrix of pre-historic myth and medieval metaphysics, the creation of its symbolic forms out of the raw material of rites and gestures, the emergence of logical functions from natural material, their gradual liberation—and therewith the self-liberation of consciousness—from sensuous encumbrances.

Symbolic forms are progressive states of the self-emergence of consciousness. That emergence may be followed in the gradual unfolding of metaphysical thought into modern science—as Cassirer has shown in the first three volumes of the *Erkenntnisproblem*—or it may be demonstrated in the gradual unfolding of the raw material and mirroring produce of the self-evolving consciousness—as Cassirer has done in his *Philosophie der symbolischen Formen*.[3]

Both forms of presentation demonstrate one and the same process of creative thought: in the first case with the emphasis on the creating mind, in the second with the emphasis on the created form. As the form, in its successive elaboration, mirrors

---

[1] *The Atlantic Monthly*, February 1943, 97 ff.

[2] Cf. *Erkenntnisproblem* I, 11 f.

[3] All references in this essay are to that work, and will be referred to by *PSF*, unless otherwise stated. The translations are my own.

the laboring mind, so the mind, in its successive effort, reflects the form wrought. In the *Erkenntnisproblem* Cassirer has shown the work of the objective spirit in its course; in the *Philosophie der symbolischen Formen* he has shown, in the evolution of its work, the course of the objective spirit. In both cases he stands at the end of the development, surveying it and focusing it within his own mind, thus re-creating the energy of cultural development and sculpturing its forms before our own eyes, a philosophical seer, whose visual, "synoptic"[4] view of philosophy—both in its historical and conceptual dimension— has rendered to us in ontogeny what the objective spirit has wrought throughout generations in phylogenic labor. Thus he has created a new symbolic form, which points beyond itself toward still higher formations. His work for us, represents what he calls "a new 'composition' of the world, which proceeds according to specific standards, valid only for itself."[5] Such a form "must be measured with its own measure. The points of view, according to which it is to be judged . . . must not be brought to it from outside, but must be deduced from the fundamental principle of its own formation."[6] No rigid metaphysical category must interfere with such "a purely immanent beginning."

Let us then measure Cassirer with his own measure. We shall be unable, within the limits of this essay, to extend our measurements into all the ramifications of the philosophy of symbolic forms. But we shall be able to follow its formative principle. From it we shall deduce, and by it justify, our own procedure. Thus we may hope to catch the spirit of that great work—the spirit of creation itself.

The philosophy of symbolic forms is a philosophy of creation. The category of creativity is the one we shall apply to and deduce from his system. In order to do so we must first clear the way and determine his philosophy negatively against its two poles, the raw-material of creation and the source of the creating act. The symbolic form is neither the one nor the

---

[4] *PSF*, III, viii.
[5] *PSF*, I, 122.
[6] *Ibid.*

other, but *represents the process of creation itself*. Confinement
to the raw-material would lead to metaphysics, confinement to
the source of the creative act to psychology. Cassirer's philosophy is neither metaphysics nor psychology; it is neither concerned with pure Being nor with pure Consciousness, but with
the context and interaction of both.

The characteristic and peculiar achievement of each symbolic form—
the form of language as well as that of myth or of theoretical cognition—
is not simply to receive[7] a given material of impressions possessing already
a certain determination, quality and structure, in order to graft on it,
from the outside, so to speak, another form out of the energy of consciousness itself. The characteristic action of the spirit begins much
earlier. Also, the apparently "given" is seen, on closer analysis, to be
already processed by certain acts of either the linguistic, the mythical,
or the logico-theoretical "apperception." It "is" only that which it has
been *made* into by those acts. Already in its apparently simple and immediate states it shows itself conditioned and determined by some
primary function which gives it significance. In this primary formation,
and not in the secondary one, lies the peculiar secret of each symbolic
form.[8]

Thus there is no "primary datum" underlying the creative
activity of consciousness. Every primary datum is already
spiritually[9] imbued, even the simplest spatial perceptions, like
left and right, high and low.[10] The same is true of the original
sensuous perceptions of time, number, and causality. If these
categories were substantial elements, they could point to an
absolute Being; but such a Being, presupposed by dogmatic
metaphysics, does not exist. Our consciousness cannot posit any
content without, by that very act of positing, setting a whole
complex of other contents. This fact cannot be explained by
dogmatic metaphysics from the presupposition of an absolute
Being; on the contrary, the existence of such a being is contradicted by that very activity of consciousness.[11] An "immediate

[7] In the sense of the Platonic "receptacle."

[8] *PSF*, II, 120.

[9] The adjective "spiritual" is used in the sense of the German *"geistig."*

[10] *PSF*, II, 120.

[11] *PSF*, I, 31 f., with reference to Kant's *Versuch die negativen Grössen in die
Weltweisheit einzuführen.*

datum" is already a material-spiritual context, it is a *creatum:* the germ of a symbolic form.

It is obvious, on the other hand, that we cannot understand the form through insight into the *natural* causes of its origination, by the method of psychology rather than that of metaphysics. What consciousness contributes to the form is as important as are the contributions of the schemata of space, time, and number; but it is as little real by itself as are the latter. There is a third "formative determination," which explains the world of symbolic forms neither from the nature of the absolute nor from the play of empirico-psychological forces. Although that determination may agree with the method of psychology in acknowledging the fact that the *subjectum agens* of the symbolic forms is to be found nowhere else than in the human consciousness, it does not necessarily have to take consciousness in either its metaphysical or in its psychological determination—but in a critical analysis which goes beyond both. "The modern critique of cognition, the analysis of the laws and principles of knowledge, has freed itself more and more determinedly from the presuppositions both of metaphysics and of psychologism."[12]

Neither from the side of an absolute being nor from that of consciousness alone can reality be comprehended. Only in the combination of both, in the symbolic form as constituted by the creative activity of the spirit, in the *produce*, the autonomous *creation* of the spirit do we have reality—and therewith truth;

for the highest truth which opens itself to the spirit is finally the form of its own activity. In the totality of its own accomplishments and the cognition of the specific rules by which each of them is being determined, as well as in the consciousness of the connection which combines all these rules into the unity of one task and one solution: in all this the spirit possesses the knowledge of itself and of reality.[13]

And that *knowable* reality alone is real.

To the question what absolute reality should be outside of that totality of spiritual functions, what the "thing in itself" might be in this sense— to this question there is no further answer. It must be understood more

[12] *PSF*, II, 15.
[13] *PSF*, I, 47.

and more as a falsely put problem, a phantom of thought. The true concept of reality cannot be pressed into the abstract form of Being, but becomes merged in the variety and abundance of the forms of spiritual life—a life on which is imprinted the stamp of inner necessity, and therewith the stamp of objectivity. In this sense each new "symbolic form," not only the conceptual world of cognition but also the plastic world of art, as well as that of myth and of language, signifies, in the words of Goethe, a revelation from the inner to the outer, a "synthesis of world and spirit," which alone truly assures us of the original unity of both.[14]

The world of symbolic forms is the world of life itself. Neither in the primitive intuition of the spirit[15] nor in the primitive perception of natural being can life be comprehended. Life has left both these states behind, it has transformed itself into the form of the spirit.[16] "The negation of the symbolic forms would therefore, instead of apprehending the fullness of life, on the contrary destroy the spiritual form, to which that fullness necessarily is bound."[17]

We must not passively contemplate these spiritual realities, but put ourselves right into the midst of their restless activity; only thus shall we comprehend these realities not as static contemplations of a metaphysical Being but as formative functions and energies. In doing so we shall discover in them, however different the "Gestalten" they produce, certain universal and typical principles,[18] the principles of creation itself. Recognizing creation we become creative ourselves: not as dogmatic metaphysicians but as artists vitalized by and vitalizing our material.

Thus, in our interpretation, Cassirer's philosophy is metaphysics as little as Rodin's figures are stone: if no creative hand had ever touched the stone it might have remained stone. The creative touch proved that mere "stone" it never was. If no creative philosophy had ever liberated the spirit from the mould of the scholastic system into which it had been "melted down,"[19] then metaphyiscs might have remained metaphysics.

14 *PSF*, I, 47 f.
15 *PSF*, I, 48 f.
16 *PSF*, I, 51.
17 *Ibid.*
18 *PSF*, I, 51.
19 *Erkenntnisproblem*, I, 11.

"Only slowly the individual moments of thought, which in that system were held together as if by a dogmatic force, step forth in freer movement."[20] From the intellectual struggles of the Renaissance, to the liberating strike of Kant's *Critique of Reason*, to Cassirer's "Critique of Culture,"[21] the life-giving touch works on and transforms metaphysics, until it culminates in the *Philosophy of Symbolic Forms*. But being capable of such transformation it shows itself never to have been mere "metaphysics." Critical philosophers, and Cassirer in particular, could vitalize metaphysics as Rodin could the stone. It may be instructive to compare the nature of Cassirer's material with that of Rodin's.

Rodin's "stone" never was just stone. Rodin only knew living surfaces. These surfaces consisted of infinitely many movements.

The play of light upon them made manifest that each of these movements was different and significant. At this point they seemed to flow into one another; at that to greet each other hesitatingly; at a third to pass by each other without recognition, like strangers. There were undulations without end. There was no point at which there was not life and movement. . . . He saw only innumerable living surfaces, only life.[22]

Cassirer's philosophy never was just metaphysics.[23] Metaphysics, as ontology, is the discipline of pure Being, but there never was pure Being. In the interaction of the thinker's mind with the raw material of his thought arises a new reality: Reality proper. That reality appears in "symbolic forms"— forms which rise under the dynamic movement of thought like Rodin's figures under the magic of his hands. Like on Rodin's surfaces, the light of reality plays on these forms, which refract it in a thousand manifestations.

When one characterizes language, myth, art, as "symbolic forms,"

[20] *Ibid.*
[21] *PSF*, I, 11.
[22] Rilke, Rainer Maria, *Rodin*, New York: The Fine Editions Press, 1945, 11 f.
[23] Somewhat doubtful in this respect is W. C. Swabey in his book-report on the *Philosophie der symbolischen Formen*, *Philosophical Review*, vol. XXXIII, No. 2, 1924, 195.

then there seems to lie in that expression the presupposition that all of them, as definite formative modes of the spirit, point back to a last primary layer of reality,[24] which is seen through them only, like through a strange medium. Reality seems to become comprehensible for us only in the particular state of those forms; in them it both conceals and reveals itself. The same fundamental functions which give the world of the spirit its determination, its imprint and character, appear on the other hand as just so many refractions which Reality, uniform and unique in itself, experiences as soon as it is being apperceived and appropriated by the "subject." The philosophy of symbolic forms is, seen under this point of view, nothing but the attempt to indicate for each of them, as it were, the definite index of refraction. It wants to recognize the particular nature of the different refracting media.[25]

Those indices determine the activity of the spirit, defining it in terms of the "modalities"[26] which the spirit assumes in each particular medium. The life· of the spirit thus is "multidimensional;"[27] there are undulations without end, movements, dynamic processes. Like Rodin's statues they grow out of the undifferentiated sensuous matrix into the determinacy of objective thought—indeed, like Rodin's own "Thought," a head growing out of the stone, or his "Thinker," shaped from himself, pondering the abundance of forms crowding "The Gate of Hell," in deep symbolism.

The process of differentiation is a process of objectivation. As Rodin followed religiously the laws of nature, the way he himself successively discovered them,[28] so Cassirer follows the laws of the spirit as he uncovers them. There are two main laws, The Law of Continuity—each phase is the fulfilment of the preceding one—and The Law of New Emphasis—each phase develops the preceding one.[29] These, of course, are nothing but the laws of growth itself. As the forms grow their "moments" change, their "accents" shift. The three stages or "dimensions"

[24] Cf. II, 50.
[25] PSF, III, 3.
[26] PSF, III, 16; I, 9 ff, 29 ff.
[27] PSF, III, 17.
[28] Story, Sommerville, "Auguste Rodin and His Work," in Rodin, New York: Phaidon Edition, Oxford University Press, 1939, 11.
[29] PSF, III, 522 ff.

of shift are Expression, Presentation, Meaning (*Ausdruck, Darstellung, Bedeutung*). These stages are not isolated from one another but contain "points" at which the forms flow into one another, greet each other hesitatingly or pass each other without recognition, like strangers. In the first stage, Expression, the subject "possesses" the environment as a variety of physiognomic experiences.[30] Long before there are "things" there is such structurization of experience. "Existence," "reality," are at that stage physiognomically manifest. The abstraction of "pure" perception, which is the starting point of dogmatic sensualism, is here already transcended. The datum which the subject experiences as being "opposite" to him is here transparent with inner life, not exterior or dumb. This is the stage at which myth and art originate, and where, with hesitating greeting, they meet language, which, in the Sentence, takes up[31] and transcends that stage, setting the new dimension, Presentation. The sentence, however, only very gradually swings itself upward into the new dimension. It remains bound to the physiognomic realm, substituting logical determination for spatial demonstration. Only gradually it expands from perceptual and emotional perspectives to full objectivation, in three steps again: the *mimic*, where it remains in the plastic world, in the spatial meanings of the copula, the demonstrative pronouns, the definite article, onomatopoetic formations, and the rendering of the physiognomic characters through voiced or voiceless consonants, higher or lower vowels; the *analogic*, where in the relation of sounds the relations of the objects are expressed; and, finally, the *symbolic*, where all similarity between the world of language and that of objects has disappeared. Only in this last form, in the distance from the lower stages, language comes entirely into its own.[32] The three stages of language are thus, as it were, steps by which the spirit passes from the physiognomic to the presentative dimension, and beyond it into that of meaning.

Whereas language and mythos partly flow into, partly greet

[30] *PSF*, III, 524; 71.
[31] *PSF*, III, 95.
[32] *PSF*, III, 525 f.; cf. I, *pass.*

each other, mythos and logos pass by each other without recognition, like strangers. The scientific concept is past the physiognomic level.[33] "Cognition" implies distance from the world, a "cut" between "nature" and the world of feeling. The concept starts its career on the level of perception, where it meets language, to ascend in harmony with it, in order, finally, to transcend it through three stages again, corresponding to the three stages of language; the *mimic*, in the platonic περιπέτεια from things to ideas,[34] with its correspondence between both; the *analogic*, in Kepler-Galileo-Newtonian science, where the correspondence between the world of objects and that of concepts has disappeared in detail but still persists in the correspondence of structures, especially in the model of a given space; and the *symbolic*, in the modern scientific concept with its purely symbolic "space" without any correspondence to the perceptual world. In this last stage the process of objectivation is completed, the symbols stand freely and in full self-consistent significance above the raw material of the world. Yet, they point to it and give it its final and culminating meaning, fulfilling in their lofty sweep the grunt, the first gesture of the man of primal times.

Rodin's "Man of Primal Times"[35] shows precisely this: the unlimited promise of that first gesture, the unfolding of thought from hand.

It indicates in the work of Rodin the birth of gesture. That gesture which grew and developed to such greatness and power, here bursts forth like a spring that softly ripples over this body. It awakens in the darkness of primal times and in its growth seems to flow through the breadth of this work as though reaching out from bygone centuries to those that are to come. Hesitatingly it unfolds itself in the lifted arms. These arms are still so heavy that the hand of one rests upon the top of the head. But this hand is roused from its sleep, it concentrates itself quite high on the top of the brain where it lies solitary. It prepares for the work of centuries, a work that has no measure and no end.[36]

---

[33] *PSF*, III, 526.
[34] *PSF*, III, 526 f.; 384.
[35] Also called "The Age of Bronze."
[36] Rilke, *op. cit.*, 24.

Gesture is the first awkward manifestation of the spontaneity of spirit which flowers forth in the full bloom of the symbolic forms. In its beginning even the primal forms of the synthetizing function of consciousness,[37] space, time, and number, are nothing but corporeal motions "that softly ripple over the body." Space arises from the demonstrative gestures of Here and There, I and Thou, and expands in concentric circles around the speaker, whose body is the first system of spatial coördination.[38] Thomas Mann's Joseph is still a mythical but also already an individual figure, as he describes his own and his Ishmaelite fellow travelers' universes:

The world hath many centres, one for each created being, and about each one it lieth in its own circle. Thou standest but half an ell from me, yet about thee lieth a universe whose centre I am not but thou art. . . . And I, on the other hand, stand in the centre of mine. For our universes are not far from each other so that they do not touch; rather hath God pushed them and interwoven them deep into each other.[39]

That body-space finally becomes the pure-brain-space of modern relativity theory. Time, originally woven into the spatial determination of Here and There as Now and Then,[40] becomes the purely mental symbol of our physical science. And number itself, "originally a hand concept, not a thought concept,"[41] develops out of its bodily encumbrance into the lofty realm it has so elaborately carved out today; now not only a content of thought but even a way of thinking,[42] a means of sharper and sharper determination of the indeterminate.[43]

Thus, like filigree work chiseled out from heavy walls, the final *Gestalten* of the symbolic forms stand out in relief against the background of metaphysics. The vertical "schemata" of the structure, reaching throughout the whole *dis-cursus* of consciousness,[44] are the formative principles: space, time, and

[37] *PSF*, III, 16.
[38] *PSF*, I, 156.
[39] Mann, Thomas, *Joseph in Egypt*, New York: Alfred A. Knopf, 1939, Vol. I, 4.
[40] *PSF*, I, 167 ff.
[41] *PSF*, III, 397.
[42] *PSF*, III, 413.
[43] *PSF*, III, 468.
[44] *PSF*, I, 167.

number. The horizontal "dimensions" are the forms of expression, presentation, and meaning. These latter are principles of differentiation, carrying forward the relief into ever finer ramifications. Thus the creative activity of the spirit resembles that of sculpture even in the method, "the process of removal,"[45] to use the words of Michelangelo. The combination of both the horizontal and the vertical principles of formation are the symbolic forms, myth, language, art, religion, theoretical cognition: peculiar energies of the spirit,[46] with their own "modalities" and their own particular "planes of reality" (*Seinsebenen*)[47]— their own position and Gestalt on the metaphysical background. Their ultimate refinement has lost all semblance to its metaphysical matrix, just as filigree on a wall, or a sculptured hand by Rodin, have lost all semblance to their own concrete material. It has lost almost even the texture of the background. It is pure symbol—either script, as the filigree on the walls of the Alhambra of Granada, or something *sui generis*, as a member sculptured by Rodin. "A hand laid on another's shoulder or thigh does not any more belong to the body from which it came—from this body and from the object which it touches or seizes something new originates, a new thing that has no name and belongs to no one."[48] It is a symbol.

The symbol, though of sensuous material, yet transcends that materiality and points toward a content in the higher forms of Meaning. Its materiality is completely absorbed, in that function of meaning,[49] its "symbolic *prägnanz*."[50] It is subjected under the sensuous; yet that subjection is at the same time freedom from the sensuous.[51] The capacity of the sensuous material to point toward a world of meanings, to symbolize it without co-inciding with it—this clothing of the sensuous with ideal meaning is indeed *"das Mysterium des*

---

[45] Cf. II, 289; *Erkenntnisproblem* I, 5 f.

[46] *PSF*, II, 284 f.

[47] *PSF*, I, 28 f.

[48] Rilke, *op. cit.*, 30.

[49] *PSF*, I, 42.

[50] *PSF*, III, 234. The similarity of Cassirer's terminology with that of Gestalt psychology is a conscious one. Symbolic forms are *"Gestalten."*

[51] *PSF*, I, 41.

Wirkens schlechthin,"[52] the mystery of creative activity *par excellence*. It cannot suddenly accrete to the sensitive faculty out of nothing, but must be part of the very nature of that faculty from its first beginnings. There is, in the sensuous itself,

to use an expression of Goethe, an "exact sensuous imagination," which appears active in the most diverse realms of spiritual and mental creativity. Each of these realms gives rise, as the true vehicle of its own immanent process, beside and above the world of perception, to a free world of images, a world which in its immediate quality still bears the hue of the sensuous, but that sensuousness is formed and therewith spiritually dominated. We do not encounter the sensuous as a simple datum, but as a system of sensuous varieties, which are being produced in all kinds of free creation.[53]

In other words, not only is there no absolute metaphysical Being, there is, on the other hand, not even an absolutely given sensuous perception. The network of meanings is present in germ, *in potentia*, in the first ripples of expression. Already *then* there is not only the substance of the material, but also the function of meaning in it. "The fundamental function of meaning is there before the positing of the individual sign, so that in that positing that function is not created but only fixated, only applied to an individual case."[54] Substance and function, material and meaning, the sensuous and the "intelligible" are originally fused in the unity of primary symbols. As the process of objectivation, of spiritualization continues, the substantial is gradually chiseled off, "in a process of removal," and the functional appears in greater and greater purity. But substance and function never lose their mutual interdependence —the filigree of the Alhambra is still on the wall, and Rodin's sculptured hand is still of bronze. That primary fusion in the symbolic, this *primacy of the symbolic function*, is the secret of all symbolic forms and all spiritual activity. There is no Outside or Inside here, no Before or After, nothing Active or Passive. Here we have a union of elements, which did not have

[52] *PSF*, III, 119.
[53] *PSF*, I, 19 f.
[54] *PSF*, I, 41.

to be constructed, but was a primary meaningful whole which belongs only to itself and interprets itself alone. In the fusion of body and soul we have the paradigm and prototype of such a relation.[55]

The moments of succession, as we find them in space and time, the connections of conditions such that the one appears as "thing," the other as "quality," the connection of successive events such that the one appears as cause, the other as effect: all these are examples of how the original fusion is gradually loosened and ramified. At the end of the development stands modern man, his intellect almost disengaged from his sensuous and social[56] background. Not without reason Cassirer's last published work had to be *An Essay on Man.*

The principles of formation, present in the gestures of the man of primal times, brought about the intellect of the man of modern times. The hand resting on the brain of Rodin's figure symbolizes the entire power of that primal gesture. That hand does not rest there any more—it has emancipated itself in the actions of that brain,[57] from which proceeded both modern science and technology, more like Ares than Athene. In the Critical philosophy the threads had been laid bare by which intellect is knitted to perception. For Kant "the intellect is the simple transcendental expression for the fundamental phenomenon that all perception, as *conscious,* always and necessarily must be *formed* perception."[58] In Cassirer's philosophy the threads are traced back to their very origin in the original skein of cultural life: the critique of reason is expanded and empirically substantiated in Cassirer's critique of culture. But, after showing the entire many-branched labyrinth of man's development to modernity, Cassirer focuses on the hero himself, a modern Theseus, who has left the guiding hand of nature and, at the end of his course, encounters a monster, the master of the maze, the Minotaur of Machinery, ready to devour him. Will man slay it or will he be slain?

[55] *PSF,* III, 117.
[56] Originally spatial.
[57] *PSF,* II, 266: Technology as "organ projection."
[58] *PSF,* III, 224.

It all depends on whether the original power of symbolization is still living in him. For symbolization is power. Rodin's
sculptured limbs are creations of a powerful energy which has
appropriated the material and bent it to its will. The power of
symbolization is a power of concentration and condensation, a
Kraft der Verdichtung,[59] active in all symbolic forms. "It is as if
through the creation of the new symbol, a tremendous energy
of thought is being transformed from a relatively diffuse into
more concentrated form."[60] That energy is the spontaneity, the
creative freedom of the spirit, a freedom not arbitrary, but
producing within the modalities of the symbolic forms.[61] It is a
power which contains within itself the entire force of cultural
evolution—the symbol concentrates in one intense moment the
entire cultural energy, diffuse in its manifold forms from past
to future: a "revelation in the material."[62] Man will slay the
monster, if he has the power of the symbol: to find his way
back to nature and at the same time to look forward into the
future, if he is able to concentrate and symbolically to divine
past and future in the present. He must become a prophet:
a symbol himself of his own origin and destination.[63]

For us Cassirer was such a "symbolic man," and so was
Rodin. Both knew the nature and power of the symbol. Rodin
saw man himself as a symbol. "When I have a beautiful woman's body as a model, the drawings I make of it also give me
pictures of insects, birds, and fishes. That seems incredible and
I did not know it myself until I found out."[64] Cassirer found
a similarly incredible content in the "symbolic forms" of the
spirit. Each of them symbolizes the totality of cultural evolution. Consciousness cannot posit anything without positing
everything; in the Goethean words, often quoted by Cassirer,

> Truly the mental fleece
> Resembles a weaver's masterpiece,

[59] *PSF*, III, 466.
[60] *Ibid.*
[61] *PSF*, e.g. I, 20.
[62] *PSF*, I, 46.
[63] Cf. *Essay on Man*, 55, 61.
[64] Story, *op. cit.*, 14 f.

Where a thousand threads one treadle throws,
Where fly the shuttles hither and thither
Unseen the threads are knit together,
And an infinite combination grows.

The symbol, the material content clothed with the ideal meaning of the whole infinite composition, is therefore the "natural" product of consciousness, the symbolic function its natural function. A healthy consciousness must in every act, to the degree and extent of that act, shuttle back and forth throughout the aeons of cultural development and knit all of them into the act. To the degree that it achieves this it is free from its sensuous origins: it is human. The essence of humanity is a free consciousness, roaming widely over cultural space and time. "Human culture taken as a whole may be described as the process of man's progressive self-liberation."[65] The more symbolic an act, therefore, the more it is a truly human act. The more it presents a cultural content, the more it must represent all culture. Ethically as well as epistemologically, the development of presentation is progressive *representation*. Man's self-liberation proceeds proportionately to his capacity for symbolic representation. Representation is the act of manifesting spiritual energy in sensuous material. It is the fundamental function of consciousness, exhibited in the primal gesture of the savage as well as in the mathematical analysis of the man of advanced studies. Between both activities is a difference of degree, but not of kind. In all intellectual activity this function is being applied, or rather, all intellectual activity *is* this function. Only in human behavior it is not yet manifest; only man himself has not yet become a symbol unto himself. In the social sphere the relationship between symbol and reality has not yet been found. It must be found; social reality must be filled with symbolic meaning. Thus the tension between symbol and reality[66] would be consummated. The other alternative of consummation would be the effacement of man, the flattening out of the spirited ripple that rose as form over the faceless deep.

The differentiation of the formless, similar to the structuriza-

---

[65] *Essay on Man*, 228.
[66] Cf. *PSF*, I, 135.

tion of the ἄπειρον by the πέρας or the articulation of ὕλη by μορφή —this is the function of Form in Cassirer's philosophy (even though limited to the field of human culture and on the level of transcendental correlation rather than that of metaphysical opposition, as it was in the philosophies of Plato and Aristotle and later in that of Hegel).[67] Form is not a static thing, a shape, but a dynamic principle, the totality of characters that transform sensuous *impressions* into intellectual and spiritual *expressions*.[68] In its totality alone the form finds truth; truth is the whole— herein Cassirer agrees with Hegel, calling part of his own philosophy a "Phenomenology of Cognition."[69]

The end, the "telos" of the spirit cannot be comprehended or pronounced, if one takes it by itself, severed from its beginning and middle. Philosophical reflection does not in this way set off the end against middle and beginning, but takes all three as integral moments of one unique total movement.[70]

In this total context, then, every element of the form, every one of its "differentials"[71] is representative of the whole. As for Rodin the beauty of the woman is representative of all creation, so for Cassirer the characteristic of one cultural unit, whether a vowel in language, a ritual in religion or an algorithm in mathematics, mirrors monadlike[72] the whole universe of forms. As Rodin's model is an end product of evolution, but as such again a middle term between the universal premise of evolution and the conclusion drawn by Rodin's pencil, so the symbolic unit is an end of the formative development preceding it, but also a mediator between that development and Cassirer's conception of it. At the same time these units are mediators between the preceding and successive stages, and focal points of the entire development.

The form of sensuous reality is based on the fact that the individual moments of which it is built up do not stand by themselves, but that

---

[67] Cf. *PSF*, III, 13, 230, and *infra* 312 ff., 322.
[68] *PSF*, I, 12.
[69] *PSF*, III, vi.
[70] *PSF*, III, vii.
[71] *PSF*, I, 40; III, 235.
[72] Cf. *PSF*, I, 102.

between them takes place a peculiar relation of "com-positing" *(Mitsetzung)*. Nowhere is here anything isolated and detached. Even that which seems to belong to a certain single spatial point or temporal moment, does not remain immersed in the mere Here and There. It reaches beyond itself into the totality of all empirical contents.[73]

The higher reality unfolds itself, the richer its pattern becomes and the fuller of symbolic functions will be the contents that offer themselves to consciousness.

The farther that process continues, the wider a circle consciousness is able to span in a single moment. Each of its elements is now saturated, as it were, with such functions. It stands in varied meaningful contexts, which again are connected and which, by virtue of that connection, constitute a whole, which we denote as the world of our "experience." Whatever contexts one may isolate from this totality of "experience" . . . always their orders will show a definite structure and a common fundamental character. They are of such a nature, that from everyone of their moments a transition is possible to the whole, just as the constitution of the whole is presentable and presented in every moment.[74]

Every phenomenon is now only a letter within the script of total reality.[75]

Thus it is possible to span the whole world in a moment. Physical science is doing that, comprehending the totality of events by representing each event through its four space-time coördinates and reducing the variation of these coördinates to (more or less) final invariant laws.[76] It thus obtains what science calls the "truth" of the phenomena, which is nothing else but their totality, "taken not in their concrete state but in the form of an ideal *coördination*."[77] That coördination is based both on logical connections and logical distinctions, on synthesis as well as analysis. The higher a symbol, that is to say the more numerous and the more complex the phenomena it refers to, the more different will be its own form, its shape, from that of the phenomena themselves, and the greater the "distance"

[73] *PSF*, III, 332.
[74] *PSF*, III, 221.
[75] *Ibid.*
[76] *PSF*, II, 80.
[77] *Ibid.*

between the sensuous and the symbolic content of consciousness
—but the greater that "distance" the greater, because the more
comprehensive, the more "universal," will be the "truth." Finally the symbol contains nothing but the *principle* of the forms
it represents, the constitutive law of their structure, the genetic
essence of their formation. It thus refers not to the similarity of
the forms, but to their inner connective law, which may or may
not express itself in similarities of form.[78] Thus the common
constructive principle of the conic sections is not betrayed in
any similarity of shape. Again we are reminded of Rodin, who
in all his work looked for the latent principles of natural movement. "Such was the basis of what is called my Symbolism.
I do not mind being called a Symbolist, if that will define the
essential principle of sculpture."[79] It was not enough for Rodin
to study nature and follow it so closely that "The Man of
Primal Times" was suspected to be cast from the living model.
He tried to find the principle of movement—by what he called
a method of "logical exaggeration." "My aim was then, after
the 'Burghers of Calais,' to find ways of exaggerating logically."[80] Indeed, what could be sensuously as well as significantly
more expressive than calling ellipse, parabola and hyperbola
"logical exaggerations" of the circle!

Logical exaggeration consists, among other things, in the
"constant reduction of the face to a geometrical figure, and the
resolve to sacrifice every part of the face to the synthesis of its
aspect,"[81] that is to say, the totality of its features. That totality
is sometimes enhanced by subtraction.

Take the Cathedral of Chartres as an example: one of its towers is
massive and without ornamentation, having been neglected in order
that the exquisite delicacy of the other could be better seen. In sculpture
the projection of the sheaths of muscles must be accentuated, the shorten-
ings heightened, the holes made deeper. Scultpure is the art of the hole
and the lump.[82]

[78] *PSF*, II, 88.
[79] Story, *op. cit.*, 14.
[80] *Ibid.*
[81] *Ibid.*
[82] *Ibid.*

The "process of removal" thus is a succession of dialectic steps in the totality of the form's movement.

Not in continuous quantitative accretion, but in the sharpest dialectic contradiction the various fundamental ideas oppose each other in the truly critical epochs of cognition. . . .[83] The myth [e.g.,] would not be a truly *spiritual* form, if its unity were nothing but oppositionless simplicity. . . . The individual stages of its development do not simply join themselves one to the other, but often oppose each other in sharp contrast. The process consists in the fact that certain fundamental traits, certain spiritual determinations of the preceding stages are not only elaborated and supplemented, but are also being negated, indeed annihilated.[84]

Whatever obstructs the law of process of the total form is being eliminated. The symbol itself cannot contain anything that is not part of the totality: it shows "hole and lump." It is not *similar* to the symbolized content, but somehow in its shape is found the principle of the totality of the represented forms, visible to the eye of the synoptic seer, whether he be of plastic imagination like Rodin or of philosophical imagination like Cassirer. Some day, perhaps, a *logic of symbolic forms* will be written, based on the combined insight of both philosopher and artist.

That logic would have to be symbolic of the entire fullness of life, its symbolism saturated with live meanings and not "sicklied o'er with the pale cast" of positivism. Cassirer's philosophy of symbolic forms is such a truly symbolic logic, culminating, as it does, in the symbols of mathematics, the "logic of invention," as it was called both by Galileo and Leibniz. But Cassirer's "*Ansatz*," the method and tendency of his work, points further: to an expansion of his method into the very field of the arts, into a logical symbolism or symbolic logic of painting and sculpture as well as of music, thus, in due time, to a method which will make these forms of consciousness as definitely and determinedly symbolic of life's fullness—maybe even in the form of communication[85]—as now are the "rational" signs of

[83] *Erkenntnisproblem*, I, 5.
[84] *PSF*, II, 289. Cf. *infra* 879 f.
[85] Cf. Langer, Susanne K., *Philosophy in a New Key*, Cambridge, Mass.: Harvard University Press, 1942, 218ff., and *passim*.

language and mathematics. Seen under this view, not of eternity but of long term development, Cassirer's "phenomenology of cognition" is as much a precursor of a new logic as was Hegel's phenomenology—only in a much wider sense, comparable, perhaps, to Leibniz' divined rather than elaborated *scientia generalis* as a precursor of modern mathematical science.

Indeed, in its emphasis on the totality of the formative process Cassirer's philosophy agrees with Hegel's phenomenology; in its emphasis on the fullness of life it draws inspiration from Leibniz' *scientia generalis*. With Hegel he has only the *"Ansatz"*[86] in common; Hegel's phenomenology "finally, so to speak, sharpens itself into a highest logical point. . . . How rich and varied ever its content, its structure is subject to a single and in a way uniform law."[87] The logic to which Cassirer points is a logic of creation, a logic of invention in a sense much wider even than that divined by Galileo and Leibniz—as wide and varied, in fact, as life itself. The structure of his work does not suffer from Hegel's shortcomings, from compression into a too narrow scheme. On the contrary, if criticism is in order, Cassirer's work seems almost too little inhibited, too artfully rambling at times in the fascinating regions it discloses, the style too ornamental sometimes to be fully effectful.[88] It is a work of art, full of life, showing, as does Rodin's work, "life in movement."[89] For Rodin it is the life of natural forms, for Cassirer the life of cultural forms. Rodin had nude models moving about in his studio,

to supply him constantly with the picture of nudity in various attitudes and with all the liberty of ordinary life. He was constantly looking at them, and thus was always familiar with the spectacle of muscles in

---

[86] *PSF*, III, vi.

[87] *PSF*, I, 15.

[88] In contrast, for example, to the condensed imagery of Bergson. Hegel's often atrocious German cannot be compared to the elegance of Cassirer's style. Although Cassirer was not as electrifying a personality as was Bergson, he was an absorbingly interesting lecturer. His classrooms, as one of his students expressed it, "seemed to be the halls where there was no life but the life of thought. In his lectures the spirit itself seemed to speak to the brains of men." This is a far cry from the utter dryness of Hegel's presentation, the effect of which seems to have been one of the riddles of his time (not only to Schopenhauer).

[89] Story, *op cit.*, 9.

movement. Thus the nude, which today people rarely see, and which even sculptors only see during the short period of the pose, was for Rodin an ordinary spectacle. . . . The face is usually regarded as the only mirror of the soul, and mobility of features is supposed to be the only exteriorization of spiritual life. But in reality there is not a muscle of the body which does not reveal thoughts and feelings.[90]

Only the highest functions of the human mind seem to express the creativity of the spirit; Kant, and in a way even Hegel, as well as most of the post-Kantian philosophers before Cassirer, were interested in them mainly. Even Cassirer demonstrated the creativeness of thought first in its highest functions, in the field of abstract science.[91] Only gradually he worked down from the brain to the lower and lowlier parts of the body, finally to the gestures of the members, the movement of the muscles, until the entire body of man stood before his eyes vibrating with spiritual life. All the forms of that life were then constantly before his view; for over thirty years he constantly looked at them. He seemed, like Rodin, "obsessed by a sort of divine intoxication for form."[92] "The living motion of the spirit must be apprehended in its actuality, in the very energy of its movement."[93] "*Procedere*" is only apprehensible through process, in its *Fortgang*. Only by constantly following the forms of the spirit and sculpturing them in their process can one apprehend them.

The true, the concrete totality of the spirit must not be denoted in a simple formula at the beginning and so to speak presented ready made, but it develops, it finds itself only in the constantly advancing process[94] of critical analysis itself.[95]

Just as the eyes of the sculptor must follow his models' motions constantly and apprehend them in motor empathy, so the spirit itself, as analysis, must follow the "*stetig weiterschrei-*

[90] Story, *op. cit.*, 13.
[91] In *Substance and Function*.
[92] Story, *op. cit.*, 26.
[93] *PSF*, III, 481.
[94] "*Im stetig weiterschreitenden Fortgang.*" The translation cannot render the plastic expressiveness of Cassirer's style.
[95] *PSF*, I, 10.

tenden Fortgang," "the steadily further striding onwalking," of the symbolic forms—parading before the philosopher's eyes like models before the artist. "The perimeter of spiritual reality can be designated, defined and determined only by pacing it off in the process."[96] The whole of the objective spirit thus reveals itself gradually as an organic unity, steadily growing and developing in a "definite systematic scale, an ideal progress, as the end of which may be stated that the spirit in its own formations and self-created symbols not only is and lives, but that it comprehends them as they are."[97] In this respect again the philosophy of symbolic forms connects with Hegel's phenomenology: "the end of development consists in the comprehension and expression of spiritual reality not only as substance, but 'just as much as subject'."[98] But there is an important difference between Hegel's and Cassirer's phenomenology, which can be illustrated by Cassirer's attitude toward Hegel's historical theory.

The concept of a history of science contains the idea of the conservation of a universal logical structure in the succession of particular conceptual systems. Indeed: if the earlier content of thought would not be connected with the succeeding one by some identity, there would be nothing to justify our comprising the scattered logical fragments then at hand, in a series of becoming events. Each historical series of evolution needs a "subject" as a substratum in which to present and exteriorize itself. The mistake of the metaphysical theory of history lies not in the fact that it demands such a subject, but in the fact that it reifies it, by speaking of the self-development of an "Idea," a progress of the "World Spirit," and so on. We must renounce such reified carrier standing behind the historical movement; *the metaphysical formula must be changed into a methodological formula.* Instead of a common substratum we only demand an intellectual continuity in the individual phases of development.[99]

That is to say, just as the sculptor is not interested in the personality of his models as such, but in their symbolic significance for the laws of nature, so the philosopher of symbolic forms

[96] *Ibid.*
[97] *PSF* II, 35.
[98] *Ibid.*
[99] *Erkenntnisproblem,* I, 16. Italics mine.

is not interested in the subject matter of the forms as such, but only their significance for the whole context in which they appear. "It is the task of philosophy . . . again and again, from a concrete historical aggregate of certain scientific concepts and principles to set forth the universal logical functions of cognition in general."[100] In this respect the histories of science and of philosophy are two aspects of one and the same intellectual process, for which Galileo and Kepler, Newton and Euler are just as valid witnesses as Descartes or Leibniz.[101] The process is an empirical logical, not a metaphysical logical process. It is the historical process by which the cultural realities have evolved.

From the sphere of sensation to that of perception, from perception to conceptual thinking, and from that again to logical judgment there leads, for critical epistemology, one steady road. Each later moment comprises the earlier, each earlier prepares the later. All the elements constituting cognition refer both to themselves and the "object." Sensation, perception, are in germ already comprehension, judgment, conclusion.[102]

Neither in the treatment of the philosophical systems nor in that of the cultural forms is Cassirer concerned with establishing a metaphysical subjective idealism. He is not dogmatic in any way; the dogmatic systems of metaphysics are in most cases nothing but

hypostases of certain logical, aesthetical, or religious principles. The more they seclude themselves into the abstract generality of principle, the more they preclude themselves from other sides of spiritual culture and the concrete totality of its forms.[103]

With that totality Cassirer is concerned, in it he finds intellectual creativity active. The existence of such creativeness thus becomes for him not a matter of principle—even though originally it was a postulate[104]—but a question of fact. In the richness of that concrete totality he finds, through the ingenious

---

[100] Ibid.
[101] Erkenntnisproblem, I, 10.
[102] PSF, I, 274.
[103] PSF, I, 14.
[104] Erkenntnisproblem, I, 18.

interpretation of the symbolic function, a whole systematic of the spirit, where each particular form receives its meaning purely by the position it has within the system, a kind of periodic system of cultural forms. Only that system is never closed, but ever active, ever in process,[105] reality thus never being but ever becoming, the ideal goal of the process rather than the process itself.

Being concerned with the universal meaning in concrete reality rather than in an abstract principle, which would only detract from that meaning, and in the sifting of that meaning from all the forms of reality itself, Cassirer is not interested only in completed philosophical systems, nor in fully grown cultural forms. Similar or even identical concepts might conceal different, even contrasting meanings,[106] and most significant features might be found in byroads hitherto overlooked. The manifold attempts and beginnings of research in all cultural forms are the trickles from which the formula of universal cultural progress must be distilled.[107] In the frozen shapes of these forms the original dynamics of their movement must be detected. Cassirer inquired into all these forms, torsos, trunks of forms, with never resting zeal, presenting not only full grown treatises like the three great master works, but a host of monographs on particular questions. In all this his reasoning was profound; he aimed to crystallize the leading idea of cultural movement, its dynamic soul. Similarly Rodin in an unheard of procedure for a sculptor, exhibited

human figures deprived of a head, legs or arms, which at first shock the beholder, but on examination are found to be so well balanced and so perfectly harmonized that one can only find beauty in them. His reason for this is artistically profound. . . . In the development of a leading idea—of thought, of meditation, of the action of walking,—his desire was to eliminate all that might counteract or draw attention from this central thought. "As to polishing nails or ringlets of hair, that has no interest for me," he said; "it detracts attention from the leading line and the soul which I wish to interpret."[108]

[105] Perhaps, in the light of the newest atomic achievements, this is also true for the periodic system of elements.
[106] Cf. *Erkenntnisproblem*, I, 10.
[107] Cf. *Erkenntnisproblem*, I, 9.
[108] Story, *op. cit.*, 13.

Just as little did Cassirer have time for the trimmings of the cultural process. His painstaking search for phenomena was the search for the essential, the symbolic in them. But, since the symbolic is never found in purity[109] but only fulfilled in the totality of the process, and the process is never finished but always proceeding, the search for the symbol itself is never ending but always asymptotic. Just as for Rodin—and for every great master—it was never Cassirer's habit "to undertake a work, complete it and have done with it. He always had by him a number of ideas and thoughts on which he meditated patiently for years as they ripened in his mind."[110] By the time he wrote the *Essay on Man* Cassirer saw the problems of the *Philosophy of the Symbolic Forms* from a different angle and in a new light.[111]

Now it was no longer so much the totality of the process that interested him, but one moment of its concrete fullness: the reference to man. The asymptotic openness of the process, the lofty culmination in merely intellectual symbols now has given place to a fuller harmony: a human universe. Now the symbolic forms were to help man to slay the monster and continue the process of life itself. Now it is no longer science which is the great culmination, but art—Cassirer has moved toward the new logic towards which we see his work tending. On the last page of the *Essay* we read the famous words of Kant, that we can learn all about Newton's principles of natural philosophy, however great a mind may have been required to discover them; but we cannot learn to write spirited poetry, however explicit may be the precepts of the art and however excellent its models. We learn that the highest of forms is not an abstract "logical function," but that it is genius himself, *homo creator*. Now the whole of science is a flat dimension as compared with the dimension of man himself. Not only *"ex analogia universi"* but, even more, *"ex analogia hominis"* we must understand the world. And it is on a note of musical harmony that this last great work of Cassirer ends:

All these functions complete and complement one another. Each one

---

[109] *PSF*, III, 142.
[110] Story, *op. cit.*, 13.
[111] *Essay on Man*, vii.

opens a new horizon and shows us a new aspect of humanity. The dissonant is in harmony with itself; the contraries are not mutually exclusive, but interdependent: "harmony in contrariety, as in the case of the bow and the lyre."[112]

The spirit of Leibniz, in the new form of warm human concern, has conquered the Hegelian aloofness in Cassirer's mind. Now spontaneity and productivity are no more prerogatives of "the objective spirit" or "the symbolic function," but are "the very center of all human activities."[113] The philosophy of symbolic forms has become the philosophy of man. Man himself now is the central symbolic form. The symbolic process is now no longer so much one of "dematerialization,"[114] "a process of removal," but of spiritualization, a process of strengthening the differentiation of matter by a new energy: the spiritual energy of harmonization. That energy combines the human world into a symphony of meanings. It strengthens itself through its wedlock with matter. Has it been an original partner of matter from the beginning? Has the harmony between it and matter been pre-established from the beginning and is the whole development of the forms nothing but the elaboration of that pre-established harmony? And is the appearance of that harmony in the logic of symbols nothing but that harmony's revelation in matter? Cassirer never answers these Leibnizian questions; although, with unconcerned assurance, he makes positive statements in all these respects—covering up metaphysical concern with reference to "miracles" and "ultimate mysteria." But he seems to be in profound agreement with Leibniz. "Leibniz was the first great modern thinker to have a clear insight into the true character of mathematical symbolism,"[115] and into the nature of symbolism in general.

For him [Leibniz] the problem of the "logic of things" is insolubly connected with the problem of the "logic of signs." The *"Scientia generalis"* needs the *"Characteristica generalis"* as its tool and vehicle. The

[112] *Essay on Man*, 228.
[113] *Essay on Man*, 220.
[114] *PSF*, III, 387.
[115] *Essay on Man*, 217; cf. *Erkenntnisproblem*, II, 142ff.

latter does not refer to the things, but their representations: it does not deal with the *res* but the *"notae rerum."* But this does not prejudice their objective content. For that "pre-established harmony" which, in accordance with the fundamental thought of Leibniz' philosophy, rules between the world of the ideal and the real: it also connects the world of signs with that of objective "meanings." The real is subject, without any limitation, to the ideal.[116]

There is no such division between ideal and real world in the philosophy of Cassirer. Critical philosophy welds the two worlds into transcendental unity. But the seam appears in the notion of the symbol. Cassirer cannot help using Leibnizian language. In that way he slides over the metaphysical problem which has been put and answered by Leibniz. With Leibniz the analysis of the real leads to the analysis of the ideas, the analysis of the ideas to that of the signs. With one stroke therewith the concept of the symbol has become the spiritual focus, the true center of the intellectual world. In it the principles of metaphysics and cognition run together.[117]

This very same characteristic can be given of Cassirer's philosophy of symbolic forms; only that the form's metaphysical ingredients, by definition, are—as metaphysical—unknowable. His philosophy is thus in a way frustrating; one would like to say, it is so by definition. The quest for a metaphysics "behind" the symbolic form is invalid. But the question concerning the nature of that energy, which welds phenomena into structural totality and thus brings about symbols, is still valid. Its answer would lead into metaphysics—a metaphysics of Leibnizian harmony with humanistic emphasis: *"the highest, indeed the only task of all these forms is to unite men!"*[118]

What a new key is sounded here! How much has totality become harmony and harmony humanism! Human harmony all over the world presupposes universal symbols. Leibniz was right: without a *Characteristica generalis* we shall never find a *Scientia generalis*. Modern symbolic logic follows the same

[116] *PSF*, III, 54.
[117] *Ibid.*
[118] *Essay on Man*, 129. *Italics* mine. Whether these forms actually do unite men is another question. See below notes 132, 133.

tendency.[119] But therewith the problem of human harmony is not solved. "In an analysis of human culture we must accept the facts in their concrete shape, in all their diversity and divergence."[120] The diversity of produced languages divide men; the unity of linguistic functions may unite them. Even more, however, may they become united by a universal logic of artistic imagination, an aesthetic logic, which is not inferior to intellectual logic, as was the one constructed by Baumgarten,[121] but superior to it, extending not only over the whole surface of things but also sounding the depths of the understanding consciousness. Only then will it truly be possible to "comprehend the world in a moment," to make actual the brotherhood of man. Science, following the Leibnizian "*Ansatz*," has conquered the totality of things. Exact science is completely under Leibniz's spell.[122] But science has diluted the metaphysical richness of his method. "For Leibniz the concept of symbol was so to speak the '*vinculum substantiale*' between his metaphysics and his logic. For modern science it is the '*vinculum substantiale*' between logic and mathematics and between logic and exact natural science."[123] For the author of the *Philosophy of Symbolic Forms* this fact implied a distinct progress and advantage. It was a fascinating discovery to find the intermediate function between the logical universal and the concrete individual,[124] the common denominator between extension and intension, to discover the world of things as a world of symbols, as representations rather than as objects,[125] and to rise, in the process of dematerialization, to the pure "conceptual sign" without any *Nebensinn*,[126] that is to say without any material appendage, in spite of the necessity of meaning to find a sensuous substratum for its actualization.[127] But for the author

[119] *Ibid.*
[120] *Ibid.*
[121] *Essay on Man*, 136.
[122] PSF, III, 54.
[123] PSF, III, 55.
[124] PSF, I, 16f.
[125] PSF, III, 373.
[126] PSF, III, 393.
[127] PSF, I, 18.

of *An Essay on Man* it is different. The fascination of intellectual discovery now seems to have given way to an endeavor of moral persuasion—a development similar to Kant's, although, in my opinion, less consciously planned for. In the *Philosophy of Symbolic Forms* it is the fascinating function of the concept to refer from the very beginning to the totality of thought, to the whole of all *possible* thought formations.[128] Precisely that which has not happened here or anywhere else is posited as norm[129] by the concept and is pre-formed in anticipation by the symbol.[130] The fascination of the *Essay on Man* is no more the all comprehensive potentiality of thought but that of man himself. The kingdom of the possible must now be actualized by man. He must make true what has never been true before, his own total harmonic life. Now a new miracle has to happen: not the miracle of the concept, "that the simple sensuous material, by the way in which it is considered, gains a new and manifold spiritual life;"[131] but a miracle of social life: that the human material, by the way in which it is considered, gains a new and manifold spiritual life. Now the question arises, how man's spiritual creations can reactively ennoble their creator himself.

This is only possible, obviously, if they do not remain merely intellectual achievements, but take hold of the whole of man's nature; if culture is integrated by the symbol not only, so to speak, horizontally, in the totality of its forms, but also in the person of its creator, vertically, so to speak, to the very foundations of his soul—in a word, if man himself is integrated into his culture. For such an achievement the intellectual logic is not sufficient. The author of the *Essay on Man* does no longer seem to find it so important that the symbolic function is the *vinculum substantiale* between logic and mathematics and between logic and exact natural science. For him it seems now to be all important that it be the *vinculum substantiale* between logic and morality.

It is one of the peculiarities of creation that the works created

---

[128] *PSF*, III, 391.
[129] *PSF*, III, 370.
[130] *PSF*, III, 197f., 211f., 234.
[131] *PSF*, I, 27.

appear as strangers to the creator. Since the essential act of
creation is a subconscious one, the miracle of encompassing the
spiritual in the material takes place in the very depths of the
creating soul; the memory of it is faint, indeed, non-existing,
and the re-cognition of the created as created almost impossible.
Herein lies the fascination of the work for the creator; but
herein also the danger of abstracting himself from his creations,
of disintegration between man and culture instead of integration. The very variety and differentiation of cultural forms, in
which lies the progress of the spirit and in the totality of which
lies its harmony, also makes for differences and separations.
"Thus what was intended to secure the harmony of culture becomes the source of the deepest discords and dissensions."[132]
This is the great antinomy, the dialectic, not only of the religious
life[133] but of all cultural life. The "process of removal" sometimes *"überschlägt sich,"* gets out of hand, and degenerates into
an urge of destruction. The great problem then is how to maintain the continuity between the soul of man and his creations,
how to weave him and the symbolic forms into one cultural
pattern, a pattern of morality. When man is identified with his
works, he is moral; for then he is identified with the works of
all mankind. How can that integration be achieved? Again let
us glance at the artist.

Rodin and his works were one.

> It was impossible to separate him from his work. His statues were the
> states of his soul. Just as Rodin seemed to break the fragments around
> the statue away from the block in which it had been concealed, so he
> himself seemed to be a sort of rock hiding various forms and crystallized
> growths.[134]

The symbolic forms are the states of man's soul. "The contents
of culture cannot be separated from the fundamental forms and
directions of spiritual creation: their 'being' cannot be apprehended otherwise but as 'doing'."[135] As the sculpture is "concealed" in the block, "pre-existent" in its shape, grain, texture,

---

[132] *Essay on Man*, 130.
[133] *Ibid.* and Chap. VII.
[134] Story, *op. cit.*, 11.
[135] *PSF*, I, 11.

"like the chicken in the egg,"[136] and the sculptor must "collaborate" with the stone to free the figure concealed in it, so man must "collaborate" with himself to free the symbolic forms within him and create culture out of himself. *Culture is* indeed *the process of man's progressive self-liberation.* "Language, art, religion, science, are various phases in this process."[137] Man is his own "matter" and his own "form." Cassirer's philosophy here completes and substantiates empirically Kant's "Copernican revolution." Matter and form

are now no more absolute *powers of Being*, but they serve the designation of certain *differences and structures of meaning.* The "matter" of perception, as it was understood by Kant originally, could still appear as a kind of epistemological counterpart to Aristotle's πρωτὴ ὕλη. Like it, it is taken as the merely indeterminate *before* all determination, which must expect all determination from the form which accrues to it and imprints itself on it. The situation changes after Kant's own development of the "transcendental topic" and his designation, within that topic, of a definite position to the opposition of "matter" and "form." Now they are no more primal determinations of Being, ontic entities, but pure *concepts of reflection*, which in the section on the "Amphiboly of the Concepts of Reflection" are being treated on the same line with Agreement and Opposition, and Identity and Difference. They are no more two poles of Being in insoluble "real" opposition,[138]

but concepts of transcendental comparisons referring to states of consciousness. They are "states of man's soul." "From the point of view of phenomenology there is as little a 'matter in itself' as a 'form in itself'—there are only total experiences, which can be compared under the point of view of matter and form, and determined and articulated accordingly."[139]

In the *Essay on Man* the transcendental "relativization"[140] of the contrast between matter and form has been applied to man; man is the sculptor of the symbolic forms—forms of his own consciousness. But the relationship already appears clearly in the *Philosophy of Symbolic Forms.* Indeed, it is the differ-

---

[136] In words of the Spanish sculptor José de Creeft.
[137] *Essay on Man*, 228.
[138] *PSF*, III, 13.
[139] *PSF*, III, 230.
[140] *PSF*, III, 13.

entiation of man's "space" by which man actually carves out the symbolic forms, pre-existent in it. Space is the universal matrix of these forms—and it is a state of man's own consciousness. Plato's πρῶτον δεκτικόν, space as common matrix of all determinations, is actually being confirmed by the philosophy of symbolic forms,[141] even though its "space," like Kant's, is very different from Plato's metaphysical "receptacle." It is a formative, dynamic principle, indeed, the formative principle of consciousness itself in its relation to the world—the form of our "outer experience." It is a living "material," living in and through the life of its shaper, just as is the "stone" of Rodin. All the symbolic forms have their particular "spatiality,"[142] their particular form of correlation[143] according to their particular modality. From empirical perceptual space develops conceptual space.[144] Perceptual space is already filled with symbolic forms and interpenetrated by them. Language forms the first space-words. In abstract geometry space is a system of topological determinations: proximity of points, distance, intersection of lines, incidence of planes and spaces. From topological develops metric and projective space. The development of space is at the same time the development of relational thought, the gradual awakening of consciousness and its world-awareness.[145]

There is no power of the spirit which has not co-operated in this gigantic process of formation. Sensation, intuition, feeling, phantasy, creative imagination,[146] constructive [!] conceptual thought—and the manner of their interpenetration create each time a new spatial *Gestalt*.[147]

At the same time there is a definitive direction of the process: "the *'Auseinandersetzung'* between world and Ego"[148]—the

[141] *PSF*, III, 491.
[142] *PSF*, III, 491.
[143] *Ibid.*
[144] *PSF*, III, 492.
[145] Cassirer refers in this connection to Carnap, Rudolf, *Der Raum, ein Beitrag zur Wissenschaftslehre*, Berlin, 1922.
[146] The German word *"Einbildungskraft"*-"power of in-forming," gives the spatial implication.
[147] *PSF*, III, 493.
[148] *Ibid.* Italics mine.

progressive "ex-position" and "ex-secution" of the separateness of man and world, their gradual differentiation. Gradually man releases space and its forms from and out of himself, until finally it seems to be an independent *Gestalt*, standing opposed to and as counter-pole of him. The mythical consciousness of space is still entirely woven within the sphere of subjective feeling, but already there appears an opposition of cosmic powers, as in the Platonic *Timaeus*, the Chinese Yin and Yang, and the innumerable forms of "cosmic bisexuality."[149] Language continues the separation and deepens it: the mythical physiognomic space becomes presentative space. Conceptual—mathematical, geometrical, and physical—thought complete the process: the anthropomorphic conditions are being pushed back in favor of "objective" determinations which result from the methods of counting and measuring. Now we have the space of pure meaning or signification.[150] A similar process of differentiation takes place within the elemental units of the symbolic forms. The flux of perceptual impressions is being subdivided into centers around which the undifferentiated variety clusters, like the diffuse matter in space, which gradually clustered into nebulae, and continues to concentrate its diffuse matter into condensed energy "through millions and mountains of millions of centuries."[151] Similarly the process of symbolic formation continues to concentrate diffuse energies as long as there is man. The diffuse matter in space is being organized by being referred to a natural center. Ever new worlds are in formation and "gain a general relation to the center, the first formative point of creation."[152] Similarly in the world of symbolic forms centers are formed as points of reference. Thus the *name* becomes name only through reference to such centers. The names "red" or "blue," for instance,[153] do not mean certain blue or red nuances, but express the specific manner, in which an undetermined variety of such nuances is seen as one and conceptually set as

---

[149] Treated symbolically in Mann's Joseph novels. Cf. Slochower, Harry, *No Voice is Wholly Lost*, New York 1945, 350 n.

[150] *PSF*, III, 493 f.

[151] Kant, *Natural History and Theory of the Heavens*, 2. Teil, 7tes Hauptstück.

[152] *Ibid.*

[153] *PSF*, III, 497.

one.[154] In physical-geometrical thought the given is not only being divided and assembled around fixed centers, but "cast into form,"[155] the harmonious form of mathematical symbols, which is as opposed to the original diffusion of formative energies as the well ordered system of planets is to the primal diffusion of matter. For Laplace Kant's theory of the heavens was the inspiration for a mathematical theory of the creation of the world.[156] For Cassirer Kant's theory of knowledge was the inspiration for a theory of the creation of the cultural world, one of whose culminations is mathematics. In both cases the world is modelled in space—a work of plastic imagination.[157] If all activity of thought expresses itself in spatial forms, then its creative activity must needs be a kind of plastic sculpturing. Cassirer himself has never, to my knowledge, drawn this conclusion, but it deduces itself logically from his philosophy.

In sculpturing the world of symbolic forms, man sculptures and forms his own soul. What he looks at in the variety of forms is his own inner life. Rodin "used to contemplate his creations lovingly, and sometimes even seemed to be astonished and contemplative at the idea of having created them, speaking as if they existed apart from himself."[158] Thus man stands wonderingly before his creations, astounded at the world, which he has created—created so unconsciously that it took several thousand years of contemplative thought until, in the mind of Kant, he recognized in it himself. This same difficulty veiled the world of symbolic forms before man's mind in a world of metaphysics. Again and again man tried to lift the veil, but the attempt was doomed to pathetic failure. As for Schiller's "Young Man of Saïs," curiosity could only yield horror: the look into the abyss of nothing—or the abyss of his own self. In

---

[154] *"In-eins-gesehen und in-eins-gesetzt." "Einsicht"* becomes *"Eins-sicht"*—"Insight" becomes "One-sight."

[155] *PSF*, III, 498.

[156] Or might have been, if he knew Kant's treatise. Whether or not he actually did is unknown.

[157] Cf. Rodin: "If we can imagine the thought of God in creating the world, we shall find that He first thought of the modelling, which is the unique principle in Nature—and perhaps of the planets." Story, *op. cit.*, 14.

[158] Story, *op. cit.*, 11.

a very real sense we are all thinkers pondering "The Gate of Hell." Thinking is fraught with shocking surprises, shocks which are dialectic hiatuses in the process of the soul's self-discovery. That process leads to successive "*crises,*" "separations" of existence, in which the unconscious and uncontemplated process of spiritual development becomes a problem to itself, in which "*Äusserung*" becomes "*Äusserliches,*" self-expression becomes the exterior world.[159] This estrangement of the symbolic forms from their creator arises from the very fundamental principle of their creation.

The acts of expression, presentation, and meaning are not immediately present to themselves, but become apparent only in the totality of their accomplishment. They *are* only by confirming themselves, and giving notice of themselves through their action. They do not originally reflect on themselves, but they look at the work which they are to execute, to the reality the valid form of which they are to build up.[160]

Hence these forms can only be described within their works and in the language of these works. Language, myth, art:

each of these exteriorizes its own individual world of *creations,* which latter cannot be understood otherwise than as expressions of the self-activity, the "spontaneity" of the spirit. But this self-activity does not proceed in the form of free reflection, and therefore remains hidden to itself. The spirit creates the series of linguistic, mythical and artistic *Gestalten,* without in them recognizing itself as creative principle. Thus each of these series becomes for it an "exterior" world.[161]

The free creations of the spirit are then regarded as "things" and the power and independence of the spirit compelled into systems of dogmatic concepts.[162] Only the Critical philosophy succeeds in prying open this dogmatism. The thing, far from being a self-sufficient being, is for it only "an intellectual partial condition of being, a single conceptual moment, which only in the complete system of our knowledge comes to full effect."[163] It is now nothing but the general principle of the series, so to

---

[159] *PSF*, II, 290.
[160] *PSF*, III, 118.
[161] *PSF*, II, 267. Cf. *Erkenntnisproblem* I, 7.
[162] *Erkenntnisproblem* I, vf.
[163] *Ibid.*

speak, its general term.[164] The whole of reality is process, and the things are condensations of that process, much as matter is in physical field theory.[165] There is now no more metaphysical absolute, but only becoming. "By regarding the conditions of science as 'become,' we recognize them precisely thereby as *creations* of thought."[166] In doing so we recognize the opposition of subject and object as a metaphysical artifice, "the characteristic procedure of metaphysics."[167] Thus metaphysics estranges man from his creations; it must be overcome if man is to become responsible for his culture. It is no wonder, therefore, that the most metaphysical people has also fallen victim to the most tremendous "crisis," the most barbaric separation of man and culture: what the German scientists of extermination strove to annihilate was the man-of-culture,[168] termed by them "the beast of intelligence"—"*die Intelligenzbestie.*" In their scientific one-sidedness they were both "metaphysical" and barbaric.[169]

To overcome this metaphysical crisis man must "collaborate" with himself as the sculptor does with his material. He must fuse his own form with his own matter. The metaphysical crisis must be transformed, through cultural critique, into harmonic responsibility of man for his world. This is only possible by man's recognizing in the cultural forms his own consciousness, by comprehending these forms as *symbolic for the unity of*

---

[164] *PSF*, III, 373.

[165] That theory should, theoretically, be deducible from Kant's *Critique of Pure Reason.*

[166] *Erkenntnisproblem* I, vi.

[167] *Substance and Function*, 271; Cf. PSF, I, 24.

[168] Cf. Kerényi, Karl, *Romandichtung und Mythologie, Ein Briefwechsel mit Thomas Mann*, Zürich: Rhein Verlag, 1945, 42.

[169] Cf. Bluhm, Heinz, "Ernst Cassirer und die deutsche Philologie," *Monatshefte für Deutschen Unterricht*, Vol. XXXVII, No. 7, November 1945, 471. Ilya Ehrenburg, *The Tempering of Russia*, New York: Alfred A. Knopf, 1944, 276, on examining the diary of a dead German who at the front continued reading philosophy and whose notebook related the philosophy and practice of extermination interspersed with quotations from Plato, Schopenhauer, and Nietzsche, wrote: "In perusing the brown notebook one is amazed at the mental poverty of these scholarly cannibals. To torture people they need philosophical quotations. . . . One feels like killing Fritz-the-philosopher twice: one bullet because he tortured Russian children; another because after murdering a baby, he read Plato."

man and his world. Symbolism is to be the vehicle of man's morality.

How else should man be able to sound the depths of his own consciousness and at the same time roam over the width of the world? The variety of forms would be too manifold for comprehension, if there were not the principle of the symbolic function to organize them. The consciousness would be too fleetingly incomprehensible, if there were not the material embodiments of its energies. How else should we be able to

penetrate to this purely inner world of consciousness as last concentration of the spiritual, if for its demonstration and description we have to renounce all the concepts and points of view, which have been created for the presentation of the concrete reality of things. Where would there be a means to comprehend the incomprehensible, to express in any way that which itself has not yet assumed any concrete form—either of the perceptual space and time order, or of an intellectual, ethical or aesthetic order? If the consciousness is nothing but the pure potentiality of all the "objective" forms, so to speak the pure receptivity and preparedness for them, then it cannot be seen how precisely this potentiality itself can be treated as a fact, indeed, as the primary fact of all spirituality itself. . . . It is obvious that this paradoxical demand can only be satisfied, if at all, mediately. We can never uncover the immediate being and life of consciousness purely as such,[170]—but it is a meaningful task to understand the process of objectivation[171]

by treating it from a double perspective, shuttling back and forth between the *terminus a quo* and the *terminus ad quem*, thus truly following the method of that weaver's masterpiece or, even better, instead of treating the objectivity of the *law* rather find the *Gestalt*[172] of cognition, thus transforming the method of psychology into that of the symbolic forms.

We start from the problems of the "objective spirit," the *Gestalten* of which it consists and in which it exists; but we do not rest there as a mere fact, but try, through a reconstructive analysis, to penetrate to their elementary conditions, the "conditions of their possibility."[173]

[170] In this connection Cassirer's criticism of Bergson's method is of importance, *PSF*, III, 42ff.

[171] *PSF*, III, 62f.

[172] *PSF*, III, 66.

[173] *PSF*, III, 67.

In other words, we look for the "various forms and crystallized growths" within the rock that is man, and then proceed to carve them out, helped by our knowledge of the grain and texture, the geology and palaeontology of those forms. Thus we would find the correspondence between the manifold of objective formations and subjective states of consciousness, a "truly concrete view of the 'full objectivity' of the spirit on the one hand and its 'full subjectivity' on the other."[174] To do so we must delve down deeply into the roots of consciousness:

> We must consider not only the three dimensions of the logical, the ethical and the aesthetic, but in particular the "form" of language and the "form" of mythos, if we want to penetrate down to the primary behavioral and formative conditions of consciousness.[175]

In this way, then, the vertical integration of man will be joined to the horizontal integration of his culture. Man must live on all the levels of his consciousness, on the deepest of myth as well as on the highest of mathematics, music,[176] and mysticism. This vertical task has only just begun, but the great minds of our age are preparing the synthesis. Bergson joins "mechanics and mysticism,"[177] Thomas Mann joins mythos and language,[178] and asks for a chair in "mythology" to join mythos and logos.[179] Cassirer joins all spiritual forms in the synthesis of cultural symbolism.

[174] *Ibid.*

[175] *Ibid.*

[176] See above note 85.

[177] *The Two Sources of Morality and Religion*, New York: Henry Holt and Company, 1935, chapter IV. Bergson's philosophy is based on the form of our inner experience, time; Cassirer's is based on that of our outer experience, space. Therefore the latter is led to the central notion of the symbol, which the former rejects, the former to that of metaphysical intuition which the latter rejects. Cassirer's philosophy can be understood in terms of the plastic arts, Bergson's in terms of music. A synthesis of both philosophies would be the true philosophy of symbolism.

[178] Kerényi, *op. cit.*, 50. According to Cassirer, *PSF*, I, 268, language as a form is between mythos and logos.

[179] Kerényi, *op. cit.*, 84, 82. The separation of the myth from logos is the immediate cause of the latest world catastrophe. The combination of both, in particular of mythos with the science of psychology, is one of the guarantees of the future. "I have long been a passionate friend of this combination; for indeed, psychology is the means to take the myth out of the hands of the fascist obscurants

In this way he has given us a tool, a "grammar of the symbolic function,"[180] a key with which to open the treasure house of our own culture. But simply to open it and wander around in it as in a museum will not solve the crisis. We must appropriate all the symbolic forms as our own creations. The symbols must not remain mute and dumb signs for us, but be charged with all the meaning of life. We must enter into their own lives and live on their level. Our survival depends on our capacity to handle symbols in communication, discussion, and agreement—in settling conflicts by handling symbols rather than the powers they stand for. We must "do away with presence in order to penetrate to representation. . . . The regress into the world of *signs* is the preparation for that decisive break-through in which the spirit will conquer its own world, the world of *idea*."[181]

We are standing before that decisive event. We must either live through symbols or die in the flesh. The symbols will be filled with life if they reach through our entire self, far above and below the merely intellectual level. We must recognize the states of our soul in them, as did Rodin in his creations; "he was the companion of these white mute creatures of his, he loved them and entered into their abstract lives."[182] So we must enter the life of human culture and lovingly develop it and us in it. In this sense the philosophy of symbolic forms may be said to be a comprehensive aesthetics, the work of an artist for artists: the vision of man as creator of all his works, the vision of culture as human creation. Indeed, it seems that Cassirer himself has had that vision very consciously; the volume on Aesthetics was to be the crowning volume of the *Philosophy of Symbolic Forms*.[183] It is the crisis itself that has separated Cassirer from

and to 'transfunction' it into the humane. That combination actually represents to me the world of the future, a humanity, that is blessed from on high, through the spirit, and 'from the depths that lie below'." Thomas Mann, Kerényi; *op. cit.*, 82. Cf. Buxton, Charles Roden, *Prophets of Heaven and Hell, Virgil, Dante, Milton, Goethe*, Cambridge: At the University Press, 1945, 29f.

[180] *PSF*, I, 18.
[181] *PSF*, III, 356; 54. Cf. III, 330.
[182] Story, *op. cit.*, 11.
[183] Bluhm, *op. cit.*, 468. *PSF*, I, 120.

the symbolic forms of the arts; his book could not be written "due to the unfavorable political conditions." Otherwise he himself might have performed that vertical synthesis of man and cast man's inner life into the forms of the new logic. Maybe he would have called that new form the form of man's "symbolic *Prägnanz*"—man's existence as symbol of his own universal thought: transcending his material confinement in universal meaning.

How Cassirer would have integrated man himself into his culture we can only guess. He has given us one lowly example for symbolic *Prägnanz:* he integrates the life of a wavy line in all fields of meaning. Let us quote that passage, not only as a symbolic review of the whole philosophy of symbolic forms, its artistic empathy and the sweep of its meaning, but also as a preview into realms to which Cassirer's philosophy points.

In the purely spatial determination there is a peculiar "mood," the up and down of lines in space contains an inner motion, a dynamic rise and fall, a psychic being and life. It is not we who feel our own inner states in a subjective way in the spatial form: but that form presents itself to us as a spirited whole, an independent manifestation of life. Its steady and calm flow or its sudden break, its roundness and wholeness or its brokenness, its hardness or softness: all this appears as character of its own being, its objective "nature." But all this recedes and seems as if it were annihilated and extinguished as soon as the line is taken in another meaning—as a mathematical design, a geometrical *figure*. Now it becomes a mere scheme, the means of presenting a universal geometric *law*. Where before we had the up and down of a wavy line and in it the harmony of an inner mood—there now we find the graphic presentation of a trigonometric function, a curve the whole content of which is absorbed in its analytic *formula*. The spatial *Gestalt* is nothing else now than the paradigm of that formula; it is only the hull into which a mathematical thought, imperceptible in itself, is clothed. And the latter does not stand by itself, but in it a universal law presents itself, the order of space in general. Every single geometric form is by virtue of that order connected with the totality of all other spatial forms. It belongs to a certain *system*—an aggregate of "truths" and "theorems," of "reasons" and "consequences"—and that system denotes the universal form by which each individual geometric figure is alone possible, that is to say, constructable and "understandable." And again the situation is different, when we consider the line as mythical *sign* or as aesthetic *ornament*. The mythical sign expresses the fundamental mythical contrast between the "holy" and the "profane." It is established in order to separate these two realms from each other, to warn and to terrify and to bar the uninitiated from approaching or entering the holy. And thereby it does not function only as a mere sign, as a mark by which the holy is being *recognized*; but it possesses a magically compelling and repelling power, which resides in it objectively. Of such a compulsion the aesthetic world knows nothing. Contemplated as an ornament the line is removed both from the sphere of "meaning" in the logico-conceptual sense as that of magico-mythical significance and warning. It now possesses its import in itself, which uncovers itself only in the purely artistic contemplation, the aesthetic intuition as such. Here again the experience of the spatial form completes itself only through belonging to a total horizon and opening that horizon up for us, . . . by standing in a certain atmosphere, in which it not only simply "is," but in which it so to speak lives and breathes.[184]

Imagine the hero of this tale to be man rather than a wavy line! How he would be seen in all realms of meaning, all forms of culture—a symbol himself of his own striving and achievement, the central system of co-ordination of all life activities. "The symbolic process is like a unique life and thought current which flows through consciousness and which in its flowing motion alone brings about the variety and continuity of consciousness in all its fullness."[185] In the unity of that flow man would become integrated, from the mythical depth of consciousness—the well of the past from which Thomas Mann brought forth his Joseph figures[186]—to the highest height of mathematics, music, and mysticism.[187]

---

[184] *PSF*, III, 231; Cf. Cassirer "Das Symbolproblem und seine Stellung im System der Philosophie," *Zeitschrift für Ästhetik und allgemeine Kunstwissenschaft*, Bd. XXI, 191 ff. Cf. *supra* 112 f.

[185] *PSF*, III, 234.

[186] Cf. Thomas Mann on the combination of psychology and myth in Kerényi, *op. cit.*, 82; also "Freud and the Future," in *Freud, Goethe, Wagner*, New York: Alfred A. Knopf, 1942, 29ff.

[187] For then the process of objectivation would not be completed in the mathematical symbols—symbols for nature rather than for human nature. It may be that those symbols will also aid in the objectivation of man toward himself, the objectivation of his own psyche: his emotions and desires. Perhaps Spinoza was

So far the highest realms of the vertical synthesis have not been reached. Cassirer's work is unfinished and waits for completion. The mysticism of the artist, the musicality of the mathematician, all these are symbolic forms and elaborations of lower forms as truly as mathematics is the elaboration of the lower symbolic forms of myth and language. Perhaps Cassirer had intended to show us these connections in his projected volume on the symbolic forms of Aesthetics. As it is, the work must be completed by us, the epigones. But we too shall only be precursors, preparers of the day "when the human intelligence, elevated to its perfect type, shall shine forth glorified in some future Mozart-Dirichlet or Beethoven-Gauss."[188] Cassirer's work points toward a future of symbolic forms so rich that man's present culture appears very primitive indeed.

In 1910, at about the time when Cassirer's first great work appeared, another great mind was concerned with the future. Leo Tolstoy, shortly before his death, dictated to his daughter Anastasia a strange prophecy. He predicted the coming of world wars, the sway of a strange figure from the North, "a new Napoleon," and finally, a "federation of the United States of nations." After that

I see a change in religious sentiment. . . . The ethical idea has almost vanished. Humanity is without the moral feeling. But then a great reformer arises. . . . I see the peaceful beginning of an ethical era. . . . In the middle of this century I see a hero of literature and art rising . . . and purging the world of the tedious stuff of the obvious. It is the light of *symbolism* that shall outshine the torch of *commercialism*.[189]

Cassirer's life was dedicated to the self-liberation of man through symbolism. Everything for him, like for Rodin,[190]

---

on the right road with his geometric ethics. But the "grammar of emotions" may have to be written, ultimately in a more fitting script: that of musical and mystical symbolism. To the latter point see *Essay on Man*, 102. Concerning the insufficiency of mathematical symbolism even for the comprehension of nature cf. Cassirer, "Goethe and Kantian Philosophy" in *Rousseau, Kant, Goethe*, 64ff., 81f.

[188] James Joseph Sylvester in a paper on Newton's rule for the discovery of imaginery roots of algebraic equations, quoted from E. T. Bell, *Men of Mathematics*, New York: Simon and Schuster, 1937, 404f.

[189] Forman, Henry James, *The Story of Prophecy*, New York: Tudor Publishing Company: 1939, 253f.

[190] Story, *op. cit.*, 17.

was "idea and symbol;" like Rodin "he sought in the energy of the human body and its symbolism for the origins of all religions, all philosophy and poetry."[191] The ethical era to come must be built to a large extent on his work. His morality was, like Rodin's,[192] the comprehensive love of life and of all its forms. Rodin "opened a vast window in the pale house of modern statuary, and made of sculpture, which had been a timid, compromised art, one that was audacious and full of life."[193] So Cassirer opened a large window in the pale house of modern critical philosophy and made of epistemology, which had been a timid, compromised discipline, one that was audacious and full of life. He prepared the horizontal-vertical integration of man's soul and culture—a symbolic cross, to which man will not be fixed in agony, but in which he will live.

ROBERT S. HARTMAN

DEPARTMENT OF PHILOSOPHY
OHIO STATE UNIVERSITY

[191] *Ibid.*
[192] Story, *op. cit.*, 11.
[193] *Ibid.*

9

Folke Leander

FURTHER PROBLEMS SUGGESTED BY THE PHILOSOPHY OF SYMBOLIC FORMS

FURTHER PROBLEMS SUGGESTED BY THE PHILOSOPHY OF SYMBOLIC FORMS

"ONE should take everything for what it is, not criticize it for not being what it is not"—such was the critical maxim of the Swedish poet-philosopher Thomas Thorild (1759-1806), on whom, incidentally, Cassirer has written an excellent book. It is, however, exceedingly difficult to criticize Cassirer for what he does say, and much easier to point to the unsolved problems which he never set out to solve. Cassirer's method in *The Philosophy of Symbolic Forms* is that of concentrating his attention on a very limited number of major problems, treating them exhaustively, adducing a great wealth of linguistic, mythological, and psychological material to prove his point. The numerous and widespread errors he refutes are disproved very thoroughly. He rarely "sticks his neck out," as the Americans say. There is a certain finality about all this and little temptation for the student to quote a passage and disagree with it. In fact, if you accept the view that all thought, in so far as it is really thought, must necessarily be true, all criticism must consist in drawing attention to omissions. Only, in Cassirer's case you rarely find the omissions mixed up with and vitiating what he does say, which latter will generally be found to be unimpeachable, as far as it goes. These introductory remarks may serve to explain the nature of the following pages, which are intended primarily to point to further problems suggested by Cassirer's philosophy. The problems suggested are: 1) the unification of the pre-scientific symbolic forms; 2) a more careful distinction between form and material; 3) an analysis of the logic of history and the logic of philosophy. I will try to show how these desiderata grew out of Cassirer's own philosophy.

I

The Unification of the Pre-Scientific Symbolic Forms

As Theodor Litt[1] has remarked, the whole of Cassirer's
philosophy of symbolic forms may be regarded as a synthesis
of Kant and Herder, or as an adoption into the former's philosophy of the wider sphere of interest represented by the latter.
Kant's epistemology, devised to explain the possibility of Newtonian physics, must be broadened so as to include aesthetics,
the theory of language, and the philosophy of mythology. It
is high time for epistemologists to rid themselves of the superior
attitude often taken towards language, myth, and especially art,
as if these things did not concern them. As Cassirer shows they
are the basis of our knowing life, the basis upon which even
science rests. Cassirer has admirably instructive studies of two of
the pre-scientific symbolic forms, language and myth. There is,
however, no volume on art, and this fact is seldom mentioned.

So far so good. We have every reason to be grateful for
these excellent books. Yet one should like to know more about
the way these pre-scientific symbolic forms are related to one
another. How does Cassirer know there are three of them?
How does he arrive at them? He simply takes over the popular delimitations without caring about the objections that
myth may be a mixture of artistic imagination and practical emotion of a certain kind, and language a crudely delimited type of
art or, alternatively, art a crudely delimited type of language.
He projects the idea that aesthetics is the general science of
pre-scientific symbolism; but he rejected it without anything resembling real disproof.[2]

In *Sprache und Mythos* (Leipzig 1925), pp. 65ff., he discusses at length the relations of language, myth and art. He
begins by pointing out that language and myth have "a common root" and are the products of an ultimately identical
mental function (*eine letzte Gemeinsamkeit in der Funktion
des Gestaltens*). They are both the products of "metaphorical
thinking." He quotes from Max Müller: "Whether he wanted

---

[1] *Kant und Herder als Deuter der geistigen Welt,* Leipzig (1930), 285f.
[2] *Die Sprache,* Berlin (1923), 120f.

to or not, man had to speak in metaphors, not because he could not restrain his poetic imagination, but rather because he had to use it to the utmost in order to find expressions for the ever-growing needs of his mind." The growth of intuition, accordingly, is correlative to the growth of poetic symbolism. The common root of language and myth turns out also to be the root of poetry; in fact, we are told, they are originally one, and the distinctions between them were gradually introduced. "Myth, language and art begin as a concrete, undivided unity, which is only gradually resolved into a triad of independent modes of spiritual creativity."[3]

The critic will remark that there are distinctions and distinctions—they need not all be of the same kind. Some may be fundamental and "real," whereas others are "merely empirical," more or less arbitrary cuts in a flowing continuum. Cassirer's Kantianism will scarcely allow him to put the distinctions between abstract and concrete, or theoretical and practical, moral good and sensuous satisfaction on a level with the arbitrary distinction between, say, a chair and a sofa, where all sorts of intermediary forms are conceivable. It is a question of logic whether you accept "real" distinctions as *ultimately* different from "merely empirical" or "pragmatic" ones. But whatever your ultimate decision on this point of logic will be, you will certainly have to admit a difference of status. Now the critic may maintain that the distinctions gradually emerging between language, myth, and art are of the "merely empirical" variety and that pre-scientific symbolism is "really" the same activity everywhere.

Cassirer describes the creation of myth and language in the very terms in which others describe the process of artistic creation. Myth arises from an emotional tension between man and his environment:

then the spark jumps somehow across, the tension finds release, as the subjective excitement becomes objectified, and confronts the mind as a god or a daemon. . . .[4] As soon as the spark has jumped across, as soon as the tension and emotion of the moment has found its discharge in

---

[3] *Language and Myth* (S. Langer translation, 1945), 98.
[4] *Ibid.*, 33.

the word as the mythical image, a sort of turning point has occurred in human mentality: the inner excitement which was a mere subjective state has vanished, and has been resolved into the objective form of myth or of speech.[5]

If anything can be objected to in this statement, it is that the additional practical emotion characteristic of myth is here overlooked in favour of a complete identification with art. The subjective practical emotion is never completely expressed in the mythical image, as is the case in pure art, but remains as terror and awe; and to this is added the practical act of "belief."

There is a profound difference between scientific symbolism on the one hand, and pre-scientific symbolism on the other. The function of the latter, according to Cassirer, is intuitive elaboration of experience (*Intensivierung* is his own term), whereas the former aims at discursive mastery, by means of rules and procedures, of a world already intuitively apprehended. Science moves on the discursive level, the level of general concepts (*Allgemeinbegriffe*) and laws. But this level of rationality could not exist by itself and must everywhere attach itself to something more basic. The intuitive level of experience is experience elaborated by means of linguistic, mythical, and artistic symbolism.[6]

---

[5] *Ibid.*, 36.

[6] In myth, says Cassirer, "thought does not dispose freely over the data of intuition, in order to relate and compare them to each other, but is captivated and enthralled by the intuition which suddenly confronts it. It comes to rest in the immediate experience; the sensible present is so great that everything else dwindles before it." (*Ibid.*, 32.) ". . . the immediate content, whatever it be, that commands his religious interest so completely fills his consciousness that nothing else can exist beside and apart from it. The ego is spending all its energy on this single object, lives in it, loses itself in it." (*Ibid.*, 33.) This would also be an excellent description of the aesthetic attitude, the common element being intuitive elaboration, or "*Intensivierung*," of experience.

"Language and myth stand in an original and indissoluble correlation with one another, from which they both emerge but gradually as independent elements. They are two diverse shoots from the same parent stem, the same impulse of symbolic formulation, springing from the same basic mental activity, a concentration and heightening of simple sensory experience. In the vocables of speech and in primitive mythic figurations, the same inner process finds its consummation: they are both resolutions of an inner tension, the representation of subjective impulses and excitations in definite objective forms and figures." (*Ibid.*, 88.) Can anyone fail

The sharp distinction between the two levels of experience—discursive and intuitive—does not imply, of course, that meanings belong merely to the discursive level. There are also meanings on the intuitive level, though of a different kind. They may be termed "felt identities," "affinities," "qualia," "characters;" as caught and held in symbols, Cassirer terms them "*Sprachbegriffe*," "*mythische Begriffe*," etc.

It appears, then, that language, myth, and art have a common task in the theoretical life of man, namely, the intuitive mastery of experience. This would seem to make it imperative to discriminate between the theoretical and the practical-emotional aspects of myth, in which case the former could hardly fail to be identified with art. A similar failure to distinguish between the theoretical and the practical vitiates Cassirer's use of the term "expressional phenomenon," by which he means the emotional qualities of phenomena. In so far as emotion is subservient to intuition, it is aesthetic; but it may also obstruct the intuitive elaboration of experience and may then be called practical. Practical emotional qualities are stimuli to immediate practical reaction: we give up the attitude of contemplation, of intuitive elaboration. Thus sudden fear, if detrimental to intuition, is practical, whereas the grandiose, the sublime and even the terrible may be aesthetic qualities. The distinction is blurred by the use of the term "expressional qualities" no less than in the phrases current among English-speaking philosophers: "tertiary qualities" and the like.

One should also note that the function Cassirer ascribes to language is intuitive mastery of experience. For one of the things that have evidently puzzled him most, is the "logical" element of language. But, when raising this problem, he invariably makes a *metabasis eis allo genos* and passes from pre-

to see that this is a perfect description of the process of artistic creation? Could there be a better proof that myth and language are aesthetic products?

If discursive thinking "tends toward expansion, implication, and systematic connection, the verbal and mythical conception tends toward concentration, telescoping, separate characterization." (*Ibid.*, 56.) "Here thought does not confront its data in an attitude of free contemplation, seeking to understand their structure and their systematic connections, and analyzing them according to their parts and functions, but is simply captivated by a total impression." (*Ibid.*, 57.)

scientific to scientific symbolism, asserting that the same "Logos" that is operative in scientific symbolism, is also at work in pre-scientific symbolism. If we ask what is here meant by Logos, we find that several different meanings are crowded together into one term. "Logos" may mean spiritual synthesis in general: and in this case it is, of course, true that Logos is operative in pre-scientific symbolism. But Logos may also mean the thinking of scientific and general concepts: and in this case it can be shown, I think, that Logos is altogether outside of intuition and of pre-scientific symbolism, although it may leave results that may be absorbed in the latter. (I shall explain presently what is meant by the last clause.)

As we have seen, meanings, according to Cassirer, are found also on the intuitive level; as caught and held in linguistic symbols they are *"Sprachbegriffe,"* not to be confused with general or scientific concepts. When he asserts that the same Logos is operative in the creation of *"Sprachbegriffe"* which on a higher level is operative in the creation of scientific concepts, this assertion is only acceptable if *Logos* means *Geist* in general. But Cassirer also means that *"Sprachbegriffe"* are a confused and preliminary creation of Logos in the sense of scientific intellect. This latter assertion seems to me untenable.

The confusion is made possible by the fact that general and scientific concepts may be "absorbed" into intuition. An electric charge is one thing for the engineer in his capacity of scientific specialist; it is a different thing for the layman and even for the engineer himself *qua* non-specialist. What was originally a mere formula, a rule of procedure, may through practice and experience of its effects be transformed into an intuitive affinity, a quale, a *Gestalt,* a characteristic physiognomy. As John Dewey puts it:

In the situation which follows upon reflection, meanings are intrinsic; they have no instrumental or subservient office, because they have no office at all. They are as much qualities of the objects in the situation as are red and black, hard and soft, square and round. And every reflective experience adds new shades of such intrinsic qualifications.[7]

---

[7] *Essays in Experimental Logic,* (1916) 17. Cf. also *How We Think,* (1933), 135 ff. ("Things and Meanings"), and *Logic,* (1938) ch. VIII ("Immediate Knowledge").

Perhaps Dewey's term "intrinsic qualifications" is better than any of those I have so far used (affinity, physiognomy, quale, etc.). Discursive procedures, then, may grow intuitive, ideas may lose their intellectual quality by habitual use. And, as a parallel process, general and scientific concepts may be transformed into *"Sprachbegriffe."* Dewey distinguishes between two types of grasp of meaning: the strictly logical type and the "aesthetic" perception of intrinsic qualifications, which is sometimes called acquaintance-knowledge. We apprehend chairs, tables, books, trees, horses, stars, rain, etc., promptly and directly; we need not think about these things in order to identify them; we cannot help seeing them as chairs, tables, etc.

Certainly logical thought-processes leave results in intuition; the starry heavens, for instance, look different to us from what they did to a contemporary of Dante. But there is also a movement in the opposite direction. "Red" meant originally an intuitively felt affinity; but when definite procedures have been developed,—*e.g.*, the colour-pyramid,—it may mean a *locus* within the system.

In spite of all this give and take, however, the intuitive and the discursive levels remain different. Since the aim and function of *"Sprachbegriffe"* is altogether different from that of general and scientific concepts, the former cannot be viewed as an inferior and undeveloped variety of the latter. Yet the interplay between the levels is certainly misleading. On the intuitive level, Cassirer says, meanings are "fused" (*eingeschmolzen*) with the concrete.[8] And he paints a picture of the poor Logos like a butterfly grovelling in the dust, until in science it disengages itself from the many-coloured intuition, rises into the air, and starts out on a proud flight in its own proper element.[9]

[8] *Phänomenologie der Erkenntnis*, (1929), 327.

[9] *Phänomenologie der Erkenntnis*, 395f. "It is true that an abyss appears to yawn between the scientific concept and the verbal concept—however, looked at more closely this abyss is exactly the same gulf which thinking had to bridge earlier before it could become verbal thought. . . . Now thought has to tear loose not merely from the here and now, from the respective location and moment, but it has to reach beyond the totality of space and time, beyond the limits of perceptual description, and of description and describability in general. . . . The 'vehicle' of word-language which served for so long a time, will now bear him no farther—but he feels himself strong and powerful enough to risk the flight which is to carry him to a new goal."

But this metaphor is objectionable. The Logos flying discursively in the air is different from that working intuitively within experience. Both are needed; but the intuitive Logos is no preliminary variety of the scientific Logos.

This panlogistic tendency is incompatible with the main body of Cassirer's thought. For he teaches that language is in essence intuitive elaboration (*Intensivierung*) of experience. And he also teaches that the "logical" element of language, in so far as "*Sprachbegriffe*" are concerned, should not be called logical at all, if we distinguish between an intuitive and a discursive, logical level of experience. Language is correlative to intrinsic qualifications, characters, physiognomies, qualia, affinities, or whatever term may be used for the meanings belonging to the intuitive level.

All this, the critic will add, proves that language is essentially an aesthetic activity. Of course, in reasoning language is the bearer of logical meanings; yet even pure mathematics has an aesthetic side, since it is an existential thought-process. The mathematical concepts are embodied in aesthetically meaningful concrete processes. Words, says Cassirer, are mere "signs" or "vehicles" of logical meanings.[10] The relation between intuitive meanings and language is that of vital incarnation. Words *express* intuitive meanings but *state*, or are mere signs of, logical meanings. On the intuitive level, says Cassirer, "the word which denotes that thought content is not a mere conventional symbol, but is merged with its object in an indissoluble unity."[11] If the lightning is *seen* as a snake, it will also be *called* "the snake of

---

"For it is precisely the 'Logos,' which was at work from the beginning in the creation of language, which, in the progress to scientific knowledge, frees itself from the limiting conditions which originally clung to it—which proceeds from its implicit form into its explicit form." (*Ibid.*, 388)

[10] "For theoretical thinking, a word is essentially a vehicle serving the fundamental aim of such ideation: the establishment of relationships between the given phenomenon and others which are "like" it or otherwise connected with it according to some co-ordinating law. . . . The word stands, so to speak, between actual particular impressions, as a phenomenon of a different order, a new intellectual dimension; and to this mediating position, this remoteness from the sphere of immediate data, it owes the freedom and ease with which it moves among specific objects and connects one with another." *Language and Myth*, (Langer tr.) 56f.

[11] *Language and Myth*, 58.

the sky:" intuitive elaboration and linguistic naming is here one and the same activity. "The spiritual excitement caused by some object which presents itself in the outer world furnishes both the occasion and the means of its denomination. Sense impressions . . . naturally strive for vocal expression."[12] Language and intuition are correlative and develop together. Intuitive meanings are vitally fused with intuition, and so they are fused with language. Scientific and general concepts, on the other hand, are externally related to intuition and have a corresponding status in its correlative, language. Since this is Cassirer's own view, why does he reject the aesthetic theory of language? He not only rejects it but misrepresents it as wanting to reduce language to mere animal expression, to mere *"natürliche Symbolik,"* mere *"Laut der Empfindung."*[13] But surely nothing of the sort has been meant by those who have held the theory in question.

A significant omission is Cassirer's failure to mention Baumgarten in his survey of the history of the philosophy of language. Certainly his view of *oratio sensitiva* as correlative to *cognitio sensitiva,* or intuition, is worthy of close attention. The "distinct" concepts, Leibniz had said, are exemplified in our conceptual methods of recognizing objects as belonging to a class; but there is also an intuitive way of recognizing them. We immediately see chairs as chairs and feel no need of proceeding by rule. This is the level of "clear but confused" categories, *i.e.,* of everyday intuition and, as Baumgarten pointed out, in its most intense form the level of art. For art is *perfectio cognitionis sensitivae, qua talis.* In the same way, ordinary speech is inherently aesthetic, *oratio sensitiva,* although the word poetry is reserved for its more intense form, *oratio sensitiva perfecta.* What Baumgarten means by "sensitive" speech might be freely expressed as follows. The nature of speech is that of "painting a picture" of something, *e.g.,* of something I want you to do, or of the field where the point is localized on which I want you to give me information. Of course, the analogy with painting must not be pressed: it only lays hold of

[12] *Ibid.,* 89. H. Usener, as quoted by Cassirer.
[13] *Ibid.,* 30f. Cf. also *Zur Logik der Kulturwissenschaften,* 37f.

the fact that the function of speech is that of conjuring up something concrete, however "thin," schematic, and bare of details it may be. Even a newspaper headline is *oratio sensitiva*, although ordinarily very far from *perfecta*.

It is strange that Cassirer, the distinguished Leibnizian scholar, should have made no use of the philosophy of language proposed by Baumgarten, the founder of aesthetics. Here is a perfect distinction between the conceptual and the intuitive levels of experience. The "affinities" or general "characters" belonging to the latter level are accounted for as "confused concepts." And language is seen to be the correlative of intuition. All this returns in Cassirer's own philosophy, even the doubtful part of Leibniz-Baumgarten, namely, the view of intuitive reason as an imperfect and preliminary form of scientific reason. Only Baumgarten's insight into the fundamentally aesthetic nature of intuition and language has fallen out of the picture. I believe it will have to be re-introduced.

II

A More Careful Distinction between Form and Material

One may note in Cassirer a certain attachment to what Dewey has termed "the museum conception of art." Dewey holds the view that any experience to the extent to which it is *an* experience, is aesthetic[14]—an idea that goes back to Baumgarten, Herder, and the romantics. From this point of view a "transcendental aesthetics" would not be the doctrine of mathematical time and space but simply aesthetics. The subjects dealt with by Kant at the end of his system, in the *Critique of Judgment*, would be placed at the very beginning of the system. Or rather, since all rationality is "absorbed" and all practical emotion is expressed in intuition, the doctrine of intuition would be at once at the end and at the beginning of the system, which would accordingly be as circular as experience itself. Theodor Litt says that if Kant had ever discovered real intuition as something very different from mathematical time and space, he would hardly have failed to place art on this level; and further,

[14] *Art as Experience*, (1934).

"he could not have been able to escape the insight which dominated a Herder, namely that aesthetic experiences stand by no means alone in this regard, but rather constitute the highest intensification of the spiritual situation which runs through all and every sensory world view."[15] In short, the true "transcendental aesthetics" is simply aesthetics; intuition and its correlative, the pre-scientific symbolism, may be divided and subdivided in many ways by means of "merely empirical" distinctions, but "really" it is one identical activity everywhere— an activity, which in its more intense form is recognized as aesthetic. A division of our intuitive acts into "more intense" and "less intense" would itself be merely empirical. "We all take some pleasure," says Dr. Barnes, "in seeing how things look, in observing their colour, their contour, their movement, whether they are moving in our direction or not. In so far as we are successful in finding what is characteristic, appealing, or significant in the world about us, we are, in a small impromptu way, ourselves artists."[16] He adds that "the artist differs from the ordinary person partly by his ability to make what he sees a public object, but chiefly in the range and depth of his vision itself."[17] A novelist spending weeks and months on working out a "great" intuition, merely intensifies an activity in which we are all engaged. We all want clarity of vision and imaginative interpretation of experience. As Cassirer points out, the poet does not "know" what he wants to say, until he has said it; he obscurely feels something working within him, but he does not know what, until he has defined it in a work of art.[18] Similarly, it might be added, workmen had no "class-consciousness" until Marx and others created their "myths" (as Sorel would say); surely there were all sorts of obscure feelings among the workmen, but they were not articulated. In the same way, we are all dependent upon poets, prophets and artists for our imaginative interpretation of experience. There is no difference of *kind* between our everyday intuitive activities

[15] *Kant und Herder*, 61.
[16] Albert C. Barnes: *The Art in Painting*, 3rd ed. (1937) 12.
[17] *Ibid.*, 13.
[18] *Zur Logik der Kulturwissenschaften*, 130.

and those of the great "seers," merely a difference of intensity and degree. Just as the science of biology deals with cells as well as elephants, so the science of intuition deals with everyday intuitive awareness, however insignificant, as well as with those greater intuitions recognized as aesthetic.

Anyone who takes such a broad view of aesthetics will almost inevitably be led to look upon the division of Art into various arts and *genres* as "merely empirical" distinctions. Surely the distinction between art and science is "real" in a sense in which the distinctions between various arts are superficial and "pragmatic." Cassirer on the other hand, not having freed himself entirely from the "museum" idea of art, believes that the main arts and *genres* are *a priori*, inherent in the very idea, the "category" of art. I do not know whether or not Cassirer would nowadays accept the "panaesthetic" conception of experience. But, even if he does, he will certainly cling to his view of certain major arts as *a priori*, categorically (not merely empirically) distinct.

The objections to such a view seem to me very strong. After all, a human race may be conceived having neither eyes nor ears and yet endowed with a type of experience resembling our own in certain general traits. Their art would be very different from ours. Further, new arts constantly arise in the course of history. Painting grew out of Byzantine mosaics; sculpture was originally an integral part of architecture—both may be an integral part of town-planning; music had no existence apart from song, etc. Recent arts are the movies and the radio drama. Art is the activity of organizing a material so as to be pleasing in perception—so as to give the perceiver an integral, rounded "experience." Since any material or combination of materials may be shaped into beauty, the number of artistic media is in principle unlimited. To what art belong good manners, a personal style of dressing and talking, pleasant conversation—the sort of aesthetic shaping that we all practice daily? Are they one art or several arts? It might seem as if all the means used to give a total unified impression ought to be considered one art. Song is not a combination of two arts, poetry *plus* music, like one cake put upon another. In dancing to music, the movements and the music are fused into one organic whole; the division into two arts is "merely empirical," whereas the aesthetic reality is an integral whole. When the Greeks painted their statues, this was not a simple addition of two arts. A church service, in so far as it is an aesthetic experience, is a whole, although numerous media may be empirically distinguished. Man, says Schiller, *"soll alles Inner veräussern und alles Äussere formen."* The emphasis should be put upon *"alles* Äussere"—*all* materials can be shaped into beauty, the possible media are infinite in number. Historical traditions arise, certain media become traditional like colours on canvas or theatrical representation. But there are always numerous media which do not fit into the classifications based upon the more important traditions. Dewey asks:

What can such classifications make out of sculpture in relief, high and low, of marble figures on tombs, carved on wooden doors and cast in bronze doors? What about carvings on capitals, friezes, cornices, canopies, brackets? How do the minor arts fit in, workings in ivory, alabaster, plaster-paris, terra-cotta, silver and gold, ornamental iron work in brackets, signs, hinges, screens and grills? [19]

All classifications can here be made, since the materials are a continuum with all sorts of intermediary forms and endless overlappings and combinations. If we distinguish between aesthetic "form" and the "material" formed, it seems evident that the differences between the various arts and *genres* belong altogether to the material side and leave aesthetic form unaffected.

If one were to accept such a theory, Cassirer objects,

one would, by so doing, be led to the strange conclusion that, by calling Beethoven a great musician, Rembrandt a great painter, Homer a great epic poet, Shakespeare a great dramatist, only inconsequential empirical marginal conditions were expressed by such assertions, conditions *aesthetically* quite unimportant and for their characteristics as *artists* entirely superfluous. [20]

In the same way, one might argue, it is no indifferent matter

[19] *Art as Experience,* p. 223.
[20] *Zur Logik der Kulturwissenschaften,* p. 130.

that Ariosto wrote a romance and Virgil an epic, or that
D. G. Rossetti wrote sonnets and Wordsworth long poems as
well as short. No such things are indifferent—or rather, the
one important thing, to which everything adds up, is that
Wordsworth was Wordsworth and Rossetti was Rossetti. Of
course, it is no matter of indifference that Shakespeare wrote
for the stage, or, in brief, all such circumstances added together,
that Shakespeare was Shakespeare. Yet aesthetically the essential point is that the stage as a traditional medium belonged to
the "material" side of his works of art, not to their "formal"
side. And on the material side there are no barriers between
media—they may merge by insensible gradations.

Cassirer is quite right in saying: "Beethoven's intuition is in
the realm of music. Phidias' intuition is in that of sculpture,
Milton's in epic poetry, and Goethe's in lyric poetry. All of this
concerns not merely the external husk, but the core of their
creative work."[21] But this only means that the imagination of
an artist works within some medium. Perhaps it was a mere
coincidence that originally presented this medium to his imagination. Perhaps he has to change and develop the medium in
order to make it a vehicle for what he wants to say. Perhaps,
having had an initial experience of various media, he chooses
the one which for some reason or other suits him best—a deaf
man, for instance, is not likely to choose music, nor a colour-
blind man painting. One puts a false interpretation upon these
facts, if one infers that the types of intuition enumerated by
Cassirer are categorial and *a priori* divisions.

One may very well, it may be added, recognize the non-
categorial and merely empirical status of the arts and at the
same time dislike the romantic confusions, rooted in a love of
suggestion for its own sake. Irving Babbitt was thoroughly
right in *The New Laokoon, An Essay on the Confusion of the
Arts* (1910). These romantics want to put us in a state of
sensuous, even voluptuous dreaming, they want to thrill us
with strange and surprising effects. There is no contradiction
between clear insight in the non-aesthetic character of such
endeavours and recognition of the merely empirical status of
the arts and *genres*.

[21] *Ibid.*, 131.

A similar tendency to apriorize merely empirical distinctions can be noticed in Cassirer's philosophy of language. When he speaks of "the form of *a* language," it is clear that the word "form" does not merely denote the nature of essence of language in general but also the fundamental and enduring linguistic habits of a particular people. Cassirer here uses the word "form" in the same way as Humboldt did when speaking of the *innere Sprachform* of a particular language. There is no objection to such a terminology, unless it leads to confusion between enduring linguistic habits (or even among these only the habits denominated grammatical) and linguistic form *per se*. For such a confusion would mean that "empirically" distinguished, historically conditioned habit-systems are apriorized into eternal subdivisions of speech as a universal form of activity.

Suppose we distinguish carefully between linguistic and artistic "form," on the one hand, and habits and traditions on the other. Suppose further that we call the "merely empirical" distinctions made among the latter: *Stilbegriffe*. Then we would have adopted a term introduced by Cassirer in *Zur Logik der Kulturwissenschaften*, using it in approximately the same sense as he does. In order to write the history of language and of art —thus Cassirer begins his exposition of what he means by *Stilbegriffe*—we need a great variety of terms describing the structure of artistic and linguistic phenomena. Open any grammar or any history of art or literature, and you will be able to grab them with both hands. Thus Wölfflin distinguishes between a "picturesque" and a "linear" style, and Humboldt introduces the notion of "polysynthetic" languages. These types of concepts, Cassirer goes on to say, differ both from those of natural science and from the concepts of value (*Wertbegriffe*).

So far no objection can be raised. Certainly history and the enquiry into general terms must keep pace; a theory of language and a theory of art are indispensable in writing the history of these activities.[22] But are the basic concepts in these theories—

[22] "On the one hand it is clear that the creation of a theory of language is not possible without constant reference to the results achieved in the history of language and in psychology of language. Such a theory can not be erected in the empty space of [mere] abstraction or speculation. But it is equally clear that empirical research in the realm of linguistics as in that of the psychology of language must constantly

the concepts of "language" and "art"—also *Stilbegriffe?* Cassirer says nothing about "art" in this context; but "language" evidently is included among the "concepts of style."[23] He says nothing about the relation of "concepts of style" to "concepts of value" and seems to have altogether forgotten that the latter have also a function in the theories of art and language. "Art" is obviously a value term, since a work of art is the better, the more it is art; on the other hand, no "picturesque" or "linear" work of art is the better, the more picturesque or linear it is. Similarly, "polysynthetic" is no value term, but "speech" is: only in so far as a person manages to express what he wants to express—and this is a question of degrees—has he achieved articulate speech.

Thus *Wertbegriffe* are seen to denote the "form" or eternal nature of art and language, whereas *Stilbegriffe* denote empirically demarcated tendencies and habits. But no such sharp distinction is to be found in Cassirer's book. The student of his thought is left with the task of working it out for himself.

III

*An Analysis of the Logic of History and the
Logic of Philosophy*

As we have seen, "Logos" in its highest, purest and most intense form is supposed to be identical with mathematical science. In *The Philosophy of Symbolic Forms* Cassirer always means mathematical science, when speaking of *Wissenschaft.*

---

presuppose concepts which can only be taken from the linguistic 'theory of forms.' If investigations are to be initiated to ascertain in which order the various classes of words occur in the linguistic development of the child, or to ascertain in which phase the child moves from the use of the 'single word sentence' to the 'paratactical' sentence, and from this latter to the 'hypotactical' sentence, it must be clear that in such procedure [of investigation] the meaning of quite definite basic categories of the 'theory of forms,' of grammar and of syntax, are laid down as basic. Elsewhere also it is shown again and again that empirical research loses itself in 'Scheinprobleme' and gets entangled in insoluble antinomies, if careful conceptual reflection concerning what precisely language 'is' does not come to the aid of such research and accompanies it constantly in the putting of its questions." *Zur Logik der Kulturwissenschaften,* 75.

[23] *Ibid.,* 75f.

History and philosophy are silently allowed to drop out of the picture.

Modern philosophers since Descartes have been chiefly interested in the thought-processes of mathematicians and scientists. They have until recently evinced little interest in those of the historians. And very few have even today discovered that their own philosophical activities might be as interesting logically as those of scientists and mathematicians. The logic of philosophical thought is a field which has not been discovered at all by the majority of philosophers. Yet it is difficult to see why general statements should not be made about the activity of philosophizing.

When exalting mathematical science to the highest place in our knowledge-getting life, Cassirer seems to have forgotten the claims of his own subject, philosophy. He has said excellent things on the activities of mathematicians and scientists, and also some good things on history. On the activity of philosophizing there is little more than a chapter on "Subjective and Objective Analysis" in *The Philosophy of Symbolic Forms*. And this chapter does not take us very far.

A brief criticism of other thinkers may be helpful. Dewey touches upon the logic of philosophy, or more specifically the logic of logical enquiry, in the Introduction to his *Logic*.[24] He believes that the philosopher's thought-processes can be accounted for by a pragmatic logic; they present no special difficulties. Similarly, logical positivists, when occasionally confronted with the problem, affirm that their own philosophy is a hypothesis of the same sort as any other scientific hypothesis. Their own philosophy, in other words, is only probable and must be verified by experience. But anyone who says: "Our philosophy is only a hypothesis," is surely talking nonsense; for in this statement is implicitly contained another one: "The criterion of verification is the ultimate court of appeal deciding the fate of each and every philosophy." An absolute, unhypothetical statement has been made. To put it in other words: *anyone who asserts that "philosophies are hypotheses," thereby affirms hypothesis-verification as the ultimate truth about our*

---

[24] *Logic: The Theory of Inquiry*, by John Dewey (New York, 1938).

knowledge-getting life. To put it in a third manner: when we
are supposed to be choosing between various systems of philosophical axioms by testing their applicability to experience, we
are also supposed already to *have* a philosophical system, of
which the idea of "applicability to experience" forms a part.
This shows that the logic of philosophy *does* present special
difficulties and does not fit into pragmatic logic.

What, then, is the logic of philosophical thinking? If philosophy is self-knowledge, the logic of philosophy is an account
of what happens in self-knowledge. That self-knowledge does
not fit into pragmatic logic can easily be shown. It is often
affirmed that all *a priori* truth is analytic and all empirical statements merely probable. But if one can be sure of an analytic
truth, one can certainly also be sure of the existence of the
thought-process in which the analytic truth is being sought; and
one can also affirm with certainty that the existential thought-
process in question belongs to a certain kind of thought-processes,
those which the theory calls analytic. Here is an element of
self-knowledge which is at once *a priori* and empirical. Further,
no verification of a hypothesis can take place, unless we can
know with certainty that we are verifying a hypothesis; an
infinite regress of verifying that we are verifying provides no
escape from nihilism—it is like lifting oneself by one's boot-
straps. Without an assertion *somewhere* there can be no probability, only a mass of hypothetical sentences; even an infinite
amount of "if-then"-sentences does not provide us with a
single probability. Self-knowledge that we are verifying is
accordingly indispensable. Similarly, the philosophical method
of analyzing linguistic statements presupposes the absolute
knowledge (at once empirical and *a priori*) that "this is a linguistic statement"—and this is a piece of self-knowledge,
knowledge of our own activity of speaking and of reconstructing other people's expressions.

In short, knowledge of our own activities and attitudes—
verifying analytic thinking, expressing oneself (speaking), reconstructing expressions (listening, reading), imagining, observing, philosophizing, etc.,—must in a sense be immediate
and direct, for otherwise the whole structure of knowledge

would break down. Self-knowledge is the basis of all other knowledge. Now self-knowledge is in one respect historical (knowledge of individual processes) and in another respect philosophical (knowledge of the general categories of activity, like those just mentioned). The history of philosophy is the history of a growing insight into the nature of our own activities. And the method of philosophy has been a sort of direct inspection of our activities, often called "reflection" upon them.

Now what has just been advanced as a criticism of pragmatism and logical positivism indicates the way I believe modern philosophy will develop.[25] And it also indicates a realm which Cassirer has left unexplored. The logical analysis of what philosophers are doing and how they do it—the logic of thinking the Idea, as Hegel would say—has become a problem to modern neo-Hegelians like Emil Lask, Theodor Litt, Richard Kroner and Benedetto Croce.[26] But Cassirer remains a neo-Kantian and refuses to venture into these problems. Abstract mathematics and unreal scientific constructions are to him the true nature of Logos. We go beyond him by identifying Logos with the Idea and interpreting philosophy as the self-consciousness of Logos.

The subject may also be approached from another angle, by a detour over the subject of "freedom and form." This was the theme of a volume of essays which Cassirer published during the first world war: *Freiheit und Form* (Berlin, 1916). The basic idea is that freely developing life finds its own law within itself, that "form" is no restriction on freedom, unless it be merely external, pseudo-classical, conventional, based upon

---

[25] Those interested in a fuller development of this criticism may read my article, "Analyse des Wirklichkeitsbegriffs," in *Theoria*, vol. IX, (1943).

[26] E. Lask: *Die Logik der Philosophie und die Kategorienlehre*, Ges. Schr. II, Tübingen, 1923.

Th.Litt: *Einleitung in die Philosophie*, 1933, p. 1-33; *Kant und Herder*, 1930, ch. 3; *Das Allgemeine im Aufbau der geisteswissenschaftlichen Erkenntnis*, Leipzig 1941 (a brief summary).

R. Kroner: *Von Kant bis Hegel*, I-II, Tübingen, 1921-1924, esp. vol. I, pp. 103ff, 289ff. Croce anticipated the Germans by several years. See his *Logica come scienza del concetto puro*, Bar. 1908.

outer pressure. In the volume mentioned Cassirer applied this idea to the fields of aesthetics, ethics, and politics.

As Cassirer himself points out, the problem of *The Philosophy of Symbolic Forms* is also at bottom a question of freedom and form. It might seem as if myth and language cut us off from reality, covering it with a many-coloured veil of "subjective" illusions. The free expansion of individuality might seem detrimental to our knowledge of reality. But Cassirer shows that this is not really the case. Pre-scientific symbolism is really a method of exploring reality, having its own type of objectivity, its own "form," in which the expansion of individuality issues.

What, according to Cassirer, is the "objectivity" or truth of myth? His answer is that the truth of myth is what myth *does* in the intuitive elaboration of experience. This view may be elucidated by a quotation from an American writer on art:

Science may seem dry and trivial or mechanical to those who have no desire to understand the world intellectually; and poetry seem tedious, futile, or trifling to those who care nothing for imaginative understanding. Each is right in his own sphere, and wrong only in supposing that his sphere leaves room for no other.[27]

The artist, he adds, is primarily the discoverer, just as the scientist is; the scientist invents abstract laws which may be used for the purposes of calculation and prediction; the artist explores reality in a different way. We see only by utilizing the vision of others, and this vision is embodied in the traditions of art. Pre-scientific symbolism, according to Cassirer, serves the purpose of imaginative, intuitive understanding. The passage just quoted corresponds to Cassirer's thought (and to the general trend of contemporary philosophy) also in another respect: in its tendency to leave out history and philosophy altogether. Failure to analyze the last-mentioned activities is indeed the weakness of contemporary thought. When this analysis has been performed, it will be clear, I believe, that individuality plays no less a rôle in history and philosophy than in art, myth, and language, and that here too the expansion of individuality is compatible with "form" and objectivity.

[27] A. Barnes: *The Art in Painting*, 37.

Only science is in substance impersonal. Of course, it takes individuals to create it, but individuality is no part of the results, which are strictly impersonal. "Freedom and form" as the *Leitmotiv* of Cassirer's philosophy cannot come into its own as long as mathematical science is taken to be the apex of our knowing life. As a system of practical procedures science is our way of controlling the forces of nature. Yet, if nature be something of the kind pictured by Alfred N. Whitehead, practical control is surely something very different from real understanding in the sense of *Verstehen*. Maybe natural history can only be dead history to us, a mere chronicle; at all events real understanding, where it is possible, i. e., in the human world, touches the rock-bottom of reality in a way that cannot be rivalled by the merely external approach of science. The apex of knowledge cannot therefore be sought in the latter; it is the self-knowledge of the mind.

If there is any truth in what has just been said, the problem of "freedom and form" is the fundamental problem of logic and epistemology. The compatibility of individuality of vision with objective truth must be established not only on the level of artistic, mythical, and linguistic symbolism but also on the level of historical and philosophical knowledge. Every philosopher has his own truths to reveal, and these truths are not mutually incompatible; only by being intensely himself, by working out his own deepest inspiration, will he bring a unique contribution to the progress of thought. Even if Cassirer has not worked out the theory of freedom and form in philosophical progress, he has, by his whole work, given us a brilliant illustration of it.

FOLKE LEANDER

HÖGSKOLA
GÖTEBORG, SWEDEN

10

M. F. Ashley Montagu

CASSIRER ON MYTHOLOGICAL THINKING

CASSIRER ON MYTHOLOGICAL THINKING

IN *SUBSTANZBEGRIFF UND FUNKTIONSBE-GRIFF* (1910) we learn that the study arose out of the attempt to comprehend the fundamental conceptions of mathematics from the point of view of logic. Cassirer found that it became necessary to analyze and trace back the fundamental presuppositions of the nature of a concept itself. This led to a renewed analysis of the principles of concepts in general.

In the course of his analysis of the special sciences it became evident that the systematic structure of the exact sciences assumes different forms according to the different logical perspectives in which they are regarded. Hence the necessity of the analysis of the forms of conceptual construction and of the general function of concepts; for it is obvious that the conception which is formed of the fundamental nature of the concept is directly significant in judging the questions of fact in any criticism of knowledge or metaphysics.

From such considerations with respect to the processes of knowing, and the conceptual formalization of that knowing as related to the pure sciences, Cassirer was led to a consideration of the more fundamental problem of the primitive origins of these processes and their development. The first fruits of his studies in this field he published in 1923, as the first instalment of a large work entitled *Philosophie der symbolischen Formen* (Bruno Cassirer Verlag, Berlin); this first volume was devoted to *"Die Sprache,"* in which the nature and function of language was considered. A second volume devoted to *"Das mythische Denken"*—which is discussed in the present chapter—was published in 1925; and the third and last volume, entitled *"Phä-nomenologie der Erkenntnis,"* made its appearance in 1929.

Of these volumes I think it is no exaggeration to say that they constitute perhaps the most important and certainly the most brilliant work in this field which has yet been published.

Before entering upon a presentation of Cassirer's treatment of the nature of mythological thinking it is necessary to present something of his views with respect to the nature of language as propaedeutic to the former.

Cassirer insists on the fact that in consciousness, whether theoretical, artistic, or linguistic, we see a kind of mirror, the image falling upon which reflects not only the nature of the object existing externally but also the nature of consciousness itself. All forms brought into being by the mind are due to a creative force, to a spontaneous act in the Kantian sense, thanks to which that which is realized is something quite other than a simple reception or registration of facts exterior or foreign to the mind. We are now dealing not only with an entering into the possession of facts, but with the lending to them of a certain character, with an integration of them in a determinate physical order. Thus, the act of consciousness which gives birth to one or the other of these forms, to science, to art, and to language, does not simply discover and reproduce an ensemble of pre-existent objects. This act, the processes which give birth to it, lead rather to this objective universe, and contribute towards constituting its being and structure. The essential function of language is not arbitrarily to assign designations to objects already formed and achieved; language is rather a means indispensable to that formation, even of objects. Similarly, in the plastic arts, the creative act consists in the construction of space, in conquering it, in opening a path of access to it, which each of these arts makes according to the manner that is specific to it. Similarly, in respect of language it is necessary to return to the theory of Wilhelm von Humboldt according to which the diversity of languages expresses the diversity of aspects from which the world is seen and conceived by the different linguistic groups, and which consequently contribute to the formation of the different representations of the world. But one cannot observe the intimate operations of the mind which are at work in the formation of language. Psychology, even after having abandoned the concepts of apperception and of association—concepts which during the nineteenth century stood in the way of the realization of Humboldt's ideas—does not provide a method which permits direct access to the specific process of the mind which ends by leading to the production of the verbal. What experimentation and introspection renders perceptible are the facts impregnated by language and by them, not the manner of formation, but the achieved state.

If one wishes to go back to the origin of language and, instead of being content with the linguistic facts and findings, one seeks to discover the creative principle, one can be satisfied only with those regions in which the formation of the language is known, in all its particulars, and to attempt by an analysis of the structure of the languages of these regions, by a regressive method, to arrive at the genetic factors of language.

Cassirer's study deals with the languages of a number of regions of this kind, inquiring into their mode of arriving at *an objective representation of the world.* According to Cassirer the lower animals are incapable of such objective representations; they find themselves enclosed in an environment, in which they live, move, and have their being, but which they are unable to oppose, and which they are incapable of viewing objectively, since they cannot transcend it, consider or conceive it. The impressions they receive do not pass beyond the level of urges to action, and between these they fail to develop those specific relations which result in a true notion of that objectivity which is essentially defined by the constancy and identity of the object. This transition from a world of action and effectiveness to the world of objective representation only begins to manifest itself, in mankind, at a stage which coincides with a certain phase in the development of language; viz., at that stage which the child exhibits when it grows to understand that a whole thing corresponds to a particular value or denomination, and at which it is constantly demanding of those about it the names of things. But it does not occur to the child to attach these designations to the representation of things already stabilized and consolidated. The child's questions bear rather more on the things themselves. For in the eyes of the child, as in the eyes of primitive peoples, the name is not an extrinsic denomination of the thing which one arbitrarily attaches to it, but it is rather an essential quality of the object of which it forms an integral part. The principal value of this denominative phase is that it tends to stabilize and to consolidate the objective representation of things and permits the child to conquer the objective world in which it is henceforth to live. For this task he needs some name. If, for a multiplicity of impressions one sets apart the same name, these different impressions will no longer remain strange to one another; in this way they will come to represent simply aspects of the modes of appearance of the same thing. The loss of this conceptual and symbolic function of the word leads to such effects as one may observe in those suffering from aphasia. That which language renders possible on the plane of objects, viz., a separation or distinction between *subjects* and *things*, it permits *equally in the domain of sentiment and volition*. In this domain also language is more than a simple means of expression and of communication; this it is only at the beginning of human life, when the infant gives expression without any reserve to the states of pleasure and of pain which it experiences; and it is language which provides the infant with a means of getting into contact with the outside world. Language prolongs these affective states, but it does not in any way alter them. Things, however, present another aspect as soon as the child acquires representational language. Henceforth, his vocal expressions will no longer be simple exclamations, nor of pure expansiveness apart from these emotional states. That which the child expresses is now informed by the fact that his expressions have taken the form of intelligible words, the child hears and understands what he himself says. He thus becomes capable of knowing his own states in a representative and objective manner, of apperceiving and looking at them as he does at external things. He thus becomes capable of reflecting upon his own affective life, and of adopting in relation to that life an attitude of contemplation. In this way his affective energies gradually lose that power of brutal constraint which it exercises, during early infancy, upon the "self." The fact that emotion attains to a consciousness of itself, renders man to some extent free of it. To the pure emotion are henceforth opposed those intellectual forces which support representational language. Emotion will now be held in constraint by these forces, it will no longer obtain an immediate and direct expression, but will have to justify itself before language, which now assumes the position of an instrument of the mind. In this connection we may recall the Greek idea that man must not abandon his passions, that these rather must be submitted to the judgment of the *Logos*, to that reason which is incorporated in language.

Thanks to its regulative powers, language transforms sentiments and volitions, and organizes them into a conscious will, *and thus contributes to the constitution of the moral self*. There is still another domain into which one can gain entry only through the medium of language, it is the *social* world. Up to a certain point in the moral evolution of humanity, all moral and intellectual community is bound to the linguistic community, in much the same way as men speaking a foreign language are excluded from the protection and advantages which are alone enjoyed by members of the community considered as equals. And in the development of the individual, language constitutes for the child, who is beginning to learn, a more important and a more direct experience than that of the social and normative bond. But when for his characteristic infantile state he commences to substitute representational language, and experiences the need of being understood by his environment, he discovers the necessity of adapting his own efforts without reservation to the customs characteristic of the community to which he belongs. Without losing anything of his own individuality, he must adapt himself to those among whom he is destined to live. It is thus through the medium of a particular language that the child becomes aware of the bond which ties it to a particular community. This social bond becomes closer and more spiritualized during the course of its development. When the child commences to pose the questions—*What is it?* and *Why?*—not only is he going to penetrate into the world of knowledge, but also into a conquest of that world and a collective possession of it. Not only does the tendency to possess a thing begin to give way before the desire to acquire knowledge, but what is still more important, the relations which hold him to his environment are going to be reorganized. The desire for physical assistance begins to transform itself into a desire for intellectual assistance; the contact of the child with the members of its environment is going to become a spiritual contact. Little by little, the constraint, the commands and prohibitions, the obediences and resistances, which up to now have characterized the relations between the child and the adult gives way to that reciprocity which exists between the one who asks and waits for a reply, and the one who takes an interest in the question asked and replies. Thus arise the bases of spiritual liberty and of that free collaboration which is the characteristic mark of society in so far as it is human.

Finally, Cassirer assigns a capital importance to language in the *construction of the world of pure imagination*, above all to that state of conscious development wherein the decisive distinction between the real and the imagined is not made. The question that has so much occupied psychologists, whether the play of the child represents for it a veritable reality or merely a conscious occupation with fictions, this question, asserts Cassirer, is malposed, since the play of the child, like the Myth, belongs to a phase of consciousness which does not yet understand the distinction between that which is real and that which merely is simply imagined. In the eyes of the child the world is not composed of pure objects, of real forms, it is, on the contrary, peopled by beings who are his equals; and the character of the living and the animate is not limited for him, to that which is specifically human. The world, for him, has the form of *Thou* and not of *That*. This anthropomorphism of the child arises out of the fact that the child speaks to the things which surround him, and the things speak to him. It is no accident that there is no substitute for dumb play; when playing the child does not cease to speak of and to the things with which he is playing. It is not that this activity is an accessory commentary of play, but rather it is an indispensable element of it. The child views every object, all beings, as an interlocutor of whom he asks questions and who reply to him. His relation to the world is above all else a verbal relation, and Cassirer asserts that *the child does not speak to things because he regards them as animate, but on the contrary, he regards them as animate because he speaks with them.* It is much later that the distinction is made between that which is pure thing and that which is animate and living. The most developed of languages still retain traces of this original state. The lack of such distinctions is strikingly evident when we study the languages, the mental instruments, of the simpler peoples, a study which is obviously necessary for any true understanding of mythological thinking.

Cassirer's approach to mythology is that of the neo-Kantian phenomenologist; he is not interested in mythology as such, but in the processes of consciousness which lead to the creation of myths. It will be recalled that he was originally concerned with inquiring into the bases of empirical knowledge, but since a knowledge of a world of empirical things or properties was preceded by a world characterized by mythical powers and forces, and since early philosophy drew its spiritual powers from and created its perspective upon the bases of these mythical factors, a consideration of them is clearly of importance. The relation between myth and philosophy is a close one; for if the myth is taken to be an indirect expression of reality, it can be understood only as an attempt to point the way, it is a preparation for philosophy. The form and content of myth impede the realization of a rational content of knowledge, which reflection alone reveals, and of which it discovers the kernel. An illustration of this effect of myth upon knowledge may be seen in the attempts of the sophists of the Fifth Century to work from myth to empirical knowledge, in their newly founded scientific wisdom. Myth was by them understood and explained, and translated into the language of popular philosophy, as an all embracing speculative science of nature or of ethical truth.

It is no accident, remarks Cassirer, that just that Greek thinker in whom the characteristic power of creating the mythical was so outstanding should reject the whole world of mythical images, namely, Plato. For it was Plato who was opposed to the attempts at myth-analysis in the manner of the Sophists and rhetoricians; for him these attempts represented a play of wit in a difficult, though not very refined, subject (*Phaedrus.*

229). Plato failed to see the significance of the mythical world, seeing it only as something opposed to pure knowledge. The myth must be separated from science, and appearance be distinguished from reality. The myth however transcends all material meaning; and here it occupies a definite place and plays a necessary part for our understanding of the world, and according to the philosophy of the Platonic school it can work as a true creative and formative motive. The profounder view which has conquered here has, in the continuity of Greek thought, not always been carried through nor had quite the same meaning. The Stoics as well as the neo-Platonists returned to the Platonic view—as did the Middle Ages and the Renaissance.

In the newer philosophy the myth becomes the problem of philosophy when it is recognized that there exists a primordial directive of the spirit, an intrinsic way of forming knowledge. The spirit (Geist) forges the conditions necessary to itself. In this connection Giambattista Vico may be regarded as the founder of the new philosophy of language and of mythology. The real and true knowledge of the unitary idea of the spirit is shown in the triad of Language, Art, and Myth.

The critical problem of the origin of the aesthetic and ethical judgment, which Kant inquired into, was transferred by Schelling to the field of myth. For Kant the problem does not ask for psychological origins or beginnings—but for pure existence and content. Myth does not make its appearance, like morality or art, as a self-contained world in itself, which may be measured by objective values and reality measurements, but it must be understood through its own immanent laws of structure and of being. Every attempt to make this world understandable by simple direct means only reveals the reflection of something else.

In the empirical comparisons of myths a distinct trend was noticeable to measure not only the range of mythical thinking but also to describe the unitary forms of consciousness and its characteristics. Just as in physics the concept of the unit of the physical world led to a deepening of its principles, so in folklore the problem of a general mythology instead of special research gained for it a new lease on life. Out of the conflicting schools there appeared no other way than to think in terms of a single source of myth and of a distinct form of orientation. From this way of treating myth arose the conception of a fundamental mythical view of the world. Fundamental and characteristic motives were found for the whole world, even where space and time relations could not be demonstrated. As soon as the attempt was made to separate these motives, to distinguish between them, and to discover which were the truly primitive ones, conflicting views were again brought to the fore more sharply than ever. It was the task of folklore in association with folk psychology to determine the order of the appearances and to uncover the general laws and principles with respect to the formation of myths. But the unity of these principles disappeared even before one had assured oneself of the existence of the necessary fullness and variety of myths.

Besides the mythology of nature, there is the mythology of the soul. In the first there are involved a large variety of myths which have a definite object of nature for their kernel. One always asked of each single myth whether it bore a distinct relation to some natural thing or event. One had to approach the matter in this way because only in this way could phantasy be distinguished, and a strictly objective position arrived at. But the arbitrary power of building hypotheses, seen in a strictly objective way, showed that it was nearly as great as the creation of phantasy. The older form of the storm and thunder mythology was the opposite of the astral mythology which itelf, again, took different forms, sun mythology, lunar mythology, and stellar mythology.

Another approach to the ultimate unity of myth creation attempted to see it not as a natural but more as a spiritual unity, expressing this unity not in the field of the object but as in the historical field of culture. Were it possible to find such a field of culture for the general origin of the great fundamental mythical motives and themes, as a center from which they eventually spread over the whole world, it would be a simple matter to explain the inner relation and systematic consequences of these themes and motives. If any such relation in a known form is obscure, it must appear at once, if one but refers to the best historical source for it. When the older theorists, e.g., Benfey, looked to India for the most important motives, there seemed to be certain striking evidences for the historical unity and association of myth forming; this became even more so when Babylonian culture became better known. With the finding of this homeland of culture the answer was also found to the question as to the home of myth and its unitary structure. The answer to Pan-Babylonianism is that myth could never have developed a consistent world viewpoint if it had been constituted out of a primitive magic, idea, dream, emotion or superstition. The path to such a *Weltanschauung* was much more likely to be there where there was in existence a distinct proof of a conception of the world as an ordered whole—a condition which was fulfilled in the beginning of Babylonian astronomy and cosmogony. From this spiritual and historical viewpoint the possibility is opened up that myth is not only a form of pure phantasy but is in itself a finished and comprehensive system. What, remarks Cassirer, is so interesting about this theory in the methodological sense is that not only does it attempt the empirical proof of the real historical origin of myth, but it also attempts to give a sort of *a priori* substantiation to the proper direction and goal of mythological research. That all myths have an astral origin and should in the end prove to be calendric, is stated by the students of the Pan-Babylonian school to be the basic principle of the method. It is a sort of Ariadne's thread, which is alone able to lead through the labyrinth of mythology. By this means it was not very difficult to fill in the various lacunae which the empiric tradition had somehow failed to make good,—but this very means showed ever more clearly that the fundamental problem of the unit of the mythological consciousness could not really be explained in the manner of the historical objective empirical school.

It becomes more and more certain that the simple statement of unity of the fundamental mythical ideas cannot really give any insight into the structure of the forms of mythical phantasy and of mythical thinking. To define the structure of this form, when one does not desert the basis of pure descriptive considerations, requires no more elaborate conception than Bastian's concept of "*Völkergedanken.*" Bastian maintained that the varieties of the objective approach do not simply consider the content and objects of mythology, but start off from the question as to the function of myth. The fundamental principle of this function should remain to be proved; in this way various resemblances are discovered and relations demonstrated. From the beginning the sought-for unity is both from the inside and the outside transferred from the phenomena of reality to those of the spirit. But this idealism, as long as it is received psychologically and determined through the categories of psychology, is not characterized by a single meaning. When we speak of mythology as the collective expression of mankind, this unity must finally be explained out of the unity of the human soul and out of the homogeneity of its behaviour. But the unity of the soul expresses itself in a great variety of potencies and forms. As soon as the question is asked which of these potencies play the respective rôles in the building up of the mythical world, there immediately arise conflicting and contradictory controversial explanations. Is the myth ultimately derived from the play of subjective phantasy, or does it in some cases rest upon a real view of things, upon which it is based? Is it a primitive form of knowledge (*Erkenntnis*) and in this connection is it a form of intellection, or does it belong rather to the sphere of affection and conation? To this question scientific myth-analysis has returned different answers. Just as formerly the theories differed with respect to the objects which were considered necessary to the creation of myths, in the same way they now differed in respect of the fundamental psychic processes to which these are considered to lead back. The conception of a pure intellectual mythology made its reappearance, the idea that the essence of the myth was to be sought in the intellectual analysis of experience.

In opposition to Schelling's demand for a tautegorical (expressing the same thing in different words, opposed to allegorical) analysis of myth an allegorical explanation was sought for (See Fritz Langer, *Intellektualmythologie*, Leipzig, 1916).

In all this is evident the danger to which the myth is exposed, the danger of becoming lost in the depths of a particular theory. In all these theories the sought-for unity is transferred in error to the particular elements instead of being looked for in that spiritual whole, the symbolic world of meaning, out of which these elements are created. We must, on the other hand, says Cassirer, look for the fundamental laws of the spirit to which the myth goes back. Just as in the process of arriving at knowledge The Rhapsody of Perceptions (*Rhapsodie der Wahrnehmungen*) is, by means of certain laws and forms of thinking, transmuted into knowledge, so we can and must ask for the creation of that form unity, the unending and manifold world of the myth, which is not a conglomerate of arbitrary ideas and meaningless notions, a characteristic spiritual genitor. We must look at the myth from a genetic-causal, teleological standpoint; in this way we shall find that what is presented to us is something which as a complete form possesses a self-sufficient being and an autochthonous sense.

The myth represents in itself the first attempts at a knowledge of the world, and since it furthermore possibly represents the earliest form of aesthetic phantasy, we see in it that particular unity of the spirit of which all separate forms are but a single manifestation. We see too, here, that instead of an original unity in which the opposites lose themselves, and seem to combine with one another, that the critical-transcendental idea-unit seeks the clear definition and delimitation of the separate forms in order to preserve them. The principle of this separation becomes clear when one compares here the problem of meaning with that of characterization—that is, when one reflects upon the way in which the various spiritual forms of expression, such as "Object" with "Idea or Image," and "Content" with "Sign," are related to one another.

In this we see the fundamental element of the parallelism, namely, the creative power of the "sign" in myth as in language, and in art, as well as in the process of forming a theoretical idea in a word, and in relation to the world. What Humboldt said of language, that man places it between himself and the internal and external world that is acting upon him, that he surrounds himself with a world of sounds with which to take up and to work up the world of objects, holds true also for the myth and for the aesthetic fancy. They are not so much reactions to impressions, which are exercised from the outside upon the spirit, but they are much more real spiritual activities. At the outset, in the definite sense of the primitive expression of the myth it is clear that we do not have to deal with a mere reflection or mirage of Reality (*Sein*), but with a characteristic treatment and presentation of it. Also here one can observe how in the beginning the tension between "Subject" and "Object," "Internal" and "External," gradually diminishes, a richer and multiform new middle state stepping in between both worlds. To the material world which it embraces and governs the spirit opposes its own independent world of images—the power of *Impression* gradually becomes more distinct and more conscious than the active power of *Expression*. But this creation does not yet in itself possess the character of an act of free will, but still bears the character of a natural necessity, the character of a certain psychic "mechanism." Since at this level there does not yet exist an independent and self-conscious free living "I," but because we here stand upon the threshold of the spiritual processes which are bound to react against each other, the "I" and the "World," the new world of the "Sign" must appear to the conciousness as a thoroughly objective reality. Every beginning of the myth, especially every magical conception of the world, is permeated by this belief in the existence of the objective power of the sign. Word magic, picture-magic, and script-magic provide the fundaments of magical practices and the magical view of the world. When one examines the complete structure of the mythical consciousness one can detect in this a characteristic paradox. For if the generally prevailing conception, that the fundamental urge of the myth is to vivify, is true, that is that it tends to take a concrete view in the statement and representation of all the elements of existence, how does it happen, then, that these urges point most intensely to the most unreal and non-vital; how is it that the shadow-empire of words, of images, and signs gains such a substantial ascendancy and power over the mythical consciousness? How is it that it possesses this belief in the abstract, in this cult of symbols in a world in which the general idea is nothing, the sensation (*Empfindung*), the direct urge, the (sensible) psychic perception and outlook seem to be everything? The answer to this question, says Cassirer, can be found only when one is aware of the fact that it is improperly stated. The mythical world is not so concrete that it deals only with psychically 'objective' contents, or simply 'abstract' considerations, but both the thing and its meaning form one distinct and direct concrete unity, they are not differentiated from one another. The myth raises itself spiritually above the world of things, but it exchanges for the forms and images which it puts in their place only another form of restrictive existence. What the spirit appears to rescue from the shackles now becomes but a new shackle, which is so much more unyielding because it is not only a psychical power but a spiritual one. Nevertheless, such a state already contains in itself the immanent condition of its future release. It already contains the incipient possibility of a spiritual liberation which in the progress of the magical-mythical world-idea will eventually arrive at a characteristic religious world-idea. During this transition it becomes necessary for the spirit to place itself in a new and free relation to the world of images and signs, but, at the same time, in a different way than formerly, sees through this relationship, and in this way raises itself above it, though living it still and needing it.

And in still further measure and in greater distinctness stands for us the dialectic of these fundamental relations, their analysis and synthesis, which the spirit through its own self-made world of images experiences, when we here compare the myth with all other forms of symbolic expression. In the case of language also there is at first no sharp line of separation by means of which the word and its meaning, the thing content of "idea" and the simple content are distinguished from one another. The nominalist viewpoint, for which words are conventional signs, simply *flatus vocis*, is the result of later reflection but not the direct expression of the direct natural language consciousness. For this the existence of things in words is not only indicated as indirect, but is contained and present in it anyway. In the language consciousness of the primitive and in that of the child one can demonstrate this concrescence of names and things in very pregnant examples—one has only to think of the different varieties of the taboo names. But in the progression of the spiritual development of language there is also here achieved a sharper and ever more conscious separation between the Word and Being or Existence, between the Meaning and the Meant. Opposed to all other physical being and all physical activity the word appears as autonomous and characteristic, in its purely ideal and significative function.

A new stage of the separation is next witnessed in art. Here, too, there is in the beginning no clear distinction between the "Ideal" and the "Real." The beginning of the formation and of the cultivation of art reaches back to a sphere in which the act of cultivation itself is strongly rooted in the magical idea, and is directed to a definite magical end, of which the picture (*Bild*) is yet in no way independent, and has no pure aesthetic meaning. Nevertheless already in the first impulse of characteristic artistic configurations, in the stages of spiritual forms of expression, quite a new principle is attained. The view of the world which the spirit opposes to the simple world of matter and of things subsequently attains here to a pure immanent value and truth. It does not attach itself or refer to another; but it simply *is*, and consists in itself. Out of the sphere of activity (*Wirksamkeit*), in which the mythical consciousness, and out of the sphere of meaning, in which the marks of language remain, we are now transferred to a sphere, in which so to say, only the pure essence (*Sein*), only its own innermost nature (*Wesenheit*) of the image (*Bildes*) is seized as such. Thus, the world of images forms in itself a Kosmos which is complete in itself, and which rests within its own centre of gravity. And to it the spirit is now first able to find a free relation. The aesthetic world is measured according to the measure of things, the realistic outlook according to a world of appearance:—but since in just this appearance the *relation* to direct reality, to the world of being and action (*Wirken*), in which also the magical-mythical outlook has its being, is now left behind, there is thus made a completely new step towards truth. Thus there present themselves in relation to Myth, Language, and to Art, configurations which are linked directly together in a certain historical series, by means of a certain systematic progression (*Stufengang*), and ideal progress (*Fortschritt*), as the object of which it can be said the spirit in its own creations, in its self-made symbols, not only exists and lives, but gains its significance. There is a certain pertinence, in this connection, in that dominant theme of Hegel's *Phenomenology of the Spirit*, namely, that the object of development lies in the comprehension and expression of the fact that the spiritual being is not only "Substance" but just as much "Subject." In this respect the problems which grow out of a "Philosophy of Mythology" resolve themselves once more to such as arise from the philosophy of pure logic. Then also science separates itself from the other stages of spiritual life, not because it stands in need of any kind of mediation or intervention through signs and symbols, seeking naked truth, the truth of "things-in-themselves," but because it uses the symbols differently and more profoundly than the former is able to do, and recognizes and understands them as such, i.e., as symbols. Furthermore, this is not accomplished at one stroke; rather there is here also repeated, at a new stage, the typical fundamental relation of the spirit to its own creation. Here also must the freedom of this creation be gained and secured in continuous critical work. The utilization of hypotheses, and its characteristic function to advance the foundations of knowledge, determines that, so long as this knowledge is not secured, the principles of science are unable to express themselves in other than *dinglicher*, i.e., material, or in half mythical form.

Every student of primitive peoples and of mythology would recognize in Cassirer's views on mythological thinking, which have here been presented only partially, a valuable contribution towards the clarification of a difficult problem. In a brilliant chapter in which Cassirer discusses "the dialectic of the mythical consciousness," he shows how interrelated and interdependent the mythical and religious consciousness are, and that there can really be no distinction between them; there is a difference in form, but not in substance. An admirable discussion of the relation of "speech" to "language" and of "sound" to "meaning" (already dealt with at length in the first volume of the *Symbolischen Formen*) leads to a brief discussion of writing.

Cassirer points out that all writing begins as picture-signs which do not in themselves embrace any meaning or communicative characters. The picture-sign takes the place rather of the object itself, replaces it, and stands for it.

This statement is perfectly true of all forms of primitive writing. One of the most primitive forms of writing, for example, with which we are acquainted is that invented and practiced by certain Australian tribes. On the message sticks which they send from one tribe to another the signs which they make fulfill all the specifications stated by Cassirer.

Cassirer also states that at first writing forms a part of the sphere of magic. The sign which is stamped on the object draws it into the circle of its own effect and keeps away strange influences.

The anthropological data lend full support to this idea. It may even be that the magicians were the first to invent writing, though it would at present be impossible to prove such a suggestion or even to prove that the magicians were among the first to use picture signs. The evidence does, however, suggest that this is highly probable.

I can only have succeeded in giving a faint indication of the value and quality of Cassirer's contribution to our understanding of mythological thinking in general and that of pre-literate peoples in particular. To appreciate Cassirer's great work at its full value the reader is recommended to go to the original work. This essay must be regarded as but a footnote to it.

M. F. Ashley Montagu

Philadelphia, Penna.

II

Susanne K. Langer

ON CASSIRER'S THEORY OF LANGUAGE
AND MYTH

ON CASSIRER'S THEORY OF LANGUAGE
AND MYTH

EVERY philosopher has his tradition. His thought has developed amid certain problems, certain basic alternatives of opinion, that embody the key concepts which dominate his time and his environment and which will always be reflected, positively or by negation, in his own work. They are the forms of thought he has inherited, wherein he naturally thinks, or from which his maturer conceptions depart.

The continuity of culture lies in this handing down of usable forms. Any campaign to discard tradition for the sake of novelty as such, without specific reason in each case to break through a certain convention of thought, leads to dilettantism, whether it be in philosophy, in art, or in social and moral institutions. As every person has his mother tongue in terms of which he cannot help thinking his earliest thoughts, so every scholar has a philosophical mother tongue, which colors his natural *Weltanschauung*. He may have been nurtured in a particular school of thought, or his heritage may be the less conscious one of "common sense," the popular metaphysic of his generation; but he speaks some intellectual language that has been bestowed on him, with its whole cargo of preconceptions, distinctions, and evaluations, by his official and unofficial teachers.

A great philosopher, however, has something new and vital to present in whatever philosophical mold he may have been given. The tenor of his thought stems from the past; but his specific problems take shape in the face of a living present, and his dealing with them reflects the entire, ever-nascent activity of his own day. In all the great periods of philosophy, the leading minds of the time have carried their traditional learning lightly, and felt most deeply the challenge of things which were new in their age. It is the new that calls urgently for interpretation; and a true philosopher is a person to whom something in the weary old world always appears new and uncomprehended.

There are certain "dead periods" in the history of philosophy, when the whole subject seems to shrink into a hard, small shell, treasured only by scholars in large universities. The common man knows little about it and cares less. What marks such a purely academic phase of philosophical thought is that its substance as well as its form is furnished by a scholastic tradition; not only the categories, but the problems of debate are familiar. Precisely in the most eventful epochs, when intellectual activity in other fields is brilliant and exciting, there is quite apt to be a lapse in philosophy; the greatest minds are engaged elsewhere; reflection and interpretation are in abeyance when the tempo of life is at its highest. New ideas are too kaleidoscopic to be systematically construed or to suggest general propositions. Professional philosophers, therefore, continue to argue matters which their predecessors have brought to no conclusion, and to argue them from the same standpoints that yielded no insight before.

We have only recently passed through an "academic" phase of philosophy, a phase of stale problems and deadlocked "isms." But today we are on the threshold of a new creative period. The most telling sign of this is the tendency of great minds to see philosophical implications in facts and problems belonging to other fields of learning—mathematics, anthropology, psychology, physics, history, and the arts. Familiar things like language or dream, or the mensurability of time, appear in new universal connections which involve highly interesting abstract issues. Even the layman lends his ear to "semantics" or to new excitements about "relativity."

Cassirer had all the marks of a great thinker in a new philosophical period. His standpoint was a tradition which he inherited—the Kantian "critical" philosophy seen in the light of its later developments, which raised the doctrine of transcendental forms to the level of a transcendental theory of Being. His writings bear witness that he often reviewed and pondered the foundations of this position. There was nothing accidental or sentimental in his adherence to it; he maintained it throughout his life, because he found it fruitful, suggestive of new interpretations. In his greatest works this basic idealism is implicit rather than under direct discussion; and the turn it gives to his treatment of the most baffling questions removes it utterly from that treadmill of purely partisan reiteration and defense which is the fate of decadent metaphysical convictions. There is little of polemic or apologetic in Cassirer's writings; he was too enthusiastic about solving definite problems to spend his time vindicating his method or discussing what to him was only a starting-point.

One of the venerable puzzles which he treated with entirely new insight from his peculiarly free and yet scholarly point of view is the relation of language and myth. Here we find at the outset the surprising, unorthodox working of his mind: for what originally led him to this problem was not the contemplation of poetry, but of science. For generations the advocates of scientific thinking bemoaned the difficulties which nature seems to plant in its path—the misconceptions bred by "ignorance" and even by language itself. It took Cassirer to see that those difficulties themselves were worth investigating. Ignorance is a negative condition; why should the mere absence of correct conceptions lead to *mis*conceptions? And why should language, supposedly a practical instrument for conveying thought, serve to resist and distort scientific thought? The misconceptions interested him.

If the logical and factual type of thought which science demands is hard to maintain, there must be some other mode of thinking which constantly interferes with it. Language, the expression of thought, could not possibly be a hindrance to thought as such; if it distorts scientific conception, it must do so merely by giving preference and support to such another mode.

Now, all thinking is "realistic" in the sense that it deals with phenomena as they present themselves in immediate experience. There cannot be a way of thinking that is not true to the reports of sense. If there are two modes of thinking, there must be two different modes of perceiving things, of apprehending the very data of thought. To *observe* the wind, for instance, as a purely physical atmospheric disturbance, and *think* of it as a divine power or an angry creature would be purely capricious, playful, irresponsible. But thinking is serious business, and probably always has been; and it is not likely that language, the physical image of thought, portrays a pattern of mere fancies and vagaries. In so far as language is incompatible with scientific reasoning, it must reflect a system of thought that is soberly true to a *mode of experiencing*, of seeing and feeling, different from our accepted mode of experiencing "facts."[1]

This idea, first suggested by the difficulties of scientific conception, opened up a new realm of epistemological research to its author; for it made the *forms of misunderstanding* take on a positive rather than a negative importance as *archaic forms of understanding*. The hypostatic and poetic tinge of language which makes it so often recalcitrant to scientific purposes is a record not only of a different way of thinking, but of seeing, feeling, conceiving experience—a way that was probably paramount in the ages when language itself came into being. The whole problem of mind and its relation to "reality" took a new turn with the hypothesis that former civilizations may actually have dealt with a "real world" differently constituted from our own world of things with their universal qualities and causal relationships. But how can that older "reality" be recaptured and demonstrated? And how can the change from one way of apprehending nature to another be accounted for?

The answer to this methodological question came to him as a suggestion from metaphysics. "*Es ist der Geist der sich den Körper baut*," said Goethe. And the post-Kantian idealists, from Fichte to Hermann Cohen, had gone even beyond that tenet; so they might well have said, "*Es ist der Geist der sich das Weltall baut.*" To a romanticist that would have been little more than a figure of speech, expressing the relative importance of mind and matter. But in Cassirer's bold and uncomplacent mind such a belief—which he held as a basic intellectual postulate, not as a value-judgment—immediately raised the ques-

[1] Cf. *Language and Myth*, 10f.

tion: How? By what process and what means does the human spirit *construct* its physical world?

Kant had already proposed the answer: By supplying the transcendental constituent of *form*. Kant regarded this form as a fixed pattern, the same in all human experience; the categories of thought which find their clearest expression in science, seemed to him to govern all empirical experience, and to be reflected in the structure of language. But the structure of language is just what modern scientific thought finds uncongenial. It embodies a metaphysic of substance and attribute; whereas science operates more and more with the concept of *function*, which is articulated in mathematics.[2] There is good reason why mathematicians have abandoned verbal propositions almost entirely and resorted to a symbolism which expresses different metaphysical assumptions, different categories of thought altogether.

At this point Cassirer, reflecting on the shift from substantive to functional thinking, found the key to the methodological problem: two different symbolisms revealed two radically different forms of thought; does not every form of *Anschauung* have its symbolic mode? Might not an exhaustive study of symbolic forms reveal just how the human mind, in its various stages, has variously construed the "reality" with which it dealt? To *construe* the equivocally "given" is to *construct* the phenomenon for experience. And so the Kantian principle, fructified by a wholly new problem of science, led beyond the Kantian doctrine to the Philosophy of Symbolic Forms.

The very plan of this work departs from all previous approaches to epistemology by not assuming either that the mind is concerned essentially with facts, or that its prime talent is discursive reason. A careful study of the scientific misconceptions which language begets revealed the fact that its subject-predicate structure, which reflects a "natural" ontology of substance and attribute, is not its only metaphysical trait. Language is born of the need for emotional expression. Yet it is not exclamatory. It is essentially hypostatic, seeking to distinguish, emphasize, and hold the object of feeling rather than

[2] See *Substance and Function*, Ch. I.

to communicate the feeling itself. To fix the object as a permanent focus point in experience is the function of the *name*. Whatever evokes emotion may therefore receive a name; and, if this object is not a thing—if it is an act, or a phenomenon like lightning, or a sound, or some other intangible item—, the name nevertheless gives it the unity, permanence, and apparent substantiality of a "thing."

This hypostasis, entailed by the primitive office of language, really lies deeper even than nomenclature, which merely reflects it: for it is a fundamental trait of all *imagination*. The very word "imagination" denotes a process of image-making. An image is only an aspect of the actual thing it represents. It may be not even a completely or carefully abstracted aspect. Its importance lies in the fact that it symbolizes the whole—the thing, person, occasion, or what-not—from which it is an abstract. A thing has a history, an event passes irrevocably away, actual experience is transient and would exhaust itself in a series of unique occasions, were it not for the permanence of the symbol whereby it may be recalled and possessed. Imagination is a free and continual production of images to "mean" experience— past or present or even merely possible experience.

Imagination is the primary talent of the human mind, the activity in whose service language was evolved. The imaginative mode of ideation is not "logical" after the manner of discursive reason. It has a logic of its own, a definite pattern of identifications and concentrations which bring a very deluge of ideas, all charged with intense and often widely diverse feelings, together in one symbol.

Symbols are the indispensable instruments of conception. To undergo an experience, to react to immediate or conditional stimuli (as animals react to warning or guiding signs), is not to "have" experience in the characteristically human sense, which is to conceive it, hold it in the mind as a so-called "content of consciousness," and consequently be able to think *about* it.[3] To a human mind, every experience—a sensation of light or color, a fright, a fall, a continuous noise like the roar of breakers

[3] Cf. *Language and Myth*, 38.

on the beach—exhibits, in retrospect, a unity and self-identity that make it almost as static and tangible as a solid object. By virtue of this hypostatization it may be *referred to,* much as an object may be *pointed at;* and therefore the mind can think about it without its actual recurrence. In its symbolic image the experience is *conceived,* instead of just physiologically remembered.[4]

Cassirer's greatest epistemological contribution is his approach to the problem of mind through a study of the primitive forms of conception. His reflections on science had taught him that all conception is intimately bound to expression; and the forms of expression, which determine those of conception, are symbolic forms. So he was led to his central problem, the diversity of symbolic forms and their interrelation in the edifice of human culture.

He distinguished, as so many autonomous forms, language, myth, art, and science.[5] In examining their respective patterns he made his first startling discovery: myth and language appeared as genuine twin creatures, born of the same phase of human mentality, exhibiting analogous formal traits, despite their obvious diversities of content. Language, on the one hand, seems to have articulated and established mythological concepts, whereas, on the other hand, its own meanings are essentially images functioning mythically. The two modes of thought have grown up together, as conception and expression, respectively, of the primitive human world.

The earliest products of mythic thinking are not permanent, self-identical, and clearly distinguished "gods;" neither are they immaterial spirits. They are like dream elements—objects endowed with daemonic import, haunted places, accidental shapes in nature resembling something ominous—all manner of shifting, fantastic images which speak of Good and Evil, of Life and Death, to the impressionable and creative mind of man. Their common trait is a quality that characterizes everything in the sphere of myth, magic, and religion, and also the

---

[4] See *An Essay on Man,* chapters 2 and 3, *passim.*
[5] *Language and Myth,* 8.

earliest ethical conceptions—the quality of *holiness*.[6] Holiness may appertain to almost anything; it is the mystery that appears as magic, as taboo, as daemonic power, as miracle, and as divinity. The first dichotomy in the emotive or mythic phase of mentality is not, as for discursive reason, the opposition of "yes" and "no," of "a" and "non-a," or truth and falsity; the basic dichotomy here is between the sacred and the profane. Human beings actually apprehend *values* and expressions of values *before* they formulate and entertain *facts*.

All mythic constructions are symbols of value—of life and power, or of violence, evil, and death. They are charged with feeling, and have a way of absorbing into themselves more and more intensive meanings, sometimes even logically conflicting imports. Therefore mythic symbols do not give rise to discursive understanding; they do beget a kind of understanding, but not by sorting out concepts and relating them in a distinct pattern; they tend, on the contrary, merely to bring together great complexes of cognate ideas, in which all distinctive features are merged and swallowed. "Here we find in operation a law which might actually be called the law of the levelling and extinction of specific differences," says Cassirer, in *Language and Myth*. "Every part of a whole is the whole itself, every specimen is equivalent to the entire species."[7] The significance of mythic structures is not formally and arbitrarily assigned to them, as convention assigns one exact meaning to a recognized symbol; rather, their meaning seems to dwell in them as life dwells in a body; they are animated by it, it is of their essence, and the naïve, awe-struck mind *finds* it, as the quality of "holiness." Therefore mythic symbols do not even appear to be symbols; they appear as holy objects or places or beings, and their import is felt as an inherent *power*.

This really amounts to another "law" of imaginative conception. Just as specific differences of meaning are obliterated in nondiscursive symbolization, the very distinction between form and content, between the entity (thing, image, gesture, or

[6] See *Die Philosophie der symbolischen Formen*, II, 97 ff.
[7] Pp. 91-92.

natural event) which is the symbol, and the idea or feeling which is its meaning, is lost, or rather: is not yet found. This is a momentous fact, for it is the basis of all superstition and strange cosmogony, as well as of religious belief. To believe in the existence of improbable or quite fantastic things and beings would be inexplicable folly if beliefs were dictated essentially by practical experience. But the mythic interpretation of reality rests on the principle that the veneration appropriate to the meaning of a symbol is focussed on the symbol itself, which is simply identified with its import. This creates a world punctuated by pre-eminent objects, mystic centers of power and holiness, to which more and more emotive meanings accrue as "properties." An intuitive recognition of their *import* takes the form of ardent, apparently irrational belief in the physical reality and power of the significant forms. This is the hypostatic mechanism of the mind by which the world is filled with magical things—fetishes and talismans, sacred trees, rocks, caves, and the vague, protean ghosts that inhabit them—and finally the world is peopled with a pantheon of permanent, more or less anthropomorphic gods. In these presences "reality" is concentrated for the mythic imagination; this is not "make-believe," not a willful or playful distortion of a radically different "given fact," but is *the way phenomena are given* to naïve apprehension.

Certainly the pattern of that world is altogether different from the pattern of the "material" world which confronts our sober common sense, follows the laws of causality, and exhibits a logical order of classes and subclasses, with their defining properties and relations, whereby each individual object either does or does not belong to any given class. Cassirer has summed up the logical contrast between the mode of mythic intuition and that of "factual" or "scientific" apprehension in very telling phrase:

In the realm of discursive conception there reigns a sort of diffuse light—and the further logical analysis proceeds, the further does this even clarity and luminosity extend. But in the ideational realm of myth and language there are always, besides those locations from which the strongest light proceeds, others that appear wrapped in profoundest darkness. While certain contents of perception become verbal-mythical centers of force, centers of significance, there are others which remain, one might say, beneath the threshold of meaning.[8]

His coupling of myth and language in this passage brings us back to the intimate connection between these two great symbolic forms which he traces to a common origin. The dawn of language was the dawn of the truly human mind, which meets us first of all as a rather highly developed organ of practical response *and of imagination,* or symbolic rendering of impressions. The first "holy objects" seem to be born of momentary emotional experiences—fright centering on a place or a thing, concentrated desire that manifests itself in a dreamlike image or a repeated gesture, triumph that issues naturally in festive dance and song, directed toward a symbol of power. Somewhere in the course of this high emotional life primitive man took to using his instinctive vocal talent as a source of such "holy objects," *sounds* with imaginative import: such vocal symbols are *names.*

In savage societies, names are treated not as conventional appellations, but as though they were physical proxies for their bearers. To call an object by an inappropriate name is to confound its very nature. In some cultures practically all language serves mystic purposes and is subject to the most impractical taboos and regulations. It is clearly of a piece with magic, religion and the whole pattern of intensive emotional symbolism which governs the pre-scientific mind. Names are the very essence of mythic symbols; nothing on earth is a more concentrated point of sheer meaning than the little, transient, invisible breath that constitutes a spoken word. Physically it is almost nothing. Yet it carries more definite and momentous import than any permanent holy object.[9] It can be invoked at will, anywhere and at any time, by a mere act of speech; merely *knowing* a word gives a person the power of using it; thus it is invisibly "had," carried about by its possessors.

[8] *Language and Myth,* 91.

[9] "Often it is the *name* of the deity, rather than the god himself, that seems to be the real source of efficacy." (*Language and Myth,* 48)

It is characteristic of mythic "powers" that they are completely contained in every fragment of matter, every sound, and every gesture which partakes of them.[10] This fact betrays their real nature, which is not that of physical forces, but of meanings; a meaning is indeed completely given by every symbol to which it attaches. The greater the "power" in proportion to its bearer, the more awe-inspiring will the latter be. So, as long as meaning is felt as an indwelling potency of certain physical objects, *words* must certainly rank high in the order of holy things.

But language has more than a purely denotative function. Its symbols are so manifold, so manageable, and so economical that a considerable number of them may be held in one "specious present," though each one physically passes away before the next is given; each has left its *meaning* to be apprehended in the same span of attention that takes in the whole series. Of course, the length of the span varies greatly with different mentalities. But as soon as two or more words are thus taken together in the mind of an interpretant, language has acquired its second function: it has engendered *discursive thought.*

The discursive mode of thinking is what we usually call "reason." It is not as primitive as the imaginative mode, because it arises from the syntactical nature of language; mythic envisagement and verbal expression are its forerunners. Yet it is a natural development from the earlier symbolic mode, which is pre-discursive, and thus in a strict and narrow sense "pre-rational."

Henceforth, the history of thought consists chiefly in the gradual achievement of factual, literal, and logical conception and expression. Obviously the only means to this end is language. But this instrument, it must be remembered, has a double nature. Its syntactical tendencies bestow the laws of logic on us; yet the primacy of *names* in its make-up holds it to the hypostatic way of thinking which belongs to its twin-phenomenon, myth. Consequently it leads us beyond the sphere of mythic and emotive thought, yet always pulls us back into it again; it is both the diffuse and tempered light that shows us the external world of "fact," and the array of spiritual lamps,

[10] Cf. *Language and Myth*, 92.

light-centers of intensive meaning, that throw the gleams and shadows of the dream world wherein our earliest experiences lay.

We have come so far along the difficult road of discursive thinking that the laws of logic seem to be the very frame of the mind, and rationality its essence. Kant regarded the categories of pure understanding as universal transcendental forms, imposed by the most naïve untutored mind on all its perceptions, so that self-identity, the dichotomy of "*a*" and "non-*a*," the relation of part and whole, and other axiomatic general concepts inhered in phenomena as their necessary conditions. Yet, from primitive apprehension to even the simplest rational construction is probably a far cry. It is interesting to see how Cassirer, who followed Kant in his "Copernican revolution," i.e., in the transcendental analysis of phenomena which traces their form to a non-phenomenal, subjective element, broadened the Kantian concept of form to make it a variable and anthropologically valid principle, without compromising the "critical" standpoint at all. Instead of accepting one categorial scheme— that of discursive thought—as the absolute way of experiencing reality, he finds it relative to a form of symbolic presentation; and as there are alternative symbolic forms, there are also alternative phenomenal "worlds." Mythic conception is categorially different from scientific conception; therefore it meets a different world of perceptions. Its objects are not self-identical, consistent, universally related; they condense many characters in one, have conflicting attributes and intermittent existence, the whole is contained in its parts, and the parts in each other. The world they constitute is a world of values, things "holy" against a vague background of commonplaces, or "profane" events, instead of a world of neutral physical facts. By this departure, the Kantian doctrine that identified all conception with discursive reason, making reason appear as an aboriginal human gift, is saved from its most serious fallacy, an unhistorical view of mind.

Cassirer called his *Essay on Man*, which briefly summarizes the *Philosophie der symbolischen Formen*, "An Introduction to a Philosophy of Human Culture." The subtitle is appropriate indeed; for the most striking thing about this philosophy viewed as a whole is the way the actual evolution of human customs, arts, ideas, and languages is not merely fitted into an idealistic interpretation of the world (as it may be fitted into almost any metaphysical picture), but is illumined and made accessible to serious study by working principles taken from Kantian epistemology. His emphasis on the constitutive character of symbolic renderings in the making of "experience" is the masterstroke that turns the purely speculative "critical" theory into an anthropological hypothesis, a key to several linguistic problems, a source of psychological understanding, and a guidepost in the maze of *Geistesgeschichte.*

It is, as I pointed out before, characteristic of Cassirer's thought that, although its basic principles stem from a philosophical tradition, its living material and immediate inspiration come from contemporary sources, from fields of research beyond his own. For many years the metaphysic of mind has been entirely divorced from the scientific study of mental phenomena; whether mind be an eternal essence or a transient epiphenomenon, a world substance or a biological instrument, makes little difference to our understanding of observed human or animal behavior. But Cassirer breaks this isolation of speculative thought; he uses the Kantian doctrine, that mind is constitutive of the "external world," to explain the *way* this world is experienced as well as the mere fact *that* it is experienced; and in so doing, of course, he makes his metaphysic meet the test of factual findings at every turn. His most interesting exhibits are psychological phenomena revealed in the psychiatric clinic and in ethnologists' reports. The baffling incapacities of impaired brains, the language of childhood, the savage's peculiar practices, the prevalence of myth in early cultures and its persistence in religious thought—these and other widely scattered facts receive new significance in the light of his philosophy. And that is the pragmatic measure of any speculative approach. A really cogent doctrine of mind cannot be irrelevant to psychology, any more than a good cosmological system can be meaningless for physics, or a theory of ethics inapplicable to jurisprudence and law.

The psychiatric phenomena which illustrate the existence of a mythic mode of thought, and point to its ancient and primitive nature, are striking and persuasive.[11] Among these is the fact that in certain pathological conditions of the brain the power of abstraction is lost, and the patient falls back on picturesque metaphorical language. In more aggravated cases the imagination, too, is impaired; and here we have a reversion almost to animal mentality. One symptom of this state which is significant for the philosophy of symbolism is that the sufferer is unable to tell a lie, feign any action, or do anything his actual situation does not dictate, though he may still find his way with immediate realities. If he is thirtsy, he can recognize and take a glass of water, and drink; but he cannot pick up an empty glass and demonstrate the act of drinking *as though* there were water in it, or even lift a full glass to his lips, if he is not thirsty. Such incapacities have been classified as "apractic" disorders; but Cassirer pointed out that they are not so much practical failures, as loss of the basic symbolic function, *envisagement of things not given*. This is borne out by a still more serious disturbance which occurs with the destruction of certain brain areas, inability to recognize "things," such as chairs and brooms and pieces of clothing, directly and instantly as objects denoted by their names. At this point, pathology furnishes a striking testimony of the real nature of language: for here, names lose their hypostatic office, the creation of permanent and particular *items* out of the flux of impressions. To a person thus afflicted, words have connotation, but experience does not readily correspond to the conceptual scheme of language, which makes *names* the preeminent points of rest, and requires *things* as the fundamental relata in reality. The connoted concepts are apt to be adjectival rather than substantive. Consequently the world confronting the patient is not composed of objects immediately "given" in experience; it is composed of sense data, which he must "associate" to form "things," much as Hume supposed the normal mind to do.

Most of the psychological phenomena that caught Cassirer's interest arose from the psychiatric work of Kurt Goldstein, who

---

[11] For a full treatment of this material see *Philosophie der symbolischen Formen*, III, part 3, *passim*.

has dealt chiefly with cases of cerebral damage caused by physical accident. But the range of psychological researches which bear out Cassirer's theory of mind is much wider; it includes the whole field of so-called "dynamic psychology," the somewhat chaotic store of new ideas and disconcerting facts with which Sigmund Freud alarmed his generation. Cassirer himself never explored this fund of corroborative evidence; he found himself in such fundamental disagreement with Freud on the nature of the dynamic motive—which the psychologist regarded as not only derived from the sex impulse, but forever bound to it, and which the philosopher saw liberated in science, art, religion, and everything that constitutes the "self-realization of the spirit"—that there seemed to be simply no point of contact between their respective doctrines. Cassirer felt that to Freud all those cultural achievements were mere by-products of the unchanging animalian "libido," symptoms of its blind activity and continual frustration; whereas to him they were the consummation of a spiritual process which merely took its rise from the blind excitement of the animal "libido," but received its importance and meanings from the phenomena of awareness and creativity, the envisagement, reason, and cognition it produced. This basic difference of *evaluations* of the life process made Cassirer hesitate to make any part of Freud's doctrine his own; at the end of his life he had, apparently, just begun to study the important relationship between "dynamic psychology" and the philosophy of symbolic forms.

It is, indeed, only in regard to the *forms* of thought that a parallel obtains between these systems; but that parallel is close and vital, none the less. For, the "dream work" of Freud's "unconscious" mental mechanism is almost exactly the "mythic mode" which Cassirer describes as the primitive form of ideation, wherein an intense feeling is spontaneously expressed in a symbol, an image seen in something or formed for the mind's eye by the excited imagination. Such expression is effortless and therefore unexhausting; its products are images charged with meanings, but the meanings remain implicit, so that the emotions they command seem to be centered on the image rather than on anything it merely conveys; in the image, which may be a vision, a gesture, a sound-form (musical image) or a word as readily as an external object, many meanings may be concentrated, many ideas telescoped and interfused, and incompatible emotions simultaneously expressed.

The mythic mind never perceives passively, never merely contemplates things; all its observations spring from some act of participation, some act of emotion and will. Even as mythic imagination materializes in permanent forms, and presents us with definite outlines of an 'objective' world of beings, the significance of this world becomes clear to us only if we can still detect, underneath it all, that dynamic sense of life from which it originally arose. Only where this vital feeling is stirred from within, where it expresses itself as love or hate, fear or hope, joy or sorrow, mythic imagination is roused to the pitch of excitement at which it begets a definite world of representations. (*Philosophie der symbolischen Formen*, II, 90.)

For a person whose apprehension is under the spell of this mythico-religious attitude, it is as though the whole world were simply annihilated; the immediate content, whatever it be, that commands his religious interest so completely fills his consciousness that nothing else can exist beside and apart from it. The ego is spending all its energy on this single object, lives in it, loses itself in it. Instead of a widening of intuitive experience, we find here its extreme limitation; instead of expansion . . . we have here an impulse toward concentration; instead of extensive distribution, intensive compression. This focussing of all forces on a single point is the prerequisite for all mythical thinking and mythical formulation. When, on the one hand, the entire self is given up to a single impression, is 'possessed' by it and, on the other hand, there is the utmost tension between the subject and its object, the outer world; when external reality is not merely viewed and contemplated, but overcomes a man in sheer immediacy, with emotions of fear or hope, terror or wish fulfillment: then the spark jumps somehow across, the tension finds release, as the subjective excitement becomes objectified and confronts the mind as a god or a daemon. (*Language and Myth*, 32-33.)

. . . this peculiar genesis determines the type of intellectual content that is common to language and myth . . . present reality, as mythic or linguistic conception stresses and shapes it, fills the entire subjective realm. . . . At this point, the word which denotes that thought content is not a mere conventional symbol, but is merged with its object in an indissoluble unity. . . . The potential between 'symbol' and 'meaning' is resolved; in place of a more or less adequate 'expression,' we find a relation of identity, of complete congruence between 'image' and 'object,' between the name and the thing.

   . . . the same sort of hypostatization or transubstantiation occurs in other realms of mental creativity; indeed, it seems to be the typical process in all unconscious ideation. (*Ibid.,* 57-58.)

Mythology presents us with a world which is not, indeed, devoid of structure and internal organization, but which, none the less, is not divided according to the categories of reality, into 'things' and 'properties.' Here all forms of Being exhibit, as yet, a peculiar 'fluidity;' they are distinct without being really separate. Every form is capable of changing, on the spur of the moment, even into its very opposite. . . . One and the same entity may not only undergo constant change into sucessive guises, but it combines within itself, at one and the same instant of its existence, a wealth of different and even incompatible natures. (*Philosophie der symbolischen Formen,* III, 71-72.)

Above all, there is a complete lack of any clear division between mere 'imagining' and 'real' perception, between wish and fulfilment, between image and object. This is most clearly revealed by the decisive rôle which dream experiences play in the development of mythic consciousness. . . . It is beyond doubt that certain mythic concepts can be understood, in all their peculiar complexity, only in so far as one realizes that for mythic thought and 'experience' there is but a continuous and fluid transition from the world of dream to objective 'reality.' (*Ibid.,* II, 48-49.)

The world of myth is a dramatic world—a world of actions, of forces, of conflicting powers. In every phenomenon of nature it [mythic consciousness] sees the collision of these powers. Mythical perception is always impregnated with these emotional qualities. Whatever is seen or felt is surrounded by a special atmosphere—an atmosphere of joy or grief, of anguish, of excitement, of exultation or depression. . . . All objects are benignant or malignant, friendly or inimical, familiar or uncanny, alluring and fascinating or repellent and threatening.—(*An Essay on Man,* 76-77.)

The real substratum of myth is not a substratum of thought but of feeling. . . . Its view of life is a synthetic, not an analytical one. . . . There is no specific difference between the various realms of life. . . . To mythical and religious feeling nature becomes one great society, the *society of life.* Man is not endowed with outstanding rank in this society. . . . Men and animals, animals and plants are all on the same level. (*Ibid.,* 81-83.)

To all these passages Freud could subscribe wholeheartedly; the *morphology* of the "mythic mode" is essentially that of dream, phantasy, infantile thinking, and "unconscious" ideation which he himself discovered and described. And it is the recognition of this non-discursive mode of thought, rather than his clinical hypothesis of an all-pervading disguised sexuality, that makes Freud's psychology important for philosophy. Not the theory of "libido," which is another theory of "animal drives," but the conception of the unconscious mechanism through which the "libido" operates, the dream work, the myth-making process —that is the new generative idea which psychoanalysis contributed to psychological thinking, the notion that has put modern psychology so completely out of gear with traditional epistemology that the science of mind and the philosophy of mind threatened to lose contact altogether. So it is of the utmost significance for the unity of our advancing thought that pure speculative philosophy should recognize and understand the primary forms of conception which underlie the achievement of discursive reason.

Cassirer's profound antipathy to Freud's teaching rests on another aspect of that psychological system, which springs from the fact that Freud's doctrine was determined by practical interests: that is the tendency of the psychoanalyst to range all human aims, all ideals on the same ethical level. Since he deals entirely with the evils of social maladjustment, his measure of good is simply adjustment; religion and learning and social reform, art and discovery and philosophical reflection, to him are just so many avenues of personal gratification—sublimation of passions, emotional self-expression. From his standpoint they cannot be viewed as objective values. Just as good poetry and bad poetry are of equal interest and importance to the psychoanalyst, so the various social systems are all equally good, all religions equally true (or rather, equally false, but salutary), and all abstract systems of thought, scientific or philosophical or mathematical, just self-dramatizations in disguise. To a philosopher who was also a historian of culture, such a point of view seemed simply devastating. It colored his vision of Freud's work so deeply that it really obscured for him the constructive aspect, the analysis of non-discursive ideation, which this essentially clinical psychology contains. Yet the relationship between the new psychiatry and his own new epistemology is deep and close; *"der Mythos als Denkform"*[12] is the theme that rounds out the modern philosophical picture of human mentality to embrace psychology and anthropology and linguistics,[13] which had broken the narrow limits of rationalist theory, in a more adequate conceptual frame.

The broadening of the philosophical outlook achieved by Cassirer's theory of language and myth affects not only the philosophical sciences, the *Geisteswissenschaften*, but also the most crucial present difficulty in philosophy itself—the ever increasing pendulum arc between theories of reason and theories of irrational motivation. The discovery that emotive, intuitive, "blind" forces govern human behavior more effectively than motives of pure reason naturally gave rise to an anti-rationalist movement in epistemology and ethics, typified by Nietzsche, William James, and Bergson, which finally made the truth-seeking attitude of science a pure phantasmagoria, a quixotic manifestation of the will. Ultimately the rôle of reason came to appear (as it does in Bergson's writings) as something entirely secondary and essentially unnatural. But at this point the existence of reason becomes an enigma: for how could instinctive life ever give rise to such a product? How can sheer imagination and volition and passion beget the "artificial" picture of the world which seems natural to scientists?

Cassirer found the answer in the structure of *language*; for language stems from the intuitive "drive" to symbolic expression that also produces dream and myth and ritual, but it is a pre-eminent form in that it embodies not only self-contained, complex meanings, but a *principle of concatenation* whereby the complexes are unravelled and articulated. It is the *discursive* character of language, its inner tendency to grammatical de-

---

[12] This is the title of the first section in Vol. II of *Philosophie der symbolischen Formen*.

[13] The knowledge of linguistics on which he bases vol. I of his *Philosophie der symbolischen Formen* is almost staggering. His use of anthropological data may be found especially throughout vol. II of that work.

velopment, which gives rise to logic in the strict sense, i.e., to the procedure we call "reasoning." Language is "of imagination all compact," yet it is the cradle of abstract thought; and the achievement of *Vernunft*, as Cassirer traces it from the dawn of human mentality through the evolution of speech forms, is just as natural as the complicated patterns of instinctive behavior and emotional abreaction.

Here the most serious antinomy in the philosophical thought of our time is resolved. This is a sort of touchstone for the philosophy of symbolic forms, whereby we may judge its capacity to fulfill the great demand its author did not hesitate to make on it, when he wrote in his *Essay on Man:*

In the boundless multiplicity and variety of mythical images, of religious dogmas, of linguistic forms, of works of art, philosophic thought reveals the unity of a general function by which all these creations are held together. Myth, religion, art, language, even science, are now looked upon as so many variations on a common theme—and it is the task of philosophy to make this theme audible and understandable.

SUSANNE K. LANGER

DEPARTMENT OF PHILOSOPHY
COLUMBIA UNIVERSITY

12

Wilbur M. Urban

CASSIRER'S PHILOSOPHY OF LANGUAGE

CASSIRER'S PHILOSOPHY OF LANGUAGE

I

A

ERNST CASSIRER is, in my opinion, the first of modern philosophers to see the full significance of the relations of problems of language to problems of philosophy and, therefore, the first also to develop a philosophy of language in the full sense of the word. Others, it is true, had made important contributions without which the more systematic treatment of Cassirer would have been impossible. In the field of linguistics itself contributions of a philosophical nature had become more and more frequent, and of these Cassirer has made full use, his erudition in this field being such as to command our admiration. In the field of the special sciences scientists had become increasingly aware of the problems of methodology which their languages and symbolisms present, and with these Cassirer is equally familiar. For these reasons, no less than because of his own philosophical acumen, he has been enabled, not only to formulate the problems of a philosophy of language in a systematic fashion but also, as I believe, in general to find the right solutions.

It is because of the outstanding character of his work that his philosophy of language becomes of great importance, not only for the understanding of his own philosophy, but for the equally significant purpose of understanding the rôle which philosophies of language play in the life of modern philosophy as a whole. It is because of this outstanding character that the present writer has learned so much from this philosophy of language and is glad, therefore, to undertake the task of presenting it for this volume. Cassirer's treatment of language is so fundamental for his philosophy as a whole that it is impossible to present it without trenching, to some extent at least, upon topics assigned to other contributors. It is to be hoped that where this is inevitable, it will serve to clarify rather than to confuse the important issues in modern science and philosophy, to the solution of which this study of Cassirer's philosophy should constitute an important contribution.

B

The chief source of Cassirer's philosophy of language is his monumental work, *Philosophie der symbolischen Formen*,[1] the first volume of which is devoted exclusively to the philosophical study of language, the second to the language of myth, and the third to the language of science. All three are, in Cassirer's terminology, "symbolic forms," and it is the interrelations of these three forms which constitute the central problem of the work as a whole.

The relation of this work to his earlier investigations will perhaps best serve to indicate its standpoint. The investigations of *Substanzbegriff und Funktionsbegriff*, so he tells us, proceeded from the assumption that the basal conception of knowledge (and its essential law) shows itself most clearly in the field of mathematics and mathematical natural science, where the highest stage of universality and necessity is achieved. The *Philosophie der symbolischen Formen*, however, goes beyond this earlier standpoint in both content and method. It seeks to show that "theoretical and form elements" are not confined to scientific construction, but are found also in the "natural world picture" and in the constructions of the imagination, mythical, aesthetic, etc.[2] This statement of the problem, formulated as it is in terms of the Kantian idiom, serves also to indicate the relation of the philosophy of symbolic forms to the critical idealism of Kant. Cassirer accepts, he tells us, the critical principles of Kant, but extends them to other spheres than the theoretical, widening the Kantian conception of "form" to the

---

[1] *Die Philosophie der symbolischen Formen* (Berlin, 1929) ; hereafter abbreviated: *PSF*.

[2] *PSF*., III, v.

more general notion of symbolic form.[3] Otherwise expressed, the *Kritik der Vernunft*, in its various forms, becomes a *Kritik der Sprache*, in its various forms and symbolic expressions. Such a critique was, indeed, like many other developments in philosophy since Kant, already implicit in the Kantian philosophy; it has been Cassirer's task, as well as his good fortune, to have made this explicit.

II

The Theme of a Philosophy of Language, according to Cassirer

A

The chief reason why Cassirer is able to develop a philosophy of language of such significance is, I believe, because he formulates the theme of such a philosophy in the main with truth and adequacy.[4]

This theme, stated in Hegelian terms,—which, as we shall see, are not foreign to Cassirer's way of thinking,—may be said to be "language as the actuality of culture." "Language," he tells us, "stands in a focal point of spiritual being, in which rays of entirely differing origin unite and from which lines run into all the realms of the spirit." Of these various realms, these ways in which culture actualizes itself, the theoretical or scientific form is that in which knowledge chiefly manifests itself, and it is with this language that philosophy is, if not solely, yet chiefly concerned; but there are other ways and other languages, and the knowledge value of these becomes also part of the problem of a philosophy of language. Thus the critique of language becomes, so he holds, the basis of the critique of knowledge, the basal theme of a philosophy of language being the "*Erkenntniswert der Sprache*."[5]

B

The theme of these three volumes is not an arbitrary pro-

[3] *Ibid.*, I, 9ff; also III, 7ff.
[4] *Ibid.*, I, Preface.
[5] *Ibid.*, I, Einleitung und Problemstellung, 1-41.

nouncement, as is the case of so many current *dicta* on language, but is shown to have developed out of the history of philosophic thought itself. Chapter I of Vol. I is entitled "Das Sprachproblem in der Geschichte der Philosophie."

Histories of philosophy have, in the main, either ignored or been unaware of the philosophies of language presupposed by the great philosophers. With his more than ordinary historical erudition, Cassirer has been enabled to rewrite the history of European philosophy from this standpoint. In making explicit the assumptions or presuppositions regarding language on the part of the philosophers, and in showing how they predetermined in various ways the results of their thinking, Cassirer has enabled us to see the central place of problems of language in the entire history of philosophy.

From Plato on (he speaks of the famous Seventh Epistle as the first attempt made to determine the *Erkenntniswert der Sprache* in a purely methodological manner) the "value of the word" becomes, either explicitly or implicitly, an essential part of the problem of knowledge. The outstanding phenomenon from this point of view, is, of course, the opposition of nominalism and realism, each representing, so to speak, a fundamental evaluation of the word.

The opposition of rationalism and empiricism in modern philosophy is, in a sense, the continuation of the same problem. The ideal of a *lingua universalis*, held by Descartes and Leibnitz, to say nothing of lesser rationalists, was an expression of the ideal of universal reason; *logos*, in the sense of language, *and* in the sense of reason, being, for all of this way of thinking, in principle inseparable. Empiricism, on the other hand, proceeds, as Cassirer tells us, from a completely opposite standpoint and reaches contrary results. Although recognizing, as did Locke, that problems of knowledge cannot be separated from language, it starts with the assumption that the primary form of knowledge is simple awarness of sense data, to which language is a mere *addendum*. The empirical philosophy of language becomes the basis for a theory of knowledge which seeks to eliminate the universal; Berkeley even proposing "to confine his thought to his own ideas divested from words," believing that thus he "cannot then be mistaken."

As the Kantian "critical" philosophy represents the mediation between rationalism and empiricism in epistemology, so philosophies of language, influenced by the Kantian criticism, represent a crucial point in connection with the speech problem in the history of philosophy. In this respect von Humboldt played an outstanding part and has consequently had a determining influence upon Cassirer himself; an entire section being given to the discussion of his main principles. For von Humboldt language is not a product (*ergon*) but an activity, (*energeia*). The Kantian principle of knowledge as synthesis is carried over into the sphere of language, "*Sprache als Schöpfung und Entwicklung,*" the title of a work of Karl Vossler to which Cassirer refers with approval, representing this "idealistic" tendency in the modern philosophy of language.

Of the relation of this general problem to current tendencies in philosophy Cassirer is fully aware, and his own position is mainly determined by his reaction to these tendencies. Modern empiricism, in its positivistic form, and the Bergsonian philosophy of organism, both proceed from a purely naturalistic and nominalistic theory of language, and to the premises and conclusions of both Cassirer is in complete opposition. There are, he tells us, in general only two ways of solving the problem of language and reality. The first of these assumes a reality known independently of language and its categories, a hypothetical pure experience to be discovered by stripping off language. The second way proposes an exactly opposite method and proceeds upon opposite presuppositions. Instead of attempting to get back of the forms of thought and language to a hypothetical pure experience, it assumes that experience is never pure in this sense and that intuition and expression are inseparable. It therefore proposes, not to deny, but to complete and perfect the principles of expression and symbolism. It proceeds upon the assumption that the more richly and energetically the human spirit builds its languages and symbolisms the nearer it comes, if not to some hypothetical original source of its being, certainly to its ultimate meaning and reality. This is the *idealistic minimum* in Cassirer's philosophy of language, as indeed it must be, in the view of the present writer, in any adequate philosophy of language.

III

Cassirer's "Idealistic" Theory of Language: Criticism of Naturalism in Linguistic Science

A

One thing which distinguishes Cassirer's philosophy of language from most contributions to this subject is his extensive use of the results of linguistic science, an advantage conspicuously absent in most discussions of the subject. Not only does he appeal to these studies in detail for the substantiation of his main theses, but he examines the postulates and method of modern linguistics.

The assumption underlying the linguistic science of the nineteenth century—and most philosophies of language had accepted this assumption—is that language is but a part of nature. As such, it was made by nature for certain natural ends—for the manipulation of physical objects or for adjustment to the physical environment. In other words, linguistic science has tended to study language, so to speak, within the bounds of naturalistic assumptions alone. Cassirer challenges this standpoint, not only from the point of view of "critical" philosophy, but from the standpoint of linguistic science itself. An important part of his entire approach to problems of language is his account of the stages in the development of modern linguistics, which not only constitutes one of the most complete pictures of that science, but also enables him to disprove many of the assumptions, regarding matter of fact, all too common in modern positivistic philosophy.

Linguistics, so Cassirer tells us, hoping to attain the same certainty and exactness as the natural sciences, moulded itself, in the first instance, on their methods and conceptions. But gradually the notion of "laws," physical, physiological, and even psychological, showed itself untenable. The entire conception of nature and natural law upon which it was sought to build, turned out to be an illusion, a wholly fictitious unity including the most disparate elements. Thus, as the naturalistic and positivistic scheme of linguistic science has tended to break up, there has been also a marked tendency towards the return to earlier conceptions of the autonomy of language. The movement within linguistics as a whole, so it seems to Cassirer, has been, methodologically speaking, a movement in a circle. A revision of the naturalistic assumptions of the science has taken place to such an extent that it is again approaching the standpoint from which it started. As under the aegis of the physical and biological sciences, it took the step from *Geist* to *Natur*, so now in a very real sense it is turning again from nature to spirit. This is the significance of the opposition of idealism and positivism in modern linguistics.[6]

B

With the return from nature to mind, the problem of meaning becomes central, and a corollary of the return movement is the methodological principle of the primacy of meaning—*der Primat des Sinnes,* as Cassirer calls it. It may be stated in the following way. The sole entrance to the understanding of language is through meaning, for meaning is the *sine qua non* of linguistic fact. Language for modern linguistics is not sound, nor again the motor and tactual sensations which make up the word psychologically, nor yet the associations called up; it is the *meaning itself* which, although conditioned by these, is not identical with any of them. This being the fact, the methodology of linguistic study is not that of the natural sciences but rather, for language, as for all symbolic forms, the phenomenological. The nature of this method, as conceived by Cassirer, will be stated more definitely presently; the significant point here is that it is interpretation from within, not merely explanation from without.

The significance of this principle of the primacy of meaning

[6] *PSF.,* I, 118 ff.

is far reaching. It means negatively, as we have seen, the denial of the adequacy of external approaches to language, whether physical, physiological, or even psychological; but it involves also, positively, significant changes in methodology. Earlier methods proceeded from the elements to the whole—from the sounds to the words, from words to sentences, and finally to the meaning of discourse as a whole. The present tendency is the exact opposite. It proceeds from the whole of meaning, as *Gestalt*, to the sentences and words as elements—the parts being understood through the whole. The spirit which lives in human discourse works as a totality constituting the sentence or proposition, the copula, the word, and the sound.[7]

Of the many important consequences of this methodological principle—a discussion of the details of which would be necessary for an adequate account of Cassirer's linguistic studies—we shall single out one which is important for all that follows, namely the nature and modes of *linguistic meaning*.

Meaning, as understood by positivistic theories, is *reference* to sensuously observable entities. "Indication" is, therefore, the essence of meaning, "in the strict sense." All other meanings are emotive in character, and the words in this case refer to nothing and stand for nothing. For Cassirer indication is indeed a primary mode, but equally primary is representation or *Darstellung*.[8] Without this element there is no linguistic meaning. This element or function is an *Urphänomen*, present in language from its simplest to its highest forms, and it is, as we shall see, the development of this mode of meaning—from copy through analogy, to symbolic representation—which constitutes the thread of Cassirer's treatment, not only of language but of the entire range of symbolic forms.

Closely bound up with this question as to what language is are the genetic problems of language, more specifically the problem of "animal language." Holding, as he does, that the *Darstellungsfunktion* is the *sine qua non* of linguistic meaning, he denies this function to the phonetic expressions of animals,

[7] *Ibid.*, I, 119.
[8] *Ibid.*, I, 126ff; III, 126ff.

even those of the higher apes. His discussion of the results of
Köhler's investigations are most enlightening, and he concludes
that recent observations of animal psychology seem to widen
rather than narrow the gulf between human and animal communication, and that what is called animal speech "seems to be
permanently held fast in the pre-linguistic stage."[9] In any
case, it is the growing conviction of linguistics that the *hiatus*
between animal expressions and human speech is widening
rather than narrowing as investigation proceeds—all of which
leads to the modern speech notion as "a human, non-instinctive
function." The step to human language is made first when the
pure meaningful sound achieves supremacy over the affective
stimulus-born sounds and this achievement has in it the character of a unique level of being. The notion of speech as an
Urphänomen, in short the autonomy of the speech notion,
seems to be more and more confirmed by the study of animal
psychology.

Cassirer's philosophy of language has been called "idealistic,"
and in the sense that it is opposed to naturalism and positivism
it is. Language is, indeed, to use an expression of Karl Vossler,
"embedded in nature," and it is out of this fact that "the illusion
of its being a piece of nature constantly arises." But Cassirer
would agree with Vossler that this illusion must be just as
constantly dispelled if an adequate philosophy of language is
to be possible. Language is indeed a part of nature and as such
it was "made" for certain natural ends. But in its development
it subserves quite other ends. Granted that it was made by
nature for a natural object, language like our intelligence, and
all the forms of culture with which it is connected, has developed along lines which are independent of natural ends,
perhaps in opposition to them. Language is not limited to the
"practical" functions for which it was primarily made, but in
its development has achieved a freedom which makes it, in the
words of von Humboldt, "a vehicle for traversing the manifold
and the highest and deepest of the entire world."

[9] *Ibid.,* I, 136 note; III, 127.

IV

*Language and Cognition: The Relation of Intuition
to Expression*

A

As opposed to purely naturalistic and positivistic theories of language Cassirer's theory is idealistic. But it may be said to be idealistic in another sense, in the Kantian sense of "critical idealism." This general "critical" position is determinative throughout; it underlies his conception of language in Vol. I, his conception of language and myth in Vol. II, and his interpretation of science in Vol. III. It is, however, with the first, the general question of the relation of language to cognition, that we are now concerned.

The problem of knowledge presents itself to Cassirer, as to all "critical" philosophers, under a double aspect, the psychological and the epistemological. In the psychological or naturalistic treatment, as in the application of the "scientific" method everywhere, the only possible standpoint is to start with the "things" or objects, as already constructed, and then ask how they acquire meaning and are known. The *petitio principii* in this method is, for Cassirer, obvious. It assumes that the things or objects are given and are then known, when actually there is an element of construction, perhaps incalculable, in the things *as* given. The epistemological treatment of the subject starts from an entirely different, perhaps opposite, standpoint. It involves a radical shift from the realm of things to that of meaning and value. It must study perception and perceptual meaning, not causally, as determined from without, but from within, as a constitutive element in cognition.[10] If it is really "meaning that transforms sense data into things," it then becomes a problem whether language and linguistic meaning are not present in the first processes of such transformation. Cassirer holds that language is thus present from the beginning, and that in this sense language first created the realm of meaning. Otherwise expressed, intuition and expression are, if not identical, as according to Croce, at least inseparable,

[10] *PSF*, III, 68ff.

In this connection we may note a term constantly used by Cassirer, the full significance of which will later become apparent, namely, the expression *Ausdruckserlebnisse*. The primary experiences (*Erlebnisse*) are at the same time primary forms of expression and constitute the "natural" world picture, as well as the picture constructed by myth. These are the original forms of knowledge and in these, according to Cassirer's "critical" principles, there are already "theoretical and form elements" which contribute their elements to knowledge. Science, it is true, tends to transcend, and in a sense "break through," these forms of expression; but that very fact creates one of the fundamental problems of a philosophy of language and of symbolic forms, namely, the *Erkenntniswert* of these *Ausdruckserlebnisse*.

B

Intuition is inseparable from expression, but in expression there is always an element of re-presentation; *die Darstellungsfunktion* is equally original—*das symbolische Grundverhältnis*, as he calls it. This is described as the bi-polar character of all knowledge and is, in Cassirer's terms, an *Urphänomen*. Empiricism, with its doctrine of presentational immediacy, proceeds on the assumption that the primary and original form of knowledge is one in which we merely *have*, or possess, the sense *data*. Such an hypothetical form of knowledge is, for Cassirer, pure myth. Without the element of polarity, and therefore of the reference of the presentation to that which is presented, that is without some element of representation, the entire notion of knowledge collapses. It follows from this that problems of knowledge and problems of language are inseparable.[11]

In connection with this fundamental principle two specific points in the development of Cassirer's thesis require special attention. They are treated by him under the two captions, *Zur Pathologie des Symbolbewusstseins* and the notion of *Symbolischer Prägnanz*, both of which serve to illuminate the general principle.

[11] This thesis is the underlying theme of the entire *Philosophie der symbolischen Formen*, but is especially developed in Vol. III, Part 1. A statement of it is found on pp. 143ff.

Under the former, the pathology of the symbol-conscious-
ness, he makes use of the phenomena of mental blindness, in its
verbal form, as studied by both psychologists and linguists.
When in certain forms of aphasia the word is not recognized or
cannot be formed, the perceptual meaning of the object itself
is absent also—facts which go far towards confirming the principle that language is part of the perceptual process itself.[12] The
significance of speech for the construction (*Aufbau*) of the perceptual world, to employ Cassirer's terms, is obvious.

The notion of *Symbolischer Prägnanz* is equally important
for his general thesis, important not only for his philosophy of
language, but for his theory of symbolism. By this term is to be
understood, he tells us, the way in which perception, as sensuous experience, becomes at the same time the means of apprehension (symbolically) of a non-intuitive meaning and brings
this meaning to immediate and concrete expression.[13] Thus a
color phenomenon is, as sense *datum,* a sensuous experience, but
it is also a symbol which stands for references and meanings
which themselves are not objects of sensuous experience. This
symbolic character is, as we shall see, present, in Cassirer's view,
on the lowest levels of experience as well as on the highest; it
extends, in his words, through every level of the world picture.
In sum, this symbolic function, like the *Darstellungsfunktion,*
of which it is an aspect, is an *Urphänomen.*

C

The function of language in the *Aufbau* of the perceptual
world is further shown by the presence of the universal in the
perceptual process itself. Everything denoted by language is
already universalized. Apart from purely formless interjec-
tions and emotive sounds, all linguistic expressions contain
implicitly this "form of thought." The universal is not, as commonly held, the product of abstraction and *then* embodied in
language; it is present in this "first precipitate of language."

[12] *PSF*, III, chapter VI.
[13] *Op. cit.,* Vol. III, p. 234. In Cassirer's own words, "Unter 'symbolischer
Prägnanz' soll also die Art verstanden werden, in der ein Wahrnehmungserlebniss,
als 'sinnliches' Erlebniss, zugleich einen bestimmten nicht-anschaulichen 'Sinn' in
sich fasst und ihn zur unmittelbaren konkreten Darstellung bringt."

The later processes of abstraction take place upon contents already thus universalized.

In developing this point Cassirer makes use of Lotze's term, "first" or primary universal, to distinguish it from the secondary or abstract universal. Nouns, verbs, adjectives are all in a sense names, and when anything is named this first universal is implicit. This first universal is intuitive, of a very different nature from the ordinary class concepts of logic, and is, indeed, presupposed by them. Perception contains this universal. It is true, of course, that it is always a particular color or tone that is perceived, always a particular *quale* and intensity. But this perception is always accompanied by the fact that every other color or tone has an equal right to function as an example of the universal. This class concept is, as he further insists, not constructed by repressing or eliminating the individual color or tone, but rather by the recognition of a common element (in the individual phenomena themselves) already intuited.[14]

This doctrine of the "double universal," as Cassirer calls it, is important for his entire philosophy of language. It also furnishes the basis for his theory of language and logic. His logical theory will doubtless receive fuller treatment by other contributors to this volume, but some comment should be made upon it in this connection.

The point at which logic and the philosophy of language, so he tells us, first touch each other is the problem of the formation of concepts; the point, indeed, "at which they disclose their inseparable character." "All logical analysis of concepts," he adds, "seems to lead in the end to a point at which the examination of concepts passes into that of words and names. From this point of view logic might be defined as the science or doctrine of the concept and its meaning."[15] Predication is a problem at once linguistic and logical and the real secret of predication is found in the doctrine of the double universal. Predication, in the logical sense, is but the conceptual expressions of relations already intuited. These form the basis for the more complex syntheses of logical thought, logical concepts

---

[14] *PSF*, I, 249ff. Also III, 135ff.
[15] *Ibid.*, I, 244ff.

having the function merely of fixing the relations already present in experience. The logical concept, so he tells us, does nothing else than fix the *"gesetzliche Ordnung"* already present in the phenomena t.&mselves; it states consciously the rule which the perception follows unconsciously.[16]

Cassirer seems to maintain a relational, as opposed to a subject-predicate logic, and his general thesis of the development from substance to function in the sphere of scientific knowledge would seem to indicate this position. It would seem also, that with regard to the issue raised by the expression "logical analysis of language," he also maintains the right of such a relational logic to exercise its critique upon the subject-predicate logic, which is the constitutive element in the natural world picture as given us by perception. And yet I am not so sure. Certainly one of his main positions is that the mathematical-logical world picture given us by science is not the only symbolic form which has knowledge value, but that such value must be accorded also to the natural and mythical pictures of the world. In any case, I cannot go into this issue here. It was one of my hopes that this ambiguity regarding logic would be cleared up in Cassirer's answers to the questions raised by the essays in this volume, before the suddenness and untimeliness of his death made this expectation futile.

D

As the *Darstellungsfunktion* is the *sine qua non* of linguistic meaning, so the nature of that function, of the relation of the "word" to the "thing"—and the nature of the truth relation in general—becomes a fundamental problem of a philosophy of language. "The function of language," according to Cassirer, "is not to copy reality but to symbolize it."[17]

In this connection his "law" of the development of language becomes of first importance. The development of language proceeds through three stages. They are (a) the mimetic or copy stage, (b) the analogical and (c) the symbolic. The characteris-

---

[16] *Ibid.*, III, 333.
[17] *Ibid.*, I, 132ff; 233ff.

tic of the first stage is that between the word, or verbal sign, and the thing to which it refers no real difference is made. The word is the thing. This initial stage is, however, broken up as soon as transfer of signs takes place. Here the relation is analogical. This relation in turn gives way to the symbolic. The characteristic of this last stage is that, whereas the element of representation (*Darstellung*), which is the *sine qua non* of linguistic meaning, still remains, the relation of similarity which conditions this representation becomes more and more partial and indefinite.

As thus briefly stated, this "law" of development is, to be sure, a mere schematism; but when it is filled in with the rich content at Cassirer's disposal, it becomes one of the most illuminating conceptions of his entire work. It becomes not only an important principle for the understanding of the *Aufbau der Sprache*, but one which also enables him to connect the development of language with other "symbolic forms," such as art, science, and religion.

As concerns language itself, Cassirer is enabled, as the result of extensive comparative studies, to show the presence of this tendency or "law" throughout linguistic phenomena. From this wealth of material I choose but one illustration to indicate the significance of the principle, namely, the phenomenon of reduplication common in primitive languages. The reduplication of sound or syllable appears, at first view, to involve merely the copying of the object or happening. Actually, however, it marks the beginning of an analogical representation which is a step on the way to the symbolic. The representation is, in the first instance, imitative and serves to conjure up the thing itself. Gradually, however, the *Gestalt* is detached from the primary material and becomes the means of representation of plurality, repetition, and finally, in many cases, becomes the form of representation or expression of the fundamental intuitions, space, time, force, etc. Cassirer develops this theme with many illustrations which cannot, of course, be given here. The important point is the presence of the representative, as well as the indicative function, from the beginning, and also the manner in which this representative function develops from representation in the sense of imitation to symbolic representation as its ultimate form.[18]

It is impossible even to indicate here the manifold applications of this principle to the development of the various speech forms. More important for his philosophy as a whole is the way in which, as he points out, the development of language through the three stages makes it possible for speech to become the medium for the expression of conceptual thought and of pure relations. It is indeed the very *Vieldeutigkeit* of the verbal signs, which appears on the analogical stage of development, that constitutes the real virtue of that stage of development. It is precisely this that compels the mind to take the decisive step from the concrete function of indication (*Bezeichnung*), which characterizes the early stage of language, to the general and more significant function of "meaning" (*Bedeutung*). It is at this point that language at the same time emerges from the sensuous husk in which it first embodied itself. The imitative and analogical expressions give place to the purely symbolic, and language thus becomes the bearer of a newer and deeper spiritual content.[19]

Of special importance in this connection is the application of this principle to space-time language, not only for the entire philosophy of symbolic forms, but more especially for Cassirer's treatment of symbolism in science. All language goes through these three stages of development, and space-time words are no exception to the rule. Into the details of his exhaustive study we cannot, of course, enter. It must suffice to give the results as summed up in his own words: "Again it is clear," he tells us,

that the concepts of space, time and number furnish the actual structural elements of objective experience as they build themselves up in language. But they can fulfil this task only because, according to their total structure, they keep it an ideal medium, precisely because, while they keep to the form of sensuous experience, they progressively fill the sensuous with ideal content and make it the symbol of the spiritual.[20]

[18] *PSF*, I, 143.
[19] *Ibid.*, I, 145.
[20] *Ibid.*, I, 208.

Thus the space and time of the immediate *Ausdruckserlebnisse* become the ideal space-time of modern physical science which, as we shall see, although keeping the forms of sensuous experience, become more and more the symbol for non-intuitable relations.[21]

E

The theme of a philosophy of language is, as we have seen, the *Erkenntniswert der Sprache*. To the question thus raised Cassirer's critical idealistic philosophy of language seems to me to be in the main, the right answer. As opposed to naïvely naturalistic and "realistic" views of language, this conception of language seems to me to be alone tenable. Nevertheless there also appear to me to be certain difficulties in Cassirer's formulation of this theory—a fundamental ambiguity in his evaluation of language which becomes increasingly puzzling as he passes from the philosophy of language *eo nomine* to other aspects of the more general philosophy of symbolic forms.

There seems to be little question of the inseparability of intuition and expression embodied in the notion of *Ausdruckserlebnisse*, that language is present from the beginning in the *Aufbau* of the perceptual world. There seems to be just as little question that language develops from copy to analogy and from analogy to symbol; that the function of language is not to copy reality but to symbolize it; and that, more and more, the symbolization of things gives place to the symbolization of relations. The problem then becomes whether, in this dialectical movement, as Cassirer calls it, inherent in language, the goal of the movement is the abandonment of language with its natural "parts of speech" and its subject-predicate logic for a symbolism of pure relations and a purely relational logic. Is there within language itself an immanental dialectic which drives it ever onward beyond itself? Otherwise expressed, are the natural categories of language, although useful for practice, wholly erroneous when applied to the sphere of theory?

On this fundamental issue Cassirer's answer seems to me to be ambiguous. In many places he appears to suggest that the

[21] *Ibid.*, III, Part III, Chap. V.

function of thought is to break through the husk of language, with its natural categories (of subject and predicate, of substance and attribute) to a "purer notation" and to a symbolism of pure relations, notably in science. In other places he seems to suggest that, although this is the ideal goal of knowledge, natural language can never be broken through completely and the categories of this language can never be completely transcended. Doubtless Cassirer is clear on this point, and my own uncertainty arises from defects of understanding. In any case, the problem here presented is one which faces all modern philosophies of language, a problem to which, in the opinion of the present writer, few have given really satisfactory answers.

V

The Philosophy of Language and The Philosophy of Symbolic Forms. Principles of Symbolism

A

For Cassirer, then, the philosophy of language leads directly to a philosophy of symbolism. If, as he maintains, the function of language is not to copy reality but to symbolize it, it becomes necessary, in order to understand that function, to understand also the nature and principles of symbolism. More than this, language is for him not the only symbolic form. In art, religion, and preëminently in "science" itself, non-linguistic symbols are employed and the relation of these symbols to language becomes one of the central problems of the philosophy of language, as viewed in its more general aspects.

Cassirer's problem, as we have seen, insofar as it is concerned with language, is the study of the *Aufbau der Sprache* in connection with the development of the varied forms of culture, more particularly science, art, and religion. The essence of culture is precisely this objectification of the "spirit" in various forms and structures. In all these, no less than in science in the strict sense of the word, theoretical and form elements are to be found.

The methodology of such a study, even in the case of language itself, obviously can not be the scientific method in the sense of natural science, as we have already seen in his critique of the assumptions and methods of linguistics. It is, for Cassirer, the phenomenological method conceived in the broadest sense. The place in his studies where the character of this method is most clearly formulated is in the Preface to Vol. III. "When," he writes, "I speak of the phenomenology of knowledge, I refer not to the modern usage, but go back to the fundamental meaning of phenomenology as finally fixed and systematically developed and justified by Hegel." For Hegel, he reminds us, phenomenology is "the fundamental presupposition of philosophical knowledge." In contrast to the scientific method, it seeks to understand the various "spiritual forms" from within, not from without. It seeks moreover "to embrace the totality of spiritual forms and to understand and evaluate them in their mutual relations," for "the fundamental presupposition of the phenomenological method is that the truth is the whole." With this conception of phenomenology, Cassirer tells us, the philosophy of symbolic forms is in accord, although in the application of these principles his procedure naturally varies significantly from that of Hegel.[22]

B

The first requisite of a general theory of symbolism is an adequate notion of the symbol and the symbolizing function. This notion must, as Cassirer rightly points out, be a broad one, if it is to be adequate. "The philosophy of symbols and of symbolic forms is not, as some suppose, concerned primarily and exclusively with scientific and exact concepts, but with all directions of the symbolizing function," in its attempt to grasp and understand the world. It is necessary to study this function, not

[22] *PSF.*, III, vi. Cassirer does not, to be sure, deny the valuable services rendered by Phenomenology in the narrower sense of Husserl. It has, he tells us, sharpened our sense anew for the variety of spiritual *"Strukturformen"* and shown us the way in which the method of their understanding must differ from the psychological. As Husserl's studies have developed it becomes ever clearer that this method is not exhausted in the analysis of knowledge, but that its task includes the investigation of the different realms of objects, according to what they mean without reference to their psychical conditions or the existence of their objects. The extension of this general point of view and method from the sphere of logic to ethics and art has, he holds, been one of the most fruitful movements of modern thought. (*PSF.*, II, 16 note.)

only in the realm of scientific concepts but in the non-scientific realms of poetry, art, religion, etc., not only on the level of the conceptual but on the cognitive levels below the conceptual.[23]

We lose our grasp of the whole, if we confine the symbolizing function at the outset to the level of conceptual 'abstract' knowledge. Rather we shall have to recognize that this function belongs not only to a single level of the theoretical world picture, but that it conditions and carries this picture in its totality.[24]

How much this warning is needed is apparent when we realize that precisely the tendency to narrow the concept of the symbol to the logical and mathematical has been a conspicuous tendency of recent philosophic thought.

The symbolic function belongs, then, not to a single level of the world picture but holds throughout. It is present on the level below conceptual knowledge, in perception itself—that is the significance of the principle of *symbolischer Prägnanz*— but it holds also for the realms of poetry, art, religion, and preëminently that of science. The philosophy of symbolic forms includes the study of the symbolizing function in all forms of the objectification of the human spirit.

One level of the world picture on which the symbolic function is most in evidence is that of myth. The second volume of the *Philosophie der symbolischen Formen* is entitled "Das mythische Denken," which is in reality a discussion of the problem of *Sprache und Mythos*. In this without question the most significant modern study of the myth, the entire problem of the nature of myth, of its *Erkenntniswert* and of its relation to religion as symbolic form, is involved. This problem is the subject of other papers in this volume, and we shall accordingly confine ourselves wholly to its significance in the context of the philosophy of language.

The essence of Cassirer's philosophy of myth is that the language of the myth represents an original form of the intuition of reality. In consequence, the individual categories of mythical thinking have their own form and structure. Space, time, number, classes, all have different meanings in mythical

[23] *PSF*, III, 16.
[24] *Ibid.*, III, 57.

thought from those of science and constitute, in their totality and interrelations, a "symbolic form" with its own immanent form and significance. Into the details of this analysis we cannot, of course, go—they are among the most admirable of Cassirer's comparative studies. It is sufficient to say that this fundamental way of intuiting the world expresses an "organic" aspect of reality which escapes the physico-mathematical categories of science. Part of this "critical" philosophy, therefore, is also the thesis that the myth is to be evaluated, not by norms taken from alien spheres, but in terms of its own form and structure as an original and primary way of intuiting reality.

The development of myth exhibits stages parallel to the stages of language—from copy, through analogy, to symbol. Here, too, an immanent dialectic drives thought on from copy to symbol.[25] It is here that the question of the relation of myth to religion is raised by Cassirer and, in the last section, entitled "Die Dialectik des mythischen Bewusstseins," is given an answer which I believe, is, in principle at least, in the right direction. According to this view, originally myth and religion (and mythical and religious symbolism) were identical, or at least inseparable and interfused. It is clearly impossible, he tells us, to make any study of religious symbols without a study of their relation to myth. There is no positive religion without these elements. The further we follow the content of the religious consciousness to its beginnings, the more it is found impossible to separate the belief content from mythical language; one has then no longer religion in its actual historical and cultural nature but merely a shadow picture and an empty abstraction. Nevertheless—and this is the important point for the philosophy of religion—despite this inseparable interweaving of the content of myth and religion, they are far from being identical. Neither the form nor the spirit of the two are the same. The peculiar character of the religious form of consciousness shows itself precisely in a changed attitude towards the mythical picture of the world. It cannot do without this world, for it is in the mythical consciousness that the immediate

[25] *PSF*, II, 292ff.

intuition of the meaningfulness of the world is given. Yet in the religious consciousness the myth acquires a new meaning; it becomes symbolic. Religion completes the process of development which myth as such can not. It makes use of the sensuous pictures and signs, but at the same time knows them to be such. It always draws the distinction between mere existence and meaning.[26]

C

This critical theory of myth and of its relation to religion seems to me the only tenable one, when all the relevant facts are taken into consideration. In contrast to positivistic theories which *identify* religion with myth, Cassirer's emphasis upon the fundamental difference between the two seems to me to be of great importance. Nor does it suffice, as in certain theories very common at the present time, to distinguish between pre-scientific myth, which is transitory, and permanent myth, which is the language of religion. There is all the difference in the world between saying that religion *is* myth, however permanent, and saying that the language of myth constitutes the indispensable source of religious symbolism; and Cassirer has grasped this fundamental difference.

On the other hand, true as this conception in principle is, it seems to me that, as formulated by Cassirer, it presents essentially the same difficulties which are encountered in his philosophy of language. Indeed the same ambiguity which there appeared is present in another form in his philosophy of religious symbolism. It concerns what he calls the dialectic of the mythical consciousness. Religion does indeed complete the process of development which myth as such can not. But what is this completion? He does tell us, to be sure, that religion makes use of the sensuous pictures and signs, but at the same time he seems also to tell us that the ideal completion of the process would be the mystical consciousness—that negative mysticism in which the pictures and symbols are transcended and ultimately abandoned. Undoubtedly, as the illustrations he gives us of the dialectic, taken from the Hebrew, Persian, and Hindu religions, indicate, every positive religion reaches a crisis

[26] *Ibid.*, II, 294.

in which it breaks with the mythical and on its higher levels seeks a direct approach to the absolute. Christianity also, as he tells us, reached this crisis and "has fought this fight." It too draws the distinction between existence and meaning. This is doubtless true, but it is very doubtful whether any form of religion—certainly not the Christian religion and theology— ever *abandons* existence for meaning. It is true, again, that the negative theology of the philosophical mystics, such as Eckhart and Tauler, might be said to have completed the dialectical process in this fashion, and Cassirer seems to quote them as representing the essence of the dialectic of religion.[27] But it is in the positive rather than in the negative mystics that the essence of Christian mysticism is to be found; and this form of mysticism, as Von Hügel has shown, includes both acceptance and transcendence of the symbol. In any case—and this is really the only point I wish to raise here—Cassirer's conception of the relation of myth to religion, however valuable it may be on the main issue, nevertheless is not wholly unambiguous, any more than is his philosophy of language as a whole. Is it, or is it not, the fate of religion to be dissolved into something else—into a philosophy which is no longer religious or into a mysticism which is no longer theological?

D

Of this critical idealistic theory of the religious symbol Paul Tillich has said that it stands in the forefront of symbol-theory today,[28] and in this he is probably right. But this is but one phase of Cassirer's more general theory of symbolism. The symbolic function belongs, as we have seen, not to any single level of the world picture, but holds throughout. By thus identifying the symbolic with the entire range of knowledge, including the scientific, the concept of the symbol and of symbolic truth has been given a tremendous expansion and a new significance. It is, indeed, on his view, only in the mathematical-physical sciences that the full significance of the philosophy of symbolic forms is seen; for, as he tells us, "no matter how high myth and art may

[27] *PSF*, II, 306ff.
[28] For a critical discussion of this problem see a discussion between Paul Tillich and myself in *The Journal of Liberal Religion*, Vol. II, No. 1, (1940).

carry their constructions, they yet remain permanently rooted in the primitive world of *Ausdruckserlebnisse*."[29] It is only in the sphere of physical mathematical science that thought, so to speak, breaks through the husk of language, with its natural forms, and creates a world of concepts which, because of the conscious recognition of their nature as symbols, and of science itself as symbolic form, makes it possible to realize the ideal immanent in knowledge from the start, namely the correlation of phenomena in a systematic whole. It is here that the step from substance to function is finally taken.

VI

The Language of Science: Symbolism as a Scientific Principle

A

The third volume of the *Philosophie der symbolischen Formen* is entitled *Phänomenologie der Erkenntnis* and the third part of this volume bears the title, "Die Bedeutungsfunktion und der Aufbau der wissenschaftlichen Erkenntnis." One chapter is entitled "Sprache und Wissenschaft, Dingzeichen und Ordnungszeichen" and the theme herein expressed is the main theme of this part of our study.

"Language and science" has, indeed, become one of the central problems of modern philosophy of science, as the problem of symbolism has become a burning issue in scientific methodology. *All* that the scientist contributes to the fact is, according to Poincaré, the language in which it is enunciated. But, if the relation of perception to language is such as Cassirer conceives it, that "all" is a very great deal indeed; for there is no "fact," in the sense of "critical" philosophy, until it is expressed, and the primary, if not the only, form of expression is language. Science, so Cassirer maintains in the introduction to *Das mythische Denken*, differs from the other stages of spiritual life not in the fact that it gives us the truth itself without any mediation through signs and symbols, but rather that science recognizes that the symbols which it uses *are* symbols and realizes this fact in a way in which the others do not.[30] This

[29] *PSF*, III, 524.
[30] *PSF*, II, 35.

"realization" constitutes the recognition of symbolism as a scientific principle and the statement of this principle—involving both the nature of the symbol and its relation to reality—becomes the central problem of "science as symbolic form."

It is in contrast with the copy or model theory of scientific concepts which characterized nineteenth century physics, that the symbolic character of these concepts is developed. If the function of language in general is not to copy but to symbolize reality, this is *a fortiori* true of scientific language. Cassirer cites a wealth of illustrations from modern physical science to substantiate this thesis, but it is in connection with the theory of light that this fundamental change from copy to symbol is perhaps clearest, and Cassirer gives an excellent picture of this development.

The corpuscular theory of Newton, according to which light consists in very small particles, proved untenable and gave way to the undulatory theory of Huygens, based upon an analogy taken from perceptible phenomena and giving rise to the construct of the ether as the substance which has these waves. Contradictions arose, however, in the predicates of this hypothetical ether which could not be eliminated. Physics was led even more deeply into paradoxes, and all *ad hoc* hypotheses invented to solve the difficulties served only to lead more deeply into the morass. Finally there came the electrodynamic theory of the field. The characteristic here is that the reality which is designated as the "field" is no longer a complex of physical "things" but an expression for a system of relations. But the important thing for us is that the notion of the intuitible is completely abandoned and therefore the entire notion of the scientific concept is changed.[31] This change, which we may take as an outstanding illustration of the movement from "schematism" to symbol in physics, illustrates also a fundamental change in the modern symbolic consciousness of science. The symbol symbolizes not things (substances) but relations (functions).

B

This symbolic theory of scientific concepts is, according to Cassirer, "the accepted theory in physical science today" and

[31] *Ibid.*, III, 542ff.

he is, doubtless, on the whole justified in calling it such. He is doubtless right also in saying that science recognizes the fact that the concepts which it uses are symbols in a way in which other symbolic forms do not. Certainly it represents in principle the standpoint of such physicists as Jeans and Eddington, to say nothing of the continental physicists he cites. For Jeans the pictures are the fables with which we deck our mathematical equations; for Eddington they are dummies in our mathematical equations. Symbolism as a scientific principle means, then, in the words of Cassirer, that

physics has finally abandoned the reality of description and representation in order to enter upon a realm of greater abstraction. The schematism of pictures has given place to a symbolism of principles. Physics is concerned no longer with the actual itself, but with its structure and formal principles. The tendency to unification has conquered the tendency to intuitive representation. The synthesis which is possible through pure concepts of law and relation has shown itself more valuable than the apprehension in terms of objects or things. Order and relation have, then, become the basal concepts of physics.[32]

To say that physical science, in the later stages of its development, is no longer concerned with the actual, but solely with formal principles and structure, is seemingly to enunciate a paradox of the most astounding sort. This view, however, Cassirer is careful to point out, does not in the least signify that science has abandoned sense experience. Science, he tells us, "starts with observable objects and is not content until it deduces from its concepts or theories objects and events which can also be observed. Without this connection with sense, however indirect and remote, there is no verification.

The meaning of the principle must be ultimately empirically and intuitively fulfilled, but this fulfilment (*Erfüllung*) is never possible directly, but only insofar as from the supposition of its validity other propositions are derived by means of an hypothetical deduction. None of these propositions, none of the individual stages in this logical process, need be capable of a direct sensory interpretation. Only as a logical totality

[32] *Ibid.*, III, 545.

can the series of deductions be referred to observation and be proved and justified by it.[33]

"Only as logical totality"—this is the significant point. Since none of the individual propositions requires reference to sensuous intuition, there is a gradual shift of the *locus* of verification from the intuitible to the meaningful. "Objectivity" in modern physics is not a problem of representation (*Darstellung*) but it is a problem of meaning alone (*"ein reines Bedeutungsproblem"*).[34]

In this last statement we have not only the heart of Cassirer's philosophy of science, but of the entire philosophy of symbolic forms, of which the scientific form is but a part. For the study of modern science shows us, what the philosophy of symbolic forms has continually emphasized, that all spiritual life and all spiritual development consist in nothing else than in such intellectual metamorphoses—and in this passage from representation to the creation of meaningful structures. Scientific knowledge repeats, in a different dimension to be sure, the same process which characterizes language and myth, a fact which, as we shall see, raises again, in an acute form, the fundamental problem of the knowledge value of all the symbolic forms.

C

In that in physical science the concept of substance has given place to that of function and the concepts of physics are found to symbolize not things but relations, mathematics, as the science of relations *par excellence*, becomes for Cassirer central in his entire treatment of science as symbolic form. His philosophy of mathematics, like his theory of logic, is a topic which belongs to other contributors, but some comment seems necessary in the present context. Here only one problem can be raised. It concerns the question of what we may call the "language of mathematics" and mathematics as symbolic form.

The main problem, of course, is that of the function of mathematical symbols in modern physical science; but this involves

[33] *Ibid.*, III, 538.
[34] *Ibid.*, III, 552.

also the problem of the philosophical basis of pure mathematics. Starting with the definition of mathematics as the science of numbers, and with the definition of numbers as symbols constructed for the ordering activities of the understanding, there is created the problem of the truth value of these symbols themselves.

Are they mere signs to which no objective meaning is to be assigned or have they a *fundamentum in re?* And if the latter is the case—where are we to seek this basis? Is it given, ready-made, in the "intuition;" or must it, apart from and independently of the intuitively given, gain and secure its validity in the independent activities of the understanding, in pure spontaneity of thought? With these questions we find ourselves in the very center of the methodological struggle which is presently raging about the meaning and content of the fundamental mathematical concepts. . . . What does this question mean for our own fundamental problem of symbolical thinking?[35]

The solution of this problem involves the entire dispute between the intuitive and the formal or symbolic theories in modern mathematics, and Cassirer's analysis of modern mathematical theory is one of the most important, as it is one of the most enlightening, phases of his work. So far as the basal problem is concerned, his answer is that the above disjunction is neither unequivocal nor complete. Mathematics, he holds, has objective significance, but that significance does not lie in any immediate correlation with the intuited world of "nature," but rather in the fact that, by constructing this world according to its own formal principles, it is enabled thereby to understand its laws. I have neither the space nor the competence to develop his solution of this problem in detail—it is but an application of the principle that the function of "language," in any form, is not to copy reality but to symbolize it—rather shall I note his comment on the opposition of realistic and idealistic theory in mathematics. A true and valid conception of the symbolic in the mathematical field, as in other fields, does not, he tells us, consort well with the traditional dualism of idealism and realism, subject and object, but rather transcends them. "The symbolic belongs neither . . . to the sphere of the immanent nor

[35] *Ibid.,* III, 414.

to that of the transcendent; its value consists precisely in the fact that it enables us to transcend these oppositions. It is not the one nor the other, but 'the one in the other' and 'the other in the one'."[36]

It is, however, as we have seen, in the transition from the schematism of pictures to the symbolism of principles that the rôle of mathematics has become increasingly significant in modern science. Order has thereby become the *"absoluter Grundbegriff"* of modern physics. For modern physical science the world presents itself no longer as a collection of entities, but as an order of happenings or events. Cassirer quotes with apparent approval a statement of Weyl in this connection.

Neither intuitive space nor intuitive time, but only a four-dimensional continuum in the abstract mathematical sense, may serve as the medium in which physics constructs the external world. If color consisted "actually" of ether-vibrations as for Huyghens, it appears now only as mathematical functional processes of a periodic character, whereby four independent variables occur in the functions as representatives of the spatio-temporal medium referring to co-ordinates. What remains, then, finally is a symbolic construction in precisely the sense in which Hilbert carried such construction through in the field of mathematics.[37]

Thus do the intuited space and time of the immediate *Ausdrucks-erlebnisse* become the ideal space-time which, as Cassirer said, while keeping the form of sensuous experience, progressively fills that form with non-sensuous ideal content and makes the sensuous form a symbol of the ideal.

D

In such fashion, then, does science, as symbolic form, find its place in Cassirer's more general idealistic philosophy of language and of symbolic forms. This symbolic theory of scientific concepts is, I suppose, not only the "accepted theory today" but one to which, as I believe, we are forced by the developments of modern scientific methodology. Nevertheless, as formulated by

[36] *Ibid.*, III, 444f.

[37] *PSF*, III, 546. The quotation from Weyl is taken from his *Philosophie der Mathematik und Naturwissenschaft*, found in *Handbuch der Philosophie*, 80.

Cassirer, it presents certain difficulties not wholly unrelated to those found in other parts of his general philosophy.

The primary difficulty arises out of an ambiguity in Cassirer's conception of science. The basal science, on his view, is the mathematical-physical, for here the essential law of all knowledge manifests itself completely; and it is for this type of science that his theory of scientific symbolism is developed. But there are other sciences ("so-called," at least), biology, psychology, etc., to say nothing of the *Geisteswissenschaften*, which, so to speak, employ other languages and exhibit very different symbolic form. Are they science or are they not? It is possible to hold, with many scientists, that they are really not science—that the universe is exhaustively analyzable into terms of pure mathematics, and only insofar as this analysis is carried out do we have science, properly speaking. This is a possible view, but it is very questionable whether the concepts of the mathematical sciences are most suitable for the biologist and psychologist, to say nothing of history and the other *Geisteswissenschaften*. Living organisms and conscious minds are, to be sure, a part of nature, but the concepts of nature developed in mathematical physics are scarcely such as to express adequately their nature as living and conscious. On the other hand, we may say that these are really science; and if that is the case the essential law of all knowledge does not manifest itself completely in the mathematical-physical sphere; nor is the concept of symbol developed in this sphere adequate to all forms of scientific symbolism. We are forced to a concept of "double symbolism" in science, such as I have developed in *Language and Reality*.[38]

It may be said, of course, that the issue here is largely verbal and concerns merely the question of the "definition" of science. But I do not believe that this is all there is to this problem. It concerns the much more fundamental question of whether the ideal of knowledge is really realized in the mathematical-physical form, whether, in short, there are not other aspects of reality the adequate expression of which requires a different kind of symbolism. Of the fact itself, of this "double symbolism," there is no doubt; the only question is whether we call this symbolic

[38] *Language and Reality*, 523ff.

form, other than that in the mathematical sciences, science or not. It is not, of course, my intention to argue these points here—I have done so in another context—but merely to suggest an important point at which Cassirer's philosophy of science leaves important questions unanswered.

Closely connected with this problem is one no less fundamental, and one which involves an ambiguity no less disturbing than the preceding. It concerns the relation of the scientific, more specifically the mathematical symbol, to ordinary language.

The ideal of science seems to be to pass from a language of things to a language of pure relations, a language which by an immanental necessity tends to become the language of mathematics. Science breaks through the husk of ordinary language, with its connotations, into a world of "pure notation." It becomes wholly *pronominal*, to use Karl Vossler's expression. The question, then, arises as to the relation of this mathematical symbolism to natural language. I am not sure as to Cassirer's position at this point; here also he seems to be ambiguous. According to him, the relation of mathematical symbols to "natural" language seems to parallel the relation of religion to myth. As the religious consciousness cannot abandon completely the mythical picture of the world, although it surpasses and transcends it, so the scientific and mathematical language never quite abandons the speech forms from which it developed. All "rigorous science," Cassirer tells us, demands that thought shall "free itself from the compulsion of the word;"[39] but this is never completely possible. The issue, as I see it, is not whether it is possible, but whether it is desirable. A mathematical equation, until it is interpreted, "says nothing," and I cannot see how it can be interpreted except in terms of "natural" language which involves inevitably those "pre-scientific" categories, of substance and attribute, which, according to this theory of science, it is the ideal of science to transcend.

I find, then, in Cassirer an ambiguity which I also find present in many modern physicists. On the one hand, we find them speaking of electrons, etc., as the symbols "with which

[39] *PSF*, III, 382.

we deck our mathematical equations;" the assumption being that the equations, the mathematical relations, express the non-symbolic aspects of reality. On the other hand, these same mathematical signs, which make up the equations, are themselves characterized as symbols—with the result that we are left uncertain as to what is symbol and what reality. My own view—which I do not, of course, wish to argue here—is that mathematical symbols *are* merely "pronominal," they merely manipulate, and, until they are translated into non-mathematical terms, "say nothing." I should be disposed to say with Brouwer that mathematics is *"weit mehr ein Thun denn eine Lehre."* Yet, whatever pure mathematics may be, mathematical physics is *not* a *mere Thun*, (activity or manipulation), but also a *Lehre* or theory—a theory of the nature of reality, a theory which, as I believe, can be stated only in terms of natural language and of the categories which naturally belong to such language. In other words, physical theory must ultimately presuppose a metaphysics which cannot be merely a symbolism of relations but must be a symbolism of things.

The questions here raised, important as they are, do not, however, affect, I think, the general critical-idealistic philosophy of science. The essence of that interpretation of science, as it is for all those who thus conceive it, is that science is one symbolic form among other symbolic forms. Science, Cassirer would say with Weyl, I think, concedes to idealism that its objective world is not given, but only propounded like a problem to be solved, and that it can only be constructed by symbols. He would also say with Eddington, I think, that the exploration of the external world by science leads not to concrete reality, but to a world of symbols beneath which these methods are not adapted to penetrating. In saying these things, *if* he says them, he would also say, by implication, that there are other symbolic forms which are more adapted—if not to *penetrate* into concrete reality (Cassirer would probably not wish to use this expression), certainly more adapted to *expressing* concrete reality. But there is a further implication of this theory of science which he could scarcely avoid, namely, that science, so understood, presupposes a metaphysics. Not only is art as symbolic form *une métaphysique figurée,* to use Bergson's terms, but science is also. The ideal of modern science, as conceived by Cassirer, is expressed in the postulate that nothing shall be admitted to science which is not resolvable into the sensible and the measurable. But this postulate presupposes that there is a metaphysical sphere not thus resolvable. If so, the question arises whether, corresponding to this sphere, there is not a language of metaphysics and a metaphysical symbolism.

VII

The Language of Metaphysics and The Nature of Philosophical Discourse

A

One of the chief problems which face any one who realizes the issues raised by the problem of the relation of language to thought and knowledge is that of the language of philosophy. The philosophy of symbolic forms is philosophy and not science; although, of course, the results of scientific investigation find their place in the phenomenology of these forms. What, then, is the character of philosophical language?

That there is such a thing as philosophical discourse, as contrasted with scientific, is recognized by Cassirer in his acceptance of the Hegelian principle that the phenomenological method is the presupposition of philosophy and in the application of this method to the philosophy of symbolic forms. It is recognized also that philosophical discourse involves a radical shift from the sphere of things (that of science) to the sphere of meanings (and values). The traditional view, of course, is that this discourse is identical with that of metaphysics—that the language of philosophy and that of metaphysics are one. This view has, however, been challenged in the modern world, not only by positivism but by certain interpretations of the Kantian "critical" philosophy. Cassirer's position is one continuous critique of positivism in all spheres of the human spirit; it is not so clear what his position is regarding Kant and metaphysics. In any case, it seems obvious that a philosophy of symbolic forms, to be in any sense complete, must include a study of the language and the form which we call metaphysical.

B

In the entire three volumes there is only one point at which the problem of metaphysics is presented at all—the section in Vol. III, entitled "Intuitive and Symbolic Knowledge in Modern Metaphysic." It is a critique of Bergson's position in which metaphysics is defined as the science which seeks to dispense with symbols—"the most radical denial," as Cassirer rightly says, "of the right of all symbol formation which has ever appeared in the history of metaphysics."[40]

Cassirer's criticism of Bergson at this point is, I believe, fully justified. Quite rightly he points out that this sharp contrast, between the way of metaphysical intuition and the way of science and knowledge, shows Bergson to be the son of a naturalistic epoch in which all activity of the intellect is reduced to the purely vital or biological. Quite rightly also he points out the impossibility of a purely intuitive metaphysics; for it would not be any kind of knowledge, even metaphysical, unless it gave us some description of the "vital force," and this too requires theoretical or form elements; in other words, metaphysical knowledge must be symbolic form also.

This criticism of a purely intuitive metaphysics seems to imply both the right to a metaphysical language and also to symbolic construction in metaphysics. We look, therefore, for a further development of the language of metaphysics and of symbolism as a metaphysical principle; but little light is thrown upon either the nature of metaphysics or the character of its language and symbolism. Just as we feel that we are about to put our hands on the key to the solution of the problem, Cassirer remarks, "Aber wir brechen an diesem Punkte ab." (III, 48) All that can be asked, he continues, is a journey round the world, the *globus intellectualis*. It would seem, then, that the philosophy of symbolic forms is intended to be just such a journey—neither penetration into the essence of "reality" nor an ultimate interpretation of its meaning. It is apparently

[40] *PSF*, III, 42ff, esp. 43 and 44.

merely a phenomenology, not a metaphysics that is offered us.

Nevertheless, it seems doubtful whether a philosophy of language and of symbolic forms can stop at this point. Even in a journey around the *globus intellectualis* the traveller will inevitably come upon a region in which men talk a language which is neither that of science, as understood by Cassirer, nor of myth and poetry—a language and symbolic form which can only be called metaphysical. That there is such a language can, I think, scarcely be denied. If the various symbolic forms, art, religion, science, all, in their several ways, constitute *une métaphysique figurée*, then there must be, it would seem, a language of metaphysics in which these symbolic forms are expanded and interpreted. As metaphysical "postulation" is necessary to round out our world of experience, so metaphysical language is necessary to make these other languages intelligible. Elsewhere I have myself attempted a study of this unique language and of the nature of the symbolic structure called metaphysics.[41] I have, of course, no intention of going into that here, but desire merely to suggest that this is one of the gaps in Cassirer's thought which I am unable to fill, and that precisely here the fundamental ambiguity in his evaluation of language is in evidence.

It would doubtless be an impertinence should I venture to indicate what, had Cassirer carried out this task, his conception of the language of metaphysics and of metaphysics as symbolic form would have been. It may be permitted, however, to suggest the point at which, in attempting to understand Cassirer, I have found myself thrown into confusion and uncertainty. If the ideal form and immanental law of all knowledge is, indeed, to be found in the mathematical-physical sciences, then it would seem that the symbolism of metaphysics must also be a symbolism of relations and that a philosophy of events, such as that of Whitehead for instance, would necessarily be the resultant metaphysics. On the other hand, if it is true, as we are told by Cassirer, that science as symbolic form has no exclusive value, but is only one way of constructing reality, and has value only from the standpoint of science, then it would appear that

---

[41] *Language and Reality*, Chap. XIII.

a metaphysics, to be adequate, must be a metaphysics of art and religion also and must have a language and symbolic form which includes these forms also—in which case it could no longer be a symbolism of relations merely, but must be a symbolism of things also.

But all this may be beside the point. It may be, after all, that it is merely a phenomenology and not a metaphysics with which Cassirer presents us. The question always remains, I suppose, whether, as in the case of Kant, the critical transcendental method is the denial of metaphysics or itself a metaphysics. This is, I believe, an ambiguity inherent in the Kantian position and one shared by the philosophy of symbolic forms itself. If so, this ambiguity must take its place beside the other forms of ambiguity which have presented themselves at various stages of the development of this philosophy. The key to the understanding of knowledge, Cassirer tells us, is the Kantian principle that we must have our eyes, not on the results, but on the processes of knowledge.[42] That may be an important key to understanding, but it is scarcely sufficient for evaluation; it may reveal to us the meaning of the process, but can scarcely determine the truth of its result. This brings us to the problem of meaning and truth in Cassirer's philosophy.

VIII

Language and Reality. The Problem of Meaning and Truth

A

How much the present writer has learned from his journey in Cassirer's company around the *globus intellectualis*, is, I hope, fully clear from the sympathetic presentation of the main points of his philosophy of symbolic forms. But that I have still much to learn is clear also from the fact that I have been forced to confess my perplexity at certain crucial points. What has puzzled me has already been suggested by the indication of certain ambiguities present in his philosophy of language *eo nomine*, and which have grown in significance as we have passed on to the wider implications of his philosophy.

[42] *PSF*, III, 7ff, esp. 8.

The critical position which Cassirer maintains throughout explicitly denies exclusive value to any one of the fundamental symbolic forms. Modern science has come to recognize, he holds, that its concepts or symbols are constructions for a special purpose, namely, "to deduce, as from models, what will happen in the external world." As such "they correspond to the standpoint of science and have no ultimate meaning outside that standpoint." Art and religion are equally symbolic forms, equally ways of representing the world. "None of these forms," Cassirer tells us, is a "direct reproduction of realistically given facts." All share in the common character of being the *media* of expression of one spiritual principle. All have meaning; do they all also have truth?

To none of these forms, therefore, does Cassirer deny meaning or significance. The question is whether this significance includes the truth-value of knowledge. I may be wrong, but on this point also Cassirer seems to me to give an equivocal answer. It is true that he *seems* to conceive them all as forms of knowledge and truth. Even to the mythical form he ascribes truth-value. From the standpoint of the problem as formulated, he maintains "relative truth" can be no longer denied, although significantly enough, he puts the word "truth" in quotation marks.[43] As for all "critical" philosophies of myth, so for his theory, the myth expresses aspects of reality which the mathematical-physical language cannot express. Obviously, then, both art and religion, which make use of mythical language symbolically, are *a fortiori* forms of truth. And yet there is another aspect of his thought. It is in science that the essential form and law of knowledge finds its supreme expression and is thus a higher symbolic form with a truth that need not be put in quotation marks. We cannot escape the suspicion that science, as symbolic form, is not only the highest expression, but one that shall supersede all other forms. Nor can we escape the further suspicion that, when "truth" is used in connection with the other forms, it is with a secret reservation which seems, to the present writer at least, seriously to threaten the stability of

[43] *Ibid.*, II, 19.

the splendid structure which Cassirer has erected in these three volumes.

Two tendencies strive for supremacy in Cassirer's thought, as indeed they do in all forms of philosophy which draw their chief inspiration from the ideals of knowledge of a scientific age, the ideals upon which Kant himself seemed at least to set his *imprimatur*. On the one hand, there is the narrow conception of truth which it seems difficult to avoid in this age of science. In many passages in Cassirer's works this seems to be the truth notion *par excellence,* as it was for Kant in one of his philosophic moods. On the assumption that the basal conception and inner law of knowledge are *completely* shown in the methods of science, this seems inevitable. On the other hand, another conception also strives for recognition in Cassirer's thought, as indeed it must in the thought of any one who is as conversant as he is with the breadth and depth of human culture—a conception which, in the words of John Dewey, is "broader and more humane"—one upon which Kant also put his *imprimatur* in another of his philosophical moods. It is the dilemma underlying all the other dilemmas into which the modern mind has been forced.

I have little doubt that Cassirer had a solution for this dilemma and that it is only my own failure to bring the many strands of his far-flung argument into a significant whole which prevents me from seeing it. None the less, I fail to see it, and it is for this reason that I ask for more light. There is, indeed, one strand of this argument which, if I understand it aright, affords such a solution.

The truth notion, Cassirer tells us, contains in itself an immanental dialectic which "drives it on unmercifully further and further forwards, beyond any boundary hitherto reached." Starting with the natural truth notion, *adaequatio intellectus et rei,* "this dialectic is content not merely with calling in question particular elements of the natural world picture, but seizes upon the fundamental truth notion itself." The outcome of this inner dialectic is a radical shift from the notion of truth to that of meaning; and, although this shift "to a realm of pure meaning and validity creates new problems and new difficulties, it nevertheless results in the subordination of the notion of truth to that of meaning"[44]—a subordination which, as we have seen, is as much a feature of the development of modern physical science as of any other symbolic form; for objectivity in modern physics is not a problem of representation (*Darstellung*), but of meaning alone (*ein reines Bedeutungsproblem*).

This subordination of truth to meaning is obviously susceptible of two interpretations. On the one hand, it may be so interpreted as to express a widespread tendency in modern philosophy—one shared by positivism and instrumentalism alike—namely, to insist upon the existence of realms of meaning or significance (such as those of art and metaphysics) in which notions of truth and falsity are irrelevant and into which, as it has been said, "truth has no right to enter." On the other hand, it may be so interpreted as to express the notion that, in the development of thought which has resulted in the subordination of truth to meaning, truth *has* a right to enter because the meaningful is already true, for truth and meaning ultimately coincide. The sum total of meaningful discourse is the truth.

This is my own solution of the problem, as developed in *Language and Reality*. I hope it is Cassirer's also, for then it would not only be true that I have learned immensely from his philosophy of symbolic forms, but also that from this learning I have not drawn consequences which would be disavowed by Cassirer himself. I hope it is his solution also, for the reason that from this solution of the problem would follow, I think, the answers to the other problems which I have felt constrained to raise in the course of these discussions.

Wilbur M. Urban

Yale University
New Haven, Connecticut

[44] *PSF*, III, 6ff.; also 328ff.

13

James Gutmann

CASSIRER'S HUMANISM

CASSIRER'S HUMANISM

CASSIRER'S Humanism is not a segment or portion of his philosophy; it is an aspect of all his writing and teaching. It permeates his thought in his historical studies and also in his theoretical and systematic works. As a student of the history of ideas, Cassirer concentrated his interest and attention on those great figures and ages of intellectual history in which the humanistic interest was especially prominent. His studies of Plato and Platonism in ancient thought and in later times, of the philosophy of the Renaissance in its ethical and cosmological speculations, and of the age of the Enlightenment are some of the evidences of his interest in the traditions of humanism. His work as an editor of Leibniz and Kant, his biography of Kant and his studies of Descartes, Kepler, Leibniz, and others, reflect a prevailing sense of philosophy's relation to other cultural interests. Even his most technical contributions to linguistics and to epistemological and mathematical theory reveal his pervasive humanistic concern. The relation of these specialized studies to his great systematic work is signally illustrated in his essay on *Language and Myth*, which was written at the very time when he was formulating the *Philosophie der symbolischen Formen*. And the significance of Cassirer's humanism in his conception of symbolic forms is definitively expressed in the synoptic version of his system, his *Essay on Man*.

The philosophy of symbolic forms starts from the presupposition that, if there is any definition of the nature or "essence" of man, this definition can only be understood as a functional one, not a substantial one. We cannot define man by any inherent principle which constitutes his metaphysical essence—nor can we define him by any inborn faculty or instinct that may be ascertained by empirical observation. Man's outstanding characteristic, his distinguishing mark, is not his metaphysical or physical nature—but his work. It is this work, it is the system of human activities, which defines and determines the circle of "humanity." Language, myth, religion, art, science, history are the constituents, the various sectors of this circle.[1]

The present paper will not, of course, attempt to review Cassirer's achievements as a humanist in all the ranges of his work. However, while stressing his contribution to the humanities, it will consider his literary and artistic interests in relation to that "philosophical anthropology" which is, after all, the equivalent—in Greek dress—of wisdom-loving humanism. The designation of "philosophical anthropology" was chosen by Cassirer himself, following in Kant's footsteps, to describe the content of the seminar in which he was engaged at the time of his death. Cassirer's use of Kant's terms in this seminar as in his *Essay on Man* showed at one and the same time his reverence for Kant and the independence with which he—unlike some of the neo-Kantians—employed the Kantian legacy.

Though Cassirer's modification of Kant raised difficulties both in his historical work and in his systematic writing, this paper, while considering some of them below, is particularly designed to show how other elements, borrowed and original, contributed to Cassirer's humanism. After considering some of these elements, notably the influence of German Romanticism, a brief review of Cassirer's own summary of the history of Western humanism will lead back naturally to certain aspects of his Kantianism, not only in its relevance to his position as a humanist historian, but also to the relation of his views on history to his other humanistic interests. That his humanism is one of the constant factors in the wide range of his interests and in all his contributions to philosophy is the thesis of this paper. Cassirer is a follower of Kant, but is surely not to be interpreted as a neo-Kantian in any limited sense. He stands in many traditions, among them, neither last nor least, in the great tradition of philosophic humanism.

[1] *Essay on Man*, 67-68.

I

It is significant that Cassirer came to philosophy as a student of literature and linguistics. Though his publications include numerous technical studies not only of mathematics but of physics and psychology, his initial interest in languages and literature remained a major preoccupation. His studies of German culture, *Freiheit und Form*, as well as some of the essays which compose his subsequent *Idee und Gestalt* anticipate *in nuce* doctrines concerning myth and language which he developed in his later writings. Goethe and Schiller, Herder, Kleist and Hölderlin, Lessing and Rousseau are figures to whom he returned again and again, not only to use them to illuminate the work of other more technical philosophers, but for their own sake. He wrote on *Goethe and Plato* or on *Goethe and Kant*, but he is as much interested in Goethe's *Pandora* and *Faust* as in Goethe's views on natural science or in Goethe and mathematical physics. He discussed Lessing and Mendelssohn or Schiller and Shaftesbury with as much emphasis on the more literary as on the more technically philosophical writer. His study of Hölderlin foreshadowed the exhaustive analysis of mythopoeic imagination in which he later developed the insights of modern romanticism and particularly of Schelling's philosophy of mythology and revelation.

Though following Helmholtz, Otto Liebmann, and Cassirer's own teacher, Hermann Cohen, "back to Kant," and though adhering to Kantian principles, Cassirer repeatedly proved his indebtedness to some of the insights of certain post-Kantian writers, notably Humboldt and Schelling. Rejecting the metaphysical absolutism which prevailed in Fichte, in Schelling's emphasis on the Infinite, and especially in Hegel, and though critical of the psychological approach made by Schopenhauer and Nietzsche, he found in Romanticism's awareness of the significance of myth, of poetic imagery and cultural continuity, elements worthy of being added to the stern and rigorous discipline of Kantianism. Never forgetting Kant's insistence that all philosophy must regard the dualism between being and becoming as a logical rather than a metaphysical dualism and that it must accept the findings of science as its data, he nevertheless concerned himself with the processes of change, of becoming, which Romanticism emphasizes. Differing from Kant and agreeing with Humboldt that speculation regarding the genesis and essence of language is not the business of the philosopher, he carried forward the study of linguistics for which Jacob Grimm had laid the foundations. Conceiving man not as *homo sapiens* nor as *homo faber* but as *animal symbolicum,* he concerned himself with symbolic forms in all aspects of man's experience.

To what extent this fusion of neo-Kantianism with interests and problems largely foreign to Kant's thought generated difficulties for Cassirer need not be questioned now. But any understanding of man as *animal symbolicum* requires at least a brief consideration of Cassirer's use of mythopoeic data. Cassirer traced the relation of myth to speculative thought from Plato and neo-Platonism to such modern writers as Giambattista Vico, Hölderlin and Schelling. Though the attitudes of these and other related thinkers differ with regard to the precise significance of mythical elements in human nature and culture, they agree in conceiving mythic apprehension as more than metaphorical or allegorical. None of them sees the symbolic function of myth precisely as Cassirer himself came to view it; but Schelling approaches this view more closely than the others. Moreover, Cassirer construed Schelling's *Philosophie der Mythologie* as being, in part, an elaboration and development of an early intuition of Hölderlin's. "Mythopoeic imagery," he wrote, "is no mere ornament which we incidentally add to our portrait of reality, but it is one of the necessary organs for the apprehension of reality itself. In it we find the world and life first truly revealed and made significant."[2]

As this statement, quoted from Cassirer's essay on "Hölderlin and German Idealism," suggests, he acknowledged this early anticipation of his conception of mythopoeic imagination as a necessary organ of apprehension which he developed especially in the second volume of the *Philosophie der symbolischen*

[2] *Idee und Gestalt,* 121.

Formen. In spite of Cassirer's diagnosis of Hölderlin's intellectual limitations, his appreciation of Hölderlin's artistic insights reveals a fundamental sympathy. If he denies Hölderlin a position of great importance in the history of philosophy, he credits him with a high degree of poetic inspiration. It is significant, moreover, that, though he bases his own estimate of Hölderlin's artistic greatness on the poet's concern with mythic imagery, he also finds this the source of his chief philosophic deficiency. He seems to be convinced that Hölderlin's absorption in mythology actually interfered with his attaining an adequate total conception of human nature and human history. Hölderlin happily reacted against those eighteenth century thinkers who treated myth only in a derogatory sense; but Cassirer finds his attainments in philosophy negligible despite Hölderlin's "lifelong earnest wrestling with philosophic problems, since he was never a systematic thinker." It remained for Schelling, who recognized myth as a product of man's collective imagination, not only to see myth as a great and indestructible force basic to all culture, but also to formulate the first systematic philosophy of mythology.

Whether or not this estimate of Hölderlin be accepted is less important, at least in the present context, than the circumstance that Cassirer's judgment is based on his insistence concerning the lack of *system* in Hölderlin's thought. It is not entirely clear whether he believes such a lack of system to be due to temperamental limitations or to the inadequacy of a humanism which fails to recognize the importance of non-literary and non-artistic elements as expressions of human nature. Be that as it may, it is evidence of the primary importance which Cassirer attached to systematic construction in philosophy.

II

However much Cassirer differed from Alexander Pope, the title of whose poem he used for his *Essay on Man,* he agreed with him that "the proper study of mankind is man." To be sure, Cassirer included in such a study many elements which would have seemed irrelevant not only to Pope but to the philosophers of his day who discussed human nature. Indeed, the history of the interpretation of human nature from the time when the Greeks inscribed "Know Thyself" on the Temple of Apollo would show striking contrasts not only with regard to the content and scope of such knowledge but also with respect to the methods of pursuing it. The anthropological philosophy which Kant fathered seems often to have been neglected by philosophers who claimed to be Kantians. It itself has undergone significant changes. Yet every example of it which is worthy of its founder combines the ethical imperative characteristic of Kant with the scepticism that underlies his *Critiques* but which is, like all genuine scepticism, the "counterpart of resolute *humanism*."[3]

"The starting point of all anthropological philosophy," writes Bernard Groethuysen in his essay "Towards an Anthropological Philosophy,"

or all philosophy of man, is the ancient maxim, 'Know Thyself.' But what is it that man wishes to know about himself? What are the questions which he puts to himself? 'Know Thyself' is the command. . . . [But this] means not simply try to define yourself by concepts, . . . but become conscious of yourself, live in the consciousness of yourself, understand yourself, come to experience yourself, be present to yourself, live in the awareness of your present, come to yourself.[4]

As Socrates interpreted the Delphic injunction, it meant not merely that the unexamined life was no life for man, but that self-knowledge by its very nature could not be achieved in isolation, that it involved a co-operative venture and that the individual, to be truly known, must be known not only in all his social relations but, indeed, required the assistance of others to achieve this very knowledge. In Socrates, "philosophy, which had hitherto been conceived as an intellectual monologue, is transformed into a dialogue. Only by way of dialogical or dialectic thought can we approach the knowledge of human nature."[5] Socrates finds his teachers among those who dwell in the city and is content to interrogate an unschooled slave boy, if only the latter can add to his knowledge of the nature of

---

[3] *Essay on Man*, 1.
[4] *Philosophy and History*, ed. by Klibansky and Paton, 77.
[5] *Essay on Man*, 5.

man. It is surely in this sense that "his philosophy, if he possesses a philosophy," is strictly anthropological.

Doubtless one of the aspects of Renaissance culture which has drawn scholars like Cassirer again and again to study its art and thought is the reaffirmation, involved in its cultural rebirth, of the validity of natural human aspiration. Contrasted with the other-worldliness of mediaevalism, the recognition that human nature is indeed natural led to the conviction that human appetites and aspirations can yield all manner of excellence. The plasticity of man's endowments not only suggested the ideal of the *uomo universale* but an increased interest in variety and differentiation as such. Though this central awareness of the Renaissance has been remarked by many students, and though Cassirer himself gave attention to its manifestation by many contrasting types, his study of Giovanni Pico della Mirandola expressed this aspect of Renaissance humanism with singular persuasiveness: What Pico

sets up as the distinctive privilege of man is the almost unlimited *power of self-transformation* at his disposal. Man is that being to whom no particular form has been prescribed and assigned. He possesses the power of entering into any form whatever. What is novel in this idea lies not in its content, but rather in the *value* Pico places on this content. . . . With Pico this inner unrest of man, impelling him on from one goal to another, and forcing him to pass from one form to another, no longer appears as a mere stigma upon human nature, as a mere blot and weakness. Pico admires this multiplicity and multiformity, and he sees in it a mark of human greatness.[6]

Clearly, for man to know himself, in this sense, is to recognize the rich and varied potentialities of his nature.

That there were limitations upon even the inclusive ideal of Renaissance humanism is evident in the comparatively small place which was allowed to natural science by humanists such as Erasmus and Vives. But in this respect, as in many others, Cassirer views the Renaissance as an age in which distinctive and original developments in the relation of science to other learning took place.

[6] In the *Journal of the History of Ideas*, III, no. 3, 331.

III

In his monograph, "Naturalistische und humanistische Begründung der Kulturphilosophie" (published in 1939) as well as in his *Zur Logik der Kulturwissenschaften* (1942), Cassirer traces in detail the complicated relationship of the naturalistic and humanistic factors in philosophy from the Renaissance to the twentieth century. In both of these essays Cassirer uses his humanism to clarify problems of the philosophy of culture. This field of study, he repeatedly points out, is perhaps the most problematic and disputed realm in the whole domain of philosophy. Not only are clear and recognized solutions lacking in this novel philosophic discipline, but there is even a lack of agreement as to the questions which may reasonably be asked. Unlike logic, physics, and ethics, which remained the three main branches of philosophy from antiquity down to the time of Kant, these newer questions lack a secure tradition and development. According to Cassirer's interpretation, Kant is here, as in so many other domains, the dividing line between fundamentally different views of the relation of nature and human nature, or, to change the metaphor, the bridge from classical humanism to distinctively modern conceptions of man and culture.

During the sixteenth and seventeenth centuries, Cassirer notes, a new preoccupation became increasingly evident among philosophers, though it could find no definite place in the traditional systems. Cultivated by philosophical humanists, the discipline which was later to be called by Dilthey the *"natürliche System der Geisteswissenschaften"* could not be assimilated to traditional philosophy, because it appeared to conflict with the natural and mathematical sciences, to which the mightiest and most productive forces, over which the modern spirit reigned, were applied. To the new scientific philosophers there seemed to be no place for a genuinely respectable philosophy apart from mathematics and the mathematical sciences, which constituted the ideal of knowledge. If the realities of humanism were to become accessible to philosophic reason, this would have to be accomplished by making them accessible to the same mathematical apprehension which had grasped the physical universe. The alternative was to leave the humanistic enterprise in mystic darkness, subject to theological traditions. Spinoza's attempt to establish a systematic unity between ethics and geometry was based upon the conviction that human nature could no longer be regarded as an enclave in an all-inclusive natural order. Man and human achievements must henceforth be viewed and described as though they were a matter of lines, surfaces, or corporeal bodies. Spinoza's doctrine of a unified nature reached its climax in his demand for a monistic view not merely as a metaphysic but as a strict method of interpreting nature. A sound philosophy will dispense with teleology and banish the notion of purpose from nature; for, if we seek the genesis of this notion, it is evident that it is merely an anthropomorphic misunderstanding and falsification, whereas only an application of mathematical law can yield the truth.

Spinoza's monistic methodology conditioned subsequent thought, and precisely this demand for unity became the decisively important motive in the revival of Spinozism at the end of the eighteenth century. Schelling linked his thought to Spinoza's at this point and expressly declared that his "Philosophy of Identity" was designed to complete what Spinoza had posited in his first, daring outline. But in spite of this assurance of complete agreement and consonance with Spinoza, Schelling could not take up the problem at the same point where Spinoza had left it. For even if he teaches that there is an absolute identity between nature and spirit, the concept of nature, one of the supposedly identical factors in the equation, has changed fundamentally for him. When Schelling speaks of nature, he reiterates that he is not thinking of a being which merely has extension and motion. He does not apprehend it as a concept of geometric relationships and mechanical laws but as a Whole having living forms and powers. The system of nature of mathematical physics is for him a mere abstraction, a shadow world. From this initial stage of being, philosophic thought ascends to the actual world of spirit—to the world of history and human culture. From theoretic knowledge of the laws of space and time, matter and force, the path of philosophy ascends through the realm of moral consciousness to the highest stage, the stage of aesthetic awareness.

That which we call nature is a poem which lies concealed in a secret, wondrous form. Yet, if the riddle could be revealed, we would recognize in it the Odyssey of the spirit, which, wondrously deceived, seeks itself while fleeing from itself, for through the sensuous world meaning can be discerned only as if through words, just as the land of imagination towards which we aim may be discerned as if through half-transparent mists.[7]

Cassirer quotes these lines of Schelling's in his "Naturalistische und humanistische Begründung der Kulturphilosophie" in an historic summary which we are following in synoptic form. He goes on to point out how Romanticism developed this view of Schelling's. In so doing he also indicated his own relationship to the Romantic movement. For Cassirer holds that the strength as well as the weakness of Romanticism are to be found in its attempt to explain by a single principle and to view in a single focus all conscious phenomena from the first dreamlike dawn of mythical consciousness, through fable and poesy up to the loftiest pronouncements of thought in language, science, and philosophy. The land of imagination, of which Schelling speaks, and the realm of strict logical knowledge constantly interpenetrate in romantic theory; they are never separated, but interlock with one another. Romanticism's greatest achievements, according to Cassirer, were derived from this imaginative power and intuition. Not only was nature seen in a new light, but, so viewed, it included all forms of the spirit. Here for the first time seemed to be revealed the most genuine and profoundest sources of myth and religion, of language and literature, of morality and law. For Romanticism the origin of all things of the spirit, which is clear and mysterious at one and the same time, is to be found in the *Volksgeist*. This is a kind of humanistic naturalism, even though it speaks the language of a spiritual metaphysics.

The weakness and danger of this position for a humanistic philosophy become clearly apparent when the veil is lifted

[7] Schelling, *System des transzendentalen Idealismus* (*Sämmtliche Werke*, III, 628).

which Romanticism had thrown over nature and history. This takes place whenever philosophy is no longer satisfied with delving by intuition into the ultimate depths of life but instead seeks to examine its view of life scientifically. This change of attitude, which occurred, for instance, in the second half of the nineteenth century, is, at least in part, responsible for the crisis in man's knowledge of himself which Cassirer pointed out in the first chapter of the *Essay on Man*. It was most clearly apparent in the circle of French thinkers who based their teaching on Comte's *Cours de Philosophie positive*. Comte's positivism not only gave them a method but also formulated the questions which they attempted to answer. But they were affected by the status of the science which they confronted even more than by the general philosophic presuppositions of positivism. For the teachings of classical physics provided them with their view of the world and, for them, seemed to possess finality. The principle of causality was axiomatic. Even critically-minded thinkers trained in Kantian philosophy did not dare to disturb the form in which the principle of causality was accepted. For example, Otto Liebmann, in his essay on *Die Klimax der Theorien*, proceeds on the basis of a strict determinism, which is presumed to apply in the same way to the several realms of thought, investigation and knowledge, without distinction or the slightest difference between the moral and the physical worlds.

As Cassirer points out, no cultural philosopher of science would dare, today, to introduce the principle of universal determinism in the form in which Liebmann used it. For if he did, he would be confronted at once by all the weighty questions and doubts involved in the development of modern theoretical physics, even though—as Cassirer adds—he does not believe that these doubts imply that the concept of causality, as such, is endangered. The French positivists, who first faced the problems which the assumption of an axiom of universal determinism posed for the *Kulturwissenschaften* and for the foundation of the *Geisteswissenschaften*, were neither mathematicians nor physicists, even if they took physics as their model. It was not the world view of Newton and Laplace but of Darwin and Spencer which characterized their outlook. Here too, as for Schelling and the romanticist philosophy of nature, culture and nature are united, insofar as both are subject to a common law, the basic law of evolution. But the direction of this unification has altered; for the difference which seems to divide human culture and physical nature is, according to positivism, no longer to be bridged by a spiritualization of nature, as in the way of Romanticism, but by interpreting culture materialistically. Not metaphysics nor theology, but physics and chemistry, zoology and botany, anatomy and physiology must, it is argued, take the lead, if a true science of culture is to be achieved.

Sainte-Beuve and Taine, too, interpreted cultural phenomena in terms of forces

not like the supra-personal unities and totalities of romantic theories, which belonged to a supersensuous world, but as the same ones which build and rule the material world. . . . Thus viewed, science is neither to justify nor to condemn but to investigate and explain. Cultural science must proceed like botany which studies the orange tree and the laurel, the pine and the birch with equal interest.[8]

If we designate one group of facts as physical and another as spiritual or moral, some sort of difference of content may then be exposed. But this circumstance is utterly irrelevant to our knowing them. For knowledge is never concerned with individual facts as such but with their inter-connections.

Cassirer considers three divergent attempts to establish a principle for interpreting these inter-connections based upon three distinct systems of postulates. In addition to French positivism he reviews the theories of Oswald Spengler and also the Hegelian philosophy of history. Spengler regarded his own views as a great advance on positivism, which he held to be narrowly naturalistic. According to him a culture is brought to birth in a way which natural science cannot comprehend, but which the philosopher should grasp by dramatizing (*dichten*) history. Thus Spengler conceived the epic-drama of *The De-*

---

[8] "Naturalistische und humanistische Begründung der Kulturphilosophie," 11; cf. Bibliography of Cassirer's Writings: 1939:3; also *Zur Logik der Kulturwissenschaften*, 87ff.

cline of the West, in which individual man, in his being and his activity, is mystically linked to the fate of civilizations whose rise and decline he can in no way control. This view Cassirer contrasts with Hegel's claim that his philosophy of history is a philosophy of freedom. But he rejects these as well as positivism. All three, he declares, are unsatisfactory as attempts to clarify history and culture, because they hold inadequate conceptions of human nature and man's activities.

IV

The preceding summary describes contrasting attitudes toward traditions of humanism before and after Kant. It indicates the extent to which his philosophical anthropology was the dividing line, in Cassirer's judgment, between the classical and Renaissance conceptions which retained their authority down to the eighteenth century, and more modern ones which have been associated especially with changes in natural science. Cassirer's historical account, which we have followed, serves also to define his own position, or, at least, to place him in the great tradition. In his humanism he has been a follower not only of Kant but of Herder and Hölderlin, of Goethe and Humboldt. Diverging from the positions of other post-Kantians, he has found sustenance in Schelling's philosophy of mythology, although rejecting his transcendental idealism.

By his distinctive interpretation of Kant, Cassirer long ago established the basis for his own doctrine of man. In so doing he illustrated not only Kant's but his own humanism. The posthumously published essay on "Kant and Rousseau" once again made clear how fundamentally Cassirer's humanism is based on Kant's view of human nature developed in his philosophical anthropology. The emphasis on this aspect of Kant's work was already evident in his *Kants Leben und Lehre.* "The man who introduced anthropology as a branch of study in German universities and who lectured on it regularly for decades"[9] was himself, according to Cassirer, much more of a humanist than scholars have generally recognized.

Herder, who during the 'sixties was Kant's pupil in Königsberg, has

---

[9] *Kants Leben und Lehre,* 25.

drawn for us a living and characteristic picture of his philosophical teaching at that time. From it we see that this teaching was by no means restricted to abstract problems, to questions of logic and metaphysics. It extended just as much to the fundamental questions of natural science, to psychology and anthropology, and it made full use of contemporary literature.[10] To be sure, this interest was essentially restricted to Kant's pre-critical period.[11]

In just that period of his life in which he was most under the influence of Rousseau from whom he "learned to respect human nature"[12] Cassirer notes that Kant was "a stylist and a psychological essayist, and in this respect he established a new standard for the German philosophical literature of the eighteenth century."[13] And he remarks "that Rousseau not only influenced the content and systematic development of Kant's foundation of ethics, but that he also formed its language and style."[14] It may not be irrelevant in this connection to suggest that Cassirer's own "language and style" reflected his study of the great figures of German literature in somewhat the way that Kant was influenced by Rousseau. In any case there need be no question that Cassirer can claim a place among the relatively small group of philosophers who were also men of letters—and the very small group of German philosophers who attained such distinction.

Some passages from Kant's writings which Cassirer quotes in his essay on "Kant and Rousseau" suggest not only the centrality of the humanistic and anthropological interest in Kant's ethical doctrine but throw further light on Cassirer's own thought. Even the conviction that the proper study for mankind is man, is reënforced by the argument which Kant uses for placing Rousseau's work alongside Newton's:

Newton was the first to discern order and regularity in combination with great simplicity, where before him men had encountered disorder

[10] See Herder's *Briefe zur Beförderung der Humanität*, 79th letter.

[11] *Rousseau Kant Goethe*, 86.

[12] Kant's *Fragmente, ed. Hartenstein*, vol. VIII, 624. Quoted in *Rousseau Kant Goethe*, 1; cf. also *Kants Leben und Lehre*, 238ff, and *Zur Logik der Kulturwissenschaften*, 113ff.

[13] *Rousseau Kant Goethe*, 6.

[14] *Ibid.*, 32.

and unrelated diversity. . . . Rousseau was the first to discover, beneath the varying forms human nature assumes, the deeply concealed essence of man. . . . After Newton and Rousseau, the ways of God are justified —and Pope's thesis is henceforth true.[15]

Kant indicated the relation of his philosophical anthropology to ethics in announcing his lectures for 1765-1766:

I shall set forth the method by which we must study man—man not only in the varying forms in which his accidental circumstances have molded him, in the distorted form in which even philosophers have almost always misconstrued him, but what is enduring in human nature, and the proper place of man in creation.[16]

Or, again:

If there is any science man really needs it is the one I teach, of how to occupy properly that place in creation that is assigned to man, and how to learn from it what one must be in order to be a man. . . . This teaching will lead him back again to the human level, and however small or deficient he may regard himself, he will suit his assigned station, because he will be just what he should be.[17]

If these quotations from Kant suggest the extent to which the influence of Rousseau led him to accept the thesis of Pope's *Essay on Man,* they also indicate how greatly Cassirer's conception of man and his *Essay* derive from this Kantian background. Cassirer writes:

For Kant man's 'assigned station' is not located in nature alone; for he must raise himself above it, above all merely vegetative or animal life. But it is just as far from lying somewhere outside nature, in something absolutely other-wordly or transcendent. Man should seek the real law of his being and his conduct neither below nor above himself; he should derive it from himself, and should fashion himself in accordance with the determination of his own free will. For this he requires life in society as well as an inner freedom from social standards and an independent judgment of conventional social values.[18]

[15] Kant's *Fragmente, ed. Hartenstein,* vol. VIII, 630, Quoted in *Rousseau Kant Goethe,* 18.

[16] *Immanuel Kants Werke,* ed. Cassirer a.o., vol. II, 326. Quoted in *Rousseau Kant Goethe,* 21.

[17] Kant's *Fragmente, ed. Hartenstein,* vol. VIII, 624. Quoted in *Rousseau Kant Goethe,* 23.

[18] *Rousseau Kant Goethe,* 23.

Kant's doctrine is, of course, based on a dualism between the world of nature and the realm of freedom, between the world of the senses and an intelligible order. Among those who learned much from Kant there were many who did not follow him along this path in the development of a more adequate conception of human nature and of humanism. Herder and Goethe discerned what they considered essential in human culture not in a mode of being but rather in humanistic achievement. Only man among all the creatures of nature is capable of such achievement. What man accomplishes according to this view is

objectification, self-recognition based upon the development of theoretical, aesthetic and ethical forms. . . . But all form requires a definite measure and is bound to it in its pure embodiments. Life in itself, as mere experience flowing freely along, cannot bring forth significant forms; it must apprehend and, in a sense, comprehend itself in order to participate in such forms.[19]

The philosophical development of Herder's and Goethe's perceptions was not advanced by the metaphysical systems of the post-Kantians, though Fichte, Schelling and Hegel repeatedly returned to these problems and sought to deal with them in their works. But it was, according to Cassirer, Wilhelm von Humboldt who made particularly significant contributions to a humanistic philosophy.

Humboldt's work at first appears much less systematic than Fichte's, Schelling's and Hegel's. As he proceeds on his way he seems more and more to lose himself . . . in questions of detail regarding his researches. But a genuinely philosophic spirit pervades all this, and he never loses sight of the inclusive purpose which his investigation is to serve.[20]

It has been conventional to treat the humanistic ideal set forth by Kant in terms of his ethics as though this constituted its entire importance. But Cassirer insists that this is a misreading of the history of ideas. According to his view the humanism of the eighteenth century which molded Kant's thought and continued its influence in Herder and Goethe, in Schiller and Humboldt, has other significance too often neglected. To be sure, they are convinced that humanistic ideals yield a distinc-

[19] "Naturalistische und humanistische Begründung der Kulturphilosophie," 17.
[20] *Ibid.*, 18-19.

tive morality and a distinctive order of socio-political life. But their vision is not directed exclusively to this goal; it extends ₁to all creative effort, no matter in what realm of life.

It appears to be the fundamental fact about all truly human existence that man is not merely a creature that absorbs the plenitude of external impressions, but that he controls this plenitude by imposing definite forms upon it which, in the last analysis, derive from the thinking, feeling, willing subject himself.[21]

Cassirer's own theory of symbolic forms may well be viewed as a development of these insights and of the humanism on which they were based. This is particularly evident in his *Essay on Man*. For though the *Essay*, as he points out, is "more an explanation and illustration than a demonstration" of the theory of symbolic forms and though students will always turn to the *Philosophie der symbolischen Formen* for the systematic formulation of Cassirer's doctrine, the briefer work sets forth most clearly his thesis that myth and religion, language and art, science and history "are, after all, only *one* subject . . . different roads leading to a common center."[22] By concentrating upon Man as this common center and thus emphasizing philosophical anthropology as the keystone of his philosophy of symbolic forms, Cassirer brings religion, art, and history into even clearer perspective than in the *Philosophie der symbolischen Formen*, where language, myth, and science were the foci of the successive volumes.

Viewing man as *animal symbolicum*, Cassirer seeks to understand human nature by exploring culture in terms of the specific character and structure of the various symbolic forms. Having denied that man can be defined by reference to an hypostatized metaphysical essence, he seeks to understand man in terms of his culture. But this understanding, in turn, is rooted in the rich soil of humanism:

A philosophy of culture begins with the assumption that the world of human culture is not a mere aggregate of loose and detached facts. It seeks to understand these facts as a system, as an organic whole. For an empirical or historical view it would seem to be enough to collect the data of human culture. Here we are interested in the breadth of

[21] *Ibid.*, 16.
[22] *Ibid., Essay on Man*, viii.

human life. We are engrossed in a study of the particular phenomena in their richness and variety; we enjoy the polychromy and the polyphony of man's nature. But a philosophical analysis sets itself a different task. Its starting point and its working hypothesis are embodied in the conviction that the varied and seemingly dispersed rays may be gathered together and brought into a common focus. The facts here are reduced to forms, and these forms themselves are supposed to possess an inner unity. . . . Here we are under no obligation to prove the substantial unity of man. Man is no longer considered as a simple substance which exists in itself and is to be known by itself. His unity is conceived as a functional unity.[23]

The common focus of all cultural forms is man—and man, in turn, must be conceived in terms of his functional unity in the development of these forms.

V

It may at times appear that when Cassirer uses the concept of symbolic forms to explain man's nature in functional terms the forms lack content. Contrariwise the specific illustrations which he employs are often familiar and, indeed, conventional, though he presents them with great originality and artistry. The interconnections between human nature and culture are constantly stressed; but Cassirer time and again appears to assume a unity and to argue for a systematic formulation which does not accord with his own practice. Indeed, the *Essay on Man* lacks systematic unity and is notable, rather, for the rich variety of the content, for the revealing insights into the researches of contemporary psychology and empirical anthropology and especially for the fruitful harvest of Cassirer's lifelong interest in literature and the arts.

If Cassirer's Kantianism seems at times to obtrude, as we have indeed seen above, this is perhaps the inevitable outcome of the neo-Kantian method of combining systematic and historical investigation which Dr. Edgar Wind pointed out in an admirable essay on Cassirer's thought, which he published in 1925. "No matter how successful the interbreeding of historical and systematic methods may prove as a means of explaining the development of science," wrote Dr. Wind,

[23] *Ibid.*, 222.

... by defending this union in general, the philosopher, who is supposed to face all problems, would seem deliberately to disregard one of them—the conflict between systematic and historical thinking as such. He must be prepared to hear the usual objections: If all standpoints are merely stages in an infinite development, how about your own standpoint? If you treat thinking as an historical matter, how about the historical limitations of your own thinking?[24]

It may well be that Cassirer had questions such as these in mind when he wrote certain passages concerning history in the *Essay on Man*. He continued to affirm the necessity of the historian writing in terms of his personal experience; indeed he finally made it the *sine qua non of* genuine historical writing.

If the historian succeeded in effacing his personal life he would not thereby achieve a higher objectivity. He would on the contrary deprive himself of the very instrument of all historical thought. If I put out the light of my own personal experience I cannot see and I cannot judge of the experience of others.[25]

It was indeed by emphasizing the humanistic significance of history and the anthropological elements in historical knowledge that Cassirer solved, to his own satisfaction, the problem of historical objectivity and answered the question of the relationship of his work as an historian to his work as a systematic philosopher.

If we bear in mind this character of historical knowledge, it is easy to distinguish historical objectivity from that form of objectivity which is the aim of natural science. A great scientist, Max Planck, described the whole process of scientific thought as a constant effort to eliminate all "anthropological" elements. We must forget man in order to study nature and to discover and formulate the laws of nature. In the development of scientific thought the anthropomorphic element is progressively forced into the background until it entirely disappears in the ideal structure of physics. History proceeds in a quite different way. It can live and breathe only in the human world. Like language or art, history is fundamentally anthropomorphic. To efface its human aspects would be to destroy its specific character and nature. But the anthropomorphism of historical thought is no limitation of or impediment to its objective truth. History is not knowledge of external facts

[24] *Journal of Philosophy*, vol. XXII, no. 18, 477ff.
[25] *Essay on Man*, 187.

or events; it is a form of self-knowledge. In order to know myself I cannot endeavor to go beyond myself, to leap, as it were, over my own shadow. I must choose the opposite approach. In history man constantly returns to himself; he attempts to recollect and actualize the whole of his past experience.[26]

And yet the ideality of history is not the same as the ideality of art. Art gives us an ideal description of human life by a sort of alchemistic process; it turns our empirical life into the dynamic of pure forms. History does not proceed in this way. It does not go beyond the empirical reality of things and events but molds this reality into a new shape, giving it the ideality of recollection. Life in the light of history remains a great realistic drama, with all its tensions and conflicts, its greatness and misery, its hopes and illusions, its display of energies and passions. This drama, however, is not only felt; it is intuited. Seeing this spectacle in the mirror of history while we are still living in our empirical world of emotions and passions, we become aware of an inner sense of clarity and calmness—of the lucidity and serenity of pure contemplation.[27]

Thus as an historian and as a humanist Cassirer once again raised the standard of self-knowledge, reaffirmed the doctrine that the unexamined life is no life for man, that the proper study of mankind is man, and asserted that man is best known and studied in his creative life. That Ernst Cassirer himself thus achieved calmness and serenity, even during the crises of the last decade, is evidence that his philosophy was, in the most significant sense, a philosophy of life. We may well salute Cassirer, the humanist, by utilizing a tribute which he himself offered to the humanism of the Cambridge Platonists: It stands to his undisputed credit that he did not allow the torch which he held in his hand to be extinguished, that in spite of every obstacle and in opposition to all dogmatism he preserved the flame of a genuinely perennial philosophical tradition and passed it on in its purity to future ages.[28]

JAMES GUTMANN

DEPARTMENT OF PHILOSOPHY
COLUMBIA UNIVERSITY

[26] *Ibid.*, 191.
[27] *Ibid.*, 205-206.
[28] Cf. *Die Platonische Renaissance in England und die Schule von Cambridge,* 141.

14

David Bidney

ON THE PHILOSOPHICAL ANTHROPOLOGY OF
ERNST CASSIRER AND ITS RELATION TO THE
HISTORY OF ANTHROPOLOGICAL THOUGHT

SYNOPSIS

ON THE PHILOSOPHICAL ANTHROPOLOGY OF ERNST CASSIRER AND ITS RELATION TO THE HISTORY OF ANTHROPOLOGICAL THOUGHT[1]

I

The Crisis in Modern Philosophical Anthropology: The Metaphysical Versus the Historical and Positivistic Approaches

IN HIS study of Wilhelm Dilthey, H. A. Hodges makes the following statement:

Modern philosophy is philosophy in crisis. Its history is one long tale of challenges, emergencies, and attempted fresh starts. As time goes on, it becomes increasingly evident that the crisis affects not this or that philosophical doctrine or principle, but philosophy itself, which is now challenged to show reason why it should continue to exist. Dilthey is one of those who have helped to bring the issue to a head, and of this he himself is fully aware. He speaks of himself as in search of a new way of philosophizing, and calls for a radical reassessment of the tradition. He draws his inspiration, as usual, from two sources: from Kant and from the Anglo-French empiricists, and his starting-point lies in what these have in common. They are united in an attack upon what had been the very heart of the philosophical tradition, upon metaphysics, the science of being and of first principles.[2]

Ernst Cassirer, whose philosophical position is essentially similar to that of Dilthey, is acutely aware of the critical position of modern philosophical thought and significantly begins his *Essay on Man* with a chapter entitled: "The Crisis in Man's Knowledge of Himself." There he writes:

[1] The research involved in the writing of this paper is part of a larger project on theoretical anthropology, which is being conducted by the writer under the liberal auspices of the Viking Fund Inc. of New York City.

[2] H. A. Hodges, *Wilhelm Dilthey: An Introduction* (New York, 1944), 88.

Owing to this development our modern theory of man lost its intellectual center. We acquired instead a complete anarchy of thought. Even in the former times to be sure there was a great discrepancy of opinions and theories relating to this problem. But there remained at least a general orientation, a frame of reference, to which all individual differences might be referred. Metaphysics, theology, mathematics, and biology successively assumed the guidance for thought on the problem of man and determined the line of investigation. The real crisis of this problem manifested itself when such a central power capable of directing all individual efforts ceased to exist. The paramount importance of the problem was still felt in all the different branches of knowledge and inquiry. But an established authority to which one might appeal no longer existed. Theologians, scientists, politicians, sociologists, biologists, psychologists, ethnologists, economists all approached the problem from their own viewpoints. To combine or unify all these particular aspects and perspectives was impossible. And even within the special fields there was no generally accepted scientific principle. The personal factor became more and more prevalent, and the temperament of the individual writer tended to play a decisive rôle. . . . That this antagonism of ideas is not merely a grave theoretical problem but an imminent threat to the whole extent of our ethical and cultural life admits of no doubt.[2a]

According to Cassirer, it would appear, the intellectual crisis of our times is a direct consequence of the fact that we have no "central power" or "established authority" capable of integrating all the sciences and the humanities in a single, unified, cultural perspective. He does not stop to consider the special characteristics of classical thought which rendered it a coherent or integrated whole. He indiscriminately lumps together "metaphysics, theology, mathematics and biology" as having at one time or another "assumed the guidance for thought on the problem of man." But what was it that made it possible for these disciplines to assume the guidance for thought, and why is this no longer possible in the present crisis?

The answer, it seems, is the one that Hodges suggests, namely, that classical thought, whatever its divergencies, agreed upon metaphysics or ontology as the foundation for its epistemology, morality, politics, and religion. By postulating a general

[2a] *An Essay on Man*, 21f. Hereafter to be referred to as *EM*.

plan of reality they found it possible to conceive all natural and cultural phenomena in relation to this master plan. The various sciences, and especially the human studies, were referred back to this center of orientation which served both as a logical starting point and as a criterion of validity. Thus, although the theologian, the biologist, or the mathematician might conceive this basic reality in different forms, once a given pattern of thought was accepted, it could serve as a norm and principle of integration for the culture as a whole. Modern thought, on the other hand, following Locke, Hume, Kant, and Comte, has denied the possibility of universal, ontological knowledge and consequently provided a favorable environment for the growth of the chaotic pluralism and mutual unintelligibility of the natural and social sciences which all the responsible thinkers of our time deplore so greatly. Not the least significant factor in the breakdown of the classical, metaphysical tradition has been the historicism and relativism of the neo-Kantian approach which swept away the last metaphysical presuppositions of the Kantian system by substituting the free or undetermined, creative, symbolic expressions of the life-process for the fixed structure of a comparatively abiding nature.

It should be noted, however, that the basic conflict in modern thought is one between diverse metaphysical approaches on the one hand, and anti-metaphysical tendencies on the other. Classical ontological thought attempted to view the phenomena of nature and life *sub specie aeternitatis*, whereas modern ontological thought tends to view cosmic reality *sub specie temporis*. It should not be an impossible task to reconcile these opposite points of view, provided there is agreement on the possibility and necessity of a comprehensive, ontological theory based on verifiable scientific knowledge, which takes account of the element of structure as well as of process in the explanation of natural and cultural phenomena.[3] But between the classical tradition of the possibility of "substantial" knowledge of reality and the "critical" idealistic position that ontological knowledge

[3] See W. H. Sheldon's *Process and Polarity* (New York, 1944) and *America's Progressive Philosophy* (New Haven, 1942) for significant analyses of this problem.

is impossible, there can be no logical reconciliation. We must choose decisively between these two contrary positions, if we are to resolve the philosophical crisis of our times. To deplore the intellectual crisis on the one hand, and yet to hold on to the very same anti-metaphysical approach which helped bring it about, as the neo-Kantians and positivists tend to do, is an irrational and hopeless procedure which only serves to make the confusion worse.

By way of indicating more precisely the nature of the conflict between classical, ontological thought and modern positivism and neo-Kantian idealism, an attempt will be made in the following analysis to present a brief survey of some aspects of the history of anthropological thought from the Greeks to modern times, referring in the process to Cassirer's interpretation of the history of the ideas involved. In relation to this background we shall be able to appreciate critically the significance of Cassirer's contribution towards a systematic philosophy of culture. Special consideration will be given to the problem of the relation of Cassirer's philosophical anthropology to that of modern and contemporary ethnology.

2

Plato's Metaphysical Theory of Man and Culture

Modern ethnology has shown that all historical societies have had cultures[4] or traditional ways of behavior and thought in conformity with which they have patterned their lives. And so valuable have these diverse ways of living appeared to the members of early human society that they have tended to ascribe a divine origin to their accepted traditions and have encouraged their children to conform to their folkways and mores as matters of faith which were above question. With the growth of experience and the development of critical thought, first individuals and then groups began to question some elements of the traditional thoughtways and practices and thereby provided a stimulus for cultural change and development.

[4] For a critical analysis of the ethnological literature dealing with the concept of culture, see D. Bidney, "On the Concept of Culture and Some Cultural Fallacies" in *American Anthropologist* 46:30-44, (1944).

The critical approach to traditional cultural expressions has varied in different societies and so has the *tempo* of cultural change. Frequently the reformers have claimed the authority of some new divine revelation and have then proceeded to institute reforms and establish new institutions to supplant the old.

What is significant in the case of historical Greek society is that the appeal against tradition was made in the name of human reason and logic rather than in the name of the gods. It was, therefore, a revolutionary event in the history of human culture when men like the Sophists, Socrates, and Plato began to question the accepted traditions and to assert boldly that "an unexamined life is not worth living." From the point of view of the conventional good citizens of the Athenian state, Socrates was indeed an "atheistic" radical, who well merited the cup of hemlock which the civilized Greeks invited him to drink for their benefit. But the amazing thing in the case of Greek society was that this critical, questioning attitude of mind, which Socrates shared with the Sophists of his day, was not entirely suppressed and was even encouraged. Self-knowledge was recognized by the Greek oracles as the highest form of wisdom.

However, self-knowledge, as Socrates and later Plato demonstrated, was not easy of attainment. It was not something to be acquired by mental introspection, since the kind of self-knowledge they were seeking was a reflective, rational analysis of the universal nature of man. To know onself in this objective sense, Plato showed, meant to have a rational knowledge of the relation of man to the whole of nature. Plato's *Republic* is based upon the thesis that the prerequisite for a scientific knowledge of man is a knowledge of mathematics and of the unchanging mathematical forms manifested in nature as a whole. The Idea of the Good, he held, was the principle of integration in the cosmos as a whole and could therefore be known and intuited only through a prior knowledge of physics and astronomy.[5] Only metaphysical, theoretical, or dialectical knowledge of this

---

[5] See F. S. C. Northrop's essay, "The Mathematical Background and Content of Greek Philosophy" in *Philosophical Essays for Alfred North Whitehead* (New York, 1936), 1-40.

kind could provide a solid foundation upon which to build the organization of man's social and cultural life. In short, genuine self-knowledge involved an ontological and theoretical analysis of nature as a whole.

The basic presupposition of Platonic (as well as of Aristotelian) philosophical anthropology is that culture, understood both as a system of education (*paedeia*) and socio-political organization (*politeia*), is to be based upon a scientific knowledge of nature. The Sophists had contrasted the uniformities of nature with the diversities of social culture and were inclined to regard the latter as a more or less arbitrary convention (*nomos*) superimposed by the rulers upon their people. Plato, by contrast, attempted to harmonize nature and culture, and held that man attained his true good and proper measure of perfection through insight into the abiding forms of being revealed through a study of mathematical science and dialectical synthesis.

Cassirer claims that "To the Sophists 'man' meant the individual man. The so-called 'universal' man—the man of the philosophers—was to them a mere fiction."[6]

Whether or not the sophists *intended* to apply the Protagorean maxim that "man is the measure of all things" to individual men only and not to universal man, the fact remains that, *as Plato interpreted it*,[7] the maxim led logically to individualistic relativism. The notion, he argued, that man is a measure of all things begs the very question it is supposed to answer, for the problem is whether it is possible to have a universal measure of human values. To say that man is the universal measure still leaves open the question how one is to determine the universal nature of man. This question according to Plato, could not be answered without a mathematical and dialectical knowledge of nature as a whole. The Platonic Socrates, in agreement with the Sophists, was certainly interested in "humanizing" philosophy in the sense of being concerned with a critical analysis of the conditions of civilized life. But he insisted, as against the sophists, that a genuine hu-

---

[6] In *The Myth of the State*, 57. Hereafter to be referred to as *MS*.
[7] See Plato's *Theaetetus;* cf. Brand Blanshard's "Current Strictures of Reason" in the *Philosophical Review* lv:670-73, (1946).

manistic education must be one based upon a rational or scientific philosophy of nature. I find it difficult, therefore, to accept Cassirer's statement to the effect that

From then on man was no longer regarded as a mere part of the universe; he became its center. Man, said Protagoras, is the measure of all things. This tenet holds, in a sense, both for the sophists and for Socrates. To "humanize" philosophy, to turn cosmogony and ontology into anthropology, was their common goal. . . . He [Socrates] is not primarily interested in the unity of Being nor in the systematic unity of thought. What he is asking for is the unity of the will.[8]

Although it is true that Socrates was primarily interested in the study of man, I find no basis for the statement that he meant to turn cosmogony and ontology into anthropology. Cassirer, it would seem, is reading a bit of Kant into the Platonic Socrates at this point.

Plato's perspective was "Copernican" and "heliocentric" in the sense that he derived his knowledge of the good for man from an objective knowledge of nature as a whole. It is significant that in the *Republic* Plato conceived the relation of the Idea of the Good to the intelligible world of ideas as similar to that of the *sun* in the physical world.[9] Cassirer himself notes that Plato's "categorical imperative" was a "demand for order and measure" and that "the triad of Logos, Nomos, Taxis—Reason, Lawfulness, Order—is the first principle both of the physical and the ethical world."[10]

Plato would acquire a knowledge of man not only through a subjective analysis of the individual, but also and primarily through an objective investigation of the natural cosmos and the political cosmos. From the study of nature and of mathematical science, he held, one derived an objective, impersonal criterion of the true good and the just social order for man, so that man the microcosm might order his life in accordance with the principles of justice and proportion which prevail in the macrocosm.[11] Furthermore, from the study of the prevailing or

[8] *MS.*, 56, 57.
[9] *Republic*, vi:508-10.
[10] *MS.*, 65.
[11] See A. N. Whitehead's paper, "Mathematics and the Good" in *The Philosophy of Alfred North Whitehead*, edited by P. A. Schilpp (The Library of Living

historical political orders (Plato did not distinguish the state from society) one may infer the psychological forces which these institutions embody and the type of personality and character which is objectively exemplified in any given society or state. Such a survey alone, however, will not tell us what is the true or ideal type of human nature or what type of personality ought to be realized.

The significance of Plato's analysis in the *Republic* for modern anthropological thought lies in the fact that here we have presented for the first time the thesis that the social culture of a given society is integrated about a given personality type, so that the individual who participates in a given cultural configuration and set of institutions takes on the social character which is exemplified in that society taken as a whole. Culturally, therefore, the individual is to be understood through the state or society of which he is a member, since the political order reflects the educational ideals. This, however, does not mean that the individual has no universal nature apart from the state. Man's ontological nature is not a socio-cultural product but rather provides the basis for any form of social order one chooses to institute. If, on the one hand, the culturally acquired personality of the individual is to be understood through the social conditioning which he has undergone from childhood onwards, it must also be kept in mind that the ontological nature of the individual is logically prior to any given social order.

Cassirer's interpretation of Plato on this point is rather ambiguous and gives one the impression that he is reading a little of Comtean sociology into Plato's thought. Thus he writes:

> We cannot find an adequate definition of man so long as we confine ourselves within the limits of man's individual life. Human nature does not reveal itself in this narrow compass. What is written in "small characters" in the individual soul, and is therefore almost illegible, becomes clear and understandable only if we read it in the larger letters of man's political and social life. This principle is the starting point of Plato's *Republic*. From now on the whole problem

---

Philosophers, Evanston and Chicago, 1941); also F. H. Anderson's *The Argument of Plato* (London, 1934), especially ch. 6 on "Microcosm and Social Macrocosm."

of man was changed: politics was declared to be the clue to psychology.[12]

Again in the *Essay on Man* he writes:

Man is to be studied not in his individual life but in his political and social life. Human nature, according to Plato, is like a difficult text, the meaning of which has to be deciphered by philosophy. But in our personal experiences this text is written in such small characters that it becomes illegible. The first labor of philosophy must be to enlarge these characters. Philosophy cannot give us a satisfactory theory of man until it has developed a theory of the state. The nature of man is written in capital letters in the nature of the state. Here the hidden meaning of the text suddenly emerges, and what seemed obscure and confused becomes clear and legible. . . .

In modern philosophy Comte was one of the first to approach this problem and to formulate it in a clear and systematic way. It is something of a paradox that in this respect we must regard the positivism of Comte as a modern parallel to the Platonic theory of man. Comte was of course never a Platonist. He could not accept the logical and metaphysical presuppositions upon which Plato's theory of ideas is based. Yet, on the other hand, he was strongly opposed to the views of the French ideologists. In his hierarchy of human knowledge two new sciences, the science of social ethics and that of social dynamics, occupy the highest rank. From this sociological viewpoint Comte attacks the psychologism of his age. One of the fundamental maxims of his philosophy is that our method of studying man must, indeed, be subjective, but that it cannot be individual. For the subject we wish to know is not the individual consciousness but the universal subject. If we refer to this subject by the term "humanity" then we must affirm that humanity is not to be explained by man, but man by humanity.[13]

Cassirer has here interpreted "the hidden meaning of the text" of Plato's *Republic,* as if the latter would define the nature of man through society and its culture. But Plato explicitly distinguishes the ontological nature of man and the psychological functions through which it is expressed from the temporal character of the political state through which it is exemplified and molded. The social order is the analogue of the individual soul; and there can be no justice in the state unless it is or-

[12] *MS.* 61f.
[13] *An Essay on Man,* 63f.

ganized on principles of justice similar to those which obtain in the soul of the individual. As Cassirer has put it:

Justice is not on the same level with other virtues of man. It is not, like courage and temperance, a special quality or property. It is a general principle of order, regularity, unity, and lawfulness. Within the individual life this lawfulness appears in the harmony of all the different powers of the human soul; within the state it appears in the "geometrical proportion" between the different classes, according to which each part of the social body receives its due and coöperates in maintaining the general order. With this conception Plato becomes the founder and the first defender of the Idea of the Legal State.[14]

And again Cassirer states:

The Platonic state gives to everyone and to all the social classes their allotted work in the common work; but their rights and duties are widely different. That follows not only from the character of Plato's ethics, but, first and foremost, from the character of his psychology. Plato's metaphysical psychology is based upon his division of the human soul. The character of man is determined by the proportion between these three elements. . . .

The different classes into which the Platonic state is divided have as many different souls—they represent different types of human characters. These types are fixed and unchangeable. Every attempt to change them, i.e., to efface or diminish the difference between the rulers, the guardians, and the ordinary men, would be disastrous. It would mean a revolt against the unchangeable laws of human nature to which the social order has to conform.[15]

Here we see that Cassirer explicitly admits that the social order of the Platonic state follows from the character of "Plato's metaphysical psychology" and from " the unchangeable laws of human nature." If this be the case, it is most difficult to accept Cassirer's interpretation that for Plato "politics was declared to be the clue to psychology" and that "philosophy cannot give us a satisfactory theory of man until it has developed a theory of the state." On the contrary, Plato's theory of the state with its rigid class differences depends on his meta-psychological theory of the natural divisions or functions of the soul.

[14] MS. 69.
[15] MS. 98f.

Cassirer, it would seem, is confusing, as Plato himself never did, the *cultural priority* of the state or society to the individual on the one hand, and the ontological priority of the individual to his society on the other.

According to Plato, an empirical, comparative survey of actual states or societies would not tell us anything of the nature of the ideal state. For the latter one would require a knowledge of "first principles" which are not derived from empirical observation. For Plato, the ideal and the actual remained forever distinct and unidentical. That is why Plato, the utopian idealist, was also theoretically a revolutionary reformer and never accepted the *civitas terrena* or *status quo* of his times. Cassirer has recognized the significance of this aspect of Plato's thought and points out: "It is one of the first principles of Plato's theory of knowledge to insist upon the radical distinction between empirical and ideal truth. . . . The difference between these two types, between *doxa* and *episteme* is ineffaceable. Facts are variable and accidental; truth is necessary and immutable."[16]

This Platonic distinction between the logical ideal and the factual or positive social situation is the direct antithesis of the Comtean approach which postulated that an empirical study of "social facts" would automatically reveal the nature of a scientific social order and the inevitable laws of social evolution. To say, therefore, that "we must regard the positivism of Comte as a modern parallel to the Platonic theory of man," is essentially misleading.

Plato's metaphysical approach implies that it is possible to envisage a universal and eternal order of nature as well as a rational, social and cultural order which is to conform to it. Plato views culture *sub specie aeternitatis* as an ideal, rational order capable of transcending the temporal and local limitations of given historical institutions. In practice, however, this metaphysical and rational ideal is extraordinarily difficult to conceive —let alone realize— and the cultural historian has little difficulty in demonstrating the limitations of his theory and general mental perspective. His conception of science, which divorced the theoretical from the practical approach, as well as his rigid

[16] *MS.* 69.

class differences reflect much of the socio-cultural conditions of his time and place. Similarly Aristotle's acceptance of slavery as something rooted in the nature of things,[17] and the general tendency of Greek intellectuals to divide the human race into Greeks and barbarians[18] demonstrate the all-too-human cultural limitations of even the most sincere philosophical idealists. This, however, does not invalidate the intellectual vision of a universally valid cultural norm which may be progressively conceived and achieved in time. The cultural limitations of a great thinker may be detected by others of a later generation coming from diverse cultural backgrounds and to that extent eliminated from their own thinking. If there is danger in not taking time seriously enough, there is even more danger in taking it too seriously.

3

Stoicism on the Rationality of Man and the Concept of Humanitas

The Stoics, while building upon the general metaphysical views of Plato and Aristotle, added two new concepts which were destined to have great influence on the subsequent history of anthropological thought and political action, namely, the concept of the intrinsic, universal rationality of man and the concept of humanity (humanitas).

In their psychology, the Stoics, unlike Plato, denied any irrational functions of the soul and regarded reason as the essential function of mind—a position which was later to find expression in the Cartesian notion of mind as res cogitans.[19] They regarded the emotions or passions as diseases which disturbed

[17] Cf. Aristotle's Politics, 1254a-55b.

[18] Cf. Plato's Statesman, 262, Jowett translation. As Plato puts it: "The error was just as if some one who wanted to divide the human races, were to divide them, after the fashion which prevails in this part of the world; here they cut off the Hellenes as one species, and all the other species of mankind, which are innumerable, and have no ties of common language they include under the single name of "barbarians" and because they have the one name they are supposed to be of one species also."

[19] For a comparative analysis of Stoic psychology see D. Bidney, The Psychology and Ethics of Spinoza (New Haven, 1940), especially ch. 1.

the apathy or calm of the rational activity of the soul. Hence they counselled that a man should limit and restrain his desires to those things within his power and should give the consent of his will to the dictates of reason only.

The significant feature of Stoic psychology in this connection is its adherence to the Platonic view of the essential dualism of body and soul. In social practice this meant that the freedom and autonomy of the rational soul could be maintained even while the body was in slavery to the state. The Stoics were concerned with the spiritual or moral freedom of the individual, his freedom from passions, but not especially with political freedom. Like the early Christians, they were content to render unto Caesar the things that were Caesar's as a matter of social tradition as well as expediency; in fact, Caesar himself, in the person of the Emperor Marcus Aurelius, was one of the chief apostles of this ethical creed. The spirit of Stoic political philosophy was one of acceptance of prevailing social conditions, since it was held that the wise man could maintain his intellectual freedom and moral integrity under any political conditions. If necessary, he could, like Seneca, commit suicide, in case he did not wish to compromise himself. Thus, although denying the Greek, aristocratic notion that some peoples were slaves by nature and insisting upon the intellectual and moral equality of all men, the Stoics did nevertheless tolerate physical slavery and political despotism. According to Seneca,

It is a mistake to imagine that slavery pervades a man's whole being; the better part of him is exempt from it: the body indeed is subjected and in the power of a master, but the mind is independent, and indeed is so free and wild, that it cannot be restrained even by this prison of the body, wherein it is confined.[20]

In view of the alleged moral and political disparity of body and mind, I find it difficult to understand the ground for Cassirer's emphasis upon the "coalescence of political and philosophic thought"[21] as characteristic of the Stoics. Stoicism, like Christianity, was originally and essentially a spiritual and moral

---

[20] As quoted by Cassirer, *MS.*, 103. The reference is to *Seneca's De beneficiis,* 111, 20, tr. A. Stewart (London, 1900) p. 69.

[21] *M.S.*, 102.

doctrine and as such was historically compatible with any political form of organization whatsover. To say that men like Cicero, Seneca, or Marcus Aurelius "admitted no cleft between the individual and political sphere"[22] simply is not in agreement with the historical facts. It is true, as later history shows, that the concept of the intellectual and moral equality of all men was a principle which could be utilized for social and political reform; but the fact remains that the Stoics themselves, in common with other philosophical schools, suffered from the cultural limitations of the Roman Empire and did not so envisage their teaching at this time. The Stoic doctrine of living in harmony with nature, far from being a revolutionary summons or an incentive to the formulation of utopian theories of the state, merely served at the time as a rationalization for accepting the *status quo*.

The concept of humanity (*humanitas*) in particular was original with the Stoics and represented an ideal alien to Greek philosophical thought which had not gone beyond the ideal of Greek unity. As Wilhelm Wundt has pointed out, the concept of humanity has a dual significance and refers to a purely logical concept as well as to a moral ideal.[23] Logically, *humanitas* refers to the unity of mankind as a whole. As a moral ideal, it is a value-attribute and refers "to the complete development of the ethical characteristics which differentiate man from the animal and to their expression in the intercourse of individuals and of peoples."[24] The concept of humanity in this latter, moral sense is not to be found among the virtues discussed in the writings of Plato and Aristotle. According to Cassirer,

The ideal of humanitas was first formed in Rome; and it was especially the aristocratic circle of the younger Scipio that gave it its firm place in Roman culture. Humanitas was no vague concept. It had a definite meaning and it became a formative power in private and public life in Rome. It meant not only a moral but also an esthetic ideal; it was the demand for a certain type of life that had to prove its influence in the whole of man's life, in his moral conduct as well as in

[22] *Ibid.*

[23] Wilhelm Wundt, *Elements of Folk Psychology* (London and New York, 1916), ch. iv on "The Development of Humanity," 470-523.

[24] *Ibid.*, 472.

his language, his literary style, and his taste. Through later writers such as Cicero and Seneca this ideal of humanitas became firmly established in Roman philosophy and Latin literature.[25]

Humanitas, as a moral-aesthetic ideal or way of life, passed over into medieval and modern European culture and became firmly established in the educational system as the study of "the humanities."

The concept of the moral and metaphysical equality of all men is logically connected with the Stoic notion of *humanitas*, since the idea of the community of reason in all men implies the notion of a community of mankind. The intellect is regarded as the universal bond of agreement between men which makes it possible for all men as rational beings to live in harmony with one another as well as with nature. Thus Marcus Aurelius writes in his *Meditations:*

If our intellectual part is common, the reason also, in respect of which we are rational beings, is common; if this is so, common also is the reason which commands us what to do and what not to do; if this is so, there is a common law also; if this is so, we are fellow-citizens; if this is so, we are members of some political community; if this is so, the world is in a manner a state. For of what other common political community will any one say that the whole human race are members?[26]

It is no exaggeration to say, therefore, that the ideal of *humanitas*, in combining individualism and universalism, prepared the way for the concept of a world culture, world history, and a world state.[27] As an ethical ideal it made the individual conscious of the personal as well as of the universal character of his rights and duties. In modern philosophical thought the ideal of *humanitas* has received its classic expression in Kant's categorical imperative as the injunction "So to act as to treat humanity, whether in thine own person or in that of any other, in every case as an end withal, never as means only."[28]

---

[25] *MS.,* 102.

[26] In *The Stoic and Epicurean Philosophers,* ed. by W. J. Oates (New York, 1940), p. 509, bk. 4, section 4.

[27] See Wundt, *loc. cit.*

[28] Kant, *Fundamental Principles of the Metaphysics of Ethics,* tr. T. K. Abbott (London, 1923), 56.

In terms of political theory, the concept of *humanitas* may be combined either with an organic notion of society and the state or with an atomistic, individualistic theory. In Marcus Aurelius we find the Aristotelian notion that man is by nature a social or political animal and that the individual cannot exercise his proper function apart from society.[29] On the other hand, the seventeenth and eighteenth century political thinkers, such as Spinoza, Locke, Kant, Jefferson, and Thomas Paine, utilized the Stoic ideal of *humanitas* in conjunction with an individualistic theory, which regarded the state as an institution organized to serve the common interests of its component citizens. As Spinoza puts it:

Nothing, therefore, can agree better with the nature of any individual than other individuals of the same kind, and so there is nothing more profitable to man for the preservation of his being and the enjoyment of a rational life than a man who is guided by reason. . . . Above all things it is profitable to men to unite in communities and to unite themselves to one another by bonds which make all of them as one man (*de omnibus unum efficiant*) and absolutely it is profitable for them to do whatever may tend to strengthen their friendships.[30]

Thus in answer to the question raised by Cassirer as to "What gave to the old Stoic ideas their freshness and novelty, their unprecedented strength, their importance for the formation of the modern mind and the modern world?"[31] it may be said: The Stoic concept of *humanitas* was combined with the atomic individualism of Renaissance science, Platonic idealism and Protestant theology to produce a revolutionary social mentality capable of questioning established authorities and institutions. Cassirer seems to assume that Stoicism alone was the primary political influence in the rise of the modern world and therefore replies somewhat enigmatically that

What matters here is not so much the content of the Stoic theory

[29] *Meditations*, bk. 8, section 34.

[30] Spinoza, *Ethics*, part iv, Appendix, sections ix, xii. The phrase "de omnibus unum" is reminiscent of the American motto "e pluribus unum." It is significant that we find *humanitas* listed among the intellectual affects in Spinoza's *Ethics* (part 3, def. 43), where it is defined as "the desire of doing those things which please men and omitting those which displease them."

[31] *MS.*, 168.

as the function that this theory had to fulfil in the ethical and political conflicts of the modern world. In order to understand this function we must go back to the new conditions created by the Renaissance and the Reformation. All the great and undeniable progress made by the Renaissance and the Reformation were counterbalanced by a severe and irreparable loss. The unity and the inner harmony of medieval culture had been dissolved. . . . . If there was to be a really universal system of ethics or religion, it had to be based upon such principles as could be admitted by every nation, every creed, and every sect. And Stoicism alone seemed to be equal to this task. It became the foundation of a "natural" religion and a system of natural laws. Stoic philosophy could not help man to solve the metaphysical riddles of the universe. But it contained a greater and more important promise: the promise to restore man to his ethical dignity. This dignity, it asserted, cannot be lost; for it does not depend on a dogmatic creed or on any outward revelation. It rests exclusively on the moral will—on the worth that man attributes to himself.[32]

Cassirer, it appears, separates the transcendental "function" which Stoicism "had to fulfil" from its actual, scientific content. He points out that the Stoic principle of the "autarky" or autonomy of human reason was the source of modern rationalism and "became the cornerstone of all systems of natural right."[33] Cassirer also attributes to the Stoics the Kantian thesis that man asserts his moral dignity by an act of moral will and that this dignity cannot be lost irrespective of the nature of one's beliefs. He omits entirely in his *Myth of the State* any reference to Galilean and Newtonian science or to the Utopian idealism which had its source in Plato.[34] The concept of natural rights is indeed related in part to the notion of natural law postulated by the Stoics, but it seems an exaggeration to base the modern theory of natural rights upon Stoic rationalism exclusively. A close analysis of the available literature of the period will demonstrate how the concept of natural rights was re-inter-

[32] *MS.* 169f.
[33] *MS.* 172.
[34] See F. S. C. Northrop's *The Meeting of East and West* (New York, 1946), especially ch. 3. Northrop provides a thorough analysis of the natural science background of eighteenth century American thought, but goes to the opposite extreme of Cassirer in neglecting Stoic influence.

preted in terms of the individualism and mechanistic science derived from distinctively Renaissance sources.[35]

4

Kant and the Anthropocentric Critique of Human Culture

Cassirer, in a passage quoted earlier, has pointed out that, in
regarding man as the measure of all things, the Sophists turned
cosmogony and ontology into anthropology. This, it would appear, is especially true of Kant. For Kant, above all, made man's
transcendental ego the measure of all things. This reversal of
the classic, objective metaphysical approach he himself regarded
as parallel to the Copernican revolution in astronomy; in fact,
however, he accomplished the exact contrary by his anthropocentric approach.[36]

It is most significant, as Cassirer observes, that Kant was
"the man who introduced anthropology as a branch of study in
German universities and who lectured on it regularly for
decades."[37] In the introduction to his *Anthropologie in pragmatischer Hinsicht* Kant informs us:

In my occupation with pure philosophy, which originally I had
voluntarily taken upon myself, but which was later on officially en-
trusted to me as an academic lectureship, I have, throughout some thirty
years, given two lecture courses whose purpose it was to transmit a
knowledge of this world, namely, (in the winter semesters) anthropology
and (in the summer semesters) physical geography.[38]

It should be noted, however, that by anthropology Kant
meant something different from the study of human culture or
comparative anatomy of peoples. For him, the term comprised

[35] See D. Bidney, *The Psychology and Ethics of Spinoza* for an example of this
fusing of ideas.
[36] See E. Gilson, *The Spirit of Medieval Philosophy* (New York, 1940), 245.
According to Gilson, "The sun that Kant set at the centre of the world was man
himself, so that his revolution was the reverse of the Copernican and led to an
anthropocentrism a good deal more radical, though radical in another fashion,
than any of which the Middle Age is accused."
[37] *Rousseau Kant Goethe*, 25.
[38] Immanuel Kant, *Anthropologie in pragmatischer Hinsicht* (Zweyte verbes-
serte Auflage, Königsberg, 1800), Vorrede, xiii-xiv.

empirical ethics (folkways), introspective psychology and "physiology." Empirical ethics, as distinct from rational ethics, was called "practical anthropology."[39] As Kant puts it:

Eine Lehre von der Kenntnis des Menschen systematisch abgefasst (Anthropologie) kann es entweder in *physiologischer* oder in *pragmatischer* Hinsicht seyn. Die physiologische Menschenkenntnis geht auf die Erforschung dessen, was die *Natur* aus dem Menschen macht, die pragmatische auf das, was er, als freyhandelndes Wesen, aus sich selber macht, oder machen kann und soll.[40]

From this it appears that, for Kant, anthropology, as a *Menschenkenntnis* or study of man, comprised two major approaches, namely, the *physiological* and the *pragmatic*. Under physiology he included all those human phenomena which may be attributed directly to nature, such as anatomy, psychology, and the relation of man to his geographical environment (ecology). Under the pragmatic approach he included all human phenomena which may be attributed to human culture, namely, those of empirical social ethics (the folkways and mores of Sumner), which he termed pratical anthropology, and rational, normative ethics, which prescribed the conditions of rational, civilized life. Kant's *Critiques* were in effect critical, anthropological treatises which investigated the *a priori* conditions of natural science and ethics as given cultural disciplines, although Kant himself did not clearly recognize this point as regards his *Critique of Pure Reason.*

Kant, as is well known, accepted the validity of Newtonian science and sought for the conditions in the human understanding which made mathematics and natural science in general possible and intelligible. His "answer" to Hume was that theoretical or pure reason was limited by its *a priori* categorial structure to the cognition and organization of phenomena. Thus Kant, in fundamental agreement with Hume, denied the possibility of an ontological knowledge of nature and more than any one else was responsible for the antithesis of science and metaphysics. He did not, however, entirely exclude the notion

---

[39] Immanuel Kant, *Fundamental Principles of the Metaphysics of Ethics*, ed. by T. K. Abbott (London, 1923), 2.

[40] *Anthropologie*, iv.

of a metaphysical or noumenal reality, but maintained that "things-in-themselves" were not the object of scientific knowledge. In effect this meant that the classic assumption of Greek, medieval, and Renaissance philosophy of an empirically validated ontology was denied. Instead Kant affirmed that "The understanding does not derive its laws (*a priori*) from, but prescribes them to, nature."[41] This meant, in sum, that Kant reduced natural philosophy or theoretical science to anthropology.

Just as Kant began his critique of scientific knowledge by accepting the fact of mathematical science, so he began his ethics and his *Anthropologie* by accepting the fact of civilization. Unlike Rousseau, Kant did not begin with "the natural man" in order to arrive at an evaluation of human culture, but, beginning with "civilized man" and accepting the reality and validity of historical cultural achievements,[42] he proceeded to outline the necessary postulates which would enable man to attain ideal moral perfection and a rational state of society. According to Cassirer,

> This beginning is indicated because in the concept of man civilization constitutes no secondary or accidental characteristic but marks man's essential nature, his specific character. He who would study animals must start with them in their wild state; but he who would know man must observe him in his creative power and his creative achievement, that is, in his civilization.[43]

Rousseau's type of approach involves a dualism or antithesis of nature and culture, and implies the possibility of a knowledge of man which is pre-cultural logically, if not historically. Kant, on the other hand, does not oppose nature to culture, but beginning with the phenomena of culture or civilization as historically given, investigates analytically the formal, logical conditions

---

[41] *Prolegomena To Any Future Metaphysics*, tr. and ed. by Paul Carus (Chicago, 1929), #36, p. 82. Metaphysics, in Kant's use of the term, refers to the *a priori* logical and epistemological conditions of experience, and hence to *a priori* synthetic propositions. This use of the term is to be differentiated from the ontological or substantial meaning as used originally by Aristotle.

[42] Kant, as quoted by Cassirer in *Rousseau Kant Goethe*, 22.

[43] *Ibid.*, 22.

which would render human cultural experience intelligible as well as rational. This explains why, in the last analysis, Rousseau was essentially a cultural revolutionary or reformer, whereas Kant remained a thinker who did not set out to change the human world but to understand it.

There is, for Kant, a fundamental difference between the object or sphere of theoretical understanding and practical reason. Nature is the sphere of mathematical, scientific law. There is an isomorphic relation between the phenomena of nature and the human understanding, such that the universal laws of nature are identical with the synthetic *a priori* rules or laws of the understanding. Human practical reason, on the other hand, is not limited by any *a priori* categories which necessarily would determine the conditions of its experience and operation; it is completely free and undetermined. Hence practical reason can issue a categorical imperative on how man as a rational, moral being ought to act, and can postulate what man ought to believe concerning such noumenal entities as God and the human soul. So far as moral culture is concerned, the maxim "Thou canst because thou oughtest" holds good; whereas in the sphere of natural science man is confronted with a necessary order of phenomena which is not determined by human will.

This explains why Kant did not postulate any *a priori* categories of practical reason, since to have done so would have meant a denial of man's moral freedom and autonomy. Nature, for him, was the sphere of necessity and required the postulation of equally predetermined categories of the understanding, but moral and religious culture was the product of human freedom and creativity, and did not, therefore, require or necessitate any fixed categories. Man does not create the order of nature of which he is a part, although the human understanding through its categories does predetermine the general modes or perspectives through which it is perceived. Man does, however, create his own moral laws and freely sets up universal moral standards for all mankind. In short, *natural phenomena are given in experience; moral phenomena are not so given, but have to be willed into existence in accordance with the dictates of practical reason and the human conscience.* This important

point seems to have been overlooked by the neo-Kantian axiologists who criticize Kant for having failed to provide categories of
practical reason and who presume to rectify Kant's failure by
providing such axiological categories.[44] These neo-Kantian axiologists, like the historical idealists, seem to confuse, as Kant
himself never did, the sphere of logical and scientific necessity
which is nature, and the sphere of moral freedom which is culture.

5

Wilhelm Dilthey's Neo-Kantian Critique of Historical Reason

In contrast to the seventeenth and eighteenth century metaphysical rationalism, the keynote of nineteenth century philosophical thought is history. Even those who accepted the "critical," anthropological idealism of Kant felt that the Kantian
approach had to be expanded so as to provide a logical and
epistemological analysis of the conditions of historical, cultural
thought. Wilhelm Dilthey gave classic expression to this point
of view and attempted to synthesize the thought of Kant and
Comte together with the historicism of the Romanticists and
Evolutionists. He proposed a "Critique of Historical Reason"
to take the place of Kant's *Critiques of Pure and Practical
Reason* in order to get to know the laws which govern social,
intellectual, and moral phenomena while following "Kant's
critical path."

Dilthey differentiated sharply between the sphere of natural
science and that of the *Geisteswissenschaften* or human studies.
Thus he writes:

> Mankind, if apprehended only by perception and perceptual knowl-
> edge, would be for us a physical fact, and as such it would be accessible
> only to natural-scientific knowledge. It becomes an object for the
> human studies only in so far as human states are consciously lived,
> insofar as they find expression in living utterances, and insofar as
> these expressions are understood. . . . In short, it is through the process
> of understanding (*verstehen*) that life in its depths is made clear to
> itself, and on the other hand we understand ourselves and others only

---

[44] See, for example, W. M. Urban's *The Intelligible World* (London, 1929),
344f.

when we transfer our own lived experience into every kind of expression of our own and other people's life. Thus everywhere the relationship between lived experience, expression, and understanding is the proper procedure by which mankind as an object in the human studies exists for us. The human studies are thus founded on this relation between lived experience, expression and understanding.[45]

In brief, according to Dilthey, the human studies have for their object life-forms which are to be adequately understood in their dynamic relationships through an inner, lived experience of the concrete expressions and symbolic meanings which constitute these forms. By contrast, natural science is said to deal with abstract or value-free objects which are known directly through observation and explained causally. Natural science is said to be "nomothetic" whereas cultural studies are "idiographic."[46]

The practical significance of this dichotomy betweeen the natural sciences on the one hand, and the human studies on the other, lies in the fact that it divorced cultural values or ends as the expression of historical reason from the value-free facts and laws provided by the natural sciences.[47] This divorce, as indicated earlier, had its source in the Kantian distinction between the inherent freedom of the practical reason and the formally-determined pure reason. All Dilthey had really done was to convert Kant's *Critique of Practical Reason* into a critique of historical reason and of human cultural expression.

Since cultural values, as the free expression and creation of historical reason were relative to one's time and society, there was on this basis no universal criterion by which they could be measured or evaluated in relation to one another. Dilthey himself was aware of this implication of his thought and accepted it. He writes:

The knife of historical relativism which has cut to pieces all meta-

[45] Quoted by Hodges, *Dilthey*, 142.

[46] *Ibid.*, 69. In his *Zur Logik der Kulturwissenschaften* Cassirer rejects this.

[47] See Howard Lee Nostrand's Introduction to José Ortega y Gasset's *Mission of the University* (Princeton, 1944) for an interesting analysis of the implications of this separation; also D. Bidney's "Culture Theory and the Problem of Cultural Crises" in *Approaches to Group Understanding*, Sixth Symposium of the Conference on Science, Philosophy and Religion, (New York, 1947).

physics and religion, must also bring healing. We only need to be thorough. We must make philosophy itself an object of philosophical study. There is need of a science which shall apply evolutionary conceptions and comparative methods to the study of the systems themselves. . . . Every solution of the philosophical problem belongs from a historical point of view to a particular date and a particular situation at that date; man, the creature of time, so long as he works in time, finds the security of his existence in the fact that he lifts his creations out of the stream of time as something lasting: this illusion gives to his creative work a greater joy and power. . . . Philosophy cannot comprehend the world in its essence by means of a metaphysical system, and set forth this knowledge in a way that is universally valid. . . . Thus from all the enormous labour of the metaphysical mind there remains the historical consciousness, which repeats that labour in itself and so experiences in it the inscrutable depths of the world. The last word of the mind which has run through all the outlooks is not the relativity of them all, but the sovereignty of the mind in face of each one of them, and at the same time the positive consciousness of the way in which, in the various attitudes of the mind, the one reality of the world exists for us.[48]

Dilthey, although accepting the historical relativity of philosophical systems and denying the validity of metaphysics, found solace in the fact of the mind's sovereignty and freedom in creating its own cultural perspectives. Thus, contrary to the naturalistic approach, historical relativity was linked, not with determinism, but with human freedom of self-expression. The idea that man is free to envisage his own world of values and to reconstruct his human world in terms of his lived experiences, is ground for optimism and faith in human progress, notwithstanding the temporal character and historical relativity of human achievements. This thesis is one which, it will appear, Cassirer also shares with Dilthey.

6

José Ortega y Gasset and Historical Vitalism

In his essay on "Wilhelm Dilthey and the Idea of Life,"[49] Ortega y Gasset has clarified and systematized the basic pre-

[48] Quoted by Hodges in his *Dilthey*, 154ff.
[49] José Ortega y Gasset, in *Concord and Liberty* (New York, 1946).

suppositions of Dilthey's theory while re-interpreting it in his own ontological terms. If one accepts the standpoint of historicism, he points out, man may not be said to possess a nature in the sense of a fixed mode of being. "Man has no 'nature;' he has history. His being is not one but many and manifold, difrent in each time and each place."[50] Summarizing and complementing Dilthey's thought Ortega y Gasset writes:

Man is historical in the sense that he has no actual and immutable constitution but assumes most varied and diverse forms. History, in the first instance, signifies the simple fact that the human being is variable. Man is historical in the sense that what he is at each moment includes a past. Remembrance of what happened to him and what he was before bears upon what he is now. History here means persistence of the past, to *have* a past, and to come out of it . . . history is the more or less adequate reconstruction which human life produces of itself . . . history is the attempt to bring to its possible perfection the interpretation of human life by conceiving it from the viewpoint of all mankind in so far as mankind forms an actual and real unity, not an abstract ideal—in short, history in the formal sense of universal history.[51]

Although appreciating Dilthey's contribution towards a genuine, historical perspective, Ortega y Gasset is critical of the the former's "spiritual anthropology." Since "consciousness cannot go behind itself," Dilthey's anthroplogy becomes a phenomenological analysis of the cognitive efforts of mankind. Although rejecting a metaphysics of fixed forms of being, he conceives of the life-process as a kind of Heraclitean flux similar to Bergson's *élan vital*. Man in particular is conceived as a sort of finite *causa sui*, as "a being creating its own entity." In his essay on "History as a System" Ortega y Gasset states:

Man in a word has no nature; what he has is . . . history. Expressed differently: what nature is to things, history, *res gestae*, is to man. Once again we become aware of the possible application of theological concepts to human reality. *Deus, cui hoc nature quod fecerit* . . . says Augustine. Man likewise finds that he has no nature other than what he himself has done.[52]

[50] *Ibid.*, 148.
[51] *Ibid.*, 166f.
[52] In *Philosophy and History*, Essays presented to Ernst Cassirer, ed. by Klibansky and Paton (Oxford, 1936), 313.

Thus Ortega y Gasset finds an ontological justification for
Dilthey's phenomenological historicism. By regarding man in
the perspective of history as literally making himself, un-
hampered by any restraints other than those man himself has
historically created for himself, Ortega y Gasset is able to combine ontological freedom with historical determinism and to attribute to man the attribute of self-creation which the classical
philosophers reserved for God alone.

It is of especial interest in this connection to compare Ortega
y Gasset's historical vitalism, as it may be called, with the existentialism of Jean-Paul Sartre.[53] Both writers are committed
to a radical humanism which postulates the self-creativity of
human life and its constantly changing modes of expression. It
would appear, therefore, that Sartre's existentialism and Ortega
y Gasset's historical vitalism share a common ontological thesis
in maintaining that life or existence determines its own essence.
Contemporary existentialism, considered as an interpretation of
man and his culture, is not quite as novel as it has been made to
appear.

7

*Cassirer's Cultural Definition of Man: Man as
Animal Symbolicum*

Cassirer also provides a historical interpretation of the concept of human nature and in this respect his view is close to the
radical historicism of Dilthey and Ortega y Gasset. The latter,
we have noted, maintains that "Man has no nature; he has
history." To have a nature would imply having a fixed form of
being, and as Ortega y Gasset, like Bergson, regards life as
essentially a Heraclitean process of becoming, he denies that
man has any fixed nature. Man is said to be always in the making, and without any fixed constitution. Cassirer, in agreement
with Dilthey's phenomenological anthropology, arrives at a
similar conclusion by the subjective route of symbolical or cultural idealism. As against Ortega y Gasset's ontological position,
Cassirer argues that

Since Kant's *Critique of Pure Reason* we conceive the dualism of

[53] Jean-Paul Sartre, *L'Existentialisme est une Humanisme* (Paris, 1946).

being and becoming as a logical rather than a metaphysical dualism. . . .
We do not regard substance and change as different realms of being but
as categories—as conditions and presuppositions of our empirical knowledge. These categories are universal principles; they are not confined
to special objects of knowledge.[54]

Thus, according to Cassirer, an ontological or "substantial"
knowledge of man is impossible, since the latter would imply
that man can have an immediate knowledge of himself as an
entity or thing-in-itself apart from his symbolical representations. Man, he argues, cannot know himself except through an
analysis of his symbolic cultural expressions or objectifications,
since all human knowledge, including self-knowledge, is organized by the *a priori*, symbolic categories of historical culture.
Man is, therefore, said to be an *"animal symbolicum"*[55] rather
than an *"animal rationale"* as he has been defined since the
time of Aristotle. As Cassirer goes out of his way to explain:

The philosophy of symbolic forms starts from the presupposition
that, if there is any definition of the nature or "essence" of man, this
definition can only be understood as a functional one, not a substantial
one. We cannot define man by any inherent principle which constitutes
his metaphysical essence—nor can we define him by any inborn faculty
or instinct that may be ascertained by empirical observation. Man's
outstanding characteristic, his distinguishing mark, is not his metaphysical or physical nature—but his work. It is this work, it is the
system of human activities, which defines and determines the circle
of "humanity." Language, myth, religion, art, science, history are the
constituents, the various sectors of this circle. A "philosophy of man"
would therefore be a philosophy which would give us insight into the
fundamental structure of each of these human activities, and which
at the same time would enable us to understand them as an organic
whole. Language, art, myth, religion are no isolated, random creations. They are held together by a common bond. But this bond is
not a *vinculum substantiale*, as it was conceived and described in
scholastic thought; it is rather a *vinculum functionale*. It is the basic
function of speech, of myth, of art, of religion, that we must seek far
behind their innumerable shapes and utterances, and that in the last
analysis we must attempt to trace back to a common origin.[56]

[54] *EM.*, 172.
[55] *Ibid.*, 26.
[56] *Ibid.*, 67f.

Thus Cassirer, in agreement with Comte, maintains that to "know thyself" individually requires that one know humanity in terms of its historical, cultural achievements, and hence he accepts Comte's proposition that "humanity is not to be explained through man but man by humanity."[57]

Cassirer, like Dilthey, would disagree with Comte's positivism only insofar as Comte applies the objective methods of natural science to human studies, on the assumption that the latter were a kind of "social physics," subject to empirical observation and explanation in terms of universal, natural laws. In opposition to this naturalistic approach, the neo-Kantians would maintain that the human studies or cultural sciences require a subjective approach which would yield *understanding* and concrete, idiographic insight into the human processes and symbols involved—a type of knowledge which no amount of external observation, causal explanation, or statistical correlation can possibly furnish.

This point is significant in that it demonstrates how closely historical idealism and sociological positivism approximate one another, and how much essential agreement there is in their conclusions, notwithstanding their professed differences in methodology. The basic reason for this agreement between historical idealism and sociological positivism lies in their common antimetaphysical perspective. In denying any ontological or substantial knowledge of man or of human nature, the adherents of both these positions are led to affirm that only a knowledge of "social facts" and historical, social achievements can provide a scientific knowledge of man. Thus both the positivists and the neo-Kantian idealists tend to reduce the category of nature to that of culture, thereby turning ontology and epistemology into "culturology" or cultural anthropology.

A careful analysis of contemporary ethnology would suggest, that both sociological positivism and cultural idealism represent extreme positions.[58] If one were to adopt a *polaristic* conception of culture and recognize that the idea of culture is unintelligible

---

[57] *Ibid.*, 64.

[58] See D. Bidney, "Human Nature and the Cultural Process" (*American Anthropologist*, 49, no. 3, 1947, 375-99.)

apart from its reference to nature, then it would follow that human nature is logically and genetically prior to culture, since we must postulate human agents with determinate psycho-biological powers and impulses capable of initiating the cultural process. In other words, *the determinate nature of man is manifested functionally through culture but is not reducible to culture. There is no necessity in fact or in logic for choosing between nature and history.* Man does have a substantial nature which may be investigated by the methods of natural science as well as a cultural history which may be studied by the methods of the social sciences and humanities. By assuming uncritically that all human phenomena pertain to the domain of cultural history, one sets up a false dichotomy or division between human studies on the one hand, and natural science on the other—a division which tends to widen the gulf between them and thus renders any effective cultural integration impossible of achievement. As Eduardo Nicol has recently put it,

> Our epoch reproduces, in the anthropological field, the situation of thought represented by Heraclitus and Parmenides in the cosmological field; we have to investigate *what the being who changes is.* It is not enough to say that man *changes,* that man is historical; it is not sufficient to say that man *is.* We must explain *how he is in change;* we must explain what constitutes the internal law of his change and how the organic structure of his being operates in history.[59]

If there were nothing relatively permanent or fixed, if there were no human nature or essence, there could be no science of man but only a sequence of descriptions for each period of history. On the other hand, if human nature were completely unmodifiable, if man were incapable of determining for himself the direction or particular form of his development in time, there could be no culture or history. *The cultural process requires as its indispensable condition a determinate human nature and environment which is subject to transformation in time by man himself.*

[59] See Eduardo Nicol, "The Idea of Man," in *The Social Sciences in Mexico,* vol. 1, no. 1, (May 1947) 62-69.

8

Ernst Cassirer and the Concept of Cultural Reality

In agreement with the Kantian position, Cassirer also holds that human thought is no passive mirror of reality but rather a dynamic agent which creates a symbolical or intelligible world of its own. In his early work on *Language and Myth* Cassirer has formulated very clearly his basic indebtedness to the Kantian approach. He writes:

Against this self-dissolution of the spirit there is only one remedy: to accept in all seriousness what Kant calls his "Copernican revolution." Instead of measuring the content, meaning, and truth of intellectual forms by something extraneous which is supposed to be reproduced in them, we must find in these forms themselves the measure and criterion for their truth and intrinsic meaning. Instead of taking them as mere copies of something else, we must see in each of these spiritual forms a spontaneous law of generation; an original way and tendency of expression which is more than a mere record of something initially given in fixed categories of real existence. From this point of view, myth, art, language and science appear as symbols; not in the sense of mere figures which refer to some given reality by means of suggestion and allegorical renderings, but in the sense of forces each of which produces and posits a world of its own. In these realms the spirit exhibits itself in that inwardly determined dialectic by virtue of which alone there is any reality, any organized and definite Being at all. Thus the special symbolic forms are not imitations, but *organs* of reality, since it is solely by their agency that anything real becomes an object for intellectual apprehension, and as such is made visible to us. The question as to what reality is apart from these forms, and what are its independent attributes, becomes irrelevant here. For the mind, only that can be visible which has some definite form; but every form of existence has its source in some peculiar way of seeing, some intellectual formulation and intuition of meaning. Once language, myth, art and science are recognized as such ideational forms, the basic philosophical question is no longer that of their relation to an absolute reality which forms, so to speak, their solid and substantial substratum; the central problem now is that of their mutual limitation and supplementation. Though they all function organically together in the construction of spiritual reality, yet each of these organs has its individual assignment.[60]

[60] *Language and Myth*, tr. by S. K. Langer (New York and London, 1946) 8f.

Thus Cassirer's Kantian thesis is that symbolic forms are not mere imitations but organs of reality and that there are a limited number of "archetypal" cultural phenomena which constitute the main categories of cultural reality. For man, all reality is ultimately cultural reality or symbolical reality which the human mind itself has created in the course of historical development, since that is the only kind of reality which it is possible for the human mind to apprehend and evaluate.

This symbolical world of objective meanings constitutes, as it were, "a new *dimension* of reality"[61] available only to man. Man literally lives in a "symbolical universe" of his own creation and imagination. As Cassirer puts it in his *Essay on Man:*

Man cannot escape from his own achievement. He cannot but adopt the conditions of his own life. No longer in a merely physical universe, man lives in a symbolic universe. Language, myth, art and religion are parts of this universe. They are the varied threads which weave the symbolic net, the tangled web of human experience. All human progress in thought and experience refines upon and strengthens this net. No longer can man confront reality immediately; he cannot see, as it were, face to face. Physical reality seems to recede in proportion as man's symbolic activity advances. Instead of dealing with the things themselves man is in a sense constantly conversing with himself. He has so enveloped himself in linguistic forms, in artistic images, in mythical symbols or religious rites that he cannot see or know anything except by the interposition of this artificial medium. His situation is the same in the theoretical as in the practical sphere. Even here man does not live in a world of hard facts, or according to his immediate needs and desires. He lives rather in the midst of imaginary emotions, in hopes and fears, in illusions and disillusions, in his fantasies and dreams.[62]

Thus, according to Cassirer, the various cultural disciplines are, as it were, the language of the spirit, the diverse modes of symbolical expression created by man in the process of interpreting his life-experiences. One cannot go behind these symbolical expressions to intuit nature or things-in-themselves directly, since experience is formally constituted by symbols which determine all our human perspectives. For Cassirer, it would

[61] *EM.*, 24.
[62] *Ibid.*, 25.

appear, the symbol takes the place of Kant's forms of intuition and categories of the understanding. The symbol is thought to constitute the ultimate element of all human culture.

Again it is interesting to note that the sociological positivists have come to a similar conclusion by a different route. In his *Cultural Reality* Florian Znaniecki argues that

> For a general view of the world the fundamental points are that the concrete empirical world is a world in evolution in which nothing absolutely permanent can be found, and that as a world in evolution it is first of all a world of culture, not of nature, a historical, not a physical reality. Idealism and naturalism both deal, not with the concrete empirical world, but with abstractly isolated aspects of it.[63]

From this it appears that Znaniecki's positivistic, historical cultural reality is identical with that of the neo-Kantian idealists, although he himself thought that he was steering a middle course between naturalism and idealism (of the Hegelian variety). Once more it may be seen how sociological positivism and historical idealism come to the same conclusion and posit a cultural reality as over against a metaphysical or ontological reality which is pre-cultural.

9

Cassirer's Critique of Kant

As pointed out in our discussion of Dilthey (Section 5 above), the neo-Kantians of the nineteenth century felt that the Kantian approach had to be modified so as to take into consideration the facts of cultural evolution. Cassirer likewise shares this view, and, in common with Dilthey, takes objection to Kant's excessive intellectualism and lack of historical perspective. In agreement with Comte, Durkheim and Lévy-Bruhl he maintains that primitive thought is pre-scientific and does not conform to our logical standards, but that it is nonetheless intelligible and orderly. Kant tended to assume that only the categories of modern science provided the necessary logical ground for order

[63] Florian Znaniecki, *Cultural Reality* (Chicago, 1919), 21. Znaniecki's formulation of the epistemological theory of cultural reality actually antedates that of Cassirer, and so there can be no question of his indebtedness to the latter.

and objectivity, whereas the facts of ethnology demonstrate the possibility of types of order and logic which are pre-scientific or non-scientific. Thus Cassirer comments:

In our modern epistemology, both in the empiristic and rationalistic schools, we often meet with the conception that the first data of human experience are in an entirely chaotic state. Even Kant seems, in the first chapters of the *Critique of Pure Reason*, to start from this pre-supposition. Experience, he says, is no doubt the first product of our understanding. But it is not a simple fact; it is a compound of two opposite factors, of matter and form. The material factor is given in our sense perceptions; the formal factor is represented by our scientific concepts. These concepts, the concepts of pure understanding, give to the phenomena their synthetic unity. What we call the unity of an object cannot be anything but the formal unity of our consciousness in the synthesis of the manifold in our representations. Then and then only we say that we know an object if we have produced synthetic unity in the manifold of intuition. For Kant, therefore, the whole question of the objectivity of human knowledge is indissolubly connected with the fact of science. His Transcendental Aesthetics is concerned with the problem of pure mathematics; his Transcendental Analytic attempts to explain the fact of a mathematical science of nature.

But a philosophy of human culture has to track down the problem to a more remote source. Man lived in an objective world long before he lived in a scientific world. Even before he had found his approach to science, his experience was not a mere amorphous mass of sense expressions. It was an organized and articulated experience. It possessed a definite structure. But the concepts that give to this world its synthetic unity are not of the same type nor are they on the same level as our scientific concepts. They are mythical or linguistic concepts.[64]

In brief, logical or scientific thought, which Kant assumed to be a native endowment of the human understanding is rather an historical achievement of man.

Thus Cassirer would transform the Kantian *Critique of Pure Reason* into a "Critique of Culture." His monumental *Philosophie der symbolischen Formen* is an attempt to demonstrate that the whole of human culture may be understood as an historical expression of the human spirit and that the diverse cul-

[64] *EM.*, 207f.

tural disciplines are functionally integrated and are all alike to
be interpreted as symbolic creations of humanity. In the introduction to the aforementioned work, Cassirer states his thesis
and main objective clearly:

> With this the critique of reason becomes the critique of culture. It
> tries to understand and to demonstrate how all the content of culture—
> in so far as it is more than merely singular content, in so far as it is
> grounded in a universal formal principle—presumes an original act
> of spirit (Geist). It is in this that the basic tenet of idealism finds its
> specific and complete validation.[65]

In sum, Cassirer's critique of culture has for its main objective "a phenomenology of human culture,"[66] and provides a
logical analysis of basic cultural disciplines in their historical and
systematic development. He takes cultural reality as given in
human experience and seeks to analyze its basic forms and the
functional interrelations of these forms with one another. Cassirer's anthropological study, like that projected by Dilthey, is
a "spiritual anthropology" and is concerned with the phenomenological analysis of cultural symbols taken as free expressions or objectifications of the human spirit. Whereas in Kant
we have an epistemological dualism of form *versus* content, Cassirer's cultural symbols are said to be concrete forms utilizing
sense material in diverse ways.[67] The symbol is thought of as an
"organ of thought" which permits of no separation of the symbol and its object. Symbols are regarded not merely as mental
constructs but as dynamic functions or energies for the forming
of reality and for the "synthesis of the ego and its world." In
sum, Cassirer stresses the autonomous creativity of the spirit
(*Schöpfung des Geistes*) and envisages life or spirit as a "function and energy of construction" which manifests a "unity of
being amidst diversity of expression."

It may be questioned, however, whether Cassirer has really
overcome Kant's epistemological dualism. So far as one can
gather, he has replaced the Kantian dualism of form and con-

---

[65] *Philosophie der symbolischen Formen*, vol. I.

[66] *EM.*, 52. Cassirer's phenomenology of culture may be contrasted with the
ontology of culture of the pre-Kantian philosophical tradition.

[67] *Philosophie der symbolischen Formen*, vol. 1, Introduction.

tent by the duality of function and content, but function as he conceives it appears to be equally formal. Thus, as we have noted, he speaks of the "function" which Stoicism had to fulfil in seventeenth and eighteenth century thought, as if the function of an idea were something distinct from its content. Similarly he speaks of the "functional bond" which binds together the various cultural disciplines irrespective of their "substance" or content. In like manner, he refers to "the true unity of langauge" as being a "functional one" rather than a "substantial one."[68] In all these instances, function and substance, end and means, are divorced as if one were quite intelligible apart from the other. In effect, function as so interpreted becomes completely formalized, since one and the same function may be performed by the most diverse cultural means or expressions. Thus, although Cassirer wishes to assure us that there is no separation of the symbol and its object, his actual procedure in separating function from substance or content demonstrates the exact contrary.

In general, it may be said that Cassirer, like the neo-Kantian axiologists referred to earlier (in conclusion of Section 4 above), reduces the sphere of nature to that of culture, but for a different reason. Whereas the neo-Kantian axiologists attempted to subordinate theoretical reason to practical reason and proceeded to endow practical reason with special value categories, the neo-Kantian culturologists, as they may be called, regarded both theoretical and practical reason as different modes of a common historical, cultural reason.[68a] In seeking to overcome the duality of Kant's *Critiques* by positing a unity either of the practical, axiological reason, or of historical cultural reason, the neo-Kantians tended to reduce, as Kant himself would never permit, the sphere of nature and natural science to that of culture and free, historical expression.

[68] *EM.*, 130.

[68a] In his monograph *Zur Logik Der Kulturwissenschaften* (Göteborg, 1942) Cassirer explicitly differentiates between his theory of symbolic forms or *Kulturbegriffe* and the *Wertbegriffe* of Rickert. Culture concepts are said to have a logical structure which differentiates them from historical as well as from value concepts (72).

10

Cassirer on Symbolism, Language, and Cultural Thought

Since the symbol, according to Cassirer, is to be regarded as the ultimate element or source of human culture, we must consider carefully his concept of symbolism and its relation to language in particular and to cultural thought in general.

First of all, it is to be noted that Cassirer distinguishes between signs or signals and symbols. A sign or signal is a sense-reference to some physical object or event. A symbol is an expression which refers to an intuited, universal meaning. That is to say, the meaning of a symbol is intrinsic to it and is not to be understood by reference to some object other than itself. Signs or signals have a practical value for behavior and may be perceived by all animals; but symbols have a theoretical function which only humans are capable of experiencing. Thus Cassirer writes:

> Symbols—in the proper sense of this term—cannot be reduced to mere signals. Signals and symbols belong to different universes of discourse: a signal is a part of the physical world of being; a symbol is a part of the human world of meaning. Signals are "operators," symbols are "designators." Signals, even when understood and used as such, have nevertheless a sort of physical or substantial being; symbols have only a functional value. . . . In short, we may say that the animal possesses a practical imagination and intelligence whereas man alone has developed a new form: a *symbolic imagination and intelligence.*[69]

Cassirer's idealistic theory of symbolism may be contrasted with the behavioristic, naturalistic theory of symbolic meaning held by contemporary linguists and anthropologists, such as, Leonard Bloomfield,[70] Edward Sapir,[71] and Charles Morris.[72] Thus Morris, whom Cassirer apparently had in mind, states that

> A symbol is a sign produced by its interpreter which acts as a substitute for some other sign with which it is synonymous; all signs not symbols

[69] *EM.*, 32f.

[70] Leonard Bloomfield, *Language*, (New York, 1933).

[71] Edward Sapir, *Language*, (New York, 1939); also article "Language" in *Encyclopedia of Social Sciences*, vol. 9.

[72] Charles Morris, *Signs, Language and Behavior*, (New York, 1946).

are signals. . . . Signals and symbols are alike signs in that they are preparatory stimuli controlling behavior with respect to other behavior; the symbol is a sign producible by the organism itself and a substitute for some other sign, but this difference, while distinguishing sign and symbol, is not regarded as a fundamental difference in their nature as signs.[73]

Morris explicitly contrasts his behavioristic position with that of the "mentalists" for whom symbols refer to concepts and not to objects or behavior.

As against this type of behavioristic, naturalistic theory, Cassirer argues that the symbolic function marks a new stage of mental development, which cannot be explained in terms of "emotionally denuded" animal cries or as a by-product of behavior. The difference, he claims,

between *propositional language* and *emotional language* is the real landmark between the human and animal world. All the theories and observations concerning animal behavior are wide of the mark if they fail to recognize this fundamental difference. In all the literature of the subject there does not seem to be a single conclusive proof of the fact that an animal ever made the decisive step from subjective to objective, from affective to propositional language.[74]

According to Cassirer, therefore, man may be defined as the symbolizing or symbol-making animal. It is this symbolic function which has enabled man to create language and culture and has opened up for him "a new dimension of reality" not accessible to the animal species. The symbolic function of language is said to be an *"Urphänomen,"* which is not to be explained causally or genetically through some antecedent order of psychobiological phenomena. This in turn presupposes a theory of evolution by "mutation" or emergence of new kinds, which may be contrasted with the Darwinian theory of gradual evolution through chance variations.[75]

Cassirer illustrates his point by reference to the development of the child:

[73] *Loc. cit.*, 25, 49.
[74] *EM.*, 30.
[75] Cf. *Zur Logik der Kulturwissenschaften*, especially part 4 on "Formproblem und Kausalproblem," 108-112.

With the first understanding of the symbolism of speech a real revolution takes place in the life of the child. From this point on his whole personal and intellectual life assumes an entirely new shape. Roughly speaking, this change may be described by saying that the child passes from a more subjective to an objective state, from a merely emotional attitude to a theoretical attitude. . . . The child himself has a clear sense of the significance of the new instrument for his mental development. He is not satisfied with being taught in a purely receptive manner but takes an active share in the process of speech which is at the same time a process of progressive objectification.—By learning to name things a child does not simply add a list of artificial signs to his previous knowledge of ready-made empirical objects. He learns rather to form the concepts of these objects, to come to terms with the objective world. . . . To the adult the objective world already has a definite shape as a result of speech activity, which has in a sense molded all our other activities. Our perceptions, intuitions, and concepts have coalesced with the terms and speech forms of our mother tongue. Great efforts are required to release the bond between words and things.[76]

The understanding and utilization of genuine, human speech are achieved when the child first acquires insight into the fact that words symbolize universal concepts or meanings. This is a revolutionary, momentous step which enables him for the first time to join the human speech community and to form a clear understanding of the objective, common cultural world in which he lives. In this sense, language is basic to all other forms of cultural activity, since the words of language mold the way in which one experiences and reacts to the objective world. In the last analysis, it is the theoretical function of linguistic symbols, the fact that they are instruments which refer to universal concepts, which makes possible their practical utilization in social communication as well as in individual thought.

It should be noted, however, that although linguistic symbols underlie all other cultural activities, they are in turn affected by the particular, cultural configuration in which they are utilized. As Franz Boas has put it:

We should rather say that language is a reflection of the state of culture and follows in its development the demands of culture. In another way, however, language exerts an influence upon culture. Words

[76] *EM.*, 131ff.

and phrases are symbols of cultural attitudes and have the same kind of emotional appeal that is characteristic of other symbols. The name of a rite, of a deity, an honorific title, a term giving a succinct expression to political or church organization, may have the power to raise the passions of a people without much reference to the changing contents of the term.[77]

Cassirer was keenly aware of the "social task" of language and its relativity to specific cultural conditions.[78] All languages, whether of primitive societies or of civilized ones, are said to be in congruity with the conditions of their cultures.

Finally, it should be noted, that the category of symbol as employed by Cassirer has a subjective as well as objective reference. Thus words are said to be symbols in the sense that they refer to universal, objective meanings which the intellect and imagination intuit immediately. This "semantic function" of words makes phenomenological analysis possible, since the ideas or meanings referred to have a subsistence which is independent of the mind which conceives them. It is because of this capacity for symbolic intuition that man may be said to be a symbol-making or *symbolizing* animal. On the other hand, symbols have a subjective function in the sense that they are expressions of human life or spirit, and of basic psychological motivations. Every cultural form is said to be a symbolic form in virtue of the fact that it is an "organ of thought" or an objectification of the spirit. Cultural symbols as objective manifestations of thought constitute a "symbolic universe" and man is described as "constantly conversing with himself." In this sense man is said to be an *"animal symbolicum"* or a *symbolized* animal, since man does not know himself directly but only through the cultural symbols which humanity has created historically.

Theoretically, however, it is quite possible to maintain the semantic thesis that man is a symbol-making or symbolizing animal without adhering also to the idealistic view that man is essentially a symbolized or symbolical animal. The former semantic point is quite compatible also with a realistic epistemology and a dualistic metaphysics which allows for the reality

[77] Franz Boas, in *General Anthropology*, edited by himself (New York, 1938), ch. iv, 142.
[78] *EM.*, 128f.

of minds as well as physical substances, whereas the latter thesis presupposes an idealistic epistemology which denies ontological knowledge. Cassirer himself utilizes both conceptions of the symbol, passing from the idealistic to the realistic view without explicitly recognizing the change in philosophical perspective.

The disparity between the subjective and objective functions of symbolic forms may be illustrated by reference to the diverse conceptions of man to which they lead. If the symbol is defined objectively, then man may be said to have a nature as well as a culture, since symbols refer to a reality other than themselves. If, however, the symbol is defined subjectively, then all reality is culturally defined and man has no nature but only cultural functions.

II

Cassirer on the Evolution of Cultural Symbolism

One of the basic tasks which Cassirer set himself in his *Philosophy of Symbolic Forms* was to trace the evolution of cultural symbolism from primitive to modern times, with a view to indicating the critical stages of development. He was, moreover, concerned to demonstrate the "unity of function" of each archetypal form of symbolism by showing how it originated in, or was motivated by, some psychological impulse which sought creative expression through a given mode of symbolism.

The act of symbolization is the initial presupposition of his philosophy of culture. In the beginning was the symbol. But originally the basic archetypal forms of symbolism were not clearly differentiated. From the start there were the elements of language, myth, and art which arose as expressions of sensation, thought, feeling, and intuition; but primitive man was not conscious of his symbolic acts as having discrete functions and objects. As Cassirer puts it in his *Language and Myth:*

Myth, language and art begin as a concrete, undivided unity, which is only gradually resolved into a triad of independent modes of spiritual creativity. Consequently, the same mythic animation and hypostatization which is bestowed upon the words of human speech is orginally accorded to *images*, to every kind of artistic representation. Especially in the magical realm, word magic is everywhere accompanied by picture magic.

The image, too, achieves its purely representative, specifically "aesthetic" function only as the magic circle with which mythical consciousness surrounds it is broken, and it is recognized not as a mythico-magic form, but as a particular sort of *formulation*. . . . Language and myth stand in an original and indissoluble correlation with one another, from which they both emerge but gradually as independent elements. They are two diverse shoots from the same parent stem, the same impulse of symbolic formulation, springing from the same basic mental activity, a concentration and heightening of simple sensory experience. In the vocables of speech and in primitive mythic figurations, the same inner process finds its consummation; they are both resolutions of an inner tension, the representation of subjective impulses and excitations in definite objects, forms and figures.[79]

As Cassirer interprets it, language and myth are originally so closely interconnected because genetically "Both are based on a very general and very early experience of mankind, an experience of a social rather than of a physical nature."[80] Just as the child soon learns that words have "magic" powers in securing attention from its mother or nurse, so primitive man is said to transfer this first elementary experience to the totality of nature, since for the latter "Nature itself is nothing but a great society —the society of life."[81] Thus for the primitive mind "the social power of the word, experienced in innumerable cases, becomes a natural and even supernatural force." In brief, myth arises originally as a magical interpretation of the power of words. Similarly image or picture magic gives rise to mythical belief. As against Max Müller's theory that myth arises as a disease of language and owing to the metaphorical use of words, Cassirer's point is that *myth arises as a result of the normal functioning of language in early childhood and in the early experience of mankind.*[82]

A crisis in the intellectual and moral life of mankind arose when primitive man first discovered that nature did not understand his language. From then on, "The magic function of the word was eclipsed and replaced by its semantic function."[83] Man

[79] *LM.*, 98, 88.
[80] *EM.*, 110.
[81] *Ibid.*
[82] *Ibid.*, 109f.
[83] *Ibid.*, 111.

discovered that words have a purely logical, symbolic function in the communication of meanings and ideas.

According to Cassirer, therefore, there is an evolutionary process of development from the mythical to the logical function of linguistic symbols. This development is produced in human experience by the functioning or exercise of language alone. Linguistic symbols must not be regarded merely as representing or referring to objective reality other than themselves; linguistic symbols create or determine the order of reality which the human mind recognizes and to which it adjusts itself accordingly. Myth, logic, metaphysics, and science are the result or product of linguistic symbolization at different stages of its development. As Cassirer puts it in his *Language and Myth:*

> Here one can trace directly how humanity really attains its insight into objective reality only through the medium of its own activity and the progressive differentiation of that activity; before man thinks in terms of logical concepts, he holds his experiences by means of clear, separate, mythical images. And here too, the development of language appears to be the counterpart of the development which mythical intuition and thought undergo; for one cannot grasp the true nature and function of linguistic concepts if one regards them as copies, as representations of a definite world of facts, whose components are given to the mind *ab initio* in stark and separate outlines. Again, the limits of things must first be posited, the outlines drawn, by the agency of language; and this is accomplished as man's activity becomes internally organized, and his conception of Being acquires a correspondingly clear and definite pattern.[84]

For Cassirer, it would appear, linguistic symbolism is primary to all other forms of cultural expression. In this sense his philosophy of culture may be said to depend upon his philosophy of language—a fact which explains the tremendous importance attached to the philosophy of language by other neo-Kantian philosophers, such as W. M. Urban,[85] who have been influenced by Cassirer's work.

In the last analysis, it would appear, Cassirer reduces ontology and epistemology to psychology and linguistics. We

[84] *LM.*, 37.
[85] W. M. Urban, *Language and Reality*, (New York, 1939).

have seen how myth is said to have originated from the normal functioning of language in the psychological history of the childhood of humanity and how gradually man discovered the logical or semantic function of words as a result of his frustrating experience with unintelligent, dumb nature. From this it follows that the very notion of an objective reality was a logical inference from man's practical, psychological experience—an argument which is reminiscent of the psychoanalytical treatment of metaphysics.

It may be questioned, however, whether Cassirer's psychological interpretation of myth and magic is not itself mythical. In the first place, Cassirer, in common with nineteenth century evolutionary psychologists, assumes a parallelism between the experiences of the child and the mental evolution of mankind—a position which modern psychologists and ethnologists have rejected. Secondly, modern psychology provides no evidence that the child originally attaches a mythical or magical significance to words. It is true that the child does assume naïvely at first that all things are equally animate and that he can communicate with them as with human beings. This, however, implies a naïve type of animism, a kind of "natural," mythical metaphysics which children everywhere tend implicitly to adopt. It may be argued, therefore, that the ontological belief of the child determines his use of language on a scale which the rational adult finds amusing. It is not his social experience with words which determines his mythical perspective upon his environment, but rather, it is his animistic perspective which determines his attempt to communicate with all things. Gradually, as his efforts at communication prove unsuccessful, the child learns to distinguish between animate and inanimate objects and to restrict his verbal communications to the former. Even then, the process is a slow one, since he has also to learn that not all animals speak his type of language and that even among humans not all speak his vocabulary. The notion that words themselves have magical supernatural powers is a rather complex and relatively sophisticated belief, which the child may acquire from folklore, but is one which he does not arrive at simply as a result of his own common experience. In other terms, the mythology and magic of words are special instances of cosmic mythology and magic, and the former cannot therefore serve as a general explanation of the latter. In the last analysis, Cassirer assumes that the will to power through words of the child as well as of early man leads them both to believe in a methaphysics of the solidarity of life—an idealistic, voluntaristic, anthropocentric assumption which does not take into consideration the empirical data of experience and the impact of man's cosmic environment upon human intelligence.

It seems no exaggeration to say that Cassirer's approach to the problem of the evolution of cultural symbolism is essentially anthropocentric. Symbols are formed in response to psychological tensions and motivations, and hence symbolic meanings are said to have a practical bearing upon the satisfaction of human psychobiological interests. As Cassirer puts it in *Language and Myth:*

> Whatever appears important for our wishing and willing, our hope and anxiety, for acting and doing: that and that only receives the stamp of verbal "meaning." . . . For only what is related somehow to the focus point of willing and doing, only what proves to be essential to the whole scheme of life and activity, is selected from the uniform flux of sense impressions, and is "noticed" in the midst of them—that is to say, receives a special linguistic accent, a name. . . . Only symbolic expression can yield the possibility of prospect and retrospect, because it is only by symbols that distinctions are not merely made, but fixed in consciousness. What the mind has once created, what has been culled from the total sphere of consciousness, does not fade away again when the spoken word has set its seal upon it and given it definite form. . . . Here, too, the recognition of function precedes that of Being. The aspects of Being are distinguished and co-ordinated according to a measure supplied by action—hence they are guided, not by any "objective" similarity among things, but by their appearance through the medium of practice, which relates them with a purposive nexus. This teleological character of verbal concepts may be readily supported and clarified by means of examples from the history of language.[86]

Cassirer's anthropocentric, pragmatic interpretation of the origin of symbolic, verbal meanings is reminiscent of Bergson's evolutionary approach to intellectual concepts. But in his

[86] *LM.*, 37ff.

emphasis upon the primacy of symbolic function over form of being, *Cassirer*, it would appear, *deserves the credit for having first formulated systematically a functionalistic theory of culture which also comprises the data of ethnology.* In the history of modern ethnology, Bronislaw Malinowski is usually credited with having first formulated such an approach, and the latter has written as if the functionalistic theory of culture were his special achievement.[87] Of course, Malinowski, as a field anthropologist, gathered his own data, especially among the Trobriand Islanders, and has undoubtedly provided the stimulus in modern ethnology for a holistic, dynamic approach to cultural phenomena.[88] Furthermore, the functionalism of Cassirer is historical and symbolic, whereas that of Malinowski is biological and sociological. It is all the more significant, therefore, that the philosophical anthropologist and the empirical ethnologist whose methods appear to differ so widely should converge upon a similar functionalistic conclusion. Cassirer himself, during his appointment at Yale University, had ample opportunity to make the personal acquaintance of Malinowski, and he soon recognized the affinity between their cultural approaches, as the many references and quotations in his *Essay on Man* and *Myth of the State* demonstrate. One may even affirm that Cassirer tended to underestimate their respective differences, especially as regards the problem of myth and the evolution of cultural mentality, thereby undermining the consistency of his own position. (See Section 14 *infra.*)

This brings us back once more to the distinction between the subjective and objective functions of symbols which we discussed earlier. We have noted that for Cassirer a symbol is an expression which refers to an intuited, universal meaning. Signs or signals may be discerned by all animals, but symbols have a

[87] Bronislaw Malinowski, *A Scientific Theory of Culture and Other Essays*, (Chapel Hill, N.C., 1944). Cf. R. H. Lowie, *The History of Ethnological Theory*, (New York, 1937), ch. xiii, "Functionalism, Pure and Tempered." See also "The Problem of Meaning in Primitive Languages" in Ogden and Richards, *The Meaning of Meaning* (first edition, London, 1923) where Malinowski interprets the significance of meaning in primitive thought and language in terms almost identical with those of Cassirer.

[88] Malinowski, *Argonauts of the Western Pacific*, (London, 1922); *Coral Gardens and their Magic*, (New York, 1935).

theoretical function which only human beings are capable of experiencing. In virtue of his intuition of the objective reference of linguistic symbols, man forms the notion of a common, objective world and is able to communicate with others who share a common cultural perspective. It is the *theoretical* function of symbols which makes possible their practical utilization in human society. On the other hand, linguistic symbols are said to have an essentially subjective, teleological reference and to reflect, not the objective character of things, but our subjective, practical interests and impulses. Reality as constituted by human symbols is a human creation or invention and serves the interests of human action or practice. Human symbols are not primarily a guide to an understanding of nature, but a reflection of human psycho-biological impulses and interests. As stated in these extreme forms, the two concepts of the nature of symbolic forms and meanings appear antithetical. Logically, it is quite possible to maintain a mentalistic theory of symbolism which would take into consideration the diversity of cultural interests and classifications. But Cassirer uses the evidence of the relativity of cultural conceptualization as an argument for his subjective, idealistic theory of cultural symbolism. That is to say, he employs a mentalistic theory of symbolism to demonstrate the concept of objective reality, and a behavioristic, pragmatic, anthropocentric theory of symbolism to demonstrate the idealistic, subjective reference of symbols.

12

Cassirer on the Unitary Psychological Functions of Symbolic Forms

In commenting adversely upon nineteenth century linguistics Cassirer writes: "The nineteenth century was not only a historical but also a psychological century. It was, therefore, quite natural to assume, it even appeared self-evident, that the principles of linguistic theory were to be sought in the field of psychology. These were the two cornerstones of linguistic studies."[89]

[89] *EM.*, 119.

Cassirer's own philosophy of language and culture provides ample demonstration of the fact that he himself participated in this historical-psychological approach, notwithstanding his professed criticism of it and his attempt to distinguish genetic from systematic, functional problems.[90] We have seen that his interpretation of the relation of language and myth depended upon uncritical, psychological assumptions as to the mythical function of words. We have found, furthermore, that he presupposes a functionalistic, voluntaristic psychology in interpreting the origin of linguistic symbols and classifications.

In general, it appears, Cassirer maintained that each archetypal form of symbolism manifested a unity of function in the subjective sense, that it was an expression of a particular psychological faculty or activity. Thus in his *Myth of the State* he remarks:

The subjects of myth and the ritual acts are of an infinite variety; they are incalculable and unfathomable. But the motives of mythical thought and mythical imagination are in a sense always the same. In all human activities and in all forms of human culture we find a "unity in the manifold." Art gives us a unity of intuition; science gives us a unity of thought; religion and myth give us a unity of feeling. Art opens up to us the universe of "living forms;" science shows us a universe of laws and principles; religion and myth begin with the awareness of the universality and fundamental identity of life.[91]

Here we are presented with a tripartite division of psychological functions or motivations which neatly correlates intuition, thought, and feeling with art, science, and religion respectively. Each psychological function expresses itself through different symbolic forms; but the underlying principle of unity amidst the diversity of objects symbolized in any one cultural discipline is its psychological motivation in the human ego. In this manner, Cassirer correlates the subjective functions of the ego with the given objective, cultural categories or types of symbols, thereby linking together man and his symbolic world.

Parallel to the cultural evolution of mankind there is a corresponding psychological evolution. Primitive man, we have seen,

[90] *Ibid.*, 118.
[91] *MS.*, 37.

is said to be motivated primarily by feelings, by emotion and desire, and his psychological motivation is reflected in myth and ritual. Only gradually, as the linguistic process develops in the course of experience, man acquires the faculty of thinking logically and rationally by distinguishing between the semantic function of words and the objective reality of objects. Similarly, art develops as an independent expression of intuition and imagination and severs its original connection with magic and myth. In each of the several cultural disciplines there is a gradual process of development from irrational and subjective to rational and objective modes of expression. In this sense the history of human culture is the record of man's progressive efforts at self-expression and self-liberation, since all culture is a manifestation of human freedom and creativity.

Cassirer's psychological approach to cultural symbolism in general is especially significant in view of his assertion that man is to be defined through humanity and not through a given psychological or metaphysical nature.[92] Again, in practice, it would appear, Cassirer does not follow his professed historical and phenomenological procedure exclusively but proceeds rather to explain the cultural achievements of humanity through man's psychological nature. Instead of choosing between humanity and man, he finds it more practicable to utilize both concepts, thereby implying that culture has a unity of function because man has a nature as well as history.

In terms of contemporary ethnological theory, the issue involved is whether culture is to be understood as essentially a "superorganic" phenomenon or whether it is to be conceived organically as a vital expression of the human organism whose individual and social needs it satisfies.[93] As a superorganic dimension of reality all cultural symbols are conceived through one another and require no further reference to the psychological nature of man. As an organic phenomenon culture cannot be understood apart from the psycho-biological nature of man. The

[92] Cf. Section 7 above.

[93] Cf. D. Bidney, "The Concept of Culture and Some Cultural Fallacies;" and "Human Nature and the Cultural Process."

superorganic theory of culture requires that man be conceived through humanity; the organic theory requires that humanity be conceived through man. Cassirer, it seems, professes the superorganic theory of Comte but in practice also leans heavily on the organic, functionalistic theory, especially in dealing with the origin and function of myth.

13

Cassirer and the Problem of the Unitary Function of Myth

Cassirer objects to the procedure of those folklorists, philologists, and psychoanalysts who attempt to ascribe a unity of object to myth, and posits instead a unity of psychological function. He assumes that the motive of myth-making is always the same and that feeling or emotion is the common functional bond, the unity in the manifold. "Biologically speaking," he claims, "feeling is a much more general fact and belongs to an earlier and more elementary stratum than all the cognitive states of mind."[94] He is opposed, therefore, to those who, like Tylor and Frazer, attempted to intellectualize myths and to interpret them as modes of logical thought and belief. Myths, he maintains, are primarily emotional in origin and their practical social function is to promote a unity or harmony of feeling between individuals as well as a sense of harmony with the whole of nature and life. In agreement with Malinowski,[95] he holds that the function of myth is not the theoretical or intellectual one of explanation, but rather the practical one of promoting a consciousness of the solidarity of all life, especially in times of crisis, through a rationalization of the social rites which preceded them.

This basic assumption of Cassirer as to the unity of psychological motivation and sociological function (the subjective and objective aspects of function) is one that leading contemporary ethnologists do not accept, since they are more inclined towards a pluralistic theory of explanation of the function as well as of

[94] *MS.*, 27.
[95] Bronislaw Malinowski, *Myth in Primitive Psychology*, Psyche Monographs, no. 6, (London, 1926); cf. also *MS.*, 28.

the object of myth. Franz Boas, for example, writes:

The fact that we designate certain tales as myths, that we group certain activities together as rituals, or that we consider certain forms of industrial products from an esthetic point of view, does not prove that these phenomena, wherever they occur, have the same history or spring from the same mental activities. On the contrary, it is quite obvious that the selection of the material assembled for the purpose of comparison is wholly determined by the subjective point of view according to which we arrange diverse mental phenomena. . . . The phenomena themselves contain no indication whatever that would compel us to assume a common origin. On the contrary, wherever an analysis has been attempted we are led to the conclusion that we are dealing with heterogeneous material. Thus myths may be in part interpretations of nature that have originated as results of naïvely considered impressions (*Naturanschauung*); they may be artistic productions in which the mythic element is rather a poetic than a religious concept; they may be the result of philosophic interpretation or they may have grown out of linguistic forms that have risen into consciousness. To explain all these forms as members of one series would be entirely unjustified.[96]

Here we see that Boas denies that any one psychological motive is sufficient to explain the origin of myth. The error of the nineteenth century anthropologists, folklorists, and philologists is said to lie, not in their limited empirical evidence, but rather in their uncritical assumption that all myth is of the same type, and that we are dealing here with homogeneous material which originates in some one psychological motive. Myths, according to Boas, may be either theoretical and explanatory, or poetic and religious; they may have a practical function and serve to rationalize a given custom, as in the case of totemism, or they may be in part philological in origin as Max Müller suggested. No one psychological function and no one type of object is sufficient to account for the various forms of myth.

Similarly Ruth Benedict, although agreeing with Boas' point that myths are not based on any one object of "fixed symbolism" and that they are not primarily explanatory, is inclined to stress the intimate connection between the play of imagination

[96] Franz Boas, "The Origin of Totemism," in *American Anthropologist*, 18: 319-26 (1916).

and wish fulfilment in a given culture.[97] Thus she writes:

Myth like secular folklore is an articulate vehicle of a people's wishful thinking. Secular heroes portray the ideal man of the culture and myth remodels the universe to its dominant desire. . . . The striking contrasts in different collections of myth are in a large measure due to the difference in the types of wish fulfilment that are characteristic of the different cultures.[98]

According to Benedict, then, the play of imagination and wishful thinking are the primary psychological factors underlying myth. The cultural function of myth is regarded as being poetic and artistic.

Thus, it appears, that Cassirer's assumption as to the unity of function at the basis of myth is one which modern ethnologists, with the exception of functionalists such as Malinowski or Radcliffe-Brown, would be inclined to question. Although they would agree with Cassirer that myths have no unity of object, they would disagree with his uncritical assumption that myths have a unity of psychological motivation or social function.

14

Cassirer, Lévy-Bruhl, and Malinowski on the Concept of Myth

The full significance of Cassirer's theory of myth and the mythical mentality may be critically evaluated in relation to modern ethnology which he investigated and by which he was influenced considerably. Among the various logical possibilities as to the nature of mythical thought there are three which are significant in this connection.

First, there is the rationalistic or intellectualistic theory, associated with the names of E. B. Tylor and Sir James Frazer, that myths are essentially rational constructions based on erroneous major premises. The native mind is said to be essentially logical and myths are regarded as the products of intellectual wonder, and logical inference. Thus animism, according to Tylor, is a logical theory which offers a plausible explanation of death on the analogy of sleep; it is a rational primitive philosophy.

[97] Ruth Benedict, article "Folklore" in *Encyclopedia of the Social Sciences* 6:288-93; also article "Myth" in same work, 11:178-80.
[98] In her article "Myth."

Second, there is the evolutionary, sociological theory of Lévy-Bruhl that the native mind is essentially "prelogical," in the sense that it is indifferent to the rules of our logic but not necessarily contrary to it. The native mind, as may be gathered from a study of the "collective representations" manifested in typical, native social culture, has not reached the stage where it differentiates clearly between the natural and the supernatural, between natural and magical powers; and hence the native mental perspective or mode of thinking differs radically from the logical, scientific mentality of civilized man. This does not mean that the native, taken as an individual, does not have a psycho-biological nature similar to that of civilized man or that he would not react and think in a given situation much the same as we do, provided he was similarly conditioned. Lévy-Bruhl's thesis is that, *culturally speaking,* the typical native, insofar as he is a product of primitive, native culture, does not think logically, that is, in accordance with the law of contradiction, and that his mind obeys instead the organic law of mutual "participation," whereby all things are thought to participate in one another in a kind of "mystic symbiosis."

As Lévy-Bruhl's theory of the prelogical character of the native mentality has been the target of much criticism on the part of modern anthropologists, and as Cassirer also takes issue with him, it will help this discussion, if we refer directly to Lévy-Bruhl's statements of his position. In his work, *How Natives Think (Les Fonctions Mentales Dans Les Sociétés Inférieures)* he writes:

By prelogical we do not mean to assert that such a mentality constitutes a kind of antecedent state in point of time to the birth of logical thought. . . . It is not antilogical; it is not alogical either. By designating it "prelogical" I merely wish to state that it does not bind itself down, as our thought does, to avoid contradiction. It obeys the law of participation first and foremost.

Essentially mystic as it is, it finds no difficulty in imagining as well as feeling the identity of the one and the many, the individual and the species, of entities however unlike they be, by means of *participation.* In this lies its guiding principle; this it is which accounts for the kind of abstraction and generalization peculiar to such a mentality and to this again we must mainly refer the characteristic forms of activity we find in primitive peoples.

As has been said, these characteristics apply only to the collective representations and their connections. Considered as an individual, the primitive in so far as he thinks and acts independently of these collective representations where possible, will usually feel, argue and act as we should expect him to do. The inferences he draws will be just those which would seem reasonable to us in like circumstances. . . . But though on occasions of this sort primitives may reason as we do, though they follow a course similar to the one we should take (which in the more simple cases, the most intelligent among the animals would also do) it does not follow that their mental activity is always subject to the same laws as ours. In fact, as far as it is collective, it has laws which are peculiar to itself, and the first and most universal of these is the law of participation.[99]

Thus, according to Lévy-Bruhl, the mentality of native peoples is prelogical in the sense that its collective representations, the mode of thought which is culturally conditioned by a given society, is indifferent to the law of contradiction and is said to be regulated instead by the law of participation. This renders the native mentality essentially mystical to our usual way of thinking. This does not mean, however, that the mind of civilized man is entirely logical by comparison. On the contrary, for Lévy-Bruhl "the rational unity of the thinking being . . . is a *desideratum*, not a fact."[100] Our mentality is said to be both rational and irrational: "The prelogical and the mystic are co-existent with the logical." In civilized society the logical, scientific aspect of thought may be dominant, but there always remain elements of prelogical mentality—a fact which accounts for the antinomies of thought and the struggle of reason with itself.

The prelogical, mystical character of native collective representations also renders intelligible the socio-cultural function of their myths. Myths are interpreted as "an expression of the

[99] Lucien Lévy-Bruhl, *How Natives Think* (*Les Fonctions Mentales Dans Les Sociétés Inférieures*, Paris, 1910), London & New York, 1926; 78f, 135f.
[100] *Ibid.*, 386.

solidarity of the social group with itself in its own epoch and in the past, and with the groups of being surrounding it, and a means of maintaining and reviving this feeling of solidarity."[101]

In opposition to Lévy-Bruhl's evolutionary conception of the prelogical, cultural mentality of the native, Bronislaw Malinowski has maintained that the native distinguishes clearly between the sphere of the natural and secular on the one hand, and the sphere of the supernatural and holy on the other. As opposed to the intellectualism and individualism of Tylor and Frazer, and in agreement with Lévy-Bruhl, he maintains that myths originate in social, practical and emotional needs and serve to strengthen the feeling of solidarity between the individual and his community as well as between the community and the forces of the natural, cosmic environment. The sociological, functional significance of myths has been emphasized by Malinowski, especially in his monograph on *Myth in Primitive Psychology*. He writes:

> Studied alive, myth is not symbolic, but a direct expression of its subject-matter; it is not an explanation in satisfaction of a scientific interest, but a narrative resurrection of a primeval reality, told in satisfaction of deep religious wants, moral cravings, social submissions, assertions, even practical requirements. Myth fulfils in primitive culture an indispensable function; it expresses, enhances, and codifies belief; it safeguards and enforces morality; it vouches for the efficiency of ritual and contains practical rules for the guidance of man. Myth is thus a vital ingredient of human civilization; it is not an idle tale but a hard-worked active force; it is not an intellectual explanation or an artistic imagery, but a pragmatic charter of primitive faith and moral wisdom.[102]

According to Malinowski, the native resorts to myth and magic, not because he fails to distinguish the natural from the supernatural, or the scientific from the magical, but precisely because he does in fact make this distinction. Myths and magic are resorted to only when all common, rational techniques and processes fail, as in time of crisis or extreme danger. As Malinowski puts it:

[101] *Ibid.*, 371.
[102] *Myth in Primitive Psychology*, 23.

Primitive man has his science as well as his religion; a myth does not serve to explain phenomena but rather to regulate human actions. . . . It is rather the recognition of his practical and intellectual limitations and not the illusion of the omnipotence of thought which leads man into ritualism, which makes him re-enact miracles, the feasibility of which he has accepted from his mythology. . . . In short, myth is not a pseudo-science of nature, it is a history of the supernatural. It invariably refers to a unique break in the history of the world and mankind.[103]

There is no need, therefore, for Malinowski to assume a mythical mentality which gradually evolved into the logical mentality of civilized man. Myths are expressions of acts of faith and as such are characteristic of man at practically all stages of human culture. Myths as beliefs in the supernatural thus complement scientific theory and practice; they are neither a substitute for science nor the antithesis of scientific thought. In Malinowski's words:

Mythology, then, is definitely the complement of what might be called the ordinary knowledge or science of primitive man, but not its substitute. . . . The so-called primitives do distinguish between natural and supernatural. They explain, not by telling a fairy-tale, but by reference to experience, logical and common sense, even as we do. Since they have their own science, mythology cannot be their system of explanation in the scientific sense of the word. Myth serves as a foundation for belief and establishes a precedent for the miracles of ritual and magic.[104]

Thus, it appears, myth is regarded as an essential element in the life of primitive as well as in that of civilized man. Myth begins where scientific knowledge ends and yet, it is pragmatically significant in providing assurance of, and faith in, the harmony of man and nature. In brief, for Malinowski, mythical thought is not prelogical but rather post-logical and post-scientific, in the sense that it involves an act of faith in the

---

[103] *The Foundations of Faith and Morals:* An anthropological analysis of primitive beliefs and conduct with special reference to the fundamental problems of religion and ethics. Delivered as Riddell Memorial Lectures, Seventh Series, 1934-5 (London, 1936).

[104] *Ibid.* Cf. also his "Magic, Science and Religion," in *Science, Religion and Reality,* ed. by J. Needham, (New York, 1928).

supernatural and miraculous which goes beyond logic and scientific evidence. It is of interest to note in this connection, that William James' *Will to Believe* provides a philosophical justification for a similar faith on the part of civilized man.

When we turn to Cassirer's own theory of mythical thought we find a rather curious state of affairs. To begin with, his description of mythical mentality is similar in all essentials to the evolutionary theory of Lévy-Bruhl, and even goes beyond the latter in positing a radical disparity between the mythical and logical stages of development. It is significant to note that Susanne K. Langer, in her preface to the translation of Cassirer's *Language and Myth*, actually refers to his "theory of prelogical conception and expression."[105] When, however, we turn to Cassirer's *Essay on Man*, we find he takes issue with Lévy-Bruhl over the latter's concept of the prelogical. Thus he states:

The thesis of Durkheim has come to its full development in the work of Lévy-Bruhl. But here we meet with a more general characteristic. Mystical thought is described as *"prelogical thought."* If it asks for causes, these are neither logical nor empirical; they are "mystic causes." . . . According to Lévy-Bruhl this mystic character of primitive religion follows from the very fact that its representations are "collective representations." To these we cannot apply the rules of our own logic that are intended for quite different purposes. If we approach this field, even the law of contradiction and all the other laws of rational thought, become invalid. To my mind the French sociological school has given full and conclusive proof of the first part of its thesis but not of the second part. The fundamental social character of myth is uncontroverted. But that all primitive mentality necessarily is prelogical or mystical seems to be in contradiction with our anthropological and ethnological evidence. We find many spheres of primitive life and culture that show the well-known features of our own cultural life. As long as we assume an absolute heterogeneity between our own logic and that of the primitive mind, as long as we think them specifically different from and radically opposed to each other, we can scarcely account for this fact. Even in primitive life we always find a secular or profane sphere outside the holy sphere.[106]

[105] *LM.*, x.
[106] *EM.*, 79f.

Similarly, in his *Myth of the State* Cassirer resumes his criticism:

> We find the very reverse of this conception in Lévy-Bruhl's well-known description of "primitive mentality." According to Lévy-Bruhl the task that former theories had set themselves was impossible—a contradiction in terms. It is vain to seek for a common measure between primitive mentality and our own. They do not belong to the same genus; they are radically opposed the one to the other. The rules which to the civilized man seem to be unquestionable and inviolable are entirely unknown and constantly thwarted in primitive thought. The savage's mind is not capable of all those processes of arguing and reasoning that were ascribed to it in Frazer's and Tylor's theories. It is not a logical, but a "prelogical" or a mystic mind. Even the most elementary principles of our logic are openly defied by this mystic mind. The savage lives in a world of his own—in a world which is impermeable to experience and unaccessible to our forms of thought.[107]

In view of the statements quoted from Lévy-Bruhl's work, one cannot regard Cassirer's criticism as valid. The latter, it would appear, has read Lévy-Bruhl too much through Malinowski's eyes. Lévy-Bruhl, we have seen, does not deny that the native is capable individually of psychological functions similar to those of civilized man. He affirms most explicitly that there is a common measure between primitive mentality and our own and that the difference between them is one of degree, not of kind. All that he claims is that a comparative analysis of the ethnological literature dealing with native thought and practice reveals a typical, collective, cultural mentality which is predominantly prelogical in character. This does not mean to say that *all* of native culture reveals this prelogical character and that it does not manifest logical, rational traits as well, but only that prelogical thought is *typical* of native culture and serves as a means of differentiating it from the typical scientific thought of civilized man. The collective representations of the native are said to reveal a cultural mentality which is indifferent to the law of contradiction as exemplified in our contemporary cultural mentality; but this does not imply that the former may

[107] *MS.,* 11.

not reveal, within limited areas, logical and empirical traits as well.

Furthermore, it should be noted, native collective representations are said to presuppose an organic metaphysics which postulates the intrinsic unity of all forms of life and the "affective category of the supernatural."[108] The collective or social character of these metaphysical representations does not, however, explain or account for their prelogical or mystical, epistemic character as Cassirer suggests it does. There is no evidence that Lévy-Bruhl regarded the social function of native representations as determining their prelogical or mystical form of expression, and it would appear, therefore, as if Cassirer were reading his own functionalistic thesis into the former's thought at this point. Our civilized collective representations are logical or scientific and the individual who participates in our form of civilization reflects the social character of our civilization, just as the native reflects the social or collective representations of pre-scientific native culture. One may indeed question, as modern ethnologists have done, the extent of the influence of social culture upon the individual in native society and whether the individual does not deviate, far more than the Durkheim school presupposed, from the social norms which are professed collectively. But Cassirer does not take into consideration this commonly accepted criticism; on the contrary, he accepts uncritically "the social character of myth," while taking objection to the theory of the prelogical.

It should be noted, furthermore, that the prelogical mentality is not, according to Lévy-Bruhl, meant to be either illogical or irrational; it simply involves a different type of logic which the scientific mind can reconstruct and infer. The issue, therefore, of the logical *versus* prelogical nature of native thought is largely verbal and originates from the tendency to identify our own Western, syllogistic logic with logic in general, and to regard any other form of thought with different ontological presuppositions as non-logical or prelogical. It may be granted, accordingly, that Lévy-Bruhl's use of the term prelogical was most unfortunate, since the real antithesis is between the pre-

[108] Lévy-Bruhl, *Primitives and the Supernatural*, (London, 1936), 36.

scientific and scientific mentality and not at all between the logical and prelogical mentality. The issue, in other words, is ultimately ontological and cultural, and not psychological or logical. If we accept the basic ontological premise of native metaphysical thought, namely, the organic unity of all forms of life and the internality of all relations, then their mode of thought appears quite intelligible and logical, even though it is, in its extant forms, hardly scientific, since it may not be verified by objective, empirical tests.[109]

Lévy-Bruhl would, therefore, be in complete agreement with Cassirer's statement that

What we, from our own point of view, may call irrational, prelogical, mystical are the premises from which mythical or religious interpretation starts, but not the mode of interpretation. If we accept these premises and if we understand them aright—if we see them in the same light that primitive man does—the inferences drawn from them cease to appear illogical or antilogical. . . . Primitive man by no means lacks the ability to grasp the empirical differences of things. But in his conception of nature and life all these differences are obliterated by a stronger feeling: the deep conviction of a fundamental and indelible *solidarity of life* that bridges over the multiplicity and variety of its single forms.[110]

This is precisely Lévy-Bruhl's thesis as any reading of the latter's works makes evident. The very argument that native thought is neither illogical nor antilogical, and that it pre-supposes "the solidarity of life" occur explicitly in Lévy-Bruhl's writings. It would appear, therefore, that for the most part Cassirer was really fighting a straw-man, a figment of his own imagination and of that of Malinowski, since he criticized Lévy-Bruhl for views which the latter never held and then proceeded to submit as his own the very thesis which the subject of his criticism had maintained. In fact, it may be shown, that Cassirer's conception of mythical thought involved, as Susanne K. Langer has said, a prelogical interpretation according to which native, mythical thought is regarded as antecedent in point of

---

[109] It is significant to point out in this connection that modern philosophical and scientific thought is also tending towards an organic type of metaphysics—a fact which explains, as in the work of A. N. Whitehead, the necessity for a radical change in our terminology and mode of thinking.

[110] *EM.*, 8of.

time to logical thought and hence as non-logical. Lévy-Bruhl, on the other hand, claims that native thought is prelogical *only* in the sense that it is indifferent to a strict adherence to the law of contradiction, but *not* in the sense that the native is incapable of logical thought. In other words, *the disparity between mythical and logical thought is much greater in Cassirer's own theory of mental and cultural development than it is in Lévy-Bruhl's work.* Cassirer has, in effect, taken over Lévy-Bruhl's interpretation of the ontological presuppositions of native thought, while criticizing the latter's use of the term prelogical to describe the native mode of thinking. But, in doing so, Cassirer has undermined his own theory of the development of human thought from a mythical or prelogical to a logical stage.

Cassirer, it seems, gives his whole case against Lévy-Bruhl away when he admits in his *Myth of the State:*

> Of course we must not understand the term "logic" in too narrow a sense. We cannot expect the Aristotelian categories of thought or the elements of our parts-of-speech system, the rules of Greek and Latin syntax, in languages of aboriginal American tribes. These expectations are bound to fail; but this does not prove that these languages are in any sense "illogical" or even less logical than ours.[111]

Once it is admitted that the term logic is not to be used in "too narrow a sense," then Lévy-Bruhl's use of the term prelogical may be regarded as an attempt to define the type of logic which is characteristic of native language and thought. Cassirer himself has employed the term "mythical thought" instead of the term "prelogical mentality;" but the meaning of the two terms is practically identical, as may be seen from the fact that the mythical mentality is said to have all the attributes ascribed by Lévy-Bruhl to the prelogical mentality. Thus, according to Cassirer, mythical thought does not clearly distinguish between reality and the symbol, accepts the principle of *pars pro toto* in magical practices, does not recognize the limits of individuality, and accepts totemistic beliefs.[112] All these modes of thought are to be found duplicated and attributed to

[111] *MS.*, 13f.
[112] Cf. *LM.*

the prelogical mentality in Lévy-Bruhl's writings.[113] Both writers also presuppose that the native mentality, whether mythical or prelogical, differs radically from the logical or scientific mentality of modern man, and that rationality in the scientific sense is a state of mind which is achieved only gradually in the process of cultural evolution.

The real difficulty in Cassirer's conception of myth lies in the fact that he has attempted to combine the antithetical ethnological views of Lévy-Bruhl and Malinowski. On the one hand, as said, he agrees substantially with the former's evolutionary conception of native mentality. On the other hand, he also professes agreement with Malinowski's thesis that the native mind clearly differentiates the category of the natural from the supernatural, the sphere of science from that of magic. According to this functionalistic theory of myth, myth and magic are not antecedent to logic and science, but rather post-logical and post-scientific mental inventions utilized in times of crisis, when scientific thought fails to achieve the desired ends of action and fails to satisfy the human longing for security. Thus whereas Lévy-Bruhl maintains that prelogical thought is something to be struggled against, something to be superseded in the development of a logical, scientific mentality, Malinowski accepts mythical thought as a means universally employed to tide societies over difficult periods of transition. Cassirer, it would appear, would have it both ways at once, maintaining that mythical thought is antecedent to logical thought, and holding with Malinowski that the native mind differentiates clearly between the sphere of science and that of myth.

15

Cassirer on the Rôle of Myth in the History of Human Culture

The practical import of Cassirer's utilization of these antithetical conceptions of mythical thought may be seen in his diagnosis of the crisis of our times as well as in his interpretation of the history of philosophical anthropology.

In the final chapter of the *Myth of the State*, entitled "The

[113] Cf. Lévy-Bruhl's *Primitive Mentality* (New York, 1923); *The Soul of the Primitive*, (London, 1928).

Technique of the Modern Political Myths," we find he again takes up Malinowski's thesis that myth-making and magic are elemental functions of the human mind, which make their appearance in times of crisis. Thus he writes:

In all those tasks that need no particular and exceptional efforts, no special courage or endurance, we find no magic and no mythology. But a highly developed magic and connected with it a mythology always occurs if a pursuit is dangerous and its issues uncertain. This description of the rôle of magic and mythology in primitive society applies equally well to highly advanced stages of man's political life. In desperate situations man will always have recourse to desperate means—and our present-day political myths have been such desperate means. If reason has failed us, there remains always the *ultima ratio*, the power of the miraculous and mysterious.[114]

Cassirer, it appears from this, regards myth as irrational and illogical (in agreement with, but going beyond Lévy-Bruhl's thesis), but at the same time agrees with Malinowski that myth fulfils a positive social function in times of social crisis. Nevertheless, myth is something to be opposed and struggled against —and not something to be welcomed as a complement to reason, as Malinowski's premises imply. The social function of myth in producing a feeling of solidarity with one's society and with nature in general is said to be evil, since it comes as a victory for the forces of irrationalism. In Cassirer's words:

In all critical moments of man's social life the rational forces that resist the rise of the old mythical conceptions are no longer sure of themselves. In these moments the time for myth has come again. For myth has not been really vanquished and subjugated. It is always there, lurking in the dark and waiting for its hour and opportunity. This hour comes as soon as the other binding forces of man's social life, for one reason or another, lose their strength and are no longer able to combat the demonic mythical powers.[115]

This statement implies that in time of crisis, at least, even modern man is no longer sure of himself and fails to differentiate clearly between reason and myth. It is not that myth complements reason but rather overcomes it and subjugates or

[114] *MS.*, 279.
[115] *MS.*, 280.

represses it. Hence, according to this psychoanalytic interpretation, myth arises in modern times as a reversion to the primitive state of mind from which mankind slowly emerged. In other words, although Cassirer professes agreement with the functionalistic thesis that the native mind does differentiate clearly between scientific reason and emotional, mystical feeling, he justifies and explains the reversion from the rational to the mythical mentality as a failure to keep this radical disparity in mind—thereby utilizing the presupposition of Lévy-Bruhl. At the same time, following the psychoanalytical approach, he also recognizes the ideal motive in modern social myth—a point Ruth Benedict had made—by suggesting that social myths serve as expressions or objectifications of "collective wishes" which are personified in the political leader who is endowed for this purpose with powers of "social magic" to fulfil the collective wish.[116]

On the whole, it would appear, Cassirer's attitude toward magic and myth is ambivalent and reflects the conflict between romantic and rationalistic traditions which he sought to reconcile. From an ethnological standpoint, he shares the view of the romanticists that myth constitutes an essential element in the evolution of human culture and thought. As a critical idealist, on the other hand, he is fundamentally a rationalist who participates in the struggle against the power of myth as an irrational, demonic force. In his *Myth of the State* Cassirer has himself well stated the antithesis between the rationalist and romantic approaches:

> That is the real difference, the deep gulf, between the period of the Enlightenment and German romanticism. . . . According to this metaphysical conception the *value* of myth is completely changed. To all the thinkers of the Enlightenment myth had been a barbarous thing, a strange and uncouth mass of confused ideas and gross superstitions, a mere monstrosity. Between myth and philosophy there could be no point of contact. Myth ends where philosophy begins—as darkness gives way to the rising sun. This view undergoes a radical change as soon as we pass to the romantic philosophers. In the system of these philosophers myth becomes not only a subject of the highest intellectual interest but also a subject of awe and veneration. It is regarded as the mainspring

[116] *Ibid.*, 280f.

of human culture. Art, history, and poetry originate in myth. A philosophy which overlooks or neglects this origin is declared to be shallow and inadequate. It was one of the principal aims of Schelling's system to give myth its right and legitimate place in human civilization. In his works we find for the first time a *philosophy of mythology* side by side with his philosophy of nature, history, and art. Eventually all his interest seems to be concentrated upon this problem. Instead of being the opposite of philosophic thought myth has become its ally; and, in a sense, its consummation. . . . In philosophy the influence of Schelling was counterbalanced and soon eclipsed by the appearance of the Hegelian system. His conception of the role of mythology remained only an episode. Nevertheless the way was paved that could lead later to the rehabilitation and glorification of myth that we find in modern politics.[117]

One may understand Cassirer's own philosophy of mythology as an attempt to reconcile the extremes of rationalism and romanticism. With the latter he shares the conviction that myths have a significant cultural value in revealing the origin and basic motivations of human language and historical thought. But Cassirer does not share the unqualified enthusiasm of the romanticists for mythology, since, as a philosopher and intellectual, he is conscious of the excesses to which mythology is inclined, once its adherents leave the realm of poetry and extend their influence into the realm of politics. In the sphere of politics, therefore, he shares the rationalistic approach and accepts the rule of reason as over against the "reason" of rule, which is the myth of the state.

It is of interest in this connection to examine Cassirer's interpretation of Plato's theory of myth. In the *Republic* (Bk. 10), Plato would expel the poets from his ideal, regimented state because, as mere "imitators," they were "thrice-removed from reality." According to Cassirer, Plato was justified in his expulsion of the poets from the ideal republic on the ground that in politics myth is the most dangerous enemy. The fact that Plato himself invented some myths of his own is explained away on the ground that Plato did not mind a few suggestive myths in metaphysics, but considered myth much too dangerous in political theory. As Cassirer puts it:

> How is it to be accounted for that the same thinker who admitted

[117] *Ibid.*, 182f.

mythical concepts and mythical language so readily into his metaphysics
and his natural philosophy spoke in an entirely different vein when
developing his political theories? For in this field Plato became the
professed enemy of myth. If we tolerate myth in our political systems,
he declared, all our hopes for a reconstruction and reformation of our
political and social life are lost. There is only one alternative: we have
to make our choice between an ethical and a mythical conception of
'the state. In the Legal State, the state of justice, there is no room left
for the conceptions of mythology, for the gods of Homer and Hesiod.[118]

Cassirer then proceeds to quote from Plato's *Republic* (377f)
a passage which demonstrates that Plato wished to "supervise
the making of fables and legends, rejecting all which are unsatisfactory." But this merely shows that Plato had no sentimental attachment for tradition as such and was prepared to
adopt a critical attitude towards it, even as Socrates had done,
accepting what appeared to him to be rational and rejecting
what he thought was irrational. The passage does not prove that
Plato decided to expel the poets from his ideal republic for
political reasons or that he considered the poets especially a
great political menace. As a philosopher Plato sought to establish a true theory of the state and in this sense he was opposed
to mere myth or fiction in political theory. One must make a
choice between a rational and a mythical conception of the state
but not between philosophers and poets.

According to Cassirer,

What is combated and rejected by Plato is not poetry itself, but the
myth-making function. To him and to every other Greek both things
were inseparable. From time immemorial the poets had been the real myth
makers. As Herodotus said, Homer and Hesiod had made the generations
of the gods; they had portrayed their shapes and distinguished their
offices and powers. Here was the real danger for the Platonic *Republic*.
To admit poetry meant to admit myth, but myth could not be admitted
without frustrating all philosophic efforts and undermining the very
foundations of Plato's state. Only by expelling the poets from the ideal
state could the philosopher's state be protected against the intrusion
of subversive hostile forces. Plato did not entirely forbid mythical tales;
he even admitted that, in the education of a young child, they are
indispensable. But they must be brought under a strict discipline.[119]

[118] *Ibid.*, 72.
[119] *Ibid.*, 67.

Here, almost in the same breath, Cassirer maintains that Plato felt compelled to expel the poets from his *Republic* because they were myth-makers, and yet admits that mythical tales, when properly censored, were considered indispensable in the education of the young. There is a decided difference between censoring the myth-makers and expelling them altogether.

In sum, it would appear, that Cassirer is reading into Plato a political motive which was alien to his thought. Plato, as a scientist and philosopher, was indeed opposed to mythology, insofar as it tended to be accepted literally as religious truth. Yet, as educator, he reluctantly admitted that myths were indispensable in educating young people and in exemplifying a metaphysical, religious truth. Myths in other words, if properly constructed and selected, were compatible with a rationalistic philosophy. Nowhere in the *Republic* does Plato suggest that the poets as well as artists whom he criticized were a political threat to his ideal state. When, towards the end of his *Republic*, he finally does suggest that poets and painters are not to be admitted into a well-ordered state, it is for epistemological and scientific reasons, and not at all for political reasons. It is because the poets and artists are dealing with "imitations of imitations" and are thrice-removed from the ideal forms which may be intuited by reason that they are not to be allowed in his scientific society.[120] In an ideal philosophical state, where the pursuit of truth and reality was the most important task, the poets and artists as such would have no place. In the actual historical state, however, they were indispensable. The non-admission of the poets and artists was, therefore, for Plato an ideal, intellectual requirement motivated by theoretical considerations. It was not motivated by practical, political considerations in the sense that the poets and artists were considered a political threat to the existence of the *Republic*.

Perhaps the issue involved regarding Plato's attitude towards the poets may be pointed up by reference to the difference of opinion between Cassirer and Jaeger regarding the ultimate

[120] *Republic*, X, 601-607.

status of Plato's *Republic*.[121] According to Jaeger, Plato regarded the Republic as the "true home of the philosopher." To this Cassirer counters, that the home of the philosopher was the *civitas divina*, not the *civitas terrena*. Yet, according to Cassirer, "Plato did not allow this religious tendency to influence his political judgment. He became a political thinker and a statesman not by inclination but from duty." The two points of view of Jaeger and Cassirer may be reconciled, if one holds that Plato's Republic was indeed an *ideal* state, a heaven on earth, for the philosopher to live in; and that it was also an attempt at a practical resolution of the social and political crises which afflicted the Greek city states of his day. The *Republic* may therefore be considered Plato's first attempt at formulating a theory of the *ideal* as well as of the *best* state.[122] As an ideal, the *Republic* was a scientific political theory which dealt with fundamental principles of social organization and culture. As the best state, the Republic was a practical social invention which took into consideration the current Greek culture and attempted to eliminate some of its objectionable features. It may be said, perhaps, that the idealistic philosopher and practical statesman in Plato were never quite reconciled and that the *Republic* reveals both tendencies. In this way, it would seem, one could account for the fact that Plato at first speaks of censoring the myth-makers and later, in the same dialogue, urges their non-admission. Cassirer, in attributing to Plato a political motive for the non-admission of the poets and artists, is not taking sufficiently into consideration the idealistic motive in Plato, which he himself has recognized in evaluating the *Republic* as a whole.

In sum, we must distinguish between a mythical conception of the state and myth-making as a poetic function. As a rationalistic philosopher, Plato rejected the former but accepted the latter. This, I take it, would be Cassirer's position as well.

The full significance of Cassirer's antipathy to political myths becomes apparent in his treatment of modern and contemporary theories of man and the state.

[121] *M.S.*, 63; cf. earlier discussion in Section 2 above.
[122] *Ibid.*, 69.

In discussing "The Myth of the Twentieth Century," Cassirer contrasts myth as "an unconscious activity and as a free product of imagination"[123] with the new political myths which are the product of a conscious, deliberate technique. As Cassirer puts it:

It has been reserved for the twentieth century, our own great technical age, to develop a new technique of myth. Henceforth myths can be manufactured in the same sense and according to the same methods as any other modern weapon—as machine guns or airplanes. That is a new thing—and a thing of crucial importance. It has changed the whole form of our social life. . . . The real rearmament [of Germany] began with the origin and rise of the political myths. The later military rearmament was only an accessory after the fact.[124]

The new political myths are fabricated through a deliberate change in the function of language from the semantic to the magical use of words,[125] from a logical to a cynically pragmatic use of words "destined to produce certain effects and to stir up certain emotions." As in primitive societies, the modern totalitarian societies supplement magic words with appropriate social rites, the neglect of which is regarded as a crime against the state. As a result, Cassirer notes,

We have learned that modern man, in spite of his restlessness, and perhaps because of his restlessness, has not really surmounted the condition of savage life. When exposed to the same forces, he can easily be thrown back to a state of complete acquiescence. He no longer questions his environment; he accepts it as a matter of course.[126]

Cassirer, it appears, does not share the naïve faith of some of the nineteenth century evolutionists in linear progress and in a steady, continuous growth in rational institutions. As in the sphere of biology, he recognizes that there may be reversions, in part, to a more primitive state, with the difference that the new primitives are far more deadly than the old, having added the techniques of modern science to the irrationalism of primitive mentality.

[123] *Ibid.*, 282.
[124] *Ibid.*, 282.
[125] *Ibid.*, 282f.
[126] *Ibid.*, 286.

Since Cassirer must have had in mind Alfred Rosenberg's *Myth of the Twentieth Century*[127] in entitling the last section of his *Myth of the State*, it will prove illuminating to consider for a moment what this Nazi "philosopher," the influence of whose work was second only to Hitler's *Mein Kampf*, meant by the term *mythus*. Myth, as conceived by Rosenberg, became transformed from a term of disparagement in the sense of being the antithesis of science, to one of positive appreciation as something which refers to a truth which transcends science. Myth became a racial or *Volk* intuition of nature and life, which reveals the special character and destiny of a given *Volk*. On this assumption, "truth" is relative to the needs and aspirations of the folk-soul; that which enhances the form and inner values of this organic life is true. Of course, only Nordic man, and in particular the late Fuehrer, was held to be qualified to determine infallibly what is true for the *Volk*, since the notion of an objective, universal criterion of truth was rejected as a perversion of Jews, Catholics, and democrats. In brief, myth was understood as an ethnocentric, mystical truth which was validated pragmatically by its social consequences for a given, chosen community.

Rosenberg's "philosophy" of mythology is a political myth in the sense that it provides a rationalization for a given pattern of political action on the part of the state and its leaders. It is a conscious attempt to undermine the presuppositions of an objective, universally normative truth in the supposed interests of a given state, thereby precluding any appeal to a common reason or to common civilized standards of value in international relations. It is this new *myth of the state* of which Cassirer voices his disapproval so whole-heartedly.

16

The Humanism and Rationalism of Cassirer

The outstanding characteristics of Cassirer's philosophy of culture are its humanism and rationalism, both of which derive from his neo-Kantian orientation.

[127] Alfred Rosenberg, *The Myth of the Twentieth Century*, (Munich, 1930). Cf. *Rosenberg's Nazi Myth*, by Albert R. Chandler, (Ithaca, N.Y., 1945).

Cassirer's standpoint is essentially anthropocentric or homo-centric. In accepting the so-called Copernican revolution of Kant he committed himself to the view that the human mind is the creative source of symbolic forces which serve as organs or instruments for the understanding of man and nature. Man is said to be an *animal symbolicum,* living in a symbolical universe of his own creation. Historically, man is said to be known through the cultural achievements of humanity. But, unlike the positivistic sociologists, Cassirer does not regard culture as a reality *sui generis, as if* culture were to be explained as a phenomenon which is conceived through itself alone and is determined entirely by itself. He always reminds us that culture consists of cultural symbols and that the function of the latter is objectification of the experiences of the human ego. Thus language is said to symbolize sense perception; myth and religion are symbolic expressions of emotion, art of intuition, science of understanding. In all instances of cultural symbolization we are reminded of the creative rôle of the human ego in the conception and formation of its cultural symbols. Thus, unlike some modern "culturologists"[128] who stress man's passivity and the predominant influence of cultural determinism, Cassirer stresses the rôle of human freedom in the development of culture. As Cassirer puts it:

Human culture taken as a whole may be described as the process of man's progressive self-liberation. Language, art, religion, science are various phases in this process. In all of them man discovers and proves a new power—the power to build up a world of his own, an "ideal" world.[129]

Cassirer, like Ortega y Gasset and Jean-Paul Sartre (see earlier, Section 6), emphasizes man's subjective freedom and power of creativity in literally making himself through the process of symbolic objectification. The so-called objective world of nature provides the stimulus or occasion for man's creative powers, but does not affect the nature and general development of this mental-cultural activity.

[128] *Vide* L. A. White, "Man's control over Civilization: An Anthropocentric Illusion," in *The Scientific Monthly,* lxvi, March 1948, 235-47.

[129] *EM.,* 228; cf. Cassirer's "Naturalistische und humanistische Begründung der Kulturphilosophie," Göteborg, 1939.

By contrast, those contemporary ethnologists or "culturologists" who hold to the "superorganic" view of culture, draw attention to the fact that culture molds or determines human personality and its modes of expression, and claim that man is not at all the free agent which he erroneously believes himself to be. As one culturologist has recently stated: "From the cultural determinist's point of view, human beings are merely the instruments through which cultures express themselves. . . . Neither as groups nor as individuals do we have a choice of rôles or of fates."[130]

Cassirer's thesis that human culture as a whole may be described as the process of man's self-liberation is thus seen to be the antithesis of the culturological view that culture is an autonomous process, subject to its own determinate laws of development, and that man is largely the instrument or vehicle of a cultural process whose direction and modes he neither controls nor determines.

According to the position proposed in this analysis, both the above views represent extreme positions. Cultural man is neither quite so free nor quite so determined as the proponents of these extremes tend to assume he is. If one accepts the polaristic conception of culture suggested earlier (Section 7), then it may be said that there is a determinate human nature which is manifested functionally through culture but is not reducible to culture. Hence man may be conceived as being in part determined by himself—by his own nature and powers—and in part by the natural forces to which he must adjust himself while utilizing them to further his own ends. Man's essence may be said to determine his functions and modes of existence in the sense of setting limits to human powers of effort and endurance in any given environment. On the other hand, human life or existence is free in the sense that man creates his own forms of cultural expression and symbolization, while adjusting himself to the conditions of his natural, cosmic environment.

The notion of unpredictable cultural freedom of expression emphasized by the neo-Kantian idealists and the humanistic existentialists is based upon a common ontological presupposition

[130] L. A. White, "Man's Control over Civilization," 244, 246. (See fn. 128.)

that life or existence is prior to its own essence, and that life creates itself progressively through its own expressions or objectifications. On the other hand, the cultural determinists presuppose that cultural essences or forms determine human existence and its dynamic modes of expression; that the *what* or essence of culture determines the function or active nature of man. This explains why the cultural positivists and cultural idealists differ on the issue of human freedom, although agreeing in positing a cultural reality as over against the notion of a meta-cultural or pre-cultural reality. Thus cultural existentialists and functionalists as well as cultural "essentialists" or culturologists end up by eliminating the category of nature and reducing nature to culture, the former in the name of human freedom, and the latter in the name of scientific determinism.

When we turn to Cassirer's philosophy of history we find him similarly opposed to the view of the historical determinists, that human cultural and social development may be described in terms of a general formula of fixed stages, and to the prophetic notion that there is a "destiny" in human culture history. Thus he writes:

> But the reality of history is not a uniform sequence of events but the inner life of man. This life can be described and interpreted after it has been lived; it cannot be anticipated in an abstract general formula, and it cannot be reduced to a rigid scheme of three or five acts.[131]

The notion of fate or destiny in human cultural history seems to him to be a mythological idea incompatible with the rationality of man as a conscious, self-determining agent. According to Cassirer,

> In almost all mythologies of the world we meet with the idea of an inevitable, inexorable, irrevocable destiny. Fatalism seems to be inseparable from mythical thought. . . . But in some of our modern philosophers this distinction [between mythical and philosophical thought] seems to be completely effaced. They give us a metaphysics of history that shows all the characteristic features of myth.[132]

On the other hand, Cassirer does not mean to say that man is

[131] *EM.*, 201.
[132] *MS.*, 290f.

absolutely free under all circumstances. It is possible for man to surrender his freedom of self-determination under the paralyzing influence of some myth of the state, so that he becomes a willing victim of his self-enslavement. Man's freedom, in other words, is manifested in his ability to surrender his freedom as well as in his efforts to retain it. As Ortega y Gasset has remarked, our present actions determine the extent of our future freedom.

Thus Cassirer reminds us that ethical freedom is not a natural fact that is given or inherited, but rather a potentiality which man himself must strive to realize and bring into practical operation. Acknowledging his indebtedness to Kant on this point, Cassirer observes that

> In the exposition of his own theory Kant always warns us against a fundamental misunderstanding. Ethical freedom, he declares, is not a fact but a postulate. It is not *gegeben* but *aufgegeben*; it is not a gift with which human nature is endowed; it is rather a task, and the most arduous task that man can set himself. It is no datum, but a demand; an ethical imperative. To fulfil this demand becomes especially hard in times of a severe and dangerous social crisis when the breakdown of the whole public life seems to be imminent. At these times the individual begins to feel a deep mistrust in his own powers. Freedom is not a natural inheritance of man. In order to possess it we have to create it.[133]

But in order to create freedom one must first have the capacity for free action by nature—a basic presupposition to which Rousseau and the rationalists who followed him have repeatedly drawn attention. Here again Cassirer confronts us with a choice between natural and cultural freedom, as if the two notions were not logically compatible. Unless freedom were a fact of nature, in the sense of being an intrinsic capacity or power of self-determination, there would be no point in postulating it as an ethical imperative.

As Cassirer conceives it, the task of the modern rationalistic philosopher is to combat the surrender of human reason and freedom to the forces of irrationalism and fatalism, by developing afresh the humanistic insight of Plato and Kant that man,

[133] *MS.*, 287f.

historically speaking, is master of his fate and can choose his *demon* in order to achieve *eudaimonia* or happiness.[134] In this sense the task of philosophy may be said to begin with itself, with the overcoming of the myth-provoking irrationalism of those philosophies (such as theological existentialism) in which reason is employed in order to accomplish its unconditional surrender in all the critical situations of human life.[135]

In the last analysis, Cassirer holds fast to his evolutionary, rationalistic faith in cultural progress and in the power of reason to keep in check the irrational powers of myth. As he expresses it:

> Yet when small groups do try to enforce their wishes and their fantastic ideas upon great nations and the whole body politic, they may succeed for a short time, and they may even achieve great triumphs, but these must remain ephemeral. For there is, after all, a logic of the social world just as there is a logic of the physical world. There are certain laws that cannot be violated with impunity. Even in this sphere we have to follow Bacon's advice. We must learn how to obey the laws of the social world before we can undertake to rule it.[136]

Here, obviously, the man of liberal faith and the prophet of rationalism is speaking and expressing his faith in the ultimate triumph of social logic in human affairs. He refers enigmatically to certain "laws" of the social world which "must" be obeyed but, like the destiny-philosophers whom he criticizes, fails to specify what these laws are or how they can be empirically established. If irrational social forces do come to the fore and do manage to gain the ascendancy, *why* "must" their triumph remain any more ephemeral than that of the opposing forces? There is more to be said for the "logic of power" than the idealistic advocates of the power of logic have yet been prepared to acknowledge. Cassirer, it would appear, was so much concerned with the power of cultural symbols that he failed to reckon realistically with the power of the objects to which the symbols referred. Furthermore, in view of Cassirer's admission that the irrational forces of myth tend to

[134] *Ibid.*, 76.
[135] *Ibid.*, 292f.
[136] *Ibid.*, 295.

predominate in times of crisis and that "it is beyond the power of philosophy to destroy the political myths,"[137] one cannot help wondering how substantial is the foundation for his faith in the ultimate victory of the rational functions of mind and of social logic.

17

Cassirer on the Problem of Cultural Unity

We return finally to the problem with which we began this analysis and ask again whether Cassirer has made any significant contribution towards the resolution of the intellectual, cultural crisis of our times. We have seen that, according to Cassirer, the crisis which confronts us is owing to the fact that modern culture lacks an intellectual center of integration. He has suggested, therefore, that what is vitally needed is a philosophical anthropology capable of comprehending man as a whole and providing a meaning and direction to all our human activities. His *Essay on Man* and *The Myth of the State* comprise his final "testament of wisdom" and may therefore fairly be evaluated with reference to this ideal objective.

In sum, it may be said, Cassirer has offered us a spiritual anthropology which reduces the category of nature to that of culture, thereby "humanizing philosophy and turning cosmogony and ontology into anthropology." The key concept to this spiritual anthropology is the symbol, which is the source of reality as well as of intelligibility in human experience. The whole of human culture is understood or interpreted as comprising the diverse modes of symbolism historically created and evolved by mankind in its efforts at self-expression and "progressive self-liberation." In the last analysis, the evolution of cultural thought is said to be dependent upon the evolution of language or linguistic symbolism, and culture as a whole is interpreted as the language of the human spirit.

Within each category or mode of culture there is a "unity in the manifold," in the sense that each cultural perspective may ultimately be conceived through some one psychological

[137] MS., 296; cf. the writer's review of Cassirer's *Myth of the State* in *American Anthropologist*, 49, (July-September 1947), 481-83.

motive or function. Thus all forms of art may be understood as
diverse symbolic expressions of intuition; myth and religion
symbolize emotions and provide a rationalization for the
identity of all forms of life; and science gives us a unity of
thought by providing a symbolic universe of laws and principles
(see Section 12 above). Cassirer thus correlates the subjective
functions of the ego with the historically-evolved cultural categories, thereby binding together man and the symbolic world of
his creation.

Similarly one may discern a common function for the whole
of human culture. Cassirer's ultimate presupposition appears to
be that the whole of human culture has a common, evolutionary
origin in human experience as well as a common end or function
in making for progressive objectification of the human spirit
and for self-liberation. Notwithstanding the diversity of cultural expressions there is said to be a "dynamic equilibrium"
and a "hidden harmony" which reconciles apparently opposing
forces.[138] As Cassirer concludes in his *Essay on Man,*

> But this multiplicity and disparateness does not denote discord or
> disharmony. All these functions complete and complement one another.
> Each one opens a new horizon and shows us a new aspect of humanity.
> The dissonant is in harmony with itself; the contraries are not mutually
> exclusive, but interdependent; "harmony in contrariety, as in the case
> of the bow and the lyre."[139]

There are then, for Cassirer, two sources of unity of function
in human culture, namely, psychological or genetic unity of
motive for each type of cultural discipline, and teleological
unity of function in achieving a common harmony for any given
historical culture as well as for the culture of humanity as a
whole.

As regards the genetic, psychological unity of function attributed to a mode of culture, we have seen, in the case of
myth, that this is open to question. Cassirer has not demonstrated that each cultural discipline may be correlated with
only one psychological function. Objectively, we find that

[138] *EM.*, 223.
[139] *Ibid.*, 228.

leading contemporary ethnologists, with the exception of the Functionalistic School, would not subscribe to the thesis that myth, for example, has one primary social function and would hold instead that it may have a plurality of functions—a criticism which may be applied to any other cultural discipline.

Furthermore, with reference to the teleological unity of function which is said to characterize a given culture and the culture of humanity as a whole, the reply may be made that this *a priori* harmony is not substantiated by the empirical evidence. Political myth, for example, has, on Cassirer's own insistence, no place in a genuinely rational culture. Obviously, then, from a historical point of view, there can be no "pre-established harmony" between myth and the rational elements of culture.

The most serious criticism, however, of the so-called functionalistic harmony of culture is that it is purely formal and provides no criterion for the evaluation of the content or "substance" of any given cultural configuration. Any one historical culture is, on this assumption, in harmony with itself, no matter what its empirical content may be. This problem becomes acute especially in the sphere of intercultural relations where we are confronted with international conflicts which may lead to world war. Obviously the assurance under such circumstances that there is an ultimate "hidden harmony" between the East and the West is of little comfort or practical significance; since what is required is a MANIFEST harmony, which may enable the nations of the world to dwell together in peace. But since there is for Cassirer no reality other than cultural or symbolical reality, there can be no meta-cultural or pre-cultural, ontological reality by which to evaluate conflicting standards of value. In the end, we are left with a plurality of empirical ethnocentric, symbolical worlds, each of which is formally in harmony with the idea of humanity but functionally and actually in conflict with the others.

As the writer has noted elsewhere,[140] the neo-Kantians are tolerant in theory to the extreme point of accepting the validity of any empirical socio-cultural system whatsoever. Any actual

---

[140] Bidney, "Culture Theory and the Problem of Cultural Crises."

perversion or "transvaluation" of concrete human values may be justified on earth, provided one acknowledges his faith in the purity and harmony of the categorial structure whose abode is Heaven.

Thus, Cassirer was led by his faith in the higher rationality of humanity to overlook the serious practical problems of cultural conflict and disunity. In other words, the very rationality of his neo-Kantian outlook led him logically and paradoxically to a toleration in theory of the irrational and mythological mentality which he strove in practice to obliterate from the social and political life of man. As a moral philosopher he did not believe in "speculative idleness" and urged his fellow philosophers to emulate the great thinkers of the past who made it their task "to think beyond and against their times."[141] But he derived his intellectual and moral courage to do so, not from his neo-Kantian theory and his egocentric, spiritual anthropology, but from the classical metaphysical traditions, from Greek culture and the *philosophia perennis* of the Hebrew-Christian tradition as well as from the humanism of the Renaissance and the rationalism of the Enlightenment which he knew so intimately and loved so well.

DAVID BIDNEY

THE VIKING FUND
NEW YORK CITY

[141] *MS.*, 296.

15

Helmut Kuhn

ERNST CASSIRER'S PHILOSOPHY OF CULTURE

ERNST CASSIRER'S PHILOSOPHY OF CULTURE

THE title "Philosophy of Culture" seems to denote a branch or field of philosophy: philosophy applying itself to the exploration of that particular fact or set of facts which we describe as "culture." This special field would have to be mapped out in terms of the total area of which it is a part, and in terms of its relation to the adjacent fields of philosophical study, such as ethics or philosophy of history.

In fact, culture is one of the themes of Cassirer's philosophy, and culture does constitute a field of study within the wider compass of his thought. But it does so only incidentally. This may seem a paradoxical assertion, flying in the face of Cassirer's own explicit statements. Does he not, in unambiguous words, distinguish between philosophy of culture and philosophy of nature as two separate, though related, domains?

Nevertheless, we rejoin, by regarding culture as a special field or theme of Cassirer's thought we choose an unpromising approach and are almost certain to miss the intent of his philosophy. Although analyzing in great detail certain forms of culture, such as language or myth, Cassirer neglects others almost completely; and this uneven treatment, far from being fortuitous, betrays the guiding and selecting interest in the philosopher's mind. This interest is not in the exploration of culture for its own sake.

Wondering what culture is and trying to describe its nature in terms as simple and straightforward as possible, the observer's mind may fasten upon certain salient features and cardinal questions. Culture, as *cultura animi*, seems to indicate a deliberate cultivation, a tending or fashioning of the mind, some kind of education. What is the nature and goal of this education? Furthermore, culture or civilization is distinguished from both

547

primitivism and barbarism, compared with which it claims to be a richer, more dignified, and more truly human mode of life. Wherein does its superiority consist and how was it achieved? Why is it as precarious a possession as the annals of mankind show? May we look forward to an as yet unattained perfection of culture in some near or distant future?

If a reader approaches Cassirer's work with these observations and questions in mind, he finds it unresponsive. The center of Cassirer's interest is elsewhere, and the student's query, which, in the opinion of the questioner, is central, is relegated to the periphery of the intellectual universe. We even begin to doubt whether the imaginary questioner correctly understands the meaning of the term "culture" as used by Cassirer. Where, then, is the center of gravity in Cassirer's world?

"Primary philosophy" (πρώτη φιλοσοφία), according to Aristotle, is a science which investigates being as being, or, in a more familiar terminology, Reality as such.[1] Cassirer's research, however radically it departs in some respects from the great current of *philosophia perennis*, is still animated throughout by the quest of "primary philosophy" as enunciated by Aristotle. Philosophy of culture is for him, first of all, philosophy, i.e., an investigation into the nature of Reality. But this investigation tends towards the study of culture as of a particularly revealing domain of reality. Culture appears the privileged document testifying with unparalleled eloquence to the adequacy of the underlying concept of "being as being."

The affirmation of the ontological primacy of culture in Cassirer's thought is borne out by a glance at his literary career. The progressive articulation of his philosophy went hand in hand with a movement towards a greater emphasis on problems of culture—a development which culminated in the *Philosophy of Symbolic Forms* (now conveniently summarized in the recent *Essay on Man*). This *magnum opus*, a boldly conceived and masterly executed philosophical interpretation of culture, completed the conquest of a domain which, though coveted before by other members of the Marburg School, had

[1] *Metaphysics*, 1003a 21.

proved inaccessible to Cassirer's predecessors. It is true, Cassirer was encouraged and aided in his undertaking by a prevailing current of thought. At the turn from the nineteenth to the twentieth century, German philosophy sought to put a check on the hegemony of the natural sciences by working out a system of *Geisteswissenschaft*. But, if we view Cassirer's achievement against the background of the co-operative effort with which he found himself in harmony, the originality of the solution he propounded becomes only the more impressive.

Following Hermann Cohen, the founder of the Marburg School, Cassirer derived his interpretation of Reality from Kant's *Critique of Pure Reason*. The *Critique* so powerfully influenced Cassirer's thinking that it determined his interpretation of culture throughout, from its principles down to the order of procedure, as shown by the tables of contents in the volumes of *Die Philosophie der symbolischen Formen*. Modestly the author takes credit only for essaying a work that was rendered both possible and indispensable by Kant, but left undone, for some reason or other, by the master. Like Wilhelm Dilthey and Heinrich Rickert, he claims to complete the Kantian architecture by giving the philosophical foundation of the science of nature as furnished by Kant a companion-piece in the philosophical foundation of the science of culture. Historically, the claim is void. The alleged supplementation requires a fresh ground-plan and, in fact, a different building. Yet the intended adherence to Kant's letter and spirit is nonetheless the salient trait of the new structure.

"For it is the same thing that can be thought and that can be."[2] With this succinct assertion Parmenides put an end to naïve reflection on the totality of real things, and philosophy as a disquisition on reality as such emerged into sight. It is made clear that "being" is related to "being thought" not as the florin is related to the purse, the cargo to the vessel, or in any other extrinsic fashion. The two terms are conjoined rather as "sight" is to "being seen" or "creature" to "being created." Despite their distinctness they form an integral unity.

Kant found a fresh formula for the Eleatic insight. In pur-

[2] Hermann, Diels, *Fragmente der Vorsokratiker*, (5th ed.), I, 231, fr. 3.

suing knowledge we put ideas together: Knowledge, the result of this process, is a synthesis. But may we, by so uniting ideas into a composite whole, expect to reveal something which, by definition, lies outside the sphere of mental operations, viz., reality? We may, Kant answers, provided the principles which direct our constructing a synthesis are identical with the principles determining the structure of reality. It will be permitted to call the totality of knowledge as based upon sense perception "experience;" to substitute for principles: "conditions of possibility," and to dub statements relating to these fundamental conditions "*a priori* judgments." With these terminological adjustments, Kant's "highest principle of all synthetic judgments" is arrived at: "We then assert that the conditions of the possibility of experience in general are likewise conditions of the possibility of the objects of experience, and that for this reason they have objective validity in a synthetic *a priori* judgment."[3]

Cassirer poses the problem in Parmenidean terms and then, for an answer, reaffirms Kant's solution.

The first point of departure for speculation is denoted by the concept of Being. The instant this concept articulates itself and a consciousness awakes of the unity of Being, as set over against the multiplicity and variety of being things, the specifically philosophical mode of regarding the world arises.[4]

With this ontological conception of philosophy in mind, Cassirer proceeds to express the Parmenidean identification in terms of a Kantian "transcendental" logic: "The concept relates to the object because and as much as it [the concept] is the necessary and indispensable presupposition of objectivation; because it is the function for which alone there can be objects, i.e., permanent basic units, amidst the flux of experience."[5] Shorter and simpler: "The logical concept is the necessary and sufficient condition for the knowledge of the nature of things."[6]

"Being," according to this transcendental logic, means "being

---

[3] *Critique of Pure Reason* (Norman K. Smith tr., London, 1929), 194.
[4] *Die Philosophie der symbolischen Formen*, I, 3.
[5] *Ibid.*, III, 368.
[6] *Zur Logik der Kulturwissenschaften*, typescript p. 37.

determined," and thinking is the process of determination. So there is no essence outside the sphere of thinking, and metaphysics as the supposed knowledge of essences is non-existent. Transcendental idealism has no room for a transcendent, i.e., super-sensible, reality, and discountenances Natural Theology and similar speculative flights. Along with metaphysics it dispenses with the "copy theory of knowledge" (*Abbildtheorie*). This theory naïvely interprets ideas "inside the mind" as copies of "things without," thus dissociating what belongs indelibly together and then reassembling the broken parts by resorting to a dubious analogy.[7]

Examining this "critical" or "transcendental" logic, we do well to remember that "naïve," i.e., pre-Kantian, metaphysics was not so naïve as to subscribe to the unphilosophical notion of knowledge as a passive image mirroring a given reality. Naïveté, of course, is undying. But it has been obsolescent in philosophy ever since Parmenides put forward his monumental identification; and traditional metaphysics as called into existence by Plato and Aristotle did not entirely fail to heed "Father Parmenides'" teaching. However, his stupendous insistence on a seemingly absurd truth, expressed in words as rigidly erect and quaintly ornate as an archaic statue, underwent at the hands of his followers a differentiation which made it supple and alive. The chief purpose of this differentiation was to find a place for the finite human knower as an integral part of reality—a part ignored by the disdainful Eleatic save, by way of compromise, in the second, pragmatic portion of his poem.

In Aristotle, the identity of "thinking" and "being" is maintained at the pinnacle of the pyramid of reality. The unmoved mover, form disengaged from matter, act free of potentiality, is described as νόησις νοήσεως—thinking returning upon itself, reality as self-comprehending intellection, a thing that is by virtue of thinking itself. But in the sublunar world inhabited by man this primordial unity bifurcates. Man the knower is confronted by things to be known—things which *are*, regardless as to whether or not he takes cognizance of their existence.

[7] Cf. *Philosophie der symbolischen Formen* (hereafter abbreviated: *PSF*), I, 5.

Yet their "becoming known" is by no means incidental to their existence in the sense in which "being portrayed" is incidental to a person. First, the kind of existence which a thing has involves a degree of knowability, depending upon the share which form has in its constitution. So a star is more knowable than a lump of clay, or the soul than the body. For cognition detaches a thing's form from its matter: the intelligent mind is the locus of forms. Second, the identity which is complete at the summit, in the form of forms, is present also in the human act of cognition, though only in a qualified way. "In the case of objects which involve no matter, what thinks and what is thought are identical" (τὸ αὐτό ἐστι τὸ νοοῦν καὶ τὸ νοούμενον).[8] The very wording is reminiscent of Parmenides.

Man may rise to intuiting forms not contaminated with matter. But he is environed by a compound reality—forms wedded to matter. Consequently the cognitive process in the human mind is, for Aristotle, an interplay and co-operation of activity and passivity. This duality corresponds to the duality of the human situation. Man, as finite, is one thing among the many things of the world, acted upon and reacting. At the same time, man, through reason, is somehow all things.

Turning now to Kant, the source of Cassirer's epistemology, we find the interplay of activity and passivity supplanted with a novel emphasis on the constructive activity of the mind. The Eleatic identification is reborn in the spirit of the modern, post-Cartesian subject. However, the scope of this idealistic motif which reverses the natural order by making objects conform to concepts[9] is strictly limited to the sensible world: to the world of phenomena as interpreted by "experience;" and this phenomenal world is not coextensive with reality. The *Critique* teaches that "the object is to be taken in a twofold sense, namely as appearance and thing in itself."[10] Beyond the pales of appearance all the essential features of the metaphysical world picture, though denied to speculative knowledge, are restored to enlightened faith. This restoration, far from being

[8] *De Anima*, 430a 3-4.
[9] *Critique of Pure Reason* (N. K. Smith tr.), 22.
[10] *Ibid.*, 28.

a mere compromise, springs from the êthos of Kant's under-taking. Rescinding the principle of happiness and dislodging contemplation from its sovereign place, he wrests man from his anchorage in nature while blocking his visionary ascent to God. But he believes he only takes away what man never right-fully possessed.

It is true, Kant disabuses man and purges his mind from speculative conceit. Yet in so humbling him he does not deliver him into the despair of metaphysical homelessness. Instead he returns the paraphernalia of the transmundane homestead, God and the *intelligibilia*, freedom and beatitude—not to man's cognitive faculty, but to his "practical belief." Man, in a chastened mood now, since he has put away his intellectual pride, is expected reverently to submit to a law that defines his place in the order of things and to which the voice of duty in his own mind bears unequivocal testimony. By the same token, the interplay of spontaneity and passivity in the cognitive process is restored. Again, the theory of knowledge is but-tressed to the idea of the finitude of man. The very act of resignation by which we disown metaphysical vision is supposed to establish the right rapport between ourselves and the objects of the metaphysical world. By a *tour de force* we thus arrive at the notion of unintelligible *intelligibilia* (νοούμενα)—unintel-ligible, we must add, to us, to man.

Following the general line of neo-Kantian thought, Cassirer adopts Kant's "highest principle of all synthetic judgments"—the identification of "the conditions of the possibility of experi-ence" with "the conditions of the possibility of the objects of experience." At the same time, again conforming to the Mar-burg pattern, he goes beyond Kant. Kant's "objects of experi-ence" are not objects as such, but "appearances" as set over against the "thing in itself." Hence, Kant's identification is a limited one. The neo-Kantian, discarding the "thing in itself," makes the identification total. He robs the object of all its sub-stantiality. To him the object is the result or the "function" of the logical process of objectivation; and the residuum which resists this "functionalization" becomes an "objective" (*Auf-gabe*)—the infinitely distant goal for further acts of logical determination. Kant's transcendental logic is made to outgrow the limited domain assigned to it by the master.

If God held in one hand truth, in the other the search for it, inviting us to choose, we should, Lessing held, beg the heavenly Father to keep the truth for Himself and let us have the search. To this Hermann Cohen objects. What truth means to God is of no concern to us; and as far as we are concerned the gifts of the two hands are actually one: truth is the quest for truth.[11] In the same vein, Cassirer quotes Faust's translation of the opening words of the Gospel according to St. John: "In the beginning was the deed."[12] *Logos* is creation, positing reality. All this goes beyond Kant in the sense that the transcendental synthesis is viewed as constituting not only "objects of experience" but objects *tout court*.

However, in so radicalizing the thesis of Kant's transcendental logic, Cassirer goes also back behind Kant—not to pre-Kantian metaphysics, but to pre-metaphysical, i.e., pre-Platonic, ontology: to Parmenides. A modern dynamic companion-piece to the immobile, self-contained Eleatic Being is achieved. This, of course, is not the avowed intent of the neo-Kantian thinker who is innocent of any archaizing inclinations. But, constrained by the logic of his transcendental identification, he comes to embrace an archaically simplified concept of Being. Incidentally, this simplification was encouraged by the scientific ideal prevalent in an industrialized civilization. Organized co-operation of vast groups, made effective by a division of labor into multiple functions,—the master-device of modern industry—was inapplicable to the intricate wholeness of metaphysics. Its "huge helplessness" (G. K. Chesterton) did not fit into the contemporary pattern. On the other hand, the neo-Kantian idea of knowledge as an infinite process of determination, suggestive as it was of the cumulative collaboration of individuals and groups, seemed more agreeable to the *Zeitgeist*.

Be that as it may (and admitting that this explanation of the pre-Socratic features so strikingly characteristic of various currents of recent philosophy is far from exhaustive), the logic

---

[11] Hermann Cohen, *Ethik des reinen Willens* (1904), 93.
[12] *Logik der Kulturwissenschaften*, 61.

of the neo-Kantian return to Parmenidian simplicity is both clear and cogent. As the transcendental synthesis, the act of objectification, wins unlimited scope, the receptivity (or passivity) in the knower is cancelled out. Along with his receptivity the knower as a finite subject is likewise lost to view; and the anthropological undergirding of the theory of knowledge, reinterpreted but preserved by Kant, is gone. The "bifurcation" of the ontological identity, which, in Plato and Aristotle, showed man as being "*of* the world," and the world as existing *for* man—this bifurcation is blotted out. We move in the self-contained sphere of a thinking that constitutes objects; and this sphere leaves as little room for man, the knower, as the Eleatic sphere of Being. The knower looks upon this sphere as it were "from outside." Never and under no circumstances is he encompassed by it.

We ask Parmenides about man and those obtrusive facts which loom large in man's life: the choice between good and evil, the cycle of birth and death, and the alternation of the seasons. In reply he puts us off with information on "the beliefs of mortals" and on the names they have decided to affix to things.[13] We ask the neo-Kantian about man, and he sends us to empirical psychology and empirical anthropology. But this, of course, is not his whole reply to our query. Man figures in his philosophy as a subject related to objects. The subject-object correlation is all-pervasive, omnipresent. However, Cassirer affirms, no hard and fast dividing line separates the two correlate spheres. Wherever a meaning is grasped, it carries with it both subject and object as polar "moments" involved in its structure; in other words, it is the result of a mediation between the two poles. "To be," in this view, means "to be a synthesis" of subject and object, or of the ego and the world. But with this definition the status of "being" or "reality" is denied to the world as well as to the ego.

Using a simile dear to Plato we may liken the synthesis to a tissue. Let us suppose a student of the weaving process, though sharp-sighted in observing the expanding pattern of warp and woof, be completely blind to loom, shuttle, and raw-material.

[13] Hermann Diels, *op. cit.*, I, 239, fr. 8, 50-61.

So he is well equipped closely to follow the progress of the work, but unable to see the tools and the thread which between them carry on this work. The puzzled student will try to make up for the lacuna in his vision by imagining hypothetical agencies which would explain the mysterious growth of the texture. Ingenious as he is he might succeed in imagining the devices invisible to him. But, instead of letting him have his way, we deepen his perplexity by adding to the defect of eyesight a mental handicap. We incapacitate him for thinking or imagining anything except in terms of a texture, and accordingly we endow him with a purely "textile" language.

The doubly disabled student of textile manufacture in our parable is man trying to study "subject" and "reality" on the line of the neo-Kantian approach. These two polar concepts are of crucial importance to him: they denote the terminal points of the axis upon which his interpretation revolves. At the same time, he finds himself debarred from ever bringing them into the purview of his analysis. By definition, one of the two, the object pole, while directing the advance of cognitive syntheses, never rises above the knower's horizon. Similarly, the ego, manifest though it is through its works, remains eternally in his back. This "evanescent nature" of both "ego" and "world," as it appears in neo-Kantian epistemology, points truly to the structure of the situation of the knower confronted with potential objects of knowledge. But the question is as to whether an analysis of the cognitive subject-object relation can provide the foundations upon which to erect a philosophical edifice. In other words, is a situation in which the world is "for man," the spectator, (while man's participation in the world as an agent is lost sight of) as prototypical for an interpretation of reality as neo-Kantianism assumes? To be sure, an understanding of culture can be won only on the basis of an adequate conception of the human agent. Hence the attempt to develop the transcendental logic of neo-Kantianism into a philosophy of culture appears a singularly unpropitious enterprise. Nature without man is imaginable, fragmentary though she may seem. But culture is clearly a man-made thing, a datum for man's inspection, too, but first of all existing through man and in man.

To find strength in weakness is the mark of a creative mind. In Cassirer's hands, transcendental logic becomes an effective tool for coping with problems of the human world. Within its limited reach, this clean-cutting tool harvests fruits which a more deeply searching instrument, or one of more sweeping grasp, would have been likely to have left ungleaned.

An analysis of the transcendental synthesis may move in either of two directions, according to the prevailing interest. The interest may be directed either towards uncovering "foundations," i.e., ultimate positing acts which afford a basis for subsequent syntheses and endow the whole process with the character of self-supporting "science" (ἐπιστήμη); or it may focus on the resulting structures. It was Hermann Cohen, the founder of the Marburg school, who took the "adventurous road" towards the discovery of origins. In his *Logic* we find him at pains to wrest Being as "aught" from a primordial "naught"—a "logogony" which forces the thinking mind through the narrow strait of an "extreme perplexity" into progressive self-determination.[14] With Cassirer, temper and direction of the transcendental enterprise have changed. Gone is the heroic passion for moving the *globus intellectualis* by the "lever of the origin;" gone also the founder's provincialism which oddly clogged his vision. Instead, we find an analyst applying himself with an open mind and heightened sensitiveness to a study of those structural features which the cognitive synthesis in its manifold forms reveals—forms abundantly exhibited by the numerous branches of actual science. This new tendency, akin in spirit to Husserl's phenomenology, bore its early fruits in the field of the logic of natural science. But gradually it gave rise to a broadening of perspective which rendered a philosophy of culture possible.

Once we have accepted the basic principle of a "critical philosophy," the primacy of the creative mind over a given reality, of "function" over "object," we need not, Cassirer argues, confine ourselves to examining the cognitive function and its objective correlate, the thing as knowable. There are other types of meaningful structures through which the mind manifests its creativity, distinct from knowledge, but no less

[14] Hermann Cohen, *Logik der reinen Erkenntnis* (3rd ed., 1922), 83f.

coherent, each forming a realm of meaning of its own, each ordered and articulated in accordance with its own laws, its own "style." Mythic thought, language, art—these are the chief instances of autonomous "structures of meaning" which Cassirer has in mind. Only by comprising these non-cognitive structures within its field of vision does transcendental idealism come into its own. "Thus the critique of reason becomes critique of culture. It seeks to understand and to show how all content of culture, inasmuch as it is not a merely particular content but one based upon a universal principle of form, presupposes a creative act of the mind (*eine ursprüngliche Tat des Geistes*)."[15]

The defeat of the naïve-realistic view of the world is incomplete as long as the idealistic analysis is confined to knowledge. While admitting that certain structural traits of the object of knowledge result from a formative activity of the mind, the realist may still maintain that there must be an independent "something," a datum, subsisting outside the subject-object relation. His contention, Cassirer holds, becomes untenable as soon as we substitute "culture" for "world." Confronted with the array of cultural forms, he must see that clinging to the idea of a self-contained non-mental substratum, a "thing in itself," henceforth will serve no purpose. Here, at last, the mind stands revealed in works unmistakably its own. There is distinctness, structure, articulate meaning, but no suspicion of an extra-mental givenness. Envisaging these structures and meaningful contexts is tantamount to discerning a variety of basic "directions" or "tendencies" of the mind, each of which issues in an object or a set of objects. And these objects are plainly products, shaped through and through by that creative "direction" from which they spring. "Being" is swallowed up in "doing." A work of art *is*. But the being we ascribe to it is derivative. It actually is nothing save what it is in relation to, and as a product of, artistic imagination. The world of aesthetic objects is a continuous and orderly manifestation of one of the mind's cosmogonic urges. And the same is true of the world of mythic thought and of language.

With its recent development modern physics has lost its grip

[15] *PSF*, I, 11.

on material reality. Models explanatory of sub-atomic structures can no longer be regarded as faithful large scale replicas of microcosmic nature. Their value is to be assessed in terms of their usefulness in rendering prediction of future events possible. These new physical concepts, instead of "picturing" facts, permit the physicist to orient himself in his dealings with nature by providing what Heinrich Hertz called "symbols." This term, signaling, so it seemed, the bankruptcy of naïve realism in physics, was seized upon and given a new and ambitious career by Cassirer. He decided to call those structures which he set out to analyze in his philosophy of culture, "symbolic forms."

The title seems appropriate. In ancient Greece old bonds of friendship and hospitality were acknowledged and renewed when the two fragments of a ring, tokens of recognition, fitted exactly together. The ring, or whatever object took its place, was called a symbol. Symbol, in the original Greek sense of the word, is a token. The cultural forms also betoken something. They express a meaning. In the symbol literally so-called the sign is clearly distinct from that which it signifies. The sign is: two physical objects fitting together; the thing signified: two minds fitting together. In Cassirer's "symbolic form" this distinction holds too. There is a perceived or imagined form: a sequel of articulate sounds, an arrangement of lines and colors, a "world picture;" and these sensible forms are designed to point to something non-sensible. They are utterances. Each one of the various "realms of forms" externalizes an inner world. Each is a language of its own.

At this juncture the metaphor of the symbol breaks down and, at the same time, gains a fresh significance. The ring is one thing, the ancient alliance of two families or clans another thing; and we find no difficulty in not only distinguishing but also separating these two types of reality. Both may exist independently of each other. This separableness is not found in Cassirer's "symbolic forms." Distinct though sign and meaning are, they belong inextricably together. They fit as neatly to each other as the broken halves of a ring fit. Like these they form an integral whole. This intimacy of the relation between "form" and "meaning" distinguishes the genuine symbolic form from conventional semantic systems such as the Morse Code or the signs used by symbolic logic. The latter provide vehicles for conveying a ready-made meaning; and they may, at any time, be supplanted with alternative, more convenient vehicles. Not so the "symbolic form." It is not exchangeable, not detachable, not arbitrarily constructed. It is not content *in* a form but content *as* form; a medium informed and animated by meaning, meaning articulating itself into form.

The mind weaves a seamless robe. A linguistic expression may be translated from one language into another, though even here the translation will never be a perfect equivalent of the original. But a content expressed in one type of symbolic form, say in language, cannot be ripped from its "connatural" manifestation and sewn to a different symbolic vesture. The meaning of languages is not expressible in painting, nor the meaning of music in terms of mythic thinking. Every realm of symbolic forms, language, art, and mythic *Weltanschauung*, must be accepted on its own terms and deciphered in consonance with the creative direction or intent which determines the structure of that particular realm. To lay bare this unique structure, neither adding nor leaving out but faithfully following in the footprints of *mens creatrix*—such is the business of a transcendental analysis of language, of mythology, of art. Philosophy appears in the rôle of a universal interpreter of the multiple "languages" through which the mind puts forth its inner wealth. It functions, in Cassirer's own terms, as "the conscience of culture."[16]

Transcendental analysis as employed by Cassirer has a special aptitude for performing precisely this task. It operates with a dynamic and highly flexible concept of "form" which is equally applicable in all spheres of symbolic expression. Kant, in the "transcendental logic," views the cognitive act as the synthesis of a diversity of sensory data. This idea of synoptic construction, stripped of the realistic ingredient which accrued to it from Kant's notion of "givenness," proves a perfect tool for an interpretation which is to range far beyond epistemology over the

---

[16] *Logik* . . ., 33.

whole field of cultural achievements. Myths and language, religious symbols and works of art—all and each show the dominance of one point of view—different in each particular field yet analogous in mode of operation to all the others; and this point of view unifies and organizes an indefinite multiplicity into an orderly Kingdom of Forms. To understand any one cultural phenomenon, be it a religious belief, an artistic motif, or a linguistic expression, means to locate it within the sphere of symbolic expression to which it belongs and from which it derives its significance. In other words, the phenomenon under analysis must be subjected to the dominant angle of vision as the principle of synthesis.

Whence do the material elements hail which are put together by transcendental synthesis in the several provinces of its operation? "From nowhere," seems the correct reply. These material elements, although affording a particular content, have no existence apart from, or previous to, the framework of forms in which they are ensconced. They owe their particularity, and, in fact, their existence, to their relation to universal form; and this assertion is reversible. Form and matter, in this view, are strictly correlate, and synthesis is diversification as well as unification. We see here Cassirer taking the path along which Fichte, Schelling, and Hegel had once moved beyond Kant and away from Kant: away from the "thing in itself" in relation to which the subject was supposed to be the suffering or receptive rather than the spontaneously active partner.

Logic, which demands the dialectical interdependence of "the one" and "the many," seems to be with Cassirer and his predecessors in radical idealism. But his resolute departure from Kant's residual realism saves the idealist from an inconsistency only to entangle him in another no less grave difficulty. If the particular content does not stem from a material datum outside the mind, it must be the mind that gives rise to it. How, then, is this infra-mental duality to be accounted for? How explain the concentration of analysis upon "form," if "form" and "matter" are of the same origin and, consequently, of the same ontological rank? Cassirer throughout uses a language which presupposes the common-sense notion of the mind exercising

itself in a world of "given" objects. This is the view which
descriptive expressions such as articulation of meaning, unification, synoptic organization, etc., imply. But the rigorous dialectics of transcendental idealism gives the lie to these and
similar terms and reduces them to the status of metaphors. No
language is available directly to express what the idealist endeavors to think.

The linguistic difficulty indicates a deep-seated quandary. We
are brought face to face with an ancient cosmogonic puzzle.
The original One, so it seems, needs a counter-force to challenge it into productivity. A metaphysical antagonist is required,

Der reizt und wirkt und muss als Teufel schaffen.[17]

In Cassirer's philosophy, cultural productivity is partheno-
genesis, parturition of the spirit that dwells in solitude. Substance, he insists, must be transfigured into function, "being"
into "doing." But function is discernible only if seen against
the foil of substance, just as doing requires something "unto
which" doing is done. The attempt to translate everything into
doing obliterates doing. Exactly this occurs in Cassirer's philosophy of culture. Total dynamism is proclaimed, the boundless liberty of the creative mind; yet the result obtained is
meaning congealed into structures rigidly static, like Parmenides' Being "immovable in the bonds of mighty chains without
beginning and without end."[18]

Parmenides was at great pains to ward off intrusions of the
non-being about which, he stoutly maintained, no assertion
can be made except that "it is not." Melissus and Zeno, armed
with the two-edged sword of Parmenidean dialectic, continued
to fight the losing battle; until in Gorgias, the prodigal son
of the Eleatic house, non-being carried the day. Plato discovered
the moral of this story. With apologies to Parmenides he laid
unfilial hands on his thesis and re-admitted non-being to some
sort of existence—the existence of "images" (*eidola*).[19] Thus he
limited the scope of Parmenides' "ontological identification" (of

---

[17] Goethe, *Faust*, "Prolog im Himmel."
[18] Hermann Diels, *loc. cit.*, 237, fr. 8, 26f.
[19] *Sophist*, 241 d.

knowledge and being) and rendered a philosophy of the finite world and the finite knower possible. Similarly, the Atomists used the void (successor to Parmenides' non-being) as an auxiliary cosmogonic principle. In our own time, while metaphysics tottered with decrepitude, neo-Kantianism reverted to the Eleatic identification; and again, at the periphery of the restored sphere of Being, the teasing presence of the unsuccessfully exorcized non-being made itself felt. Its name, in Cassirer, is "the flux of experience," out of which the symbolic forms are said to crystallize. This matrix of Being, itself non-being, however indispensable it seems, is inassimiliably alien within the transcendental scheme. It is supposed to be objectifiable. But it is not objectified. Hence it is not.

As the "flux of experience" looms as that which, a passive substratum, is as yet to be objectified, so, at the opposite pole of the transcendental axis, the active partner becomes just discernible: that which objectifies but has not yet passed into objectivity. And again, according to the rigid laws of transcendental logic, this still, so to speak, "fluid" creativity is kept lingering at the outer confines of the universe of philosophical discourse. To mingle with transcendentally respectable concepts it lacks the stamp of objectivity which can be imprinted upon it only by a synthesis. This but dimly perceived creativity resembles the Christian God rather than the Platonic demiurge who, with the Eternal Model before him, persuades the "errant cause" into submission to his formative will. There is, according to the "critical" view, no malleable stuff to be fashioned. Creation is *creatio ex nihilo*. But, of course, the creative mind which reveals itself in symbolic forms has vacated its transmundane heaven to take up quarters in the human sphere. It is alternately called "life," a name which denotes its present abode, and "spirit" which is reminiscent of its exalted origin. Life or spirit in Cassirer's philosophy is akin to Hegel's *Weltgeist*. But, whereas the latter unfolds itself in history, baring the rhythm of its movements for our inspection, Cassirer's "life" is known by its fruits alone. At the same time, the element of transcendence, maintained in Hegel, is discarded. Cassirer's philosophy is plainly "immanentist." Its principle of creativity is conceived in the spirit of an era whose implicit faith found a classic expression in Auguste Comte's "worship of humanity."

We remember here that student of textile manufacture to whom we likened the follower of "critical" or "transcendental" idealism. This student, we agreed, was to be blind both to his tools and to his raw material. He has an eye only for the web itself. Loom and shuttle, in our simile, stand for "life" (or "spirit"), the thread as raw material for the "flux of experience." We could not prevent our student from casting about uneasily for surmises concerning these to him invisible agents. In the same way, the ideas of "creative life" and the "flux of experience" intrude upon the attention of the critical analyst. But a further stipulation we agreed upon cannot, as we now see, be upheld. We tried to cast upon the victim of our experiment a spell which would force him to think everything (including tools and material) in terms of texture. This proves more than human blood and flesh can bear. In non-metaphorical language: metaphysics is not to be expelled by a vow of abstinence. Drive it out with the critical pitchfork: *tamen usque recurret*. Definite metaphysical tenets underlie Cassirer's philosophy of culture. His determination to refrain from metaphysics is itself dictated by his immanentist metaphysics—a self-denying metaphysics, condemned to suffering atrophy.

The common denominator of the divers symbolic forms is their character as principles of objectivation. They are non-cognitive variants of the Kantian "synthesis of transcendental apperception." But this is not the only bond between them. They bear, as it were, a family likeness to each other. Although they form different "languages," they show analogies of "syntax" and treat identical themes. This analogous structure of the various "realms" is reflected in the parallel order followed by the argument in the three volumes of the *Philosophie der symbolischen Formen*. The analysis of language (in volume I), the analysis of myth (in volume II), and the analysis of the cognitive process (in volume III) begin with a treatment of space and time. This, of course, is done in adherence to the pattern set by Kant's "transcendental aesthetics," the opening part of the *Critique of Pure Reason*. But Cassirer adds a discussion of number which has no pendant in the *Critique*.

For Kant self-consciousness and time are intimately related to each other. Time is "the form of the inner sense." So, in letting an examination of the ego follow on the heels of his "transcendental aesthetics," Cassirer still is guided by the spirit though not by the table of contents of Kant's work. The latter part, in all three volumes, corresponds roughly to the master's "transcendental logic," insofar as it rises above the outlines of the sensible world to more abstract relationships.

The significance of these analogies is obvious. Language, myth, knowledge are different media, all three of them refracting rays emitted by one and the same luminary; or to use another more closely "transcendental" figure of speech: they are different idioms which express an identical conception. This pervasive conception or pattern is of triadic structure: the sensible world, the ego, the ego orienting itself in the world. The world, a temporal sequence of events, extended in space, exhibiting a prodigious wealth of qualities—this world is reflected in linguistic signs, intuited by mythic consciousness, interpreted by religion and art, known by science. In its passage from one medium to another, it is, and is not, the same, comparable to a tune played on different instruments. And what is true of the first unit of the triad, the sensible world, holds likewise of the ego, and of the relations between self and world.

Space, for instance, as a feature of mundane existence, is found in mythic thought as well as in a scientific interpretation of reality. There are not two different spaces: a mythic and a scientific space. Wherever space is apprehended, it shows certain persistent traits: it has dimensions, and it is the locus in which things are placed as "here," or "there," as inside one thing, distant from another thing, etc. In another sense, however, there are indeed different spaces or rather types of space. In mythic thought no clear distinction is made between the place and the thing that fills the place. The "here" and "there" are conceived of as properties of objects. Things have their "natural" place and displacement may destroy them.

Likewise spatial directions coalesce with features of reality: north is air, and it is also war and hunting; south is fire, and also medicine and agriculture, and so forth. The nature of this "mythic" space does not greatly differ from space as we all perceive it in everyday life. But only remotely does it resemble the strictly homogenous space of Euclidean geometry which is "the locus of loci," totally detached from localized objects. Time, number, relation, ego—they all show a similar plasticity. Although retaining their nature, they suffer modifications in conformity with the realm of meaning in which they appear. They are "polyglot" in the sense that they express themselves in different "languages," such as religion, art, or science.

The tripartite pattern which recurs in each of the symbolic forms mirrors a more basic triad. The triptych: world—ego—categorial relations, forms within the sphere of constituted structures the counterpart to a triune constituent structure "higher up," in the sphere of transcendental origins. "World" corresponds to "flux of experience," "ego" to "life," and the "categorical relations," which straddle over this dichotomy, to "transcendental synthesis." The former are to the latter as the non-lingual conditions which render language possible (voice, communicable meaning) to a universal grammar.

The "universal grammar," which shows the uniformity of all types of symbolic expression, is diversified into a number of "languages" by principles of specifications; and the specific structure combines, in every particular field, with the all-pervasive structure into a complex pattern. So there is one *differentia specifica* which modifies the "universal grammar" into what is literally called language, another specifying principle constitutes the type of expression called "religion," a third one constitutes art, and so forth. The principles of specification are not arrived at by deduction. Cassirer even refrains from enunciating them *in abstracto*. The analyst of culture, he holds, should not rival with natural science in the attempt to formulate universal laws which determine causally connected events. Instead he must seek to "make visible" a "totality of forms," held together by unity of "style." The concepts through which a style is comprehended do not "determine"—they "characterize." From the point of view of Cassirer's own methodology, the "structural analysis" which he brings to bear on culture holds a middle-ground between natural science, which aims at the discovery of universal laws, and historiography, which emphasizes the individuality of facts.[20] With this logical topology Cassirer puts on record his own contribution to that prolonged and dust-raising battle of books for which Wilhelm Windelband, as long ago as in 1894, sounded the opening flourish with a timely and successful platitude, the distinction between generalizing knowledge (*Erklären*) and individualizing knowledge (*Verstehen*), and whose prize was *Geisteswissenschaft*, philosophically justified.

In order to make visible that unity of style which characterizes one type of expression as myth, another as art, a third as religion, and so on, the conceptual instruments traditionally used by neo-Kantian thinkers were of no avail. Neither Hermann Cohen's rhapsodic construction nor Heinrich Rickert's painstaking diaeresis could have helped Cassirer solve the problem at hand. Long enough Windelband's terms "idiographic" and "nomothetic" had been bandied about by argumentative methodologists. Cassirer came, through his affiliation with Marburg stamped as a man of vastest generalities, and possessed himself of that subtly individualizing art of understanding which had been evolved in the camp of his intellectual antipodes: in the Historical School and by Wilhelm Dilthey. With Cassirer, neo-Kantianism, originally given to rigidly constructive methods, became sensitive to the finest shades of style and structure—to a type of order which reveals its secret to the observant physiognomist rather than to the classifying logician. In Cassirer's work, transcendental construction and empirical interpretation come to a fruitful understanding.

Mythic thought is dominated by what Cassirer describes as "the concrescence of related terms."[21] The wound suffered in combat is considered not merely an effect related to the foe as to its cause: somehow it *is* the foe, the presence of his malignant power in the stricken man's body. Similarly, the parts are seen not only as composing the whole, but each part stands for, and

---

[20] *Logik* . . ., 89-93.
[21] *PSF*, II, 83.

to some extent *is*, the whole. A man's footprints, or his nails, are in a way the man himself, carriers of the "real power" which centers in a person. This coalescence of related but distinct elements runs through all strata of the mythic world picture. Together with other features it forms the "specific difference"— that which defines myth as myth and sets it off against other types of symbolic expression such as religion or art. However, Cassirer does not deduce the nature of myth from "participation" or "concrescence" as from a principle, but proceeds in a manner which might be described as "constructive empiricism." He first surveys his assemblage of data, an astonishingly rich harvest gleaned from a thorough study of anthropological literature, then fastens upon some salient features which bring out the structure of the field under investigation. These features he follows into their finer ramifications until he finally succeeds in hammering out the rich relief of a coherent and balanced "totality of forms."

Naturally this structural interpretation, with all its scrupulous attention to facts, is ultimately guided by the principles of transcendental philosophy. But to a large extent, this philosophical orientation, far from imposing ready-made concepts upon a recalcitrant material, serves as a critical catalytic. We are prone to cast our experiences in a number of streotyped forms which are most handy to us because of their usefulness in practical life; and in so doing we readily overlook the unique character of these experiences. To this "pragmatic fallacy" the analysis of symbolic forms offers an effective antidote.

In ancient Greece, language, as a system of phonetic signs, was made the object of a famous controversy. Those who regarded these signs as existing "by nature" (φύσει) joined issue with others who considered them conventional (νόμῳ); and even today, as the emergence of Semantics in our midst shows, the hoary "conventionalism" is not yet extinct. Here is a test case for Cassirer's method of arbitration. The study of linguistic form, conducted under the auspices of transcendental philosophy, establishes language as a unique type of expression. This "symbolic form" of language *qua* language is adequately described neither by linguistic naturalism with its emphasis on onomatopoetic links between sign and signified objects, nor by conventionalism with its insistence on the arbitrary character of signs. Another illustration is furnished by the debate between imitation theory and expression theory in aesthetics. Again a unique creative direction, incarnate in works of art, is unduly assimilated to that type of objective existence with which we are most familiar in our workaday world. And again, the analyst of symbolic forms, with his eye upon the *differentia specifica* of the aesthetic form *qua* aesthetic, may arbitrate between the disputants by discarding their false disjunction.

Up to this point, the symbolic forms have been treated by us as autonomous domains, of analogous structure, but otherwise insular, unrelated among themselves. Yet there are, over and above their generic features as "forms," certain specific ties and interrelations between them. As we now focus on the links connecting form with form we come across another factor, neglected hitherto. Eleatic immobility has seemed to characterize the symbolic structures. Studying their interrelations we catch a glimpse of their subdued dynamism.

Some of the symbolic forms as distinguished by Cassirer can, others can not, coexist in the same mind or in the same cultural environment. Language, e.g., lives together with religion peaceably and in fruitful co-operation; whereas scientific knowledge is intolerant of myth. This observation furnishes a clue for uncovering the configuration of Forms in a field of mutual relatedness.

Significantly the philosophy of the symbolic forms opens with language. Language, in effect, occupies a unique place within the scheme of cultural structures. It is the one form that associates with all other forms. Be he a primitive, his mind beclouded by magic and superstition, or a specimen of *homo sapiens*, consumer and fabricator of books on philosophy, as human, man is, according to Aristotle's definition, "an animal endowed with speech."[22]

Cassirer distinguishes three linguistic phases, characterized severally by the prevalence of mimetic, analogical, and symbolic expression. At the stage of mimetic expression, the word is

[22] *Politics*, 1253a 10.

an imitative gesture clinging closely to what it denotes. The primitive Ewe language, for example, has no less than 33 "phonetic images" for various modes of "walking;" and we may believe that, beside the mimetic power and evocative vividness of each of them, even so picturesque English verbs as "stagger," "lumber," "strut," and the like, appear sicklied over with the pale cast of thought. In modern languages this primitive type of expression survives in those linguistic fossils which we call onomatopoetic.[23] The analogical stage is reached, where the arrangement of phonetic signs corresponds to the arrangement of denoted events. The resemblance between event and phonetic signal is here superseded with the analogy between the order of things and the order of sounds. So a difference in pitch of voice may be used to signal a difference of distance; or reduplication (as in *do, dedi*) serves to express the past tense. With the attainment, finally, of the symbolic stage, the heterogeneity of sign and fact is understood and fully exploited. The phonetic symbol is made to "signify" (*bedeuten*) instead of merely to "denote" (*bezeichnen*), and the mind now moves with supreme freedom in the fully mastered medium of linguistic expression.

The trend of the movement from stage to stage is, it appears, towards greater "spiritualization" or "etherialization" (*Vergeistigung*). At the same time, it becomes clear why one, and only one, of the symbolic forms, language, "mingles" with all its peers. In its development from mimetic to symbolic expression it covers the entire rising scale on which each of the other forms occupies a fixed point. Language evolves through all phases of the mind's progress towards freedom, whereas the other forms are located each within one phase; and this is why, to some extent, they are mutually exclusive. In addition to being autonomous provinces of expression, they mark "stages on life's road."

With the mythic world picture, we find ourselves at the starting point of the road. Owing to the operation of the principle of "concrescence," meaning exists here only as materialized, fettered to a sensuous substratum. At a point farthest removed from myth, knowledge is located, the road's terminus. Here

[23] *PSF*, I, 137f.

spiritualization has reached its consummation; and the philosophy of symbolic forms, itself a type of knowledge, endeavors to give adequate expression to this crowning achievement. With its emphasis on the creative deed of the intellect in "positing" its objects, and with its fight against the "copy theory" of knowledge, it claims for the spirit its finally accomplished freedom. Recognizing itself in its works, the mind has won the prize of its longest journey.

Two intermediate stages link beginning and end. They have not been given a full treatment by Cassirer. But the intimations of volume two, in the concluding section, entitled "The Dialectic of the Mythic Consciousness," are sufficiently revealing to help us round off our "dynamic chart" of the forms of culture. The life which animates the mythic consciousness tends to burst into a freedom beyond the world of myth. In religion this new freedom is attained. But, although shedding the materiality which the principle of concrescence imposes upon mythic consciousness, religion still cleaves to a sensuous substratum. Its spirituality, insisted upon by a trend towards mysticism, is counterbalanced by an equally vital attachment to the world of sacred imagery. This tension between disembodied spirituality and imaginative concreteness is set at rest, though not fully resolved, in another type of symbolic expression, in art. Through the work of art, meaning builds itself an appearance, filling it with expression to the brim without overflow and making it wholly alive. But at the same time, this appearance offers itself as nothing but an image, as "semblance." It renounces the claim to objective reality in the context of practical life.

Myth appears as a prelude followed by a triadic sequel: religion, art, knowledge. Unmistakably this is the rhythm of the "Absolute Spirit" according to Hegel.[24] At the same time, it becomes plain why the evolutionary impetus which sweeps through Hegel's philosophical vision must remain a subordinate and undeveloped feature with Cassirer—a "subdued dynamism," as we have called it. Given full scope, this dynamic element, a corrosive power, would wash away the foundations from under the Symbolic Forms.

[24] Cf. Hegel's *Encyclopädie*, §§553-577.

Cassirer's symbolic forms are primarily independent structures, viewed in juxtaposition, each animated by an immanent, unique "direction of creativity." Once we stress the dynamic feature, envisaging a succession of forms, this immanence, autonomy, and static self-sufficiency of the Form singly taken is called in question. Cassirer is well aware of this danger and warns us not to confuse his "three phases" with Auguste Comte's law of the *trois états*.[25] The latter schema, he writes, does not permit a purely immanent evaluation of the achievements of the mythic-religious consciousness. In fact, it is a perilous undertaking for Cassirer even to moot the problem of a dynamic self-transcendence of the Symbolic Forms. By doing so he himself encourages us to relinquish his principle of a "purely immanent evaluation" and thus brings down upon himself a host of disconcerting questions. How can the co-ordination of Form as equals be upheld in the face of the fact that one of them, knowledge, encompasses all the others? What of the truth which religion, or rather every particular religion, claims for itself? Does not transcendental analysis, although attributing to religion a certain meaningful structure, tacitly nullify this claim? Furthermore, is not the passage from myth to religion, and perhaps also from religion to science, or from a primitive to a pure religion, a progress from the misery of error and superstition to wisdom and to the felicity, precarious and yet real, of a civilized life? And would not progress, so understood, be a greater thing than what it appears in Cassirer? Not a tenuous dialectic which wafts the spirit from one insular Form to another, but man's Promethean deed which made him human— culture in the full sense of the word?

In these questions we readily recognize the voice of the importune questioner who, at the beginning of our analysis, came out with his naïve query concerning culture only to find Cassirer's philosophy unresponsive. An explanation of this unresponsiveness is now at hand.

The field within which the dynamic interrelatedness of the Symbolic Forms unfolds, the dimension, we might say, of their orderly combination into a comprehensive pattern of co-opera-

[25] *PSF*, II, 291.

tion—this field is the mind of the concrete individual, living his own life and participating, at the same time, in the life of a civilization. On him, poor wretch, is incumbent the choice between good and evil. For him, happy man, for his enjoyment, the works of civilization are produced. He will not be content with learning that the story of Faust, as a myth, exhibits certain features typical of "mythic thought." He is interested in knowing whether, perchance, it prefigures a truth. That religion wavers between mystic spirituality and imaginative concreteness will be, for him, only a preliminary statement leading up to more relevant problems such as: Is the idea of "original sin" as taught by one particular religion, Christianity, in conformity with what we know about human life? It is he, the concrete living individual, who asks all the importune questions. It is he, also, for whose enlightenment and betterment Socrates, Plato, and Aristotle labored, and following them, the philosophers of the Middle Ages and the Modern Era, including, of course, Kant. But never and under no circumstances is he admitted to the precincts of neo-Kantian thought. Where is, we wonder, a place for ethics and political philosophy in the frame-work of the Symbolic Forms? For Cassirer, life comes into view only as *vita acta*, "life that was lived," never as *vita agenda*, "life as it is to be lived." This accounts for the calm perfection of his thought, and also for its ineluctable limitations. He is not in the mêlée, forever breathing the cool air of contemplative detachment. But how such serenity is achieved his philosophy does not tell.

For once, Cassirer sounds a sombre note. At the conclusion of his analysis of the logic of *Geisteswissenschaft* a thoughtful chapter is devoted to the "Tragedy of Culture." We are invited to survey the vast panorama as disclosed by "critical philosophy." With one glance we embrace the Symbolic Forms, a solemn array of structures which outline the timeless possibilities of the creative mind. Their rigid architecture rises above an element of infinite mobility, a whirl of incessant change: the temporal flux of life. At brief creative moments this flux is arrested. It crystallizes into shapes that temporarily fill the vessels of timeless possibility with the actuality of life: languages become articulate, religions seek and find credence, works of art spread delight, philosophies express truth. But life is alternation of building up and breaking down. Man's creations, the works of culture, bask for awhile in the broad daylight of history only to return whence they came. Such is "the tragedy of culture," according to Cassirer.

Is this transience truly tragic, the reader asks. Surely, it lies in the nature of things, and it leaves intact the grandiose perdurance of the Symbolic Forms. The philosophical complaint on mortality recalls a well-known earlier treatment of the theme:

> "Mark ye the leaves, for men are like thereto.
> When leaves by winds into the dust are whirled
> Soon the green forest buddeth millions new,
> And lo, the beauty of Spring is on the World.
> So come, so pass, all that are born of Man."
>
> *(Iliad,* vi, 146-149 tr. Gilbert Murray)

Again we ask why the transitoriness of man should be a subject for mourning. The forest endures, and so does mankind, and both forest and mankind can live only through suffering numberless deaths.

The answer to our query will be the same, or nearly the same, in both cases. For the Ionian poet, singing at the dawn of Hellenic culture, the passing of generations is tragic, because in him the self-conscious individual with his thirst for eternity just awakens. For the twentieth century scholar, the timeless validity of symbolic structures is not enough to forestall tragedy, because the old imperious desire for "world without end" is not entirely put to sleep. The individual is not wholly banished. His ghostlike presence suffuses the great unconcern of the philosophy of Symbolic Forms with an elegiac mood.

HELMUT KUHN

DEPARTMENT OF PHILOSOPHY
EMORY UNIVERSITY

16

David Baumgardt

CASSIRER AND THE CHAOS IN MODERN ETHICS

CASSIRER AND THE CHAOS IN MODERN ETHICS

THERE is, in Ernst Cassirer's vast work, one example above all of penetrating analysis, dealing with the chaos of contemporary ethical thought and indicating a way out of its Babel of confusion. It is a pregnant chapter in Cassirer's *Axel Hägerström*, 1939. This work, analyzing the philosophy of a Swedish thinker, seems hardly the place in which to find a masterpiece of contemporary ethical research. But the fact that Professor Cassirer chose just this inconspicuous place for his main contribution to ethics shows, I think, the degree of his affection for that nation which offered him a real home at the time of a gigantic homelessness of the spirit. In *Axel Hägerström*, and in widely scattered reflections in his other writings, Cassirer's own ethical views evolve out of brief examinations of a considerable number of contemporary theories: ethical neo-intuitionism and the ethics of absolute values, as well as ethical relativism and utilitarianism.

I. THE PLURALISTIC ETHICS OF ENGLISH NEO-DEONTOLOGISM

Although Sir W. D. Ross is fond of appealing to the authority of Kant's concept of moral duty, Cassirer, who set out from Kant, has in his ethics very little, almost nothing in common with Sir David's neo-deontologism. Professor Prichard, Professors Broad and Ross obviously think that their ethical teachings on *prima facie* duties, on "imperatives . . . which are here and now categorical,"[1] and on particular self-evident moral "obligations"[2] are still somehow in line with the Kantian ethics of duty. All these moralists believe that they remain in far-reaching agreement with Kant despite their "pluralistic" tendencies, i.e.,

[1] C. D. Broad: *Five Types of Ethical Theory*, (1930), 123.
[2] See H. A. Prichard, "Does Moral Philosophy Rest on a Mistake?," *Mind*, January (1912), New Series, vol. XXI, 36f.

despite their supposition of a multitude of genuine *a priori* duties. Professor Broad, in his defense of a definite pluralism of ethical principles, even went so far as to maintain that Kant himself presupposed "imperatives which are here and now categorical for certain persons;" and that, with this Kantian thesis, justice is done to "an important psychological fact which moralists like Spinoza and Hume tend to ignore." In contrast to this pseudo-Kantian pluralism, Professor Cassirer is doubtless correct when he emphasizes that, in Kant at least, "categorical" has the meaning of *universal validity*, and that for Kant the uniqueness and universal validity of his ethical axiom are at least as essential as, if not more essential than, its imperative character.[3]

Kant frequently expressed the meaning of his categorical imperative in non-imperative terms, and without explicit reference to the concept of duty, but he never agreed to a plurality of categorical imperatives. All the duties of which he speaks in his *Metaphysik der Sitten* are applications of one categorical imperative. Any supposition of a multiplicity of ethical axioms would destroy the whole epistemological basis of Kant's ethics. Such a supposition is incompatible, not only with the letter of what Kant wrote, but also with the spirit of all that Kant's "Typik der pracktischen Vernunft" and his numerous discussions of moral casuistry stand for. Henry Sidgwick, Alexander Bain, and other English or German Kant interpreters of the 19th century were certainly right when they denied that there is any pluralism in Kant's doctrine of duties. Kant's aim was "to show that they (the duties) may be all deduced from the single imperative."[4] His intention was "to deduce a complete code of duty from a purely formal principle."[5]

[3] See e.g. E. Cassirer, *Axel Hägerström* (Göteborgs Hogskolas Arsskrift XLV), (1939), 79.
[4] Alexander Bain, *Mental and Moral Science* (1868), 731.
[5] See H. Sidgwick, *The Methods of Ethics* (1884), 207. Note discussion in Thomas K. Abbott's *Critique of Practical Reason and other Works on the Theory of Ethics*, Memoir of Kant p. li. Cf. H. Sidgwick, *The Methods of Ethics*, (1901), 209. I have dealt with these questions in detail in my book, *Der Kampf um den Lebenssinn unter den Vorläufern der modernen Ethik*, (1933), and shall, therefore, not repeat myself here.

But no matter whether contemporary English moralists do or do not have truly Kantian tendencies, the main question is: do their pluralistic theses deserve any preference to a "one-principle ethics,"—the Kantian or any other? Out of the extreme complexities involved in this question, I should like to take up only a few points for summary discussion.

Cassirer agrees with Kant that, in the theory of nature as well as in ethics, the "demand for greatest unity" must be placed constantly in the center of philosophical reflection.[6] Contemporary ethics, however, is generally pluralistic, and this for a number of complex reasons. But there seems little doubt that one of the main reasons is the fear of oversimplification so frequently expressed by modern moralists and their disdain for the "sweet simplicity" of utilitarians who perhaps represent the most marked type of a one-principle ethics. In the eyes of the best known contemporary English ethicists, it obviously would be an oversimplification to presuppose the universal validity of a single ethical principle. To believe in the validity of several moral axioms or *prima facie* duties seems to be much more *"gegenstandsnah;"* it seems to do far more justice to concrete ethical situations. Is this implicit methodological consideration justifiable?

I think not, for at least three reasons. First, it is by no means self-evident that in ethical reasoning, as in simple induction, the way leads from evident *particularia* to less evident *generalia*. If, on the contrary, as Professors Prichard and Ross assure us, we have immediate insight into the validity of concrete moral obligations comparable with the insight into mathematical truth, then we have every reason to assume that, as in mathematics, the general axiom is less complex and more immediately given than any concrete, particular mathematical relation. If ethical insight is, in fact, of the same structure as mathematical, then here too the principle applies that *totum est ante partes*.

Secondly, even if the methodological procedure in ethics were not merely deductive, a mere analogy to mathematical reasoning, even if it were, as in natural science, a complicated combina-

[6] E. Cassirer, *Axel Hägerström*, (1939), 79.

tion of deduction and induction, even then—as in meteorology —the general principles may be well established and ascertained, although their application to concrete cases may be extremely complex and, in many circumstances, actually impossible. If this be the case, then again, as under the first mentioned supposition, it would be a gross oversimplification to begin with seemingly evident particulars instead of general principles or hypotheses. Although this may appear paradoxical to common sense, in a science of ethics, as well as in mathematics or physics, the validity of general principles may be much more elementary and more easily ascertainable than the validity of particular concrete rules.

Thirdly, the concrete duties which Sir David considers *a priori* obligatory, such as keeping a promise, telling the truth and giving aid to victims of accidents, are by no means obligatory as such, as concrete duties. Contrary to his presuppositions, the moral validity and obligatory character of these duties are highly controversial. In a consistent morality of power, the very same duties are not binding either as *prima facie* duties or in any other way. The moral validity of these *particular* obligations can be assured only after the general validity of a morality of altruism, a Jewish, Christian, Buddhist ethics, or something similar, has already been accepted; and this is by no means a matter of course in any critical ethics.

Sir David thinks it essential to deal with the questions of the "good" and the "right" separately, and to avoid in this way a great amount of entanglement in ethics. For the same reason Professor Broad breaks up his analysis into even more elements when he discusses the intuitively given essence of the "useful" and the "fitting" of every phase of any act. Only in this way, he states, can decision about the morally right act be composed, namely, through moral decisions on many more elementary points. "The rightness or wrongness of an action in a given . . . situation is a function of its fittingness in that situation and its utility in that situation;" we have to estimate "total rightness from total fittingness and total utility."[7] It probably did not occur to either of these subtle thinkers that, although abhorring

[7] C. D. Broad, *op. cit.*, 221f.

oversimplification at the end of the inquiry, one may nevertheless fall into it at the very start. As I have tried to hint, I think
that such seemingly simple questions as "is keeping a promise a
prima facie duty?" or even "is this phase of this action morally
fit?" contain highly complex ethical problems and by no means
the most elementary ones.

Only in an early stage of the development of physics could it
have been considered self-evident that the fall of a particular
body in a definite time was a less complex phenomenon than the
general laws of equally accelerated movement and of friction, or
than the most general law of the verification of scientific statements by sense data. Why epistemological conditions in ethics
should be the opposite of those in science has never been explained or justified by contemporary English ethics and I do
not think that it can ever be justified.

Of course, it must be admitted that, psychologically speaking,
the genius of Galileo was able to decipher the meaning of one
particular observation in such a way that he intuitively read out
of it the general law of the free fall of bodies, and even the
univeral law of the necessity of verifying all hypothetical laws
in physics by minute observation. Any modern physicist is now
able to interpret any particular phenomenon of a free fall, so
to speak, intuitively by immediate insight. In the same way the
moral genius and, after a long period of conscious or unconscious
training, the plain man may be able to make decisions on highly
complex and particular moral rules instantly, by immediate
ethical insight, without even being aware of underlying general
principles.

Epistemologically speaking, however, an insight into the essence of the universal law of verification, or even an insight into
the law of free fall, can never be won by a merely inductive
piling up of particular observations or particular rules. On the
contrary, from the epistemological standpoint any adequate interpretation of particular cases of free fall must be preceded by
the adoption of the universal law of verification of scientific
statements, and by the hypothesis that the free fall of bodies is a
case of equally accelerated movement. If the validity of such

general laws is not acknowledged first, there would be no reason to prefer the Galilean analysis of free fall to Franz Baader's mythological interpretation, or to Hegel's metaphysical, dialectical explanation.

Seen from the psychological point of view, particular *prima facie* duties may appear to represent elementary moral issues, whereas general moral laws, or one universal law, may seem to involve far more complex and perhaps insoluble or unnecessary complex difficulties. But, if the problem is viewed epistemologically, certain general laws or one universal principle must form the indispensable precondition of the validity of any particular moral rules or duties. To replace the epistemological point of view by the psychological would be what I should like to call a "psychologistic fallacy." It does not seem to me entirely impossible that this kind of confusion or fallacy may have played some part in the foundations of Sir David's and Professor Broad's ethical reasoning, despite the admirable acuteness of the superstructure of their work. In any case, Cassirer's ethics has kept itself free from the psychologistic fallacy and free, also, from the other uncritical presuppositions just mentioned.

II. The Ethics of Non-Natural Intrinsic Goodness and of Absolute Values

Professor G. E. Moore's ethical analyses concentrate mainly on the concept of "good," though he grants, in his "Reply to my Critics" in 1942, that the following not very lucid relation exists between the concept of good and that of duty:

To say of anything, A, that it is "intrinsically" good is equivalent to saying that, if any agent were a Creator before the existence of any world, whose power was so limited that the only alternatives in his power were those of (1) creating a world which consisted solely of A or (2) causing it to be the case that there should never be *any world at all*, then, if he knew for certain that this was the only choice open to him and knew exactly what A would be like, it would be his duty to choose alternative (1), provided only he was not convinced that it would be *wrong* for him to choose that alternative.[8]

[8] "The Library of Living Philosophers," vol. IV: *The Philosophy of G. E. Moore*, ed. by P. A. Schilpp (1942), 600.

From this statement one might infer first that it seems hardly possible to break through all the reservations enumerated in this one sentence. On second thought, however, from this and other statements of Professor Moore's one might draw at least the inference that his ethics more than that of English neo-deontologists is on the whole in favor of one unifying principle—the principle of the good which does not seem to be in need of supplementary principles of the morally right or morally fit, of prima facie duties and of utility. In truth, however, he is in other respects probably no less of an ethical "pluralist" than the Provost of Oriel and Professor Broad.

If I understand Professor Moore aright, his opinion is that there are a multitude of ethical goods, as there are a multitude of yellows or reds. But there is no universal principle which determines what is morally good; "good" is indefinable and ultimately independent of anything else existing or given by experience. The main thesis of this ethics is, obviously, that a large plurality of morally good things or motives or acts do exist, each case being isolated and independent of the others, good by itself. If this thesis were correct, then, as Professor Moore and the neo-deontologists imply, it would of course be superfluous to carry on the age-old attempts to determine what may be good by some general elementary criterion. Moreover, these attempts would be not only useless but misleading and futile, as misleading and futile as are all efforts to determine or to define the nature of a concrete sense-datum. One may be able to speak of relations existing between different data of the senses; and one is able, according to Professor Moore, to speak of a very complicated relation existing between "good" and duty. But in neither case can a general principle determine the nature of good or of a sense datum; and no critical justification of the validity of our propositions on "good" is thought to be possible or needed. For what "good" is, no less than what is a sense datum, is believed to be known already by an unfailing insight of common sense; and therefore, to Professor Moore, ethics does not seem to demand any general principle for a critical distinction between morality and immorality.

I wish to hint at least at a few reasons why, in my view,

Professor Moore's analyses lead to such embarrassing problems that perhaps, as he says himself, he has "not gone about the business of trying to solve them in the right way." Moore himself admits that "it is a just charge against me that I have been able to solve so few of the problems I wished to solve;" and I see no reason why one should take this statement as a mere flourish of modesty or irony in a thinker who often shows most definite self-assuredness. But, if Professor Moore's self-criticism is not without foundation, his failure to answer fundamental questions in ethics satisfactorily is certainly not due, as he adds, "partly [to a] sheer lack of ability."[9] There is no doubt of the subtlety of Professor Moore's ethical analyses, i.e., of all the superstructures which he built up on his common-sense ethical beliefs; but the basis of these superstructures, which seems to him so undoubtedly firm, "realistic," and unassailable in its common-sense quality, seems to me amazingly weak.

(a) Intrinsic Goodness and Values in Themselves

In Professor Moore's ethics, and similarly in modern ethics of values in general, the following concepts are basic: intrinsic, non-natural goodness; intrinsic value; things good by themselves and existing by themselves "in absolute isolation."[10] In about the same sense moral values are self-evident in Max Scheler's, Nicolai Hartmann's,[11] or Wilbur M. Urban's ethics of values. Everywhere in these ethical systems the morally good and all values are values, not in consequence of any "external" relations to other things or experiences or principles, but only on the ground of their "intrinsic nature."

Professor H. J. Paton protested, in "The Library of Living

[9] *The Philosophy of G. E. Moore*, ed. by Paul A. Schilpp (1942), 677.

[10] See G. E. Moore, *Principia Ethica* (1903), 37, 6ff, 21, 110f; *Philosophical Studies* (1922), chapters VIII, X; *Principia Ethica*, 187, 184, 27ff, 95; chapter VI; *Ethics* (1912) chap. VII; cf. William K. Frankena in *The Philosophy of G. E. Moore* (1942), 93f.

[11] For a more detailed criticism of Max Scheler's and Nicolai Hartmann's ethics of values see my essay on "Some Merits and Defects of Contemporary German Ethics" in *Philosophy* (The Journal of the British Institute of Philosophy), (1938), 183ff.

Philosophers," against this alleged independence of goodness. He pointed out that, to say the least, "the goodness of a thing . . . must stand in some necessary relation to a rational will . . . and . . . may vary in different circumstances."[12] In his reply to this, Professor Moore admitted only "that the existence of some *experience* is a proposition which does follow from the hypothesis that there exists a state of affairs which is good;" but, as he adds, "I cannot see" that logically the hypothesis of the existence of a good state of affairs "entails any proposition to the effect that a *mental disposition*" such as rational will exists.[13] Certainly this is absolutely correct according to the principles of formal logic. Unless it is granted first by explicit definition or implicitly by experience that scarlet is a particular shade of red, I cannot conclude from the concept of scarlet that it includes the concept of red.

But the question at issue, the particular question which Professor Paton obviously has in mind, is not this problem of drawing a merely logical inference. It is the epistemological question of whether, in the world of reality, it is possible to think of goodness without any relation to rational will. This question has not been answered by Professor Moore.

The question is not how to define moral goodness. The question is whether the meaning of moral goodness in reality can be clarified without taking into account the concept of rational will—a concept which, it is true, from the merely logical point of view or from the standpoint of linguistics is not connected with the concept of goodness. That is, to approach this controversial point from a slightly different angle, can the meaning of moral goodness be clarified without taking into account more than particular, isolated states of affairs of goodness? Are not some general principles, or is not one universal, unifying rational principle needed for determining rationally whether certain states of affairs can rightly be called good, or whether certain concepts, such as honor or love, really deserve to be called values? Has any isolated particular state of affairs

[12] *The Philosophy of G. E. Moore*, 113.
[13] *Ibid.*, 618.

"by itself" the "intrinsic nature" to be good without being related to anything "outside" itself?

Cassirer answers this question in the following way: It "is and remains . . . in any case a questionable metaphor . . . to speak of 'values-in-themselves';" every ethical "evaluation" includes "a form of retrospect, of preview, and of survey, which is lacking in feelings; since these [latter are] merely given phenomena."[14] As we may add, in the spirit of Cassirer's whole neo-Kantian outlook, this kind of preview, retrospect and survey is a necessary precondition of true statements in all knowledge of nature as well as in morals. That there is any truth or moral validity built up dogmatically on the perception or the analysis of a particular state of affairs, isolated from all others—may be a seemingly plausible common-sense view; but it is by no means self-evident and is scientifically untenable.

To Professor Moore this "method . . . of isolation" is "the only safe" one.[15] Even his "organic unities" are unities separate from each other; and no conclusion has for him "any weight whatever failing a careful examination of the (separate) instances which have led" him "to form it."[16] But this method of generalization—a generalization by mere induction of separate instances is certainly not the method of exact science, and, above all, it seems to me by no means "the only safe" method in ethics.

Professor Moore is absolutely right in saying that "to search for 'unity' and 'system,' at the expense of truth, is not, I take it, the proper business of philosophy, however universally it may have been the practice of philosophers."[17] Certainly it is entirely unphilosophical, if unity and system are sought at the expense of truth. But does this statement exclude in any way the possibility that the concept of truth itself is closely tied up with the "right kind" of unity and system? Contrary to Professor Moore's and Ross' presuppositions, might it not be im-

---

[14] E. Cassirer, *Axel Hägerström* (1939), 65.
[15] G. E. Moore, *Principia Ethica.* (1903), 94; cf. 91.
[16] *Ibid.*, 223.
[17] *Ibid.*, 222.

possible to arrive at any worth-while truth by analyzing only isolated phenomena, even if they are analyzed with the greatest acumen?

A similar question has been raised by Professor Paton in the following piece of analysis: "When Sir Philip Sidney in dying resigned to a wounded soldier the cup of water which had been offered him, I take it that his action was a good action and that its goodness depended partly on the circumstances;" if, however, one would "evaluate in isolation, not the action in itself, but the action in the relevant circumstances together with its motive and intention," then "the main contention would . . . be reduced to the view that the goodness of an action is independent of the circumstances irrelevant to its goodness—which is a mere tautology."[18] To this argument Professor Moore simply replies that "these 'when-clauses' " in Professor Paton's example do not express external "*circumstances* under which the choice we admire was made: they form part of the description of the *intrinsic nature* of that choice," which is morally good; these so-called circumstances are "an essential part"[19] of Sidney's good action; they belong to its intrinsic nature.

Again, this method of "solving" problems is certainly correct from the point of view of formal logic. But how similar is this manner of overcoming philosophical difficulties to that of Molière's "Le malade imaginaire"! In Molière, too, certain "external" relations are "explained" by elevating them to the rank of "intrinsic" ones. Here, too, the external causal connection between poppy and its making people sleep is explained by taking this causal relation as an "intrinsic" attribute, as a part of the "essence" of poppy, by bringing that causal relation into the "intrinsic nature" of poppy and calling it the "essential" dormitive power of the plant.

Apart from this reminder, I should say that, even if all these circumstances mentioned by Professors Paton and Moore are interpreted as forming the intrinsic nature of Sidney's good action, I fail to see why a choice of exactly this intrinsic nature

[18] *The Philosophy of G. E. Moore*, 126.
[19] *Ibid.*, 619.

is morally good on the ground of self-evidence, as is evidently implied in Professor Moore's argument.

My trouble—and obviously the trouble of only too many contemporaries—is that questions of just this type, questions of why Sidney's action is good, occupy my mind even more than the logical subtleties of Moore's ethics. And while I try to follow his minute, logical, step-by-step procedure, which often admittedly leads to nothing, I am afraid that I cannot follow him when he suddenly indulges in sweeping assertions which concern not merely logical problems but questions of obvious psychological and ethical importance, e.g., whether Sidney's choice is intrinsically good, and as such needs no further qualification or justification; or when Professor Moore states that "Americans are more generally and markedly friendly" than the English,[20] it seems to me that not only Lord Baldwin, who called the English the most friendly people on earth, but also many Americans may feel some hesitancy on this point; nor can one, I think, accept the similarly bold statement of Professor L. S. Stebbing, that "anyone who has been able to learn something of Moore's way of thinking . . . could not . . . succumb to the muddle-headed creed of Fascism or National-Socialism."[21] There is no doubt that it should be one of the primary aims of any ethical teaching to protect us from succumbing to any kind of Machiavellianism. But I fear that hardly any ethical doctrine developed so far has succeeded in reaching this high aim.

To return to Sidney's action: in order to show why his choosing is morally good it seems to me indispensable to show, first, why the general principle of altruism or any kind of altruism is moral, and to clear up numerous other preliminary questions which present the most fundamental ethical difficulties. If for the sake of argument one granted all the presuppositions of Professor Moore, the "when-clauses" which he thinks essential for the intrinsic goodness of Philip Sidney's choice would by no means be sufficient. Contrary to Professor

[20] *Ibid.*, 39.
[21] *Ibid.*, 532.

Moore's assumption, far more would be needed as an essential part of the good choice than that "the cup should be given to another man, when he (Sidney) himself was in pain and thirsty and knew that the other man was in pain and thirsty."[22] It would be essential, also, that the dying man who refused the cup of water was not, for example, an ancient Egyptian. For if he were, his refusal of the cup would have implied a lack of faith in the doctrine of immortality. He would have been guilty of an act of impiety. He would have shown by his choice that, contrary to the rules of Egyptian piety, he obviously thought he would be able to go on after death without food and drink. Or, if the wounded soldier to whom the cup of water was later offered had shared the not-uncommon superstition that to take away food and drink from a dying man brings misfortune upon you, or if the dying man himself had shared the same superstition, would the choice of the dying man still have been morally good, even if one grants additionally that altruism is always good? It seems to me that, if one adopts Professor Moore's teaching about assimilating "when-clauses" to the intrinsic nature of a moral choice, the "when-clauses" would have to be extended so far that the "isolation" of the intrinsic nature of any moral choice would grow utterly hopeless.

(b) Is Moral Goodness a Non-Natural Property or Has It Only an Emotive Meaning?

The most outstanding and most influential contribution which Professor Moore has made to the development of modern ethics is in all probability this: he insisted, in his *Principia Ethica*, on denying that "morally good" is a natural intrinsic property or characteristic. To speak of good as if it were a natural property of things or acts or motives would be what Professor Moore termed, in 1903, a "naturalistic fallacy;" and it was certainly most illuminating when he unearthed this naturalistic fallacy in some well-known ethical theories. This was a vigorous, lucid application of an old truth in a new and striking formulation.

[22] *Ibid.*, 619.

The "idealistic" moralist, who does not share uncritically every "realistic" common-sense opinion, should not find it too difficult to adhere to a clear-cut distinction between natural and non-natural characteristics. Such moralists (including a really consistent utilitarian) can explain the difference in question in about the following way: natural properties are those which are given us immediately in our various experiences such as sweetness, hardness, redness, and even pleasantness. Non-natural properties such as "true" or "good" concern properties of judgments built up on the comparing and ordering of immediately given data of experience. Professor Moore has never accepted any definition along these lines, probably because it would not conform to the principle of his "common-sense" reasoning.

In his essay of 1932 "Is Goodness a Quality?" he states that ethical good means "an experience which is worth having for its own sake."[23] This is a view which obviously fits the "isolationist," "pluralistic," "common-sense" tendencies which he has always maintained, despite his principle of "organic wholes." It fits these trends far better than does any such "idealistic" explanation as that morally good is not an immediately given quality at all, but a quality bound up with judgments which, at least, try to "unify" experiences universally.

In his "Reply to My Critics," however, in 1942, even his own view of 1932 is evidently no longer "realistic" enough for Professor Moore. He now explicitly rejects the explanation of good he had given in 1932 and suggests, instead of this, the following explanation of non-natural properties, such as good, in general:

Properties which are intrinsic properties, but *not* natural ones, are distinguished from natural intrinsic properties, by the fact that, in ascribing a property of the former kind to a thing, you are not describing it *at all*, whereas, in ascribing a property of the latter kind to a thing, you are always describing it *to some extent*.[24]

[23] *Proceedings of the Aristotelian Society*, Supplementary Volume XI, (1932), 121ff.
[24] *Ibid.*, 591. See also 555.

Concerning this account of the cardinal distinction between natural and non-natural properties Professor Moore himself says that it is "certainly" a "vague and not clear . . . account."[25] This is, as Professor Moore states himself with regard to a similar thesis of his, "at least an honest statement."[26]

Yet it is certainly most discouraging to see that an ethics which set out only to "clarify" problems leads finally to explanations which are admittedly "vague and not clear." One may readily grant Professor Moore's main contention, that what we need first (and obviously, in his view, what is often our only need) is not to solve problems but to clarify their meaning. If, however, these strenuous efforts at clarification end in a definite lack of clearness even on a most fundamental point, one may perhaps be allowed to make use of Professor Moore's most radical prescript in philosophy. *I.e.*, one may ask whether the question itself which he seeks to clarify is not a confused question, which stands in need neither of clarification nor of solution, but of dissolution.

In other words, to ask how to distinguish natural from non-natural properties on the ground of a realistic common-sense philosophy is to ask a question which can be asked only on the ground of an illusion—Moore's fundamental illusion—that, despite all differences between non-natural and natural properties, the non-natural properties "exist" on the same level and show the same character of "givenness" as the natural ones given by sense data. Without going into any critical analysis of Professor Moore's ethics, or of any other ethics of values, Professor Cassirer has briefly, and I think rightly, stated that non-natural ethical characteristics are not to be found on the same plane of "existence" or "givenness" as natural properties, and are, therefore, not comparable to each other on the same plane. "The question concerning the possibility of an 'objective' morality can, consequently, not be whether in this field, qualities in themselves correspond to our judgments—qualities which are comparable to physical qualities theoretically statable."[27] "The

[25] *Ibid.*, 591.
[26] *Ibid.*, 545.
[27] E. Cassirer, *Axel Hägerström*, 74.

question ... is ... not ..., whether there are any empirical things or thing-qualities, which correspond to our value-judgments."[28]

There is, however, one way left open by Professor Moore to avoid the fatal conclusions which can be drawn from his "vague and not clear" accounts of non-natural properties such as the morally good. It is, of course, possible to doubt that there are such properties at all. In another statement, which Professor Moore characterizes explicitly as "at least honest," he makes a definite concession to this effect. He asserts:

I must say again that I am inclined to think that "right" in all ethical uses, and, of course, "wrong," "ought," "duty" also, are, in this more radical sense, not the names of characteristics at all, that they have merely "emotive meaning" and no "cognitive meaning" at all: and, if this is true of them, it must also be true of "good," in the sense I have been most concerned with. I am *inclined* to think that this is so, but I am also inclined to think that it is not so; and I do not know which way I am inclined most strongly. If these words, in their ethical uses, have only emotive meaning, . . . then it would seem that all else I am going to say about them must be either nonsense or false (I don't know which).[29]

As we have seen, if right and good have cognitive and no merely emotive meaning, then they are, according to Professor Moore, of necessity non-natural properties. However, the best account which Professor Moore can give of these non-natural characteristics must, in his own words, remain vague and not clear. Therefore, it may seem preferable to consider morally good and morally right as being without cognitive meaning and as not being "the names of characteristics at all."

But if we follow this second suggestion left open by Professor Moore, the consequences are in my view no less unattractive. First, if this suggestion is accepted—if morally good, morally right, morally wrong, and moral duties have no cognitive but merely emotive, meaning—then again, in Professor Moore's own words, "all else I am going to say about them

[28] *Ibid.*, 72.
[29] *The Philosophy of G. E. Moore*, 554, 545.

must be either nonsense or false (I don't know which)." In truth, then, the whole basis on which Professor Moore's past and present ethical reasoning rests is cut away from under his feet. Second, if one should nevertheless say in favor of Professor Moore's whole argument that it is, after all, instructive, close reasoning, though proceeding under the mistaken supposition that good has a cognitive meaning, then in any case the titles of his main works are completely misleading. His first book *Principia Ethica*, his *Ethics* and his essay on "Ethics" in 1942 are, then, by no means treatises on ethics. They are not even preliminary remarks to prolegomena toward an introduction to *Principia Ethica*. They are complicated scholastic exercises in logic, built up on an untenable basis, and fail to represent themselves clearly as such.

As Moore reports in his autobiography, Henry Sidgwick once called McTaggart's dissertation, and probably also that of Professor Moore himself "nonsense of the right kind."[30] I am afraid that what Professor Moore wrote on ethics after his dissertation may perhaps be termed, not quite inaptly, "best common-sense of the wrong kind." To use once more one of Professor Moore's own witty remarks about a fellow moralist, throughout his ethical work he hits the nail on the head, but unfortunately not "the right nail."[31] We witness in his ethics the grandiose spectacle of a mighty air armada of arguments successfully destroying a few mosquitoes by blockbusters, but leaving untouched the real targets of the enemy.

III. ETHICAL RELATIVISM AND ETHICAL RELATIVITY

That morally good and right have merely emotive meaning is a thesis generally advanced by ethical relativism, by the anthropological school in ethics, or in our days by logical positivism in so far as logical positivism takes any interest in morals. As do most of the representatives of the modern ethics of values, Professor Moore denied in his two main works, *Principia Ethica*

[30] *The Philosophy of G. E. Moore*, 21.
[31] *Ibid.*, 546.

and *Ethics,* that morally good has a merely emotive meaning. He insisted that "this choosing is morally good" does not mean that I or someone else emotionally approve of it. It means that this choosing is good, independent of anyone's emotive approval. Later, in his "Reply to my Critics" in 1942, Professor Moore admitted that morally good may have merely emotive meaning; and I should prefer this later attitude to the almost complete ignoring by modern neo-deontologism of the mighty problems of ethical relativity.

In 1939, on the eve of world war II, just after the spokesman of the most powerful state of that time had declared the morality of Berlin and of London to have nothing in common, neo-deontologism comforted itself with the "time-honoured" belief that there is, in morals, a *consensus omnium* or at least an agreement between all those men whom neo-deontologism would call "wise." The "common knowledge," the "common opinions," about morality and the ethical judgment of wise men were believed to be in perfect harmony, and all the clashing differences in the moral outlook of hostile economic classes and political ideologies were calmly said to be only the result of "different perspectives" in facing the same truth.[32] Even in the eighteenth century it was somewhat out of date, among the leading moralists, to use that "time-honoured" belief as the basis of ethical inquiry. Even Kant, who shared that belief, did not regard its dogmatism as the proper basis of a critical ethics.[33] But in the middle of the twentieth century it seems to me the height of—*wishful* thinking to disregard the arguments of Nietzsche, Marx, Freud, Durkheim and Lévy-Bruhl as irrelevant on the very first pages of a work entitled *Foundations of Ethics.*

Strangely enough, even the examples which these most skillful and experienced thinkers use to apply their teachings to life smack more of the atmosphere of the European and American classroom than of real life. They are, unfortunately, the mani-

[32] See W. D. Ross, *Foundations of Ethics* (1939), 1ff.

[33] See D. Baumgardt, *Der Kampf um den Lebenssinn unter den Vorläufern der modernen Ethik* (1933), I. Teil.

festation of a rather dubious and certainly unjustifiable pride in the "narrow" range of experience of a "don."[34] In contrast to the neo-deontologists, Professor G. E. Moore in some of his publications and Nicolai Hartmann in his ethics of 1935 tried to take into account the far-reaching relativity of moral valuations. But they do so only with much hesitation and reserve.

Professor Cassirer, despite his neo-Kantian extraction, takes fully into consideration the "widely called upon relativity of moral ideas."[35] He takes even the radical moral scepticism of Axel Hägerström most seriously and admits that it is critically superior to the naïve dogmatic belief in an ethical agreement between all plain men or all wise men. In agreement with modern comparative ethnology, Cassirer holds that there is a lively and far-reaching contrast between the moral ideas, the particular ethical rules and customs of different groups of men. Following Hägerström, he cites Herodotus' story about the moral horror with which the ancient Greeks regarded an Indian tribe which considered it their duty to eat the corpses of their fathers and the moral horror with which those Indians regarded the Greeks, who burnt such corpses.[36] Unlike most of the ethicists of the last three decades, Cassirer invokes Kant's partial praise of scepticism, and applies it not only to the field of theoretical, but also to that of "practical," philosophy. He quotes from the *Critique of Pure Reason* the following daring passage: "All sceptical polemic should properly be directed only against the dogmatist, who, without any misgivings as to his fundamental objective principles, that is, without criticism, proceeds complacently upon his adopted path; it should be designed simply to put him out of countenance and thus to bring him to self-knowledge."[37] In the greatest possible contrast

---

[34] See C. D. Broad's self-characterization in his *Five Types of Ethical Theory*, xxiv.

[35] See E. Cassirer, *Axel Hägerström*, e.g. 69.

[36] *Ibid.*, 67f.

[37] *Ibid.*, 63; the above given quotation is the Norman Kemp Smith translation of the passage, which, in the Original German of Kant's *Kritik der reinen Vernunft*, reads as follows: "Alles sceptische Polemisiren ist eigentlich nur wider den Dogmatiker gekehrt, der, ohne ein Misstrauen auf seine ursprünglichen objec-

to contemporary neo-intuitionism, Cassirer emphasizes that the days have definitely gone when the evidence of moral insight could be compared with mathematical evidence in the way that, up to the nineteenth century, scientists believed in simple, unproblematic, and immediate mathematical intuition. In the seventeenth century the rationalist Leibniz, and even the empiricist Locke, drew this parallel between ethical and mathematical science.[38] But, at least since the age of Hume and Kant, a critical ethics should not longer rely on such over-optimistic presuppositions.

There is hardly anywhere a more flagrant dissension than in the case of the so-called *prima facie* duties of men or of seemingly intrinsic values. This has led ethical relativism to the conclusion that, as Axel Hägerström puts it, "the word 'value' . . . is . . . only an expression for a feeling or a desire, not an expression of a thought."[39] Logical positivism, in one of the statements of Rudolf Carnap, has arrived at a similar conclusion, asserting that it is meaningless to speak of any possible philosophical ethics. At best there can be, according to Carnap, the possibility of a "psychological ethics."[40] Yet such a psychological ethics, of course, is no ethics at all. It would be nothing but psychology. For it would deal only with the psychological analysis of certain feelings which are wrongly thought to impart an alleged ethical insight. Of the logical positivists, it is probably Mr. Ayer who has formulated the ethical attitude of the group most bluntly: ethical concepts are, in his opinion, "mere pseudoconcepts."[41] "Sentences which simply express moral judgments

tiven Principien zu setzen, d.i., ohne Kritik gravitätisch seinen Gang fortsetzt, bloss um ihm das Concept zu verrücken und zur Selbsterkenntniss zu bringen." Kant, *Kritik der reinen Vernunft*, 2nd ed., (1787), 791; *Kants Gesammelte Schriften*, herausg. v.d. Königlich Preussischen Akademie der Wissenschaften, I. Abtheilung, Bd. III (1904), 498; N. Kemp Smith tr. (1929), 608f.
[38] E. Cassirer, *Axel Hägerström*, 63, 100.
[39] *Die Philosophie der Gegenwart in Selbstdarstellungen*, ed. by Raymund Schmidt, Band VII (1929), 44.
[40] R. Carnap, *Philosophy and Logical Syntax* (1935), 25.
[41] A. J. Ayer, *Language, Truth and Logic* (1936), 158; cf. 168, 170. Cf. Bertrand Russell, *Religion and Science* (1935), 24: "Since no way can be even

do not say anything . . . they are unverifiable for the same reason as a cry of pain or a word of command is unverifiable—because they do not express genuine propositions."[42] According to Mr. Ayer we may evince certain subjective feelings by making value judgments; but in doing so we do not say anything which can be subject to the criterion of objective truth.

Cassirer describes Hägerström's moral scepticism thus: The object of ethics has

no real but only a nominal existence. "Values," understood in an objective sense, are nothing else and can be nothing more than words. With this assertion there seems to be denied to all objective value-judgments not merely their strict validation and demonstrability, but also every graspable sense [and meaning]. If we continue to prefer any practical conduct to some other and to characterize it as "better," such judgments, according to Hägerström, lack every foundation.[43]

However, although Professor Cassirer wishes to do full justice to this and other types of ethical scepticism, he does not agree with them.

In his *In Quest of Morals* (1941), Henry Lanz has tried to show with special emphasis, why a moralist who fully acknowledges the relativity of factual moral valuations is by no means obliged to end in moral relativism or nihilism. There is no doubt that even the sense data experienced by different individuals may differ widely; but this fact in no way undermines the possibility of true judgments concerning the world "represented to us by our senses." Subjectivity and relativity of value experiences in no wise render impossible the objective validity of certain judgments concerning morality and immorality. On the contrary, "it is precisely relativity, defined as invariance in transformation, which renders moral standards objective."[44] Similarly, Cassirer stresses the point that "an ever so great difference of moral *percepts*, with which experience confronts us, . . . does

---

imagined for deciding a difference as to values, the conclusion is forced upon us that the difference is one of tastes, not one as to any objective truth."

[42] A. J. Ayer, *Language, Truth and Logic*, 161.
[43] E. Cassirer, *Axel Hägerström*, 64.
[44] H. Lanz, *In Quest of Morals* (1941), 159.

not necessarily lead to a divergence of the underlying concepts."[45] "The liberation from metaphysics in ethics need by no means sacrifice . . . the concept of 'objective mind' with that of 'absolute mind'."[46]

Modern science insists that there can be no truth about nature, no objective judgment on nature, which is not in one way or another ultimately verifiable by data of the senses. Nevertheless, science does not deny that "isolated" sense data are by no means "in themselves" of objective validity. They may differ radically and contradict each other with different individuals or with the same individual at different times; and many of these data of the senses are stripped of all immediate objective value, although they remain related to the same object. But there remains, unshaken by contradictory sense data related to the same object, an objective criterion of truth as to the knowledge of nature. This criterion enables us to determine which data of the senses fit a coherent, i.e., true, interpretation of nature and which are unfit for this purpose, although all common-sense evidence may speak in favor of the data unfit for immediate scientific use. In a similar way, the radical relativity of human valuations in no wise excludes the possibility of an objective criterion of morality. This criterion would enable us to determine what truly valuable, i.e., moral, conduct is, and would allow us to distinguish objectively between morally valueless and valuable behavior.

IV. UTILITARIANISM

Professor Cassirer has not so far outlined a positive theory of morals. He has limited his task to showing why it should not be impossible to build up an objective theory of ethics, even if the isolated moral ideas of different men seem to have only emotive meaning and are widely at variance.

Obviously he does not approve of utilitarianism; but he grants that utilitarianism does not teach ethical relativism and scepticism. Utilitarianism aspired, at least, to erect an objective

---

[45] E. Cassirer, *Axel Hägerström*, 67.
[46] See *ibid.*, 62.

theory of morals which is meant to overcome the mere relativism of moral judgment and the uncritical belief in the moral validity of particular values or duties. Consistent utilitarianism, such as that of Bentham, denies that we have any evidence of the intrinsic goodness of any particular isolated choice and any evidence of the obligatory character of particular duties. Nevertheless, utilitarianism suggests at least the "hypothetical" validity of a universal and objective moral principle which would enable us to make particular judgments of objective validity.

Utilitarianism affirms throughout the objectivity of moral ideas and judgments. It sets up a supreme goal: "the greatest possible happiness of the greatest possible number," and it utters its "yes" or "no" to the actions which advance or retard this goal. There reigns here, then, throughout a social *teleology*, which declares a certain condition of human society as valuable, whereas it rejects another. In a very acute fashion Hägerström proved, in his own research, that Marxism too, irrespective of its economic materialism and despite its loathing of all "ideology," contains such a teleology within itself and that, in this sense, Marxism contains a "morality" for which it claims objective validity.[47]

Professor Cassirer shares, with utilitarianism, the view that we are confronted with contradictory claims of particular moral views and can, nevertheless, maintain that universal objective validity of moral judgment is possible.

Both sides of this fundamental issue are stressed by critical utilitarianism and by Cassirer with equal emphasis.[48] In agreement with Bentham's utilitarianism Professor Cassirer does not even reject fanaticism offhand.

Fanaticism has not only at all times proved its power in the life of mankind, but it also has ever and again been represented and proclaimed as an ideal; and today it is actually being praised in many quarters as precisely "the" moral ideal as such. . . . For a purely descriptive

[47] E. Cassirer, *Axel Hägerström*, 73f.
[48] As to consistent utilitarianism, see especially Vol. II of my *Jeremy Bentham and the Ethics of Today*, which Princeton University Press will publish early in 1949.

ethics . . ., which wants to be nothing else and nothing more than a science of the factual moral evaluations in their historical status and growth . . . there would obviously exist no reason

for the rejection of fanaticism.[49] "If the . . . humanities and social sciences had to do only with feelings," with moral value feelings, with feelings of justice, with feelings of beauty, then "a logic of the humanities" would be . . . "nonsense."[50] "Anthropocentricity is even much more difficult to overcome in ethics than in the knowledge of nature."[51] But, like utilitarianism, Professor Cassirer proclaims the possibility of securing objective truth in morals as well as in natural science, despite the relativity of particular sense data and particular moral observations.

Again and again he points out that "in morals and in jurisprudence as in language there . . . reigns . . . a strange function of objectification."[52] "The copy-theory of concepts must be surrendered in favor of a purely functional theory."[53] "The direction towards something not given . . . cannot be described as a mere deception, as an empty fiction,"[54] which is as important to note in morals as in science. "The principal emphasis of the concept of objectivity lies . . . not on the . . . given as such, but on its coherence and consistent order."[55] "Conceiving the idea of systematic jurisprudence, the Romans carried through a great new synthesis, which in a certain sense is of value and significance equal to the Greek view of 'natural law,' as this latter developed from the time of Leucippus and Democritus on."[56] The task of "the psychology and sociology of law," of the psychology and sociology of morals, "could appear completed" when the factors are described which are operative in the formation of law and morals: "religious intuitions, the so-called 'judicial consciousness,' class-interests, the general tendency to

[49] E. Cassirer, *Axel Hägerström*, 81.
[50] *Ibid.*, 114.
[51] *Ibid.*, 78.
[52] *Ibid.*, 105f.
[53] *Ibid.*, 97f.
[54] *Ibid.*, 108.
[55] *Ibid.*, 72.
[56] *Ibid.*, 102.

yield to existing circumstances, the fear of anarchy, . . . but for a real 'philosophy' of culture the question . . . is not thus settled."[57] In morals and "in the philosophy of culture . . . metaphysics . . . must . . . in turn be succeeded by criticism . . .; but criticism need no more turn into scepticism, into doubt concerning the possibility of an objective foundation, in this area then it does in that of theoretical knowledge."[58] How this "objective foundation of ethics" is to be secured, Professor Cassirer has not as yet developed in detail.

Moreover, he seems not at all satisfied with the result of any attempt yet made in this direction. He goes so far as to say:

It is no secret that no other philosophical discipline is so far removed from the ideal of an honest-to-goodness scientific foundation as is [true of] ethics, and that superstition has as yet been no more extirpated from the philosophy of morals than from everyday morality. Coming centuries, when looking back upon many a moral doctrine which even today is being widely proclaimed as "wisdom's ultimate conclusion," may perhaps pass the judgment that such doctrines have exactly the same relation to genuine ethical knowledge which alchemy has to chemistry or astrology to scientific astronomy.[59]

I cannot conceal a cordial agreement even with this far-reaching criticism of highly reputed contemporary ethics and have tried to give some reasons for my agreement. Strange to say, quite independently of this remark by Professor Cassirer, I drew the same analogy between contemporary "time-honoured" methods of ethics and alchemy in a book not yet published, and I further compared the ethics of the "plain man," developed in contemporary neo-deontologism, not with astrology but with Ptolemaic astronomy as regards their methods.

On this point, however, I should add a few remarks concerning which I am not at all sure that Professor Cassirer will agree. I should compare the status of modern ethics with that of alchemy and Ptolemaic astronomy in another respect as well. As, up to the beginning of the nineteenth century, alchemy and

[57] *Ibid.*, 95f.
[58] *Ibid.*, 83.
[59] *Ibid.*, 63.

even Ptolemaic astronomy did not die out with the development of scientific chemistry and Copernican astronomy, so old scholastic "time-honoured" methods of ethics still survive the beginning of a science of ethics which I see developed in hundreds of painstaking and almost unknown arguments in Jeremy Bentham's writings and unpublished papers.

There is not the slightest doubt that we must reject the bulk of Bentham's psychological teaching, and any naïve hope of a concurrence between self-interest and the maximization of happiness—a hope which was J. S. Mill's far more than it was Bentham's. Bentham held extremely narrow views on metaphysics, religion, the arts, poetry, and the philosophy of history. All such narrow-mindedness definitely impairs, in my opinion, the importance of any ethicist. But, because of the critical subtlety of his ethical method, I think Bentham for many reasons superior to any modern moralist.

Of course, it must be granted that Bentham changes intentionally (and not by a naturalistic fallacy) the common-sense meaning of "morally good" as much as the common-sense meaning of "truly existent" has been changed in science. Therefore, in so far as contemporary ethics wishes to maintain, at all costs, the common-sense meaning of the moral *ought* and of the morally good, Bentham's concept of morals has to be rejected with as much reason as Copernican astronomy had to be rejected by astronomers who were not willing to sacrifice the common-sense meaning of sunrise and sunset.

The price which Ptolemaic astronomers as well as contemporary moralists must pay for the maintenance of their common-sense views is a more and more complicated and embarrassing arrangement in the superstructure of their theories. But, paying this price, they may go on for a long time, and neither contemporary ethics nor Ptolemaic cosmology can as such be "refuted" by its opponents. In due time mankind knew how to grow out of the views of "time-honoured" astronomy and will, in all probability, learn to outgrow time-honoured ethics without endlessly deploring the loss of the common-sense meaning of fundamental astronomical or ethical concepts.

Kant once said that the senses are to be acquitted from the charge of betrayal.[60] Kant himself carried out this acquittal in his *Critique of Pure Reason* by an equally reasoned opposition to uncritical rational metaphysics and uncritical sensationism and relativism. Bentham did the same in the field of ethics.

Bentham acquitted all subjective, relative "feelings of positive and negative tones" from the charge of betrayal; and, nevertheless, by reference to merely subjective emotions of pleasure and pain, he tried to establish an objective theory of morals in a great number of most acute discussions of ethical method in general. I believe that no one should write on ethics without having become familiar with these discussions.

I am well aware that even the most guarded defense of consistent hedonistic ethics sounds outrageously shallow to practically all contemporary schools of ethics and to critics of the possibility of any scientific ethics. Therefore I do not wish to burden Cassirer with even these hints at my defense of Bentham's ethical method.* I wish to build up my type of "consistent hedonism" entirely at my own risk; it is, however, especially gratifying to me that, in one of his letters, Cassirer expressed his heartfelt approval of my principal ethical ideas.[61]

DAVID BAUMGARDT

LIBRARY OF CONGRESS
WASHINGTON, D.C.

[60] See Kant, *Anthropology in pragmatischer Hinsicht*, § 8ff; *Werke*, ed. by E. Cassirer, Band VIII (1922), 28ff.

* *Editor's Note:* As the reader will see from footnote 61, this essay was not merely written before Professor Cassirer's death, but had been submitted by its author to Cassirer in time to elicit a reply from the latter.

[61] In his letter of March 15th, 1944, Cassirer wrote me: "Für Ihren Aufsatz fühle ich mich Ihnen zu herzlichem Dank verpflichtet. Er hat mich besonders erfreut, weil ich aus ihm ersehen habe, wie nahe wir uns in unseren ethischen Grundanschauungen stehen. Über Ihre Kritik an G. E. Moore und anderen englischen Ethikern kann ich wenig sagen,—da Sie diese Dinge sehr viel genauer kennen als ich."

17

Katharine Gilbert

CASSIRER'S PLACEMENT OF ART

CASSIRER'S PLACEMENT OF ART

ART is not one of the subjects to which Professor Cassirer devoted an independent volume, as he did to language, myth, and to the scientific and philosophic categories of substance and function. But this fact by no means proves a lack of important views on art present in the body of his writings. The precedent of many great names reminds us at once of the congruity of philosophical reflection on art, and its relatively incidental placement. Cassirer's latest book, *An Essay on Man*, contains a chapter on "Art;" the volumes on language and myth as symbolic forms carry a pervading consciousness of art as a parallel symbolic form; and the genius and work of certain great artists, especially Goethe, have undergone extensive analysis at his hands. Having edited Kant and Leibniz, he remains conscious, in all references to their philosophy, of the service they performed for aesthetic theory. In his *Individuum und Kosmos in der Philosophie der Renaissance* implications concerning art stand in relief. Pregnant phrases and notions meet the reader again and again as he follows an historical argument—phrases and notions that contain in germ the lacking independent volume. For instance, Cassirer connects the origin of plastic art with a mutation in the idea of immortality. He relates how among the Egyptians the soul was first cherished toward its immortal destiny by preserving its mortal house, the body; how, then, a second way of ensuring human survival was discovered. Beside the mummy a statue was placed. Thus art was born.[1] Again he notes how hostile to art is a certain tendency in religion—the tendency to introverted pietism. The food gone

[1] *Philosophie der symbolischen Formen: Zweiter Teil*, 205.

on which art lives—contact with the outside world—art can
beget only monotonous songs of soul-ecstasy. It takes the gift of
a Bach, he says, to restore art's vitality. Bach elaborated a new
language of musical forms, and thus made the new intensity of
feeling articulate.[2] Such compact insights on the relation of art
to other elements of culture are scattered throughout Cassirer's
volumes.

Cassirer's method in respect to art is the philosopher's. He is
neither critic, psychologist, nor an artist celebrating his own
way of life. As a philosopher, Cassirer accepts the task of placing
art among the realms of spirit (language, myth, religion, and
science particularly) and of tracing within the history of culture
the growth of appreciation of art's autonomy. He always keeps
awareness of the wider cultural and cosmic context, though
there is abundant reference to the concrete, particularly to
Goethe, who is the star example. Learned historians of art
could hardly have fitted, as they have done, their detailed researches to his intellectual frame, if he had not commanded
wide expanses of fact. Nevertheless, his purpose remains philosophical, i.e., he defines the sphere of art among the forms of
the spiritual life, and does not to any great extent sharpen and
validate images—the general function of the art-critic. As a
philosopher, he emphasizes the truth that a language of relevant
sensuous forms is indispensable for the larger part that art wills
to play in social life. But he is not an original investigator of
these forms and their ultimate elements.

Art is placed by Cassirer among the "symbolic forms." In a
contribution to a symposium on the nature of symbol in 1927,[3]
he developed the emphasis laid in 1887 on the idea of symbol
by Friedrich Theodor Vischer. Vischer had asserted its centrality for all the philosophical disciplines, its protean character,
and its tendency to assume new meanings at its core when applied to a new field. Symbols are made when man learns to
separate himself from nature and to use independent carriers

[2] *Freiheit und Form,* 274.

[3] "Das Symbolproblem und seine Stellung im System der Philosophie," *Zeitschrift für Ästhetik und Allgemeine Kunstwissenschaft,* XXI, 295-319.

to hold his meanings. A symbolic form in general is an active interpreter, binding an intellectual content to a sensuous show. Its mediating power is the heart of it. Wherever a symbol is present, there is polarity operative and yet somehow overcome. The opposites that are reconciled by the offices of symbol are many: meaning and sensuous embodiment; the intelligible world and the world of time and change; contemplation and action; freedom and form; spirit and nature; divine essence and human need. In speculative aesthetics in particular, says Cassirer, from Plotinus to Hegel, the problem of symbol has always come up in connection with such reconciliation. The relation of painted shows to the intelligible world, of the semblance on the stage and in the singer's lay to the values of truth and goodness—such problems are continually provoking inquiry.

The beautiful is essentially and necessarily symbol because and in so far as it is split within itself, because it is always and everywhere both one and double. In this split, in this attachment to the sensuous, and in this rising above the sensuous, it not only expresses the tension which runs through the world of our *consciousness*,—but it reveals by this means the original and basic polarity of Being itself; the dialectic which obtains between the finite and the infinite, between the absolute idea and its representation and incorporation inside the world of the individual, of the empirically existent.[4]

The aesthetic symbol is, then, for Cassirer, symbol at its height. It is bordered below by religious symbolism where the communication is still opaque, and above by the scientific sign where the sensuous sign is often arbitrary.

We may briefly outline Cassirer's ideas concerning the symbolism of art. Art as symbol requires for the unfolding of its meaning a two-fold movement of thought: a purification of its conception from confusing adhesions and then a restoration of it to the family of human functions. (1) Art begins to be conscious of itself in the process of its disentanglement from a pre-aesthetic existence where its mode is bodily and its charm magical. Even after art begins to emerge from its religious, mythical,

4 *Ibid.*, 296,

and biological matrix, it still leads for centuries a servile life; first, as a servant of things, when it is interpreted as imitation; second, as a servant of reason, when interpreted as analogue. It is also less than its free self when it is still largely governed by instinct or emotion. Art only becomes a characteristic symbolic form when it stands forth as a free entity, declaring itself.

(2) The second part of the defining movement reinstates liberated art once again within the circle of the activities of spirit, and sees it as part of man's total functioning in his world. Art, freed from patronage and models, from alien patterns of order and from dark urges of instinct, tends to become undisciplined genius expressing itself lyrically out of and into a void. This tendency is a false excess. Though loosed from irrelevant adhesions and dominions, art has a work and place committed to it. As imaginative penetration into the nature of things, Cassirer teaches, art swings rhythmically between the realm of objects and of subjects, and bears witness to the ultimate solidarity of the two. Hence the "polarity" or "tension" in all art-symbols and the favorite definition of beauty as harmony.

Besides being witness to the harmony of man and his world in polarity, art as symbol is a peculiar microcosm of the age. In it are reflected as in a mirror the concerns of time, place, and social habit. This is the essential historicity of the symbol. In its historical setting art is a free collaborator with science, philosophy, religion, the formulations of social and political values, and other cultural functions.

We may now expand the accompanying outline which we have constructed to suggest the form of Cassirer's thought. Art begins its fight for self-subsistence by struggling free from substantial nature.[5] Although the student of culture sometimes thinks himself able to point to a moment when detachment occurred, on the whole art loosened its bonds gradually. Before man deposited his intention in a free-standing form, he mixed it obscurely with things, and myths and magic grew up hybrids. In these earlier forms of symbolism there was no sharp line

---

[5] The paragraphs sketching pre-artistic symbols in space, time, and language are based on *Philosophie der symbolischen Formen: Erster Teil: Die Sprache; Zweiter Teil: Das Mythische Denken.*

separating man's intentional act from the natural world which he molded to convey his will. Before the architect or sculptor submitted matter—the element spread out in space—to his euplastic engine, the hand, in order to make a god after his own image or build a god's house, he accepted as his medium the heavy earth as it stretched out beneath him, and made it bear in its raw state the distinctions that his feelings and desires sought to place. Right and left, high and low, near and far achieved moral sense as well as plain, physical sense. They all reflected the body's station, and the direction toward which he faced or reached or looked, or the forefeeling or memory in his limbs of an effort of movement. Man committed to the surface of the earth his pride or awe in the sacred field marked off from the indefinite stretch of common ground. Gradually he projected into the given earth and heavens his main qualitative

---

PLACEMENT OF ART

Object		*Subject*
Substantial things	Myth	Soul's magical fusion with things
	Expression	Instinct; Affects
Appearance	Imitation	Perception; feeling
	Analogue	Obscure processes

Symbolic Synthesis

Religion	Social Values	Art	Philosophy	Science

genera: colors, animals, organs of the body, seasons of the year, totemic classes for marriage and inheritance purposes, his religious attitude. The divisions of space were drafted as they lay to carry the order man had achieved for the conduct of his life. But man was not an original artificer of spatial form in all this. His feelings and sensuous perceptions accepted the shape and color of nature's regions and toned these givens into harmony with affective attitudes. Spatial determinations at this level are the carriers of human propensities. Here we have the thing-like opaque symbol of mythology and religion.

As space still inheres in things on the mythical level and has not become an inspired form or a constructed relation, so also with time. Time was not in primitive experience a relation of periods measured in terms of a system of referents, nor even the rhythm of poetry or music, but the very process of the torches of time: sun, moon, and stars. It was real passage incarnate in the agents of passage. The same incompleteness of the human shaping act was present when speech symbols first appeared. A word is not in the first instance a coin minted by a creative spirit out of the indefinite flux of sound to express an intent. A word, though symbol, is also for primitive thought a thing—the thing that is named with cryptic potency. The Word of God was a phase of the God-head and not his title merely. Or, in its half-brutish beginnings, language was interjection, cry of pain or joy, gesture of welcome or defiance, echo of some natural marvel. When language jets without pause for reflection, then it is an aspect of primitive organic behavior as well as the forerunner of intelligible speech. Though it is the indistinct mythical habit that thus confuses name with the named and the statement of meaning with organic response, even the art of poetry has to work its way free from the immediate lyrical impulse of nature. It is, for Cassirer, a proof of Goethe's constant mastery of his art that even in his youthful storm and stress period, when he liked to lie on the earth and court the sun and small creatures crawling through the grass, when the rhythms in his lyrics were the rhythms of waves and winds, he was not absorbed. He never confused his mind's ways with nature's ways. In just this assurance about the indispensable formative function of art does he stand apart from the poets who discharge natural impulses with primitive directness or make themselves sensitive plates of nature.

In his most recent statement of the nature of art, Chapter IX in his *Essay on Man*, Cassirer has once more illustrated the distinction between the symbolic function in art, where a material is transformed by the spirit of man, and that pre-artistic relation of man to his world where the content is imposed largely from outside. This time he has the naïve contemporary spectator of art in mind. He chooses the example of the enjoyment of landscape. For the simple awareness of the natural man, agreeable physical qualities operate on the passive organism: bright colors, fragrant, mild airs. The "meeting soul" takes in the pleasant scene as a whole and half suffuses it with a life and tone of its own; but what is present is things not forms. "But I may then," writes Cassirer,

experience a sudden change in my frame of mind. Thereupon I see the landscape with an artist's eye—I begin to form a picture of it. I have now entered a new realm—the realm not of living things but of "living forms." No longer in the immediate reality of things, I live now in the rhythm of spatial forms, in the harmony and contrast of colors, in the balance of light and shadow. In such absorption in the dynamic aspect of form consists the aesthetic experience.[6]

Art to be art must not only extricate man's concern from ingredience in things, magical or sentimental; it must stop reproducing the shows of things. The conception of art as imitation has been historically so persistent that Cassirer was bound to take account of it, little as he agrees with it. The neo-Kantian idealist who denies any element of pure datum even in the perception of a patch of color could never admit an art that repeats a given. The simplest item of common sense experience points beyond itself for him, and thus involves an act of spirit, if and in so far as it has meaning. But the symbolizing acts of artists (and of all builders of culture) imply a higher and more complex human entrance. In art man builds a disentangling frame to hold and relieve the item.[7]

[6] *Essay on Man*, chapter IX on "Art," 151f.
[7] *Philosophie der symbolischen Formen*, I, 41.

Cassirer notes here and there in his historical surveys and analyses variants of the *mimesis* doctrine. Each of these altered without redeeming it. The concept of imitation is still dominant in that view of art which identifies it with the extraction for preservation of the beautiful elements of things. In noting the contribution of the Swiss literary critics, Bodmer and Breitinger, to the progress of aesthetic theory, Cassirer remarks that they could not draw out the implications of the notion of a heightened energy in individual vision, prepared by Leibniz's metaphysics. Rather they marked off a region of the actual as good poetical material. "How," they asked, "can a painting of a peasant and his beasts of burden charm us, if the original scene does not draw our gaze?"[8] The assumption here is the familiar one that art is imitation, though selective. It derives, as is always told, from the famous story of the painting of the maidens of Crotona by Zeuxis, and is but a feeble change in the ape doctrine. It leaves the two factors in the situation standing over against each other. However, the selection is up to a point evidence of human valuation.

The next refinement—one developed by Shaftesbury and Lessing—is simply an intensification of the first. Artists select for perpetuation the pregnant moment in a scene. The artist lets his spatial fancy grow in responding to the center of movement in the piece of nature he is contemplating. He and his object are both alive; they are both in labor with something new and important that is to be brought forth. Cassirer reminds us that this marks a progress in the artist's view from the content of the given to its form and relations. The pregnant moment reaches before and after itself and by a half-revealed energy extends its sphere of existence into what the spirit alone sees and knows.[9]

A third variant of the imitation doctrine Cassirer finds in the values of omission, and binds it with the second. "The artistic sketch becomes such, and distinguished from mechanical reproduction, by virtue of what is dropped out of the immediately given impression."[10] In this imitation through negation there

---

[8] *Freiheit und Form*, 116-117.
[9] *Philosophie der symbolischen Formen*, I, 44.
[10] *Loc. cit.*

is restriction of the dominance of the particular model, but increase in its symbolic potency.

A fourth variant is the recognition of the importance of individual style in imitation. Certain thinkers, e.g., Diderot, may conceive art as imitative, and yet have a most lively feeling for the special individualities of different languages. Diderot is endowed with a feeling for the finest nuances of words, for their tone and clang, for their untranslatable moments.[11] This marks the passage of any art, whether an art of words or an art of images, from the stage of social utility and rational generality to an unquestioned aesthetic level. There was in the eighteenth century a whole strain, starting with Leibniz, which clarified more and more the importance for art and culture of individuality and eccentricity, sensuous detail, passionate aberration. Cassirer attaches this enrichment of theory to Hamann and Herder after Leibniz and sets it for purposes of contrast over against the new assertion of orderly classicism in Winckelmann.[12] Indeed, Cassirer is always watching for the moment of individual variation in the essence of art. Emphasis on individuality is, however, sometimes combined with the unacceptable imitation doctrine.

Besides being taken as a servant of things in its mode of imitation, art is servilely treated (though less so) as a dependent of reason in its phase as analogue. We owe the beginnings of this interpretation to Leibniz. It came about in this way.[13] Leibniz entertained the logical ideal of submitting all the work of mind to the standard of clear and compelling order. The reduction worked without much difficulty so long as rational truths and abstract categories, such as substance and cause, were in question. To all the ideas that fell within this circle Leibniz applied the strict law of consistency: of identity and difference. But both for completeness and system, and in conformity with the law of continuity in which he believed, he was obliged to make the effort to handle in the light of the same goal the less clear notions furnished by perception, memory, and

[11] *Ibid.*, I, 82.
[12] *Freiheit und Form*, 170-221.
[13] *Ibid.*, 99-218.

the aesthetic activities. He had to try to satisfy the demand for reason, law, and order in the inferior faculties and obscure regions of the soul. He accomplished this by postulating a progressive scale of clarity. In the scale the earlier confused stages implied but did not reveal the coming distinctness. Out of the I itself, from which he made all mental facts flow, he drew an anticipating and accumulating sequence, dim at first, but exhibiting even in the semi-darkness intimations of form and rule. Leibniz placed music and painting then among the analogues of reason. He interpreted them as big with their own rational explanation, though conceived on the sensuous plane of feeling and taste. One might perhaps say that they prophesy their own clarification and that they instinctively correspond with their own ratios and proportions. Art, then, for Leibniz no longer imitates, but presses toward, without attaining, its own logical fulfilment.

In spite of the advance of the concept of analogue over the concept of imitation, there is still unfitness in the new notion. As in the phase of imitation art defers to a model, so in the rôle of analogue art is measured by the superior excellence of reason. Therefore art is not yet autonomous nor handled in terms of wholly relevant categories.

In the building up of the artistic function of man, Cassirer says there is a general law of three stages: the mimetic, the analogical, and finally, the symbolic.[14] We have been noting in what way art falls short of self-determination in so far as it is copy or analogue. Cassirer also ties in the imperfection of these early stages with the fragmentary conative views. Language was interpreted by Vico as half rooted in interjection,[15] and art recurrently offers itself as the immediate utterance of nature. Cassirer passes in review the variants of this definition of art as expression of genius. For him they seem all to be either romantic theories which overemphasize feeling, emotion, or god-like creativity, or, on the other hand, play-theories which overemphasize primitivism and release.[16] As an idealist, Cas-

---

[14] *Philosophie der symbolischen Formen*, I, 136, 137.

[15] *Ibid.*, I, 91.

[16] *Essay on Man*, 140ff, 163ff.

sirer never loses awareness of the spirit's being there. No field
of reality nor region of culture exists for him which is not
stamped by the energy of mind. However, the phrases employed by the Schlegels and Schelling implying the unrestricted
rights of genius Cassirer would temper and balance. Cassirer
believes that the "genius" theory of art or the emphasis on
soul-discharge does justice to only one pole of the artistic situation. It is a pole that will always be highly charged when art
has been subjected to rules or models, as by Boileau and the
neo-classicists generally. The neglected jet of the human imagination will spring up when it is suppressed. It was Kant—the
Kant who for Cassirer marked the culmination of the cultural
passage from Leibniz in the eighteenth century—who gave once
for all the proportions to Genius and Nature in Art. "Art can
be called beautiful only if we are conscious that it is Art although
it looks like Nature." "Genius is the talent through which
Nature gives the rule to Art." "Nature by the medium of
Genius . . . prescribes rules to Art."[17] Therefore where a
Rousseauist urges the rights of feeling, Cassirer counters with
the claims of form and repose. And the various biological
theories of the nineteenth century, which featured the play
instinct, needed, according to Cassirer, to humanize the concept
for art, so that play is seen as productive and structural.[18] Even
the play theory of Schiller, though far closer to the balanced
view of art as living-form, gives too much to the unordered
sport of innocent childhood.

In the group of theories which make art less than free and
less than complete because of over-emphasis on the emotional
thrust, Cassirer places those of Croce and Collingwood.[19] He
complains that those thinkers limit the whole of art to the lyrical impulse and leave out the contribution made by medium and
structure. Undoubtedly there are many passages in the writings
of these two philosophers which support the adverse view of
Cassirer. But with respect to medium one must remember the
famous passage in Croce's *Essence of Aesthetic,* in which he cer-

[17] *Kant's Kritique of Judgment,* trans. J. H. Bernard, 188-190.
[18] *Essay on Man,* 164ff.
[19] *Ibid.,* 141f.

tainly demands the realization of intuitions: "A thought is not thought for us, unless it be possible to formulate it in words; a musical image exists for us, only when it becomes concrete in sounds; a pictorial image, only when it is coloured."[20] The apparent failure to provide a place in his system for sensuous medium is the result of a prohibiting metaphysic. As one might say that a modern physicist who denies the old concept of solid matter, substituting the current one of fields of force, left no room for cans and kidneys! As for form, one remembers the statement in Croce's most recent general article: "The problem for aesthetics today is the reassertion and defense of the classical as against romanticism: the synthetic, formal theoretical element which is the *proprium* of art, as against the affective element which it is the business of art to resolve into itself."[21] It seems definitely inappropriate to regard a theory which involves such a statement as instinctive. Both in the case of Croce and of Collingwood the importance of structure and medium is recognized in the long and intricate treatment of language. Collingwood says that the experience of art involves the change from affect in the lower level of the psyche to the activity of conscious awareness, from impression to imagination, from brute giveness to domination by thought.[22] These marks of art are hardly consistent with the sentimentalism and exhibitionism implicitly charged by Cassirer.[23]

Although Cassirer rejects the notions of art as imitation, lyricism, or analogue, he carries over elements from these into the one he accepts. Art for him is a symbolic form: a living shape worked out in a sensuous medium, expressing tension and release. The tension holds man over against the world; the release means reconciliation with it. In Cassirer's latest statement of what art is various expressions are used rather than "symbolic form" to convey both the autonomy and the richness of the idea as he holds it: "constructive eye,"[24] "con-

[20] Benedetto Croce, *The Essence of Aesthetic*, 42-43.
[21] Croce, article on "Aesthetics," *Encyclopaedia Britannica*; 14th edition (1946).
[22] R. G. Collingwood, *Principles of Art*, 234-235.
[23] *Essay on Man*, 142.
[24] *Ibid.*, 151.

templative creation,"[25] "intuitive form,"[26] "sympathetic vision."[27] In each of these phrases it is obvious that the opposition between the subjective and objective contributions to the act and fact of art is meant to be resolved. Something is saved, to be sure, from the imitation doctrine, as the words "contemplative," "intuitive," and "vision" suggest. Cassirer points out that when Leonardo da Vinci said that the function of art was to teach men how to see (*saper vedere*) he uttered an inexpugnable truth.[28] Art does not imitate the world of men and things, but it penetrates it with the faculty of imagination and restates its essential character in revealing and beautiful forms. A painter interprets the spectacle which it is contrary to his genius to retrace dumbly line for line. He discriminates and communicates delicate aspects of the nature whose gross appearance bores him. Intensive and concentrated vision is a main attribute of an artist and this is what is left of the discarded doctrine of *ars simia naturae*.

There is value to be conserved also in the variants of expressionism. The force of genius, the lyrical thrust is the inception of art. But the value in emotional theories has to be balanced by values taken from the rationalistic school, the values of measure and order. In all contexts the Kantian Cassirer asserts the primacy of the spontaneity of consciousness. In the context of art this general idea becomes the interpretation of art as man's deed. Art, in fact any cultural symbol, he is never tired of saying, is *energeia* and not *ergon*.[29] Every symbolic form, art, myth, or speech is a revelation proceeding from within outwards. One of the insights of Leibniz, important for aesthetic theory, was just this revaluation˙ of reality in terms of force. In interpreting the aesthetic significance of Hogarth's line of beauty Cassirer traverses the lower levels on which it is a mere sensuous impression, and then an optical structure. As one looks at it, Cassirer writes, the thin perceptual experience be-

---

[25] *Ibid.*, 162.
[26] *Ibid.*, 167, 170.
[27] *Ibid.*, 150, 170n.
[28] *Ibid.*, 144.
[29] *Philosophie der symbolischen Formen*, I, 104.

gins to move and become a self-shaping energy. It has then
arrived at the stage of aesthetic form; it becomes definite
ornament, with artistic intent and place. For, although as beautiful ornament it is timeless, even so it belongs to the history
of style and can be placed in an epoch. "In the concrete experience of the simple linear track, there comes now into being at
a single blow, just a particular style, just the comprehensive
characteristic 'art will' of the time pregnant and living before me."[30]

But, though art begins as spontaneity, act of will, or expression of emotion, it is great in proportion as it is the expression
not of a feeling but of the gamut of human feelings, thereby
attaining universality and subtlety. If various emotions in their
responsiveness to multiplied occasions, and fortune's turns, are
represented, the work of art rises to wholeness and sloughs violence. Emotion converts to motion, i.e., to rhythm, measure,
and design. Tension deepens to the center's stillness. Cassirer
makes use of the idea of *catharsis* to prove how inadequate
unshaped passion is for the purposes of art. Art must operate
to convert the passive burden of pity and fear into an active
state of soul. Cassirer answers the question: Of what is man
freed by art? thus: So long as fear is a real dread of a real
state of affairs man feels his dependence. But, if he remolds
this fear into the art of tragedy—whether he writes it or
relives it as a fit spectator—he is emancipated by the form of
art from the material load of existing danger, be it a tyrant's
menace or the approach of death, poverty, or disease.[31] In such
ways Cassirer limits the idea of the absoluteness of genius.

Having brought to a point the positive and negative elements
in Cassirer's theory of art as symbol or intuitive awareness of
living form, we turn to Goethe for concrete demonstration.
"The life and the poetry of Goethe gives us the best and most
typical example of the mutual penetration of all those elements
that constitute a work of art."[32] Particularly we find there on a

---

[30] *Zeitschrift*, XXI, *op. cit.*, 299.

[31] *Essay on Man*, 148f.

[32] *Ibid.*, 10. The page-reference here is to Cassirer's original typescript pages;
I have been unable to locate the above sentence in the printed chapter on "Art"

grand scale and in clear outlines the swing from originative lyrical thrust to compensating objective vision of beauty, both in nature and in the human form. We find this tension over-ruled by the mastery of Goethe's poetical power which holds all in seamless unity. We will avail ourselves of typical observations made by Cassirer on this master illustration.

The early lyrics and dramatic sketches of Goethe convey the Prometheus motive, the youthful accent of energy, generosity, and love of nature and thus express the first subjective stage of symbol clearly. They were written in the *Sturm und Drang* period of Goethe's life, when he felt the liberation wrought by Rousseau, when he was overwhelmed by the gigantic strength of a Gothic cathedral, and when his own mounting genius found dramatic counterparts in Götz von Berlichingen, Mohammed, and Caesar. Like the early lyrics the *Urfaust* is an expression of the first thrust of a great spirit's power and dream. In the first scenes of the Faust poem, which conserve the early force, one remembers how the young world of the on-coming Renaissance, its experimentation and ferment, and the unbounded eagerness and ambition of a scientific explorer show themselves in epithets, figures and scenes. Faust's ecstatic wonder in the awareness of his god-like powers, his thirst for contact with the very springs and breast of nature, his intoxicated yearning after the fire and loom and ocean of Being all reflect the onset of symbol as such. However important the swaying middle position of symbol and its reconciling function, a work of art as symbol is born on the side of spiritual freedom and power; it is autonomous creation.

In *Faust* the objective pole is represented by Helena, her beauty and implications. To the extent that subject and object can be perfectly balanced in a work of art the union of Faust and Helena stands for that total compensation. But this would be too static a name for the living, dynamic conception of symbol that Goethe employed and Cassirer expounds. Helena herself, though she represents the beauty of the ancient world and of nature, and most of all, of the fair human shape, is a

---

in *An Essay on Man.* However, the main source for Cassirer's use of Goethe is *Freiheit und Form*, 271-421.

shifting, shimmering, many-visaged, and finally poignantly fading form. She shows in a mirror, she incarnates in Gretchen, she leaps ages and mountains. The too humbly Teutonic Gretchen gives place under the growing aesthetic ideal to the nobler form of Menelaus' wife. But in total conception the classic heroine answers to that firm objective beauty which Goethe found and celebrated on his Italian journey. He wrote from there that his early Titanic ideas were only airy shapes and that before the serene beauty of the human form in antique art he had first learned to see.[33]

The peace of the aesthetic sense, resting in its formed counter-part, is for this view, as we have said, only the limit and cross-section of a process. The admiration of Helena becomes a function. For Faust it acts as a fluid standard in terms of which his many admirations may be measured. German shapelessness, though dear through kinship, becomes relatively unsympathetic. He returns to it indeed: Gretchen is envisioned again. But pain mixes with the pleasure of the experience of Helena throughout. In her phantom-quality she symbolizes the instability of all embodied loveliness. Hers and Faust's child, Euphorion, who shared with his father vaulting ambition, dies like Icarus. Thus the subjective moment, Faust's ambition, and the objective moment, Helena's beautiful form, interweave and change. In their interaction and growth they compose the poetized image of Goethe's own life in the sense of the law of the form of his life, and beyond this, of the history and tragedy of humanity.

While analyzing the symbolism of *Faust* Cassirer makes a cross-reference to the *Pandora* in which, he says, Goethe's symbolic meaning has received its purest poetical stamp.[34] He also devoted a separate study to the Pandora fragment.[35] Though unfinished and more difficult to analyze, it is almost a symbol of the symbolic function itself. As it is the business of symbol to harmonize tensions, so with Pandora here. For Cassirer explains that the Pandora Goethe has in mind is the

---

[33] *Freiheit und Form*, 409f.

[34] *Ibid.*, 412.

[35] "Goethe's Pandora," *Zeitschrift für Ästhetik und Allgemeine Kunstwissenschaft*, XIII, (1919), 116.

"all-gifted and all-giving one," the loving dispenser of goods to man, the kind and beautiful force that draws men into communion and fellowship. Like Love, the great ascending and descending *Daimon* of Plato's *Symposium*, Pandora is the arch-mediator, "destined to connect together poverty and plenty, finite and infinite, mortality and immortality, and by so doing to cement the universe into a whole."[36]

Cassirer watches the Pandora symbol grow, and by following the illustration we may get fresh light on this basic interpretation of art. The tensions that are stated and harmonized mount in intensity and depth of meaning. In most general terms the opposition running through the whole is that between deed and reflection, subjective force and objective seeing, the active and contemplative forces in life and being. At one point, where Cassirer himself almost turns poet, he suggests that we hear in our mind's ear the individual dramatic parts as voices brought together contrapuntally in a magnificent fugue. Early in the poem where the tension is at its most uncompromised stage the active pole, Prometheus, represents man's primitive self-reliant effort to work nature for his basic needs. Measuring all values in terms of tangible utilities, Prometheus has no sympathy for sabbath rest or aesthetic contemplation. The early reflective pole, Epimetheus, receives from Pandora a floating vision of beautiful natural forms, on water and land, in youth and woman. But because form, *Gestalt*, is at this point sheer gift and not achievement, the lovely shapes disintegrate and pass away with the passing of natural light. As the contrapuntal music thickens, the active moment becomes purposive and enlightened cultivation of the arts and sciences; the reflective moment brings justice and the loving co-operation of communal life. Then another character, *Elpore thraseia*, strengthens the reality of the good gifts of Pandora, by bringing confident hope. This optimism, however, Cassirer finds balanced near the end by the expression of an old man's serene renunciation, renunciation of the belief in the possibility of steady maintenance of classic peace and harmony. But there is mastery by form even though classic harmony passes. Goethe realizes

[36] *Ibid.*, 116.

and expresses the realization that the forces that generate the changes in being spring within man as well. He accepts the fact of his own decline as linked with the larger rhythms in things and yields more place to the idea of passage and individuality.

The application to Goethe illuminates Cassirer's conception of true art as symbolic form. We understand more vividly after the projection on to the Goethean plane how a great poem figures forth the conciliating office of living form; how the impetus of Faustian, Promethean spirit needs for completeness the quieting influence of Helena's and Hellenic beauty and the scope and objectivity of Nature's inner rhythm; how the self-assertive tendency needs to be controlled by the contemplation of beauty; how social bonds are insufficient without enlightenment, confidence without resignation; how even beautiful irenic love and classic ideals are subject to time—how beauty is one aspect of the total life of form.

Cassirer's application of his concept of art remains on the whole within the field of the art of words. For the other arts he furnishes us only a general program and occasional allusions. We are not, however, without indication of the direction his applications might easily have taken in the field of the visual arts. In several places the art-historian, Dr. Erwin Panofsky, borrows Cassirer's usage of the term "symbolism," praising its aptness; and one may, I think, make so bold as to assume that this art-historian's rich iconographical studies in the main illustrate what Cassirer would like to have understood as the application of his theory of art to painting and sculpture. The best locus for our desired application to the spatial arts is *Die Perspektive als "Symbolische Form"*[37] where the very wording of the title shows Cassirer's influence. In this learned study Panofsky traces the handling of perspective in painting and drawing from classical times to the present and ties the spatial treatment throughout with the general *Weltanschauung*. He demonstrates how man's pictorial and plastic portrayals reflect through the ages his primary orientation to his environment—his place in the world—his set toward things—his middle position be-

[37] *Vorträge der Bibliothek Warburg*, (1924-1925), 258-330.

tween the heavens above and the pit at the center—his physical consorting with nature—what he fundamentally means by here and there, between, outside of, near, far—all under the influence of a changing ultimate sense of values.

Examples from Panofsky's study should make this clear. For period after period he matches the artistic handling of spatial relations, the particular variant of perspective worked out by a period's artists, with wider tendencies in philosophy and science. Thus, while he is converting spatial symbols into historic monuments, he is at the same time relating these monuments to the other major contemporary activities. This is that reinstatement of autonomous art to its position among its human kindred which Cassirer believes in and which is illustrated in the expanding movement of our initial schematic outline.

Panofsky begins with classical antiquity. The artists of this time saw their material world loosely held together. The objective scene was made up of a plurality of bodies with shapes determined by function, and with 'tactile values.' Empty space was in this style a nothing—simply a remainder. The whole field of vision was thus a sum of separate spaces. Now the world of the philosopher Democritus was just such an aggregate: atoms plus a void within which the atoms could move. If Democritus be thought not central enough in Greek philosophy to be taken as the significant background of Greek artistic symbolism, then Plato and Aristotle can be drafted. Plato with his triangles and receptacle, Aristotle with his nest of forms made the space of nature a sum of the places of bodies and forms. Neither for classical Greek thought nor for art was there an envisioned space that could master and fuse the contents of space.

The quasi-impressionism of Hellenistic landscape and architectural interiors cracked the atomistic independence of classical forms, but, being inconsistent and inconclusive, achieved no federating, spatial continuum. In the realm of art this was like the Pyrrhonic scepticism which shook the simple positiveness of earlier philosophy, but achieved no system of its own. Passing on to the Middle Ages, we find there the gradual conquest of spatial unity in art corresponding to the many-sided movement of Christian philosophy. In the manuscript illuminations and mosaics there was the rhythmic interplay of pure gold and colors correspondent to the metaphysics of light —a metaphysics at first pagan, but then central in Christian theology. When St. Thomas made Christian thought Aristotelian in outline, he added a divine outer body, spiritual in essence and infinite in power, to Aristotle's set of starry orbits. This may be claimed as the analogue of the rising dominance in architecture of arched roofings and canopies over lesser sculptured forms—still a great body ruling lesser bodies, and to this degree pluralistic—but a kind of unity for all that.

With the great painters and architects of the Renaissance conscious unity arrived. A mathematical theory of perspective was constructed in terms of sectioned visual pyramids, and expressed itself through chess-board tiled-floors, ground plans, etc. Thus a whole of space definitely replaced a space-aggregate. The philosophical rationalism of the seventeenth century, with all its subsidiary mathematical disciplines, stands in the wide world of theory for the perfected system of perspective in art. A natural continuum, dispensing with a supernatural over-lord, a homogeneous infinite extension of which all particular bodies are determinate modes, is contemplated and analyzed. Space at last signifies an unbroken web, not a sum of entities.

Why was this apparent conclusion of the problem of space, for art and for philosophy, not a final resting-place? One knows that the naturalistic perspective style of the High Renaissance yielded to others; and that the Substantial Extension of Descartes was no last word in Nature-philosophy. We remember that symbols are polar, and always retain at their heart an ambiguity. The symbolism of naturalistic perspective painting carries within it the typical tension. The reason that Dürer's "St. Jerome" or De Hooch's interiors look like a slice of reality set on the canvas is because, paradoxically, the subjective point of sight has been so perfectly reckoned with. Where the phenomenon of art seems most real, there the subjective factor enters in most penetratingly. The perspective system of Alberti and Piero della Francesca is both a triumph for the reporter of fact and for the egotist whose will to power subdues the fact to the individual point of view. Once the process of perspective representation was mastered, artists began to adapt the cross-cut of nature freely to their fancy. The Italian baroque painters played freely with the possibilities of an emphasized high-space; Altdorfer with oblique space; Rembrandt with near space. This variety of space-emphasis in art corresponds once more to modern subjectivism in thought. Coming still nearer to our own day, everyone knows how in the last few decades the model of naturalistic space has been fundamentally defied by Abstractionists, Futurists, Surrealists, Dadaists, Suprematists. Such control of the organization of the artist's space by an arbitrarily accented motive is in harmony with new psychological tendencies, and a late pervasive irrationalism. There have also been sympathetic symptoms from non-Euclidean pangeometry.

The purpose of this brief summary has been not only to exemplify Cassirer's notion of the art-symbol in its characteristic form, but to indicate the way art can be both recognized as an autonomous activity of spirit and yet restored to the family of human functions. There is a typical organization of space in painting in the Renaissance; but this treatment of space has an underlying kinship with the naturalistic philosophy and mathematical sciences of the same centuries. Even so in expounding Goethe's *Pandora*, Cassirer keeps the poem Goethe's own, yet points out the kinship with Schelling's metaphysics. What came out of genius in that day could hardly miss the flood-tide of romantic influence. There is in any case in any age a world-outlook characteristically coloring both art and philosophy. The most sensitive and profound spectator of a picture will, Panofsky thinks, penetrate to what he defines as its philosophical layer, where the total habits of the time bear subtle witness to themselves. His analysis of the layers of meaning in a work of art provides, first, for a superficial layer of recognizable and expressive objects and events; a secondary layer of literary types; and an ultimate basis of philosophical meaning. In his exposition of this last layer Panofsky cites Cassirer: ". . . the intrinsic meaning . . . may be defined as a unifying principle which underlies and explains both the visible event and its intelligible significance, and which determines even the form in which the visible event takes shape."[38] "In this conceiving of pure forms, motifs, images, stories, and allegories as manifestations of underlying principles, we interpret all these elements as what Ernst Cassirer has called 'symbolical values'."[39]

The spectator of symbolical values, the third philosophical layer, being in his own person aware of the "essential tendencies of the human mind,"[40] intuits their presence in what is before him. He senses the artist's half-conscious communication of a habit of spirit, a dominant attitude toward men and things, and responds to it, is articulate about it. This fine awareness of philosophical habit and spiritual sense, Panofsky, in agreement with Cassirer, makes complex. He who intuits it, intuits a many-in-one, and an atmosphere surrounding the one. Within the "symbolic form" are condensed "symptoms" of the political, scientific, religious, and economic tendencies of the age that produced the work. The philosophical interpreter reads the many symptoms compact in a single frame and knows their echoes and analogues. It is the whole life and tone of an age that pulses in the image.

The art-historian will have to check what he thinks is the *intrinsic meaning* of the work . . . against what he thinks is the *intrinsic meaning* of as many other documents of civilizations historically related to that work . . . as he can master; of documents bearing witness to the political, poetical, religious, philosophical, and social tendencies of the personality, period, or country under investigation. . . . It is in the search for *intrinsic meanings* or *content* that the various humanistic disciplines meet on a common plane instead of serving as hand-maidens to each other.[41]

The work of art as symbolic form is in the middle position of a spiritual circuit which runs from personal creator to the whole cultural scope of the age, back and forth, and round and round. It is the chief home of the busy messenger Eros— Eros here himself a symbol.

[38] Erwin Panofsky, *Studies in Iconology*, 5.

[39] *Ibid.*, 8.

[40] *Ibid.*, 15.

[41] *Ibid.*, 16.

We have now completed the account of that two-fold movement of thought in the course of which Cassirer frees art from alien domination, defines it as an autonomous symbol, and then recharges its connection with the principal human activities.

Such a theory of art as Cassirer's, instructed as it is by the movement of culture, the history of aesthetic theory, and the phenomena of art, is bound to be largely satisfactory. It provides for the two main classical factors of clear control and sensuous richness. It stands by art's autonomy. In adding to the notions struck out by the thought of the great German classical period later ideas of historical style and tragic transience, Cassirer leaves in the main little to be desired by the traditional lovers and students of art. But the question does arise whether the philosophy of overcome polarity, of subject and object, their tensions and syntheses, furnishes—not a possible frame of art-critical reference for recent developments in art, for this it obviously does—but at present the most appropriate and illuminating one. I am not clear whether Cassirer would say: "My view is elastic enough to receive recent experiments," or would say: "My view cannot and ought not so to do. For the recent achievement is wandering rather than a genuine advance." At any rate the polar pattern of Cassirer's symbol seems a little too balanced and full of grace when approached from immersion in Eliot, Auden, Picasso and Stravinsky. The very meaning of polarity derives from common-sense perception and the ordinary interplay of organism and environment. Sapient seeing itself and reconstructed interplay leave normal vision and normal practice as axes of reference. However, one guesses that Cassirer's own thought feels the impact of the less contemplative and more electrically and experimentally generated symbolism of recent years, as he writes his latest chapter on the subject of art. He speaks of the "new force" as well as of the "new form" of art;[42] he quotes Leibniz's definition of perfection as "enhancement of being" and is at pains to note the contribution of Leibniz's functionalism to the newer aesthetics. "It is," he says, "the intensification of our dynamic energies that we seek and find in art." This last phrase certainly marks the

[42] *Essay on Man*, 154.

direction in which recent art has moved. The art of the generation between the wars yielded more intensity and force than harmony and centralized form. Its experiments in denser packing of tones and metaphors and its series of cubistic experiments, have excited interest, but the results have oftener maintained suspense and deepened art's resources than resolved tensions. A deeply boring curiosity and demonic wit have finely fractioned and strangely fused the old vocabulary and grammar. One feels that Cassirer increasingly savors the qualities of the new aesthetic ways and would recognize the place of today's art beside the new physics and psychology in the social picture and humanistic circle. Would he find wanting the completion of its own peculiar task: the achievement or promise of a symbol, after war and exploration, of peace and a valid humanism?

KATHARINE GILBERT

DEPARTMENT OF AESTHETICS, ART AND MUSIC
DUKE UNIVERSITY

18

Harry Slochower

ERNST CASSIRER'S FUNCTIONAL APPROACH TO ART AND LITERATURE

18

ERNST CASSIRER'S FUNCTIONAL APPROACH TO ART AND LITERATURE

ART and literature occupy a more pervasive location in the writings of Ernst Cassirer than they do in any other modern philosopher since Nietzsche. Four of his books are largely devoted to theories of aesthetics and to studies of Hölderlin, Lessing, Schiller, Kleist and Goethe. Furthermore, questions involving the nature and process of art-forms are also raised in his other more general works.

A study of Cassirer's view on art and literature requires an examination of its context in his system as a whole. Even as Cassirer writes that the various cultural functions "cannot be reduced to a common denominator," he insists that they "complete and complement one another."[1] Indeed, a striking feature of Cassirer's philosophy, as developed in *Philosophie der symbolischen Formen* and in *An Essay on Man*, is its strategy of showing that science, language, myth, religion, history and art form an organic unity located in a common structural framework. Although, following Kant, Cassirer ascribes to art a degree of autonomy, he views it as a phase in the process of human culture and bound up with its basic directives. Thus, he would show the principle connecting Greek drama with Greek philosophy, classical and romantic literature and aesthetics with the systems of Leibniz, Newton, Shaftesbury, Kant, Fichte, Rousseau, and Hegel.[2]

However, art-problems are not simply an integral part of

---

[1] *An Essay on Man*, (New Haven, 1944), 228.

[2] *Logos Dike Kosmos in der Entwicklung der griechischen Philosophie*, Göteborgs Högskolas Arsskrift XLVII, (Göteborg, 1941), 4, 15ff. *Die Philosophie der Aufklärung*, (Tübingen, 1932). *Freiheit und Form. Studien zur deutschen Geistesgeschichte*, (Berlin, 1922). *Idee und Gestalt. Goethe, Schiller, Hölderlin, Kleist* (Berlin, 1924). *Rousseau Kant Goethe*, (Princeton, 1945).

Cassirer's philosophy, but offer the most *characteristic* amplification of his method and system. This essay will attempt to demonstrate that an understanding of Cassirer's view on art and literature is indispensable for gaining the full import of his basic category, "function," in which a dialectic method is applied to and verified by concrete, material forms leading to a free social act. The point will be developed by an analysis of

1. Cassirer's strategy and leading principles.
2. Their objectification in his approach to
   a. Art and aesthetic theory
   b. Literary personalities, particularly Goethe.

Finally, we shall indicate the limitation and the fruitfulness of Cassirer's approach with reference to contemporary problems of art and literary criticism.

METHOD

The initial impression gained from some of Cassirer's works is that they are learned treatises on the history of philosophy, science, culture, and art. Indeed, Cassirer has been criticized for showing greater interest in citing other men's theories than in stating a position of his own. It is true that his writings contain extensive quotations from a great number of sources, and that his studies on aesthetic theory, on Goethe, etc., trace their historical development. However, this documentation is not merely a matter of scholarly learning. Cassirer's specific employment of the historical method, as we shall see, is a characteristic function of his philosophic method.

Cassirer's primary concern in all of his investigations is *method.* "All unity of the intellectual form which comprises a system," he writes, "is finally grounded in (method)." Method is "the most objective and the most personal element in every philosophy." Cassirer is persuaded that a difference in method makes a difference in the direction taken by content. This is the point he would establish in discussing Lamprecht's philosophy of history, Schiller's and Kleist's manipulation of Kantian concepts, etc. In these analyses, Cassirer is less concerned with content and conclusion than with the method through which they are reached and in which they are grounded.[3]

Stated generally, Cassirer's method consists in examining the interplay of the particular and the universal in a dialectic dynamic process. He investigates the individual perspective in its interaction with the over-all view reached, and its merging with a philosophic tradition. The essay on Hölderlin, for example, would demonstrate that the poet shares many of the tenets held by German idealism, but that they take on a different significance and color for him, because in his case they are rooted in other intellectual presuppositions. For the same reason, Hölderlin's own contributions vary from the tenets which he took over from the founders of idealism. Throughout, it is this "dual process of taking and giving" which Cassirer traces, as in discussing the relations of Goethe to Plato, Spinoza, Newton, of Rousseau and Kleist to Kant, etc.[4] Everywhere, he moves in a dialectic rhythm to establish what separates and what unites different personalities and movements.

This centering on method is, however, not in the interests of denying basic assumptions and principles. To be sure, Cassirer keeps himself aloof from the traditional metaphysical substance. In the manner of the Marburg School, to which he belongs, he converts Kant's thing-in-itself into a dynamic unending process. Yet, Cassirer also rejects the traditional brands of positivism, empiricism, and rationalism. Enumeration of empirical data, he notes, can establish no law, and the rationalistic law gained by abstracting from particular manifestations is to him an "impoverishment of reality." Nor may Cassirer's focus on method be linked to Dewey's instrumentalism; for he is opposed to the pragmatic denial of substance and certainty. In so far as pragmatism identifies truth and utility, it is but "a philosophic catch-word." Progress in knowledge is not determined by variations in need, "but by the universal intellectual

[3] *Idee und Gestalt*, 83, 97ff., 178ff. *Essay on Man*, 201f.
[4] *Idee and Gestalt*, 118, 33ff., 178ff., *Rousseau Kant Goethe, loc. cit., Goethe und die geschichtliche Welt*, (Berlin, 1932).

postulate of unity and continuity." All forms of human activity must be traced back "to a common origin," must be imbedded in their "general structural principles." A philosophy of culture involves viewing facts "as a system, as an organic whole." Philosophy must hold to the idea of invariance.[5]

The idea of a leading principle requires that, in some sense, the part represents the whole. The specific nature of Cassirer's problem, however, is to find a methodology through which the part would represent the whole and by which it would in turn be represented *in* the whole. Stated summarily, his method aims at discovering principles manifested in their function and form.

SERIAL ORDER AS FUNCTIONAL STRUCTURE

Cassirer's term for this principle is "serial order" ("Reihenordnung"). The question posed is not what characteristics are common to various elements, but what are the conditions according to which one element is arranged and connected with another and follows from it. As formulated in *Die Philosophie der symbolischen Formen:*

A series of terms a, b, c, d, . . . are to be perceived as "belonging" together, are to be connected by a rule on the basis of which the "issuance" of the one from the other can be determined and predicted. . . . The elements a, b, c, d, . . . are arranged in a manner that they can be . . . regarded as terms in a series x_1, x_2, x_3, x_4 . . . which is characterized by a definite "general member."[6]

The most elementary sensory plane presents structural elements, such as congruence or opposition, similarity or dissimilarity. The point is also illustrated by the phenomenon of memory. More is required for memory than mere repetition of former events and impressions. These must be ordered and

[5] *Substance and Function*, (Chicago-London, 1923), 317, 319; *Essay on Man*, 68, 69, 172, 222. Article on "Substance," *Encyclopaedia Britannica*, 14th ed., (1928), vol. XXVI.
[6] The principle "stellt ein Neben- und Nach-Einander auf, das fortschreitend in ein In-Einander umgesetzt werden soll." *Philosophie der symbolischen Formen*, Dritter Teil, (Berlin, 1929), 482.

located in time. "Such a location is not possible without conceiving time as a general scheme—as a *serial order* which comprises all the individual events." What is sought are analogous correspondences within empirical variations. Both *Substance and Function* and *Philosophie der symbolischen Formen* emphasize that the whole must not be conceived as an absolute outside of all possible experience. "It is nothing else than the ordered totality of these possible experiences."[7] Serial order makes for a philosophic system "in which each separate form gains its meaning purely by the position which it occupies, where its content and import are marked by the wealth and the individuality of relations and implications through which it is connected with other human forces, and finally with their totality." The analogous "inner form" of culture lies in "the conditioning principle of its structure," in which the individual relation does not lose its uniqueness by its interrelation with other human energies. This produces an abiding unity of basic patterns (*Grundgestalten*). The very relational network in which separate contents of consciousness are interwoven contains a reference to other contents. These references mean that there are certain forms (*Gebilde*) of consciousness. The form-principle which finally emerges lies above—but not beyond—the material forms from which they originally stem.

The unity thus achieved is "a functional unity." It involves change which is "directed toward *constancy*, while constancy reaches consciousness in *change*." Objectivity is determined functionally, that is in "the manner and form of its objectification." The "thing in itself" apart from its function is a false problem. The life of Reality is constituted by the manifold fullness of human forms which has the stamp of functional objectivity. The problem of Reality issues into a phenomenology of human culture.[8]

Cassirer's functional unity is not one of specific *materials*, of products or effects. It involves a concept of causality which, in

[7] *Ibid.*, 494; *Essay on Man*, 51; *Substance and Function*, 292.
[8] *Philosophie der symbolischen Formen*, Erster Teil, (Berlin, 1923), 14, 12, 41ff., 47-8. Dritter Teil, 19. *Essay on Man*, 52

contrast to the mechanistic and teleologic, probes "the creative process" itself. From this approach, the "distinguishing mark" of man "is not his metaphysical or physical nature—but his work. . . . It is the system of human activities which defines and determines the circle of 'humanity'." Cassirer's philosophy transforms substance into function and essence into relation.

The creative value in the method of functional structure lies in that it permits us not only to maintain order in the relationship of the "real" with the "real," but to pass from the "real" to the "possible." It enables us, for example, to foresee what color-nuance belongs to a given series of colors, even if we never experienced it before. Cassirer cites the scheme of Heinrich Wölfflin as a structural view in the history of art. From his study of different art-modes, Wölfflin derived the categories of "Classic" and "Baroque." These terms do not simply describe, nor are they exhausted by particular historical periods, but designate general structural patterns. Wölfflin naturally refers to the works of Raphael, Titian, Rembrandt and Velasquez; yet, what he analyzes is "the schema" which their works embody. It follows from Cassirer's stress on the creative process of man's work that reality can never be exhausted. In the spirit of Hermann Cohen's notion of an "*unendliche Aufgabe*," it is a question of "an ever progressive process of determination."[9] It is here that the historical method emerges as an integral aspect of Cassirer's functional approach.

HISTORICAL PROCESS AND FREEDOM

Cassirer's historical procedure is based on an idealistic orientation translated into the constructive act. Basing himself on neo-Kantian epistemology, Cassirer holds that forms of culture, from language to art, do not refer to physical objects, but are expressions of human feelings and concepts. The latter have a

---

[9] *Essay on Man*, 71, 70, 68, 69. *Philosophie der symbolischen Formen*, Dritter Teil, 496. Here, Cassirer opposes Hume on the basis of a relational and Gestalt-psychology. In a similar way, he analyzes the Theory of Relativity as functional objectivity. *Ibid*, 551ff. *Philosophie der symbolischen Formen*, Erster Teil, 22.

productive and constructive function, and must be studied, not simply in their final products, but in their process. Instead of viewing concepts in their static completed form, "we want to, so to speak, grasp them in *statu nascendi*." Historical process is the vehicle through which the creative-dynamic and functional-dialectic nature of man's world becomes concretized in time. It is not simply a review, but a construction or a "prophecy of the past." Symbolic reality itself requires "symbolic reconstruction." Because its subject matter is human life and culture, history is not an exact science, and its "last and decisive act is always an act of the imagination."[10] Genuine historical time is not biological, as Bergson thought, but involves an act of will as well as a contemplative moment. Cassirer also opposes Nietzsche's argument that the study of history enfeebles our activistic powers. Rightly employed, history "strengthens our responsibility with regard to the future." We study the past, not in order to escape into a lost paradise. On the contrary, "only to the extent the human mind . . . develops in a futuristic direction can it find itself in the framework of the past." As Goethe puts it, genuine longing must here too be 'productive:' It should seek out the past "in order to grasp and view it as a symbol of the lasting and enduring."[11] The study of history is determined by our futuristic perspective. Cassirer's own analysis of the historical connection between Logos, Dike and Kosmos in Greek philosophy is motivated by "anxiety over our human freedom. We know that (our) future is most heavily endangered unless we succeed to link truth and justice, Logos and Dike in the same way as the Greeks linked them in the history of man." Historical form involves the element of freedom.

This element prevents history from being an exact science. Yet, it is not therefore subjective idiosyncrasy. It is not ego-

---

[10] *Essay on Man*, 131, 178, 177, 191, 69, 204. *Logos Dike Kosmos*, 4.

[11] *Philosophie der symbolischen Formen*, Dritter Teil, 210f., 218. *Freiheit und Form*, 575; *Essay on Man*, 179. See also *Wissenschaft, Bildung, Weltanschauung*, (1928), 30, quoted in *Philosophy and History*, Essays presented to Ernst Cassirer, (Oxford, 1936), 141-42.

centric, but anthropomorphic. The rules which bind the scientist hold for the historian as well. History too has "a general structural scheme" by means of which it can classify, order, and organize disconnected facts. What history aims at is an "objective anthropomorphism."

The historical method which Cassirer uses in his analysis of art and other cultural activities follows from his general functional approach. History is the form in which the laws of human behaviour are *enacted* by way of symbolic construction and reinterpretation. To know the whole, we must present it in its functional acts. Conversely, the parts represent the whole. This is the character assumed by the "natural" symbolism of consciousness.[12]

THE DIALECTIC OF FUNCTIONAL STRUCTURE

Cassirer's historical procedure contains the dialectic notion that all creative effort contributes towards the dynamic process of reality by its very dramatic location in that process. Cassirer agrees with Whitehead in opposing the method of "simple location." Older methods are not to be eliminated, but referred to "a new intellectual center." He sees no either-or between the descriptive and the exact procedures, but would relate both to two different aspects of a general problem. Nor would he choose among the psychological, sociologic and historic methods, between the proponents of *l'art pour l'art* and the opposing method of I. A. Richards. Likewise, he rejects the theory of Windelband and Rickert that history is a logic of individuals, whereas natural science is a logic of universals. Cassirer points out that "thought is always universal," and that a judgment also contains an element of particularity. Where others see irresolvable antinomies, Cassirer seeks the plane from which they may be viewed as partial aspects of a more inclusive whole. "It is characteristic of the nature of man that he is not limited to one specific and single approach to reality but can choose his point of view and so pass from one aspect to another." Thereby,

[12] *Logos Dike Kosmos*, 23; *Essay on Man*, 69, 191. *Philosophie der symbolischen Formen*, Erster Teil, 43.

the general and the particular, content and form, element and relation become reciprocal correlates. Such union of the typical with the specific provides "a kind of grammar of the symbolic function as such."[13] The point is bound up with Cassirer's concept of "theory."

In *Substance and Function,* the form of knowledge was seen as identical with that of the exact sciences. *Philosophie der symbolischen Formen* enlarges the concept of "theory" to show that genuine theoretical forms and motivations also obtain for the world of perception. Yet, even the earlier work draws a distinction between the universality obtained in mathematics and mathematical physics and that gained in fields where perception enters. The former uses an abstractive procedure, "selecting from a plurality of objects only the similar properties and neglecting the rest." Herein lies its limitation. "Through this sort of reduction, what is merely a *part* has taken the place of the original sensuous *whole*. This part, however, claims to characterize and explain the whole." Selection, on the basis of the similarity-principle, is one-sided, for it disregards "things and their properties." Thus, in passing from the particular to the universal, we reach "the paradoxical result . . . that all the logical labor which we apply to a given sensuous intuition serves only to separate us more and more from it." For this reason, modern logic opposes abstract universality by concrete universality as in the logic of the mathematical concept of function. And, even though this form of logic is not confined to mathematics, but is applicable to other fields, a distinction remains between the space of sense-perception and the space of geometry. In the former, space-differentiation is connected with the *content* of sensation. This is not the case in geometrical space. Here, "the principle of absolute homogeneity of spatial points denies all differences, like the difference of above and below, which concern only the relation of outer things to bodies, and thus belong to a particular empirically given object." The logic of mathematics and of mathematical physics "forbids any . . . identification of the

[13] *Essay on Man,* 50, 68, 50, 166f., 186f., 170. *Substance and Function,* 314. *Philosophie der symbolischen Formen.* Erster Teil, 18-19, 32.

exact and the *descriptive* methods." Here lies the contrast between science and árt. Even as the work of the great natural scientists has an element of "spontaneity and productivity," their particular type of abstraction impoverishes reality. Science is concerned with the uniformity of laws, rather than with the diversity of intuition, with conceptual depth, tracing phenomena back to their first causes, rather than with visual, audible, and tactile forms.[14]

Art as the Dialectic of Concrete Totality

Cassirer regards the Platonic dialogue as the basic intellectual form of all dialectics. And he pays tribute to Hegel as the organizer of this method. But he sees Hegel's limitation in that the resolution in his dialectic issues from the pure movement of thought, and in that it pretends to be final. Hegel, to be sure, did speak of the "concrete universal," and in the second part of his *Phenomenology*, his *Philosophy of History*, and elsewhere, attempted to show the location of physical and individual existence in the dialectic scheme. Yet, Cassirer regards Hegel's dialectic as moving mainly in the realm of the speculative idea. Furthermore, in its pretense at exhaustive "syntheses," it violates the process of human acts and feelings.

Cassirer's insistence is on the *concreteness* and *materiality* of cultural forms. Traditional metaphysical dualisms are bridged insofar as it can be shown that "the pure function of the spiritual must seek its concrete fulfillment in the physical." And, it is because art is in the most favorable position to fulfill this task that Cassirer finds in it the richest function of reality. Cassirer's philosophy itself reaches its own most eloquent expression in his discussion of art and literature. Here his writing is at its most engaging and animated, metaphor, style, and imagery moving in rhythm with the subject discussed.

Art gives us "a richer, more vivid and more colorful image of reality" than science.[15] This is so because artists and writers

[14] *Philosophie der symbolischen Formen*, Dritter Teil, V. *Substance and Function*, 6, 16, 18f., 21, 105. *Essay on Man*, 220, 169.

[15] *Idee und Gestalt*, 108f., *Philosophie der symbolischen Formen*, Erster Teil, 19. *Essay on Man*, 170, 207.

replace an abstract-conceptual dialectic by the material-content-ual dialectic. Furthermore, they are nearer to reality in that they do not pretend to offer a final resolution of conflict, but present this conflict practically in its entire depth. On this account, Cassirer pays tribute to Hölderlin's "dialectic of feeling," Kleist's "dramatic dialectic" which issues from forms and characters, rather than from tendencies and ideas. Whereas other forms of symbolic activity combine the universal with the particular, art comes nearest to this goal because it communicates through an *immanent* symbolism. Its immanence appears two-fold: every work of art has specific individuality, and it has sensuous form. This holds not alone for the arts which manipulate materials (architecture, sculpture, painting, etc.), but also for poetry and music which work in a sensuous medium, in images, sounds, rhythms. For Cassirer, the mode and design are "necessary moments of the productive process itself." An artist does not merely "feel"; he must *externalize* what he feels and imagines in visible, audible, or tangible embodiment. He works not simply "in a particular medium—in clay, bronze, or marble—but in sensuous forms, in rhythms, in color patterns, in lines and design, in plastic shapes. . . . Free from all mystery, they are patent and unconcealed." Shakespeare illustrated this aspect of poetic imagination in *Midsummer Night's Dream:*

> And, as imagination bodies forth
> The forms of things unknown, the poet's pen
> Turns them to shapes, and gives to airy nothing
> A local habitation and a name.

In that the realists of the nineteenth century concentrated on "the material aspect of things," they had a "keener insight into the art process than their romantic adversaries." Likewise, Croce errs in minimizing the material factor as having only technical, not aesthetic importance.[16]

The concept of "form" is central to Cassirer's scheme. And, in character with the nature of his philosophy, the term itself

[16] *Idee und Gestalt*, 155, 201. *Essay on Man*, 207, 170, 141f., 154, 157, 153.

appears in varying functional imports. We can distinguish four different and overlapping meanings:

1. Form as material embodiment.
2. Form as organized construction.
3. Form as imaginative reconstruction and transcendence.
4. Form as Law, or as the unifying functional principle among different phenomena.

Cassirer's high evaluation of art is due to the fact that it combines these various aspects of form. We have already spoken of the art-form as material embodiment. But art is more than material form: it *organizes* and *shapes* this material. It is not simply an "imitation" of reality, as the naturalists claim, and it is more than emotional "expression," as Croce and Romantic theorists argue. It expresses emotion in a *disciplined* way and through an act of construction. Yet, this act of construction does not render art subjective. Great works of art "reveal a deep unity and continuity" which reside in their structural unity by which they organize and reconstruct experience. The process of selection is also a process of objectification.

Law in art-form does not preclude but contains the element of transcendence or freedom. As the most anthropomorphic of cultural pursuits, art possesses a teleologic structure, and expresses "an activity of the mind." This activity does not receive sense impressions passively, but gives them a dynamic life of forms. The symbolic nature of art moves it beyond mere expression and mere representation towards "an intensification of reality." Whereas art conforms to the same fundamental task as other forms of culture, unlike science, it does not eliminate but intensifies the personal and the individual element. Art-forms are specific, but not static. Their concretion is a continuous process revealing a mobile order which is the dynamic process of life itself. "Pregnant with infinite possibilities which remain unrealized in ordinary sense experience," they transform our passions into "a free and active state." Freedom is once more Cassirer's final value, freedom to shape and construct human life in accordance with the limits imposed by the structural forms of our world.[17]

[17] *Essay on Man*, 151, 143, 144f., 149. A stimulating view of art along

The functional and dialectic aspect of art also appears in genuine aesthetic experience. Here too a dialectic relationship must obtain where we would understand a work of art, involving an element of empathy and a ready attitude to enter into the artist's perspective. It is not simply a question of extracting "pleasure" from art, as the hedonistic theory claims, but to gain a sense of freedom through absorption in dynamic forms, and in turn by reconstructing them towards new emerging functions.

AESTHETIC THEORY

Cassirer's category of function appears in his own analysis and demonstration of particular materials. That is, it becomes more completely meaningful in its own concrete functioning. In the field of art and literature, his studies comprise analyses of aesthetic theories, examination of individual critics and artists, and consideration of specific art-works. Throughout, Cassirer's principle of functional objectivity makes itself felt through the manner in which the general thesis appears in its particular form, and the central argument is ever felt amidst the rich multiplicity of detailed historical data.

The problem set in Cassirer's historical account of aesthetic (as well as philosophic and moral) theories is to show their gradual development to the point where the ideas of freedom and form appear as reciprocal functions.[18] Before Kant, Cassirer points out, German aesthetics (Gottsched, Bodmer, Breitinger) was dominated by rationalistic categories. Alexander Baumgarten's *Aesthetica* does distinguish between the logic of the imagination and the logic of reason, but relegates the former to a lower plane. The aesthetic is conceived as the lowest logical, not as an extra-logical function. The notion of form dominant here and in the Italian and French neo-classicists is a form of

---

similar lines is offered by G. Kepes in *Language of Vision*, (Chicago, 1944), 12ff. "The experience of an image is . . . a creative act of integration. . . . Here is a basic discipline of forming, that is, thinking in terms of structure. . . . This new language can and will enable the human sensibility to perceive space-time relationships never recognized before. . . . Visual language . . . must absorb the dynamic idioms of the visual imagery, to mobilize the creative imagination for positive social action, and direct it toward positive social goals."

[18] Particularly in *Freiheit und Form, loc. cit.*

reason, not of sensuous matter. Art is but to reproduce the beautiful in nature, leaving no room for freedom or for the power of the imagination. The romantic theory, on the other hand, stressed almost exclusively the free poetic imagination as the clue to reality. And by dissolving the distinction between poetry and philosophy, art became a universal product, rather than the work of an individual artist. By this emphasis on art as a symbolic representation of the infinite, the Romanticists left no place for the finite world of sense experience. Their universal freedom was beyond the world of finite and determined form.

The discussion of historical aesthetic movements is supplemented by analysis of specific writers on aesthetics. It extends from the general philosophic and aesthetic examinations of Shaftesbury, Leibniz, Kant, Fichte, Schelling, Rousseau, Herder, Hamann and Wincklemann to concrete exemplification of art-theory in the drama and poetry of Lessing, Hölderlin, Schiller, and, above all, Goethe. Everywhere, Cassirer would show what connects and what distinguishes the various writers. And faithful to his strategy, he employs a different method in each case.

In Lessing, Schiller and Goethe, Cassirer finds the nearest dialectic fusion of freedom and form in German classical literature, with Kant as the most potent stimulant.[19] Lessing held that drama must be examined not only for its climax and conclusion, but for the *law* of its construction. Foreshadowing Kant, Lessing saw in the freedom of creative genius the source of artistic necessity. The genius does "freely" what objective formal rules demand. And, in his stress that action is the primal ingredient of poetry, Lessing stated the objective of art itself to be that of producing inner movement.

---

[19] Through his rejection of English empiricism with its doctrine of "receptivity," Shaftesbury is credited with providing the seeds for a philosophic aesthetic which helped shape German intellectual history. Following English Platonism instead, Shaftesbury sought the beautiful not in the realm of the *formed*, but in activity, in the creative principle of *forming*. ("The Beautifying not the Beautify'd is the really Beautiful."—Shaftesbury). Cf. Cassirer's *Die Platonische Renaissance und die Schule von Cambridge*, (Leipzig, Berlin, 1932), 112ff., 138f.

In the case of Schiller, Cassirer traces his development from a eudaemonistic and rationalistic ideal of truth to the point where art appears as autonomous, not as a means to truth or ethics. Through Kant, Schiller came to realize that art finds its form and purpose in itself, and that the aesthetic acts as a mediator between the theoretic and practical realms. But, whereas Kant demands or *postulates* this mediation, Schiller, as artist, *knows* it as such. Kant's *principles* become *"Triebe"* for Schiller. He sees the tension and resolution not as a static relation of concepts, but as a dynamic process. It is precisely here that Kant's transcendental methd begins to go over into the dialectic method of his followers. "In setting up the basic opposition between stuff and form, receptivity and spontaneity, Kant proceeds as a transcendental analyst, . . . Schiller as dramatist." Schiller's *"Spieltrieb"* synthesizes *"Formtrieb"* and *"Stofftrieb"* which belong to the realm of Ideas without however leaving the sensuous world. Beauty for him is "freedom incarnate" (*Freiheit in der Erscheinung*). The analogy between the genuine work of art and the living organic form lies in that both are determined by a self-given rule. Herein Schiller reveals the highest degree of sensuous dialectic thought.[20]

GOETHE

Cassirer's treatment of historical personalities and theories is such that at times one feels that he is identifying himself with them. This flows from his notion that the past is to be treated as a living force, not merely effective in the present, but closely interlocked with it. Still, Cassirer does distinguish between greater or lesser historic truth and error, validity and limitation, and we can thereby distinguish Cassirer's own position from those he presents. In one instance, however, this distinction almost disappears. It is in Cassirer's discussion of Goethe that one senses something like complete identification between author and subject. Indeed, some of Cassirer's very formulations on the rôle of form in art are identical with those

---

[20] *Rousseau Kant Goethe*, 87; *Freiheit und Form*, 156, 421ff.; *Idee und Gestalt*, 81ff., 90, 102.

ascribed by him to Goethe. Likewise, Cassirer's principle of "serial order" appears completely illustrated in his presentation of Goethe's own method in the natural sciences. The same holds for other problems, such as causation, the rôle of hypotheses, etc.[21] Cassirer is here at one with the German tradition, particularly from Nietzsche to Thomas Mann, which looks to Goethe as the inspiring prototype.

Goethe appears, in Cassirer's studies, as the highest development in the historical relation between form and freedom.[22] For Schiller, natural law is in conflict with the idea of freedom; for Goethe, it is in harmony with nature. Hence, Schiller regards the ethical *imperative* of freedom as the most inclusive category. For Goethe, objective existence itself provides the material for freedom.

Cassirer's method avoids the traditional approach to Goethe in terms of "phases" and "periods," which gives parts instead of a whole. The problem is to show the inner unity and basic forms of Goethe's life, poetry, drama, science, etc., "to show how the same law operates in all . . . that they are various symbols for one and the same living connection." This is the method Goethe himself employed in striving to find a central "pregnant point." Moreover, appreciation of Goethe's work requires more than seizing on his conclusions. The approach must be functional: the results are to be shown as they were arrived at through the concrete process of his life and art.

It was Hellenic art which helped shape the substance of Goethe's thought. It taught him that the content and essence of art and nature are analogous.

> Wie Natur im Vielgebilde
> Einen Gott nur offenbart,
> So im weiten Kunstgebilde
> Webt ein Sinn der ew'gen Art.

From then on, Goethe's view on art struggles towards the typical, or the "*Urbild.*" This type is not a fixed schema, but "a norm which cannot be known and grasped except through

---

[21] *Essay on Man*, 140; *Freiheit und Form*, 321ff.; *Idee und Gestalt*, 48ff., 57f.

[22] Cassirer sees Greek philosophy and tragedy as the first to have expressed the connection between freedom and law. *Logos Dike Kosmos*, 22.

the regulated changes from one individual structure to the next." This does not exclude the method of abstraction—a method Goethe did not reject, but use. Yet, Goethe's abstractive method does not detach itself from individual phenomena, but presents the totality in all of its combinations. It is not a pragmatic norm, for it seeks the structural processes in which various distinct moments interpenetrate. Cassirer gives something like a restatement of his own logical method when he writes that Goethe leaned towards that method in logic in which a law is based on the continuity of individual parts—rather than of *classes*—, which gives a *series* bound together by firm principles. He calls attention to Goethe's term "ultimate phenomenon" (*Urphänomen*), as combining the Platonic concept of eternal Ideas with the notion of sensuous "phenomena." The *Urphänomen* appears in a dialectic play of antitheses (*Polarität* and *Steigerung*), ultimately reducible to the basic antithesis of rest and motion. Every complete poem of Goethe's shows this blending of motion and structure, of individuality and totality, of freedom and form. All Being finds its fulfillment in Becoming, and there is no Becoming in which Being is not present. In that we think of the two (the "simultaneous" and the "successive") as united, we reach the plane of the "Idea."

However, only the direction of this process, not its goal, is knowable. The essence of all true symbolism lies precisely in that here the particular represents the general—not as a dream and shadow, but in Goethe's formulation "as a living and immediate revelation of the unfathomable."[23] Here, Goethe is at one with the greatest artists, such as Leonardo da Vinci. His notion that "the beautiful is a manifestation of secret natural laws which would be eternally hidden from us, if they did not come into concrete appearance," is altogether in Leonardo's sense.

This reveals Goethe's relation to traditional metaphysics. In his essay "Goethe und Platon," Cassirer points out that, whereas in Plato becoming was the limit of knowledge, in Goethe it is transformed into a presupposition and a form of knowledge. As

[23] *Idee und Gestalt*, 137. *Freiheit und Form*, 277-79, 307, 311, 327, 378f., 412. Cf. the essay, "Goethe and the Philosophic Quest," by Slochower, H., in the *Germanic Review*, vol. VIII, No. 3, (July, 1933).

an artist, he saw no antinomy between idea and experience. A work of art *demands* sensuous concretion of the Idea. With Plato, Goethe also saw the beautiful as an expression of truth and law. But for him, this truth cannot be measured or replaced by another. Its truth is that of the image, the highest moment of appearance. Plato rejected art, since it does not drive from nature to the Idea, but stays at the reproduction of the image. But to Goethe art was the realm where man both stays aloof from and also binds himself most firmly to the world. In it, we are no longer in the sphere of the sensuous, yet still stand within the periphery of the perceptual. It is the real mediator between idea and appearance.[24]

Goethe's "corporeal" (*gegenständliches*) thinking is again shown in Cassirer's discussion of specific works, such as *Pandora* and *Faust*. His analysis of *Pandora* would demonstrate "how the artistic image gradually takes on the stamp of the idea and the idea takes on the stamp of the image and the sensation." In contrast to Platonic thinking (to which this poetic drama bears an inner relation), the idea has sensuous form. And "form" does not pertain to a transcendental plane, but emerges in the midst of the dynamics of life. Yet, the final truth is that man can never grasp the realm of form. His real formative power is not in the contemplation but in the creation of form which gains life and reality in the realm of action. In this way, Goethe reconciles the formless world of action (Prometheus) and the inactive visionary world (Epimetheus). The same point appears in *Faust*. Helen's veil dissolves in Faust's hands. His final wisdom is that the meaning of life lies in human co-operative work. His liberation takes place not in the world of beauty but in that of action. The highest goal lies in the liberation of mankind. "The world of freedom," Cassirer concludes, "arises from the world of form . . . a freedom which exists only in that it continually *becomes*." As against the individualistic idealism of German humanism, we have here a new social ideal.[25]

[24] *Individuum und Kosmos in der Philosophie der Renaissance*, (Leipzig, 1927), 168. *Goethe und die geschichtliche Welt*, 114f.
[25] *Idee und Gestalt*, 11, 27. *Freiheit und Form*, 415.

One of Cassirer's more notable contributions are his essays on Goethe's scientific studies. He does not agree with those who dismiss these studies as poetic fancies. Following Geoffroy de St. Hilaire, Helmholtz and others, Cassirer regards them as containing a vital contribution to methodology. He is concerned with showing that Goethe's conflict with the method of mathematical physics is not merely a historical phenomenon, but is permanently relevant.

To begin with, Cassirer would establish that both Goethe's method and that of the mathematical physicist aim at finding "an analogy of form." In his studies on optics and morphology, Goethe too employs the idea of continuity and the method of genetic construction. He also recognizes the value of general formulation, and his morphological cognition is never identified with sensuous particularity. However, beyond this, there is a differentiation in their methods, as becomes apparent in Goethe's controversy with Newton. Newton's theory of color reduces differences of color to numerical differences. It is concerned with the *general*, not the *real* form of color. Goethe directs his problem to the world of *vision*, rather than to color. He too would introduce a definite principle; yet, he would not reduce it to numbers which *represent* things merely conceptually, but to a principle which would *signify* and *be* this order. The mathematical formula aims to make phenomena *calculable*, Goethe's principle to make them *visible*. Actually therefore, the two views are not in conflict. Goethe was concerned with the physiological, Newton with the physical aspect of color.

Goethe's scientific studies are an organic mode of his poetic productions as well. Likewise, there is an analogy between Goethe's critique of eighteenth century science and of eighteenth century poetics. He condemns Boileau's philosophy of art and Linné's philosophy of botany from the same angle: both slighted particular phenomena in their quest of the general.

Goethe was persuaded that phenomena themselves were the final formula, insofar as they are regarded in their genetic connection which preserves their perceptual *quality*. The *Urphänomen* is Goethe's "final" principle beyond which he does not try to penetrate to ask for *its* "why." The nearest equivalent for the *Urphänomen* is "life." It follows that this principle is not a final solution and resolution, but only a final and highest problem. Goethe knew only one way in which this problem could be "resolved": *practically*, in the realm of action. He avoids the either-or of a mystic-pantheistic method and that of scientific abstraction. Nor does he urge an eclectic reconciliation of the "middle way" between the two. Instead, Goethe transforms the *problem* into a *postulate* to be resolved through the act. Cassirer quotes Goethe's maxim: "Theory and experience stand in perpetual conflict. All unity arrived at through reflection is illusion; only through activity can they be united."

The value of Goethe resides in his significance for us. "The problems which he posed live among us and await decision: we feel them to be *our* problems." Our norm in approaching Goethe should not be in terms of praise and celebration. In Goethe's words: "The true celebration of the genuine man is the act."[26]

CRITIQUE

Evaluation of Cassirer's work might well apply the functional method to "locate" his own system. Cassirer's neo-Kantian orientation places him in the idealistic "serial order." His notion that man is a "symbolical animal" with powers of reconstruction postulates that reality is basically constituted by thought. This confronts us with a number of problems and ambiguities in Cassirer's work.

1. The stumbling block of idealistic systems arises from their difficulty in being able (or, more precisely unable) to account for evil and error. Despite Cassirer's modifications of traditional idealism through his concept of concrete functional objectivity, his analysis is heavily weighted towards regarding all historical creativeness as retaining validity through its location and order, by which it finally contributes to the whole. That is, Cassirer tends to identify history with value, *what is*

---

[26] *Idee und Gestalt*, 37, 44. *Goethe und die geschichtliche Welt*, 121, 99f. *Freiheit und Form*, 326. Similarly, Cassirer writes that his study of the Enlightenment is for the purpose of finding "the courage to compare ourselves with it and to come to terms with it inwardly . . . to free the original forces which produced and shaped this form." *Die Philosophie der Aufklärung*, (Tübingen, 1932), xvi.

with *what is good*. To be sure, in his actual analysis, Cassirer's sensitive discrimination leads him to occasional criticism and rejection.[27] But such critique is infrequent and generally tempered with the suggestion that even a narrow perspective contributed towards an evolving truth. Thus there arises an ambiguity between what *does* develop and what *should* develop. Cassirer rarely views any pattern or doctrine as in basic opposition with another. Cassirer's dialectic is, in the main, one of *reconciliation*. Although he criticizes the logical approach to art, Cassirer credits the rationalistic aesthetics of Leibniz with containing elements which were later developed in the notion of the manifold in art. In reviewing the relation of Heraclitus to Parmenides, Cassirer focuses on the fact that they meet in centering on Logos and Dike. The discussion of Goethe and Plato begins by contrasting Goethe's conception of truth in terms of the image and Plato's notion of truth as a pure Idea. Yet, Cassirer notes that Plato also had recourse to the images of the sun and the cave to represent the Idea of the Good and the State, and that, in his later dialogues, Plato taught that motion and becoming penetrated the sphere of pure Being. A similar approach is used by Cassirer in his historical analyses of science, language, mythical thought, religion, and culture. "Only in such relations and in such contrasts," Cassirer concludes, "does truth have its concrete historical being. . . . Whoever grasps history intellectually and the intellectual historically hears everywhere this solemn-friendly sound of the bell—and it becomes a consoling bass-sound which assures the inner harmony of . . . world history in all its chaotic entanglement of outer happenings."[28]

2. Cassirer's dynamic concept of the dialectic clearly transcends his Kantian heritage. It also does greater justice to the material aspect than does Hegel's dialectic. Cassirer's functional methodology provides a general lever for examining the social along with the intellectual conditions for the conception and the

---

[27] Some of these have been noted earlier. Cassirer also speaks of Hellenic influence as having endangered the development of the dynamic form-concept. He criticizes Tolstoy's suppression of form in art, and rejects deterministic theories as "full of metaphysical fallacies." *Essay on Man*, 141f., 147, 192ff.

[28] *Logos Dike Kosmos*, 11. *Goethe und die Geschichtliche Welt*, 124f., 141f., 148.

reception of culture. Yet, the material aspect which Cassirer stresses is generally restricted to material *form* which art and other cultural expressions manipulate. He does view art as part of life and sees in "work" man's outstanding characteristic. But, in his specific analyses, "life" and "work" are considered mainly apart from *social* "life" and "work."[29] Similarly, Cassirer's general formulations recognize the reciprocal relationship between the subjective and objective factors. What becomes of the beams which philosophic ideas send out, he writes, "depends not only on the character of the source of light, but also on the mirror they encounter and in which they are reflected." Yet, Cassirer examines this source and mirror primarily in their intellectual and formal nature. His study of the Enlightenment aims to show the connection between its philosophy and its science, history, law, and politics. But, to Cassirer, it is philosophy which provides the "living breath, the atmosphere in which alone they can exist and function." Throughout his analyses, the conditions for "influence" are considered in terms of the "*geistige*" situation. Questions such as why Goethe, Schiller, and others were ignored in certain periods, despite their stature, are not raised. Cassirer does not analyze the social reference to revolutionary innovations in art and literature which condition their acceptance or nonacceptance, the specific accents in their development and related features. His discussion of Lessing, Schiller, Goethe, and others focuses on their formal or humanistic dialectic. He is less concerned with their rebellious social rôles. Perhaps this predilection explains why Cassirer steers clear of the great literary rebels of the 19th century.[30]

[29] However, some passing references should be noted. Cassirer speaks of the "narrowness of German life" which determined the rationalistic view of art. Language is said to have also "a social task which depends on the specific social conditions of the speaking community." Likewise, the classification of its idioms is dictated by needs which "vary according to the different conditions of man's social and cultural life." In discussing Diderot, Cassirer writes that his thought "moves within and is bound up with a specific social order . . . the atmosphere of the Paris salons." See *Freiheit und Form*, 103f., 217f. *Essay on Man*, 128, 136, 178. *Rousseau Kant Goethe*, 8.

[30] *Rousseau Kant Goethe*, 98. *Philosophie der Aufklärung*, x. Yet, Cassirer's orientation must be distinguished from that of Wilhelm Dilthey, to whom some

3. If Cassirer slights the rôle of social materials, he all but ignores the weight of personal psychic elements. This is particularly striking in his study of Kleist, whose personality and work are a clear expression of unconscious motivation and psychological estrangement. Cassirer would prove that Kleist's so-called "Kant-upheaval" was due, not to Kant, but to Fichte's *Vocation of Man* and to its doctrine of the subjectivity of perception. He demonstrates that Kleist's plaint over the relativity of knowledge could not have its source in Kant's transcendental idealism, which proved the validity of experience as against Berkeley's psychological idealism. Cassirer argues further that, through Kant, Kleist was induced to abandon his monistic teleology. Yet, whereas this shift produced an intellectual upheaval in Kleist, it also made for a profounder objectivity in his art. Finally, the disciplinary impact of Kant's ethics appears in Kleist's last years in his drama "The Prince of Homburg." Now, shortly afterwards, Kleist committed suicide. Yet, Cassirer's study does not contain a single reference to this act, nor to the inner motives which were driving Kleist towards his tragic end at the very stage when he appeared to have found an intellectual center in Kant's ethics. Cassirer merely writes of the "immediate living force" which Kant exerted on Kleist, and notes that Kleist's nature was averse to compromise. There is no examination of Kleist's social context, involving factors such as his equivocal societal location as a member of a pauperized nobility in the era of the Stein-Hardenberg reforms, nor of his psychological dilemmas, the great attraction for his sister Ulrike

---

have linked him. Dilthey saw the greatest task of the historian and artist in "understanding" and "reliving" experience. Although requiring passionate immersion into inner experiences, his *"Verstehen"* and *"Erlebnis"* were essentially a pious non-reactive homage to historical "lived experience." Hence Dilthey's prototypes were the German Romanticists, such as Novalis and Schleiermacher. Cassirer's concept of the historian and artist has a much more active and reactive tenor. His approach to the Romanticists is more critical, and he identifies himself most readily with writers preceding and following the Romanticists, with Shakespeare, Lessing, Schiller, and Goethe, who viewed art and the genius in terms of their recreative, not merely relived, capacities. See Wilhelm Dilthey's *Das Erlebnis und die Dichtung*, 10th ed. (Leipzig and Berlin, 1924), Cf. H. A. Hodges' *Wilhelm Dilthey. An Introduction*, (N.Y., 1944).

and for men-friends, evidence of sublimation and compulsion in the relation to his bride,—all of these factors which enter into the pattern comprising Kleist's complex emotional reaction to Kant, Rousseau and Fichte, and his final suicide.

In his study of Rousseau and Kant, Cassirer similarly confines himself to speaking of Rousseau's "fundamental trait," of the turmoil in the man who was "always fleeing from himself." Kant, on the other hand, is termed "the man of the clock," whose "being" was guided by order and law. Cassirer's whole point in drawing the contrast in their personalities is to indicate that Kant's attraction for Rousseau's ideas can not be accounted for on the basis of their individual structures, but that the influence was of an intellectual and moral nature. It was in these spheres that they met "at some profound stratum of their beings."[31]

Although Cassirer places the "symbol" into the center of human activity, the term is used solely in an honorific sense. Its imaginative transcendence is seen only as *good* transcendence. It stands in overlapping harmony with, never in opposition to other elements. Metaphorical expression is analyzed to the extent that it is more than the object referred to, but not in terms of its *conflicting* variations. The dissociative and oppositional disparity in the relation between art and society is ignored, as is the complex interplay between public demands and private desires within the individual. In short, the whole problem of psycho-social alienation falls outside the framework of Cassirer's investigations.[32] This introduces a troubling problem for Cassirer's category of freedom. Freedom in Cassirer's work lies in creative reconstruction and in the preservation of the individual-concrete form within the presentation of the universal. Hence his high elevation of art, which can fulfill this task most adequately. He does not press towards the question of the realistic conditions which can offer the widest possibilities for art to exercise this ideal function. Cassirer blurs the adverse situation (in

[31] *Idee und Gestalt*, 164-188. *Rousseau Kant Goethe*, 3, 56, 4, 57.

[32] Compare the chapter on Marx and Freud in Harry Slochower's *No Voice Is Wholly Lost. Writers and Thinkers in War and Peace*, (N.Y., 1945).

its personal and public forms) from which man might free himself. By slighting the factor of conflict, Cassirer's concept of freedom loses much of its own functional import.[33]

However, Cassirer's eighteenth and nineteenth century perspectives not only mark the limits of his approach. They also make possible his distinctive contributions. The pyscho-social function which Cassirer neglects is today provided, and sometimes over-provided. On the other hand, such analyses often lose sight of the broader intellectual and aesthetic forms. Here, Cassirer's work offers a much-needed corrective. His very classical standards separate him from the secessionist vogue of our time. The era of "division of labor" has developed split and compartmentalized motivations in which man appears separated from tradition, divided within himself, and lacking the basis for integrating the new complexities. Cassirer is not altogether unaware of such disturbances, as shown in his analysis of psychical disturbances in *Philosophie der symbolischen Formen*. Yet, he is persuaded that men live in a common world and respond similarly to similar conditions. Cassirer's thinking in terms of organic centers is a wholesome antidote to the divisionism in the critical fashion which would analyze art simply in terms of "form," where form is divorced from content and historical motivation. Here technical factors, such as plasticity, line, color, relief, are viewed as things in themselves, detached from subject matter and the artist's creative imagination. This has resulted in the phenomenon which Toynbee has called "etherealization." A similar emphasis violates denotation in art in the interests of maximum connotation. To be sure, all art is connotative insofar as it has general import. But art differs from philosophy and science in that it aims at maximum denotation, which it is in a position to approximate because of the particularity and sensuousness of its material. Cassirer's functional objectivity offers a welcome alternative to such unreal dilemmas.

Another signal value is the crucial weight Cassirer places on process and form. One of the melancholy aspects of much art-

---

[33] Relevant to this point is Helmut Kuhn's criticism of Cassirer in *The Journal of Philosophy*, vol. XLII, no. 18, (August 30, 1945).

criticism is its focus on the "what," "the point of view," or "purpose" of the artist. It seeks out a writer's "conclusion" and praises or condemns him on that score. This method blurs the distinction between an essay and a painting, between a logical exposition and a musical motif to the extent that it singles out what they "stand" for. This procedure obviously violates the specific character of the material. Moreover, it contains a fallacious assumption as to what constitutes "conclusions" in art. The "message" is identified with the moral exhortations of the "good" characters and the fate which overcomes the "sinners." This type of analysis leaves out almost everything that is peculiarly relevant to a work of art, which makes its "point" by way of imagery, metaphor, irony and, above all, the *dramatic process*. Cassirer's functional approach shows that to get at the artist's "what" we must enter into his "how," that its whole meaning lies precisely in the manifold of its form. Examining art from this angle, we may find that a writer's ostensible "conclusion" is at least modified by the "sympathy" in the artist's form. Such sympathy appears in the relative *enthusiasm* revealed by the power and richness of depiction, by ironic reservations introduced in motivating the context of "bad" acts, and similar structural and formal devices. The same principle holds for an evaluation of literary criticism itself, insofar as the latter is not mere documentation, but attempts reconstruction of literary material. Cassirer makes an analogous point when he refers to the discrepancy between Taine's explicit formulation of naturalism in his *Philosophie de l'art* and his actual investigation and description which corrects this formulation. It follows that appreciation of creative works requires entering into the process *through* which the conclusion is reached, requires attention to the formal elements involved, which are "part and parcel of the artistic intuition itself," —in short, calls for something of the same temper and equipment which is exhibited by the art-work which is being evaluated. In Cassirer's formulation, "we cannot understand a work of art without, to a certain degree, repeating and reconstructing the creative process by which it has come into being."[34]

[34] *Essay on Man*, 194f., 155, 149.

In conclusion:

Cassirer's functional analysis sees man as a dialectical complex of a triadical unity: Man as history, Man as permanence, and Man as *animal symbolicum*. In the latter capacity, man recreates his world by means of his symbolical tools of which art is the most enriching. Cassirer's dialectic is not content with establishing "ambivalence,"—a favorite resting ground for contemporary truncated criticism—, but penetrates towards the underlying *valence*.

The stimulation and fertility of Cassirer's work stems from the dynamic concatenation of these elements. In his mastery of detailed knowledge, his catholic learning, his calm reasoning approach, and in some of his underlying logical framework, Cassirer reminds one of Morris R. Cohen.[35] To it all, Cassirer brings high imaginative sensitiveness and a synthesizing vision. The whole makes for living history, for life as art and art as life. The lines of the Earth-Spirit in *Faust* which Cassirer quotes for Goethe's method apply to his own:

> Wie alles sich zum Ganzen webt,
> Eins in dem andern wirkt und lebt . . .
> Harmonisch all' das All durchklingen!

The final contribution of Cassirer's functional method lies in its own functional value for us: the extent to which it sets up, suggests and stimulates analogous waves of ideas and images, and helps us to reshape the world in accordance with new emerging materials. This is in spirit with Cassirer's own supreme value—the liberating social act.

HARRY SLOCHOWER

DEPARTMENT OF GERMAN
BROOKLYN COLLEGE

[35] See, in particular, chapters II, III, IV of Cohen's *A Preface To Logic*, (New York, 1944).

19

Konstantin Reichardt

ERNST CASSIRER'S CONTRIBUTION TO LITERARY CRITICISM

ERNST CASSIRER'S CONTRIBUTION TO LITERARY CRITICISM

IN HIS *Essay on Man,* Cassirer—in the form of a paradox—defines the historian's aspiration as "objective anthropomorphism."[1] Whereas the process of scientific thought shows a constant effort to eliminate "anthropological" elements, history appears not as a knowledge of external facts or events, but as a form of self-knowledge: man constantly returns to himself attempting to recollect and actualize the whole of his past experience. The historical self, however, aspires to objectivity and is not satisfied with egocentricity. In his discussion of the various methods of historical research Cassirer expresses greatest warmth when speaking of the work of Ranke, who once voiced the desire to extinguish his own self and to make himself the pure mirror of things. This wish, clearly recognized both by Ranke and Cassirer as the deepest problem of the historian, remains at the same time the historian's highest ideal. His feeling of responsibility and his ethical standing will determine the value of his results according to the definition of "objective anthropomorphism." Cassirer reveals Ranke's ethical conception and his universal sympathy for all ages and all nations as his principal merits and he contrasts Ranke's basic attitude with that of Treitschke's Prussian school.[2]

According to Cassirer, history belongs not to the field of natural science, but to that of hermeneutics. Our historical knowledge is a branch of semantics, not of physics.[3] Cassirer stands closer to Dilthey than to Taine. Submitting the "scien-

[1] *Essay on Man,* 191.
[2] *Ibid.,* 187ff.
[3] *Ibid.,* 195.

tific," statistical and psychological methods of Taine, Buckle, and Lamprecht to criticism he maintains that history, not being an exact science, will always keep its place and its inherent nature in the organization of human knowledge, and the speeches in Thucydides' work will retain their historical value, because they are objective and possess ideal, if not empirical truth.[4] Cassirer asks for greater susceptibility in exactly this sense: "In modern times we have become much more susceptible to the demands of empirical truth, but we are perhaps frequently in danger of losing sight of the ideal truth of things and personalities. The just balance between these two moments depends upon the individual tact of the historian. . . ."[5] In order to achieve the high task, the last and decisive act is "always an act of the productive imagination." "It is the keen sense for the empirical reality of things combined with the free gift of imagination upon which the true historical synthesis or synopsis depends."[6]

In other words, the just balance in historical research postulated by Cassirer will depend upon two basic elements: on the historian's ethical conception of his duties and on the disciplined greatness of his productive imagination,—the full knowledge of the material being self-understood. Thus conceived, history becomes a sister of art. Art turns our empirical life into the dynamic of pure form; history molds the empirical reality of things and events into a new shape and gives it the ideality of recollection.[7]

We could make psychological experiments or collect statistical facts. But in spite of this our picture of man would remain inert and colorless. We should only find the "average" man—the man of our daily practical and social intercourse. In the great works of history and art we begin to see, behind the mask of the conventional man, the features of the real, individual man.[8]

In August 1943 I had the opportunity to read a—then unpublished—manuscript by Cassirer on Thomas Mann's Goethe

[4] *Ibid.*, 205.
[5] *Ibid.*, 205.
[6] *Ibid.*, 204f.
[7] *Ibid.*, 205.
[8] *Ibid.*, 206.

novel *Lotte in Weimar.* I began to read the manuscript with a special kind of expectation. Knowing Cassirer's stern demand for the highest degree of objectivity in historical research, including literary criticism, and the complete absence of humor, irony, or any lighter tone in general in his writings, I was eager to see if Cassirer would make an exception in this case, which—as I thought—would tempt even the most serious and objective critic to some application of Thomas Mann's own and possibly most characteristic style element, his "loving irony." However, Cassirer had written his critical essay in the Cassirer mood: sympathetically and without one deviation from full seriousness. This consistency throughout all his publications shows how deeply his general demand for ethics and tact in historical research are rooted in his personality, and it also explains the almost complete absence of polemics in his contributions to the field of literature. Compared with many of his German contemporaries Cassirer distinguishes himself by the objective spirit of his work. He seems to be urged to write whenever he feels able to improve or to elucidate, and not because he would like to correct or to attack. Thus, his own discussions appear usually as an investigation of a point without an edge. "Man cannot live his life without constant efforts to express it,"[9] this would be Cassirer's general answer to a question about the value of literary documents in the past or present. Every document requires, from a historian, a sympathetic and expert reading, and the true historian will remain sympathetic, since every document will be a contribution to his "self-knowledge" and the knowledge of man. How he himself will express his own attitude and beliefs will be a matter of ethics and tact. It is highly revealing how gently and without a trace of irony or impatience Cassirer treats far-fetched theories in aesthetics or the immature statements on art by the young Schiller.[10] They receive his serious attention as historically logical efforts of man to express the fact that he is living. And without sympathy significant interpretation is impossible.

[9] *Ibid.*, 184.
[10] *Die Philosophie der Aufklärung,* 368-482. *Die Methodik des Idealismus in Schillers philosophischen Schriften,* 86ff.

Cassirer considered himself a philosopher, not a literary critic. With the exception of one article, all his publications in the field of literature appeared either in independent form or in strictly philosophical periodicals. The scope of his contributions is wide: the German enlightenment period and German classicism and romanticism stand in the foreground; however, there are many valuable chapters, passages, or remarks on Classical, French, English, Swedish, etc., literature in his work. They all deal with literary-philosophical questions and they are all directed toward an understanding of the relation between certain literary personalities and certain philosophers or systems of philosophy; however, Cassirer's ideal problem seems never to be merely that. His investigations always exceed the concrete question of influences or individual works of art, and his deepest interest seems to lie elsewhere. Although Cassirer, as far as I can see, nowhere makes a statement to this end, his publications concerned with literature are of greater interest for the aesthetician than for either the philosopher or for the literary critic in general. Whenever Cassirer writes about a writer X in relation to a philosopher Y, he seems to be—in spite of all his attention to X and Y—more interested in Z, and Z is the individual essential poetic element (*dichterisches Wesenselement*) of X.

In the introductory part to his essay on Hölderlin[11] Cassirer expresses the aim of his investigation most significantly. I translate the passage:

It [the investigation] will have to try to draw from Hölderlin's poetic essence, as it belongs to him originally and as it precedes all abstract reflection, the interpretative conclusion in regard also to those trends which manifest themselves more and more distinctly in the totality of his theoretical attitude toward the world and life.[12]

This means clearly that Cassirer considers it the first duty of his investigation to clarify the character of Hölderlin's "poetic essence" which he regards as Hölderlin's "original property," before any possible statement about the development of his theoretical attitude can be made. Cassirer's wording looks like a

---

[11] *Hölderlin und der deutsche Idealismus.*
[12] *Idee und Gestalt,* 118.

sanctification of deductive method; however, the essay itself gives clear proof of the opposite and his other publications on literature support it. An inductive analysis is always made—as far as such an analysis can go. The final evaluation of the material, however, is no longer a matter of scientific method.

Thus, Cassirer's task here and elsewhere is a two-sided one. He does not limit himself to the never quite satisfactory investigation of certain philosophical influences on certain elements or periods of an artist's work, but tries to find a concrete picture of the artist's essence *qua* artist before the question of the artist's reflective world is raised. As a matter of fact, Cassirer—without mentioning it—has the tendency to protect the artist both from literature and from philosophy as these fields are usually represented in criticism. Cassirer, the philosopher, shows his greatest sympathy for the world of creative art and its individual rights.

The essay on Hölderlin may serve as an example for Cassirer's general attitude and method in the realm of literary-philosophical problems. The ideal subject for this purpose would be Cassirer's intensive occupation with his master, Goethe. However, this latter would greatly exceed the scope of our contribution.

Before Cassirer wrote his Hölderlin essay, three modern and important works on Hölderlin had appeared,—Dilthey's famous essay, Zinkernagel's book, and Gundolf's deep analysis of Hölderlin's *Archipelagus*. The result of Cassirer's essay shows, besides important additions, intensification of Dilthey's views, agreement with Gundolf, and a sharp contrast to Zinkernagel's method.

One of the foremost questions in regard to Hölderlin had been the exact determination of his position within the philosophy of German idealism. That Hölderlin had been greatly and constructively influenced by Platonic reflections, Kantian criticism, and Spinoza's system was known. However, Hölderlin's relation to Fichte, Schelling, and particularly to Hegel had not been clarified. In this respect, Professor Zinkernagel had tried to reach results by an analysis of Hölderlin's foremost work *Hyperion* and had offered a very thorough appearing list of "influences" which seemed to make Hölderlin a receptive organon of all kinds of stimulations. A reader of Zinkernagel's book, in spite of all possible admiration for the author's knowledge and minute scholarship, would ask in vain why Hölderlin, as both poet and philosopher, shows such remarkable and generally acknowledged unity, and proved at the same time to be able to survive all these "influences" as an individual and to maintain his artistic personality to such an extent that today he is considered one of the most consistent and full grown lyric poets in world literature. It is in connection with Zinkernagel's book that Cassirer made his statement that Hölderlin's artistic personality was to be the *res prior* of his investigation and all other questions were to be regarded as *res posteriores*. The reciprocity between Hölderlin's imaginative and rational world was to be investigated.

Since Hölderlin's poetry as a whole is an expression of his personal conception—or philosophy—of nature, Cassirer chooses at first to characterize Hölderlin's peculiarity in contrast to Fichte and Schelling. Hölderlin, seeing in Kant's Critical philosophy a propaedeutic step towards a "system" and finding the ideal form of a system represented in Spinoza, tried —as did Fichte and Schelling—to establish an idealistic counterpart of Spinoza's construction. However he distinguished himself from Fichte and Schelling by regarding the One not as the supreme principle of deduction but as a ἓν διαφερόμενον ἑαυτῷ conceived in direct relation to his conception of nature. The study of Plato contributed greatly to Hölderlin's peculiar mythical imagination; however, myth never was and to Hölderlin never became a mere symbol or a poetic ornament; but it was a necessary organon to apprehend reality. Myth and mythical phenomena appear in all of Hölderlin's works, including his letters and philosophical fragments, as sensuous-spiritual realities in which he believed without any noticeable sense of dualism. Hölderlin's conception of nature manifests an intertwinement of the reflective and perceptive elements without any break or inconsistency, and what Schiller tried to evoke sentimentally (*sentimentalisch*) in his poem "Die Götter Griechenlands," Hölderlin achieved naïvely and faithfully: to him the gods of Greece were not welcome poetical elements, but realities and therefore means towards the cognition of truth. The contact with Fichte's writings stimulated the depth of Hölderlin's reflective thinking, however—again—he reached his independent conclusion: nature, for him, was not matter but form.

Zinkernagel's belief that Schelling's influence was telling for Hölderlin's repudiation of Fichte's doctrine is denied by Cassirer. Moreover, Cassirer is able to provide almost irrefutable proof for the opposite. Disregarding the fact that Schelling had been Fichte's follower until 1796,—the year in which the "influence" was supposed to have taken place,—we have (with Cassirer) to take into consideration that Schelling's later philosophy of nature reminds one of Hölderlin's earlier general attitude. A document made available in 1913 seems to correct all former interpretations of the Schelling-Hölderlin relation. In 1913, the Royal Library at Berlin acquired a folio-sheet which shows Hegel's hand and contains a brief outline of a philosophical system. The editor called it "the oldest systematic program of German idealism" and was able to prove that the manuscript is a Hegelian copy of a Schelling text.[13] The text expresses a demand for a system of philosophy that would combine "the monotheism of reason" with "the polytheism of imagination," in order to develop a "mythology of reason." This is exactly what Hölderlin in his more imaginative rather than rational way of thinking had felt and fought for. Cassirer's conclusion seems good enough: the widely discussed meeting between Hölderlin and Schelling in 1795 had not brought about a Schelling influence on Hölderlin, but had given Schelling an opportunity to find stimulation from the side of Hölderlin and to formulate rationally what had already been in Hölderlin's mind.

The result is the historically significant fact that Hölderlin had been the responsible agent implanting the thoughts into the man who was to become the most Romantic representative of German idealism. Cassirer was able to supply the proof for this contention because of his correct basic presumption that

[13] F. Rosenzweig, *Das älteste Systemprogramm des deutschen Idealismus* (1917).

Hölderlin's imaginative world was clearly outlined before any outside influences came upon his reflective world. What follows in the last part of Cassirer's essay is an intensively compressed description of Hölderlin's pantheism. After giving one of his masterly surveys of the dialectic method in Kantian and Romantic philosophy, Cassirer shows that Hölderlin, who used the categories and terms of philosophical idealism, transformed them gradually but consistently into a dialectic of feeling—the simultaneously consistent and antithetic essence of every lyric poet. Hölderlin did not try to solve the dialectical problem concerning the relation of the general and the particular; he only expressed the depth of the problem as an artist.

I do not find sufficient reason for divergence from Cassirer's interpretation and, in particular, from his discussion of Hölderlin's "artistic essence." Newer and fuller investigations, carried through with greater ambition in regard to completeness, have enlarged on the material; however, they have not improved our understanding in general.[14] Yet, I should like to take up one specific statement in Cassirer's essay, a statement which makes me uneasy.

In the introduction to his brilliant last section Cassirer expresses himself rather apodictically about the general character of a lyric poet.[15] According to him the peculiarity of a lyric poet is to be found in two elements: his individual conception of nature (*Naturgefühl*), and his individual feeling for form and development (*Ablauf*) of spiritual occurrences (*seelisches Geschehen*). When these two elements meet and determine each other reciprocally, the peculiar lyric form of expression arises. In other words, the individual conception of nature and of the human soul is the basic condition for a meeting which—in the world of an artist—makes lyric art. The important attribute here seems to be "individual," since all art shows the interrelationship of nature (all manifestations of nature, from a flower to a slum dwelling) and man (the life of soul in all

---

[14] See W. Böhm, *Hölderlin* I-II (1928-30), K. Hildebrandt, *Hölderlin; Philosophie und Dichtung* (1939).

[15] *Idee und Gestalt*, 136.

possible aspects). Therefore, what does "individual" mean? In the following passages Cassirer speaks lucidly of Hölderlin's tragic efforts to find objectivity, and he manages, very methodically, to leave the impression that Hölderlin as an individual was one of the unusual artistic phenomena who were both influencing and being influenced in regard to their philosophical or cognitive achievements. However, this did not make Hölderlin a lyric poet, and his individuality as such—if we accept Cassirer's two conditions—does not differ in principle from other artists who were not lyric poets, but, for instance, dramatists.

I do not believe that Cassirer, in his statement about the lyric poet, and speaking of his "individual" conceptions, was entangled in the still rather common belief that subjectivity is one of the foremost elements of lyrics. Many years after he wrote his Hölderlin essay Cassirer expressed himself clearly in this respect. After a discussion of Croce's aesthetic theories,[16] he says:

It is of course true that the great lyrical poets are capable of the deepest emotions and that an artist who is not endowed with powerful feelings will never produce anything except shallow and frivolous art. But from this fact we cannot conclude that the function of lyrical poetry and of art in general can be adequately described as the artist's ability "to make a clean breast of his feelings." . . . The lyric poet is not just a man who indulges in displays of feeling. . . . An artist who is absorbed not in the contemplation and creation of forms but rather in his own pleasure or in his enjoyment of "the joy of grief" becomes a sentimentalist. Hence we can hardly ascribe to lyric art a more subjective character than to all the other forms of art. For it contains the same sort of embodiment, and the same process of objectification. . . . It is written with images, sounds, and rhythms which, just as in the case of dramatic poetry and dramatic representation, coalesce into an indivisible whole. In every great lyrical poem we find this concrete and indivisible unity.[17]

There is an interval of twenty-six years between the Hölderlin essay and the Essay on Man. Yet I cannot find any basic inconsistency between the quoted passages from the latter and

[16] Essay on Man, 141f.
[17] Ibid., 142f.

Cassirer's general attitude in the former. However, the statement about the principal elements of a lyric poet still remains unexplained. Perhaps, Cassirer used a cliché—an unusual process in his writings—in order better to express the content of the directly following statement about the peculiarity of the German lyric poets in the period of Idealism, their desire to become conscious of their actions as creative artists, and their further desire to verify these actions philosophically. This is, to be sure, not a singular incident in the history of lyrics—the French symbolists and their successors show a more than general parallel—, but it is true.

There are many relations between philosophy and literature which have been noticed surprisingly late[18] or have not as yet found a satisfactory explanation. Those cases appear most puzzling in which there exists a deep similarity between a philosophical system and the expression of a poet without permitting the assumption of a "physical" influence. In the case of Hölderlin the existing material is such that his development simply could not be understood after eliminating the surrounding philosophical situation. In the case of Corneille, however, and his position in relation to the Cartesian system, the problem is much more involved. In consideration of the methodically different approach, Cassirer's attitude seems to be significant.

G. Lanson[19] expressed the situation very well in a few words: "*Il y a non seulement analogie, mais identité d'esprit dans le Traité des passions et dans la tragédie cornélienne.*" The curious facts are that Descartes and Corneille were contemporaries—Descartes' *Discours de la Méthode* appeared in 1637, immediately after the first performance of the *Cid* at the Théatre du Marais in Paris—, that they represented a school of thought which was new and individual, and that yet a direct relation between them cannot be established. G. Krantz tried to show Descartes' constructive influence on the aesthetic theories of French classicism, and Faguet[20] made the attempt to establish reasons

---

[18] I am thinking especially of Plotinus' influence. See Franz Koch, *Goethe und Plotin* (1925).

[19] G. Lanson, *Etudes d'Histoire Litteraire* (1930), 58ff.

[20] G. Krantz, *Essai sur L'Esthétique du Descartes* (1882). Faguet, *Dix-septième siècle*, 175.

for a possible influence on Descartes by Corneille,—both in vain. Lanson, who is certainly right in not trusting either theory, explains the similarity between Descartes' and Corneille's psychological and ethical aspects from their physical environment and tries to ascertain that the spiritual-moral reality in French seventeenth century life was reason enough to stimulate both the philosopher and the poet toward the same end; that the active-intellectual type of man, then representative in France, gave both of them an object of experience which contributed to the results in their respective attitudes.

In his book on Descartes, Cassirer devotes a chapter to the discussion of Descartes and Corneille.[21]

Cassirer does not assume any direct influence. A Cartesian influence on Corneille is impossible chronologically, and a Corneillean influence on Descartes highly improbable because of Descartes' well-known attitude toward literature in general and modern literature in particular. Since Lanson's explanation does not appeal to Cassirer, he directs his efforts towards finding reasons which may have brought about something like a pre-established harmony between Descartes and Corneille. His method is *geisteswissenschaftlich*,—the essence in Descartes' reflective and in Corneille's poetic psychology and ethics is to be defined and explained in their connection with the historically preceding or simultaneous philosophical development.

According to Cassirer, both Descartes and Corneille were dealing with an object of thought which had been one of the foremost topics since the early Renaissance: the relation between Ego and World. They both express the "pathos of subjectivity," theoretically-ethically or poetically, and—a striking parallel —they have the same theory of freedom in contrast to their contemporaries.

Essential for both Descartes and Corneille was their occupation with the world of passions. Descartes tried to investigate his object as a physicist (*en Physicien*); only through cognition of the passions can we master them and use them to our ethical advantage. In Descartes' scale of values the highest ideal is

[21] *Descartes*, 71-117.

represented by the combination of full energy of will and perfect judgment, although Descartes does not deny the existence of a relative ideal besides the absolute one, which ideal would consist of a combination of full energy of will and not perfect judgment. Corneille, in his plays, shows an exactly equivalent attitude and was attacked by his contemporary critics as immoral because of his opinion that the application of great will power, no matter whether the aim is good or not, has its own value.

Furthermore, Cassirer shows clearly that the Stoicism, as it appears both in Descartes' and in Corneille's work, experienced a significant transformation, losing its passive attitude (*sustine et abstine!*) and its moral characteristic as a doctrine for "bodiless beings." Descartes' psycho-physical interpretation of the passions and Corneille's similar attitude distinguish them both from the classical and the Christian conception.

Cassirer succeeds very well in pointing out sharply the general parallels which, without any doubt, are essential. In addition to it, his literary discussion of Corneille's tragedies is of high value because of its historical objectivity. Corneille's *dramatis personae* will seem unreal or psychologically improbable to anyone who has not been initiated into the essence and the laws of the poet's individual world; yet they regain their ideal truth as soon as the doors to this world have been opened. Then, and then only, is it not a question of liking or immediate appreciation any more, but a case of following a creative poet on his excursions through his imaginative world.

All this granted, we are still waiting for an answer to the original question. There can be no doubt that certain lines of development can be traced down to Descartes and Corneille which will make them appear as historically "logical" personalities; yet their peculiar conformity in reaching the same conclusions in regard to such specific objects as human passions and the scale of values has not been explained by Cassirer. In his interpretation, Descartes and Corneille still remain lonesome giants, having many clear connections with the past and, at the same time, with modern views, yet lacking any significant connection with their own time. The clarification of their philosophical or poetic systems is helpful for our understanding of *them;* however not sufficient for the understanding of their positions in their time.

Lanson's idea that Descartes and Corneille were basically influenced by the peculiarity of their time is enticing in its methodical aspect. Cassirer finds the connection between them in the past; Lanson stresses their immediate relations as not resulting from any direct physical influence but from the source of life surrounding them. And Cassirer himself, in a different chapter of his Descartes book, offers new material which seems to give Lanson substantial support.

In the chapter about Descartes and Queen Christina of Sweden, Cassirer discusses the question whether Christina might have been acquainted with Corneille's writings.[22] There is no conclusive answer; yet Christina's interest in contemporary thought and art is established so well that her ignorance of the first great French dramatist would seem unbelievable. Cassirer goes farther; he not only shows that Christina in her reactions and actions resembles greatly the heroines in Corneille's plays, but also gives a highly interesting, concrete example which manifests a deep affinity between one historical reaction of the Queen of Sweden and a poetic one in Corneille's *Pulchérie:* Christina's decision to dissolve her engagement to Karl Gustaf and the parallel Pulchérie—Léon. Corneille wrote his play twenty-five years after Christina had made her famous decision. Therefore, no fantastic hypothesis about the influence of poetry on life can be offered in this case.

Queen Christina, after Cassirer's very valuable interpretation, appears as an addition to the list of seventeenth century personalities who, according to Lanson, showed Corneillean character *in concreto.* It is surprising that Cassirer, in spite of this, reacts so indifferently to Lanson's theory in his Descartes-Corneille chapter. Descartes and Corneille would become fully comprehensible, if not only their common roots in the past but also in their own time could be shown. Great philosophers and artists, I think, never stand apart from their own time, no matter

[22] *Ibid.,* 251-278.

whether they act as friends, enemies, or prophets. The sociological aspect of both philosophy and literature should never be forgotten, and in the case of Descartes' and Corneille's "strange" affinity it should be applied in full. Therefore, Lanson's treatment of the question, although deplorably incomplete, shows the way to future research. I am not at all in favor of giving the sociological method a prominent position in literary research; however, I think that the physician should know which medicine to use in each specific case.[23]

A completely different problem appears in connection with the most controversial German romanticist, Heinrich von Kleist.

Kleist's relatively small artistic output stands in no quantitative relation to the amount of work dedicated to him in literary criticism. The Kleist-specialization in Germany has resulted in research conditions which have made every element in Kleist's life and work an object of passionate discussion.[24] The phenomenon Kleist represents an in many respects interesting riddle which, in order to be solved, seems to require a co-operative effort on the part of rather broadminded literary critics, historians, and psychiatrists. The limitations of critics manifest themselves almost necessarily in regard to Kleist. To make things worse, Kleist has some national importance for his country, and we need hardly enlarge upon the almost inevitable results in criticism. The most significant example of misunderstandings in regard to Kleist, however, is in my eyes the *Kätchen von Heilbronn* interpretation in F. Gundolf's book on Kleist,[25] in which this truly exceptional and far-sighted critic manifests a complete lack of hermeneutic ability in this particular respect. All the difficulties of interpretation *in re* Kleist arise from Kleist's own super-nervous and chaotic personality more than from his artistic work. He is one of the best examples both of the inability of the soul of man to master absolute ideal demands and also of a psychopathic condition together with a capacity for exceptionally creative and lucid artistry.

---

[23] The sociological method has been applied with good results in modern Russian criticism; see especially P. N. Sakulin, *Die russische Literatur* (1927).

[24] See *Jahrbuch der Kleist-Gesellschaft*, 1921ff.

[25] F. Gundolf, *Heinrich von Kleist* (1922).

Kantian philosophy, as generally acknowledged, had a great influence on Kleist as a man and as a writer. Obvious records, among them his letters, give a solid basis for this contention; and his artistic works show Kleist's symbolical transformations of philosophical (and other) problems. However, the exact significance of Kant's philosophy for Kleist as an artist has not been clarified as yet, and certain gaps of understanding prevailed when Cassirer enlivened the Kleist research by his daring essay on Kleist and the Kantian philosophy.[26] Among other contributions to the point, Cassirer advanced a new hypothesis which—if accepted—would, even though it would not change our general attitude toward Kleist, compel us to take new data into consideration.

In his letters to his sister Ulrike and his fiancée Wilhelmine von Zenge, young Kleist gave an intimate account of his state of mind and his general views. The letters are sometimes so expressive and self-interpreting that many a statement in them has been taken for granted without due regard to Kleist's general characteristic of being very inconsistent and versatile in his moods, predilections, and self-expression. In his plays and short stories Kleist offers a magnificent example of his creative ability to transform a moment into a life. However, his letters suffer from the dualism between his creative, and therefore practically not always reliable imagination, and the attempt of giving an empirically realistic account of his life. This is likely to be a rather general situation in an artist's letters. Yet in this case it is more prominent than in others, perhaps because of the constant efforts in the Kleist research to establish the empirical truth instead of pursuing the wiser way towards the ideal truth.

In a much discussed letter of March 22, 1801, Kleist, in utter despair, describes to his fiancée the annihilating effect of his occupation with the Kantian philosophy and gives a vivid picture of his total apathy after learning that "We cannot decide, whether what we call truth is really the truth or only appears to us as such." Kleist's world of ideals, for which he had lived and from which he had received his strength, seemed to

[26] "Heinrich von Kleist und die Kantische Philosophie," in *Idee und Gestalt*, 159-202.

be destroyed. This letter is a masterpiece of writing and could, without a change, fill the place of a monologue in any suitable tragedy.

At least three specific questions arise directly from this letter. First, Kleist gives the impression that he had begun his occupation with Kant's philosophy "a short time ago" ("*vor kurzem*"), although we know that he had already studied Kant in 1800. Secondly, speaking of Kant, Kleist uses the strange expression "the more recent so-called Kantian philosophy" (*neuere sogenannte Kantische Philosophie*). Thirdly, Kant's Critical method and philosophy seem to have been misunderstood by Kleist.

The discussion of these three points is the backbone of Cassirer's hypothesis in the first part of his essay: that Kleist in this letter had in his mind not Kant's transcendental idealism but Fichte's *Bestimmung des Menschen*.

The question is not of great importance outside the circle of the professional Kleist experts. However it has methodical significance. We know that in 1800 Kleist had occupied himself with Kant without experiencing any disastrous results. On the other hand, it is easy for Cassirer to show that Kant's Critical method did not imply the denial of the objectivity of man's cognitive efforts. These two facts, in connection with the strange formula "so-called Kantian philosophy," leads Cassirer to the possibility that Kleist, in 1801, had read Fichte's *Bestimmung des Menschen*, which had been published in 1800 in Berlin— where Kleist lived—under circumstances which made this book immediately one of the most widely discussed in Prussia's capital. Kleist must have known the book; and it contained ideas which would make his reaction very plausible.

Cassirer's hypothesis may be correct. However, I think that it represents one of the very few instances in his writings on literature where he presses a point less from necessity than from his own status as a Kant expert. It is certainly strange to observe that Kleist, who in November 1800 had written his sister that he would like to go to France in order to spread there the new (i.e., Kantian) philosophy, would have had such a shocking experience on account of this same philosophy less than half a year later. The explanation that Kleist was shocked after reading the *Critique of Pure Reason* is not sufficient, since this work does not express an attitude that would have been basically different from Kant's earlier works. On the other hand, Fichte had become such a well-known personality in Germany, after his "atheism controversy" and his leaving Jena for Berlin, that it is hardly comprehensible that Kleist should have hidden Fichte's name in his letter, if it was Fichte and not Kant whom he had in mind. Cassirer sees that the acquaintance with Fichte's *Bestimmung des Menschen* would have been—without any misunderstanding—a sufficient cause for Kleist's despair; however, he does not sufficiently take into consideration a possible misunderstanding by Kleist as to the meaning of Kant's philosophy. Strong inconsistencies and quick impulsive reactions were characteristic of the violently emotional Kleist, and these two letters of 1800 and 1801 may be just other examples of this sort of conduct. If Fichte, a "Kantian" philosopher, misunderstood Kant, why should not Kleist, certainly not a professional philosopher, have made a similar mistake? And his desire to spread Kantian philosophy in France is no proof by itself that Kleist, in 1800, had an intimate knowledge of Kant's transcendental idealism.

To prove either opinion is, of course, impossible; and it was to be expected that critics of Cassirer's hypothesis were split into two camps. Oskar Walzel, one of the foremost experts in the field of German romanticism, remarked: "Among the numerous discussions of Kleist's 'Kant experience,' only . . . [Cassirer's essay] needs to be emphasized."[27] Eugen Kühnemann, in his lecture on "Kleist und Kant," took the stand against Cassirer.[28]

The discussion of Kleist's confusing letter is only a part of Cassirer's essay. Its second half deals with the significance of transcendental idealism for Kleist as a creative artist, and shows in an exemplary manner how Kleist's artistic work received a constructive impetus from Kantian thoughts. Kleist's personal tragedy, experienced by him consciously in continuous philo-

[27] O. Walzel, *German Romanticism*, translated by A. E. Lussky (1932), 302.
[28] E. Kühnemann, "Kleist und Kant," in *Jahrbuch der Kleist-Gesellschaft* (1922), 1-30.

sophic reflections, expressed itself in his art. Cassirer may be right in stating that Kleist is perhaps the only example of a great poet whose creative power had been awakened by a reflective experience (*gedankliches Erlebnis*); at least I do not find any striking parallels. In this connection Cassirer, after his adventure into the realm of empirical truth, is again searching for the ideal truth and is, consequently, at his best.

I do not want to leave the Kleist essay without calling attention to a brief passage in it[29] which is very characteristic of Cassirer as a historian. In the history of German literature there is one of those rather common little events which, *sub specie aeternitatis* would appear as mere trifles but which come up again and again and are discussed with much satisfaction: I am speaking of those numerous examples of apparent pettiness in great men. Our example concerns Goethe and his relation to Kleist and refers to the simple fact that Goethe had no understanding for the tragic genius of his younger colleague. We know some examples of Goethe's not exactly admirable reactions in similar cases; but we do not think their discussion particularly valuable. However, if a discussion were necessary, the only possibly fruitful method is that used by Cassirer in his essay. His brief analysis appears to me to be a perfect example of the ideal method of procedure. Showing Goethe's individual views and his certainly broad, but naturally limited, i.e., defined, personal requirements for what he would have considered great art, Cassirer puts Goethe's lack of understanding for Kleist in the light in which it needs to be seen. There are worlds of thought and of art where friendship is not possible, and that is all. Another sober interpretation of one of Goethe's peculiar reactions was given by Cassirer in his essay, "Goethe and the 18th Century."[30] Goethe astonished Mr. Soret, Prince Karl Alexander's educator at Weimar, in August 1830, by his total indifference to the fact of the July revolution in Paris and at the same time by his very strong interest in the fact that his, Goethe's, synthetic method in scientific research had just been

---

[29] *Idee und Gestalt*, 186ff.

[30] *Zeitschrift für Aesthetik* XXVI (1932), also in *Goethe und die geschichtliche Welt* (1932), 86ff.

accepted by Geoffroy St. Hilaire. In this context Cassirer is able to give an objective and, to me, doubtlessly correct interpretation. Goethe believed in "representative moments" in history. To him the July revolution was less representative than the victory of his synthetic method. As we know today, Goethe was right.

In the history of literary criticism Cassirer is one of the representatives of the field and methods of *Geisteswissenschaft* —the study of the development of ideas. Usually the work of the individual in this line of endeavor shows individual concentration, since what is investigated is not ideas *par excellence* but ideas in their relation to something else. Our survey of a few of Cassirer's contributions shows that his main concern is to be found in the investigation of the relation between the reflective and the imaginative world of the artist. Cassirer is most explicit and most eloquent when recreating the life of the artist's imaginative conceptions which manifest themselves as transformations of his reflective life. His most significant contribution seems to me to be in the neighborhood of this particular point. I find it in the gap which Cassirer leaves unexplained, because he does not want to make a pretentious statement without offering the scale of processes which would solidify it. In spite of everything, Cassirer's apparent interest in the clarification of historical items—Kleist and Fichte or Kant—, or in the truer understanding of a poet's philosophical contribution— Hölderlin and Schelling—, or a better psychological interpretation of a great individual's momentous reactions—Goethe and Soret—, he dedicates his greatest effort to re-telling the story of artistic imagination in those individual lives which caught his fancy. There is no doubt that Goethe is for Cassirer the most significant phenomenon since he is the broadest; a phenomenon which, in the rare combination of pure artistry, profound understanding of the sciences, and peculiarly unacademic philosophizing, represents an object of investigation beyond the usual scope. In his writings on Goethe[31] Cassirer has the opportunity to apply his own wholly constructive, positive, and synthetic

---

[31] See especially *Freiheit und Form* (1916), *Goethe und die geschichtliche*

mind better than anywhere else. But here also a lacuna remains. Cassirer expresses with great penetration his conception of Goethe's artistic essence as he sees it, and the discipline of his knowledge and thought restrains him from overstepping the limits of the material at his disposal. However, here also a point appears again and again where I would ask for further objective penetration; Cassirer would probably reply that the remaining part is a matter of experience, tact, and taste. The demand for more becomes consequently so urgent that,—if the demand is followed by a new investigation,—Cassirer surely would have stimulated it. The investigation ought to be directed toward a more objective foundation of our conception of the artist's creative world.

To be sure, Cassirer has never published a statement referring to what I shall try to express. He knew, however, that such a demand is a logical consequence of his writings on literature; and in conversations he liked to dwell on this point. Fortunately, Cassirer has published a comprehensive chapter on "Art" and there has given a clear picture of his aesthetic views.[32] There is no inconsistency between his general theoretical discussion and the method used in his more practical contributions.

We must mention a few of Cassirer's statements, in order to clear the ground.

Cassirer conceives art in general as a reality of the same value as, for example, science.[33] *"Rerum videre formas* is a no less important and indispensable task than *rerum cognoscere causas."*[34] Art has its own rationality, the rationality of form.

Art is not fettered to the rationality of things or events. It may infringe all those laws of probability which classical aestheticians declared to be the constitutional laws of art. It may give us the most bizarre and grotesque vision, and yet retain a rationality of its own—the rationality of form.[35]

Welt (1932), "Goethes *Pandora"* (in *Idee und Gestalt,* 7-32), "Goethe und die mathematische Physik" (in *Idee und Gestalt,* 33-80), *Rousseau Kant Goethe.*
[32] *Essay on Man,* 137-170.
[33] *Ibid., passim.*
[34] *Ibid.,* 170.
[35] *Ibid.,* 167.

The artist who discovers the form of nature is philosophically equal to the scientist who discovers nature's laws. Moreover, "language and science are abbreviations of reality; art is intensification of reality. Language and science depend upon one and the same process of abstraction; art may be described as a continuous process of concretion."[36] "Science gives us order in thoughts; morality gives us order in actions, and art gives us order in the apprehension of visible, tangible, and audible appearances."[37] And—"We cannot speak of art as 'extrahuman' or 'superhuman' without overlooking one of its fundamental features, its constructive power in the framing of the human universe."[38]

These incomplete quotations help us to summarize Cassirer's attitude. Cassirer believes in a creative world of art as a fundamentally independent world of human behavior, with its own conditions and laws. The essence of the artist's mind is different from the reflective mind of the scientist or philosopher. The scientist deals with phenomena and makes the intellectual attempt to bring order into them, renouncing to the highest possible extent an interference of anthropomorphic elements. The artist offers the principal human example of free creative action. The scientist's work comprises a reciprocity of the phenomenal and his intellectual world; his reflective activity has the form of conquest: he becomes master of the phenomena by fully conscious induction, trying (never quite successfully) to reduce the exciting but dangerous combination by means of an always threatening semi-conscious deduction. The artist, on the contrary, uses his intellect rather as a function than as a condition, in order to express the results of his creative imagination.

The transformation of the "real" world which takes place in every great work of art shows something else which may be called intensification or concretion, a something which otherwise does not make an unhindered appearance in the regions of human behavior. In art, and only in art, a decade can be made an hour, and a life made a mere moment.

[36] *Ibid.*, 143.
[37] *Ibid.*, 168.
[38] *Ibid.*, 167.

The intellect's interference manifests itself most clearly in literature, because literature is a linguistic art. However, the total work of literary art does not always have any, and sometimes has very little, direct relation to the world of reflection. The main characteristic of art, in contrast to philosophy and science, is its inherent particularity not to be basically dependent upon the laws of scientific reflection. Since form is the only common rational factor of every art, and the form of each art manifests a specific order, the order and form of the arts are to be investigated, if we want to examine the artist's imagination at work and the architecture of the world of art.

This has certainly been done again and again; however from a different methodical point of view. Since, in this context, we are not interested in the biographical, psychological, or general historical implications of an artist, nor in a more or less casual or accidental investigation of certain elements in the work peculiar to a certain artist, our task should be a complete investigation of the artist's formative tendencies which result in the total of his artistic creation. Art's main element is not the content; it is the creation of a form which—in all its dimensions—offers us the cognition of a content. The formative tendencies may vary in one or in all artists.

When Cassirer speaks of poetic essence (*dichterisches Wesenselement*), he does not use simply a general term for an unclear conception, but thinks of the full essence of the artist's creative and created world. The method of finding it remains undiscussed. Aesthetic judgment, experience, taste, and tact combined in a mind of methodical strength and constructive imagination reach,—as we know and as Cassirer himself shows, —remarkable results. However, the stimulation to a "more" is given at the same time, since the road toward subjectivity is wide open and the question arises whether among the aesthetic opinions of several experts some may not approach the "ideal truth" more closely than others. As long as the object of investigation is not the function of pleasure but the formative conditions of a work of art, an objective method should, at least, be visualized. That such a method can never consist of the traditional formidable computations of, for instance, rhymes, influences, or new words, is obvious.

In literary research we find some of the finest examples of hermeneutic ability. The changes and the continuous development of evaluation do not necessarily make the quality of the preceding or following critical opinions appear weak, because the liking of individuals, groups, and generations may differ. This will remain so forever. However, we are not dealing with a sociology of art or with a history of taste. We may not "like" a certain artistic creation. However we ought to find a method of discovering whether our dislike is simply a dislike or whether it is based on the fact that the work in question is not a work of art. We ought to have the methodical means of finding the characteristics of the numerous "essences" or "worlds" of art as objectively as possible. Acknowledging that form and order in art are a *conditio sine qua non*, we certainly should be able to reach a better understanding of all the forms and orders appearing in the history of art. This has been achieved quite admirably in one of the non-linguistic arts—painting.

An ideal work of art may be compared with a sphere, every external and internal point of which stands in a meaningful connection with every other point. To determine the connections and the necessity of their full reciprocity is the aim of an investigation in regard to the form of art. Obviously, such an ideal example may be found best in an artistic genre which by necessity lends itself to a relatively easy analytical approach, for example in music and also in painting. Linguistic art is far more complex. A lyric poem or a drama can be approached much more easily than for instance a novel, a widely changing and only superficially definable object which, because of the lack of formal limitation, appears as the most difficult possible problem in this respect.

The enervating element in literary research, as in all arts, is the difficulty of determining why an apparently good work of art is good. Here Cassirer says: "It is the task of the aesthetic judgment or of artistic taste to distinguish between a genuine work of art and those other spurious products which are indeed playthings, or at most 'the response to the demand of entertainment'."[39] I believe that more concrete results can be reached. A novel may be good, because it manifests profound psychological insight in spite of bad style; and another novel may be bad, because it shows superficiality of content in spite of a very good style. But it is not psychology or style or content which make a novel good or bad; it is something else. We should try to find this "something else." We should find the conditions under which art manifests itself in literature. We should, in every work of real or presumed art, investigate and define those elements which make it art.

Experience shows that certain results can be achieved very quickly, for instance in the field of the novel. An initial two-sided attempt usually clarifies the ground. A novel combines, under normal circumstances, the description of man with the description of man's environment—nature in any kind of variation. A minute investigation of the formative elements pertaining to the representation of man is the foremost aim. What literary research has done so far is only a part of the whole task. In discussions of paintings we are accustomed to point out every detail of a depicted being's characteristics; in literary research we are usually satisfied with less. It is not a question of physical colors,—an artist's language transforms ideas and feelings into its own colors; "it is written with images, sounds, and rhythms . . . which coalesce into an indivisible whole." The character of a person in a novel as concerns his actions, feelings, and thoughts is the most obvious, although not the artistically most important part of it. A look at the formative tendencies of a novelist shows numerous, but not innumerable, pecularities in making a person come, go, think, speak, impress, yawn, weep, live, and die. A thorough examination of these peculiarities will tell us something rather important about, not the mere technique, but the creative activity of the artist. A complete analysis of a novel will give us a fairly objective comprehension of his formative action. The literary critic should become a neighbor of the fine arts, since literature, in its greatest performances, manifests the same purity of form and order as does great painting. The reason why a complete analytical

[39] *Ibid.*, 164.

investigation of a novel or even of a short story has never yet been made lies in the apparent enormity of the task. The task *is* great. However, considering the immense amount of time spent on other—and sometimes hardly worthwhile—types of literary research, one may be permitted to think this and similar objects worthwhile.

Remaining with our subject, the novel, we may say that an investigation of nature as a formative element is much easier than is that of man. In literary criticism we are accustomed to find statements about the particular tendency or ability of certain artists to describe nature. Very little has been said of the various types of nature descriptions in prose works and still less about the part which descriptions of nature play as a constructive power, necessary for the understanding of the total essence of the work, or as a mere embellishment with no other reason than that of serving the pleasure of the reader. In the first, artistically significant, case there are various patterns or types of form, and in each individual example an objective picture of the artist's aim and creative ability can be found. The results may sometimes be surprising; here I am able to offer a small but concrete example, since a concrete analysis has been published.[40]

In the history of the German novel, Theodor Fontane holds an eminent place. Fontane's descriptions of North German landscape, an inherent and distinct element in his best novels, were praised by critics as creative achievements of high quality. An analysis of these descriptions, however, showed that Fontane used a superficial pattern, introducing the descriptions without necessary inner connection, phrasing them rather monotonously, and using them as a kind of background music. Fontane was clever, but not a creative artist in his descriptions of nature. His quality in other respects has thus far not been investigated. In his technical dealing with nature he shows a tendency toward ornament or embellishment. In the history of human taste, in regard to literature, fine arts, and music—technical ornamentation has been one of the safest steps to popularity and has often been mistaken for true art.

"So long as we live in the world of sense impressions alone we

[40] Max Tau, *Der assoziative Faktor in der Landschafts- und Ortsdarstellung Theodor Fontanes I* (1928).

merely touch the surface of reality. Awareness of the depth of things always requires an effort on the part of our active and constructive energies."[41] The active and constructive energies have not yet been used sufficiently for our better understanding of the means which make it possible for a creative artist to show, in a symbol, a concretion of his poetic world. Better understanding does not mean destructive analysis or hair-splitting. I believe with Cassirer that creative art is the noblest activity of man. The investigation of the formative elements of poetic creation is a noble task.

KONSTANTIN REICHARDT

DEPARTMENT OF GERMANIC LANGUAGES
YALE UNIVERSITY

[41] *Essay on Man*, 169.

20

John Herman Randall, Jr.

CASSIRER'S THEORY OF HISTORY AS ILLUS-
TRATED IN HIS TREATMENT OF
RENAISSANCE THOUGHT

CASSIRER'S THEORY OF HISTORY AS ILLUS-
TRATED IN HIS TREATMENT OF
RENAISSANCE THOUGHT

> Die Aufgabe der Geschichte besteht nicht lediglich
> darin, dass sie uns vergangenes Sein und Leben kennen
> lehrt, sondern dass sie es uns deuten lehrt. . . . Was uns
> tatsächlich von der Vergangenheit aufbewahrt ist, sind
> bestimmte historische Denkmäler: "Monumente" in
> Wort und Schrift, in Bild und Erz. Zur Geschichte wird
> dies für uns erst, indem wir in diesen Monumenten
> Symbole sehen, an denen wir bestimmte Lebensformen
> nicht nur zu erkennen, sondern kraft deren wir sie
> für uns wiederherzustellen vermögen.
> —*Zur Logik der Kulturwissenschaften*, 85, 86.

IN THE work of Ernst Cassirer, historical and systematic studies were not only carried on side by side, they were woven together and used to illuminate each other. From the outset he brought his great gifts for historical interpretation to bear on strengthening and extending the philosophy of humanism he found in Kant. The autonomy of reason, the creativity of the human spirit, *der Wille zur Gestaltung*—this was Cassirer's central vision. It gave him a consuming interest in all the products of the human mind and in the processes by which they have been created—in what he came to call "the universe of symbols." "History as well as poetry is an organon of our self-knowledge, an indispensable instrument for building up our human universe."[1] The autonomy of thought was the lesson he learned from history; it was also the principle of interpretation he brought to the past to make it speak to us.

Hence his special interest and love went out to those periods

---

[1] *An Essay on Man*, (1944), 206.

in the past when men were most keenly aware of their own productive powers and responsibility—to those periods in which a creative humanism was most alive, and was forging its weapons. Closest to his heart was the great humanistic movement in the classic literature and philosophy of eighteenth-century Germany. In Goethe and in Kant he found the culmination at once of an emancipated imagination and an autonomous reason; here poetry, science and philosophy had at last reached maturity and began to realize their *"unendliche Aufgabe."* Dear also was the Greek humanism of antiquity, above all of Plato, which classic German humanism had used as an instrument to build its own human universe. And dear was the emancipating thought of that Renaissance which had earlier turned to antiquity to win its liberation from the theocentric world of the Middle Ages, and to create its own *"freies weltliches Bildungsideal."*[2]

All three of these creative humanistic movements of the past, Cassirer held, can furnish inspiration and sources of power for creating further forms of culture in the future. When by careful historical study we have learned to understand their language, they can free us both from the optimism of a Hegel and from the fatalistic pessimism of a Spengler. Once we have achieved "a humanistic foundation for culture," we shall find that "action once more has free scope to decide by its own power and on its own responsibility, and it knows that the direction and future of culture will depend on the way it decides."[3]

"A humanistic foundation for culture"—thus Cassirer had come to see his task. How then can we explain the central rôle he always gave to natural science in human thought and in his historical studies? How can we reconcile his humanism with his major contribution to the history of philosophy, his making the history of scientific thought an integral part of it? How was it that Cassirer the humanist became one of the outstanding historians of science of our times?

[2] *Freiheit und Form* (1916), 3.
[3] "Naturalistische und humanistische Begründung der Kulturphilosophie," *Göteborgs Kung. Vetenskaps- och Vitterhets—Samhälles Handlingar*, Femte Földjen, Ser. A, Band 7, No. 3 (1939), p. 28.

This seems a paradox only so long as we remain with the conventional opposition between the humanist and the scientist. As William James pointed out, "You can give humanistic value to almost anything by teaching it historically. Geology, economics, mechanics are humanities when taught with reference to the successive achievements of the geniuses to which these sciences owe their being." Natural science Cassirer always looked upon as the highest and most characteristic expression of the powers of the human mind. Even when, as a young student, he was most under the spell of Kant's scientific interests, with his teacher Hermann Cohen he emphasized this humanistic import of the exact sciences. Mathematics and mathematical physics were always for him great creative enterprises of the human spirit, forms of Socratic self-knowledge. In analyzing precisely the concepts and methods by which men have constructed their natural science, we are really analyzing the nature of man himself. Hence from his earliest work on Leibniz down to the penetrating studies he wrote in Sweden and in this country, the history of natural science, the meaning and interpretation of its epoch-making creative achievements, formed the core of his investigation into the nature of man.

We have only to consider his interpretation of the humanistic movement of the Renaissance. Of his favorite historical periods, this is the one in which science is conventionally held to have played the most minor rôle. From Burckhardt down, the controlling interests of the Renaissance have been thought to be irrelevant to, if not actually opposed to the development of natural science. Historians of science, like Lynn Thorndike, have in turn even questioned the existence of any significant "Renaissance."[4] But for Cassirer, the "discovery of the individual," that humanistic task of Renaissance thought, "as the Renaissance pursued it in poetry, in the plastic arts, in religious and political life, found its philosophical conclusion and its philosophical justification" in the scientific achievements of Galileo and Descartes.[5]

But highly as Cassirer esteemed man's self-expression

<hr />

[4] "Renaissance or Prenaissance?" *Journal of the History of Ideas*, IV (1943), 65-74.

[5] "Descartes' Wahrheitsbegriff," *Theoria*, III (Gothenburg, 1937), 176.

through natural science, the Kantian limitation of truth to mathematical physics was from the beginning far too narrow for him. As early as the *Substanzbegriff* in 1910, he attempted a further analysis of the concepts and methods of chemistry. More recently he did the same for biology.[6] But his outstanding theoretical achievement was to carry through a similar methodological analysis of all those other "symbolic forms" which man makes and which make man known to himself. An analysis of the "logic of the cultural sciences"—of the categories and concepts, the methods and notions of truth and of objectivity by which men interpret these symbolic expressions of their life— came more and more to occupy the center of his attention. Only by sharpening these tools of interpretation can we make a knowledge of what man has created in his culture in the past into a genuine "humanistic foundation for the culture" of the future.[7]

Cassirer saw the "cultural sciences" as embracing primarily linguistics, the sciences of art, and the sciences of religion. And with them belongs history, so fundamental a part of them all. Cassirer did not attempt to formulate with precision the distinctive concepts and methods of historical investigation and interpretation until the latter part of his life. He then developed his analysis in critical opposition to most of the theories of history of the last generation in Germany, and against the background of his general philosophy of symbolic forms. But his thought is also obviously his own aims and procedures come to critical self-awareness; he tested other views by what he had already learned during his own practice as an intellectual historian. With a thinker so conscious of method as Cassirer, it is doubly important to start any examination of his actual historical work from his own statement of his theoretical views as to the nature and procedure of the historian's enterprise. "Nobody," he says, "could ever attempt to write a history of mathematics or philosophy without having a clear insight into the systematic problems of the two sciences. The facts of the philo-

---

[6] *Zur Logik der Kulturwissenschaften* (Gothenburg, 1942), 100-104; see also the forthcoming fourth volume of the *Erkenntnisproblem*.
[7] See *Zur Logik der Kulturwissenschaften*.

sophical past, the doctrines and systems of the great thinkers, are meaningless without an interpretation."[8] Likewise, no one can hope to understand Cassirer's historical practice without a knowledge of what he conceives to be the questions and problems the historian is trying to answer.

Consequently, the best way to understand what Cassirer has done as an historian is in terms of his own analysis of the historian's aim. This makes clear not only why he has proceeded as he has; it answers the questions as to why he has not done other things, why he has left out what many other intellectual historians would want to include, and minimized what they would make central. We shall start, therefore, with a statement of Cassirer's analysis of history.

I

Cassirer belongs with those who find a sharp difference between natural science and history. Physical facts are not like historical facts, though neither are brute, "hard" data—both depend on theoretical construction, and their objectivity is established only by a complicated process of judgment. Physical facts are determined by observation and experiment; they become part of the physical order only if we can describe them in mathematical language. "A phenomenon which cannot be so described, which is not reducible to a process of measurement, is not a part of our physical world."[9] But historical facts are not established by observation and experiment, nor are they measured and expressed in mathematical terms. They have to be given "a new ideal existence." "Ideal reconstruction, not empirical observation, is the first step in historical knowledge."[10] A scientific fact is always the answer to a question; the object is always there to be questioned. But the historian's questions cannot be directed immediately toward the past he is trying to understand; they must be addressed rather to documents or monuments. His data, indeed, are not things or events, but symbols with a meaning; he confronts a world of symbols to be

[8] *Essay on Man*, 179.
[9] *Ibid.*, 174.
[10] *Ibid.*

interpreted. The task of the historian is thus not the mathematical expression of observed events, but the interpretation of symbols.

Cassirer rejects, however, those distinctions between natural science and historical knowledge which have been most popular in recent discussion of historical knowledge and historical truth, especially in Germany. History has no distinctive "logic" of its own. Logic

is one because truth is one. In his quest of truth the historian is bound to the same formal rules as the scientist. In his modes of reasoning and arguing, in his inductive inferences, in his investigation of causes, he obeys the same general laws of thought as a physicist or a biologist. So far as these fundamental theoretical activities of the human mind are concerned, we can make no discrimination between the different fields of knowledge. . . . Historical and scientific thought are distinguishable not by their logical form but by their objectives and subject matter.[11]

But again, the difference does not lie in the fact that the objects of historical knowledge are past. Science too is concerned with the past: the astronomer, the geologist, the paleontologist, all succeed in disclosing a former state of the physical world. Nor does the difference consist in the historian's concern with individuals—the view of Windelband and Rickert, who held that science aims at general laws and universals, history at unique events and particulars.

It is not possible to separate the two moments of universality and particularity in this abstract and artificial way. A judgment is always the synthetic unity of both moments; it contains an element of universality and particularity. These elements are not mutually opposed; they imply and interpenetrate one another. "Universality" is not a term which designates a certain field of thought; it is an expression of the very character, of the function of thought. Thought is always universal.[12]

On the other hand, many natural sciences, like geology, determine concrete and unique events. Thus, in distinguishing history from natural science, Cassirer avoids many of the theoretical difficulties of those who have sharply divided the two realms. Above all, he does not rule scientific procedures out of

[11] Ibid., 175f.
[12] Ibid., 186.

the historian's method, but makes them necessary if not sufficient conditions.

The real difference, Cassirer concludes, is that the historian's object is human life and human culture.

History can make use of scientific methods, but it cannot restrict itself only to the data available by these methods. No object whatever is exempt from the laws of nature. Historical objects have no separate and self-contained reality; they are embodied in physical objects. But in spite of this embodiment they belong, so to speak, to a higher dimension.[13]

The historian must use the concepts of science in reconstructing the past from its present traces, just like the geologist. But "to this actual, empirical reconstruction history adds a symbolic reconstruction."[14] Its documents are not dead remnants of the past but living messages from it to us. The historian must make us understand their language. Not the logical structure of historical thought, but this special task of "interpretation," is his distinguishing mark.

What the historian is in search of is the materialization of the spirit of a former age. He detects the same spirit in laws and statutes, in charters and bills of right, in social institutions and political constitutions, in religious rites and ceremonies. To the true historian such material is not petrified fact but living form. History is the attempt to fuse together all these *disjecta membra*, the scattered limbs of the past and to synthesize them and mold them into new shape.[15]

The historian thus aims at a "palingenesis," a rebirth of the past.

. . . an understanding of human life is the general theme and ultimate aim of historical knowledge. In history we regard all the works of man, and all his deeds, as precipitates of his life; and we wish to reconstitute them into this original state, we wish to understand and feel the life from which they are derived.[16]

All human works are forever in danger of losing their meaning.

Their reality is symbolic, not physical; and such reality never ceases

[13] *Ibid.*, 176.
[14] *Ibid.*, 177.
[15] *Ibid.*
[16] *Ibid.*, 178, 184.

to require interpretation and reinterpretation. . . . In order to possess
the world of culture we must incessantly reconquer it by historical
recollection. But recollection does not mean merely the act of reproduction. It is a new intellectual synthesis—a constructive act.[17]

The historian, consequently, is a kind of "retrospective prophet." He interprets the *meaning* of the past; and the category
of meaning is not to be reduced to the category of being. It is,
in fact, an *Urphänomen*, in Goethe's sense; its "origin" is an
insoluble question. It is a kind of "mutation" in evolutionary
development that must be accepted with natural piety.[18]

If we seek a general heading under which we are to subsume historical
knowledge we may describe it not as a branch of physics but as a
branch of semantics. The rules of semantics, not the laws of nature,
are the general principles of historical thought. History is included in
the field of hermeneutics, not in that of natural science.[19]

In this work of historical interpretation of the meaning of
the past, the historian must take his point of departure from
his own times.

He cannot go beyond the conditions of his present experience. Historical
knowledge is the answer to definite questions, an answer which must
be given by the past; but the questions themselves are put and dictated
by the present—by our present intellectual interests and our present
moral and social needs.[20]

The questions we put to past thinkers are determined by our
understanding of our own problems. Hence the need for continual reinterpretation.

As soon as we have reached a new center and a new line of vision in
our own thought we must revise our judgments . . . we have a Stoic, a
sceptic, a mystic, a rationalistic, and a romantic Socrates. They are
entirely dissimilar. Nevertheless they are not untrue; each of them gives
us a new aspect, a characteristic perspective of the historical Socrates
and his intellectual and moral physiognomy. . . . We have a mystic
Plato, the Plato of neo-Platonism; a Christian Plato, the Plato of

[17] *Ibid.*, 185.
[18] *Zur Logik der Kulturwissenschaften*, 109-112.
[19] *Essay on Man*, 195.
[20] *Ibid.*, 178.

Augustine and Marsilio Ficino; a rationalistic Plato, the Plato of Moses Mendelssohn; and a few decades ago we were offered a Kantian Plato. We may smile at all these different interpretations. . . . They have all in their measure contributed to an understanding and to a systematic valuation of Plato's work. Each has insisted on a certain aspect which is contained in this work. . . .[21]

When we turn from the history of ideas to "real" history —to the history of man and human actions, the same holds true. In political history we wish to understand not only the actions but the actors. "Our judgment of the course of political events depends upon our conception of the men who were engaged in them. As soon as we see these individual men in a new light we have to alter our ideas of these events."[22] Hence what Cassirer is emphasizing is a *personal* interpretation of history, in which the key is in the last analysis the *personality* and character of outstanding men. And history is for him "personal" in a double sense. Not only does the historian look for "a human and cultural life—a life of actions and passions, of questions and answers, of tensions and solutions." He must also give a "personal" interpretation of these other personalities, a "personal truth."

He infuses into his concepts and words his own inner feelings and thus gives them a new sound and a new color—the color of personal life. . . . If I put out the light of my own personal experience I cannot see and I cannot judge of the experience of others. Without a rich personal experience in the field of art no one can write a history of art; no one but a systematic thinker can give us a history of philosophy.[23]

Cassirer cites Ranke as his model—not the Ranke of the familiar precept of impersonality, but the Ranke who actually wrote history with a universal "personal" sympathy—a sympathy which was intellectual and imaginative, not emotional.

The procedure of the historian, therefore, is that of the interpreter of another human personality. Thus, to understand Cicero's rôle in the events in which he took part, and to under-

[21] *Ibid.*, 180.
[22] *Ibid.*, 181.
[23] *Ibid.*, 187.

stand those events themselves, we must first of all understand his personality and character.

To this end some symbolic interpretation is required. I must not only study his orations or his philosophical writings; I must read his letters to his daughter Tullia and his intimate friends; I must have a feeling for the charms and defects of his personal style. Only by taking all this circumstantial evidence together can I arrive at a true picture of Cicero and his rôle in the political life of Rome. Unless the historian remains a mere annalist, unless he contents himself with a chronological narration of events, he must always perform this very difficult task; he must detect the unity behind innumerable and often contradictory utterances of a historical character.[24]

In this delicate task he must be selective; but not necessarily of those events which have had important practical consequences, as Eduard Meyer held; he will single out those acts or remarks which are "characteristic," whose importance lies not in their consequences but in their semantic meaning, as "symbols" of characters and events.

The true historian must thus be not only a trained scientific investigator, he must be an artist as well.

But even though we cannot deny that every great historical work contains and implies an artistic element, it does not thereby become a work of fiction. In his quest for truth the historian is bound by the same strict rules as the scientist. He has to utilize all the methods of empirical investigation. He has to collect all the available evidence and to compare and criticize all his sources. He is not permitted to forget or neglect any important fact. Nevertheless, the last and decisive act is always an act of the productive imagination.[25]

I well remember a conversation with Cassirer, in which I was trying to establish some continuity between the procedures of the scientist—whom I do not take in strictly Kantian terms as the mathematical physicist alone—and of the historian. He admitted that the closest parallel in natural science to what the historian has to do is the physician's diagnosis of the ailment of his patient, in which all his scientific knowledge is brought to

[24] *Ibid.*, 182.
[25] *Ibid.*, 204.

bear upon a particular case. But he went on to insist that the
historian must proceed always like the biographer of a man. He
must gather together all his evidence—evidence which is "symbolic" of the character of the man he is considering—and then
try to find that unifying focus or "center" from which all the
manifestations of that character can be understood—what he is
at bottom trying to do. This is, of course, to try to interpret a
thinker in terms of his central problem—in terms, as Ebbing-
haus put it, of *"was er eigentlich will."* This seems, indeed, the
height of wisdom in interpreting the thought of any individual.
But it is significant that Cassirer used this example as the way
to interpret all history. It illustrates what I have called his
"personal" view of the historian's enterprise; and it throws a
flood of light on what he does not do in his historical studies—
on his complete indifference to any economic interpretation of
intellectual history, for example.

Cassirer's analysis of the aim and function of the historian is
well summed up in the following passage from *Zur Logik der
Kulturwissenschaften:*

> The task of history does not consist merely in making us *acquainted
> with* past existence and life, but in showing us how to *interpret its
> meaning.* All mere knowledge of the past would remain for us a "dead
> picture on a board" if no other powers than those of the reproductive
> memory were involved. What memory preserves of facts and events
> becomes historical recollection only when we can relate it to our inner
> experience and transform it into such experience. Ranke said that the
> real task of the historian consists in describing *"wie es eigentlich
> gewesen."* But even if we accept this statement, it is still true that
> what has been, when it comes into the perspective of history, finds there
> a new meaning. History is not simply chronology, and historical time
> is not objective physical time. The past is not over for the historian in
> the same sense as for the investigator of nature; it possesses and retains
> a present of its own. The geologist may report about a past form of
> the earth; the paleontologist may tell us of extinct organic forms. All
> this "existed" at one time, and cannot be renewed in its existence and
> actual character. History, however, never tries to set before us mere
> past existence; it tries to show us how to grasp a past life. The content
> of this life it cannot renew; but it tries to preserve its pure form. The
> wealth of different concepts of form and of style which the cultural

sciences have worked out serves in the last analysis a single end: only through them all is the rebirth, the "palingenesis" of culture possible. What is actually preserved for us from the past are particular historical monuments: "monuments" in word and writing, in picture and in bronze. This does not become history for us until in these monuments we see symbols, through which we can not only recognize definite forms of life, but by virtue of which we can restore them for ourselves.[26]

II

This is Cassirer's statement of the fundamentally humanistic task of the historian. By entering into the spirit of former ages, he can reveal man to himself, and in so doing enlarge man's imaginative sympathies beyond the narrow limits of the present cultural expressions of what man is.

Like language or art, history is fundamentally anthropomorphic. . . . History is not knowledge of external facts or events; it is a form of self-knowledge. . . . In history man constantly returns to himself; he attempts to recollect and actualize the whole of his past experience. But the historical self is not a mere individual self. It is anthropomorphic, but it is not egocentric. Stated in the form of a paradox, we may say that history strives after an "objective anthropomorphism." By making us cognizant of the polymorphism of human existence, it frees us from the freaks and prejudices of a special and single moment. It is this enrichment and enlargement, not the effacement, of the self, of our knowing and feeling ego, which is the aim of historical knowledge.[27]

With this statement of a humanistic historical enterprise, of its emancipating function in liberating us from the provincialism of the present, and of the imaginative enrichment and enhancement it can bring, no sensitive man could quarrel. Nor could the methodologist seriously doubt that Cassirer's procedure is appropriate to this goal of his. Not even the embattled proponent of the unity of intellectual method could take real issue with that added "dimension" which Cassirer finds in history, or with the "artistic element," the final work of the "productive

[26] *Zur Logik der Kulturwissenschaften*, 85.
[27] *Essay on Man*, 191.

imagination," which he sees it demanding. Cassirer has no scorn for "mere" science. He is only too anxious to make use of all the help which "scientific methods" can furnish.

Philosophic reflection upon the fact of history and upon the ways in which it can be construed and understood might, indeed, point out that these ways are many and diverse. Cassirer's humanistic enterprise is but one of many types of historical investigation, each of which has its own function and validity. Like most of those who have given thoughtful consideration to historical goals and methods, especially if they have been men who have themselves long and fruitfully pursued the interpretation of the meaning of the past, Cassirer is too ready to set up his own distinctive conceptions and working principles as the sufficient model for every approach to the past. But it is not only human existence that exhibits a "polymorphism"; so likewise does men's concern with their living past. It is doubtless a "prejudice of the moment" to identify one's own historical enterprise with the task of "history" in general. In the historian's house are many mansions; and a comprehensive analysis of the ways in which history may be understood, and in which that understanding may illuminate human life today, would have to examine the specific functions and contributions of each. That task Cassirer has not attempted.

What the historian, even the intellectual historian, is likely to find most questionable in Cassirer's "symbolic reconstruction" of the spirit of past ages in terms of the achievement of great men, is his almost total lack of concern with any questions of historical causation. Men and ages in the past thought differently from each other, and from ourselves; to realize this elementary fact is an enhancement of our knowledge of man. But no mention is made that it might be a valid problem for historical investigation to ask why; there is not even a reasoned defense of a negative position on causation in history, as in theories like those of Croce or Collingwood. So far as Cassirer's analysis goes, thought might well be operating in a vacuum. The Hegelian cast of the passage quoted above about the non-individual self actualizing the whole of its past experience is obvious. But there is not even the Hegelian concern with the "immanent" development of thought.[28] All those questions which are certainly central in the "spirit" of our own age, as to the "dynamics" in history, are simply omitted. There is, in fact, no place in Cassirer's discussion where it would be fitting even to raise the problem of a possible influence of technological or economic factors in determining the issues which confront thinkers. It is significant that in criticizing historical determinism, Cassirer examines three forms: the physicalistic determinism of the French positivists, the 'psychologistic determinism of Spengler, and the metaphysical determinism of Hegel.[29] Economic determinism is not so much as mentioned. Indeed, it is hard to ascertain whether the social sciences and their subject matters enter into Cassirer's thought at all. Certainly neither as symbolic forms nor as heuristic principles do they figure in his historical enterprise, nor are they ever mentioned as "*Kulturwissenschaften.*"

Cassirer, however, is surely right in pointing out that the questions the historian puts to the past are the questions that are central in his own philosophic understanding of the world. As he maintains, only a philosopher can write a significant history of philosophy; and what he finds significant in past philosophies will depend on his own. Hence Cassirer's statement of his conception of the task of the historian is so intimately bound up with his systematic philosophy of symbolic forms that a searching examination would have to come to grips with that philosophy. This is not the place for such an undertaking. We can only be grateful that any set of leading principles, when applied by a mind with a scholar's equipment and scrupulous conscience before facts, is bound to shed a great light and reveal new rela-

---

[28] Cf., however, *Essay on Man*, 180: "The history of philosophy shows us very clearly that the full determination of a concept is very rarely the work of that thinker who first introduced that concept. For a philosophical concept is, generally speaking, rather a problem than the solution of a problem—and the full significance of this problem cannot be understood so long as it is still in its first implicit state. It must become explicit in order to be comprehended in its true meaning, and this transition from an implicit to an explicit state is the work of the future."

[29] "Naturalistische und humanistische Begründung der Kulturphilosophie," *op. cit.*, 12-14.

tions and meanings. It is not necessary to share Cassirer's extension of the Kantian approach in order to appreciate his actual historical achievement.

III

But it is necessary to understand Cassirer's approach and his theory of history in order to understand why that achievement is what it is. Whatever our judgment of the importance of his humanistic conception of history, or of the validity of the philosophy on which it ultimately depends, it remains true that that conception does state the aim and method he himself pursued. It makes clear why he devoted himself with such success to the particular historical task he undertook, and why he set about that task in the particular way he did. It also makes clear the reasons for the self-imposed limitations of his historical work —why he disregarded the problems he did, and why he gives no answer to many questions that have interested other intellectual historians. If his theory of history grew out of his own practice, that practice in turn can be taken to illustrate the theory; and the theory will furnish his own *apologia*, his own answer to the criticisms that have been directed against the practice. I wish, therefore, to turn now to an examination of Cassirer's treatment of the Renaissance, to show how that treatment illuminates his theory and how it can be understood in terms of his systematic views.

As an historical interpreter, a "retrospective prophet," Cassirer aimed to recreate the past, to recapture the spirit of a former age and to understand and feel it from within. In the Renaissance as a whole, or in any of the figures who represented its different facets, he was consequently concerned to grasp what was most distinctive and original, not what was merely traditional and received as a legacy. His studies abound in phrases like "a wholly new feeling," "a completely different conception." The Middle Ages serve as the foil, the contrast; they have for him little existence in their own right as themselves expressions of the human spirit and its achievements.[30]

[30] For Cassirer, the fundamental trait of medieval thought, which sets it off

Cassirer was not a medievalist, and when he first embarked on his pioneer studies of Renaissance thought the later Middle Ages were, as he has pointed out, largely a *terra incognita*.[31] That a closer first-hand acquaintance with the complex currents of fourteenth and fifteenth century thought—an acquaintance won only during the past generation, and still in great need of enlargement—would have led to some modification of his interpretation of Renaissance figures, especially of the scientists, is certainly true. But it is doubtful whether that knowledge would have altered fundamentally his judgments. For the tracing of continuities and antecedents played a very minor part in his own historical enterprise. What interested him was rather the other side of history's shield, its novelties and new achieve-

---

sharply from that of the Renaissance, is its subjection of reason to an external standard and authority. "In order to find an unchangeable, an absolute truth, man has to go beyond the limit of his own consciousness and his own existence. He has to surpass himself. . . . By this transcendence the whole method of dialectic, the Socratic and Platonic method, is completely changed. Reason gives up its independence and autonomy. It has no longer a light of its own; it shines only in a borrowed and reflected light. If this light fails, human reason becomes ineffective and impotent. . . . No scholastic thinker ever seriously doubted the absolute superiority of the *revealed* truth. . . . The 'autonomy' of reason was a principle quite alien to medieval thought." *The Myth of the State* (1946), 83f; 95. "The discovery of truth and the foundation of truth [in Thomas Aquinas] is withdrawn from individual thinking and instead handed over to the Church as a universal institution." "Descartes' Wahrheitsbegriff," *Theoria* III (1937), 174. Speaking of Galileo, he says: "Just this character of the completeness, the self-sufficiency, the autonomy of natural knowledge the medieval system of doctrines and beliefs could not recognize. Here there could be no possible compromise: had the Church accepted Galileo's new conception of truth and his new conception of nature, it would have been giving up its own foundation. For what Galileo is demanding, not indeed explicitly but implicitly, is the abandonment of the dogma of original sin. For him there is no corruption of human nature through which it has been led astray from its goal of the knowledge of truth and of God." "Wahrheitsbegriff und Wahrheitsproblem bei Galilei," *Scientia*, LXII (1937), 130; cf. 191-3.

That this formulation of the "medieval conception of truth," in the light of the many different and shifting views from the 13th century on, is hardly adequate to the complexity or even the "autonomy" achieved by reason in medieval philosophical discussion, no impartial student of medieval intellectual life would be likely to deny.

[31] "Some Remarks on the Question of the Originality of the Renaissance," *Journal of the History of Ideas*, IV (1943), 50.

ments; this concern is implicit in his whole enterprise of "palingenesis." He had a genius for seizing on what was geninely original in a thinker, and lifting it out of its context in what was merely traditional. The traditional he freely recognized; but that was not what he was looking for. And, having no interest in causal questions, he was not concerned to show how a man, working with traditional materials upon new problems, had managed to strike off original ideas. He loved sharp contrasts, the setting off of a "wholly new" idea against its background. Thus his symbolic reconstruction aimed ultimately at a description, an intellectual portrait of a man's ideas, not a genetic analysis.

He stated the general problem:

Even if it were possible to answer all these psychological, sociological, and historical questions, we should still be in the precincts of the properly "human" world; we should not have passed its threshold. All human works arise under particular historical and sociological conditions. But we could never understand these special conditions unless we were able to grasp the general structural principles underlying these works. In our study of language, art, and myth the problem of meaning takes precedence over the problem of historical development. . . . The necessity of independent methods of descriptive analysis is generally recognized. We cannot hope to measure the depth of a special branch of human culture unless such measurement is preceded by a descriptive analysis. This structural view of culture must precede the merely historical view. History itself would be lost in the boundless mass of disconnected facts if it did not have a general structural scheme by means of which it can classify, order, and organize these facts. . . . As Wölfflin insists, the historian of art would be unable to characterize the art of different epochs or of different individual artists if he were not in possession of some fundamental *categories* of artistic description.[32]

For Cassirer, it is clear, the "spirit of a former age" is caught in a descriptive analysis, not in a causal or genetic explanation.

Cassirer kept in touch with all the major secondary interpretations of the medieval background of Renaissance thought. He did not dream of questioning these discovered antecedents. But

[32] *Essay on Man*, 68f.

he brushed them aside with some impatience; they did not affect the fundamental question, as he saw it. Typical is a statement about Galileo:

The antecedents of Galileo's science are now much more precisely known than they were a few decades back. When I began my studies in Galileo forty years ago, this field was largely a *terra incognita*. A turning-point here came with the investigations of Duhem. . . . The antecedents of Galileo's theory of method have also been thoroughly and intensively examined. . . . But can all this historical evidence seriously shake our conviction of the incomparable scientific originality of Galileo? I believe that it can only serve to strengthen this conviction and to support it with new arguments. . . . A work like the dynamics of Galileo could not come to birth all at once, like Athene from the head of Zeus. It needed a slow preparation, empirically as well as logically and methodologically. But to all these given elements Galileo added something completely new. . . . All this is wholly new and unique—and unique not only as a particular discovery, but as the expression of a scientific attitude and temper.[33]

Or take his judgment of Descartes:

That between Descartes' philosophy and the scholastic systems there are close relations, that the break between the two is by no means so sharp as it often appears in the traditional conception and presentation of his ideas: this cannot be contested after the fundamental investigation of Gilson. But no matter how many points of contact we may find between medieval and Cartesian thought, the whole *accent* of knowledge still changes when we pass from one to the other. The scholastics and Descartes can agree completely in assuming and establishing definite particular "truths"—as in the ontological proof of God—but in the conception of truth itself, in the explanation of its "nature" and its real meaning, there is an ineradicable, a radical difference. . . . The new in Descartes is not that he used doubt as the means by which alone we can arrive at truth. In this respect Augustine had preceded him. But

[33] "Some Remarks on the Question of the Originality of the Renaissance," *Journal of the History of Ideas*, IV (1943), 50, 51. Cf. his comparison of Galileo with Machiavelli: "Recent research has taught us that both Machiavelli and Galileo had their precursors. . . . They needed a long and careful preparation. But all this does not detract from their originality. What Galileo gave in his *Dialogues* and what Machiavelli gave in his *Prince* were really 'new sciences.' . . . Just as Galileo's Dynamics became the foundation of our modern science of nature, so Machiavelli paved a new way to political science." *Myth of the State*, 130.

Augustine's maxim: "Noli foras ire, in te ipsum redi, in interiore homine habitat veritas" had another significance from Descartes' return to the "Cogito." The inner experience that is here denoted is not that of pure knowledge, but that of the will and of religious certainty. . . . The principle of doubt becomes for Descartes the real synthetic constructive principle of knowledge.[34]

Or, in another field, take Cassirer's illuminating distinction between Luther and medieval mysticism:

Here there is the closest connection between Luther and the religious individualism of the Middle Ages, as it is expressed in mysticism in particular. But on the other hand it is clear that the conception in which this connection is above all presented contains also the decisive difference. . . . Together with the dependence on objective things, mysticism destroys at the same time every principle of objective imposition of form: the "self" that it seeks is wholly without form, it is a "self" that has divested itself of all finite measure and limitation. . . . In contrast, Luther's conception of freedom and of individuality contains not the mere principle of the denial of the world, but in that principle and because of it the principle of world transformation. The value of "working" itself is not destroyed along with the intrinsic value of particular works.[35]

And finally:

The Platonism of the new age, as it appears in the Florentine Academy, remains in its beginnings still completely bound up with Augustinianism and, as it were, merged in it. Relying on the authority of Augustine, Ficino himself acknowledges, he first dared to combine Christianity with Platonism. Hence it is not the *discovery* of the "self" that is distinctive for the Renaissance, but rather the circumstance that a fact and content which the Middle Ages acknowledged only in its religious psychology the Renaissance removed from this connection and exhibited in independence.[36]

IV

These instances make clear just what Cassirer meant by "recreating the spirit of a former age." They also illustrate the

[34] "Descartes' Wahrheitsbegriff," *Theoria* III (1937), 173-5, 178-9. Cf. *Individuum und Kosmos* (1927), 135.

[35] *Freiheit und Form* (1916), 19-21.

[36] *Das Erkenntnisproblem*, I (1922; third ed.), 78.

way in which another of his historical principles entered in to modify and give direction to his aim of symbolic reconstruction. This re-creation is to be no mere passive act of reproduction, we recall.[37] It is rather a new intellectual synthesis, a new *Gestaltung*, a new creative, constructive act. For, though the answers to the historian's questions must come from the past, the questions themselves depend on his own interests and systematic problems.[38] Cassirer's central concern with the autonomy of thought, the creativity of the human spirit, not only directed his attention to the Renaissance in the first place, but made him devote to its thinkers a detailed study which he gave only in a derived sense to the medieval philosophers. It also determined the creative achievements and ideas he would single out.

This is most apparent in his great *Erkenntnisproblem*. The first volume includes a careful and penetrating analysis of almost all the major Renaissance thinkers, beginning with Cusanus. Its successive editions (1906, 1910) brought to light a great wealth of material then nearly unknown. The problem of knowledge is very broadly construed, and upon it is hung an analysis of most of the major themes of Renaissance thought.[39] The store of otherwise inaccessible quotation from the sources has made it for a generation one of the most useful books for the student of the period.

But the volume is unmistakably the work of a neo-Kantian philosopher. The reader gets at times the impression that the Renaissance was populated largely with *Vorkantianer*. It is not that Cassirer actually distorts the thought of the men he is dealing with; for that he is too honest and scrupulous a scholar, and too largely endowed with a vivid historical sense. His interpretations have stood up remarkably well. It is rather that the problems he singles out for analysis are those which interest the Kantian.

[37] *Essay on Man*, 185.

[38] *Essay on Man*, 178.

[39] Cf. *Erkenntnisproblem*, I, 13: "In general, the history of the problem of knowledge will mean for us not so much a *part* of the history of philosophy—for with the way in which all the elements in a philosophical system are internally and mutually determined, any such separation would remain an arbitrary limitation—as rather the total field from a definite point of view and a definite approach."

For the *Erkenntnisproblem*, of course, was undertaken to furnish historical confirmation of "the power and the independence of the mind." It was designed to exhibit all scientific concepts "as the means by which thought wins and makes secure its dominance over appearances." It belongs with the learned and penetrating historical studies of that other "critical idealist," Léon Brunschvicg, as an historical proof that science is a construction and creation of "reason"—the reason embodied in the concrete social enterprise of science. By an analysis of the development of scientific thought it establishes the same position which the *Substanzbegriff* reaches by its systematic analysis. "In regarding the presuppositions of science as *having come about*, we are at the same time recognizing them as *creations* of thought; in discovering its historical *relativity* and conditions, we are opening up the prospect of its never-ending progress and its ever-renewed productivity."[40]

History becomes the completion and the touchstone of the results which the analysis and reduction of the content of the sciences gives us. . . . The analytic task imposed on modern thought finds its logical conclusion in the system of Kant. Here is taken the final and conclusive step; knowledge is based completely on itself, and nothing further in the realm of being or of consciousness is prior to its own legislative activity.[41]

As Cassirer moved beyond the limits of a narrow Kantianism —he came to be provoked that the label was still attached to him—this apologetic aim and direction of his historical studies became less intrusive. He had reached "a new center and a new line of vision." But his fundamental humanism remained, and continued to dominate his interpretation of the Renaissance, and of what in it was of significance and importance. The *Individuum und Kosmos* is not a neo-Kantian book, in the same sense as the *Erkenntnisproblem*. If anything, as its very title suggests, it is Burckhardtian.[42] But it is uncompromisingly "humanistic" in Cassirer's sense.

[40] *Erkenntnisproblem* (3rd ed., 1922), I, vi.
[41] *Ibid.*, 6, 13.
[42] This is also especially true of the brief sketch of the Italian Renaissance in the Introduction to *Freiheit und Form*, with its emphasis on the "new relation to politics," and "the state as a work of art."

That Cassirer should have interpreted Renaissance thought from the standpoint of his own philosophic vision was inevitable. What is more important, it is also completely consistent with his considered conception of the very nature of historical interpretation. If it be a shortcoming, it was an intentional one. Like all perspectives, to be sure, it is a limitation: it excluded other aspects of the Renaissance from the center of his attention. From a less partial point of view—perhaps merely from a different perspective, one that I happen to find more illuminating—Cassirer was prevented by his Kantian humanism from realizing the full significance of at least one of the major currents of Renaissance thought. He appreciated its Humanism, and he analyzed brilliantly its Platonism. But he failed to see the rôle of its Aristotelianism. He did not, like other great students of Renaissance thought—like Gentile, for instance—dismiss that Aristotelianism as a mere survival of "scholasticism." His analyses of Pomponazzi[43] are suggestive; and he was the first to call attention to the great importance of Zabarella.[44] But he naturally saw in Renaissance Aristotelianism primarily its new humanistic element—which was great—and not its still greater naturalism. And since he did not adequately bring out the significance of that Aristotelianism, he did not contrast it effectively with the Platonistic movement, and thus failed to reveal the full significance of the latter.

The contrast between the Platonism and the Aristotelianism of the Renaissance is at bottom one between a modernistic and a naturalistic humanism. Both focused attention on man and his destiny; both emphasized individual and personal values.[45]

[43] *Erkenntnisproblem,* I, 105-17; *Individuum und Kosmos,* 85-7, 108-12, 143-49.

[44] *Erkenntnisproblem,* I, 117-20, 136-44.

[45] Cf. *Individuum und Kosmos,* 148: "Both men, Pomponazzi as well as Ficino, are wrestling with the problem of individuality; both are trying to make the phenomenon of the 'self' the center of psychology. But they pursue this goal in ways that are completely separate. For Ficino it is the purely intellectual nature of man which can alone form him into a 'self' in the strict sense, and elevate him above the realm of all that is merely corporeal. . . . For Pomponazzi, on the contrary, individuality is not to be asserted against Nature, but is to be derived and proved *from* Nature. . . . Just as Ficino in his fight for the rights and the uniqueness of the individual self calls for help upon supernaturalism and transcendence, so Pomponazzi in the same fight calls upon naturalism and immanence."

In this sense both were humanistic. But where Ficino and the Platonists, to support their religious modernism and "liberalism," went back to the Hellenistic world, to Plutarch and Alexandria, Pomponazzi and the greater Zabarella went to ancient Athens to find inspiration in its naturalistic and scientific thought. Their scientific humanism is much more original than the religious humanism of the Florentines. Where the Platonists vindicated the dignity of the individual soul by elevating it in freedom above nature, the Aristotelians made the soul a natural inhabitant of an orderly universe. Not until Spinoza and the eighteenth-century Newtonians is there another figure who effects so "modern" a blend between humanism and scientific naturalism as Pomponazzi and Zabarella. They are, in fact, the spiritual fathers of Spinoza's religious naturalism. The historical influence of the Platonists was great. But the Renaissance Aristotelians have a more original as well as a much sounder philosophy, and one which much more closely foreshadows later modern thought.

This is hardly the place to substantiate this interpretation, made from another perspective than Cassirer's, or to maintain —as I think can be done—that it is closer to the problems of Renaissance thought itself. It is easier to show that Cassirer overemphasized the influence of Platonism and underemphasized that of the Aristotelian tradition on points of detail, especially in the development of science. Galileo, for instance, was much closer to the scientific Aristotelianism of the Italian schools, and much farther from Plato, than Cassirer realized.[46]

---

[46] For Cassirer's view of Galileo's "Platonism," see *Individuum und Kosmos*, 178; "Galileo: a New Science and a New Spirit," *American Scholar*, 12 (1943), 10; "Descartes' Wahrheitsbegriff," *Theoria*, III (1937), 168. Cassirer has been very cautious in asserting the Platonism of Galileo's thought. It is mentioned only once in the *Erkenntnisproblem* (I, 389), and does not appear in "Wahrheitsbegriff und Wahrheitsproblem bei Galilei" (*Scientia*, LXII [1937]) at all. In contrast to A. Koyré, e.g., who speaks of Galileo's work as "an experimental proof of Platonism," and identifies any mathematical science of nature with "Platonism," ("Galileo and Plato," *Journal of the History of Ideas*, IV [1943], 428; cf. also his *Ètudes Galiléennes* [Paris, 1940]), Cassirer emphasizes instead the differences between Galileo's and Plato's views. "Galileo had still another dualism to overcome before he could found a science of nature. Plato had based his philosophy upon the presupposition that we cannot speak of a science of nature in the same sense as we can of a science of mathematics. . . . It was most difficult for Galileo to combat the authority of Plato. . . . But he was convinced

And Cassirer likewise fails to give due importance to the Aristotelian background of the Nature philosophies of the Italian Renaissance. On the development of both science and Nature philosophy he underestimates the influence of the tra-¹ dition of Ockhamism. And he undoubtedly overestimated that of his favorite Cusanus, as he came reluctantly to admit.⁴⁷

---

that in his own work, in the new science of dynamics, he had removed the barrier Plato had erected between mathematical and natural science; for this new science proved nature itself a realm of necessity rather than of chance." "Galileo: a New Science and a New Spirit," *American Scholar*, 12 (1943), 10. Cf. also "Descartes' Wahrheitsbegriff," *Theoria*, III (1937), 168: "So long as the philosophical orientation was directed toward Plato *alone*, and to a certain extent committed to him, there was a weighty obstacle opposed to the carrying through of the ideal of an exact science of nature." And Cassirer distinguished sharply between the "mathematical mysticism" of much of the Pythagoreanizing Platonism of the Renaissance, and the "mathematical science of nature." Cf. "Mathematische Mystik und mathematische Naturwissenschaft," *Lychnos* (Upsala, 1940). In his final judicious analysis ("Galileo's Platonism," *Studies and Essays in the History of Science and Learning offered in homage to George Sarton* (1947)), Cassirer identifies Galileo's very novel "physical Platonism" primarily with the hypothetical *method* of "problematical analysis" he found in the *Meno* as well as in Euclid and Archimedes, and best described in his letter to Carcaville.

But if, as Cassirer emphasizes, Galileo insists that the subject-matter of knowledge is not an intelligible, "ideal" world dubiously related to the world of natural events, but is rather the intelligible structure of that world; and if he also insists that it is arrived at by the intellect through the careful analysis of instances of it encountered in sense experience, as Aristotle had suggested and the Italian methodologists more precisely formulated—how can this be called a "Platonism" rather than an "Aristotelianism"? There is no evidence that Galileo was in any sense touched by Platonic metaphysics, or that he is any more of a Platonist than Aristotle himself. On the fundamental issue in any philosophy of science, the relation of discourse to knowledge and to the subject-matter of knowledge, Galileo was one with the Italian tradition of realistic Aristotelianism. Galileo's distinction was his startling illustration that the best human knowledge is mathematics, and that the intelligible structure of things which that knowledge, when clearly formulated, is able to grasp, is mathematical in character. Cf. my "Development of Scientific Method in the School of Padua," *Journal of the History of Ideas*, I (1940), 204-6.

⁴⁷ "I avail myself of this opportunity to revise a former statement made in my *Individuum und Kosmos*. In the second chapter I tried to show that Nicholas of Cusa's philosophy exerted a strong influence on the general development of Italian thought in the Quattrocento. I still think this to be highly probable, but I should perhaps have spoken with more caution. I quite agree that, on the strength of new historical evidence, we can not give a direct and definite proof of this thesis. It is possible that Ficino conceived his general theory independently of Nicholas of Cusa. In this case the close relationship between the two thinkers

But when all this has been pointed out, it remains true that, in importing the issues of a later day into his study of the Renaissance, Cassirer had instruments with which to ask questions. Even should we end by drastically modifying his interpretation of Renaissance thought, his questions have taught us an immense amount. What he learned forms the basis on which we have asked our own questions. And in the course of putting his questions to the Renaissance, Cassirer was led much nearer to the problems of the Renaissance itself. There is a vast difference between the *Erkenntnisproblem* and late studies like those of Pico, Ficino, Galileo and Descartes.[48] The closer we can get to the problems of the Renaissance itself, and the farther we can get away from viewing them in terms of problems of a later incidence, the more likely we are to arrive at a genuine historical understanding. May our perspectives give us an equal chance to learn!

V

The illustrations already given show also how Cassirer himself followed his third major principle, that historical interpretation must always center on individual persons, and understand events in terms of such personalities. His analyses are always carried out as the intellectual portraits of men, even when those men have been selected as "symbols" of an age, or of characteristic answers to a problem.[49] His interest in intel-

---

would be all the more important and interesting from the point of view of the general history of ideas. For it would show us the common background of the philosophy of the fifteenth century—the general intellectual and religious atmosphere of the Renaissance." "Ficino's Place in Intellectual History," *Journal of the History of Ideas*, VI (1945), 492n.

[48] "Giovanni Pico della Mirandola," *Journal of the History of Ideas*, III (1942), 123-44, 319-46; "Ficino's Place in Intellectual History," *Journal of the History of Ideas*, VI (1945), 483-501; "Wahrheitsbegriff und Wahrheitsproblem bei Galilei," *Scientia*, LXII (1937), 121-30, 185-93; "Galileo," *American Scholar*, 12 (1943), 5-19; "Descartes' Wahrheitsbegriff," *Theoria*, III (1937), 161-87.

[49] This is true of the one book Cassirer wrote specifically about the Renaissance, *Individuum und Kosmos* (1927). After quoting the major criticisms of the "concept of the Renaissance," Cassirer goes on: "What is needed is the universality of a systematic point of view and a systematic orientation, which by no means coincides with the universality of merely empirical generic concepts, commonly

lectual personalities is so great that it quite bursts the frame of the context for which an idea has been introduced. It is the history of "thinking," of *Denken*, that he definitely gives us, not of ideas divorced from the minds that have entertained them. His analyses of ideas are beautifully lucid, but they aim to convey the feel of those ideas to the men expressing them— he is true to his "personal" interpretation. He is at his best in such a "contextual" analysis, in pointing out how an idea in one man's thinking differs from what seems to be the "same" idea in another's. All this, of course, lends added value to Cassirer's work, and makes the reader quite forget the limitations originally suggested by his own intellectual framework. Thus whatever his shortcomings in appraising the significance of the Aristotelian movement as a whole, Cassirer cannot help but do a great measure of justice when he comes to individual Aristotelians like Pomponazzi or Zabarella. This is reinforced by the wealth of judiciously selected quotations—quotations which are always "symbolic" of far more than the point for which they are introduced.

In this art of portraiture, Cassirer's method is clear. He seeks above all for that "central focus" in terms of which everything the man says will form an "organic whole." His comment on the work of another historian, P. O. Kristeller, states this well. In the last article Cassirer wrote, he quotes Kristeller: "If we are to understand Ficino's metaphysics," he declares,

we must start from the phenomenon of "internal experience." Here we find the real clue to Ficino's philosophy—the fundamental fact and

---

used to divide history into periods and to delimit conveniently its individual epochs. Toward this goal the following considerations are directed. . . . They remain within the history of philosophical problems, and seek to find an answer there to the question whether and in how far the intellectual movement of the 15th and 16th centuries, in all the multiplicity of its ways of putting problems and all the divergence of its solutions, forms a self-contained unity." *Individuum und Kosmos*, 5, 6.

But the book itself is far from a unity. It is a collection of studies of the views of different men grouped around a few central problems—ultimately, as the title suggests, those raised by Burckhardt. Its organization is far from clear, it is full of digressions, and its enduring value is undoubtedly its presentation of the "intellectual portraits" of men looking at these problems.

principle on which all his special doctrines depend. . . . If we accept this starting-point of Kristeller's interpretation—and to my mind he has proved his point by conclusive arguments—we have won a new perspective, a vantage-point from which we may see the whole of Ficino's system in a clearer light. Many questions that were highly controversial can now be answered in a better and more satisfactory way. . . . He gives us a much more "organic" view of Ficino's philosophy than we find in other writers. Kristeller makes no attempt to conceal the contradictions inherent in Ficino's doctrine. But he shows convincingly that in spite of all. its discrepancies Ficino's work preserves its systematic unity. It is centered around a few fundamental problems which complete and elucidate each other.[50]

What Cassirer thus praises in the method of Kristeller he himself tried to do in his own. Thus, facing the apparent contradictions in the thought of Pico della Mirandola, he says:

Pico . . . was trying to assert the validity of his own *principle of knowledge*. . . . The distinctive category under which he subsumed his doctrine of God, of the world and of man, his theology and his psychology, is the category of *symbolic thought*. Once we ascertain this central point of his thinking, the different parts of his doctrine immediately coalesce into a whole. . . . Pico is no longer trying to exhibit the Many as the *effect* of the One, or to deduce them as such from their cause, with the aid of rational concepts. He sees the Many rather as *expressions*, as *images*, as *symbols* of the One.[51]

Cassirer's method appears in a little different form in connection with Galileo:

If we wish to comprehend Galileo's nature and activity, we confront the same problem we encounter in almost every portrayal of one of the great geniuses of the Renaissance. We cannot remain within a single area of his activity, however significant and consequential it may appear, and we cannot take our standards from this area *alone*. We must rather proceed, as in concentric circles, from the center of his intellectual activity to its ever wider and more comprehensive expressions. Here is revealed a definite scale: the extent of the problem becomes greater and greater, and embraces a richer and richer area, while the typical

[50] "Ficino's Place in Intellectual History," *Journal of the History of Ideas,* VI (1945), 485-7.

[51] "Giovanni Pico della Mirandola," *Journal of the History of Ideas,* III (1942), 137-8.

form in which the question is put as such remains the same. The following consideration has to do with no special content of Galileo's science, but rather with this universal type of his investigation and questioning.[52]

This procedure is clearly applicable to the thought of a single intellectual personality, where something like an "organic unity" with a discoverable "center" may reasonably be expected. Even here, one sometimes suspects, there may be more of conflict and tension, even in a great thinker, than Cassirer allows for; his heroes emerge uniformly as intellectually integrated. For many philosophers, especially those facing problems of reconciliation, one could find equal illumination in an interpretation that took the strife of incompatibles as central.

But the difficulties are greater when the method is extended to a group of men, and greatest of all in attempting to characterize an entire "age." Cassirer applies it to the Cambridge Platonists:

> With all this we have won only partial aspects; we have illuminated the *work* of the Cambridge School from different sides, but we have not grasped the real intellectual principle it represents, in setting forth and carrying through which it alone deserves a place in the history of the modern mind. To lay bare this principle and in it the real ideal center of the intellectual work of the Cambridge School is the task of the following investigation. . . . It is a unified and total view that is represented by the Cambridge circle: a view which is maintained and carried through as a constant basic theme amidst all the individual differences of the particular thinkers and all its extension to the manifold and disparate areas of problems. . . . What is embodied in it is a definite type of thinking of independent power and significance.[53]

The applicability of this search for a unifying "type of thinking" grows more doubtful when we begin to seek for the "center" from which to interpret an entire age. In the *Erkenntnisproblem* Cassirer is aware of the difficulties:

> In Jacob Burckhardt's portrayal, which first made the total picture

[52] Wahrheitsbegriff und Wahrheitsproblem bei Galilei," *Scientia*, LXII (1937), 125.
[53] *Die Platonische Renaissance in England und die Schule von Cambridge* (1932), 4.

of the Renaissance live once more in its individual traits, philosophical efforts and achievements recede completely into the background. While everywhere else they represent the structure and the real measure of the intellectual progress of a period, they here stand as it were outside the common pattern. Nowhere does there appear at first glance a recognizable unity, nowhere a fixed center about which the different movements are ordered. The conventional traits and formulae with which we are accustomed to indicate the character of the Renaissance fail us when we honestly consider the individual philosophical currents and their multiplicity.[54]

This raises the question whether we can hope to find any unifying formula in structural or morphological terms for the thought of the Renaissance as a whole—the entire problem of "styles" of thought, a conception German *Kulturgeschichte* has taken over from the historians of art. As a conscientious scholar, Cassirer's attitude is very cautious and reserved.

That in a mere chronological sense we cannot separate the Renaissance from the Middle Ages is obvious. By innumerable visible and invisible threads the Quattrocento is connected with scholastic thought and medieval culture. In the history of European civilization there never was a break of continuity. To seek for a point in this history in which the Middle Ages "end" and the modern world "begins" is a sheer absurdity. But that does not do away with the necessity of looking for an *intellectual* line of demarcation between the two ages.[55]

At times Cassirer was willing to use this notion of "style" in a definite non-temporal sense.

Our controversy as to the originality of the Renaissance and as to the dividing-line between the "Renaissance" and the "Middle Ages" seems to me in many ways rather a "logical" dispute than one about the historical facts. Ideas like "Gothic," "Renaissance," or "Baroque" are ideas of historical "style." As to the meaning of these ideas of "style" there still prevails a great lack of clarity in many respects. They can be used to *characterize* and *interpret* intellectual movements, but they express no actual historical *facts* that ever existed at any time. "Renaissance" and "Middle Ages" are, strictly speaking, not names for historical

[54] *Erkenntnisproblem*, I, 74.
[55] *Myth of the State*, 130.

periods at all, but they are concepts of "ideal types," in Max Weber's sense. We cannot therefore use them as instruments for any strict division of periods; we cannot inquire at what temporal point the Middle Ages "stopped" or the Renaissance "began." The actual historical facts cut across and extend over each other in the most complicated manner.[56]

The meaning of these ideas of "style" Cassirer tried to clarify and analyse in his *Zur Logik der Kulturwissenschaften:*

Jacob Burckhardt gave in his *Kultur der Renaissance* a classic portrait of "the man of the Renaissance." It contains features that are familiar to us all. The man of the Renaissance possesses definite characteristic properties which clearly distinguish him from "the man of the Middle Ages." He is characterized by his joy in the senses, his turning to nature, his roots in this world, his self-containedness for the world of form, his individualism, his paganism, his amoralism. Empirical research has set out to discover this Burckhardtian "man of the Renaissance"—but it has not found him. No single historical individual can be cited who actually unites in himself all the traits that Burckhardt considers the constitutive elements of his picture. "If we try," says Ernst Walser in his *Studien zur Weltanschauung der Renaissance,*[57] "to consider the life and thought of the leading personalities of the Quattrocento purely inductively, of a Coluccio Salutati, Poggio Bracciolini, Leonardo Bruni, Lorenzo Valla, Lorenzo Magnifico or Luigi Pulci, it is regularly found that for the particular person being studied the traits set up absolutely do *not* fit. . . . And if we bring together the results of inductive research, there gradually emerges a new picture of the Renaissance, no less a mixture of piety and impiety, good and evil, longing for heaven and joy in earth, but infinitely more complicated. The life and endeavor of the whole Renaissance cannot be derived from a *single* principle, from individualism and sensualism,—no more than can the reputed unified culture of the Middle Ages."

I agree completely with these words of Walser's. Every man who has ever been concerned with the concrete investigation of the history, literature, art, or philosophy of the Renaissance will be able to confirm them from his own experience and add many further instances. But does this refute Burckhardt's notion? Shall we regard it, in the logical

[56] "Some Remarks on the Question of the Originality of the Renaissance," *Journal of the History of Ideas,* IV (1943), 54-5.

[57] Ernst Walser, *Studien zur Weltanschauung der Renaissance,* now in *Gesammelte Studien zur Geistesgeschichte der Renaissance* (1920; Basel, 1932), 102.

sense, as a null class—as a class into which no single object falls? That would be necessary only if we were here concerned with one of those generic concepts which are arrived at through the empirical comparison of particular cases, through what we commonly call "induction." Measured by this standard, Burckhardt's notion could indeed not stand the test.

But it is just this *presupposition* that needs logical correction. Certainly Burckhardt could not have given his portrait of the man of the Renaissance without relying for it on an immense amount of factual material. The wealth of this material and its reliability astonishes us again and again when we study his work. But the kind of "conspectus" he draws up, the historical synthesis he gives, is of a wholly different kind in principle from empirically acquired natural concepts. If we want to speak here of "abstraction," it is that process which Husserl has characterized as *"ideirende Abstraction."* That the result of such an *"ideirende Abstraction"* could ever be brought to cover any concrete particular case: this can neither be expected nor demanded. And "subsumption" also can never be taken here in the same way as we subsume a body given here and now, a piece of metal, under the concept of gold, because we find that it fulfills all the conditions of gold known to us. When we indicate that Leonardo da Vinci and Aretino, Marsiglio Ficino and Machiavelli, Michelangelo and Cesare Borgia are "men of the Renaissance," we do not mean that there is to be found in them all a definite particular trait with a fixed content in which they all agree. We shall perceive them to be not only completely different, but even opposed. What we are asserting of them is only that regardless of this opposition, perhaps just because of it, they stand to each other in a definite ideal connection; that each of them in his own way is co-operating to construct what we call the "spirit" of the Renaissance or the culture of the Renaissance.

It is a unity of *direction*, not a unity of *existence*, that we are thus trying to express. The particular individuals belong together, not because they are alike or resemble each other, but because they are co-operating in a common *task*, which in contrast to the Middle Ages we perceive to be new, and to be the distinctive "meaning" of the Renaissance. All genuine notions of "style" in the cultural sciences reduce, when analyzed more precisely, to such notions of "meaning." The artistic style of an epoch cannot be determined if we do not bring to a unity all its different and often apparently disparate artistic expressions by understanding them, to use Riegl's term, as expressions of a definite "artistic will."[58] Such notions indeed *characterize*, but they do not *determine*; the particular that falls under them cannot be derived from them.

But it is equally incorrect to infer from this that we have here only intuitive description, not conceptual characterization; it is rather a matter of a distinctive manner and direction of this characterization, of a logico-intellectual work that is *sui generis*.[59]

This passage hardly possesses the clarity we are accustomed to expect from Cassirer. Is it only an elaborate way of saying that we "perceive" certain common "tendencies" running through Renaissance thought, though fidelity to facts demands that we recognize its wide diversity? Or is Cassirer trying to indicate something deeper by his "ideal types," his "unities of direction," his "common task" and "will"? In saying that such "unities" are not historical *facts* discoverable in the web of history, that they can be used to "characterize" and "interpret" the facts, but do not "determine" them, Cassirer is of course, being faithful to his general Kantian epistemology. "Unities" in that theory of knowledge are applied to the materials of knowledge, they are not discovered in those materials. In Kantian terms, Cassirer is saying that these "unities," these concepts or historical "style," are not constitutive but regulative principles. They are closest, perhaps, to the idea of teleology as it appears in the *Critique of Judgment*. In any event, we should remember that for Cassirer the act of "interpreting" any symbolic forms is creative, productive of a new synthesis; the historical "meaning" that results from it is as much a creation of the historian as a deliverance of the past. It is a genuinely new "*Gestaltung.*" In less Kantian phraseology, all such unities are working hypotheses employed to explore the facts.

Cassirer's labored distinctions are thus involved in all the dubieties of his philosophy of symbolic forms. That there are discoverable unities in history, and in the thought of the Renaissance in particular, I should myself maintain. That thought, I should suggest, is unified in the light of the problems men were

---

[58] Alois Riehl, *Stilfragen* (1893), and *Spätrömische Kunstindustrie* (1901).
[59] *Zur Logik der Kulturwissenschaften* (Göteborg, 1942), 79-81.

then facing. And there is much in Cassirer which points to such a unification in terms of problems, rather than in terms of the vague and indeterminate notion of "meaning." To be sure, his further notion of a common "task" is rather blind. In the *Erkenntnisproblem,* however, he puts the matter much more precisely. "It is the fight against 'substantial form' that is above all characteristic of the Renaissance."[60] This suggests that the problems of the Renaissance were primarily negative: intellectually, men were seeking to escape from earlier views, just as in their social life they were seeking to escape from the forms of medieval society which had outlasted their usefulness and were now felt to be constricting rather than directing. The vexed question of Renaissance "individualism" also, I think, is soluble if that "individualism" is construed in terms of the specific social organizations from which men were seeking to escape, rather than in terms of any positive content. Like the Romantic movement, the Renaissance is to be understood in the light of what it was revolting against. Being, like Romanticism, a reaction and a revolt, it naturally expressed itself in a wide variety of alternatives.

Such a "functional" interpretation, I submit, is really closer to Cassirer's own fundamental position than the "structuralism" —the attempt to find some common structural or morphological "meaning"—into which he was occasionally seduced. Cassirer is at his best when he insists that the originality and novelty of a period, or a thinker, lies not in the statement of *"eine neue Thematik,"* but in the serious confrontation of *"eine neue Problematik."*[61]

Whatever weight Cassirer was inclined to give to "styles" or unities as he reinterpreted them as regulative principles, in his last statement on this problem he returned to his fundamentally "personal" conception of history. "What we learn from this discussion," he says in his final paper on Ficino, referring to the symposium on the originality of the Renaissance,[62]

---

[60] *Erkenntnisproblem,* I, 76.
[61] *Die Platonische Renaissance in England,* etc., 5.
[62] *Journal of the History of Ideas,* IV (1943).

is only the fact that the period of the Quattrocento and Cinquecento is too subtle and too complicated a phenomenon to be described by any simple term or abstract formula. All such formulae are bound to fail. When we come to the real question, when we begin to deal with any special problem or any individual thinker, we must forget them. They turn out to be inadequate and misleading. In every particular investigation the question must be raised anew and answered independently.[63]

The question of novelty and originality, so important in all of Cassirer's studies of the Renaissance, remains. What is it which in that period can be called really "new"? Surprisingly enough, in view of his sharp distinction between the concepts of the natural and the cultural or symbolic sciences, in good Kantian fashion Cassirer often uses metaphors drawn from the science of mechanics—"forces," "center of gravity," new "equilibrium." Thus in speaking of Machiavelli he says: "When Machiavelli conceived the plan of his book the center of gravity of the political world had already been shifted. New forces had come to the fore and they had to be accounted for—forces that were entirely unknown to the medieval system."[64]

The fullest and most illuminating use of such a mechanical figure occurs in his discussion of the originality of the Renaissance:

Nevertheless the distinction [between Middle Ages and Renaissance] has a real meaning. What we can express by it, and what alone we intend to express, is that from the beginning of the fifteenth century onward the *balance* between the particular forces—society, state, religion, church, art, science—begins to shift slowly. New forces press up out of the depths and alter the previous equilibrium. And the character of every culture rests on the equilibrium between the forces that give it form. Whenever therefore we make any comparison between the Middle Ages and the Renaissance, it is never enough to single out particular ideas or concepts. What we want to know is not the particular idea as such, but the importance it possesses, and the strength with which it is acting in the whole structure. "Middle Ages" and "Renaissance" are two great and mighty streams of ideas. When we single out from them a particular idea, we are doing what a chemist does in analyzing the water of a

[63] "Ficino's Place in Intellectual History," *Journal of the History of Ideas*, VI (1945), 483-4.
[64] *Myth of the State*, 133.

stream or what a geographer does in trying to trace it to its source. No one denies that these are interesting and important questions. But they are neither the only nor the most important concern of the *historian of ideas*.

The historian of ideas knows that the water which the river carries with it changes only very slowly. The same ideas are always appearing again and again, and are maintained for centuries. The force and the tenacity of tradition can hardly be over-estimated. From this point of view we must acknowledge that there is nothing new under the sun. But the historian of ideas is not asking primarily what the *substance* is of particular ideas. He is asking what their *function* is. What he is studying—or should be studying—is less the *content* of ideas than their *dynamics*. To continue the figure, we could say that he is not trying to analyze the drops of water in the river, but that he is seeking to measure its width and depth and to ascertain the force and velocity of the current. It is all *these* factors that are fundamentally altered in the Renaissance; the dynamics of ideas has changed.[65]

More often, however, Cassirer employs not a metaphor drawn from the natural science of dynamics, but the more appropriate conception that a new *problem* has been insistently posed. This conception of a new *"Problematik"* dominates his major treatments. In the *Erkenntnisproblem* he says:

The philosophical character of an epoch cannot be judged merely by its achievement in fixed doctrines; it announces itself no less in the energy with which it conceives and maintains a new intellectual goal. The unity of the different directions which stand opposed to each other in the thinking of the Renaissance lies in the new attitude which they gradually come to take toward the problem of knowledge.[66]

In *Freiheit und Form* he says: "In destroying the whole medieval system of religious beliefs, the system of religious mediation through fixed, objectively communicable means of salvation, Luther imposed upon the individual an immense new task. Union with the Infinite must now be accomplished in himself without the aid of any assistance in material means."[67]

---

[65] "Some Remarks on the Question of the Originality of the Renaissance," *Journal of the History of Ideas*, IV (1943), 55.

[66] *Erkenntnisproblem*, I, 75-6.

[67] *Freiheit und Form*, 18.

The *Individuum und Kosmos*

remains within the history of philosophical problems and seeks to find
there an answer to the question whether and in how far the movement
of thought in the 15th and 16th centuries, in all the multiplicity of its
ways of putting problems and in all the divergence of its solutions, forms
a self-contained unity.[68]

And again:

What characterizes and distinguishes the Renaissance is the new *relation*
in which individuals place themselves toward the world and the form
of community which they establish between themselves and the world.
They see themselves facing an altered conception of the physical and
the intellectual universe, and it is this conception that imposes upon them
a new intellectual and moral demand, which requires of them an inner
transformation, a *reformatio* and *regeneratio*.[69]

VI

When Cassirer goes beyond the attempt to analyze the intellectual personality of an individual thinker to essay the portrait of an age, to try to reconstruct its spirit as a whole, he
wavers between two rather different conceptions. On the one
hand, he tries to introduce a unity into a mass of divergent
currents of thought by constructing a synthesis in terms of a
characteristic "style" or "ideal type" of thinking. On the other,
he finds unification in terms of the new problems forced on
men—forced primarily, in his interpretation, by the advance
of scientific knowledge and the new conceptions of truth to
which that advance leads. Combining something of both conceptions is the notion he most commonly employs, that the
unification can be constructed in terms of a new "task," a new
"*Aufgabe*." The first idea is morphological, a descriptive analysis, though of a sort Cassirer claims to be not "merely empirical," but *sui generis*, appropriate to the human universe of
symbolic forms. The second idea is equally appropriate to a
human world: it finds understanding in terms of ends, goals,

[68] *Individuum und Kosmos*, 6.
[69] "Wahrheitsbegriff und Wahrheitsproblem bei Gaillei," *Scientia*, LXII (1937),
122.

and purposes, it is teleological and functional. Is it too much to say that the first was impressed on Cassirer by Burckhardt and Dilthey, whereas the second came from his own more original thought? The first can be called, in his own terms, a "substantial" or "structural" conception; the second is "functional."

The structural unification has the disadvantage that when worked out with complete honesty in the face of facts, as Cassirer had to work it out, it leads to a conception that is unique and without parallel—a conception, furthermore, that Cassirer has great difficulty in trying to formulate. It is a conception which by definition eludes public confirmation; it depends on the "productive imagination" of the historical interpreter not only for its discovery, as do all hypotheses, but also for its validity. And it opens the way to no further inquiry as to its causes and conditions. The functional unification in terms of new problems forced on men by their changing social experience, on the other hand, introduces nothing that is not already familiar in human life. It is clear and precise, and it can be confirmed by public evidence. It suggests the further investigation of the many and complex causes, intellectual and social, which have led men's social experience to change.

Cassirer quotes from Kant, in speaking of Plato:

It is by no means unusual, upon comparing the thoughts which an author has expressed in regard to his subject, . . . to find that we understand him better than he has understood himself. As he has not sufficiently determined his concept, he has sometimes spoken, or even thought, in opposition to his own intention.[70]

Cassirer himself adds:

The history of philosophy shows us very clearly that the full determination of a concept is very rarely the work of that thinker who first introduced that concept. For a philosophical concept is, generally speaking, rather a problem than the solution of a problem—and the full significance of this problem cannot be understood so long as it is still in its first implicit state. It must become explicit in order to become comprehended

[70] *Critique of Pure Reason* (2nd ed.), 370. Tr. N. K. Smith, 310.

in its true meaning, and this transition from an implicit to an explicit state is the work of the future.[71]

Is it not possible that we may be able to understand the idea of a truly functional interpretation of history better than Cassirer understood it, and that we may hope to make the problem which he introduced more explicit than he was able to do himself?

JOHN HERMAN RANDALL, JR.

COLUMBIA UNIVERSITY

[71] *Essay on Man*, 180.

21

Walter M. Solmitz

CASSIRER ON GALILEO: AN EXAMPLE OF
CASSIRER'S WAY OF THOUGHT

CASSIRER ON GALILEO: AN EXAMPLE OF CASSIRER'S WAY OF THOUGHT

"Als wie der Tag die Menschen hell umscheinet
Und mit dem Lichte, das den Höhn entspringet,
Die dämmernden Erscheinungen vereinet,
Ist Wissen, welches tief der Geistigkeit gelinget."

—Hölderlin.*

I

THE following passage may be regarded as a typical "Cassirer" text. It can call to mind a few characteristics of Cassirer's philosophical style.

Galileo emphasized unceasingly that the law which rules the phenomena, and their underlying reasons *(ragioni)*, cannot immediately be read off of the phenomena by sensory perception. What is required for the discovery of those laws is rather the spontaneity of mathematical reasoning. For we learn to know the eternal and necessary in things not by means of mere piling up and comparison of sense experiences; rather the mind must have grasped it "from within itself" in order to be able to find it again in the phenomena. Each intellect knows from itself *(da per sè)* the true and necessary things, i.e., those which could not possibly be [or act] otherwise;—or else it is impossible for the mind ever to know them.[1]

There is nothing very extraordinary about this passage. It is an historical passage from an historical book, written in a rather

* "Bright is broad day that beams around the man,
    Uniting with the light that comes forth from the heights
    The various things appearing in the dusk.
    Thus too beams knowledge that has blessed the spirit's depth."
[1] *Individuum und Kosmos in der Philosophie der Renaissance.* Studien der Bibliothek Warburg, vol. X, (Leipzig, 1927), 173.

conventional manner. The reader is carried along easily and pleasantly; his intellectual imagination is helped by a rhetorical antithesis in the form of "not this; but that." Moreover, when read in the (original) German it recalls the pleasant rhythm of Cassirer's prose. You read through it almost without realizing that you have read some statement which might set you thinking. As it stands, it looks rather trite, more or less a matter of course; but, if you read it in the context of the book, you are sustained by the very rhythm of the prose, expecting somehow that the real thing is yet to come, and is, so to speak, just around the corner.

Now let us read the few sentences over again. And let us keep in mind that this is an historical statement, a fairly close paraphrasing of Galileo's text (as is quite common in Cassirer's historical books). Cassirer's writings can often be read as an anthology from an author or various authors—an anthology, to be sure, with a very definite purpose in mind. (Cassirer was once asked what it was that made his books so readable; his reply was that this was due to the simple fact that he had read the authors themselves about whom he wrote.)

In the present instance also we have an historical report. The strange thing, however, is that one is inclined to read historical reports by Cassirer, such as this, as if they were "systematic" statements; i.e., as if they were reports not about a thinker who lived several centuries ago, but as if they were reports about presently stated and perceived truth.

If read with these facts in mind, the passage here under consideration—even when thus isolated from its context—makes a significant, if not actually bold assertion. As a matter of fact, those few sentences state a fairly radical form of rationalism.

For what is it that the sentences say? First of all, they say something about the *methodology of science*. In this respect they express and demand resignation as well as encouragement. They teach resignation by saying: we cannot know the world immediately, by unreservedly giving ourselves up to it, by just looking at it and faithfully observing it. We might be inclined to do so; we may desire to have the phenomena speak for themselves and by themselves—so that we may listen to them faithfully, passively, and without prejudice. That cannot be done. In order to understand them and to arrive at some knowledge about them, our mind must work actively. But there is also the encouraging assurance that our mind can proceed in this fashion and still arrive at (some) objective knowledge. In fact, it cannot proceed otherwise—else it will not be able to know anything at all.

These methodological maxims depend on the *theory of knowledge*. Scientific knowledge consists of mathematical equations, not of sense perceptions. Mathematical equations cannot simply be read from the stars or from whatever moves around on our own planet; the phenomena do not carry mathematical equations as labels pasted on their backs. One has to search for mathematical equations; they are found not by continuously looking outside, but only by turning "inside," by questioning ourselves, and by drawing from the well of our own mind.

Does this reliance on our own mind not compel us to recognize that science is something completely subjective and therefore merely a product of some arbitrary constructions? On the contrary, without mathematics there would not be such a thing as objectivity in this respect at all; we would not even be able to distinguish the subjective from the objective.

This, then, is a definite statement of Galileo's view; but it is definitely misleading, if taken in isolation. In the context in which the statement occurs the passage is preceded by one which emphasizes Galileo's "empiricism" and the fact that Galileo was always fighting against a scholastic method which concentrated on the exposition of books instead of concerning itself with a description and interpretation of the phenomena themselves.

Which statement, then, is true? In Cassirer's opinion, is Galileo an empiricist or is he a rationalist? The point is that *both* interpretations are *true*—or, rather, that *each* of them is wrong, when taken by itself. It is only against the background of the passage on Galileo's empiricism that the antithetical assertion about his rationalism appears in its intended meaning;— and the passage on Galileo's empiricism is meant to lead up to the surprising statement of its opposite. In other words, from the point of view of Cassirer, Galileo's empiricism is the empiricism of a rationalist.

Each of the apparently contradictory statements, then, is true. They are true, however, only in that both of them, thesis and antithesis, are but preparing the way for the synthesis. One arrives at definite knowledge only by means of empirical, experimental proof. But what is an experiment? An experiment is a method by which Nature is made to answer with "yes" or "no" to a question put to it. Without such a question there is no experiment. This question is an intellectual act. It is with my mind that I conceive (*"mente concipio"*) an "hypothesis." This hypothesis is an anticipation of what is the objective law of Nature. Such an hypothesis needs confirmation by experiment; but it is only such an hypothesis that can be either confirmed or refuted by the experiment.

2

The historical statement quoted does not read as if it were a statement concerning the opinions of a scientist of several centuries ago; rather it reads "as if it were a present true statement." In reading a novel or in seeing a play and listening to it, you are tempted to forget that you are witnessing only a "story;" moreover, this is quite as it should be. A novel or play is supposed to exert this kind of temptation, and you are expected to yield to it. But, if the same kind of experience is encountered in a scholarly book on the history of philosophy, you are apt to feel a little uneasy afterwards. You were fascinated and caught by the thought itself: you were following the several steps, and led to ask yourself: Is Galileo right? And, in asking this question, you look around for Cassirer's assistance: What does *he* think? Was Galileo right or not? But you look in vain for the author's assistance. You suddenly realize that it was not a present truth-assertion you were reading, but only a "story"—the history of a philosophical opinion. The more you were fascinated and caught by the thought itself, the more quickly you are likely to lose interest. From the enthusiasm which your excursion—or escape—into history may have produced, there is almost bound to result a kind of intellectual hangover. You ask yourself: But where is truth? And what is truth?

Indeed, the context from which the above passage is taken makes it clear that we are faced with an *historical* statement. The passage serves as an illustration of some characteristics which were common to the period of the Renaissance, to its scientists as well as to its artists. This particular passage is included in a discussion of Leonardo da Vinci's theory of the arts; and Galileo's empiricism and rationalism are introduced only to show that Leonardo's views were of something more than individual significance; that they were indeed a characteristic of the period. Accordingly, this short discussion of Galileo's theory leads to the statement that Galileo's theory about the relationship between thought and experience is in strict analogy to that relation which, according to Renaissance aesthetic theory, exists between the imagination (*Phantasie*) of a painter and the "objective" reality of things. The power of the mind, of artistic as well as scientific ingenuity, consists not in unrestrained or arbitrary procedure, but in the fact that only the mind can teach us to *see* and to recognize the "object" in those factors which are its highest determinants. The genius both in the artist and in the scientist discovers the necessity of Nature.

There is considerable intellectual pleasure in being led from strict empiricism to rationalism, and from there to a comprehensive synthesis of both, and again further to an interpretation of scientific method as something "artistic." In spite of the enjoyment of this intellectual process, however, we stop at this point, and ask: Does Cassirer really mean to say that science is founded on no firmer ground than the imagination of a painter? To be sure, one realizes that this is a statement which is meant to apply only to the period of the Renaissance. At the same time, however, the passage on Galileo recalls some of Cassirer's own views. Consequently, the reader's uncertainty is only increased: Is this statement of the historian supposed to be "true," i.e., is it at the same time an assertion by the present philosopher himself? The best way of getting an answer to this question is to look at some of the passages in which

Cassirer discusses Galileo in his systematic philosophical treatises.

3

There is no doubt that the above passage from Galileo is a very "Cassirerian" passage. The keen paradox that the individual mind, out of itself, (*da per sè*) knows the objective laws of nature—or rather the fact that this is not regarded as a paradox—reflects the ideas one is accustomed to in Ernst Cassirer to such an extent that one almost expects to hear the ring of his voice, and to see the statement emphasized by his own personality.

Indeed, the passage expresses Cassirer's basic epistemological position—and at the same time it does *not* do so. The famous words come to mind in which, in the Preface to the second edition of the *Critique of Pure Reason*, "Kant tried to appraise the consequences of empiricism and rationalism." These words denote in general terms the starting point of Cassirer's own theory of knowledge; and the way in which he quoted them in one of his latest remarks on Galileo[2] suggests that they were also the starting point of Cassirer's own historical work, and especially of his history of the *Erkenntnisproblem*. "When Kant . . . tried to appraise the consequences of empiricism and rationalism, he was obliged to go back to the source of this development." One is greatly tempted to substitute here Cassirer's name for Kant's.

When Galilei let balls of a particular weight, which he had determined himself, roll down an inclined plane . . . a new light flashed on all students of nature. They comprehended that reason has insight into that only which she herself produces on her own plan, and that she must move forward with the principles of her judgments, according to fixed law, and compel nature to answer her questions. . . . Reason holding in one hand its principles . . . and in the other hand the experiment, which it has devised according to those principles, must approach nature in order to be taught by it: but not in the character of a pupil who agrees to everything the master likes but as an appointed judge who compels the witnesses to answer the questions which he himself proposes. . . . Thus only has the study of nature entered on the secure method of a

[2] "Galileo: a New Science and a New Spirit," *The American Scholar*, (Vol. 12) 1943, 6.

science, after having for many centuries done nothing but grope in the dark.[3]

These lines show where Kant and Cassirer (in so far as the latter was a Kantian) agree with Galileo. At the same time, these same lines, and the context from which they are taken, point out those principles in regard to which their thought moves in a direction diametrically opposed to that of Galileo. There is nothing in Galileo which suggests that Reason acts as the "legislator to Nature" and "prescribes its laws to Nature." On the contrary, Cassirer frequently quotes Galileo's statement, which says that the word of God is written in Nature, in mathematical language; Reason is capable of sharing the divine knowledge in kind, though not in extent. This claim of possessing divine knowledge, the claim of having an absolutely certain knowledge of Being-in-itself—these ontological claims are irreconcilable with those 'Critical' views which Cassirer never ceased to share with Kant.

The same vacillation between taking sides both "with" and "against" Galileo can be found in Cassirer's systematic writings on the philosophy of science.

In order to testify for Cassirer's own views, Galileo is called in, e.g., when Cassirer discusses the problem of *induction.*[4] Among the many theories of induction there are essentially two types; one of them is represented by Bacon and John Stuart Mill,—the other one by Galileo, both in his capacity of a scientist and as a theoretician of science. In Galileo's 'classical' and 'a-prioristic' view the experiment answers a question; i.e., it answers *only* a question, and this question *qua* question is limited; it is defined by the "mental conception" which makes us raise the question. But, although it is *only* to a *question* that the experiment gives an answer, it *does* give an *answer*, and it

---

[3] Immanuel Kant, *Critique of Pure Reason*, Preface to 2nd Edition. Translated by F. Max Müller, London, Macmillan and Co., (1881) Vol. I, p. 368. Quoted by Ernst Cassirer in his article "Galileo: a New Science and a New Spirit," published in *The American Scholar*, (Vol. 12) 1943, 6.

[4] E.g., *Substance and Function*, Engl. Translation (1923) pp. 237-270, esp. 252-270. *Determinismus und Indeterminismus in der modernen Physik* (hereafter abbreviated: *Determinismus*) pp. 103, 118. "Goethe und die mathematische Physik," in: *Idee und Gestalt*, 1st ed., 42.

answers the question once and for all. Every experiment can be made only under particular circumstances, and these circumstances change from hour to hour, or even from one split second to another, and from place to place. The particular event which is observed can serve in the rank of an *experiment* only to the extent to which one abstracts from the particular circumstances; one can abstract from them only by taking them into consideration; in order to take the accidental circumstances into consideration, however, the decision must have been made beforehand as to what in the particular case *is* accidental and what is essential and necessary. That is to say, the criterion for the abstraction is '*a priori*,' and it is this *a priori* criterion which makes the *universal* validity of the experiment possible; i.e., makes the experiment an *experiment*.

This universal validity of the experiment is contested by the doctrine of induction which Bacon and Mill represent; and with its universal validity they also question its *a priori* character. The "induction from particular to particular," from which Mill stated his canons, gives up the *a priori* claim of universal validity, since, according to this conception, one experiment is always a set of experiments, the function of which is to discover the *constant* factor. Instead of stating *a priori* something *about* the phenomena with preconceived notions, it is necessary to come to and to remain in constant touch with them; if, through a great number of variations in various ways, two factors remain uniformly connected, then a constancy and uniformity is shown in the connection between those two factors. This uniformity is proved strictly only for the number of cases for which it was shown to exist; there is no reason why this uniformity should last beyond the number of tested cases; the uniformity of nature, which we rely on, is itself supposed to be based only on an "induction" of this type. The disclaimer that such a theory of induction lacks a *logical* justification can not well be raised against it; for it is precisely one of the purposes of the theory to bring into sharp relief the fact that human knowledge does not have any such independent foundation, but remains ultimately exposed to the uncertainties of the unknown. It gives up the claim to universal laws. If physics, on the other hand, has shown that phenomena can not only be stated and measured, but that they can be subsumed under laws, then such a theory of induction is not sufficient for physics.

Against Mill's notion that a natural law can always be only an "aggregate of specific truths" a decisive objection was raised by Galileo at the very beginning of modern science. Galileo declared: If this were so, then any general judgments concerning reality would be either impossible or useless. They would be impossible, if the series of the individual cases which are observed is infinite; for such a series cannot be exhausted by means of enumeration *(per enumerationem simplicem)*; and they would be superflous, if the series were finite; for in this case we could be satisfied with ascertaining the fact specifically in the case of each of the members of the series. Mill's declaration "All inference is from particulars to particulars" is therewith declared void, at least for the field of exact physics.[5]

In other words, what Bacon's and Mill's type of induction can establish are statements of information which in the ideal (and unattainable) case of perfection, would have the form of: "Whenever X, then Y." The form of physical laws, as established by Galileo, has the form: "If X, then Y"—whereby it is completely irrelevant whether X ever "happens." On the other hand, "if X ever happens, then Y must necessarily be the case too."

Cassirer, as far as I can see, never in the least questioned the usefulness of the methods of induction as a means of finding "correlations" between two sets of phenomena between which so far no relation had been discovered. If I do not have any idea with what factors a certain phenomenon P might be connected, then, in my desperate need for a good idea, I look around and may try by the methods of trial and error, as improved by Mill's canons, to "get an idea," or any "suggestion" as to where to look for any relevant factors. Also, the other way around; suppose I have an idea, a "suspicion" that two phenomena, which have never before been related, may have something to do with each other; then again, by means of "induction," such as stated by Mill's canons, I can find out

---

[5] *Determinismus*, 51. (Cf. Galileo, *Opere*, ed. Albèri. XLI, 513).

whether there is any basis for my suspicion and whether there is any *possibility* (and in *this* sense, any likelihood or probability) of its being true. But such a suspicion is not an "hypothesis," and its "try-out" is not an experiment in the strict sense of the word. To be sure, it is merely a verbal question whether such a "try-out" is called an experiment. What *is* important is this: that the small, but immensely significant difference is recognized which exists between the "testing a suspicion" and an experiment in the, strict sense, i.e., an experiment which serves to confirm an hypothesis.

A "suspicion" in the sense in which the word was used here refers to a matter of some factual information, something that may happen to be the case, it can be proved completely, or rather replaced, by an observation; in fact, it makes sense only in the absence of an observation, as its substitute. An hypothesis represents an insight, and may be true even though there might never again occur a case to demonstrate the insight. As an *insight* it is not "derived" from experience, but is only *provoked* by an experience. (Plato's term is παρακαλεῖσθαι). In the establishment of an hypothesis, in the strict sense of the word, "experience" plays, so to speak, only the rôle of a trigger action. As one illustration out of many others in the history of science, Cassirer discusses in detail the very accidental "experience" which led Robert Mayer to the first statement of the principle of the conservation of energy. Similarly, the study of the case of *one* single patient may give a physician the insight into the intrinsic and universal connection between some "mysterious" symptoms, which so far had remained unexplained, and some relevant condition.[6] Cassirer quotes Goethe's criticism of Bacon's inductive method, and his comparison with that of Galileo.

He who is not capable of becoming aware of the fact that often one case is worth thousands of them and includes them all, will never be able to promote anything for his own enjoyment and benefit, and that of others. . . . "Through Bacon's method of dispersion natural science seemed to be scattered forever. But through Galileo it became at once united and concentrated. Galileo proved in his early youth that for a

[6] Cf. *Determinismus*, 59.

true genius, one case may stand for a thousand cases, inasmuch as he developed the theory of the pendulum and of the fall of bodies from the observation of a swinging lamp in a cathedral." . . . In the sciences everything depends on what is called an aperçu, and on becoming aware of what lies at the basis of the phenomena. Such an awareness goes on to be productive ad infinitum.[7]

It is seen from these instances that in Cassirer's systematic writings Galileo appears in an extremely un-historical fashion. Galileo is pictured in discussion with John Stuart Mill, and Goethe is called in to aid him; no attempt is made to excuse the chronological anachronisms (as was done even by Plato, when he had old Parmenides meet young Socrates). Galileo has to dispute with the theoreticians of modern statistical physics, and even then is made to carry the day. He comes in to defend himself (and Cassirer) against Exner's questioning of the ultimate validity of the laws of dynamic physics. From the "classical" point of view, any statistical arguments are regarded simply as preliminary, temporary statements which are supposed to be replaced eventually by "dynamic" statements. In the case of all "irreversible" processes, however, statistical statements must be regarded as final. If both the dynamic and the statistical forms of laws are required, then it seems necessary to consider the statistical laws of the general concept, and to subsume the classical form of dynamic laws under it as a special case. The laws of the kinetic theory of gases do not have any "exact," but only statistical validity, and offer average values gathered from a great number of observations.

Is it different with the rest of the laws, with the laws of classical physics? Does the formula which Galileo has established for the free fall of bodies really apply *always* and everywhere? How can we decide about the universal validity of a law, since our experience can always cover only the "average" of a phenomenon during a long, but limited stretch of time?[8]

[7] *Ibid.*; cf. also "Galileo: A New Science and A New Spirit," 16. The internal quotation is taken from Goethe's *Zur Farbenlehre*, Historischer Teil, Weimar edition, Part II; Vol. 3, 236, 246ff.

[8] *Determinismus*, 102 (the quotation stems from Exner, *Vorlesungen über die physikalischen Grundlagen der Naturwissenschaften*, Wien, 1919; 86th & 87th Vorlesung, 647ff.).

Could it not be that the average laws would not apply within very small stretches of space and time? To this question Galileo answers with an extensive quotation from one of his letters,[9] to this effect: his arguments would not lose the least of their force and conclusiveness, even if the bodies of Nature did not happen to fall with a strictly uniform acceleration; for these arguments claim only a hypothetical and not an assertive validity.

This shows, according to Cassirer, that Galileo's equations are not supposed to give a collective description of "all" individual cases. "One could express this, somewhat paradoxically, by saying that Galileo's equations do not claim to be *true* because they apply always and everywhere, and because this 'always' and 'everywhere' had been experimentally *proved*—but because, strictly speaking, they never apply anywhere."[10]

4

And now something very strange happens, and something very unhistorical and antihistorical indeed—although what Cassirer did here to Galileo is, from the historical point of view, probably not any worse than what Plato did occasionally to the historical Socrates. After having brought the argument to this point with the aid of Galileo, Cassirer takes it up again himself, and leads it to a point which represents the very opposite of what Galileo could ever have thought. There is, however, not the slightest historical misrepresentation. Galileo, so to speak, has left the room without his departure being noticed; and the stream of thought, within which he had emerged for a few "interviews," has gone on so rapidly and so smoothly that if and when you come to stop for a moment, and ask yourself: "Yes, but what about Galileo?", you notice that he has been left behind long ago.

What Cassirer does is to take up Exner's argument, and in general the argument of "induction from particular to particular," in a more radical form—only in order to outdo it in its radicalism. It should be said at once that, in a later chapter on

---

[9] *Ibid.*, 103 (Galileo to Carcaville, *Opere*, ed. Albèri, VII, 156f).
[10] *Ibid.*, 103.

the logical analysis of probability, Cassirer stresses the fact that judgments of probability are just as "true" (or false), and just as "objective" as any judgments of the classical form. But here he considers Exner's objection to Planck's position of maintaining dynamic laws as an ideal of knowledge. Exner expresses very strongly that mood of the philosophy of empirical induction in which man is regarded as a stranger in this world, insignificant as compared with the universe, and out of touch with it. Can we ever be quite sure whether what happens in Nature "really" corresponds to what we assume and establish in our general laws?

Nature does not care whether man understands it or not; also, it is not appropriate for us to construct a Nature which is adequate to our understanding; the only thing for us to do is to become resigned to accepting it as it is given to us. . . . The actual empirical confirmation of the results of the calculus of probability demonstrates that "chance" must be something that is completely independent, something that is given in Nature. Otherwise, it would not be possible that physical laws could be derived on the assumption of chance.[11]

The argument of Exner does not concern Cassirer; he considers the question dealt with therein as a pseudo-problem. He replies with the counter-question: on what grounds may we assume that there does not prevail a complete chaos, but a certain regularity which is expressed in objective—statistical—laws?

Cassirer, as has already been intimated, is more radical than Exner. Not only does Nature not care, but there is not any Nature which could either care or not care. For any scientific experience there is no Nature which "exists," as an absolute being, outside of a system of experience; the system of experiences *by* which we know phenomena may be called Nature. After having realized that we know *by* (the conception of) Nature rather than know Nature, it no longer makes sense to ask for laws "in" Nature. The boldness and efficiency of Kant's "Copernican Revolution" on which Cassirer insists is apparent in a context like this.

[11] *Ibid.*, 108 (the quotations are taken from Exner, *loc. cit.*, 697, 667).

Thus, there does not "exist" any Nature, but there is *objectivity*. Not Nature "cares" and "asks," but "knowledge" asks whether and to what extent it may be possible to find an objective order and determination within the phenomena: and all its individual concepts are but partial expressions for this one basic problem. If physical research, starting from some general hypothetical presuppositions, is able to link them together in such a manner that a more and more perfect knowledge of the particular phenomena will result, then we have all that can be meant by and expected from strict dynamic lawfulness *(Gesetzlichkeit.)*[12]

The very analysis of the problem is offered as its complete solution.

But would Galileo accept *this* solution? He is not mentioned, and a little reflection shows that, if Galileo were confronted with Exner's problem, he would not have considered it as a pseudo-problem as Cassirer did. For, whereas for Galileo the book of Nature is written in mathematical language, it is the book of an *independent* Nature that is written in this language; Galileo's doctrine is just as "ontological" as is Exner's; and Exner's "ontological" view is not more so than that of Galileo —whom Cassirer had quoted against Exner.

5

Let us consider this case of "Galileo versus Galileo;" a brief consideration of this somewhat disturbing phenomenon may give us some insight into the structure of Cassirer's thought.

The case *is* disturbing, for several reasons. First of all, it is disconcerting, to say the least, to find that, whereas the witness is called in order to testify when he is needed to speak *in favor* of the cause, he is not called in at any other occasions. Perhaps it was assumed that he did not have anything relevant to say. But it has already been pointed out that what he has to say *is* relevant to the matter, and that he would be opposed to Cassirer's views here. And thirdly, it can easily be shown that Cassirer *knew* that what Galileo would have to say here would be contrary to his (Cassirer's) own views.

[12] *Ibid.*, 108f.

If this is so, then the counter-argument could have been omitted only for didactic or stylistic reasons of simplification. A psychological after-effect, however, may remain as the result of such procedure: namely, one might begin to distrust Cassirer's quotations, of which there are many. (As to this, however, there is no reason for concern, either in this particular instance, or, for that matter, in general.) In the *present* case, one can easily convince himself that neither the historical truth nor the argument suffers from the fact that on occasion the evidence to the contrary has been withheld, whereas that "in favor" has been given.

Although the psychological after-effect may, then, be dismissed, the "objective" question remains all the more disturbing. How is it possible that Cassirer agrees and disagrees with the same author at the same time and in the same respect?

If one is familiar with Cassirer's thought, one is so used to the fact that Cassirer can agree and disagree at the same time that he no longer wonders about it.

In his investigations into "Einstein's Theory of Relativity" Cassirer's problem is in part this: Kant's transcendental deductions refer to the classical physics of Newton and Galileo. If classical physics is superseded by modern physics, are Kant's transcendental deductions also out of date?[13]

Since, in some respects, Cassirer is a Kantian, one might (if one did not know him well) expect him to tend to minimize the difference between modern and classical physics. However, the very opposite is the case. The reason for the insufficiency of classical physics lies in its very concept of "mechanism," and in the metaphysical and *ontological* basis on which Galileo's, Newton's, and Leibniz' discoveries were based. As for Galileo, it is recognized that his foundation of dynamics is due to his conception of mathematical *hypothesis* (which we mentioned), which enabled him to "abstract" from the happenings in phenomenal or empirical space to which absolute being, ontological reality, is ascribed. At the same time, his own *new* concepts

[13] Cf. *Einstein's Theory of Relativity*, in: *Substance and Function* (Engl. transl.), 355.

do not abandon the idea of such an "absolute reality" altogether; this is the reason, as Cassirer sees it, why Galileo's idea of mechanism is faulty and insufficient.

. . . The way is open to Galileo's foundation of dynamics: for since place has ceased to be something real, the question as to the *ground* of the place of a body and the ground of its *persistence* in one and the same place disappears. Objective physical reality passes from *place* to *change of place*, to motion and the factors by which it is determined as a magnitude. If such a determination is to be possible in a definite way, the identity and permanence, which were hitherto ascribed to mere place, must go over to motion; motion must possess "being," that is, from the standpoint of the physicist, numerical constancy. This demand for the numerical constancy of motion itself finds its expression and its realization in the law of inertia. We recognize here again how closely, in Galileo, the mathematical motive of his thought was connected with an ontological motive, how his conception of *being* interacted with his conception of *measure*. The new measure, which is found in inertia and in the concept of uniform acceleration, involves also a new determination of reality. In contrast with mere place, which is infinitely ambiguous and differs according to the choice of the system of reference, the inertial movement appears to be a truly intrinsic property of bodies, which belongs to them "in themselves" and without reference to a definite system of comparison and measurement. The velocity of a material system is more than a mere factor for calculation; it not only really belongs to the system but defines its reality, since it determines its *vis viva*, *i.e.*, the measure of its dynamic effectiveness. In its measure of motion, in the differential quotient of the space by the time, Galileo's physics claims to have reached the kernel of all physical being, to have defined the intensive reality of motion. By this reality, the dynamic consideration is distinguished from the merely phoronomic. The concept of the "state of motion," not as a mere comparative magnitude, but as an essential element belonging to the moving system intrinsically, now becomes the real mark and characteristic of physical reality. . . . In all these examples, it is evident how sharply, on the one hand, the physical thought of modern times has grasped the thought of the relativity of place and of motion, and, on the other hand, how it has shrunk back from following it to its ultimate consequences.[14]

So much then is clear: the fact that Galileo does not always

[14] *Substance and Function*, 362f.

agree with Cassirer's views is clearly understood and fully recognized by Cassirer. Cassirer finds that he cannot agree with Galileo because Galileo bases his theories on ontology and metaphysics.

This is clear and simple. What remains puzzling is the fact that Cassirer *can* agree with Galileo after all. The simplest solution of this would, of course, be to say that he just happens to agree with some of Galileo's views and to disagree with some others. But Cassirer does not give such a superficial answer; and he cannot give it because he sees much too clearly how intimately Galileo's achievements, which Cassirer admires, are connected with Galileo's metaphysical doctrine, which Cassirer rejects.

Galileo's (as well as Newton's and Leibniz') "error" consists in their mathematical metaphysics, i.e., in the fact that they were convinced of the identity of Mathematics and Nature. Their views in this respect are summarized in this manner:

He who thinks and makes inferences mathematically, does not play around with empty thoughts; he does not move in a narrow world of self-made concepts, but he is in contact with the fundamentals of reality themselves. Here we are at the point in which thinking and being are in immediate touch with one another, and where, accordingly, there is not noticeable any difference between "finite" and "infinite" understanding any more. For the divine intellect has this privilege: it knows the objects not because it looks at them and observes them from the outside; it knows them because it itself is the very reason of their being. Its thought grasps Being because and in so far as it *creates* Being; and this original of creation is determined by magnitude, number, and measure. Far from being mere copies of reality, these concepts are the very originals, the everlasting and unchangeable "archetypes" of Being. On this assumption there rests Kepler's doctrine of "cosmic harmony," . . . and the same idea permeates Galileo's representation and justification of the Copernican system. In his Dialogues . . . Galileo emphasizes that with regard to mathematical knowledge there is no basic qualitative difference between the human and the divine intellect.[15]

This is, as Cassirer remarks, a point which gave offense to the church and which, for dissimilar but related reasons, offends

[15] *Determinismus,* 19.

Cassirer's critical-philosophical mind. Nonetheless, as this passage shows, Cassirer always has "the fullest understanding" for the ideas of other thinkers—a human understanding and a historical understanding; sometimes it looks, therefore, as if this "understanding" enabled him to "agree and disagree at the same time;" i.e., as if he could forget his disagreement because he was always making allowance for "extenuating circumstances." In the views of these mathematical metaphysicians and metaphysical mathematicians, and in their identification of mathematics and Nature,

there is expressed the characteristic subjective "pathos" which inspires the first founders and champions of the classical rationalism. . . . It is the first exuberant enthusiasm and, as it were, the intoxication with the newly founded and established mathematical knowledge which coined this language.[16]

It is true, the word "language" in this connection, in a book by Cassirer, has a special connotation: he wrote a philosophy of language, and this philosophy of language is part of what could be called a philosophy of languages, or of "Language"— in the sense and the effect that *every* form of world view can be regarded as one complete and consistent "Language" in the "words" or symbols of which every content can be expressed. Whereas "Language" becomes something very important (—there is no world-view without such a "Language"—), the importance of the "vocabulary" of every world-view declines somewhat: in short, what Galileo and the "rationalists" had to say in metaphysical terms is no longer very important. But (—and, in describing Cassirer's thought, the word "but" must be used again and again—), having made this statement, we notice at once that this is only half the truth, and that the very limitations of this metaphysical "Language" caused the insufficiency and faultiness of the great systems of mathematical rationalism.

Hence a passage like this, which reveals Cassirer's willingness and ability to achieve "full understanding" of historical and human limitations, must not be taken too seriously in a strictly

---

[16] *Ibid.*, 18.

philosophical sense. It serves as a kind of protection, so to speak; it is as a sheath which is used for both purposes: for protecting the "human interest" from being hurt by the crystal-hard edge of the core of the argument—and also for protecting the most sharply cut edges of the argument from being blunted by some inappropriate use. The core of the intellectual argument in the case "against Galileo" remains unaffected, even though the sentence passed on the "human" factor has been mellowed by granting "extenuating historical circumstances."

In his mechanistic metaphysics Galileo did not know what he was talking about. In drastic words, this is what Cassirer says in more urbane terminology, when he says that only the subsequent periods of science *recognized* what Galileo had meant.

In the progress of mechanics the principle of inertia is *recognized* with increasing distinctness as what it *meant* fundamentally to Galileo.[17]

6

In a very agreeable manner, then, Cassirer disagrees with Galileo the metaphysician; but the agreeable manner does not change the fact of extreme disagreement; it is a *fight* which is going on—or is it only a tournament?

As has been shown, the reconciliation between Galileo, the defender of the principle of "hypothesis," and Galileo, the metaphysician, is made possible only on the assumption that one can understand Galileo better than he understood himself. An adequate interpretation of this assumption and what it meant to Cassirer could be given only in a discussion of his theory of history. It sometimes looks as if Cassirer were inclined to give an answer, in terms of an optimistic rationalistic theory of history, to the effect that the "dim" ideas of former generations are freed from their metaphysical make-up by the following generations. Sometimes Cassirer does seem to come close to the "organic" interpretations of a mathematical metaphysics as advanced by Whitehead. All this, however, and all that has to do with the convictions and motives of Cassirer's philosophy must be disregarded in the present discussion which attempts

[17] *Einstein's Theory of Relativity* in *Substance and Function*, 364.

only to sketch briefly the formal schematism by which Cassirer's thought proceeds.

Galileo, the defender of "hypothesis," and Galileo, the defender of metaphysics, can be "reconciled" only because they are not treated impartially. What the defender of "hypothesis" has to say is accepted and believed; what the defender of metaphysics has to say, however, does not receive such acceptance. The judge knows better than the witness himself what the witness "means" to say; his statement is discarded as unessential and accidental. As far as the *form* of the argument goes, this is the basic factor: the metaphysical statement is regarded as accidental.

Hypothesis is an expression of *Necessity*. *Metaphysics* is *accidental*.

If we give Cassirer's judgment this form then we recognize its formal connection with another pair of basic concepts of reflection in Cassirer's philosophy: "Function" is an expression of Necessity, "Substance" is accidental.

On the other hand, and when more closely studied, we also see the formal connection with a paradox around which Cassirer centers his discussion on this point, a paradox which he found in Kant: the paradoxical conception of *the contingency of necessity*.[18]

What does this paradox mean, and how does Cassirer arrive at it? Stated in simplest terms it is this: if we are to have the concept of necessity, we need the concept of contingency. We do have and use the concept of necessity; therefore, we need the concept of contingency. Contingency is a requirement for necessity. The two concepts are correlates. This correlation can be expressed in different and more significant ways: The question, "Why?" can be answered and makes sense only within a certain system. If we ask for the "why?" of the system itself, it no longer makes any sense. The system itself remains contingent; without such a contingent system we could not ask or answer the question: "why?" Thus Kant says that there is no apodictical proof for the principle of causation. It can be "deduced"

18 Cf. *Determinismus*, 128f.

only through its relationship to something contingent, namely, "possible experience." Cassirer puts its as follows:

The general principle of causation can be called both necessary and contingent with equal justification—depending on the point of view which we happen to choose. The principle is necessary, since every empirical statement is based on it, and since, as a "synthetic judgment *a priori*" it precedes all empirical judgments. On the other hand, however, it is "accidental" since the totality of experience, to which it refers and on which it depends for its justification, is itself given as purely factual.[19]

This interpretation of Kant appears to be very characteristic of Cassirer indeed. I am not sure whether it is possible to interpret and exhaust its real significance; quite apart from the question whether it is "defensible." A little metaphorical circumlocution may lend some help to the imagination, if not to thought. Experience is intrinsically "necessary," and it is something which in itself is "moving." But it is moving only within itself—self-contained, and well-rounded—suspended, as it were, in a vacuum, without support, kept in balance and kept in motion only by itself. Although such a metaphorical circumlocution certainly does not help with the technical explanation, and although in its vagueness it would not be acceptable to Cassirer himself, it may help the imagination to realize, if not the logical ground, then at least the *ideal* of knowledge which Cassirer seems to have in mind.

What needs to be stressed within this context is the following: if we fully realize the significance of the idea that experience as a fact is accidental, then Kant's transcendental deductions appear in a light which is different from their customary and historically well-founded interpretation. The transcendental deductions lose some of the pragmatic "weight" which they usually have. More simply expressed, we may describe the principle of the transcendental deduction in a somewhat "pragmatic" fashion as follows: "there is the fact of experience; and the pure concepts of the understanding are the necessary conditions or instruments of this fact." By emphasizing the contin-

[19] *Determinismus*, 128.

gency of this "fact," Cassirer takes away from the solid "factualness" and what I have called the "pragmatic weight" of such a formulation; he has made experience a "structure;" or, in a metaphor he used to employ occasionally during the last two decades, he has made the "fact" of experience "transparent." In proceeding thus, Cassirer conceived of experience as of a Platonic Idea.

Only if we keep in mind this "transparence" and ideality of experience can Cassirer's following argument appear in its proper light and function. As soon as pragmatic or teleological expressions appear in Cassirer's arguments, one has to interpret them as metaphors which are supposed to express "ideal" relationships which cannot be expressed "directly." This is a feature Cassirer's thought has in common with Plato's thought.

In such half-metaphorical language Cassirer can now say that both concepts, necessity and contingency, are "required for" and "justified by" the fact of experience.

On the whole the isolation of formal structures which has been attempted in these remarks is not at all in line with the tendency of Cassirer's work. Cassirer not only holds the theory that there is no form without content, and vice versa, but he never actually deals with a form without its corresponding content. It is perhaps for this very reason, however, that a paradoxical formulation like that of the *contingency of necessity* can be used in interpreting various levels of Cassirer's thought, and in this respect presents a key to many of his doctrines.

Out of the many variations of this theme in Cassirer's philosophy, only a few examples from our context may be cited.

1. The necessary and the contingent are not two different "powers" or "things," but correlates.

2. There is no "system of experience" (mythical thought, theoretical thought, or systems of individual philosophers) without these concepts.

3. In this respect they represent something which is common to all systems of thought—and a principle of unity,—

4. —and diversity, since the accentuation of what is necessary and what is contingent varies in every system.

5. Therefore this paradox is applicable to itself: for just what *is* necessary in every system *is* contingent.

6. Thus there is a dialectic, according to which every "succeeding" system regards as contingent (and rightly so) what was regarded as necessary in the "preceding" system.

7. This applies to Cassirer's own system too; so that its most fundamental concept (the concept of "understanding," "*verstehen*") is also regarded as contingent—as an expression of an ultimate problem rather than as a definite "being."

Applications to Galileo are easily made:

1. *Within* Galileo's system the necessary is represented by the equations of motion; the contingent is represented by the subjective sense qualities.

2. The concept of determination in Galileo has the form $y = f(x)$. That is to say, y is precisely determined by x, and in that sense the relationship is "necessary." An equation of this form answers the question "how does y change?" but it does not answer the question "*why* does y change?" (in the sense of one of the four Aristotelian causes). Because the *kind* of determination is not expressed, there is an element of indetermination and contingency.

3. There is no answer to the question *why* the equations of motion are as they are. They are to Galileo ultimate metaphysical realities; but as such they are contingent.

From these schematic remarks, it may be seen why "Galileo the metaphysician" could be "rejected," and yet be "reconciled" with "Galileo the defender of hypothesis." In this sense the "case" of Galileo is an exemplification of the principle of the *contingency of necessity*.

Upon reflection, the more one considers the formulation of the "contingency of necessity" with respect to all fields and aspects of Cassirer's philosophy, (as well as in itself), the more one realizes the intellectual impetus which such a "symbolic" concept provides and the more one experiences the suggestive power and fascination which comes from it. Yet, perhaps, a more serious and sober reflection would now seem to be called for. The question arises: Have we not fallen victim to a splendid performance of subtle sophistry? If a theory, such as mathematical metaphysics, is first rejected and then accepted on a different level, is this not exactly "making the weaker cause the stronger?" Furthermore: is a concept like that of "the contingency of necessity" not simply a device of sophistic jugglery? What does it really mean to say that "contingent" and "necessary" are correlative concepts, and that in order to have a necessary system of experience the idea of contingency is required? Is this different at all from saying that for the preservation of health some sickness is required? This may be true in some special sense, but the suspicion of a sophistic trickery cannot be repressed. Brought to more abstract formulation: would such a thesis not correspond to the postulate that the concept of Non-Being is required in order to have a concept of Being?[20]

As soon as we arrive at this more general formulation, however, we become aware that it might be advisable to become suspicious of our suspicion. At any rate, the central problem is indicated: Is there a possibility that "in looking for the Sophist we have encountered the Philosopher unaware?"[21]

This is possible; and the contrary is also possible: in looking for and believing ourselves to be following a philosopher, we may have caught (or may have been caught by) a sophist. This question does not yet admit of a ready answer; but it certainly needs at least to be raised whenever one undertakes to understand and examine the philosophy of Ernst Cassirer.

In this region [of dialectic] we shall discover the philosopher now or later or whenever we shall look for him; like the sophist, he is hard to recognize precisely, although the difficulty with him is different from the difficulty one has with the sophist.—The sophist runs away into the darkness of not-being where he is used to feel his way by routine; and because of the darkness of the place he is hard to recognize.—The philosopher who has his mind and thought fixed to the idea of Being is also hard to recognize, because of the shining brightness of the place.[22]

---

[20] Cf. "Zur Logik des Symbolbegriffs," *Theoria*, IV, 145-175, *Geschichte der griechischen Philosophie* (in: *Lehrbuch der Philosophie*, ed. M. Dessoir), 129 and frequently.

[21] Plato, *Sophist*, 253ff.

[22] Plato, *Sophist*, 254a.

Just as the student is blinded by a philosopher no less than by a sophist, there is a deceptive resemblance between the two. A sophist appears like a philosopher, and a philosopher appears like a sophist, as a dog resembles a wolf, and, as we may add, a liar may resemble a poet, or the tyrant may resemble the philosopher-king. There is an infinitely fine and yet immensely decisive difference between the two. Both the philosopher and the sophist employ the same means and tricks, both use the playful joke.[23] In fact, the philosopher is the "good" sophist. Diotima speaks ὥσπερ οἱ τέλεοι σοφισταί, like one of the accomplished sophists.

The criterion lies in their concepts of Being. Until these are analyzed, the issue between Sophist and Philosopher remains in suspense. Yet, in the case of Ernst Cassirer, whoever thinks of his person and his style may be confident about the outcome, "because of the shining brightness of the place."

7

The present illustrations, loosely knit as they are, may have at least suggested that the very rhythm of Cassirer's prose reflects his philosophical dialectics. A statement by Cassirer, valid in itself, must yet be seen within its dialectical context. Furthermore, in addition to the horizontal dialectics, there is a kind of vertical dialectics: a historical statement by Cassirer has a systematic significance at the same time. The fact that Cassirer could "revive" and "re-present" Galileo on the contemporary intellectual scene is obviously due to the special form of Cassirer's systematic interest in Galileo.

Cassirer does not simply write a detached historical report about Galileo nor does he really enter into an intimate discussion with him. His relationship to Galileo is much more and much less close than is that of two persons talking to one another: either Cassirer agrees with Galileo and then speaks "through" Galileo, somewhat like a dramatist speaks through a historical character; or else he disagrees with him and then he makes Galileo the object of his comprehensive and extremely liberal understanding in such a manner that even where Galileo seems

---

[23] *Phaedrus*, 277e; *Sophist*, 235a.

to "disagree" he is also made to "express" the truth—in a different language. (Cassirer had started from the ahistorical neo-Kantian approach; but he combined Hegel's method and that of a historical relativism in order to arrive at what may be called a new timelessness in history.)

In fact, the ways in which Galileo is made to reflect Cassirer's thought are far more manifold than could be indicated in this sketch. Cassirer tried to find a theoretical synthesis of scientific and aesthetic understanding[24] just as he tried to find a synthesis of historical and systematical understanding; and his own actual understanding has definitely an artistic note in addition to, and in combination with, its scientific and historical character. These manifold relationships are apt to be implicitly present in what he says, and a statement by Cassirer can often be read on various levels, just as symbols can be in a work of art. What may appear as an ambiguity is in fact a multiplicity of meanings which, however, do not necessarily impair one another at all. The spell which emanates from Cassirer's style (as it did from his person) fascinates his reader and student; its recognition must make one wonder whether *what* Cassirer taught should and could be separated from *how* he taught it.

Cassirer's art is that of the Platonic philosopher, playful and used with that irony and sovereignty which is owed to the Idea of the Good. With the *cunning* of this idea, in Hegel's term, its light "unites the various things appearing in the dusk." Cassirer's synthesis, unifying through that understanding and reconciliation of opposites which made him an extremist of universal liberalism, is basically Platonic. If Plato found it difficult to distinguish between a sophist and a philosopher when he met one, we need perhaps not be ashamed if we require a little more time and space to arrive at a full view of, and a clear distinction between, the scientific, historical, and aesthetic elements in the structure of Ernst Cassirer's philosophical thought.

WALTER M. SOLMITZ

DEPARTMENT OF GERMAN
BOWDOIN COLLEGE

[24] Cf. "Goethe und die mathematische Physik" in *Idee und Gestalt* (Berlin, 1921), 27-76.

22

William H. Werkmeister

CASSIRER'S ADVANCE BEYOND
NEO-KANTIANISM

CASSIRER'S ADVANCE BEYOND
NEO-KANTIANISM

WHEN critics of the Marburg School of neo-Kantianism argued that the theories of Cohen and Natorp had little in common with the original views of Kant, Paul Natorp replied[1] that it had never been the intention of the Marburg School to revive orthodox Kantianism; that, on the contrary, the step back to Kant had been taken only in order to gain a more profound understanding of the genuine insights of the Sage of Königsberg, and to advance from his position in a direction more in conformity with the developments of modern science; that, finally, the spirit of Kant, rather than any one of his propositions, was to be preserved. A poor student of Kant is he, Natorp stated, who understands the meaning of "critical philosophy" in any other way.

In the same spirit in which Cohen· and Natorp advanced beyond Kant, Ernst Cassirer seems to have advanced beyond the neo-Kantians.

When Cassirer published his monograph, *Zur Einsteinschen Relativitätstheorie*, several critics, although agreeing with his conclusions, doubted that he was justified in drawing them, unless he relinquished at the same time his neo-Kantianism. Readers of Cassirer's later works—in particular, readers of his *Philosophie der symbolischen Formen*, and of his *Determinismus und Indeterminismus in der modernen Physik*—may experience similar doubts. Cassirer himself, however, feels that the ties which connect him with the founders of the Marburg School have not been loosened, and that the "debt of gratitude" he owes them has not been diminished; although he may now

---

[1] "Kant und die Marburger Schule," *Kant-Studien*, Vol. XVIII (1910).

interpret the foundations of modern science in a way which differs in some essentials from the interpretations given by Hermann Cohen and Paul Natorp.[2]

It will be our task to examine briefly the extent to which Cassirer's views still fall within the general framework of neo-Kantianism, and to describe those points of doctrine which constitute a definite and decisive modification of the original position of the Marburg School.

This task is formidable and can be fully accomplished only in a detailed study which far exceeds the space available in this volume; for Cassirer has been a prolific writer. His interests are truly catholic and his books deal with a great variety of problems. Even if we restrict our considerations to questions of epistemology, Cassirer's discussions range from the foundations of mathematics and modern physics to an approach to art, religion, and a general philosophy of culture.

Our task is somewhat simplified, however, by Cassirer's own recent statement[3] that the essentials of his philosophy of science have undergone no significant change since the publication in 1910 of his book, *Substanzbegriff und Funktionsbegriff*, and that today he still adheres to the point of view of that work. In view of the developments of modern physics he has been able to formulate more clearly and demonstrate more effectively the basic ideas expressed more than thirty years ago; but his philosophical position remains substantially unaltered and, in the opinion of Cassirer himself, has been confirmed by what has happened in the sciences. It is therefore possible for us to disregard the problem of a gradual evolvement of Cassirer's philosophy, and to concentrate on its most adequate and most recent formulations, leaving to the historian of philosophy the additional task of determining to what extent, if any, these formulations modify Cassirer's earlier position.

Our discussions will be concerned primarily with Cassirer's views as expressed in his monograph, *Determinismus und Indeterminismus in der modernen Physik,* and in his three-volume work, *Die Philosophie der symbolischen Formen.* These views

---

[2] Cassirer, *Determinismus,* viii.
[3] *Ibid.,* vii-viii.

we shall compare with Natorp's position as formulated in *Die logischen Grundlagen der exakten Wissenschaften* (1910) and, for the sake of completeness, with certain sections of Cohen's *Logik der reinen Erkenntnis* (1902). Such a comparison should reveal the extent to which Cassirer has advanced beyond neo-Kantianism and should disclose also the affinities he still has with the founders of the Marburg School.

In order to facilitate our task further, we shall restrict our comparison to a consideration of a few basic concepts; all minor issues can have only a secondary bearing upon our problem. We have chosen for our analysis the concepts "object," "space-time," and "causality," and the general problem of an epistemological basis of the cultural sciences or *Geisteswissenschaften*.

We begin our discussion with a consideration of the concept "object."

I. "Object"

We must understand from the start that the founders of the Marburg School were interested primarily in scientific knowledge, and that they saw in scientific cognition the prototype of all cognition worthy of the name. Scientific cognition, moreover, they identified in all essentials with mathematics and mathematical physics. Epistemology, therefore, became for them an analysis of "the logical foundations of the exact sciences;" and this limitation of the scope of their analyses became decisive for their whole point of view. We shall return to this in Part IV of our essay.

If, for the time being, we accept the restrictive definition of knowledge as given by Cohen and Natorp, the question arises: What is the "factum" of science? What is the ultimate basis of validation of scientific cognition, and what are the "objects" concerning which science gives us "knowledge"?

The "factum" of science, Natorp maintains, is neither "given," ready-made and complete in itself; nor is it some "completed or definitive knowledge;" for every cognition which provides the answer to a given problem leads to, or implies, new and even greater problems. Plato, therefore, was right in the opinion of the neo-Kantians when he saw the task of science in an infinite process of determining the indeterminate. And since the infinite process of determination may move in two directions—toward the determination of particulars as well as toward the determination of an all-inclusive universal—there can be no absolute or definitive starting-point of the process of cognition any more than there is an absolute or definitive terminal point. The process is unending in either direction.

In order to get the process going at all, that is to say, in order to have some anchorage, some vantage-point from which to begin the determination of the indeterminate, it is necessary to "posit" or "fixate" something in experience as our point of departure and then to advance from it as far as possible on logically justifiable grounds. We must remember at all times, however, that our starting-point was "posited" or assumed and that it is subject to revision as soon as such revision seems possible or necessary in the light of subsequent experiences. The individual "factum," therefore, originally posited as our starting-point or "discovered" in the process of advancing cognition, is never an isolated datum, but must needs be an element within a context—within the context of cognition itself.

Mathematics provides the most clear-cut example of what is meant; for the basic concepts of mathematics are "posited" concepts which find their justification and validation only within the orderly process of mathematical thinking. This reference to mathematics, incidentally, also makes it clear that the "progress" here meant is essentially not a progress in time, not a merely psychological or historical progress, but a logical progression, a system of implications. Time itself is but one aspect—and by no means the most fundamental one—of the systemic progress with which epistemology is concerned.

If it is true that the "factum" of science finds justification and determination only within the systemic context of which it is an element, then we can no longer speak of "objects" as "given," ready-made and complete, or of cognition as an "analysis of the given." On the contrary, the "object" itself is now a "problem," something which we may attain at the end of the cognitive process but which we certainly do not possess at its beginning. And cognition, in so far as it is concerned with "objects" is necessarily "synthetic" in Kant's meaning of the term, i.e., it is the enlargement of, or the continuous progress in, our context of experience.

From the above it follows also that there is not and cannot be a "favored" starting-point of cognition. The integration of experience according to law may be started, ideally, wherever one wishes. The context of experience can be established no matter what we posit at the beginning so long as we remember that this starting-point, being only assumed to begin with, is subject to constant revision as we progress. Only one condition is indispensable. The context of cognition must be grounded in a unitary origin of thought.

This unitary origin (*Ursprungseinheit*), however, is not an undifferentiated logical One. Such a One could never provide an adequate basis for a variegated context. The unitary origin, furthermore, is neither a psychological nor a metaphysical entity whose "existence" would have to be assumed. It is rather the logical ideal of the all-comprehensive context of experience in and through which each "posited" element leads to all other elements of that context. It is the ideal of "systemic" thinking, the idea that all thinking ultimately strives toward systemic unity.

But this context, as unitary origin, is also not "given" in actual concreteness. It is an implied but as yet unrealized goal. All cognition begins with the implicit assumption that the establishment of a systemic context is the logical task ahead of us. The unitary origin, in other words, is neither a system *in nuce* nor a first element within a system. It is in itself not even "systemic" but is only the demand for a system.

Hermann Cohen, in particular, attempted to clarify the demand for a starting-point of cognition. He argued that, strictly speaking, all cognition would have to start from "nothing." From "nothing," however, nothing can be derived, and if the starting-point of cognition were strictly interpreted as "nothing," cognition itself would be impossible. The "nothing"

Cohen speaks of must therefore be only a "relative nothing." In Cohen's own argumentation it turns out to be the "possibility of transition, of logical progression (or regression)" which, in Natorp's terminology, is identical with the ideal of an all-inclusive cognitive context, the ideal of the context of logical proof, logical interdependence.

As has been mentioned before, this context may be "traced" in two directions: toward the unification of differentiated elements, or toward the differentiation of what is unified. This double-faced context of logical interdependence is, for the neo-Kantians, the basis of all cognition.

Context, as here understood, must mean and imply the preservation of the logical significance of each individual element and, at the same time, the unification of elements in a higher logical unity; and, vice versa, it must mean the preservation of the logical unity of the context and, at the same time, the diversification and preservation of the individual elements. The particulars must be preserved within the context, and the context must be maintained despite all differentiations. Logical context, as exemplified in mathematics and mathematical physics, fulfills both requirements.

This context is encountered in its most elementary form in the relationship of a question and its answer. The question anticipates its answer; the answer fulfills or satisfies the question. Both belong indissolubly together.

The relationship of question and answer, however, also defines the problem of the "object;" for the "object" is an answer to a question. Its primary meaning is that of an answer, that of an element within a context determined by a question. The fact that the "object" seems to lie "outside" cognition and that it is "appropriated" by cognition is fully explained, according to Natorp, by the idea of anticipation which we encounter in the question. It is the context defined by a question which, in and through its anticipation, defines or determines the "object." As in the case of mathematical equations the unknown variables x, y, z have meaning for the equation and within the equation only by virtue of the meaning of the equation itself, i.e., in relation to the "invariables," the assumed "variables," and the "roots" of the equation, just so, and only so, is the great X of cognition, the "object," meaningful and understandable only as an element within the context of cognition.

So interpreted, the "object" of cognition becomes an anticipation, a "projection," and ceases to be an unapproachable "thing-in-itself," a something which literally and in the absolute sense transcends all cognition. There is no longer any need for the assumption that "objects" exist in and by themselves. All we need to accept now is the possibility of an orderly progress of cognition, the possibility of establishing an all-comprehensive context according to law, the method of securing scientific cognition. The "object" becomes the ultimate goal of that process, the ultimate determination of the X in our initial question.

The unity of context is unity of thought. To think, so Natorp maintains, is to unify. That which is to be unified, however, is not something beyond or outside of thinking. It is, rather, something "posited" as a terminal of synthetic relations and therefore is a product of thought itself. The psychologist may still speak of "sense impressions," "images," and the like; but so far as logic is concerned, we can speak only of "contents" and "content relations" which are determined and defined in and through thinking. From a strictly "critical" point of view it is meaningless to speak of a "manifold of the senses" which exists prior to, and independent of, thinking and which is "unified" in cognition through a secondary thought process. For the neo-Kantians, to think means to posit that something "is." What this something may be prior, or in addition to, our thinking, is a question which cannot be asked legitimately within the framework of thought itself, for the demand for a meaning, the demand that the "something" mean something within the context of thought, is already a demand for a justification of it in and through thought, a demand for its validation as a content of thought. For thought, all "being" exists only in and through thought itself. Logically there is nothing prior to thinking. The X of cognition may be determined as an A or a B or a C; but as X it is only the "pure expression of a question" and not an entity, psychological, metaphysical, or otherwise.

If thinking, and thinking alone, creates the comprehensive context which, through its unity or interrelations, determines or defines the X of cognition as an A or a B or a C, then the epistemological problem reduces to a problem of the ultimate logical functions of thinking. The problem of cognition, in other words, will have been solved as soon as we solve the problems of the "categories" which govern and determine the basic functions of thought.

Natorp finds that, to begin with, the categories "quantity" and "quality" are indispensable. Wherever an X is to be transformed by thought into a determinate A or B or C, we must think that X in terms of quantity and quality at least. Neither one of these categories by itself is sufficient as a determination of X, for the "quantum" is only the quantum of a quale, and the "quale" is but the quale of a quantum. Both together, and in their interpenetration only, constitute magnitude—the first product of thought, the first synthetic or integrational unity of experience. They determine X as an "object," but only in a general way. They certainly do not yet determine the interdependence of "objects" within a determinate context of experience.

The next step in cognition is to advance from such simple and primary syntheses to a new level of unification, to a synthesis of the elementary syntheses, i.e., to the construction of a system of interrelations. The interrelations to be established are the "relations" of Kant's *Critique of Pure Reason;* that is to say, they are "relations of dependence according to law;" they are "functional relations."

The goal of cognition, so we have seen, is the universal and complete determination of the "object" of cognition which leaves nothing undetermined in the original X. The method by means of which alone this can be achieved is, according to Natorp, the method of establishing functional relations which are integrated into a contextual system of experience. Upon such integration depends the very meaning of our term "nature" —the possibility of conceiving "nature" as a system of laws or dynamic interrelations.

The complete integration is, of course, not attainable at once and at one stroke. Only little by little does our thinking move toward the all-comprehensive context of the whole of experience. At every step, however, "nature" or "reality" is encountered and understood to exactly the same degree as univocal interrelations of the diverse elements have been established, or to which, for any given field of investigation, the choice between possible kinds of functional interrelations has been restricted. Admittedly, every fixation of interrelations thus achieved raises new problems and does not constitute a definitive terminal of integration; but we are not interested in definitive terminals anyway. Our concern is with the discovery of a method of progressive determination which will lead toward the ultimate goal of cognition, the one univocal context.

This progressive determination must be defined by the basic law of synthetic unity, i. e., by the generic law of the synthetic process itself. This law involves or presupposes, first, a "starting-point" or an "anchorage" as the foundation or reference point of the integration. It presupposes, secondly, the possibility of unrestricted progression from one element to another. And it implies, lastly, a relative termination of the process for each level of integration reached. Natorp identifies these three "indispensables" of the generic law with the "basic series," with the "space-time" schema, and with "causality," respectively.

The possibility of arranging experience in series presupposes a secure basic series as reference point and foundation of the whole schema of order—a *fundamentum relationis* or basic scheme which provides a univocal and unchanging standard for all subsequent series, a sequence of positions or a "scale" in terms of which the progression of all other sequences can be determined. This requirement of the generic law gives rise to the age-old demand for something constant or permanent as the basis of all change, for a *subjectum* (in the Aristotelian sense).

Since the required "invariable" subjects are not provided by sensuous things, we must construct them—as science has always done. The unchangeable basic constants of science are the permanent relations which, in our various equations, take the place of "things." Science, in other words, deals with "mass," "energy," "gravitation," or whatever it may be, but these concepts represent, not "things," but ultimate relations which have been posited hypothetically for the sake of the laws based upon them. In especially favorable cases these "posits" serve well, for a time at least, the purpose of integration. But as soon as the field of experience is broadened it may be necessary to revise our original hypotheses and to employ different "constants." In any case, however, it remains necessary to posit *something* as ultimate, for without any "positing" of some constants it would be impossible to deal with "nature" scientifically or to determine events in accordance with laws; and only such determination can lead to the conception of one all-comprehensive "nature." Only through the assumption of some basic constants will it be possible to determine "nature" univocally and as a whole.

The one sequence of order which is basic and common to all experience is *time*. Time is the clearest form of the type of scale requisite to a progressive synthesis. But it must at once be supplemented by space, as the basis for an interrelation of parallel series. Together, space and time provide the relational foundation for every possible progression from one element of experience to another.

Since we shall deal with Natorp's interpretation of space and time more fully in Part II, we refrain here from giving further details. Suffice it to say that through the relations involved in the space-time schema we can now define "change" as well as "permanence." Every change which occurs in a definite time and at a definite point in space must be representable as the univocal result of the continuously changing spatial distribution of a "substance." "Substance," therefore, is nothing "given" as independent or as existing in and by itself; it is "posited" as required by the "relations according to law" which describe observable changes.

Space and time, being infinite, cannot by themselves determine any particular "object." They provide only the "possibility of progression" from one element to another. The actual synthesis is achieved through the "law of causality" which defines the order of relation as an order of "antecedent" and "consequent": If x, then y; "y" is now regarded as in some manner dependent upon, or conditioned by, "x." And this relation of dependence is posited as a permanent relation. Whatever determinateness an object possesses must be derivable from this general law through the means of cognition; it must be "constructable" on the basis of the law of causality.

According to Natorp, the first and primary means of the "construction" is the positing of "rectilinear uniform motion" as the one unchangeable factor in all our calculations which are meant to describe events in nature. Upon this "posit" the validity of Newtonian mechanics depends, and upon it also depends the integrative success of classical laws.

Newton's three laws of motion do not describe directly and as such the events in nature; they only formulate the broadest and most fundamental presuppositions in accordance with which an interpretation of motion is at all possible in systemic integration. Together they provide the framework within which an "object" may be specifically determined in accordance with the law of causality, the schema in and through which the X of experience may be described as an A or a B or a C.

Newton's first law of motion, the "principle of inertia," fulfills only the demand for substantiality; for mass, strictly speaking, is nothing but the measure of inertia. As yet no reference is made to "forces" which might determine change.

Newton's second law provides the rule in accordance with which all "forces" must be posited—the rule, namely, that "forces" must be posited in proportion to determinate accelerations.

To state this matter differently, the first law formulates the general presupposition of an underlying "substance" of all motion. The second law corresponds to the law of causality which, according to Natorp, makes it at all possible to fulfill the demand for substantiality.

Newton's third law, stipulating that for every action there exists an equal and opposite reaction, expresses a more profound conception of causality. The mere "chain" of events has been transformed into a "system" of interactions.

But this third law, too, is only another version of the first. Both express the same factual situation from different points of view. We attribute the n-fold mass to a body which gives to another body (chosen as unit) an acceleration n-fold of that which it itself would receive from the latter. The proportionality of the masses can thus be defined through the negative and inverse proportion of the counter-acceleration. Mass, in other words, is not "given" prior to the dynamic or functional relations of causation but in and through those relations, for mass is the proportion of force to acceleration.

Mass, however, is an indispensable factor in all calculations through which the principles of pure mechanics are specifically applied to concrete physical situations. Mass ties the equations to physical "reality." Mass itself and "mass-points," nevertheless, have no "physical existence." It is not permissible to say that bodies "consist" of masses or of mass-points. Masses and mass-points are only the conceptual integrals of "bodies;" they are what scientists mean by "objects."

It is clear from the above statements that, according to Natorp, laws are not derived from "objects" by a process of abstraction, but that "objects" are posited in requirement of certain functional or dynamic relations according to law. They are the product of progressive integration.

Hamilton's principle of energy extends this procedure of integration to the whole field of physics. In the realm of electricity the "ponderable masses" of classical mechanics are dissolved into "forms of energy," but the epistemological procedure is unaltered. Such at any rate is the theory of Natorp and of the neo-Kantians in general.

We shall now try to understand Cassirer's view with respect to this problem.

To begin with, Cassirer, like all neo-Kantians, asserts "the epistemological primacy of the concept of law over the concept of things."[4] "Understanding" the world is not a purely passive process, a mere copying of some "given" structure of reality, but is a free and constructive activity of mind. "Objects" as such are not "given," ready-made and rigidly fixed in themselves; they do not exist prior and external to the synthetic unity of comprehension, but are "constituted" through that

[4] *Philosophie der symbolischen Formen*, III, vii.

unity, are the result of an integration in and through consciousness. Every picture or conception of the world which we have has been achieved through some kind of "objectification," some kind of synthetic transformation, which changes mere "impressions" into determinate and integrated "representations."[5] Even the most elementary sensuous content of experience is already permeated with a "tension" between "content" and "representative function," is not "mere" content but content pointing beyond itself. It is not simply "given" in isolated independence but is already viewed *sub specie* and in a certain "respect;" and this "respect" alone gives meaning to the impression. Just as any word of a language can be understood only within the totality of a sentence, so each individual impression has meaning and significance only in and through the context within which we view it.[6]

The cognitive process begins when in the flux of sensuous impressions certain "units" are "fixed" and retained as centers of integration. Individual phenomena receive their characteristic meaning only through their relation to such fixed centers or points of reference.[7] The "incisions" which determine the "fixed units" are the product of thought, the first determinations of the X of experience, and obviously correspond to the "posits" of Natorp's terminology. They provide the anchorage for the progressive determination of the "objects" of experience.

Every individual content is determined "objectively" and as an "existant" when it is brought into a space-time order, a causal order, and a thing-attribute order. Participation in the contextual interrelations of these "orders" assures each particular phenomenon of "objective reality" and "objective determinateness"[8] or, as Natorp said, it changes the X into a specific A or B or C. For Cassirer, as for Natorp, any object as determinate existant "is" only in so far as it is an integral element of a relational context established by cognitive thought.[9] It is

[5] *Ibid.*, II, 39.
[6] *Ibid.*, III, 149-155; II, 40.
[7] *Ibid.*, III, 165.
[8] *Ibid.*, 235-236.
[9] *Ibid.*, II, 40.

Cassirer's contention that this fact becomes perfectly clear when we consider sensuous impressions in various space configurations.

The relation of externality and spatial separateness, i.e., the relations of co-existence, Cassirer argues, are not "given" along with sensuous impressions; they are highly complex and mediated results of constructive thinking. When we attribute to things in space a specific magnitude, a specific position, or a specific distance from one another, we refer to no simple data of sense impressions but place the sensuous elements into a context of relations, into a system, which, in the end, is a context of judgments, a product of pure thought.[10]

Throughout our discussion of Cassirer's point of view we have repeatedly spoken of "sense impressions" and "sensuous element," as Cassirer himself does; and it seems that, with respect to this reference to "sense data," Cassirer has already forsaken the position of the orthodox neo-Kantians, for it was Natorp's contention that as far as epistemology is concerned there is nothing prior to thinking. To think is to posit that something "is." Upon analysis we find, however, that the difference between Cassirer and Natorp on this point is verbal rather than real. Natorp admitted that the psychologist might speak of "impressions," "perceptions," "images," etc., but maintained that neither "impressions" nor "perceptions" could be thought without being taken up into thought, without being permeated with thought; that their very meaning depended upon their being elements within the context of thought. What he repudiated was the idea of "impressions," "perceptions," and the like, existing by themselves in complete separation from thought and having meaning or epistemological significance in and by themselves. Cassirer, if I understand him correctly, is saying the very same thing because, as he puts it, even the simplest sensuous impressions are already permeated with an "internal tension" involving elements of thought. He would join Natorp in repudiating the idea that sensuous elements are significant or meaningful for cognition prior to and independent of systemic thought.

[10] *Ibid.*

But let us return to our main theme.

The transition from the level of sense impressions to the mediated world of spatial representations is made possible by the fact that within the sequence of fluctuating impressions certain constant relations can be fixed and defined and can be asserted as something permanent and independent of the flux itself.[11] Each impression must then prove its objective significance by becoming an integral element of these relations or, rather, of the totality or the system of these relations. Its fusion into the systemic context, and this alone, gives objective meaning to the individual impression. From the very first, every formation of concepts, irrespective of the field in which it is carried through, points toward one ultimate goal, the one goal of all cognition, namely, the fusion of all specific "positings," of all particular conceptual structures, into one unique and univocal all-comprehensive context of thought.[12] This complete synthesis, this absolute systemic unity, is the goal and driving force impelling the process of cognition—and it is this for Cassirer no less than for Natorp and Cohen. Only at the end of the process of integration is the object of experience fully determined, and only then has truth, absolute and unchanging truth, been attained.

However, before the contents of experience can be integrated as here demanded they must be transformed. The "sense data" or "immediate impressions" must be "resolved" into elements of theoretical thinking. They must be "posited" as such elements.[13] Without this transformation, carried through most effectively in the physical sciences, it would be impossible to formulate the laws which describe and determine the context of experience. And without attaining at least in some measure the systemic unity according to law we could not even speak about "nature." "Nature"—for Cassirer as well as for Natorp —is the unity according to law, the systemic context of all particulars in experience, the totality of progressive integra-

[11] *Ibid.*, 41.
[12] *Ibid.*, III, 331.
[13] *Ibid.*, II, 43.

tion and objective determination of the "objects" of experience.[14]

In the field of physics the "transformation" referred to involves a change from the quale of immediate impressions to concepts of measure and number. The laws of physics are stateable only with respect to such transformed "objects." And, *vice versa*, the significance of an "object" *as object* now depends exclusively upon the clarity and univocality with which it reflects or represents the law or the determinateness of the context, upon its inclusion within a system of law. Cassirer and Natorp would agree on this point. They differ, however, in their reference to the specific laws determining the content. Natorp based his interpretation exclusively upon Newtonian mechanics; Cassirer, on the other hand, took into consideration more recent developments in the field of physics. For Natorp, "existence" means the complete and absolute determination of an "object" with respect to space and time.[15] Cassirer, contemplating the conclusions reached by quantum mechanics, knows that such complete determination is impossible even in theory, and that we must rest satisfied with a less rigid demand.[16] Let us follow Cassirer's argument in greater detail.

Cassirer finds that quantum mechanics has confirmed rather than disproved the general position of the neo-Kantians. At least it has cut the ground from under all realistic interpretations of reality. "Things" no longer provide the starting-point of cognition but are the ultimate goal of our interpretations. Laws can no longer be derived from "things" through a process of abstraction; they constitute the basis upon which alone we can assert the existence of "things." The concept of law is logically prior to the concept of thing.[17] Our knowledge of "nature" extends only so far as does our concept of law. Objective "reality" can be asserted only in so far as there is order in accordance with law. "Things" are the "limit," the ultimate goal toward which the process of cognition moves but which it never

[14] *Ibid.*, II, 65; III, 367.
[15] *Logische Grundlagen*, 341 ff.
[16] *Determinismus*, 236.
[17] *Ibid.*, 163.

actually reaches. The "object" of experience is not something completely determined in itself but something determinable without end in the process of cognition.[18] Except through the medium of laws, no "object" is "given" or known.[19]

So far Cassirer is in complete agreement with Paul Natorp. But, whereas Natorp believed that Newtonian mechanics provided the means, in principle, for a complete determination of an object in space-time, Cassirer points out that this thesis involves an over-simplification of the facts. "Field" theories, the phenomena of "entropy," and the "uncertainty relations" of quantum mechanics involve problems which cannot be solved within the framework of classical mechanics.

"Fields of forces," for example, are not "entities" in the classical sense of "material bodies." As far as such "fields" are concerned, "mass" can no longer be regarded as "ponderable reality" but must be resolved into electric "charges." The whole conception of a "physical body" must therefore be redefined.[20] The "field" is not a "thing," but a "system of effects."

Similarly, the "atom" can no longer be conceived as a "thing." It has turned out to be an intricate "system" of dynamic relations and can be described only through the laws which express its effects.[21] To assert that "electrons" exist within the atom and that they move in definite orbits actually means only that certain laws, formulated to describe observable phenomena of cathode rays and line spectra, are valid; that they are descriptive of the phenomena.[22] Neither the "electrons" nor their "orbits" are "things-in-themselves," mere "stuff," "given" to us prior to cognition. They are, rather, terminals within the integrative process of cognition.[23] The electron "exists" only relative to a "field," relative, that is, to a "system of effects," and as a particular "place" of that field.[24]

[18] *Ibid.*, 164.
[19] *Ibid.*, 178.
[20] *Ibid.*, 163.
[21] *Ibid.*, 165.
[22] *Ibid.*, 168.
[23] *Ibid.*, 171.
[24] *Ibid.*, 222.

The laws of classical mechanics are so formulated that they are valid only under two assumptions. First, all physical objects must be reducible to mass-points; and, second, these mass-points must be definitely localizable in space at any given time and with any given momentum. Quantum mechanics shows, however, that it is impossible to determine the exact location of an electron if we determine its momentum at the same time with an accuracy required by the classical laws. The impossibility here involved is not merely of a practical nature but is one in principle. We must therefore conclude that the individuality of an electron can no longer be defined or determined as that of a "thing" in space and time.[25] If we continue to speak about individual electrons we can do so only indirectly. That is, we can speak of their "individuality," not as something "given," but only as constituting specific focal points of relations, "intersections" within a system of effects.[26] All formulations of quantum mechanics are systemic formulations concerning functional dependencies, not statements concerning individual "things" called "electrons."[27]

The situation, in brief, is something like this: Classical mechanics assumed that the "state" of a "thing" in space can be completely determined at any given moment and in every respect. The possibility of such determination was regarded as so certain that it became the basis for the definition of the "reality" of a thing. Only an object that could be determined completely in space-time was said to be "real."[28] Now this definition of "reality" must be relinquished, for we now know that the "picture" of an object which we obtain is inescapably conditioned by the process of observation. If we carry out one type of experiments, we can locate the electron in space-time and can regard it as a "particle;" but its momentum cannot be determined with accuracy. If we resort to a different type of experiments, we can determine the momentum of the electron with complete accuracy, but we cannot locate it in space; we

[25] *Ibid.*, 224.
[26] *Ibid.*, 225.
[27] *Ibid.*, 228.
[28] *Ibid.*, 235.

must then consider it as a "wave." What an electron "is," in the absolute sense and independent of specifically defined conditions of observation, we cannot say.[29]

If we insist upon an absolute determination of the "object," we retain nothing but a shadowy abstraction. If, on the other hand, we relinquish the demand for an absolute determination and are satisfied with a relative one, then we find that this relative determination can be achieved with great accuracy.[30] This means, however, that we must abandon the cognitive ideal which, for Natorp, was the goal of all science. Cassirer is willing to take this step; and there is no question in my mind that Natorp himself would have taken it had he lived long enough to come in contact with modern quantum mechanics. The spirit of Natorp and the whole conception of his theory of knowledge warrant such a conclusion; for there is nothing involved in this step which in the least challenges the idea of the primacy of law over things. On the contrary, Cassirer is perfectly right when he sees in the development of quantum mechanics a confirmation of the neo-Kantian thesis. Just as in mathematics "point" and "straight line" are implicitly defined by the relations which govern them, so, in quantum mechanics, "atoms" and "electrons" are defined by the laws and relations of the system as a whole.[31] The only difference between physics and mathematics is that the axiomatic assertions of mathematics are replaced in physics by hypothetical "posits" of such a type that their interrelations constitute the most complete system, the most comprehensive context, of the phenomena of experience. In neither case are the laws derived from existing "objects" by a process of abstraction, but the "objects" are constituted and determined through the laws of integration. Cassirer and Natorp are equally emphatic on this point.

II. "Space" and "Time"

Our second point of comparison involves the interpretation of space and time as given by Natorp and Cassirer, respectively.

[29] *Ibid.*, 238.
[30] *Ibid.*, 239.
[31] *Ibid.*, 243.

For Natorp, "time" is a "mode of order," just as "space" is such a "mode." "Time," however, is the one "mode" common and basic to all happenings, whereas "space" is the "order" of coëxistence. The definite co-ordination of specific points in space with successive points in time enables us to define all change as "motion," i.e., as "change of position in time."

But if "time" is only an "order of position," it is essentially a "parameter" in the purely mathematical sense—in the sense, that is, in which all space co-ordinates also are such "parameters." As "modes" of arranging the manifold phenomena of experience in specific ways, space and time are of exactly the same logical significance for cognition.[32] They represent the "form," i.e., the kind of order according to law, in accordance with which alone the manifold of experience can be viewed concretely and in relations of succession and coexistence; they represent a certain "mode" in which the integration of the phenomena can be accomplished, a "condition" which restricts the activity of synthetic thinking in its dealings with sense impressions by imposing upon it certain laws of relations.[33]

As we have seen in the previous section, the cognition of an "object" means, for Natorp, the progressive determination of an undetermined X; and univocality of cognition means complete determination. Such determination, Natorp believes, can be achieved with respect to space and time, giving rise to the concept "existence." We must, however, examine more closely the meaning and nature of space and time.

To begin with, space and time may be considered from two points of view, namely, as mathematical structures and as indispensable conditions of the existential determination of all possible experience. Viewed from the point of view of pure mathematics, space, like time, is but an order of position and is without content. Time and space, as mathematical structures, are "empty." They are, however, subject to one and the same type of law—the law of any order of position, the law of "number"—and, in this sense, are inseparably interrelated.[34]

[32] Natorp, op. cit., 72-78.
[33] Ibid., 268-269.
[34] Ibid., 280.

As mathematical structures, space and time are subject only to the laws of integrative thought and their qualities depend exclusively upon that thought. The "directions" and "dimensions" of space, for example, may be arranged in complete freedom. All types of non-Euclidean geometry are acceptable so long as they fulfill the logical requirements of coherent systems.[35] Natorp, in other words, fully accepts the modern developments in geometry[36] and he approves of Cantor's "transfinite" numbers. Indeed, he sees in both developments a verification of his neo-Kantian position.

However, when we leave the realm of pure mathematics and attempt to determine the X of experience through the "forms" of space and time, a specific restriction in the development of space-time relations must be accepted. This restriction may be formulated as the demand that the directions and dimensions admitted must constitute a univocal and closed system of relations, and that no greater number of dimensions be introduced than is necessary and sufficient to establish a complete, univocal, homogeneous, and continuous context of spatial determinations for the contents of experience.[37]

This demand for a limitation of the free creativeness of mathematical thought does not arise from any need or implication of mathematics, but solely from the nature of our judgments of existence. In their epistemological significance, "dimensions" are means of determination; but an infinite number of dimensions would determine nothing.

If the limitation of the dimensions of space be carried through in conformity with the stipulation that only such a number of dimensions is to be admitted as is necessary and sufficient for the univocal determination of "objects," then, Natorp argues, we are at once restricted to three dimensions of Euclidean constitution. The space within which our manifold experience can be arranged in univocal and complete order is a continuous, homogeneous, and three-dimensional space; it is the Euclidean space.[38]

---

[35] *Ibid.*, 304.
[36] *Ibid.*, 308.
[37] *Ibid.*, 305.
[38] *Ibid.*, 306-308.

Natorp points out, however, that the Euclidicity of physical space is neither an absolute necessity for pure thought nor a fact of pure experience. It is only a "necessary presupposition" for the integration of experience in the sense that it is required as the basis for a univocal determination of the "objects" of experience. It is a requisite for thought only when thinking is concerned with the actual integration of "objects," with their univocal determination as coexisting entities within the context of experience.[39]

Consequently, if relations of objects are discovered which deviate from the assumptions implicit in Euclidean space, it may be necessary to modify our geometrical presuppositions. If non-Euclidean geometries offer technical advantages in the integration and determination of experience, so Natorp maintains, it would be foolish not to employ them.[40] Every empirical datum can be reconciled mathematically with every type of geometry if proper assumptions are made,[41] and only the demand for univocality of description and the stipulation that no unnecessary assumptions should be made can guide us in our choice of the geometrical system which we regard as constitutive for the world of experience.

For Natorp, the univocal determination of the "objects" of experience can be achieved only through the establishment of "causal" relations in space and time—of relations, that is, as exemplified in the laws of classical mechanics; and these laws presuppose and imply the Euclidicity of space.[42] Physics, however, as actual cognition, can never fully attain the ideal of absolute determinateness, for we can measure only with empirical means. The degree of determinateness achieved depends in every case upon the accuracy of our measurements. This being the case, we must employ, as the basis for measurement, that empirical value which most closely approaches the ideal limit. For contemporary physics this value is the constant

[39] Ibid., 312.
[40] Ibid., 315.
[41] Ibid., 316.
[42] Ibid., 339-347.

velocity of light in empty space[43] as disclosed in the Michelson-Morley ether-drift experiment and as "posited" in the Einstein-Minkowski theory of relativity.

Natorp, who published his *Logische Grundlagen* in 1910, i.e., five years prior to the publication of Einstein's generalized theory, sees in the Einstein-Minkowski theory the reconciliaton between pure, absolute, and mathematical space and time on the one hand, and empirical, relative, and physical space and time determinations on the other.[44] That is to say, he sees in the "special" theory of relativity the completion of Newton and Kant, the reconciliation of the ultimate ideal of absolute determination with the restriction of all knowledge to relative determinateness. Instead of achieving absolute determinateness, science must now rest satisfied with a determinateness in space and time which depends upon the value c as upon the last univocal measure empirically attainable.[45] The laws of motion and the principle of the conservation of energy must be restated in somewhat different form, but they appear again in classical form if, instead of c, we posit ∞ as the ideal constant.

It is obvious from this line of reasoning that Natorp accepts the special theory of relativity and maintains that, far from impairing the basic position of the neo-Kantians, this theory actually confirms the epistemological views of the Marburg School.[46] The ideal of absolute and univocal determination of the "objects" loses nothing of its attractiveness or of its logical validity; only the possibility of its empirical fulfillment has been restricted in a very specific way. The theory of relativity stipulates a freedom of choice so far as space and time co-ordinates are concerned which was not found in classical mechanics; but this freedom does not endanger the integrated unity of our cognition of nature because it does not impair the univocality of the laws of nature. On the contrary, the recognition of the "invariance" of the laws of nature despite the relativity of the

[43] *Ibid.*, 398.
[44] *Ibid.*, 399.
[45] *Ibid.*, 400.
[46] *Ibid.*, 401.

space-time factors (as expressed in the Lorentz "transformation equations") is, according to Natorp, the most important result of the relativity theory.[47]

What is Cassirer's view with respect to this point?

Natorp, we repeat, published his book, *Die logischen Grundlagen der exakten Wissenschaften,* five years before Einstein's general theory of relativity became known. Cassirer, on the other hand, published his monograph, *Zur Einsteinschen Relativitätstheorie,* six years after the general theory first appeared in print. This circumstance alone, I believe, is sufficient to account for whatever difference concerning the interpretation of space and time there may be in the writings of these two men.

In accord with Natorp's view, Cassirer maintains that "the doctrine of space and time developed by the theory of relativity is a doctrine of empirical space and empirical time, not of pure space and pure time,"[48] and that to this extent the relativity theory constitutes "the most definite application and carrying through of the standpoint of critical idealism within empirical science itself."[49]

Space and time, by themselves, "signify only a fixed law of the mind, a schema of connection by which what is sensuously perceived is set in certain relations of coexistence and sequence."[50] That is to say, time is, like space, a schema in which we must arrange events, if the flux of our subjective impressions is to have objective order and significance. The actual arrangement of impressions, however, can be accomplished only upon the basis of measured relationships. And, as the theory of relativity shows, two observers in relative motion to each other will make the arrangement in different ways. Each will regard his own system of reference as the starting-point in relation to which the space-time order of events is to be established, but each order will be different.

Nevertheless, both arrangements, if carried through consistently, will have objective significance, since it is possible to

---

[47] *Ibid.,* 403.

[48] Cassirer, E., *Substance and Function, and Einstein's Theory of Relativity* (W. C. and M. C. Swabey, trans.), 409.

[49] *Ibid.,* 412.

[50] *Ibid.,* 412.

deduce from each the particular arrangement valid for the other observer. The old idea of a unitary time and a unitary space has been abandoned, but its place has been taken by a one-to-one correlation of space-time values in empirically different systems. The dynamic unity of temporal and spatial determinations has been retained, but only as a postulate of relations which are validated in and through a system of laws other than that of Newtonian mechanics.

Following Newton, Kant assumed that the three laws of motion of classical mechanics provided the sole and sufficient basis for an integration of experience; and these laws presuppose absolute space and absolute time. In the special theory of relativity, the principle of the constancy of the velocity of light was accepted as the basic presupposition of our integration of experience. Natorp and Cassirer agree on this, and both modify the Kantian position accordingly.

In the general theory of relativity even this principle is replaced by a still different one—by the principle of the equivalence of gravitational and inertial fields; and it follows from this principle that "all Gaussian co-ordinate systems are of equal value for the formulation of the universal natural laws."[51] We must still conceive an absolute space and an absolute time, i. e., an absolute unity of all space-time determinations; but this unity is not the unity of some "real" object. It is, rather, an Idea (in the Kantian sense) which serves as "a rule for considering all motions in it as merely relative." "The logical universality of such an idea," Cassirer argues in complete agreement with Natorp, "does not conflict with the theory of relativity."[52] On the contrary, it alone assures the validity of the empirical laws. All motions in space must be regarded as merely relative because only in this way is it possible to combine them into a definite concept of experience which unifies all phenomena. "The one valid norm is merely the idea of the unity of nature, of exact determination itself;"[53] and this the theory of relativity safeguards by guaranteeing the "invariance" of the laws of nature despite the relativity of all space-time co-ordi-

[51] *Ibid.*, 415.
[52] *Ibid.*, 416.
[53] *Ibid.*, 416.

nates. Cassirer and Natorp are in complete agreement on this point; although Natorp did not know the generalized theory of relativity when he wrote his *Logische Grundlagen.*

When Natorp's book was republished without revision in 1923, Cassirer's interpretation of relativity was well known, and Natorp, in the new preface to his book, referred his readers to Cassirer's monograph, saying that this monograph provided a substitute for Natorp's own interpretation, since it "contains much of what I myself might have said concerning this matter."[54]

III. Causality

Our third point of comparison involves the interpretations of causality as given by Natorp and Cassirer, respectively.

According to Natorp, experience is integrated and the "order" of experience is established in conformity with the ideas of succession and simultaneity. Through the idea of succession, impressions are related in series, and these series, in turn, are related in sequence until the whole of experience has been incorporated into one unitary system of series. Through the idea of simultaneity, parallel series are interrelated in accordance with a law of progression which establishes a mutual dependence or interdependence of coexisting series. The arrangement involving succession is carried through on the basis of "causality;" the arrangement involving interdependence presupposes "interaction."

The "law of causality," according to Natorp, asserts that a result attained under certain conditions at a time t will be attained again under the same conditions at a time t' but it does not stipulate what the specific conditions are in any given case.[55] In other words, the "law of causality" affirms merely the dependence of a consequent in general upon an antecedent in general. It affirms an "orderliness according to law" which involves immediately and directly only an order of succession.

In so far, however, as we deal not only with a single series in time but with the interrelation of parallel series, the general

[54] Natorp, *op. cit.,* vii.
[55] *Ibid.,* 80.

relationship of antecedent and consequent does not adequately represent the idea of causality.[56] A comparison of various parallel or "co-ordinated" series of changes shows that the law which determines the specific sequence of each series is determinable only through a law which defines the relation of co-ordination—a law, that is, which defines a "totality of order," a system of interrelations, within which each individual series is determined by all other series, and in which each series contributes to the determination of all others. Such a law, however, is nothing but Kant's "principle of interaction," the culmination of our conception of "nature" as a dynamic system, i.e., as a singular and all-comprehensive functional context of events.[57]

The demand for a general law of causality has been fulfilled, according to Natorp, through Newton's formulation of the three basic laws of motion. The second of these laws, in particular, is an expression of the most general demand for a dependence of a consequent upon some antecedent. The third law provides the more profound interpretation of causality as "interaction."[58]

Through the application of the law of causality in its most profound sense, a totality of order, a system of order, is established—the totality or system which we call "nature." The nature of the law itself is such that the mathematical term "function" describes it most adequately. We may say, therefore, that only through the idea of "function" can the demand for an all-inclusive and orderly context of experience be fulfilled. "Nature" or "reality" is known or "understood" only to the extent to which such a "functional" or "dynamic" context has been established.[59]

Cassirer, I am sure, would agree with Natorp that only the "functional" or "dynamic" context according to law discloses to us the reality and the essence of "nature." His earlier book, *Substance and Function,* is sufficient proof for this. But, whereas Natorp argues that the functional equations of classical me-

[56] *Ibid.,* 81.
[57] *Ibid.,* 81.
[58] *Ibid.,* 371.
[59] *Ibid.,* 67.

chanics, as based upon Newton's three laws of motion, are the sole means through which that context can be established universally, Cassirer maintains that these classical equations must be supplemented and that even new types of laws may be required for the establishment of an all-comprehensive context.

According to Cassirer, the "law of causality" must be clearly distinguished from the specific equations of the empirical sciences. It is logically on a different level. The equations express particular interrelations of various magnitudes, but the "law of causality" is the general demand that the cognitive process of transforming the data of observation into concise expressions of measure, the process of synthesizing the results of measurements in functional equations, and of unifying these equations in conformity with certain uniform principles, shall be possible without end. The "law of causality," in other words, is the axiomatic demand that the progressive functional interpretation of experience can and must be carried through.[60]

The "law of causality" is in so far *sui generis* as it is not a statement about "things" or "events," but a statement concerning laws and principles. It is the axiomatic assertion that the results of our measurements, the laws governing these results, and the principles of interrelating those laws can be integrated in such a manner that they constitute one coherent system of cognition, one unitary and univocal integration of "nature."

If I understand Natorp's arguments correctly, they imply this very same conception of the "law of causality;" for does not Natorp maintain that the law of causality in its profoundest sense is the demand for the homogeneous functional system, and not some specific equation describing "events"? But so far as Natorp is concerned, this demand for a system is completely realizable through the equations of classical mechanics. These equations, for Natorp, express the prototype of relations which fulfill the demand for causal interdependence.

Cassirer admits that the "law of causality" has been decisive for the development of classical physics, that it has given impetus and direction to this development.[61] But Cassirer shows

---

[60] Cassirer, *Determinismus*, 76.
[61] *Ibid.*, 82.

that the statistical treatment of entropy, as given by Boltzmann, has introduced into physics a new type of "law," a new type of equations of interdependence, which must be given equal status with the dynamic laws of Newtonian mechanics. A dualism has thus been introduced into the conception of "physical laws."[62]

Natorp, in agreement with most of his contemporaries, seems to have regarded the "statistical laws" as approximations which did not affect the ideal of a rigid functional interpretation. According to this view, the "fate" of individual particles is strictly determinable through classical laws, but it is not always convenient or possible for practical reasons to ascertain all the "conditions" requisite for a complete functional interpretation. In principle, however, the demand for a complete determination remains unchallenged.

Cassirer argues in a somewhat different manner. He points out that even Galileo claimed unconditional or complete exactness for his laws only in so far as these laws are hypothetically exact formulations, not in the sense that they describe actual events with absolute exactness. They are expressions of an "if-then" relation rather than descriptions of the "here-and-now" of events. They apply, strictly speaking, to "ideal" cases, not to empirically given situations.

What is true of Galileo's laws, Cassirer points out, is true also of all laws formulated in conformity with the Galilean model. It is true, in particular, of the equations of Newtonian mechanics.[63]

The laws of classical mechanics, however, involve only "reversible" processes. The principle of entropy, on the other hand, deals with processes which are not reversible; and such processes, Cassirer argues, require a new type of "law," statistical laws, and laws involving the calculation of "probabilities."[64]

The "probabilities" involved in these laws are not of a subjective nature but are objective in their significance and meaning. Once the factors present in a cognitive situation have been analyzed, our probability calculations determine rigidly what

[62] Ibid., 96.
[63] Ibid., 103.
[64] Ibid., 111.

is a probable (or improbable) result under those conditions, and they determine this probability or improbability of the event in complete independence of our subjective opinion in the matter.[65]

Probability calculation is a branch of pure mathematics and leads to definite conclusions in accordance with strict rules once we apply it to certain assumed or stipulated empirical conditions. And, Cassirer argues, in so far as this is true, statistical expressions have the same epistemological significance as the laws of classical mechanics. They can and must therefore be co-ordinated with those laws.[66]

This co-ordination is easily accomplished if we remember that the classical laws expressing specific causal relations pertain to the *course* of an event, whereas probability concerns our knowledge of the *initial conditions* which give rise to that event. The idea of causality in conjunction with the conception of probabilities results in the special laws of "statistical mechanics" which strictly determine an event as a consequent of the assumed or stipulated conditions but which, when applied to actual events, constitute the prototype of a physical hypothesis.[67] Only through the interpenetration of causality and probability is the general form of "order in conformity with law" at all conceivable. Newton's law of gravitation, for example, tells us exactly what will happen under condition of some specific distribution of matter in space, but the actual state of that distribution is not determined by the law of gravitation and can be ascertained only through measurements and calculations involving probabilities.

So far, therefore, no radical change of the epistemological position of neo-Kantianism is required to accommodate the statistical laws. So far Cassirer was not compelled to modify Natorp's view in any radical manner. The question arises, however, to what extent and in what sense the significance and meaning of the "law of causality" have been affected by the transition from classical mechanics to quantum theories. Natorp, so we have seen, died before quantum mechanics came into its own. Hence,

[65] *Ibid.*, 113.
[66] *Ibid.*, 118.
[67] *Ibid.*, 130.

if Cassirer's views differ essentially from those of orthodox neo-Kantians, this difference should become noticeable at this point.

It is Cassirer's thesis, as it was Natorp's, that the principle of causality is not a proposition dealing directly with things or events but is, rather, a stipulation concerning the means through which things and events are constituted in experience. This general meaning of causality, according to Cassirer, remains unaffected by quantum mechanics. It is true that Heisenberg has shown that specific "uncertainties" are unavoidable whenever we deal with individual electrons or similar particles, and that therefore "probability equations" alone adequately describe the observed processes. But, as Heisenberg himself has pointed out, these "probabilities" are by no means indeterminate. They are derivable from the principles of quantum mechanics and are strictly and univocally determined by them.[68] The "uncertainty relations," therefore, do not imply a lack of precision in quantum mechanical laws.[69]

To put it differently, quantum mechanics, like every other branch of science, makes certain stipulations from which it proceeds and upon which the validity of its formulations depends. It no longer accepts all the stipulations of classical mechanics and has abandoned the hope that all propositions of physics can ultimately be reduced to one type of functional laws; but, within the framework of its own stipulations, the equations of quantum mechanics reveal objective interrelations of events with exactitude and precision.

When Heisenberg rejected the "law of causality," his arguments were directed only against a narrowly conceived version of that law, not against the general idea of "orderliness in accordance with law."[70] But "causality" in the narrow sense, Cassirer maintains, had been invalidated even before the advent of quantum mechanics. It had lost status in classical physics, because the equations of classical mechanics could be applied to actual situations only on the basis of probability considerations.

[68] *Ibid.*, 144.
[69] *Ibid.*, 146.
[70] *Ibid.*, 143, 153.

If we discard this narrow conception of causality and adhere only to the general demand for "orderliness according to law" *(Gesetzlichkeit)*, Cassirer argues, then the "uncertainty relations" of Heisenberg "do not constitute a contrary instance."[71] The very demonstration of the validity of the "uncertainty relations" presupposes the validity of the generalized law of causality. Moreover, the basic postulates of quantum mechanics are inseparably tied up with the principles of conservation of energy and conservation of momentum, with principles, that is, which are "pure and typical statements of causality."[72]

The general principle of causality demands in general the dependence of a consequent *y* upon an antecedent *x:* If *x*, then *y*. Even traditional logic reveals (1) that the falsity of *x* does not necessarily imply the falsity of *y*, and (2) that the universal validity of the conditional proposition is unaffected by the falsity of the antecedent, or by any restriction of its truth. Hence, if the "uncertainty relations" imply that in the field of physics some judgements of causality rest upon false premises or upon premises of restricted truth, nothing is said thereby concerning the pure form of the hypothetical syllogism or concerning its formal validity. The schema, *If x, then y*, as purely formal schema, loses nothing of its force or of its validity. If, however, the schema is to be applied to some concrete situation, it is necessary to ascertain whether or not the values to be inserted for *x* can be determined by measurement with complete and absolute accuracy. The problem, in other words, pertains not to the causal relation as such but to the "empty places," the measured variables, which make the general principle applicable in concrete cases. The values of *x* must be "admissible" if the principle of causality is to have specific and univocal meaning in some particular situation.

From the point of view of physics, only such values are "admissible" which can be definitely ascertained through determinate and definable methods of measuring. This restrictive interpretation of the conditions under which the law of causality becomes applicable alone assures the physical significance of

[71] *Ibid.*, 153.
[72] *Ibid.*, 154.

that principle. Natorp, I am sure, would agree with Cassirer on this point, for the idea as such is not new. Newton already included it in his *regulae philosophandi*. The new aspect is that quantum mechanics reveals, through its "uncertainty relations," that it is forever impossible to obtain experimentally certain pairs of magnitudes—such as the place and momentum of an electron—with complete accuracy. Through this discovery the application of the principle of causality is subjected to a condition of which classical physics knew nothing; but the restriction in applicability does not entail the suspension of the principle itself.[73]

So far as quantum mechanics is concerned, the law of causality stipulates that, if at any time certain physical magnitudes have been measured with the greatest accuracy possible in conformity with the "uncertainty relations," then there exist at some other time certain other magnitudes the measurable qualities of which can be predicted with accuracy. It is impossible, however, to describe completely in space and time the actual connections expressed by the functional law, just as it is impossible to construct a mechanism on the basis of classical laws which reveals the quantum theoretical connection between waves and particles. Such a representation and description in space and time is, however, not needed for the application of the principle of causality. The formalism of quantum mechanics itself provides all necessary "functional" connections. So long as empirical events can be measured and, on the basis of these measurements, can be described in mathematical terms and by means of mathematical equations, the postulate of the "comprehensibility of nature" is fulfilled. Moreover, inasmuch as this "comprehensibility" rests upon the principle of causality in its broad sense, this principle, too, has lost nothing of its epistemological significance.[74]

Natorp, I feel certain, would endorse wholeheartedly this conclusion of Cassirer's argument. Had he lived to see the advent of modern quantum mechanics he would have moved on beyond the position of orthodox neo-Kantianism in the same direction in which Cassirer has actually moved. The initial posi-

[73] *Ibid.*, 157.
[74] *Ibid.*, 234.

tion taken by Natorp with respect to the presuppositions of scientific cognition implies this. In developing his interpretation of quantum mechanics, Cassirer has not broken with neo-Kantianism but has adapted its established principles to the latest results of scientific research. He has carried out a program first enunciated by Natorp, and he has carried it out in the very spirit of Natorp. In one essential respect, however, Cassirer has gone far beyond the orthodox neo-Kantians. We shall consider this point in our next section.

IV. Foundations of the "Geisteswissenschaften"

Up to now we have considered Cassirer's views only in so far as they pertain to the epistemological basis of the exact natural sciences. We have found that in all these matters Cassirer has advanced beyond orthodox neo-Kantianism only in a very restricted sense. However, in the course of his many-sided investigations, Cassirer became convinced that the traditional epistemology in its usual limitation to "scientific cognition" does not provide a basis for the *Geisteswissenschaften* or cultural sciences.

If all types of knowledge are to find epistemological justification, then the basic principles of epistemology itself must be radically expanded or generalized[75] and must be conceived in such a manner as to admit knowledge differing in kind, not only in degree, from that obtained in the natural sciences. And with this demand for a generalized epistemological basis of all knowledge Cassirer departs radically from the position of orthodox neo-Kantianism; for Natorp is committed to the idea that the prototype of all knowledge is found in the mathematical sciences. The cultural sciences find no consideration in the *Logische Grundlagen* or in Natorp's other epistemological writings. The epistemological problems of these sciences are not recognized as such—unless we are to accept Natorp's explicit restriction of analysis to the foundations of the so-called *exact* sciences as an implied admission that other sciences may require a different treatment.

Despite this break with the orthodoxy of the Marburg School,

---

[75] Cassirer, *Philosophie der symbolischen Formen*, I, v.

Cassirer has by no means abandoned the essence of Kantianism. On the contrary, he finds ample room for the new generalization within the framework of that position.

Starting once more from the premise that the basic concepts of science are obtained, not through a process of abstraction, but through an integrative or synthetic act of mind, Cassirer argues that this integrative activity of mind permeates all types of knowledge. Our concepts, whatever they may be in any given field of investigation, are man-created intellectual symbols by means of which experiential contexts are established; they are integral parts of logical systems and are defined and determined in and through the logical structure of their respective systems.

But if this is true, then our basic concepts participate in, or "share," the logical structure of the system to which they belong. And if an "object" of experience is constituted only through these concepts, then "we cannot reject" the idea that the variety of such constitutive logical means produces a variety of "objective" contexts, a variety of differently integrated "objects."[76] Even within the realm of "nature" the "physical" object is not strictly identical with the "chemical" object, or the "chemical" object with the "biological" object, for "physical," "chemical," and "biological" cognition, respectively, involve specifically different points of view from which the questions are raised which guide our inquiries, and from which the phenomena of observation are subjected to interpretation and integration.[77]

The One Being, presupposed in all realistic epistemologies, the thing-in-itself as it exists in and by itself, recedes more and more from the field of investigation and becomes the unknowable X. It is not encountered at the beginning of cognition as something "given," but only at the end, as the fulfillment of completed cognition, the culmination of all integration. Our basic concepts of cognition cannot be obtained from this X through a process of abstraction. All Kantians agree on this. But is it possible to take the opposite view and to interpret all intellectual symbols, irrespective of the field of their application, as expressions of one and the same basic function of mind?

[76] *Ibid.*, 6.
[77] *Ibid.*, 7.

Natorp maintains that all cognition, no matter how different its ways and modes may be, aims ultimately at an integration of experience in terms of causality, at the complete subsumption of all objects of experience under the law of causality. The particular is not to remain an isolated particular but is to be merged into a context determined and defined by causal interrelations. Cassirer, on the other hand, finds that the causal mode of integration is only one of many which are equally possible and equally actual. "Objectification" is carried on, and the particular is fused into context, by means quite different from that employing logical concepts and laws of logical relations. Art, mythology, and religion exemplify these other types of integration.

No work of art, no mythology, no religion merely reflects an empirically "given." All of them constitute their "objects," their "world," in conformity with some independent principle of integration. Each creates its own symbolic forms, forms which are not of the same type as the "intellectual" symbols of science but which, nevertheless, considering their origin, are epistemologically equivalent to them. Not one of these different types of symbols can be fully represented by any other, or can be translated into, or derived from, any other. Each type represents a distinct approach to, and a distinct mode of interpretation of, experience and thus constitutes in and through itself a specific aspect of the "real." These types of symbols are not different ways in which one and the same "thing-in-itself" reveals itself to us, but they are modes through which mind accomplishes its "objectification" of experience.[78] Kant's "Copernican revolution" must therefore be extended to all of them.[79]

The question in all cases of "objectification" is this: Is the function of the "symbol" derivable from the "object," or does the "object" presuppose the functional significance of the "symbol"? Does the "symbol" find its validation through the "object," or is the "object" constituted through (or by means of) the "symbol"? Since this question arises in every field in which symbols are employed, it represents the intellectual bond, the methodological unity, which holds these fields together.

[78] *Ibid.*, 9.
[79] *Ibid.*, 10.

Answering this question in the basically Kantian sense of the primacy of "functions" or "laws" over "objects," Cassirer finds that it is possible to transcend the narrowly conceived position of the neo-Kantians without discarding the essence of Kantianism itself. As he now sees it, the integrative activity of mind is not restricted to a purely cognitive function. In addition to the logical integration of experience we can discern a "function of linguistic thinking," a "function of mythico-religious thinking," and a "function of artistic intuition." Each one of these integrating functions leads to a particular type of integration and is therefore constitutive to its own specific context of experience, to its own "objective totality."[80]

Interpreted in this way, the critique of reason becomes a generalized critique of culture, showing how all content of culture presupposes and involves a primordial act of mind, an act of creative integration. And in this generalized critique the basic thesis of idealism finds its proper and complete validation.[81] The varied products of culture—language, scientific cognition, myths, art, and religion—despite their diversified character and despite the difference in method and aim of integration, now are conceived as being one in ultimate purpose—in the purpose, namely, of transforming the passive world of mere impressions (in which mind seems at first imprisoned) into a "world of pure spiritual expression."[82]

If we insist upon the complete logical unity of all integrations, the universality and exclusiveness of the logical form tend to destroy the specificality and uniqueness of the objectifications in non-logical spheres of integration. If, on the other hand, we acknowledge the specificity of these integrations without advancing at the same time beyond it to an all-inclusive principle of integration, we are in danger of losing ourselves in particulars.[83] But, if we accept the expansion of Kant's "Copernican revolution," then, according to Cassirer, both of these fatal alternatives can be avoided. We can then admit the greatest

[80] *Ibid.*, 11.
[81] *Ibid.*, 11.
[82] *Ibid.*, 12.
[83] *Ibid.*, 16.

diversity of forms without being forced to relinquish the demand for ultimate unity in the creative function of mind. For example, the synthesis in which the succession of tones is transformed into the unity of a "melody" is quite different from the synthesis through which the manifoldness of linguistic sounds is integrated into the unity of a "sentence;" but common to both is the fact that the sensuous elements no longer remain isolated particulars but are fused into a context in and through which each element receives its real meaning and significance.[84] Each field of integration is characterized by its own approach and procedure; each involves its own specific integrative principle. But all of them are, nevertheless, only functions of the same integrating mind,[85] and in and through its diversified products this mind reveals itself and reveals the world of experience as an expression or manifestation of mind.[86]

Such is the essence of Cassirer's thesis. That it involves a step beyond orthodox neo-Kantianism is obvious. It is true, furthermore, that in all cultural achievements—in language, art, religion, and science—creative and integrating minds reveal themselves. Whenever we deal with "symbols," a creative mind which integrates and interprets them may be assumed to be at work. The use of "symbols" is an act of synthesis, of construction, not of abstraction or passive reception. To this extent at least Cassirer's thesis may be regarded as validated.

However, Cassirer's three-volume work, *Die Philosophie der symbolischen Formen,* still leaves many questions unanswered.

The epistemological problem of the exact sciences (mathematics, mathematical physics, and chemistry) may be regarded as solved, for the principle of integration is evident in each case. It may be granted likewise that the epistemological problem of "mystical" thinking (mythology and religion) has found its solution. Its integrating principle seems to be identical with what Lévy-Bruhl has called the principle of "participation." Both mathematical science and mythology (religion) have, however, in common that they aim at an integrated totality of

---

[84] *Ibid.,* 27.
[85] *Ibid.,* 31.
[86] *Ibid.,* 25.

experience. Language and art, on the other hand, do not share this aim.

No "object of art" claims to be an all-inclusive totality of experience, nor do all "objects of art" together constitute such a totality. The creative synthesis in a work of art is undeniable, but in intent and method it is not on the same level with a law or theory of science or with an "explanatory" myth.

Language also is the product of creative synthesis; but it, too, is, epistemologically speaking, not on the same plane with science or mythology (religion). Both science and mythology represent distinct world-views, intellectual positions from which the manifold of experience is to be integrated into comprehensive contexts. Language, on the other hand, despite its symbolic character, is but a means to be employed in such integration. It may reflect in its forms and vocabulary predominantly the point of view of mythology or that of science (and usually is a fair mixture of both), but in itself it provides no "point of view" from which experience is to be integrated. This is not to say that the development of language remains unaffected by the purpose for which linguistic symbols are employed. My contention is merely that language as an instrument useful in integrating experience cannot be set in strict parallel with science or mythology as "point of view" and as mode of integration. Cassirer's "philosophy of symbolic forms" needs clarification at this point.

Cassirer, as will be recalled, generalized the position of the neo-Kantians in order to provide an epistemological basis for the cultural sciences. But neither in his *Philosophie der symbolischen Formen* nor in his other books does this problem find further consideration.

It may be granted that the general thesis of the primacy of the integrative functions of mind over all "objects" of experience implies a suggestion of the direction in which an answer to this problem must be sought. But the task of carrying through the required analysis of categories and principles of integration still remains to be done. What, for example, is the principle (corresponding to the law of causality in the exact sciences) which determines objectification and integration of historical knowledge? Upon what basis is the historical context of experience to be established? If in the field of history, too, the basic principle of integration is to be a law of causality, then, it seems, this law must be even more generalized than it was in the field of quantum mechanics—and generalized in a different manner. It may have to be transformed into a "principle of relevancy"— a principle, that is, the application of which involves value judgments. If so, new questions arise, questions which transcend the field of history proper. We must then ask: What are values? What is the epistemological basis of value judgments? What is the principle of integration in the general field of axiology? All these questions must be answered before the epistemology of *Geisteswissenschaften* is complete; but none of them are answered by Cassirer. His radical step beyond the neo-Kantians of the Marburg School is also a step away from specifically epistemological problems and from the type of analyses which such problems demand.

WILLIAM H. WERKMEISTER

DEPARTMENT OF PHILOSOPHY
UNIVERSITY OF NEBRASKA

23

Fritz Kaufmann

CASSIRER, NEO-KANTIANISM, AND PHENOMENOLOGY

SYNOPSIS

CASSIRER, NEO-KANTIANISM, AND PHENOMENOLOGY

I

The Historical Conjunction

IT IS NOT the purport of the present paper to pin down to any 'Ism' so rich and distinguished an individuality as Ernst Cassirer's. I am convinced, however, that the encyclopedic nature of his thought, of his learning and empathy and the peculiar lucidity of his style are partly due to the sound philosophical tradition and scholarly discipline of "Marburg neo-Kantianism" (just as, for instance, the followers of Hegel were privileged to harvest the fruit of their master's systematic achievements and historical wisdom).

Yet, although Cassirer, skillfully and conscientiously at once, cultivated and transformed his teachers' heritage, he remained closer to the original Idealism than even Cohen and Natorp themselves in their last writings. Their turn toward religious metaphysics took place at a time when Cassirer's ideas had already crystallized in a form which he continuously developed without ever reaching a breaking-point such as Cohen did in the religious personalism of his *Religion der Vernunft* (1919) or Natorp in the religious mysticism of *Praktische Philosophie* (1925).

Cassirer's Kantianism has to be seen against the background of Hermann Cohen's *Logik der reinen Erkenntnis* (1902) and Paul Natorp's *Einleitung in die Psychologie nach Kritischer Methode* (1888), the original version of the *Allgemeine Psychologie* of 1912. Hence we shall have to make particular reference to these classical writings of the school. This will be especially fitting in our context, since Husserl's Phenomenology also profited very much from his ponderings over Natorp's *Psychologie* and the preceding article "Ueber objective und subjective Begründung der Erkenntnis" (*Philosophische Monatshefte*, 1887).[1] These are the main sources for any attempt at defining and evaluating anew the relationship between neo-Kantianism and phenomenology proper. Cohen's breaking away from an orthodox neo-Kantianism had its effect primarily on the Jewish philosophy of religion (Franz Rosenzweig), and Natorp's thoughtful *Praktische Philosophie* has not yet attained the productive recognition which it deserves, i.e., the status and dynamics of a historic philosophical motive. As regards phenomenology, only the grandiose syncretism of Heidegger's *Sein und Zeit* seems to show traces of the metaphysical philosophy of language in Natorp's posthumous work.[2]

In German philosophy, the beginning of the twentieth century was marked by the appearance of three classic works: Edmund Husserl's *Logische Untersuchungen* (1900/01), Hermann Cohen's (already mentioned) *Logik der reinen Erkenntnis* (1902) and Heinrich Rickert's *Die Grenzen der naturwissenschaftlichen Begriffsbildung* (1902)—the third of which, the foremost exponent of the so-called Southwestern neo-Kantian School, does not fall within the scope of this study.[3] Whereas Cohen's *Logik* climaxed a movement which lost more and more ground in the following decades, Husserl's *Untersuchungen* was the beginning of a philosophical enterprise which was to make proselytes from all schools of German philosophy. This success it owed not only to its inner strength and radical method: it was also favored by the tendencies of

[1] Cf. Husserl, *Logische Untersuchungen* (2nd edition) II, 1, 353f; *Ideen zu einer reinen Phaenomenologie*, 109f; Natorp, *Allgemeine Psychologie*, 33ff; 280ff. Husserl's relation to Natorp's early writings is carefully studied in Marvin Farber's *The Foundation of Phenomenology* (1943).

[2] Cp. Natorp's *Praktische Philosophie*, 249ff, 261 with Heidegger, *Sein und Zeit*, 160f.

[3] Besides, a phenomenological criticism of Rickert's position was set forth both by the present writer in *Geschichtsphilosophie der Gegenwart* (1931) and Eugen Fink in *Die Phaenomenologische Philosophie Edmund Husserls in der gegenwärtigen Kritik* (1934).

the age.[4] Husserl put to philosophical use the descriptive method introduced in psychology by Brentano, James, Dilthey and Lipps. He contributed also to the rise of the new morphological trends which—heralded by the disciples of Burckhardt, Nietzsche and Stefan George—came to prevail, first, in the analysis of the forms and products of culture. But from the interpretation of poetry, art, religion, etc., these trends began to expand and invade all realms of being and experience, psychological as well as biological and physical: they all were to unfold the variety and articulation of their forms and show their specific, irreducible natures. Phenomenology served the self-understanding of all these movements by providing them with a methical foundation and bestowing upon them a systematic unity.

When we analyze the implications of this phenomenological approach to the facts and problems of world and life, the points of contact with neo-Kantian thought as well as those of contrast to it (and, hence, the mixture of alliance and tension between the two movements) will immediately come to the surface. It should be stated, however, from the outset that this relation was not static, but seemed to lead toward a qualified *rapprochement* to which the later writings of Natorp, Husserl and Cassirer bear witness.[5] The present article, too, was intended to advance a closer co-operation between the thinkers of both schools: a purpose which is now largely frustrated by the untimely death of my eminent partner in the originally contemplated dialogue.

Husserl found himself in a common front with the Marburg scholars in his victorious struggle against the psychologism of 1900. As a matter of fact, the anti-psychologism which domi-

[4] It is symptomatic that, in the late twenties, most of the teachers in the Department of Philosophy at the University of Marburg itself (Heidegger, Mahnke, Loewith, (Gadamer), Krueger) claimed to be adherents of phenomenology.

[5] Historically the germs for such an understanding were present from the beginning in the profound admiration for Leibniz which the author of the *Untersuchungen* has in common with Cassirer (whose book, *Leibniz' System*, appeared in 1902) as well as in Husserl's grateful interest in Natorp's *Psychologie*—an interest which shows not only in Husserl's writings, but also in the fact that Natorp's book was repeatedly the subject of discussion in Husserl's (and later, Heidegger's) seminars.

nates the first volume of the *Logische Untersuchungen* proved so successful that only few readers, like Dilthey, realized the methodological importance of what the second volume offered under the somewhat misleading title "descriptive psychology:" this 'psychology' was as little a piece of merely empirical research as was the psychology that played its part in the philosophical systems of Cohen and Natorp. At the same time, the systematic function of Husserl's 'psychology' was not that of studying the unity of human culture or reconstructing the original unity of consciousness—the tasks set for "psychology according to the critical method" by Cohen and Natorp respectively. In the terms of Natorp's philosophy, the complementary methods of direct construction and psychological reconstruction express the correspondence between two procedures —that of objectification and subjectification (a difference said to be logically prior to the determination of object and subject proper). According to Cohen and Natorp the unity of the subject, i.e., of the concrete living consciousness, this unity directly enjoyed, but not directly grasped, has to be regained through a reversal of the processes of objectification—through fusing what, under the theoretical, ethical and aesthetic aspects, had been separated in the pure forms and normative products of science, art, and the moral "kingdom of ends." The unity of the mind is said to consist in the unity of these aspects, i.e., of these types of objective synthesis and legislation which make up the worlds of pure science, pure morals, and pure art.

In neo-Kantianism the search for this unity of conscious life and its world—the life and world wherein these different attitudes (*Einstellungen*) pervade one another—is not the first step to be taken. It is preceded by the investigation into the constitutive principles (the "inner forms") through which objectivity in one sense or the other can be achieved. The critical distinction between the different ways of objectification and between the corresponding realms of culture is intended to secure the autonomy of these realms, ascertain the both irreducible and limited variety of the 'styles' of human experience and overcome the dangers of one-sided naturalism (including psychologism), moralism, and aestheticism.

What distinguishes this neo-Kantian philosophy from the phenomenological approach are (1) the different rôles assigned to the element of *form*, (2) the different concept of *subjectivity* and (3) the *greater variety of experiences* accounted for by phenomenology.

II

Variety of Experience vs. Autonomy of Cultural Realms

It is advisable, perhaps, to begin with the discussion of this third factor. Neo-Kantianism is a "philosophy of human culture:" even the latest important document of the school—Cassirer's *Essay on Man*—has "philosophy of culture" in its subtitle. The philosophical interest is centered in the foundation, forms, and products of human civilization. The traditional tripartition of the realms of culture tended, at first, to determine, i.e., both to fix and to limit the various types of human experience. The religious experience, e.g., does not fit into this schema: the very possibility of a philosophy of religion is denied by Natorp—at least in his capacity as a transcendental criticist;[6] in Cohen's last works its recognition comes close to destroying the framework of critical idealism; and in Cassirer's thought religion occupies a somewhat precarious position between myth and morals: in his *Essay on Man* it seems almost restricted to the moral, positive revaluation of the ancient taboo system.[7]

To be sure, following Natorp's own suggestion, Cassirer enriched the neo-Kantian system by a variety of symbolic forms and, with their help, by the systematic interpretation of an enormous wealth of relevant phenomena. We shall turn later on to this new phase of a more versatile transcendental method. For the moment, it may be stated, first, that the very rise and attraction of phenomenology was greatly due to its insist-

---

[6] Cf. Natorp, *Praktische Philosophie* (1925), 534f (in partial revision of *Allgemeine Psychologie*, 94).

[7] Cf. Cassirer, *Essay on Man*, 105ff.—In his *Philosophie der symbolischen Formen* (II, 16, n. 1) he lists, however, with chivalrous praise "amongst the epochal merits of Husserlian phenomenology that it has sharpened our eyes for the differences between the 'structural forms' of the mind and, in a departure from the method of psychological inquiry, has shown us a new way of viewing them," viz., through analysis of their essential meanings.

ence on, and exhibition of, a manifoldness of experiences and types of being—an open-mindedness which was not narrowed down by the preconception of three spheres of objective experience. To survey and divide the otherwise boundless field of investigations, Husserl used tentatively the different formal and material ontologies (of nature, soul, spirit, etc.,) as "guiding clues" for the analysis of the different types of phenomena. But these ontologies functioned as mere "indicators," and their establishment was in itself a philosophical task. To the phenomenologist there are no pre-established "transcendental facts" like the fact or even *fieri* of science—data which have only to be resolved into their constitutive factors.

Phenomenology is not a philosophy of culture in the sense that it takes orders from any canonic standard. It is free not only to criticize the actual state of our culture, but to delimit even the idea and claims of culture as such.[8] It does not accept Cohen's identification of the subject, i.e., the unity of consciousness, with the unity of the human culture—an identification through which the *objective* mind comes to account for the whole sphere of the human spirit.

III

The Nature of the Subjective

In the neo-Kantian interpretation subjectivity is 'nothing but' the system of objectifying functions read from the cultural documents in which they have manifested themselves and in which alone they are said to have their true life and being.[9] Οὐ γὰρ ἄνευ τοῦ ἐόντος, ἐν ὧι πεφατισμένον ἐστίν, εὑρήσεις τὸ νοεῖν: "You will not find thought apart from the objective content wherein it found its expression" (Parmenides).

My purpose cannot be to discredit the great Parmenidean tradition which is still alive in Kant and his followers. The

---

[8] Cf., e.g., Husserl, *Formale und Transzendentale Logik* (*Jahrbuch für Philosophie*) X, 161; *Die Krisis der Europäischen Wissenschaften und die Transzendentale Phaenomenologie* (*Philosophia*, I) 79ff. But even Natorp eventually comes to criticize Cohen's reliance on the transcendental facts of physics, jurisprudence, etc.: Cf. *Praktische Philosophie*, 208ff.

[9] Cf. e.g., Cassirer, *Philosophie der symbolischen Formen III*, 59.

primacy of the positive—Leibniz's conviction that people are right in what they see and aver, although they may be wrong in what they deny only because they do not see it—is a leading principle of phenomenological interpretation. The quasi indirect, hermeneutic approach to human being—the discovery of this being in its most characteristic expressions—is the rightful method of moral sciences (*Geisteswissenschaften*). It has been analyzed and practiced as such in an admirable way by a thinker like Wilhelm Dilthey. All we know and all we need to know, e.g., of Shakespeare, lives, indeed, in his works and has not passed with the passing of his private life nor been buried in the archives of London and Stratford-on-Avon. Still, the historical and *geisteswissenschaftliche* approach is not the only way of human self-concern and self-knowledge. Cassirer's main methodical principle—that "only by expressing itself the spirit reaches its true and perfect inwardness (*Innerlichkeit*)"[10] has its historical foundation in idealistic thought, but represents an indisputable truth only if it is properly qualified and understood: it cannot be simply presupposed; the roots it has in the structure of our being must be bared. That introspection would yield only "a very meager and fragmentary picture of human being"[11] is not borne out by the *Confessions* of Augustine, the *Thoughts* of Pascal or the *Journals* of Kierkegaard.

Yet, man's true and direct self-knowledge is not even confined to these religious confessions or to the existential re-flections of men who are thrown back upon themselves—that type of 'immanent perception' in which consciousness and conscience may become one. In addition there may well be a scientific research for the essence of subjectivity and for the different types of what Brentano and Husserl called the intentionality of consciousness. By the nature of its subject such analysis will grow in intensity so as to uncover the innermost springs of conscious life—including those of philosophy itself as a way of life leading toward the appropriation of our very own essence. In this regard Heidegger's existentialism (biased and one-sided

[10] Cassirer, *Philosophie der symbolischen Formen*, II, 242; cf., e.g., 193, 229, 246, 267.

[11] Cassirer, *Essay on Man*, 2.

as its execution proved to be) is no mere deviation from Husserl's thought, but its rather unorthodox pursuance into a sphere of problems which Husserl considered a *cura posterior* of the phenomenologist.

Husserl has shown how the 'noetic' processes of the mind (e.g., the synthetic actions of judging) are to be studied parallel (1) to its 'noematic' contents (e.g., the meaning of judgments—the subject-matter of *apophantic logic*) and (2) to real or ideal facts judged of (and studied, first of all, in the system of formal and material ontologies). The neglect of the noetic studies (which are prefigured in Kant's "Subjective Deduction," i.e., in an approach that was long somewhat discredited in the Marburg school) deprived neo-Kantianism of such fundamental insights as are worked out in Husserl's analysis of time-consciousness (*"Vorlesungen zur Phaenomenologie des inneren Zeitbewusstseins,"* Jahrbuch IX, 367-496).

This neglect may have been caused partly by the fear of falling prey to psychologism, partly by the adherence to the Cartesian dogma that the mode of consciousness (*Bewusstheit*) is always the same, and that consciousness differs only in its contents, objects, and their respective orders.[12] Following Husserl,[13] Adolf Reinach[14] had already protested against leveling all functions of consciousness, and asked how, without the awareness of functional differences, the indistinct hearing of a loud tone could be distinguished from the clear and distinct hearing of a low one. As a matter of fact, the differences of attention and the distinction between intentional *experiences* in general—like just seeing and hearing things—and intentional *acts* in particular—like the explicit looking at, listening to something—have played an important part in phenomenological analysis. Yet they are far from being the only themes of noetic investigations: the centrifugal or centripetal ways of experience; the looking upward, downward, or straight forward at things or persons; the variations in pace, temper, genuineness,

---

[12] Cf. Cohen, *Logik der reinen Erkenntnis*, 363ff., Natorp, *Allgemeine Psychologie*, 27ff., 40ff.

[13] *Logische Untersuchungen* (2nd edition) II, 1, 362.

[14] *Gesammelte Schriften*, 359ff.

etc., represent additional ways of dealing with things, i.e., particular modifications of "intentionality." They can be overlooked only by one who identifies without reservation the "being conscious of" with the appearance of a thing, with the φαίνεσθαι itself—this "most wonderful phenomenon of all" (Hobbes), behind which allegedly no question can reach, which is no problem itself, but gives to all questions an unquestionable foundation.[15] And, indeed, consciousness cannot be deduced and explained; but why should it not be explored in its modes as well as in its contents?[16]

Failing the recognition of this possibility, the life and nature of the subject appear only by way of interweaving the diverse principles to which all types of objects owe their existence and *re-constructing* thus, at the bottom of all specific experiences, the original, formative unity of consciousness as such (Kant's unity of the transcendental synthesis of apperception). The construction of the object is temporally and logically prior to its reversal, the reconstruction of the subject.

As a matter of fact, even according to Husserl, the method of reflection which gives us access to pure consciousness is but the reverse of the primary, natural attitude (*natürliche Einstellung*) and its orientation. Still, reflection is to him a way of immanent intuition; it is no bare reconstruction of the subjective, does not presuppose the whole work of objectification and is not restricted to the Penelope-labor of undoing the careful syntheses of the mind. It starts from distinctive unities of experience (phenomena in this sense) and is free to go back all the way through the synthetic processes and actions which lead upward to these appearances or else to go on to objective unities of a higher level. The given experience appears thus

---

[15] Cf. Cohen, *Logik*, 365; Natorp, *Allgemeine Psychologie*, 29, 35; Cassirer, *Das Erkenntnisproblem, II*, 67f.

[16] To be sure, it is a remarkable fact that in as early a writing as *Substanzbegriff und Funktionsbegriff* (32f) Cassirer refers to Husserl in acknowledging a variety of the most different acts of thought. Each of them is a mode of consciousness which represents "a specific way of interpreting its content, a peculiar intentional relation to the object." Still, he continues to study the life of consciousness only in the dialectics of its formations, in the objective meaning which the sensory material acquires and in the transformation of meaning which it undergoes; in Husserlian terms the analyses remain within the 'noematic' realm.

as the product of a phenomenological genesis which can be verified by retracing the whole process—springing back from a given point to a more primitive state and following from there the stream of consciousness—just as in the case of living reminiscence we are drawn back into the past to embark once more on the path toward the present. The phenomenological research never loses the color of life, the dynamics of consciousness which it is in search of—the concrete experience from which mere objectification and subjectification, mere construction and reconstruction are alienated. (So much so that in his *Practical Philosophy* Natorp would like to describe the process of transcendental synthesis entirely without any reference to the Kantian Ego, to subject and consciousness.[17])

Even so, Natorp considers himself faithful to the spirit of Kant's basic intentions. And Cassirer is at one with him in emphasizing that the process of experience as such—not only of theoretical experience as described in the first *Critique*—antedates the distinction between the objective and the subjective, between being and consciousness. Self and object are not presupposed from the first, nor is one the foundation of the other and its knowledge, "but in one and the same process of objectification and determination the whole of experience comes to be divided for us into the 'spheres within and without,' into 'Self' and 'World'."[18]

This may be compared with Husserl's conception of pure consciousness as the sphere of origin within which alone the real person and his real world are to find their "phenomenological constitution." The absoluteness of the latter constitutive process, however, is not so remote as to make it a mere dialectical construction. Even where intentional experience (*intentionales Erlebnis*) is not a matter of personal activity, it is still borne and animated by living consciousness. And, whereas Natorp speaks of a quasi-automatic and utopian "movement of the categories" as such, taken to enjoy a sort of mythical super-being, Husserl

---

[17] Natorp, *Praktische Philosophie*, 241. Cf. also Cohen, e.g., *Logik der reinen Erkenntnis*, 415, *Ethik des reinen Willens*, 130.

[18] Cassirer, *Kants Leben und Lehre*, 209. Cf. *Philosophie der symbolischen Formen III*, 59.

deals not only with the categories, but with the καπηγορεῖν itself, the very acts of determining things. Here the procedures of objectification as such are followed out and not merely fixed as to their results at the different stages of their evolution.

The function of *objectification* certainly plays an important part in Husserl's transcendental phenomenology—the very title 'transcendental" refers to the self-transcendence of the subject towards the object. But it does not cover the whole of conscious life and is not the only concern of the phenomenologist. This fact would have come out even more clearly, if the second and third parts of Husserl's *Ideas* had ever been published. While speaking of the subjective side of a phenomenon as well as of the objective one, i.e., "that experiential content which points away from the Ego," Husserl gives in the first part of the *Ideas* preference to the latter—to the "objectively oriented aspect, since it is this aspect which is most familiar to us from our natural attitude."[19] Yet even in the description of the synthesis in which an identical object comes to be realized, Husserl does not confine himself to the spontaneity of the intellect and the process of "categorial constitution."[20] He studies also the more primitive fusion of appearances, the work of what he calls *primary passive syntheses*, i.e., syntheses in which the Ego is still latent, just as there is a secondary passivity into which each previous activity is likely to fall back: a judgment, for example, after having been actively built up, lives on in a sedimentary state in which it enters new connections, new passive syntheses.[21] In this way the formative power of pure consciousness can be exhibited and analyzed, whether or not the subject *qua* agent is openly on the stage and personally engaged in performing any synthetic activities.

[19] Husserl, *Ideen* I, 160; cf. also 192, 219, 232.

[20] Natorp, *Praktische Philosophie*, 212ff, 222. Cf. Cassirer, "Paul Natorp," *Kantstudien*, XXX (1925) 280.

[21] Cf. Husserl, *Méditations Cartésiennes:* § 38, "Genèse active et passive" (65ff); *Erfahrung und Urteil*, pass. (e.g. § 16, 74ff). These problems are intimately connected with Dilthey's attempt to lay a foundation for *formal* logic and its categories through a logic and categories of *life:* cf., especially, Dilthey, *Schriften* VII, 228ff; Georg Misch, *Lebensphilosophie und Phaenomenologie* (1930), *pass.*

IV

The Form (in Construction and Intuition)

The confrontation of Husserl's "passive syntheses" with the ideals of "construction and re-construction" in neo-Kantianism can serve very well to characterize the difference in the tenor of these two types of philosophy. Neo-Kantianism, attributing to construction a foremost place in the growth of all experience, pursued a constructive method in its own procedure. Cassirer always insisted on the paradigmatic importance of Kant's "Copernican revolution" in philosophy:

In each and every sphere of objects—the viewpoint of "ectypal reflection" (*nachbildende, copeyliche Betrachtung*) has to be abandoned for that of 'architectonic ordering.' . . . Even outside of the realm of pure theory we ought to see that the object of a certain synopsis is constituted rather than copied by this form of unification, the synopsis.[22]

As a matter of fact, this unqualified emphasis on the archetypal function of the forms of our experience makes neo-Kantianism border on anti-Kantianism. It is not balanced by the recognition of the finiteness of our knowledge in contradistinction to an *intuitus originarius* which brings the *Ding an sich* into being. In this neo-Kantian interpretation the *Ding an sich* is not determined in itself; it is not qualitatively different from the objects and products of experience; it is reduced to a methodological idea—the sum total of experience—and has become relative to the process of objective determination; as an ideal limit it marks only the point of complete determination of things in every possible way—a point never reached, but always striven for. Leibniz's principle of a continuous scale of representation has gained the upper hand over the transcendental contrast between the two forms of representation (sensory and intellectual) in Kant.

This is why the procedure in the different ways of cultural

---

[22] Cassirer, "Das Symbolproblem und seine Stellung im System der Philosophie" (*Zeitschrift fuer Aesthetik* XXI (1927), 311). For thought *qua* determination cf. Natorp, *Die logischen Grundlagen der exacten Wissenschaften* (1910), 38f: "To think does not mean anything else but to determine. . . . Thought does not recognize any determination prior to that which is of thought's own making." Cf. Kant, *Kritik der reinen Vernunft*, B, 375.

life, as described by Cassirer, resembles so much the building of the Tower of Babel: it seems to reach into the void, governed as it is exclusively by internal principles, without being oriented toward anything or controlled by anything independent of this whole process and without being animated by the messianic spirit of Cohen. The constructive schemata designed by thought "do not *borrow* their hold and support from the empirical world of things, but *create* this support themselves" by way of a context of *signs* contrived to represent a system of universal relations.[23]

The full meaning of this contention comes to light by the help of its negative counterpart: the rejection of sense-perception as a mediating link in a causal chain between subject and object. The relation between object and consciousness being that of "intentionality" (Husserl), no causal relation can prevail between them, since causality, according to Cassirer, has its place exclusively within the realm of things. This statement neglects, however, the variety of causal experience and narrows causality down to a phenomenologically derivative type, the relation between physical events. Even the Kantian category had been much more comprehensive. Cassirer insists that sensation can be only the sign, the representative of its 'intentional' object, never the effect of a transcendent *Ding an sich* which affects our mind.[24]

---

[23] Cassirer, *Phaenomenologie der Erkenntnis*, 331f.

[24] *Ibid.*, 365ff, above all 376ff. In his *Essay on Man*, however, Cassirer actually did employ such biological terms as 'stimulus' and 'response' to characterize the dynamic, i.e., causal relations between man and world. At the same time, thought appeared as a refined means to regulate this rapport as well as conquer a new dimension of reality. In this way Cassirer seems to have accommodated himself to the American scene. But this adaptation to Dewey's thought ought not to be over-rated: there has always been a bridge between panmethodologism and instrumentalism. Moreover, Cassirer does not take these biological and instrumental aspects to be distinctive of man. In the formation of his symbolic worlds man still enjoys perfect autonomy and is left to what we may call his inner genius. As regards, finally, the organic correlation between stimulus and response, we must consider, first, that affection by way of stimulus is not simply identical with sensation, and then that things must not needs be treated alike in philosophical anthropology, on the one hand, and a logic of pure knowledge and other transcendental disciplines, on the other. Unfortunately, the systematic locus of *An Essay on Man* is nowhere sufficiently clarified from the viewpoint of transcendental idealism.

Hence sensation is not backed by reality: its own ontological status is not defined with respect to a reality which is more than the final product of objectification. Only because in his philosophy sensation had such support by the *Ding an sich*, could Kant make the "being bound up with sensation" the criterion of actual existence.[25] That an idea is right when its consequences agree with the data of our senses—this explanation may be satisfactory within the peculiar framework of Leibniz's metaphysics;[26] it may accurately describe the way of scientific verification—hence it appears in Heinrich Hertz's famous *Prinzipien der Mechanik* (a passage which Cassirer quotes repeatedly[27]): but, on new-Kantian ground, it is hardly sufficient to bear out the full meaning of real truth.

The neo-Kantian thinker cannot want to have a theoretical assertion verified by mere reference to immediate sensation— for the simple reason that to him pure, formless sensation may be the methodical presupposition of all objective determination as well as (*mutatis mutandis*) the ultimate result of psychological reconstruction, but never an immediate and self-evident datum of consciousness. Referring to the findings of modern psycho-pathology, Cassirer takes great and well rewarded pains in showing the conceptual ingredient in all sense perception. Sensation itself remains a mere hypothesis; its possibility is never accounted for. In phenomenology, on the other hand, the Kantian *affection* has found its revaluation in Husserl's analysis of the field of passive pre-acquaintance, affective tendencies, and the receptivity of the Ego—studies to which, in the present essay, I can only refer.[28]

If the objective validity of a theoretical, moral, or aesthetic idea is to mean more than its consistency with other ideas and its quasi-stylistic purity according to the inner rules of procedure, Cassirer does not seem to have set forth the solution to this problem. The concluding thoughts of his *Phaenomeno-*

[25] Kant, *Kritik der reinen Vernunft*, B 266ff.
[26] Leibniz, "*Quid sit Idea*," *Philosophische Schriften* (ed. Gerhardt) VII, 263f.
[27] Cf., e.g., *Philosophie der symbolischen Formen* I, 5f.
[28] Cf. Husserl, *Erfahrung und Urteil*, §§ 16f with Cohen's declaration (*Logik der reinen Erkenntnis*, 402:) "We have nothing to do with . . . sensation. This is our logical direction."

logie der Erkenntnis (552ff) can hardly be taken as the proper fulfillment of a promise to this effect given previously,[29] yet finally postponed—perhaps for an additional volume which has never been published. Meanwhile, in the *Philosophie der symbolischen Formen* as well as in *Substanzbegriff und Funktionsbegriff* and in some later articles, Cassirer understands "objectivity" to abide in the invariability of universal relations. This is a problem to which we shall return later on.

Whereas to Kant knowledge is essentially intuition,[30] the strict imperceptibility (*Unanschaulichkeit*) of the object of knowledge is proclaimed (from Cohen to Cassirer) as the true corner-stone of the "critical" theory of knowledge.[31] In Cassirer's youth this problem had been the very point of dispute between the neo-Kantianism of the Fries-school and that of Marburg. The same question arises again in relation to phenomenology and its revised and enlarged concept of intuition (the paramount importance of which does not prevent us from recognizing the impossibility of giving a perceptual illustration to the key concepts of modern physics.)

The idea of construction as the general character of mental life on the whole is so strong in neo-Kantianism that it makes knowledge also exclusively a matter of constructive or reconstructive determination. Since the form-matter relation and correlation—witness its original meaning in Aristotle—is most congenial to this idea of 'poietic' activity, it dominates the neo-Kantian theory of knowledge to such a degree as to make its repeated application somewhat dull and monotonous in the long run—even more so in the form-matter hierarchy characteristic of the school of Rickert and Lask than in that of Marburg. This accounts for the fact that in the early stages of phenomenology the uniformity and recklessness of this constructive procedure ("matter does not deserve any forbearance") was most suspicious to us young phenomenologists who felt committed to do justice to the variety of phenomena: the opposition to

[29] *Phaenomenologie der Erkenntnis*, 27n, having reference to a (non-existent) Book III, ch. 6.
[30] Kant, *Kritik der reinen Vernunft*, B 33.
[31] Cassirer, *Phaenomenologie der Erkenntnis*, 367.

neo-Kantian criticism thus became focussed in the polemics against "construction"—a term which came close to being an invective.

The form-matter relationship is too useful a pattern not to play an important rôle even in Husserl's philosophy—e.g., under the title of syntactic forms and syntactic materials.[32] But it did so only within the frame of a much more comprehensive and flexible pattern of interpretation—that of intention and fulfilment. A first 'empty' intention of the mind was to be given an original fulfilment in direct intuition. I take it that this conception of knowledge, of which Cassirer also availed himself occasionally,[33] was much more both in the letter and in the spirit of Kant (who spoke of thought as a mere means for direct intuition[34]) than was this type of neo-Kantianism itself. It is partly true that in Husserl also "the content of perception depends on thought, 'fulfilment' on 'intention,' presentation on representation and that the perceptual aspect is fundamentally determined" by the conceptual outlook.[35] Yet a given intention is no ultimate with Husserl, but an intellectual habitude which, in *genetic phenomenology*, can be accounted for as an outgrowth of (1) processes of "associative synthesis" and (2) the still more primitive syntheses of the "immanent time-consciousness."[36]

In the eyes of the phenomenologist, the fulfilment given to our intentions by way of intuition makes the process of knowledge as much a process of discovery and explication as of determination. To apprehend is not identical (as it is in Cassirer[37]) with the *establishment* of relations—even the *recognition* of

[32] Cf. Husserl, e.g., *Formale und Transzendentale Logik*, 259ff.

[33] E.g., in the necrology on Natorp (*Kantstudien*, XXX, 287).

[34] Kant, *loc. cit.*

[35] Natorp, *Allgemeine Psychologie*, 287. But cf. *Praktische Philosophie*, 210ff for the final recognition of the primacy of content.

[36] At this point I must content myself with these terms indicating problems with which Husserl dealt, e.g., in *Ideen*, 73f, *Méditations Cartésiennes*, 65ff, in the "Vorlesungen zur Phaenomenologie des inneren Zeitbewusstseins" (*Jahrbuch*, IX, 252ff); *Erfahrung und Urteil*, 74ff, 460ff.

[37] Cf. Cassirer, *Phaenomenologie der Erkenntnis*, 346. In *Zur Logik der Kulturwissenschaften* (80f), Cassirer comes closer to adopting the descriptive aims of phenomenology, namely with regard to the concepts of *style*, which (he says) are reached by way of *ideation* and *characterize* rather than *determine* their objects.

relations is only a part of it. To equate knowing with relating is a dangerous oversimplification, which cannot but have detrimental consequences in epistemology and is implicitly refuted by the careful way in which Husserl distinguishes, within the course of knowledge, phases of simple apprehension, explicative study, perception of relations, determinative and relational judgment (*bestimmendes und beziehendes Urteilen*), etc.[38] Altogether, 'intentional experience,' as it appears in Husserl, is not restricted to noesis in the sense of actively *constituting* a certain meaning (*Sinngebung*): it is always *acknowledgment* of meaning (*Sinnfindung*) at the same time; and it is only in one specific stratum of transcendental phenomenology that the former character appears all-dominating.[39]

[38] Cf. Husserl, *Erfahrung und Urteil*, §§ 23ff, § 54.

[39] It is worth mentioning that the language of Cassirer's last work—*Essay on Man*—is far less rigorous in maintaining the panmethodology of the Marburg school. The diction of critical idealism is often abandoned in favor of terms which have their proper place in epistemological realism. He stresses the fact that material objects exist independent of the scientist (185); speaks of the symbolic systems as links between man and reality (24f.); characterizes knowledge as interpretation (138, 146, 170) and even as discovery and abbreviation (143, 156) of reality, art as an intensification of it (143); and, in a phrase which reminds one of objective idealism (in Dilthey's sense) rather than of neo-Kantian criticism, he sees in art the apprehension of "the dynamic life of forms" by "a corresponding dynamic process in ourselves" (151)—a formula which may reveal the growing influence Kant's *Critique of Judgment* in its more metaphysical prefigurements had on Cassirer's mind. (Cf. *Kants Leben und Lehre*, 354). Pointing in the same direction is his emphasis on the Stoic maxim of the "sympathy of the whole" as "one of the firmest foundations of religion." (*Essay on Man*, 95).

The trend away from the earlier logical idealism of the Marburg school toward objective idealism is strongly accentuated in Natorp's *Praktische Philosophie*. But it is also noticeable (though less pronounced) in Cassirer's discussion of Scheler's philosophical anthropology: first at Davos in 1929, in the following year in an article of *Die Neue Rundschau:* "'Leben' und 'Geist' in der Philosophie der Gegenwart."* Here Cassirer tries to resolve the alleged opposition of Life and Spirit into two complementary forms of movement within life as a whole—spirit representing a later phase of life itself. This idea of immanent transcendence is closely akin to the rôle which I myself have assigned to 'absolute consciousness'

---

* EDITOR'S NOTE: The interested reader will find this essay from Cassirer's pen reprinted—in English translation—as Part III of the present volume, under the title: " 'Spirit' and 'Life' in Contemporary Philosophy," (855-880 *infra*).

The objectivistic ingredient in the phenomenological concept of knowledge is expressed by the mistakable and often mistaken watchword of the movement: "back to the things themselves;"[40] and it is also evidenced by the term "eidos" (essence) as the object of this discovery, i.e., as the correlate of ἀ-λήθεια (truth in the predominantly objectivistic view of the Greek mind). It is symptomatic that the tribute which the thinkers of Marburg paid to Plato's idealism was more in the enthusiastic recognition of the *idea* than in that of the *eidos*. Natorp's *Platons Ideenlehre* begins with the distinction of these terms: the latter is said to stand for the sight a thing offers, whereas the former is said to mean the aspect, the point of view from which this thing comes to be seen.[41] The emphasis on the *eidos* in Husserl's phenomenology thus betrays a genuine interest in the nature of *things*—as much as the praise of the idea shows Cohen's, Natorp's, and Cassirer's primary concern with the nature of *thought*, i.e., "with the immanent laws according to which thought does not accept its object as simply given, but constructs it in conformity with thought's own way of looking at things."[42]

In the sharpest contrast to this declaration is what Husserl announces as "the principle of all principles," i.e., that "whatever presents itself in 'intuition' directly and as it were in bodily reality has to be accepted just as it shows itself, though only within the limits of such self-presentation."[43] Whereas the panmethodology of neo-Kantian philosophy cannot but abolish

---

within the sphere of the 'Absolute'—an attempt at broadening Husserl's concept of the absolute sphere as being identical with the sphere of immanent consciousness. (Cf. "Art and Phenomenology" in *Philosophical Essays in Memory of Edmund Husserl*). But the self-transcendence of life, which is here in question, underlies and is by no means one with, the inner dialectics of the categories or that of the pure forms of culture, which is in the foreground of Natorp's and Cassirer's interest (cf., e.g., *Praktische Philosophie*, 209; *Essay on Man, pass.*). Logical idealism and phenomenology may converge, but they never coincide.

[40] In its true and original meaning this word occurs in the Introduction to the second volume of *Logische Untersuchungen* (second edition), 6.

[41] Natorp, *Platons Ideenlehre* (second edition, 1921) p. 1.

[42] *Loc. cit.*, cf. Cassirer, e.g., *Phaenomenologie der Erkenntnis*, 347ff.

[43] Husserl, *Ideen zu einer reinen Phaenomenologie*, § 24 (*Jahrbuch*, I) 43f.

the definition of truth as *adaequatio* (*rei et intellectus*), this definition was to be restored in a new sense through the *Logische Untersuchungen:* by conveying an ultimate intuitive fulfilment of a certain intention a thing may present itself as it is—at least as regards its general nature. At this point the *essentia formalis* and the *essentia objectiva* of the thing will coincide. Complete evidence, i.e., the experience of adequate fulfilment, and true being thus become correlative terms. Actually such consummate evidence cannot be obtained for each and every type of being. The adequate knowledge of outer reality, above all, exists only (but actually) as an ideal in the Kantian sense. This fact, however, does not detract from the *meaning* of truth: truth is experienced wherever that which is meant is fully 'covered' by that which is *given*—given in the mode of perfect self-presentation.[44]

To be sure, the adequacy of knowledge which phenomenology is seeking is not that of faithfully copying mere *facts*—phenomenology deals with the *essence* of things—but neither is it mere faithfulness to the purity of its methodical principles. It consists in the adequate fulfilment of original intentions. As mentioned above, there is a mutual dependence between intention and fulfilment (cf. *supra,* p. 816). On the one hand, the intentions are charged with expectations marking out the ways and types of intuitive experience in which a proper fulfilment may be sought and found. Intuition thus responds and corresponds to intention and varies with it. This relation accounts for that broadening of the concept of intuition in phenomenology of which we spoke before—*sense*-perception exhibiting only one peculiar (though peculiarly important) mode of intuitive fulfilment. On the other hand, an intention is to be verified (or disproved) by subsequent perception. In its objective orientation it represents an aspect which, as experience goes on, is continuously adjusted to the things that are to be disclosed from this point of view. It needs must be congenial to the inner essence (*sachhaltiges Wesen*) of the phenomenon in question.

[44] Husserl, *Logische Untersuchungen* (second edition, 1921) II, 2, 115ff; *Ideen zu einer reinen Phaenomenologie* (*Jahrbuch,* I) 125ff., 282ff.

Thus it is under the dictate of the experiental content just as much as this content appears in the forms in which it is apprehended 'as' such and such a thing, as a chair or a table, as H_2O or a drink, i.e., according to the meaning that is carried by a certain intention.

Consisting in this adequacy of intention to its stuff, truth has a dimension of depth: it does more or less justice to the inner nature of the material in question. Philosophical truth, at least, is not exhausted by the alternative 'right or wrong.' The higher or lower degree of adequacy of interpretation becomes particularly relevant in phenomenological philosophy, devoted as it is to the disclosure of the essential structures within the world of conscious life. For it is the nature and experience of life which give rise to the use of the term 'depth' in connection with the truth of being. Phenomenology as the analysis of the original constitution of consciousness tries to penetrate into the very depths from which the various formations of consciousness originate.

The search for these original springs, modes and structures of life presupposes and sharpens a *sense* of the original, a capacity of retracing familiar appearances to their sources, of renewing and intensifying insights of the past and piercing through conventional interpretations so as to understand where and why they veil rather than unveil the essential truths of life. In this way a phenomenological description will pass through different strata and become more and more profound as it reaches more and more original depths. This procedure has been inaugurated in Husserl's *Ideen* starting as he does from the naïve, worldly attitude of life to discover then its true origin in the stream of pure, transcendental consciousness. Yet this " 'Absolute' again is not truly ultimate but constitutes itself in a certain hidden and most peculiar sense, having its original source in an ultimate true Absolute."[45] This latter dimension is only hinted at in the *Ideen:* it is that of inner time-consciousness which has been analyzed by Husserl in courses, parts of which were published by Heidegger in the *Jahrbuch*, IX (1928).

[45] Husserl, *Ideen zu einer reinen Phaenomenologie*, 163.

Heidegger's own *Sein und Zeit* betrays both in its title and its composition his dependence on Husserl's approach and results: he too tries to identify 'absolute being' with the being or rather welling up (*Zeitigen*) of time; he too advances from the workaday world, the world of tools, and from Everyman's attitude to the original mode of true temporality. In the academic courses of both, Husserl and Heidegger, the term "*Abbau*" (destruction) marked this regress from the established positions of conscious life to its sources, although it had a much less aggressive note with Husserl.

The inner historicity of consciousness can be sounded by what Husserl called 'genetic phenomenology'—a splitting up, as it were, of given experiences and formations into the different layers and sediments of meaning which they imply and the processes through which this meaning came to be constituted and settled. Each phenomenon has a coming into being (a γένεσις εἰς οὐσίαν) the style of which is prescribed by its very nature. Thus the discovery and descriptive analysis of these implications is, on the whole, independent of empirical studies of the primitive mind or of psycho-pathology such as are accumulated in Cassirer's *Das mythische Denken* and *Phaenomenologie der Erkenntnis*. In saying this, I do not deny that findings of this kind can be used to good advantage by the phenomenologist. In fact, they have been employed this way, e.g., by Max Scheler. They help to enlarge the scope of variations which are indispensable for the control of phenomenological intuition (cf. *infra*, pp. 827-830); and mental deficiencies—as in aphasia—or deviations from the norm may be referred to in order to place the very norm into bolder relief. On the other hand, a preknowledge of the norm is obviously the condition without which the abnormal cannot be characterized as such.

It may be added that the phenomenological re-search after the sphere of origin, although bearing some analogy with Natorp's 'psychological reconstruction' of the original unity of consciousness, cannot be identified with it either. The leaping back from objective units to the underlying manifoldness of the contents of consciousness remains a mere inference with Natorp: how can this manifoldness be regained from the synthetic unity

of the objects by which it seems absorbed (whereas an infinity
of perspectives is of the very essence of the phenomena which
are the primary concern in Husserl's analyses)? Above all,
however, the true meaning of 'original life' does not lie in the
dimension and hierarchy of contents and objects at all: it
denotes a distinctive *mode* of experience which Natorp cannot
account for because he denies all distinctions of modes in consciousness (*Bewusstheit*), trying to reduce them to mere differences in the order of contents (cf. *supra*, p. 808). In the same
vein Cassirer also neglected somewhat the problems of the How
of Experience (*Vollzugssinn*) in favor of its What (*Gehalts-
sinn*—to use two terms of Husserl and, especially, of Heidegger): he showed the 'subject' only in the ways in which it rises
above impressions, not in those in which it is subjected to them.

Finally (and this, perhaps, marks the disparity in the outlook
of the two schools most clearly) the phenomenological research
into origins is not the laying of a foundation in the sense of a
rational principle as in Herman Cohen, where the "principle"
and the "judgment of origin" give rise to the physical object
(in *Logik der reinen Erkenntnis*) and to the human individual
(in *Ethik des reinen Willens*). This difference must be stated,
not to disparage the sagacity in which the *Logik* shows how the
something originates in the relative nothing (the μὴ ὄν) of the
"infinitesimal number" (the "differential"), nor to discredit the
moral wisdom which seeks the origin of the Self in the recognition of the *Alter Ego*, but to prove the different atmospheres
in which phenomenological and neo-Kantian thought, including
that of Cassirer, came to grow. The feeling of this dissimilarity
could be even intensified by comparing the way (just mentioned) in which Cohen reaches Being "through the detour
of the Nothing"[46] with that of Heidegger, who finds the
original revelation of Being in the "clear night of Nothingness"[47] (the nothingness of dread)—an extreme, but also, for
this very reason, exaggerated contrast. (It would appear much
milder, even as far as Cohen and Heidegger are concerned,
if we took account of the concepts of origin, Being, and Non-

---

[46] Cohen, *Logik der reinen Erkenntnis*, 69.
[47] Heidegger, *Was ist Metaphysik?*, 19.

Being in the religious function they obtain in Cohen's posthumous work *Religion der Vernunft*.[48])

In short, the paramount difference between the two movements which we are trying to present consists in their different philosophical ethos: in the self-reliance of reason as a systematizing power, the passionate interest in the purity of method on the one hand, and the faithful devotion to Being in all of its manifestations on the other. It must be admitted, however, that this latter *amor intellectualis* has sometimes been lacking in humility and trustworthiness even in the case of some of the most gifted phenomenologists—men who proclaimed this love most fervently (as, e.g., Max Scheler)—whereas the school of Marburg was always distinguished by a spirit of admirable scholarly discipline.

V

The Rapprochement between neo-Kantianism and Phenomenology

The discussion between Marburg neo-Kantianism and phenomenology has always been carried on in an exemplarily fair way. The gap between them did not and could not be bridged, but it was narrowed in the second and third decades of the present century. Whereas in *Logische Untersuchungen* the ultimate philosophical decisions were still in a state of suspension, Husserl's *Ideen* made the transition to transcendental idealism and accepted Natorp's concept of the Pure Ego—although in a sense vastly different from that of the neo-Kantians: Husserl's Pure Ego is individual in character and not identical with the pure unity of objective thought represented by "pure apperception, i.e., the pure 'Ego'," "the ideal subject as such (*Subjekt überhaupt*)."[49] The famous debate between Cassirer and Heidegger at Davos (Switzerland) in April 1929 was preceded by a series of lectures which showed a curious crossing in

[48] Cohen, *Religion der Vernunft*, 48, 51, 76ff.

[49] Natorp, *Allgemeine Psychologie*, 244f. The contrast to phenomenology is much milder in Cohen's ethics and, especially in his philosophy of religion; also in Cassirer's account of the aesthetic experience; cf., e.g., *Essay on Man*, 228.

themes—Cassirer speaking on Philosophical Anthropology, Heidegger on Kant.

But, again, Cassirer's conception of man was far from being Heidegger's (it was actually in striking contrast to it); and Heidegger's interpretation of Kant stressed the importance of the first *Critique* for the foundation of metaphysics and not, as the neo-Kantians did, for the theory of scientific knowledge.

It may be profitable to study the rapprochement in question with specific regard to the problems discussed in the preceding sections of this essay. In his old age, when death intervened with his purpose, Natorp was about to supplement the formalism of his earlier thought with an increased emphasis on the *content* of experience[50] taken as an "actuated individual factor."[51] Struggling beyond the limits of his original neo-Kantian position, he began to realize that the actuality and the meaning of a thing (its *Dassinn* and *Wassinn*) were to be acknowledged rather than posited. Knowledge *qua* determination no longer meant to him imposing a unifying form on a variety of materials: it was now supposed to ascertain and fix the intrinsic meaning of given phenomena.[52] He came to disclaim the creativity of knowledge by what amounts almost to a play on words—by re-interpreting the ambiguous German word *"Schoepfen:"* instead of meaning "to create" it was now taken to mean "to draw from the source of being."[53] (It is to be regretted that all this did not lead to any serious revision of Cassirer's own theory of being and knowledge).

On the other hand, Husserl's own writings and particularly those of the following generation bore witness to the legitimate rôle construction can play as an element of phenomenological interpretation. With so widely varying representatives of phenomenological thought as Heidegger or Felix Kaufmann, 'construction' (Heidegger's *'Entwurf'*) has ceased to be a sort of phenomenological bogy. "There is no meaning"—says Felix

[50] Natorp, *Praktische Philosophie*, 211f; cf. Cassirer, "Paul Natorp," *Kantstudien*, XXX, 291.

[51] Natorp, *Praktische Philosophie*, 198ff.

[52] Cf. *op. cit.*, 240, 261.

[53] *Op. cit.*, 212.

Kaufmann—"either in scientific thinking or in pre-scientific thinking, that does not imply a mental construction (synthesis)."[54]

Cassirer's own attitude toward phenomenology cannot be read simply from the growing use he made of the term 'phenomenology' itself: this use is greatly influenced by Hegel's description of the spirit's way from naïve consciousness toward knowledge proper.[55] Such a dialectical movement, from mythical to scientific thought, is the theme of Cassirer's *Phenomenology of Knowledge*, the third volume of the *Philosophie der symbolischen Formen*. In the same sense he describes his *Essay on Man* not only (in the subtitle) as an "Introduction to a Philosophy of Human Culture," but equally as a "phenomenology of human culture."[56]

This dialectic proceeds in articulated steps and passes through well distinguished stations. In other words, each of these steps represents a specific form of consciousness and cultural expression. Thus genetic interest and genetic description are supplemented by the morphological ones in a phenomenology of the "main forms of the objective mind."[57] This procedure is somewhat analogous to the way in which the problems of static and genetic constitution combine in Husserl's later works.[58] And 'phenomenology' stands here not only for Hegel's conception of this term, but also for Husserl's eidetic description of the phenomena.

Hence there are not only occasional points of contact between phenomenology and Cassirer's theory of symbolic representation—such as when he refers to the analysis of "expression and signification" in the second volume of Husserl's *Logische Untersuchungen*[59] or even relates his own concept of representa-

---

[54] Felix Kaufmann, *Methodology of the Social Sciences* (1944), 34.

[55] Cf. Cassirer, " 'Geist' und 'Leben' in der Philosophie der Gegenwart," *Neue Rundschau* (1930), 260 (cf. translation of this article in the present volume, p. 875); *Philosophie der symbolischen Formen*, I, 15; II, xf; III, vi.

[56] *Essay on Man*, 52.

[57] *Philosophie der symbolischen Formen*, III, 58.

[58] Cf., e.g., Husserl, *Méditations Cartésiennes*, 115.

[59] Cf. *Philosophie der symbolischen Formen* III, 375.

tion to Husserl's idea of intentionality.[60] It is also methodically important, but not yet decisive that his theory of perception and expression has much in common with Max Scheler's phenomenology of inner and outer perception,[61] etc. But over and above all this, the common morphological interest creates a general affinity between the two ways of philosophizing. Through his whole description of the forms of human culture, his analysis of the structures of linguistic, mythical, and religious thought, Cassirer draws close to phenomenology and its descriptive analysis of the essential forms. In this spirit Cassirer emphasizes, e.g., the fundamental difference between "the genetic question" and "the analytical and phenomenological" one as regards the nature of language.[62]

This affinity is given another expression in Cassirer's philosophical *group-theory*—dealing with the universal relations which remain invariant throughout the transformation of structures in both the perceptual and conceptual realms. The unity of the manifold, which in this way comes to the fore, gives to the particulars a community of being (*Wesen*) which must not lie in external resemblances, but consists in an analogy of function within a context of relations.[63]

This theory is, in a certain way, an application of Poncelet's "principle of the permanence of mathematical relations." Within its original realm it enjoys, therefore, the privilege of mathematical exactness. In recent publications, however, Cassirer was anxious to show that essentially the same procedure can take place even where this privilege has to be renounced, i.e., in non-mathematical realms such as perception[64] and language.[65]

---

[60] Cf. e.g., Cassirer's article on Paul Natorp, *Kantstudien*, XXX, 287; *Philosophie der symbolischen Formen*, III, 227ff.

[61] Cf. *Phaenomenologie der Erkenntnis*, 100ff.

[62] *Essay on Man*, 30.

[63] Cf. *Substanzbegriff und Funktionsbegriff*, 18ff; *Philosophie der symbolischen Formen*, III, 341ff, particularly 352; 463ff.

[64] Cassirer, "Group Concept and Perception Theory," *Philosophy and Phenomenological Research*, V (1944), 1-35.

[65] Cassirer, "The Influence of Language upon the Development of Scientific Thought," *Journal of Philosophy*, XXXIX (1942), 309-327.

Thus he emphasizes the importance of the ideal 'schema' (in the Kantian sense) for the establishment of perception and the constitution of our world. With reference to Ehrenfels' concept of *Gestaltqualitäten* (the *'Einheitsmomente'* of Husserl's *Philosophie der Arithmetik*) he points out that the identity of a perceptual form—e.g., a melody—throughout the change of all its elements is but what, "in a much higher degree of perfection," prevails in the domain of geometrical concepts. "What we find in both cases are invariances with respect to variations undergone by the primitive elements out of which a form is constructed."[66] The reason for such a perceptual invariance is the 'goodness' of a certain exemplary 'form.' "The 'true' color, the 'true' shape, the 'true' size of an object are by no means that which is given in any particular impression, nor need they be the 'sum' of these impressions." "The *constitutive* factor . . . manifests itself in the possibility of forming invariants."[67] The 'true' impression is that which is transformed into a fixed value able to build up a knowledge of constant reality.

These ideas are not only in agreement with Husserl's analysis of perception and, e.g., with his emphasis on the rôle of perceptual *optima,* they go far in the direction of Husserl's *Wesensschau* (intuition of essences). Cassirer's statement that "the intentional reference to an object is not, to the extent to which it is realizable at all in perception, fulfilled all at once, but gradually only"[68] is couched in the terms of both Husserl's phenomenology of perception and of his phenomenology of intuition. Nothing is ready made and given *uno intuitu*; the intuition of essences is as much in need of verification and elucidation as any individual perception. Far from being an uncontrolled mystical or a dogmatic rationalistic concept, Husserl's idea of intuition and *eidos* is bound up with a process of methodical discovery (ideation). And the pith and marrow of this ideation is nothing else but variation in a sense not altogether different from that in Cassirer's writings.

[66] "Group Concept and Perception Theory," 25.—For the whole problem of this paragraph cf. Husserl, *Ideen,* §§ 71-75.

[67] Cassirer, "Group Concept and Perception Theory," 34.

[68] Cassirer, *ibid.,* 30. Cf. Husserl, *Ideen,* § 67.

In what amounts to a mental experiment, Husserl shows how
to vary a certain given phenomenon by way of free imagination
while preserving the unity of the original intention. Without
being restricted by the limits of real experience (or even of
experience *possible* within the frame of our real world), he
moves through all possible dimensions of change implied within
the horizon of the same phenomenon. Thus he manages to grasp
the identical content—the general essence—at the bottom of an
infinitude of possible varieties. This 'ideational abstraction' can
do with one (preferably one pregnant) example and thus differs
radically from inductive abstraction, which is dependent on the
accumulated evidence of many instances.[69]

Husserl's method of ideation was to be applied to all types
of experiences and attitudes—perceptual, social, historical,
moral, aesthetic, religious, etc. A large stock of *a priori* knowledge of this morphological type has thus been gathered by Husserl himself, by his friends and disciples, but also by scholars like
Litt, Riezler, and many others who never belonged to the
inner circle of the phenomenological movement. I restrict myself to the quotation of one recent statement:

We cannot hope to deal scientifically with any problem of social or
cultural change if we tie our concepts to particular and changing conditions. As our variables must at least aim at universality, they cannot
be defined in terms of mutable institutions. If we do not eventually
succeed in finding universal variables that constitute a pattern of all
patterns, containing in itself the principles of its variations, social change
will continue to engulf the meaning of the concepts in which we pretend
to formulate its laws.[70]

Thus the concept and method of variation figure as a link
between Cassirer and phenomenological thought. The value of
this rapport at first seems to be limited, however, by his specific
way of approach. Motivated as he is by mathematical prece-

---

[69] A much more thoroughgoing description of this method is given in Husserl's
Erfahrung und Urteil, III. Abschnitt, II. Kapitel (402-442). Cf. also my article
"In Memoriam Edmund Husserl," *Social Research*, February 1940, especially
74-76.

[70] Kurt Riezler, "What is Public Opinion?" *Social Research*, November 1944,
397f.

dents, he insists that the "form of logical *systematization* which is both possible and necessary in the domain of geometrical thought is once and for all inaccessible to perception."[71] This is contrary to the convictions and practice of phenomenologists like Husserl, Scheler, Schapp, Leyendecker, the two Conrads and others. They concentrated on studying the *a priori* structure of the perceptual sphere—as, for instance, the essential relations between impression, retention and protention in every perception (Husserl). They could expand the span of the *a priori* without falling prey to intellectual hybris because in phenomenology the *a priori* forms are not imposed on the phenomena, but (by way of ideational abstraction) abstracted from them. Cassirer, on the other hand, leaves the constancies in the perceptual realm to the empirical observation of the psychologist: "here no *a priori* judgment is possible."[72]

This attitude may account for the abundant use he makes of psychological, psycho-pathological and anthropological material both in the *Philosophie der symbolischen Formen* and in his *Essay on Man*. Even so, his philosophical practice is somewhat different from his methodological theory. Just as his *Geschichte des Erkenntnisproblems* is not only an inestimable source of authentic historical knowledge, but interprets modern science and philosophy on the basis of a principle which is truly congenial with them (the concept of function over against that of substance), so—besides being a mine of information—his *Philosophy of Symbolical Forms* bears out general philosophical convictions and is interspersed with analyses which are of an *a priori* character and phenomenological in a broad sense, even though they remain fragmentary and are not ruled by so strict and clear a method as that of Husserl's eidetic and phenomenological reductions. There are, e.g., in the *Essay on Man*, the sections on experienced space and time; in the *Phaenomenologie der Erkenntnis*, the investigation into the inner unity of perception and conception; in an (unpublished) essay on Thomas Mann's *Lotte in Weimar*—one of the masterpieces of Cassirer

[71] Cassirer, "Group Concept and Perception Theory," 26.
[72] *Ibid.*

as a literary critic—an appreciation of the formative power of (symbolic) memory.[73] In "The Influence of Language upon the Development of Scientific Thought" (*Journal of Philosophy*, XXXIX, 309-327) and elsewhere, he investigates the nature of speech—those characters which are independent of a specific situation or the medium of a particular language; and with reference to Buehler's "*Organmodell*" (cf. Karl Buehler, *Sprachtheorie*, 1934), he points out how, in all speech as such, speaker, hearer, subject matter, etc., combine to form an intrinsic unity.

Moreover, though established on the basis of innumerable scientific findings, his 'symbolical forms' have an inner consistency and almost self-containedness which give even to prerational structures a quasi-rational cogency. Their components are related to one another in a way which is empirically discovered, but intuitively evident; and this super-factual evidence resembles that which illumines the relations between essences (general qualities), like color and extension, or red, orange and yellow (to give some primitive examples of the 'relation of ideas' which are a main subject of phenomenological inquiry).

The essential *forms* of language, myth, etc., come thus to complement the general *laws* in which the earlier neo-Kantianism had been too exclusively interested. Science is not the only transcendental fact which can be analyzed by way of transcendental philosophy. Even if ethics, aesthetics, and philosophy of religion were concerned with nothing but universal and necessary laws, "does the same hold true of their spiritual *content*, that is to say of morals, art, religion *themselves?*"—this is the question in terms of which Cassirer objects to the pan-nomism of Cohen and Natorp.[74] He did not try—as Natorp did—to identify "phenomenology of consciousness" with the psychological "description of ethical, aesthetic, religious *knowledge.*"[75] He realized the heterogeneous natures of these different ways of

---

[73] For this latter point cf. also *Philosophie der symbolischen Formen*, I, 22f; *Essay on Man*, 52f.

[74] *Philosophie der symbolischen Formen*, III, 66. It must be said, however, that Natorp himself rectified his earlier attitude in *Praktische Philosophie*: cf. especially 209.

[75] Natorp, *Allgemeine Psychologie*, 241; cf. 72, 94.

objectification and gave 'structuralism'[76]—the investigation into the 'inner forms' of language, myth, religion, etc.,—its place alongside the 'legalism' of knowledge, i.e., the search for general laws. By this way of aiming at a philosophical morphology he countenanced the phenomenological attempt to bare the inner nature, the typical structure of the acts, objects, and contents of consciousness.

To be sure, this convergence with phenomenology was more or less incidental in Cassirer's development. It was not only, and not even so much, phenomenology which stood behind his new version of neo-Kantian philosophy—Cassirer's emphasis on the 'inner form' derives, first of all, from the artistic ingredient of his own nature, the Goethian element of his being, and tallies with the Goethe revival in his generation. (Whereas Natorp, and above all, Cohen represented much more the moral idealism of Kant, Schiller and Fichte, ethics plays a very minor rôle in Cassirer's systematic writings). It is connected with the "wholism" of the later nineteenth and the twentieth centuries, which expressed itself in the mathematical group-theories as well as in the field-theories of physics and psychology, in Wölfflin's analysis of fine arts[77] as well as in the biology of thinkers like Kurt Goldstein, on whom Cassirer drew heavily for his *Phaenomenologie der Erkenntnis*. (In his theory of the organism Goldstein makes use of the concept of essence in a combination of Goethian and phenomenological thought which could not fail to strike a sympathetic vein in Cassirer.)

VI

The Symbolical Forms
Neo-Kantian and Phenomenological Philosophies of Man

The 'symbolical forms' figuring in a scale of representations —Cassirer distinguishes between the expressional, the strictly representative, and the significatory dimensions of the symbol[78]

---

[76] Cassirer, *Essay on Man*, 121.

[77] Cf. Cassirer, *Essay on Man*, 69.

[78] Cf., e.g., "Das Symbolproblem und seine Stellung im System der Philosophie," *Zeitschrift fuer Aesthetik und Allgemeine Kunstwissenschaft*, XXI, 303ff.

—remind us of the gamut of representations in Leibniz. Since the beginning of his philosophical career Cassirer was deeply familiar with Leibniz's philosophy; and this fact was doubtless instrumental in Cassirer's peculiar relation to Goethe, in so many regards an heir to Leibniz's mode of thinking.

In *Freiheit und Form* Cassirer had shown how the founder of modern philosophical aesthetics, Alexander Baumgarten, employed and transformed the Leibnizian schema of representation. Baumgarten inserted between the lower pole of obscure and confused perception and the highest point of clear and distinct conception a stage of singular perfection in clarity, yet without distinctness: the *perfectio phaenomenon*, the *cognitio perfecte sensitiva* of aesthetic experience. This is analogous to the rôle the non-scientific symbols of language and the myth have in Cassirer's philosophy: while showing a perfection of their own, they are, at the same time, preconditions of scientific and philosophical knowledge. "Each genuine and fundamental function of the spirit has one decisive feature in common with knowledge: in every one of them resides an archetypal power, not only an ectypal one."[79]

To vary a famous verse of Schiller's: we enter the land of knowledge only through the morning-gate of the myth. In a similar way language is said to figure in a dialectical movement in which it heals its own (logical) defects by setting itself "different and higher tasks." "Man can proceed from ordinary language to scientific language, to the language of logic, of mathematics, of physics."[80] And as regards religion—its ultimate *truth* seems ascertained only in a philosophy of religion like that of Schleiermacher (we shall see presently that its ultimate *aim*—the perfect balance between meaning (*Sinn*) and image (*Bild*)—is reached only in art).[81] In all this there are tokens and remnants of that scientism which is of the original dowry of neo-Kantian thought. The questions, how far theoretical knowledge can accept the honors assigned to it, how

[79] *Philosophie der symbolischen Formen*, I, 8.

[80] Cassirer, "The Influence of Language upon the Development of Scientific Thought" (*op. cit.*), 327.

[81] Cf. *Philosophie der symbolischen Formen*, II, 318ff. Cf. *infra*, 850ff.

congenial it is to the original impulses that live in language and religion, how much of these primitive motives will be lost on the way of their intellectual transformation—such questions are either not asked at all or answered in an unduly optimistic vein.

To be sure, the critic of each dialectical movement—and, therefore, of each dialectical treatment—is on difficult ground. His subject will always offer an aspect complementary to that under which he tries to attack it. In our case, the preliminary character of certain symbolical forms is made up for by their indispensable function: they are autonomous constituents in the system of culture. They have structural laws of their own which we ought to recognize, even if they do not fully participate in the canonic authority which Cohen's classicism attributed to the topmost formations of the objective mind. The phenomenologist will be inclined to challenge this whole dialectical construction of a self-contained cultural process. He will question the strange synthesis between the autonomous perfection of the forms of culture on the one hand and, on the other, the reduction of most of them to mere prefigurations of final truth—the truth of knowledge. This is, indeed, the tenor of Heidegger's review[82] of *Das mythische Denken,* the second volume of the *Philosophie der symbolischen Formen.* He argues that the systematic unity of the symbolic forms ought to be sought for, more radically than Cassirer does, in the original make-up of human existence (*Lebensform*); and intimates, for instance, that mythical thought is not fully elucidated by making it an expression of human creativeness. A fundamental concept like that of 'mana' betrays as its ultimate motive man's perplexity in the face of his tasks and his feelings of being overwhelmed by the world around him. Man does not extricate himself from such a predicament by acknowledging it in this fashion. The myth may thus testify to his resigning himself to the domination of uncontrollable powers as well as exhibit his constructive capacities. The world of the myth, though being in one sense the work of his creative imagination, may still fail to be man's proper world—the world in which he feels at home. The needy man, the man dependent

---

[82] Cf. *Deutsche Literaturzeitung* (1928), 1000-1012.

on mercy and subject to renunciation, disappears (here as well as elsewhere in Cassirer's writings) behind the screen of his specious cultural achievements.

With all its wealth of new materials, the *Philosophie der symbolischen Formen* is still neo-Kantian in its method. This can best be shown by tracing its plan back to suggestions contained in the tenth chapter of Natorp's *Allgemeine Psychologie*. Natorp recognizes as one "mighty and central province" of general psychology a

description of the formations of consciousness . . . which must not be restricted to the pure forms of knowledge, volition, and art, and, furthermore, to the pure foundations of religious consciousness, but may be extended to the . . . imperfect objectifications of opinion, belief, and imagination—regardless of, and unlimited by, their inner relation to truth and the realm of laws. . . . Even the most irresponsible opinion, the darkest superstition, the most boundless imagination make use of the categories of objective knowledge; they are still ways of objectification, however poor the means and impure the performance of this process may prove to be.[83]

And as regards "the almost inexhaustible fund of primitive knowledge" stored in the words and syntax of higher languages—there we have even "objectifications which, within the limits of their specific purpose, do not fall very short of the exactness and precision of scientific knowledge."[84] Almost the same applies to other subject-matters of "differential psychology"—the special social classes and orders and the ways in which the sexes and ages of man assert themselves.[85] In the terms of Natorp, it is largely to these "lower stages of objectification" that Cassirer's phenomenologies of language, the myth, etc., are devoted although he tried to distinguish them and their genuine value more clearly from the particular form of *intellectual* synthesis than Natorp may have done in his earlier writings.[86]

[83] Natorp, *Allgemeine Psychologie*, 241f.
[84] *Ibid.*, 99.
[85] *Ibid.*, 221.
[86] Cf. *Philosophie der symbolischen Formen* I, 8; III, 64ff. Cp., however, Natorp himself, *Praktische Philosophie*, 209.

The interpretation of life as a contest of objectifying functions tends to bear out the hermeneutic nature of neo-Kantian idealism. The way to man leads through the analysis of human expressions. Although testifying once more, to its great value, I have to hint at the limits of this procedure which cannot serve as a philosophical *passe-partout*.

Our discussion will be under the restriction set by the title of the present article. It cannot deal with the cardinal problem whether nature and function, locus and scope of the symbolic are defined by Cassirer in a way radical and consistent enough to make this idea of the symbol the firm corner-stone of a philosophical system.[87] Instead of probing these depths, I confine myself to such methodological remarks as are invited by our previous considerations.

Cassirer emphasizes that he deals with the *world* of man above all in order to pass through it to the *being* of man which is expressed in such a "world of his own—an 'ideal' world."[88] Perhaps, he is not quite consistent in speaking of 'ideal' worlds as links between man and "physical reality"—[89] terms which presuppose a concept of the real which neo-Kantianism fails to provide. Cassirer is always inclined to think of physical reality as reality proper. This attitude, however, is by no means an essential part of transcendental idealism: Cohen's conception of reality, e.g., is much more plastic and corresponds to the different ways of the human outlook. Take, e.g., the following passage from Cohen's *Jüdische Schriften* (III, 142):" Real, eminently real is what is not yet actual, but anticipated by way of hope so that its actuality is postulated in the vision of hope. Hope, the future, humanity belong together: they are the protest against taking reality only as what is actual in nature and history."

However this may be, it is quite in the neo-Kantian style of thought to see and define man according to the ways in which

---

[87] I have discussed this question in my review of *An Essay on Man*, see *Philosophy and Phenomenological Research*, VIII, 2 (1947), 283-287.

[88] Cassirer, *Essay on Man*, 228. Cf. *Philosophie der symbolischen Formen*, III, 104.

[89] Cf. *Essay on Man*, 24f.

he realizes himself in worlds of his own making. He is not seen in the ways he faces a reality and moves in a world in which he is never quite at home. "No longer," says Cassirer, "can man confront reality immediately, he cannot see it, as it were, face to face. Instead of dealing with the things themselves, man is in a sense constantly conversing with himself."[90] If that were really the case, we would know only objectifications, projections of our own being, and no objects at all—no things which may 'object' to us and to our existence. As a matter of fact, we come to deal with objects even through these objectifications. Just as it seems of the very nature of things in space to manifest themselves in certain spatial perspectives, thus in our intercourse with things they may present themselves in mythical, historical, linguistic, and other perspectives. Although qualifying our views, neither the spatial nor these personal aspects are separated from, and block the sight of, the things themselves. This is almost admitted by Cassirer in one of the following sentences: man "cannot see or know anything except by the interposition of this artificial medium," *sc.* the symbolic forms—; but even here we must take exception to the figurative use of the term "medium" which is as likely to be misunderstood as is the epithet "artificial" used in connection with it.[91]

That things present themselves in more or less adequate forms of appearance and modes of interpretation does not do away with the fact that they present *themselves.* On the other hand, the fact of this self-presentation is not incompatible with the recognition of something beyond cognition—beyond it, because it is ἐπέκεινα τῆς οὐσίας, beyond any definite form of being: the Alpha as well as the Omega of our life, i.e., not only the final point of all ways of determination, but also the dark yet everpresent ground from which all beings seem to rise, against

[90] *Essay on Man*, 25.

[91] *Ibid.* The same incongruity appears, e.g., in " 'Geist' und 'Leben' in der Philosophie der Gegenwart," *Neue Rundschau*, 1930, 254-259. Cf. pp. 870-874, *infra.* According to this passage reality can be reached only after passing through the sphere of the ideal. But, although this contention may be borne out by reference to mathematics, some fields of art, etc., it is far from being universally valid. The ideal factors are not always so separable from the real ones as to allow such a dialectical movement to take place between them.

which they stand out for some time and into the embrace of which they seem to return after their time is over (κατὰ τὴν τοῦ Χρόνου τάξιν). This principle of origin is of a metaphysical order, not a logical one. It lays a foundation which cannot be laid by such a principle of thought as Cohen tried to establish.[92] The pathos of this metaphysical experience—the fountain-head of all religious feeling—is conspicuously absent in Cassirer's work.

The neo-Kantian pan-methodology[93] is the complement of the "critical" attitude which separates reality proper from the forms of appearance and leads many of its representatives to an anti-metaphysical position, an unconcern with reality *par excellence*. It is partly for these reasons that the chapter on "History" in *An Essay on Man* fails to deal either with historical reality as such or with the historical nature (the 'historicity') of man—problems which have played a more and more prominent rôle in the phenomenology of the last twenty years. Cassirer takes here a somewhat belated part in the methodological discussion, which took place, around 1900, between historians and neo-Kantian philosophers such as Karl Lamprecht, Eduard Meyer, and Heinrich Rickert. In contrast to Natorp (*Praktische Philosophie*, §§ 66ff), he treats history almost exclusively as historical science, not so much historical science as a variety of historical consciousness and as continuous with historical life and historical tradition.[94]

History as found in classical writers like Ranke stands with science among the refined, perfected forms of civilization, "an indispensable instrument for building up our human universe."[95] These regions are the birth-place of logical idealism. We have seen, however, that Cassirer tried to deal not only with the super-structure of highest objectifications, but also with the primary phenomena of human life. The intermediate forms of the myth, language, etc., are closer to naïve life and cannot

---

[92] Cf. Cohen, *Logik der reinen Erkenntnis*, 32.
[93] "There is not any difference more radical than that of method," says Cohen (*Jüdische Schriften*, III, 143).
[94] Cf. *Essay on Man*, 206.
[95] *Ibid.*

claim the universal validity of the exact sciences.[96] But whatever
may be the character of the forms he takes as his starting point,
they represent *eo ipso*, i.e., by their very nature as forms and
objectifications, certain human achievements. Thus, they put
man from the very beginning into a, perhaps, too favorable
light. The image of man is not independent of the setting in
which it appears. To be sure, there is a distinction to be made
between a form itself and its content. Through scientific history, e.g., we become more thoroughly acquainted with man—
man's joys and sorrows, possibilities and dangers, his passions
and sufferings, his greatness and defects. Still, the objectivity
of this representation has an effect similar to the mastery of the
artist: the wonderful polish of the mirror reconciles us with the
sadness of the image; the perfect representation succeeds in
outbalancing the imperfections of what is represented in such a
way.[97]

Cassirer's own philosophy of man, moreover, shows a quasi
superhuman aloofness by which he seems to outdo even the
composure of the historian and the artist. At first glance, neither
the tenor nor the themes of the *Essay on Man* betray any effect
of the crisis of man in our eschatological age—not to speak of
the experiences of the author himself who was driven from land
to land as a victim of racial persecution and global war. Only on
second thought does the reader come to realize that Cassirer's
interest in myth is partly prompted by a present day revival of
mythical thought, and that his studies in mythology may well
serve to understand the effectiveness of mythical symbolism
and check its misuse. On the other hand, the economic problems
of human existence are scarcely mentioned at all; and even the
forms of political life are passed over as being "a late product
of the civilizing process."[98] The process of civilization, the
movement of self-propelling pure forms (so to speak), seems
to be something like a metaphysical absolute; it goes on

---

[96] Cf., e.g., *Philosophie der symbolischen Formen*, III, 14, 357f.

[97] Cf. *Essay on Man*, 149. Cf., however, in qualification of what follows,
Cassirer's posthumous writing, *The Myth of the State* (1946).

[98] *Ibid.*, 63.

smoothly and essentially undisturbed by the regrettable accidents of our own life.

Whereas as early as in 1902 a William James dared to remind his audiences that "our civilization is founded on the shambles, and every individual existence goes out in a lonely spasm of helpless agony,"[99] Cassirer's happy eyes saw man even as late as 1944 only in the light of his cultural products, not in the darkness of his earthly struggle, nor in the hours of his despair and in the loneliness of his death. In difference from Aristotle, Cassirer defines man somewhat loosely as the *animal symbolicum*—in the sense of the *animal symbola formans* or, as we would have preferred to say, the *animal imaginativum*. This latter formula would imply an allusion to imagination as the central root of human nature, "our destiny, our being's heart and home;" but, although being in accordance with ideas of Hume and Kant,[100] of Coleridge and Wordsworth, to give to 'imagination' so dominant a place would meet with Cassirer's aversion to any 'image' theory of knowledge.[101] Although he stressed its importance repeatedly,[102] imagination did not become a patent factor in his definition of man.

The noble Aristotelian tradition of defining man by his highest capacity—reason—is slightly modified by Ernst Cassirer. The latter's definition of man gives a specific difference—the symbolizing power—which is said to extend further down than does reason.[103] His statement fails, however, to grasp the true significance of Aristotle's approach to the problem. Aristotle does *not* offer a *pars pro toto* definition.[104] In his psychology Aristotle tries to show how reason functions as the formal cause of our whole being, and how man's development is to be understood as the growing self-assertion of reason.

[99] W. James, *Varieties of Religious Experience* (Modern Library), 160.

[100] Cf. Cassirer himself, e.g., in " 'Geist' und 'Leben' in der Philosophie der Gegenwart," *Neue Rundschau* (1930), 257 (cf. 871 *infra*).

[101] Cf. Cassirer, *Essay on Man*, 57.

[102] Cf. Cassirer's "Kant und das Problem der Metaphysik," *Kantstudien*, XXXVI (1931), 8f., 18; "The Concept of Group and the Theory of Perception," *Philosophy and Phenomenological Research*, V (1944), 32f.

[103] *Essay on Man*, 25.

[104] *Ibid.*

Moreover, Cassirer loses the great advantage of the Aristotelian definition—its dynamic possibilities. Whereas 'animal symbolicum' adds only a specific difference to the generic one, 'animal rationale,' by showing man between the heights to which he can attain and the depths to which he can sink, may indicate the permanent tension and strife between man's animal and rational natures, the promise as well as the danger of human freedom. To be sure, Aristotle himself did not exhaust the dramatic potentialities implied in his definition. The instability of the human condition in the realm between the two poles—pure rationality and mere animality—is seen in contrast to the blessedness of the divine being, but this contrast is not fully developed in its tragic implications. He is more interested in normal mentality, in the organic health of human life than in its extremities and conflicts. The same may be said of Cassirer. He was not a tortured soul. Both in his writings and in his appearance he made the impression of an Apollonian nature. He was a neo-Kantian in the sense that his intellectual temper was congenial to the Kant whom he loved and admired. What he said of Kant, applies to himself and explains the high pleasure we experience in reading his works: He "is and remains a thinker of the *Enlightenment*—in the most radiant and sublime sense of this word: he aspires toward light and clarity even when reflecting on the darkest depths and 'radices' of being."[105] Yet, we cannot help feeling that the darkness of these depths is not sufficiently represented in Cassirer's own philosophical outlook. Thus he extolled the positive aspect of existence: the self-transcendence of life into spirit, of πρᾶξις into ποίησις, of organic formation into the formation of ideas and symbols: he remonstrates on the metaphysical hypostatizing of Life and the Spirit, on their being taken for two hostile entities (as in Klages) or for two heterogeneous powers which are on precarious terms with one another (as in Scheler).[106] Yet, like Aristotle, he sees human freedom too exclusively in the growing

---

[105] Cassirer, "Kant und das Problem der Metaphysik," *Kantstudien*, XXXVI, (1931), 24.

[106] Cf. " 'Geist' und 'Leben' . . .", *op. cit.*, 244-264; also Part III of the present volume, 862-880.

independence from the senses—manifested as it seems by the processes of symbolization. He does not really plunge into the abyss of freedom in the human soul—that freedom which is, at once, man's distinction and his temptation, man's pride and his torment—and he does not ask how human freedom can coexist with human finiteness. He is so engrossed by the dialectics of the spirit as "a new turn and conversion of life itself" that he all but forgets about the labor-pains of such a dialectical turn—this perennial turn and, therefore perennial crisis of human existence.

It is of the very nature of human freedom that the outcome of this crisis and, therefore, the continuation of the objectifying process can never be foreseen. We know it again: just as the individual person, so is the whole of cultural life threatened by death. But in the radiance of his own being and in his admiration for the triumphal procession of culture, Cassirer was inclined to neglect its sad, tragic, even suicidal traits. Yet life creates idols as well as true symbols; the work of the spirit drains man's vital energies; there are all the frustrations of human endeavor; and man chokes to death in the very shelters (Jaspers' *Gehäuse*) and is slain by the very arms he built himself. Cassirer's philosophy suffers from too much light; still it is a noble and finished account of *come l'uom s'eterna*. "The various modes of [his]expression . . . . have a life of their own, a sort of eternity by which they survive man's individual and ephemeral existence."[107]

A corollary to their assertion of the autonomous course of the objectifying process is Natorp's and Cassirer's insistence that, both genetically and systematically, individual self-knowledge is a very late product of consciousness. Cassirer agrees with Max Scheler's theory in the contention that experience is at first quasi anonymous and only subsequently attributed either to myself or to other Egos.[108] This phenomenological description may be correct as to the origin and qualification of the *contents* of *human* consciousness; but it applies neither to the noetic side of ex-

---

[107] Cassirer, *Essay on Man*, 224.
[108] Max Scheler, *Wesen und Formen der Sympathie*, 284ff. Cf. Cassirer, *Philosophie der symbolischen Formen*, III, 100-107.

periences, i.e., to the actualization (*Vollzugsmodus*) of these contents, nor to the pure Ego of phenomenological reflection, which is to be distinguished from the inner perception, the 'natural' self-knowledge of man.[109]

In Cassirer the two levels of analysis—that of empirical or even eidetic psychology of human life and that of transcendental philosophy of pure consciousness—are not always as clearly separated as these subtle problems require. But, although in the case of empathy psychological findings are played off against the data of original constitution (as these appear in the light of transcendental reflection), usually the transcendental process of objectification is given the upper hand over anthropological facts.[110]

We have seen that Cassirer's pre-occupation with the boundless objectifying process almost blinds him to the essential limitations of human life. This applies, above all, to the life of the individual.[111] Cassirer's main concern is, like Kant's, with the

---

[109] Cf. the dissertation of Husserl's assistant Edith Stein, *Zum Problem der Einfuehlung*, 1917, 30-39. Edith Stein reproduces fairly well Husserl's own teaching on empathy. I regret that in the present article references to Husserl's work must be brief and may appear, therefore, in spots somewhat cryptical or dogmatic. But it is obviously impossible within the framework of this essay even to attempt to render Husserl's subtle analyses with any degree of adequacy.

[110] With the neo-Kantians Cassirer used to distinguish very carefully between the transcendental and the psychological or anthropological methods. (He did it as late as in 1931—in his discussion of Heidegger's "Kant und das Problem der Metaphysik:" *Kantstudien* XXXVI, 15f. But whereas the *Philosophie der symbolischen Formen* was thought to conquer new territory for transcendental idealism, *An Essay on Man*—for the most part an abstract of the former work—is obviously an experiment in philosophical anthropology. Is the purity of the transcendental method impaired by the anthropological material of the *Philosophie der symbolischen Formen*, or is the anthropological turn in the *Essay* impeded by the demands of neo-Kantian transcendentalism?

[111] Husserl's position differs from that of Cassirer in so far as Husserl's transcendental Ego, although not being essentially finite either, is from the outset a single Ego, not a universal subject as such: this Ego apperceives itself only afterwards as a member of a monadic universe, i.e., of an intersubjective sphere of transcendental Egos, and ends with identifying itself in a certain way with a particular and finite human being—part of the transcendentally constituted human world (cf. the fifth of *Husserl's Méditations Cartésiennes*). The analysis of intersubjectivity was complemented in Husserl's *courses* (e.g. on *Ethics*) by that of interpersonal relationships which have their ultimate end in constituting the real world of true humanity. It must be admitted, however, that neither

'intelligible substrate of humanity,' not with human existence.[112] The problems of individual birth and death—personal problems rather than merely creatural ones—are scarcely handled at all (death only in a negative way). While—under the influence of Kierkegaard, Jaspers, and Heidegger—the second generation of phenomenologists was almost obsessed by this latter problem, inclined as they were to see life only in the light (and the shadow) of death, Cassirer adhered to a tradition that prevails from Descartes to Eucken and Caird: he recognized in man's *knowledge* of his finiteness the very dawn of the infinite.

This was in fact not only the general tenor of his discussion with Heidegger at Davos; it was also his main objection to the sort of existentialism which Oskar Becker tried to build into the very foundation of mathematics. Whatever the truth-value of either position may be, it is symptomatic that in the well-known definition of the mathematical procedure—'the mastery of the infinite through finite means'—Becker stressed the element of the finite, Cassirer that of the infinite.[113]

To introduce a philosophical anthropology under the subtitle of a "philosophy of human culture" implies (as indicated above) a foregone conclusion: it anticipates the answer to the first question of the *Essay on Man:* "What is man?" It eliminates in one stroke from the field of research such profound experiences as love and hatred, fear and trembling, shame and repentance, guilt and sin, and such revealing traits as concentration and distraction and innumerable others—so far at least as their existential meaning is not exhausted by their contribution to the forms of cultural life. It neglects man's inability to express certain experiences in an adequate way as well as his unique capacity

---

Husserl nor Cassirer fully developed all three dimensions implied in the idea of self-realization—which are (1) the awareness of the individual Self as determined and limited by the Other (Thou); (2) the fulfilment of one's own being in this very relationship; and (3) finding one's place in the real world by way of interpersonal communication.

[112] Cf. Cassirer, "Kant und das Problem der Metaphysik," *op. cit.*, 18; H. Cohen, *Ethik des reinen Willens*, 3.

[113] Cf. Oskar Becker, *Mathematische Existen* (1927); Cassirer, *Philosophie der symbolischen Formen*, III, 469ff. It ought to be acknowledged, however, that at this point the difference is one of two generations rather than of two schools.

for going into hiding by the very means of communication.

Cassirer did not and could not proceed the way Kierkegaard, Jaspers and, within their sphere, the great tragedians and also such novelists as Joseph Conrad and Franz Kafka did: he could not 'define' man with a view to the extreme situations (*Grenzsituationen*) in which man's true being, his greatness and weakness come out—most eloquently in the very moments of his growing silent and succumbing to destiny. (Personal 'destiny' is not a category that fits into a dialectical schema of the objective mind.)

Why should philosophy rely entirely on previous objectifications without doing some objectifying of its own? Why should it be confined to the conceptualization of previous expressions? It may well discover and even prefigure new human possibilities or reveal moods and modes of life which—*von Menschen nicht gewusst oder nicht bedacht*—waited for the penetration and the candidness of a great thinker to be unearthed. The claim to make such a new, original beginning, to lay a new, absolute foundation not only of thought, but (through thought and even a very abstract thought) of life itself, was the secret behind Husserl's increasingly priestly and almost prophetic attitude. His phenomenology was designed to overcome "the radical crisis in the life of the European man."[114] And due to the specific phenomenological impulse and approach to things, a similar absolute claim lives (*mutatis mutandis*) in the phenomenological philosophies of Scheler, Heidegger, and Nicolai Hartmann. Cassirer, on the other hand, remained in accordance with the hermeneutic principles of critical idealism when he restricted himself to the noble task of a sovereign interpreter of given expressions. He felt far too modest for the rôle of a path-finder of life—and was far too honest for that of a false prophet.

Cassirer's definition of man as the *animal symbolicum* is intended to absorb both of the Aristotelian definitions—man as the rational and man as the social animal. He considers the first definition too narrow, the second too broad: the social character of human life needs to be specified by reference to language,

---

[114] Cf. Husserl, "Die Krisis der europäischen Wissenschaften und die Phaenomenologie," *Philosophia*, I (1936), 77ff.

myth, art, religion, science as "the elements and the constitutive conditions of this higher form of society."[115] But since this remark appears only in the 'Summary and Conclusion' of the *Essay on Man*, its implications are not sufficiently elaborated. The different symbolical forms which are meant to establish the specific difference of human social life are not really evinced as *means* of *personal intercourse*. The communicative function of language, e.g., is much less prominent in Cassirer's writings than its representative nature, i.e., its relation to things, its inner form, its prefiguring of scientific concepts.[116]

Besides, it is questionable whether the cultural media in which human relationships develop are the only distinctive marks of intersubjective and, above all, interpersonal life. There are many modes and dimensions of these relationships which are, of course, reflected and evolved in myth and language, religion and art, but have a structure and dynamics of their own in the very actuality and, as it were, welling up of human intercourse. These original relations between I, Thou, and We, the essential attitudes prevailing between the first, the second and the third person, the specific characteristics of social, socially conditioned, socially addressed acts, etc., are studied in the often masterly descriptive analyses of Husserl, Reinach and Scheler, Pfaender and Geiger, Edith Stein and Dietrich von Hildebrand, Theodor Litt and Karl Loewith. The approach of these scholars is more direct, their patience and subtlety of description greater than Cassirer's, even though he may be superior to them in the careful evaluation of the most modern scientific results.

VII

Philosophy and Religion

Since, according to Cassirer, to know means to relate, the whole of being is defined as a net of relations. Man, however, is not (or not primarily) defined by his peculiar relationships—by

[115] Cassirer, *Essay on Man*, 25f., 223.

[116] This impression is slightly modified but not overthrown by the discussion of the I-Thou relation in *Zur Logik der Kulturwissenschaften* (particularly 44), a book published in Sweden in 1942 and not available when the present article was written.

the ways he relates himself and finds himself related to things,
to his fellows—perhaps to God. He is not defined in these ways,
i.e., his limits are not delineated, his concrete determination is
not given through the correlations which prevail between re-
sponsive and responsible beings.

Since the dialectical, more or less anonymous and almost
mythical process of objectification and transformation is always
considered first[117] (even in aesthetics[118]), *personalism*—also
personalism in religion—has little chance to be embraced in
this form of anthropology. To be sure, Cassirer recognized religion as giving scope to the feeling for individuality;[119] and,
following Cohen's example, he saw as the meaning and merit of
Jewish prophetism the insistence on a moral and spiritual relationship between God and man—the most intimate correlation
of two persons—I and Thou. But, just as in Cassirer the prophetic spirit is a theme and not an element of thought (as it
was in H. Cohen), the I-Thou relationship—either between
God and man or within the human sphere proper—never became a pivot of Cassirer's philosophy (in contradistinction to
Cohen in his old age, Ferdinand Ebner, Franz Rosenzweig,
Martin Buber, and the theologians around Karl Barth[120]).
The nature of this relationship was not expounded by him in
the thoroughgoing way we find, e.g. (on the basis of suggestions by Pfaender, Scheler and Reinach), in Kurt Stavenhagen's
Absolute Stellungnahmen (1925). Cassirer does not see nor, as
it were, locate man in this paradoxical and precarious relation

---

[117] Cf. e.g., *Philosophie der symbolischen Formen*, II, 289f.

[118] *Essay on Man*, 141ff, 154, 164; but cf. 226ff.

[119] *Essay on Man*, 96.

[120] The relation between Kant and Cohen on the one hand, the school of Karl
Barth on the other, is mediated through Kant's distinction between the noumenal
and the phenomenal worlds, corresponding to that between the infinite intellect
of God and the finite intellect of man, and through Cohen's principle of origin
(Prinzip des Ursprungs) which is no longer the central problem in Cassirer's
philosophy. For this relation cf. Heinrich Barth, *Das Problem des Ursprungs in der
platonischen Philosophie* (1921), Emil Brunner, *Erlebnis, Erkenntnis und Glaube*
(1923) and *Religionsphilosophie evangelischer Theologie* (1927), Max Strauch,
Die Theologie Karl Barths (1926), H. W. van der Vaart Smith, "Die Schule Karl
Barths und die Marburger Philosophie," *Kantstudien*, XXXIV (1929), 333-350.

between the finite and the Infinite. Without annihilating altogether the duality involved in any relation as such, he pushes it into the direction of a mystic union, where nothing happens *to* the soul that did not happen *in* it eternally, and where the I and the Thou are poles of a movement in which neither of them has the status of an independent value.[121]

This account of religious experience, however, neglects the essential inequality between the terms of a relation which man does not feel able to determine himself, whereas he himself feels determined by it; a relation, moreover, in which God is grasped by man only when man is 'grasped' by God, and as far as God deigns to reveal himself to man. (That is the reason why in the Bible man is entitled to give names to all living creatures, whereas only God Himself can disclose His own name, i.e., His very essence.)

According to Cassirer man learns to recognize his own capacities as a free agent by projecting them into the figure of his God.[122] In this way it is *man* who is understood in the symbol of his God, instead of God's being approached, however inadequately, through the human symbols. The God-man relationship in which man is confronted by another, infinitely superior (if not altogether different) being is re-absorbed by one of the forms of the cultural process, one of the modes of objectification. Offerings and prayers, e.g.,

are typical forms of religious expression which do not *lead* from a previously determined and well described sphere of the Ego to an equally fixed sphere of the divine, but serve to *determine* either sphere and draw the limits between them in always different ways. What the religious process takes to be the spheres of the divine and the human are not two strictly exclusive realms of being rigidly separated from one another at the outset by spatial and qualitative boundaries: rather we are dealing here with an original form of the religious spirit's *movement* the opposite poles of which do not cease to flee from and seek one another.[123]

But what is this spirit, if it is not the spirit of man? And

---

[121] Cf. *Philosophie der symbolischen Formen*, II, 283ff, 307.

[122] *Ibid.*, 252, 261.

[123] *Ibid.*, 283.

what is this movement, if it is not the "performance of the mythical-religious consciousness" bent on building up its own symbolism without recognizing anything beyond itself?[124] These ideas are contrary to the development neo-Kantianism has taken, for instance, in the later Natorp. He protested against "drawing the divine into the human realm, the realm of human culture." And he revised his own former *Religion within the Limits of Humanity* by "seeking religion not any longer within, though just as little without the limits of humanity, but precisely in its very limit"—the one ultimate limit which marks man's difference from the absolute One.[125]

To proclaim the religious experience a form of cultural achievement runs counter to two of its mainsprings. First, to the neediness of the individual to whom the presence of God is proved by—yea, consists in—His gracious assistance (this is implied in the Eheje Asher Eheje of the God of the Bible). This dependence on God finds a more specific expression in the second motive: man's reliance on divine mercy because he realizes his incapacity to perform satisfactorily the moral task of 'objectification' which is assigned to him as a moral agent— the establishment of the "kingdom of ends." Although man is honored by his *moral* responsibility—as a moral agent he bows only to the moral law within himself—,he is humbled by the facts of his *religious* consciousness—and rehabilitated only from above (a statement which needs to be qualified differently in different religions).

These facts have been in the forefront of Cohen's philosophy of religion. They recede into the background in Cassirer's analysis of religious thought. He took religion for the new moral form of ancient mythical contents—the spiritualization, e.g., of the external purity prescriptions and prohibitions of the taboo system.[126] They are not abolished; but what counts in religion is only the purity of the heart and the inner obligation. Yet this dialectical description will not do. Religion is not only the moral transformation—*Aufhebung*—of the naïve mythical

---

[124] Cf. *Ibid.*, 291f.

[125] Natorp, *Platos Ideenlehre*, 2nd edition, 512; cf. 468.

[126] Cf. *Philosophie der symbolischen Formen*, II, 294; *Essay on Man*, 103ff.

consciousness and a declaration of man's moral freedom; it is also man's abdication of moral autarchy, his declaration of absolute dependence.

But even the purely ethical correlation between I and Thou, between man and the Highest in person (the pure and eternal form of religious consciousness which Cassirer seemed to recognize with H. Cohen, presenting as it does the highest transfiguration of formerly mythical motives[127])—this concrete personal relation comes to be weakened and quasi-'neutralized' at the end: Cassirer makes it a relation between man and the *Whole*—or, rather, between man and the principle(s) of the Whole, the laws of the Universe. Thus he shifts the consummation of religion to a realm beyond the limits of religious consciousness itself—to the realm of systematic thought: he finds it in Leibniz's monadism and in his *characteristica universalis,* and in Schleiermacher's philosophy of religion. Now

an event derives its religious significance not any longer from its content, but merely from its form; its character as a symbol does not depend on what it is and whence it directly comes, but from the spiritual aspect under which it is placed, from the "reference" to the universe which it bears thanks to the religious feeling and religious thought.[128]

The neo-Kantian primacy of the method reasserts itself once more over against the "inner form" of the original contents of experience, and against the very insight which he, like Natorp, gained in the nineteen twenties: that the character of any synthesis depends on the peculiar nature of its material contents, and that "the specific 'form' of the mythical 'meaning' as well as of the theoretical one is expressed, more profoundly and more clearly than in any complex formation, in the relatively simple, the truly 'primitive' structures."[129]

In a similar way the existential tension which the finite individual feels in view of the infinite God is, as it were, shifted to the objective sphere: we are told that the religious attitude differs from the mythical one by clearly recognizing the in-

---

[127] Cf. *Philosophie der symbolischen Formen* II, 278ff.

[128] *Ibid.,* II, 319.

[129] Cassirer, "Zur Theorie des Begriffs," *Kantstudien,* XXXIII (1928), 136.

commensurability between religious image and religious meaning.[130] The inadequacy of the religious *symbol* is emphasized by Cassirer almost to the point of neglecting the insufficiency of the human *being*. The gap between the human and the divine is said to be *"created"* by consciousness itself in order to be closed again by the same consciousness.[131]

As mentioned above, the shortcomings (not of man but) of religion are to be made up for by another form of cultural creativity—by philosophy and art. The tension between image and meaning, the fact that the symbol (*Sinnbild*) cannot wholly surpass the limits of sensory appearance (*Sinnenbild*) is of the very nature of religious experience. In art, however, a perfect equilibrium is reached between the spheres of the sensory and the spiritual. Here "the image does not appear as a thing by itself which, in turn, affects the mind, but has become a pure expression of one's own creative power for the mind."[132]

As represented by the *Philosophy of the Symbolical Forms*, the dialectics of consciousness seems to proceed beyond the religious level to issue in philosophy of religion on the one hand, and in art on the other. It is doubtful, however, whether either art or philosophy is fully equipped to play the superior part assigned to it. A phenomenology of art and religion, e.g., will have to ask whether the alleged dialectical movement from religion to art is not, at least, counterbalanced by a corresponding movement leading from art to religion. In an article on "Art and Religion" I have tried to indicate such an aspect, from which art can be considered a prefigurement of religion, and the fruit of religious experience appears the ultimate fulfilment of the specious promise which is embodied in the flower of art.[133]

[130] *Philosophie der symbolischen Formen*, II, 290ff.

[131] *Ibid.*, 284.

[132] *Ibid.*, 320. I refer, however, to note 39 as regards the slightly different attitude in a passage of the *Essay on Man* (151): there "the sense of beauty" is taken to be "the susceptibility to the dynamic life of forms."

[133] Fritz Kaufmann, "Art and Religion," *Philosophy and Phenomenological Research*, I (1941), 463-469. A somewhat similar position can be found in Paul Haeberlin, *Allgemeine Aesthetik* (1929).

It is quite true (as Cassirer stresses repeatedly[134]) that a work of art is the more universal in character, the more deeply individual it proves to be. Yet this universality is not only flavored, but also qualified by the individual point of view. The work of art incarnates the spirit of the artist's world—the world which is the common denominator of his impressions and the objective correlate of his productive reaction. This universal representation gives to his work an inner infinitude which is, neverthless, (to speak with Spinoza) an *infinitum in suo genere*, rather than the *absolute infinitum*. While his point of view serves to integrate the phenomena into a whole, the artist cannot but sift them, accenting what is essential under his aspect, while neglecting what does not add to his image of the world. The artist conjures up what may be called the genius of the universe; but this genius speaks the language and voices the experience of the author. Man succeeds in mastering his impressions as far as he can extend the mastery of his expression.

The religious prophet, on the other hand, is not the author of his speech nor does he find 'composure' in the 'composition' of his masterwork. He feels himself to be the mouth-piece of a voice which is no more his own and speaks in terms which may be beyond his grasp. Through the voice of man sounds here that of his God. This is a difference of type, of meaning and of claim which is to be acknowledged whether or not the disparity between the aesthetic experience and the religious one derives from two really different existences—God and man. This difference between the Absolute and the finite is more radical than that between two poles within a movement whose dynamics is the true Absolute in Cassirer's philosophy.

The two types of experience in question have to be recognized as heterogeneous, even though they may be found in a personal union. There is the element of poetic fascination in all religious expression, since in God himself the *mysterium fascinosum* is one with the *mysterium tremendum*. And religious art may bear witness not only to some congeniality be-

[134] Cf. *Freiheit und Form*, 312ff, 363ff; *Kants Leben und Lehre*, 354; *Essay on Man*, 143.

tween the artist and the *Creator Spiritus mundi,* but also to man's personal response to this spirit and its claims and to his trustful invocation of it. In ecstatic experiences, such as Rilke's at the time of the *Sonnets to Orpheus* and the *Elegies of Duino* (experiences which almost destroy the framework of human nature), the artist's state of mind comes close to that of the prophet—though even here the measure of man comes finally to prevail. *"Denn das Schöne ist Nichts als des Schrecklichen Anfang, den wir noch grade ertragen."*[135] The poet as such is always victorious in his work, whereas the religious person conquers only in his absolute surrender.

Although the essential differences are clear, the actual boundaries between both states are often hidden—so as to leave a man like Kierkegaard tragically uncertain whether he has only the talents of a religious poet or the call of a religious witness. But the thirst of the religious person is not satisfied by the draughts of poetical imagination. The distinctive gift of man, the gift of thinking in terms of open possibilities,[136] needs to be complemented by the recognition of an ultimate reality which is not a product of objective determination, but the very origin, the *fiat* behind both facts and *fieri* of experience.

The reliance on the autonomy of culture with all its symbolic forms is challenged by the religious experience in which man ceases to exploit his own possibilities. In this experience man sees himself determined not only by what amounts to a process of self-realization (and self-liberation)[137] or by that anonymous process of the "categorial constitution" whose secret author and hero he actually is himself, but fundamentally by a power which is not only beyond the empirical self but also beyond the multiform unity of transcendental synthesis.

All this had to be said—not in order to substitute for Cassirer's never fully developed philosophy of religion a sketch of our own making, but to show how the implications of this cultural immanentism compare to the claims of religious experi-

---

[135] R. M. Rilke, from the first of the *Duineser Elegien.*
[136] Cf. *Essay on Man,* 56-62.
[137] Cf. *ibid.,* 228.

ence. We do not shut our eyes to the possibility that these
claims cannot be ultimately verified; but their eventual fulfilment has to be true to the very nature of the religious intentions. This is not only a necessary postulate of the phenomenological method—a principle which Cassirer would have been
the last to repudiate; it is an ideal to which Husserl's phenomenology has actually tried to live up even on this point, i.e., in
spite of his own emphasis on the absoluteness of the process of
pure consciousness. I am referring to the modest hypothetical
reflections on the theological problem in the *Ideen*.[138] They
have been acclaimed even by so strictly Christian thinkers as
Theodor Haecker[139] and proved instrumental in the beginnings
of a genuine phenomenology of religion.

Husserl speaks of God's transcendence in contradistinction to
that of the Ego and that of the world. None of the three is an
immanent part of consciousness as such. But, whereas the pure
Ego and pure consciousness cannot be disconnected, it is different with God and consciousness. Consciousness is confronted by
God just as it is confronted by the world; yet these two forms
of transcendence belong to opposite dimensions: God's transcendence is "as it were the polar opposite to the transcendence
of the world." But whereas, according to Husserl, the real
world is relative to pure consciousness, God as the ordering
principle of absolute consciousness would be absolute himself[140]
—though again in a different sense both from the absoluteness of
myself *qua* Ego of the phenomenological reduction and from
that of the *Alter Ego*, or rather, all the other "transcendental
Egos" who are "constituted" within my consciousness by way
of empathy, yet recognized as being essentially my equals.[141]
The divine being "would be an 'Absolute' in a sense entirely
different from the absoluteness of consciousness—while, on the
other hand, it is a transcendent being in an entirely different

---

[138] Husserl, *Ideen zu einer reinen Phaenomenologie und phaenomenologischen
Philosophie*, 96f, 110f.

[139] Cf. e.g., Haecker's *Nachwort* to Kierkegaard's *Der Begriff des Auserwählten*,
344f.

[140] Husserl, *Ideen*, 96.

[141] Husserl, *Méditations Cartésiennes, Méditation V*.

sense from that in which the world is understood to be transcendent."[142]

What holds for "absolute consciousness" in Husserl's sense,
applies *a fortiori* to finite human consciousness. The recognition
of such an absolute transcendence would doom the enterprise of
a predominantly 'humanistic' anthropology like Cassirer's. It
would make it impossible to write an *Essay on Man* with exclusive regard to a 'Philosophy of Human Culture' and would,
thus, prevent an idolization of the cultural process—the danger
which threatens this neo-Kantian idealism. Man's true nature
would not be seen in his cultural achievements alone, but in his
failures and limitations as well. And—but this assertion has to
be *made* true, in order to *be* true—man would be at his best
where culture becomes cult again: a praise of the Highest and an
offering to Him:

> "... *die Erde grünt*
> *Und stille vor den Sternen liegt, den*
> *Betenden gleich in den Staub geworfen,*
>
> *Freiwillig überwunden die lange Kunst*
> *Vor jenen Unnachahmbaren da; er selbst*
> *Der Mensch mit eigner Hand zerbrach, die*
> *Hohen zu ehren, sein Werk der Künstler.*"[143]

FRITZ KAUFMANN

DEPARTMENT OF PHILOSOPHY
THE UNIVERSITY OF BUFFALO

[142] Husserl, *Ideen*, III.
[143] Hölderlin, "Stimme des Volks."

Ernst Cassirer

"SPIRIT" AND "LIFE" IN CONTEMPORARY PHILOSOPHY

"SPIRIT" AND "LIFE" IN CONTEMPORARY PHILOSOPHY*

I

AMONG the minor works of Heinrich von Kleist may be found a brief essay in which the author has succeeded in setting forth one of the philosophical problems of his era with all the brevity and succinctness, all the cogency and penetration which mark his incomparable prose style. Kleist attains this pregnancy of thought by capturing content of it in the form of a tale by the telling and creation of which the whole art of the epic poet is revealed. He starts out from the recollection of an occurrence which he depicts as one experienced by himself. A youth, excelling not only in physical beauty but also in the naturalness of his whole bearing and demeanor, comes to lose this attractiveness the moment he accidentally becomes aware of it; and once lost, it proves to be irrecoverable by will-power or by any conscious effort. The consequence which Kleist draws from this is that nature and consciousness, beauty and reflective thought belong to different realms and stand in a relation of polar tension and opposition to each other. Insofar as the one comes to the fore, the other must give way. Confronted by the bright daylight of consciousness, by reflection's piercing ray which strikes it to the heart, beauty must needs pale and vanish. "We can see that just insofar as reflection grows weaker and more obscure, in the organic world, beauty emerges all the brighter and more overpowering. Nevertheless, just as two lines diverging from a point, extended to infinity, will suddenly come together again on the other side; or, just as the image in

---

* From the original German essay, " 'Geist' und 'Leben' in der Philosophie der Gegenwart," which appeared in *Die Neue Rundschau* (Berlin und Leipzig, 1930—I, pp. 244-264), translated specifically for this volume by Robert Walter Bretall and Paul Arthur Schilpp.

a concave mirror, when extended to the infinite, suddenly emerges again directly before us: even so, when knowledge has, so to speak, traversed the infinite, beauty once again will disclose itself, so that simultaneously it will appear in its purest form in that human organism which either is without consciousness at all or has an infinite consciousness—*i.e.*, in the marionette or in God." For man, once driven from the paradise of immediacy—man who has once partaken of the tree of knowledge and therewith has forever left behind the limits of merely natural existence, of life which is unconscious of itself —for man it follows that he must traverse his appointed orbit, in order at the end of his road to find his way back again to its beginning. That is the fate imposed by our "circular world." "Paradise is bolted fast, and the cherub far behind us; we must travel around the world and see whether perchance an entrance can be found somewhere from the rear."

Kleist's essay, "The Marionette Theatre," appeared in the *Berliner Abendblätter* in 1810 and is thus well over 100 years old. But if some one came upon it today who did not know its original author, he might well imagine that the writer belongs to our own time—so clearly does he mirror the problematic character of our anthropology today, of our philosophical doctrine of man. At once all the well-known names and works of present-day philosophy press for comparison: in this trend we see once again how deep the roots of our "modern" and most up-to-date philosophical thinking go down into the soil of Romanticism, and how, consciously or unconsciously, they all depend upon Romantic prototypes. Today anew the great antithesis of "Nature" and "Spirit," the polarity of "Life" and "Knowledge," looms as the very centre of philosophical speculation—and it is still in terms of Romantic concepts and Romantic categories that the problems are posed and their solution is sought. But really the conflict seems to have been sharpened, and the contradiction stands before us even more definitive and inexorable than in the days of Romanticism. For in order to meet this contradiction, however sharply it might be set forth, Romantic philosophy has always held ready a definite metaphysical solution and reconciliation: in the last analysis, by way of various mediations, the contradiction runs squarely into the underlying concept of the "Identity philosophy." "What we call Nature," as Schelling puts it in his *System of Transcendental Idealism*, "is a poem which lies locked up in a wonderful, secret script. Yet the riddle could be solved, if we would but learn to recognize the spirit's Odyssey as, wondrously deceptive, it seeks itself in continual flight from itself." From any such solution of the riddle, from any such aesthetic harmonizing of the contradiction between Nature and Spirit, modern philosophy is far removed. It recognizes and permits, on this point, no purely aesthetic compromise, but rather seeks to apprehend and to tear open for us the chasm between the two worlds in all its yawning depth. Thus especially in the writing of Ludwig Klages, where the problem has been given its most pointed expression, Spirit appears as a power which in the very depths of its being is anti-divine and hostile to Life. "Consciousness" and "Life," "*cogitare*" and "*esse*" remain sundered from each other at the very root of their being. Having given himself to the domination of Spirit, man sets himself at variance with Life and entrusts himself to vampiric forces which enter into the music of the spheres as a piercing dissonance.

One feels it almost as a redemption from this magic-mythical web in which Klages' theory of consciousness threatens to entangle us, when we shift our attention from this to the basic doctrines of Max Scheler's "Anthropology," as developed in his latest philosophical writings, particularly in his book, *Die Stellung des Menschen im Kosmos*.[1] A presentation, and interpretation and critical examination of these basic doctrines remains indeed an audacious undertaking. For Scheler's Anthropology remained fragmentary; we still do not know whether we shall ever possess it in all the breadth and fulness in which he himself had originally planned and conclusively envisaged it. Only a few brief sketches of the project as a whole were published by Scheler himself; only a few of the major lines

---

[1] First appearing under the title, "Die Sonderstellung des Menschen," in the collection of essays, *Mensch und Erde*; now published separately (Otto Reichl Verlag, Darmstadt).

of demarcation were drawn and firmly laid down. We must try to hold to these lines of demarcation in order to use them as guide-posts to the new world of ideas which opened up to Scheler during the last few years of his life. What makes Scheler's solution so distinctive, and also, at first glance, so paradoxical and foreign to our customary thought-patterns, is this: in no wise does he seek to reconcile "Life" and "Spirit"— or to overcome the dualism between the two; but he succeeds nonetheless in drawing a totally different picture of the real meaning and significance of this dualism, of this original cleavage of Being within itself, from that presented by traditional Western metaphysics. From this tradition he parts company in two respects. On the one hand he absolutely forswears any and all attempts at a monistic "identity-philosophy," whether of the speculative or of the empirical-scientific variety. According to Scheler there is no such thing as an evolution leading from bare Life to Spirit, no such thing as a gradual emergence of the latter out of the former. "The new principle," he emphasizes, "which makes man truly man, is something that stands entirely outside the realm of what can be called 'Life' . . . in even its most inclusive sense. That which makes mankind truly human is a principle standing in direct opposition to all Life *qua* Life, and which, as such, cannot in any way be traced back to 'the natural evolution of life'." That this is so, that in all those activities which are usually embraced under the term "Spirit," what we have is not any simple extension of the functions of Life as such, nor so to speak any tranquil emergence therefrom, but on the contrary a resolute reversal of Life's basic direction: according to Scheler this much is shown, above all, in that just the aforementioned activities, measured in terms of bare Life, are not positive but negative in kind. What makes itself felt in them is no intensification of Life's natural forces, but rather their obstruction, a giving pause and a turning aside from everything toward which Life is oriented, when Life is conceived purely as impulse, purely in its own sphere and according to the principle of its own dynamic motion. Man is not wholly man until he executes this turning aside—until he is no longer tied and bound fast to the wheels and engines of purely vital events, but is able to view them from a vantage-point outside and above.

The basic determination of a spiritual being, according to Scheler, is consequently his existential disengagement, his freedom, his release from confinement, from compulsion, from dependence upon the organic. "Such a 'spiritual' being is not longer bound to impulse or to his environing world, but free from it and, as we should like to call it, *open* to the world. Such a being may be said to *have* a 'world;' he is able to raise to the status of 'objects' those centres of resistance and reaction originally presented to him by his environment (in which environment the animal ecstatically loses itself), and even to grasp the very quintessence of these 'objects' in their essential being, without the limitations of experiencing this world of objects or its 'givenness' via the apparatus of vital impulses and via its sense functions and organs. Hence Spirit is objectification, the capacity of determination through the essence of things as such. And such a being is a 'carrier' of Spirit, whose principal intercourse with reality outside itself has dynamically reversed itself completely in its relation to the animal." By means of highly original and epistemologically weighty and fruitful trains of thought Scheler seeks to show how precisely the fundamental cognitive functions—those functions to which we are indebted for the construction of an "objective" world in any proper sense—measured purely by reference to Life's relational system, exhibit a *negative* prefix. "Pure" space and "pure" time, for example, are nothing but *schemata—i.e.*, empty forms of cognition. Manifestly neither one has any positive content; neither are they "objects" in the sense that effects flow from them or can be wrought upon them. On the other hand, they are clearly not a mere nothing: rather it is in this their very negativity,—in this basic opposition of theirs to anything real,— that they possess an entirely definite meaning, which is a necessary function for the theoretical formation and for the theoretical cognition of reality. This function depends upon the fact that empty space and empty time are pure *forms of order*—forms which apply not only to the actual, but extend beyond that to the possible. Space—as Leibniz already defined it—is the order of all *possible* togetherness, just as time is the order of all *possible* successiveness. This concept of the possible—which Leibniz first used to open up the realm of the Ideal, the region of "eternal truths"—from the standpoint of philosophical anthropology now reveals itself as a quite peculiar, a specifically *human* concept. What perhaps differentiates man most sharply from the beast, according to Scheler, is just this, that he is not fast bound to the actuality of the moment which surrounds him, and that he is not held by it, but is capable of the free contemplation of the Possible. "The animal is as little able to separate the empty form of space and time from the specific content of things in its environment, as it is to abstract 'number' from the greater or lesser 'quantity' of things themselves. It lives entirely in the concrete *actuality* of its specious present. Only when the instinctive expectations, transforming themselves into motivating impulses, gain the *ascendancy* over everything which is [merely] *factual* instinctive fulfilment in perception or sensation, does there take place in man the exceedingly unique phenomenon that spatial and also temporal *emptiness* appear to precede and to be the foundation of all possible contents of perception and of the whole world of material objects."

Thus again we see the antithesis between "Life" and "Spirit" stressed as sharply as possible and rigorously carried out—nevertheless, in the definition of the basic relationships of the two to each other, the prefix, so to speak, has now been changed. For Scheler has not the slightest doubt concerning the superiority and sovereignty of the spirit in the metaphysical hierarchy and order of values. One thing only he emphasizes—that this superiority in point of *value* be in no way equated with superiority in point of *existence* or *efficacy*. Rather we encounter here another peculiar antithesis, and one which seems at last destined to trace the dualism of Life and Spirit down to its very deepest roots. Scheler most resolutely opposes the doctrine that the higher *value*, in the totality of being and becoming, must also be endowed with the *greater strength*. Over against this optimistic viewpoint he sets the sharply contradictory thesis: the Spirit, or the Idea, in which a supreme value seems collected and concentrated, is, precisely because of this fact, by no means commensurable in terms of power, of immediate actuality and efficacy, with Life and with the merely vital forces. As we have seen, man was defined by Scheler as the living being who is capable of assuming a *primarily ascetic* attitude toward his own life. Compared to animals, who always say "Yes" to whatever happens to be, even when they are repelled and are running away, man is "the being who is able to say 'No'," "the ascetic toward Life," the everlasting protestant against sheer actuality.

"Here, however, arises the decisive question: does the Spirit *arise* out of *ascesis*, repression, and sublimation—or does it merely derive its *energy* from these? In the answer to this question lies a radical parting of the ways. It is my own conviction that the *being* of the Spirit in no way hinges on this negative activity, this 'No' to actuality, but only, as it were, its supply of energy and therewith its ability to manifest itself." Hence the Spirit, as Scheler understands it, is at the outset absolutely powerless. All the power of which it can avail itself in its struggle with Life stems not from itself; it must rather, in a unique roundabout way, wrest it from the realm of Life itself, step by step, through just that act of asceticism and impulse-sublimation. Erroneous, according to Scheler, is that theory which originates in the Greek conception of Spirit and of the Idea—the doctrine of the "inherent power of the Idea," its inner strength and activity, its independent efficacy. True, the Spirit may gradually attain power to the degree that Life's impulses enter into its lawfulness: "but to begin with and in its original form, the Spirit has not energy of its own." Hence the Spirit must be content with pointing Life's forces toward a definite goal, in terms of its own ideational structures and meanings; but it is not the Spirit's own task to produce this goal. The promised land to which it points is and remains a land of mere promise. At no other point, perhaps, does Scheler's theory diverge so clearly from that of Hegel, which comes to a focus precisely in this *one* thought, the conviction that the Idea is not merely a task, but a "substantial power." "Human spirit and human volition"—Scheler emphasizes, over against Hegel—"can never mean more than guidance and direction." And this means simply that the Spirit, as such, presents Ideas to the

impulsive forces; but not that it introduces any original potency
of its own for the realization of these Ideas. Consequently, this
is how the goal and the true meaning of human evolution now
appear: "the mutual *penetration* of the originally impotent
Spirit and the originally demonic Impulses (*i.e.*, one which, as
over against all spiritual Ideas and values, is blind) . . . and
the simultaneous empowering, *i.e.*, enlivening, of the Spirit is
the final End and Goal of all finite being and becoming—which
Theism mistakenly posits as the point of departure."

II

Here, however, two questions arise to which, as far as I can
see, this firmly joined and internally coherent system of
Scheler's anthropology no longer affords any answer. First of
all: if Life and Spirit belong to entirely disparate worlds—if
they are completely foreign to each other in their nature as well
as in their origin—how is it possible that they nevertheless can
accomplish a perfectly homogeneous piece of work, that they
co-operate and interpenetrate in constructing the specifically
human world, the world of "meaning"? Is this interpenetration
—to use a word which Lotze once coined in another epistemological connection—nothing more or less than a "happy accident"? How can it be explained that the forces of Life—the
purely vital, impulsive urges in Scheler's sense—permit themselves to be diverted from their own paths and to take that
other, precisely opposite direction, which the law of the Spirit
demands? True, Scheler emphasizes the fact that the Spirit by
no means directly breaks in or infringes upon the world of Life
—that it has no force of its own to set over against the force of
Life's impulses, but that it is content to function in a purely
symbolic manner, by pointing and showing the way. The Ideas
are not efficacious; they merely lead and direct; they illumine
the course of Life, but they do not compel it to take a certain
direction. But in spite of all this: how is Life capable of even
seeing the Ideas which the Spirit holds up to it and of directing
its way by them, as by starry constellations, if its pristine nature
be defined as mere impulse, *i.e.*, as spiritually blind? If we are

to gain an answer to this question, within the framework of Scheler's anthropology, we must, it seems, risk a leap into the dark; we must refer back to the unity of the metaphysical world-ground—the ground which nevertheless unites what to us is and remains manifestly heterogeneous and knits it into a single whole. Scheler himself, at one point in his essay on "Die Stellung des Menschen," has pointed the way toward some such solution. He stresses the idea that the Spirit absolutely never can be derived from Life or explained in terms of Life, since it is rather a principle standing in opposition to all Life as such, so that it must fall back, if on anything at all, upon the supreme Ground of things themselves. However widely Spirit and Life may diverge, for us, in all their phenomenal forms and appearances, there always remains nonetheless the possibility that the two may meet at some infinitely distant point— that they may, in some manner unknown to us, be held together in that X which is the ultimate ground of the universe. But with such an answer the Gordian knot is really not so much untied as cut. It is remarkable that Scheler, with all the evident originality and excellence of his last philosophical works, is here thrown back upon problems which belong to the very oldest stratum of the metaphysical thinking and self-reflection of mankind. Already his conception of "Spirit" as such, in its very wording and original definition, is unmistakably reminiscent of Aristotle's, and Scheler confronts us with the same internal difficulties in which the Aristotelian doctrine of Spirit finally ensnares us. Aristotle's Spirit, or νοῦς, is related to the lower mental faculties, to the forces of the purely vital sphere—to sense-perception, memory and ideation—not as an additional member of the same evolutionary series, but rather as super-ordinate to them all: it enters into the world of Life and of psychical being "from without." Here, however, burst upon us all those questions with which the entire metaphysics and the whole psychology of the Middle Ages, and thereafter the psychology of the Renaissance, wrestled on and on, and which even today, as the structure of Scheler's anthropology shows, seem not yet to have been definitively silenced. How is the Spirit able to exert any effect on a world to which it does not itself belong; —how can the *transcendence* of the *Idea* be reconciled with the *immanence* of *Life?*

For Aristotle himself the answer to this question is supplied by his system of *teleology*. The Aristotelian God—who is conceived as pure Spirit without admixture of anything material, as *actus purus,* as "thought thinking thought"—nevertheless moves the world: but he does so not in a mechanical way, not through any external impetus, but rather because, as the Supreme Form, he also constitutes the purpose towards which the universe itself is striving as the goal of its own self-realization. Thus God moves the world not through physical force, but "as the beloved object moves the lover." This interpretation (so profound and beautiful in itself) of the relation between God and the world, between Idea and Life, is, however, no longer useful to Scheler in the last phase of his philosophy; it is, for him, antiquated and superseded. He charges the "classical theory" of the Spirit, as developed in ancient Greece, with precisely this, that in its consequences it has led "to the untenable nonsense of a so-called teleological *Weltanschauung*," as it has dominated the whole theistic philosophy of the Occident. But failing this classical, theistic-teleological solution of the problem—what other solution remains? How is it to be explained that Life follows the pattern set before it by the Idea— if there is not contained in Life itself an immanent "trend toward the Idea"—if (to speak in Platonic terms) a yearning for the Idea and striving toward it were not already prevalent in the phenomenal world? May not Life, after all, be something other and something more than mere impulse, more than a drive into the indeterminate and the aimless? Does there not exist originally within Life itself the Will to attain its own self-portrayal, its own self-objectification, its own "visibility"? And on the other hand: must not the Spirit—even if one ascribes to it no original energy of its own and confines its activity merely to the inhibiting of the natural, purely vital forces—must not the Spirit, even in this inhibiting, still be something positively determinate and something positively effective? How could even this stoppage, this unique damming up of Life's forces and impulses ever succeed, if, from the very beginning, the Spirit were entirely impotent? The problem of the opposition between Life and Spirit, as posed in modern metaphysics, is strikingly reminiscent in more ways than one of that set of problems in the older metaphysics which centered around the mind-body problem. As greatly different as is the mere *content* of the questions in these two cases, the essential, purely *methodical* motives repeat themselves in both instances in a peculiar way. Thus immediately alongside Scheler's answer to the question concerning the unification of Life and Spirit we may place Descartes' answer to the question of the unification, the *"union"* of body and soul. Descartes begins with the proposition that the soul can neither beget any new force in the field of bodily events, nor destroy any force already extant: for the realm of bodily events constitutes a homogeneous, tightly closed causal system, which is determined by a strict law of conservation, by the law of constancy of momentum in the universe. Thus the soul, of itself, can neither create any physical energy nor can it destroy any already in existence. Only *one* possibility remains to the soul, according to Descartes, and this is that it may determine and under certain conditions alter the *direction* of these movements operating in the physical realm; and it is supposed to be precisely this change of direction, which marks the soul's influence upon the body, and to which this effect is confined. The objection which remained standing against this solution of the mind-body problem, and which was at once raised by Leibniz, lay just in the fact that even this mere change of direction necessarily demands a certain definite expenditure of energy, without which it is inconceivable. Quite analogously, even that process of mere inhibition—which, with Freud, Scheler calls the sublimation of life—would be incomprehensible and impossible, were the Spirit, which is to effect this result, in its essence to be thought of as totally impotent. Even this inhibition must ultimately go back to some sort of positive factor and to some positive impulse. If one takes the "Spirit" exclusively in the sense of Scheler's original definition, it will never be able in any way to effect anything beyond itself. Of it, Faust's saying would hold strictly true:

> The god that dwells within my soul
> Can stir to life my inmost deeps.
> Full sway o'er all my powers he keeps,
> But naught external can he e'er control.[2]

When Life is once defined as the "wholly other," as the contradictory opposite of Spirit, it becomes impossible to see how this contradiction can ever be resolved—how the Spirit's summons is not to die away in emptiness, but is still to be heard in the sphere of Life and to be understood there.

III

Herewith we at once arrive at a very general question which must be put to Scheler's projected philosophical anthropology. Does there really obtain this relationship of strict opposition, *i.e.*, a genuine logical *disjunction* between the "classical" doctrine, which Scheler combats, and his own basic point of view —between the view which grants the Spirit absolute substantial power over all actuality and, on the other hand, that which sees it as a principle "powerless" from the very beginning? Such would only be the case, if the concept of "power" itself were a completely definite, logically entirely unambiguous concept, so that we could be quite certain it was being taken in exactly the same strictly circumscribed sense in both theses of the disjunction. But it is precisely this presupposition which seems not to be fulfilled in this case. A keener analysis of Hegel's, as well as of Scheler's, concept of "power" seems to me to indicate that there exists here an equivocation which must first be cleared up, if we wish to lay bare the distinctive, the fundamental problem which is in question at this point. Scheler himself does not distinguish between *efficient* energy and that kind which might be called *formative* energy or energy of pure formation. Yet between the two there is an essential and very specific difference. Efficient energy aims immediately at man's environment, whether it be in order to apprehend it as it actually is and take possession of it, or in order to alter its course in some definite direction. Formative energy, on the other hand, is not aimed

---

[2] Lines 1566 to 1569 (incl.) of Goethe's *Faust*, First Part, as translated by George Madison Priest (Alfred Knopf, New York, 1941), 46.

directly at this outer environment, but rather remains self-contained: it moves within the dimension of the pure "image," and not in that of "actuality." Here the human spirit does not directly turn against objects, but rather weaves itself into a world of its own, a world of signs, of symbols and of meanings. And herewith it really forfeits that immediate oneness which, in the lower animals, unites "observing" and "effecting." This is perhaps one of the most characteristic traits of the animal world, of its organic firmness and its inner organic health, that in it this unity is most strictly preserved. The world of the Spirit, on the contrary, does not come into existence until the stream of Life no longer merely flows freely, but is held back at certain points—until Life, instead of unceasingly giving birth to new Life and consuming itself in these very births, gathers itself together into enduring forms and projects these forms out of and in front of itself. Herein seems to me to lie the truth of Scheler's fundamental position: that by no mere quantitative increase, enhancement or intensification of Life can we ever attain the realm of the Spirit, but that in order to gain entrance into this sphere a turnabout and return, a change of "mind" and of direction are necessary. But from this it by no means follows that in its peculiar, constitutive principle the Spirit would have to be understood as completely powerless, as utterly static and as "the ascetic of Life." Indeed the Spirit would not be capable of bringing Life to this relative stand-still, which in a certain sense marks the beginning of all "understanding," if it did not have some power of its own to set over against Life, power which is not borrowed from Life, but which it draws from the depths of its own being. The mediate activity of form-creation, to be sure, differs from the immediate activity of work and deed in the direction which it takes and in the goal at which it aims; but it is, no less than the other, pure activity, *actus purus*. The genuine "ideas"—according to Spinoza, and this is true not only of the ideas involved in pure cognition, but also of the creations of language and the arts, of myth and religion—stand there not like silent pictures on a blackboard; they bring themselves into being, and in this their act of self-generation they afford at the same time a new intuition into "objective" reality.

From this functional character of pure Form—*i.e.*, from the circumstance that it ever *exists* only insofar as it continually *re-creates* itself—it first becomes wholly clear how and why each form is antithetical in itself—why a necessary polarity must reside therein. It is always a double movement that works itself out here: a continuous alternation of the forces of attraction and repulsion. "There is no surer way of evading the world than through art,"—so says Goethe,—"and there is no surer way of binding oneself to it than through art." This double determination applies to every kind of creative activity and of "symbolic formation." This formative activity always begins by holding off the world, as it were, at a distance and by erecting a barrier between the I and the world. In the purely vital sphere no such division has yet taken place. Here action immediately follows action; effect is followed by counter-effect, from which again a new effect arises. Even relatively very complicated instinctive actions of animals appear to be nothing other than such "reflex chains." But with the first dawning of spirituality in man this kind of immediacy is a thing of the past. Henceforth, the tension between the I and its environment is not resolved with a single stroke, the spark between the two no longer leaps over directly; rather it is mediated in a way which, instead of leading through the world of event and action, proceeds by way of creative formation. Only at the end of this long and difficult way of inner formation does actuality again come into the purview of man. In his research into anthropoid intelligence Köhler has shown that the highest achievement which can possibly be expected of an animal is the art of the "detour"— and that even the highest animals learn this art only with great difficulty and to a very limited degree. Compared to this, the world of the human Spirit, as built up in language and in the use of tools, in artistic representation and conceptual knowledge, is nothing other than the persistent, continuously expanding and refined "art of the detour." More and more man learns to set the world aside, in order to draw it to himself—and more and more these two basic antithetical directions of efficient action come to melt, for him, into one homogeneous activity, both sides of which, like inhaling and exhaling, reciprocally condition one another. Man must retreat into the world of "unreality," into the world of appearance and of play, in order therein and thereby to conquer the world of reality. For aesthetic theory, this basic insight was set forth above all by Schiller, and developed by him in all its ramifications. From this point of view Schiller's *"Letters on the Aesthetic Education of Mankind"* looms up as one of the fundamental writings on which modern philosophical anthropology is also based. Here is the root of that famous idea (*Begriffserklärung*) in which Schiller seeks to express man's essential nature: "Man only plays when he is man in the fullest sense of the word, and he is only fully man when he plays." This pregnant explanation of man's being is, however, expressly limited by Schiller to the aesthetic sphere: according to him man should only play with beauty, but also he should play *only* with beauty. But if we take the concept of play as broadly as possible, this limitation [to aesthetics] turns out to be unsound and unnecessary. Rather one may venture the paradox that not only the sphere of beauty but also that of *truth* is first wholly disclosed to man by the play-function. In one of the deepest and most fruitful sections of Kant's *Critique of Pure Reason,* it is shown that the function of pure reason, if it is not to remain empty, has need of another function as its completion and necessary correlative—a function which Kant designates by the name of "productive imagination." And he went on to infer that everything we are accustomed to call simple sensory "perception" is most closely bound up with this function—that the productive imagination also forms an "ingredient of every possible perception." If this is so, then what we call the intuition of "the actual" does not occur without the outlook and prospective glance into "the possible"—then furthermore, the construction of the "objective" world of experience is dependent upon the original formative powers of the Spirit and upon the fundamental laws according to which they act.

IV

It is impossible to enter into the weighty and decisive consequences for *epistemology* which follow from this basic viewpoint.[3] If we return, instead, to our starting-point once more,

[3] I have tried to draw these consequences in another place, the third volume of my *Philosophie der symbolischen Formen* (published by Bruno Cassirer).

to the way in which the problem is posited in Scheler's philosophical anthropology, we shall then be able to define more sharply the basic thesis of this anthropology, both positively and negatively. What Scheler saw and what—even in the brief sketch of his anthropology which is all we have had until now —with his extraordinary dialectical power and mastery, he has succeeded in working out, is precisely that tension, that irreconcilable difference, that antithesis which holds between the region of "Spirit" and that of "Life." Here he successfully dismisses every attempt at a comfortable "monistic" solution. Scheler, however, does not stop with the primary and methodical contradiction herein demonstrated: he goes on immediately to another, *metaphysical* contradiction which for him arises out of the former—an antithesis not between functions but between real powers of Being. The metaphysical concept of "being," however, is marked by this peculiarity, that it possesses a strongly absolutistic character. Within it there is basically no room for "being" of a different stamp and different *type of meaning*. Rather we are led sooner or·later to a simple "either-or"—to that "crisis" between being and non-being by which the first great thinker of Western metaphysics, Parmenides, already found himself confronted. In Scheler's philosophical anthropology, too, this fate of metaphysics is borne out anew in a rather singular and remarkable way. What Scheler gives to the Spirit he must take away from Life; what he allots the latter he must deny the former. Thus for him originally a Spirit hostile to Life and a Life blind to Ideas stand confronting one another—only in order then to be drawn to each other after all, and, as if by a miracle, to "find their way back to each other." The Spirit, powerless in itself, and without drawing upon its own resources, but sheerly through its presence (*Dasein*) and nature (*So-Sein*), at last steers Life into its own orbit; and Life yields itself to the Spirit, it follows the Ideas which are held before it, even though these Ideas, seen purely from the standpoint of Life, mean nothing more than a diversion from its own goal and consequently a definite weakening and obstruction. The supreme, yes indeed the only power which man can bring to bear, in order to outgrow the realm of mere vitality and attain his distinctive being and his specific worth, is accordingly the power of asceticism. That Scheler should impute to asceticism this moral-spiritual power is perhaps the only, yet at the same time a most significant symptom of the fact that even the final "atheistic" phase of his philosophy is still bound as by invisible threads to the earlier period of his thinking. But just here it seems to me that the actual inner logic of Scheler's fundamental position clearly points even beyond the stage to which he himself had pursued it in his last works on anthropology. For it would indeed be comprehensible that asceticism might, so to speak, break the path for energies already at hand and standing on their own; but not that it could call these energies forth, as it were, out of nothing, or that it should be able to endow with real strength, in the first place, an inherently impotent principle. For in truth that asceticism which is viewed by Scheler at the pre-condition and the point of departure for all basic phenomena of the Spirit, more closely scrutinized, bears not so much an absolute as a definitely *relative* character. Plainly it is no turning away from Life as such, but rather an inner transformation and about-face experienced by Life itself. This about-face—this pathway from "Life" to "the Idea"—is not marked by rest as opposed to motion; it is no quietistic, inherently inactive principle as contrasted with restless becoming. Rather it is energies of a different order and, as it were, of a different dimension which here stand confronting one another. The most comprehensive definition of "Spirit" set down by Scheler is to the effect that for him Spirit means objectivity, "determinability through the essence (*So-Sein*) of things as such." In his activity man is presumed to be determined not, like the animals, by the mere reaction to opposing forces, but by the intuition of objects—and this elevation above the circumstantial to the realm of the objective, this pure object-existence is supposed to be the most formal category of the logical aspect of the Spirit. But as soon as this definition has been agreed to, the further question must at once be raised, how precisely this fundamental act of objectification is itself possible, and by what it is conditioned. The totality of its conditions, it seems to me, can be surveyed and exhibited only by entering

into the "in-between" realm of the "symbolic forms," by viewing the many-sided image-worlds which man interposes *between*
himself and reality, not in order to remove and thrust the latter
from him, but in order, by thus gaining distance, to bring it
properly within the purview of his vision—in order to elevate it
from the merely tangible sphere, which demands immediate
proximity, to that of the visible. Language and the arts, myth
and theoretical knowledge, all work together, each according to
its own inner law, at this process of spiritual "setting at a
distance:" they are the great stages on the way which leads
from the Space of grasping and doing, wherein the animal lives
and remains, as it were, imprisoned, to the Space of intuition
and thought, to that of the spiritual "horizon."

Viewed in this perspective, the polarity of Spirit and Life,
which constitutes the basic idea of Scheler's anthropology, is by
no means cancelled; but, systematically considered, it now appears in a different light. Even in his last works, however
radical a transformation of his views they may contain, Scheler
still speaks the language of a definitely realistic metaphysics. He
sets Spirit and Life over against each other as primeval powers
of being—as real forces which, in a certain way, contend with
one another for dominion over the whole of reality. In doing
this, however, a purely functional antithesis is transformed into
a substantial one—from a distinction exhibitable in phenomena
we are suddenly led to an assertion about the transcendental,
initial cause. To be sure, Scheler even here remains far removed
from Klages' mythicizing and demonizing of the Spirit. For
Scheler the Spirit is demarcated and distinguished precisely by
the fact that it can never be exhibited as a substantial entity, but
only in its pure act of functioning, in its living actuality. Just
because it represents the principle of objectification it can never
itself become objective, it cannot be defined and comprehended
in the manner of any objective entity. But in spite of this disclaimer and this critical delimitation, the Spirit, even for
Scheler, still remains, as it were, a kind of substantive. In him
too the metaphysical interest in the end takes precedence over
the purely phenomenological: the Spirit becomes a *Being sui*

generis, standing over and above the being of mere Life. If, instead, one understands Life and Spirit not as substantial essences set over against one another, but takes both of them in the sense of their pure functional activity, the antithesis between the two immediately acquires a different meaning. No longer need the Spirit be viewed as a principle foreign or hostile to all Life, but it may be understood as a turning and about-face of Life itself—, a transformation which it experiences within itself, insofar as it passes from the circle of merely *organic* creativity and formation into the circle of "form," the circle of *ideal* formative activity.

At this point the fundamental thesis of "Objective Idealism" completely maintains its ground, in the face of all the criticism which the nineteenth and twentieth centuries', "philosophy of life" has urged against it. Especially as concerns Hegel, it would be a complete misunderstanding of his system to bring against it the reproach that by reason of its panlogistic tendency it denies the rights of Life—that it has sacrificed the vital sphere to that of logic. Even a mere glance at the historical development of the Hegelian doctrine is sufficient to invalidate this objection: for it is precisely in the writings of Hegel's early period that, in connection with his investigations in philosophy of history and philosophy of religion, a new, systematically most fruitful concept of Life is coined. In the introduction to his *Phenomenology of Spirit,* however, Hegel then, in propositions of truly classical formulation, proceeded to carry out the advance and to make the definitive break. He now demands that the self-contained and closed substantiality of life open up, that it spread out and reveal itself: for only in this process and by virtue of it can mere substance achieve its "Being-for-itself" and become a "subject." "The strength of the Spirit is only as great as its expression; its depth only as deep as in its revelation it dares to expand and lose itself." The realization of this principle demands not only that Spirit and Life come to know themselves as opposites; but that, at the same time, on account of this very opposition, they seek and demand each other. The polarity between the two remains, but it loses its appearance of absolute estrangement. Indeed, if we pass in review the whole series of accusations which the modern "philosophy of life" has raised against the usurped supremacy of the Spirit, one objection immediately obtrudes itself. Who exactly—it must be inquired—is the plaintiff, and who the defendant in the trial here getting under way? It seems as if Life were here brought to the bar against the Spirit, in order to defend itself against the latter's enroachment, against its violence and its conceit. And yet this impression is deceptive—for Life as such is self-imprisoned, and in this self-imprisonment is speechless. It has no language other than that which the Spirit lends it. Hence, wherever it is summoned against the Spirit, the latter in truth is always both assailant and defendant, plaintiff and judge in one. The real drama takes place not between Spirit and Life, but in the midst of the Spirit's own realm, indeed at its very focus. For every accusation is a form of predication; every condemnation is a form of judgment; predication and judgment, however, are the basic and time-honored functions of the *Logos* itself. In connection with this we may recall that in Greek it is one and the same word, one and the same term—the term κατηγορεῖν and κατηγορία—which expresses accusation as well as predication in general. All of the passionate speeches of accusation against the Spirit, in which modern philosophical literature is so rich, cannot make us forget, therefore, that here in truth it is not Life striving against the Spirit, but the latter striving against itself. And this internal conflict is really its appointed fate, its everlasting, inescapable pathos. The Spirit *is* only, insofar as it turns against itself in this manner; its own unity is thinkable only in such contrariety. Hence the Spirit is not only —as Scheler defines it—the ascetic of Life, not only that which is able to say "No" to all organic reality; it is the principle which *within itself* may negate itself. And the paradox of its nature consists precisely in the fact that this negation does not destroy it, but first makes it truly what it is. Only in the "No" with which it confronts itself does the Spirit break through to its own self-affirmation and self-assertion: only in the question which it presents to itself does it become truly itself. *Montaigne* said once that man is the enigmatic animal who is capable of hating himself: an anomaly and a contradiction for which no precedent exists anywhere else in the realm of nature. Nature knows suffering and death, destruction and annihilation; but it knows nothing of that self-disintegration whereby man turns against himself. As the being who alone is capable of questioning, man is also the being who is and remains to himself thoroughly problematical, the being eternally *worthy* of questioning. In this sense all those who, in the name of Life, bring the Idea into court, remain,—to use Hegel's expression—the "agents of the Idea," for just this passing of judgment upon itself is nothing but a primeval phenomenon and an imperative, a categorical demand of Spirit; and from this setting of the problem it necessarily follows that precisely the Spirit's own accusers must in the end become its custodians and its witnesses.

V

This fundamental situation emerges most clearly and most definitely perhaps, if we endeavor to grasp it by way of Language and to throw light upon it from the basic and peculiar spiritual structure of the latter. It can be said that as long as there has been philosophy of language, so long has there also been *critique* of language—that the insight into the positive strength and the positive meaning of language has always been followed by scepticism, as by a shadow. And this doubt about language, indeed this despair regarding it, remains by no means limited to philosophy; it is not even foreign to the great poets and to the greatest coiners of language in the realm of poetry. In a well-known Venetian epigram Goethe complained of the fact that, bound as he was to the medium of the German language, he unfortunately had to corrupt both life and art by having to use this "worst of material." But among his works there is also to be found another poem, entitled "Language," which, compared with this epigram figures as its polar opposite and palinode:

> What's "rich," what's "poor"! What's "strong" and "weak"!
> Is rich the treasure in the buried urn?

Is strong the sword within the arsenal?
Grasp gently, then, and benign fortune
Flows, Godhead, out from Thee;
T'ward victory, might, reach for the sword
And glory o'er thy neighbors.[4]

Here again the feeling of the true language-coiner breaks through: the feeling that, essentially, language is only what the momentary impulse, the animating and life-giving moment, makes out of it. Its meaning and value depend not on what it may be "in itself," in its metaphysical nature, but on the manner of its use, its spiritual employment. For it is not the rigid substance of language, but its living, *dynamic* function, which determines this meaning and value. Language is mis-judged if it is taken in some way or other as a thinglike being, as a substantial medium which interposes itself between man and the reality surrounding him. However one were then to define this medium more precisely, it always appears neverthe-less—while wanting to be the *connecting link* between two worlds—as the barrier which separates the one from the other. However clear and however pure a medium we may then see in language, it always remains true that this crystal-clear medium is also crystal-hard—that however transparent it may be for the expression of ideas, it still is never wholly penetrable. Its transparency does not remove its impenetrability. But this misgiving vanishes the moment we remember that basically we are dealing here with a self-created difficulty—that the antinomy is grounded not so much in the nature of language itself as in an inadequate metaphorical description of its essen-tial nature. If, instead of likening Language to an existing thing, we understand it rather in the sense of what it really does,—if

[4] The German original reads as follows:

> Was reich, was arm! Was stark und schwach!
> Ist reich vergrabener Urne Bauch?
> Ist stark das Schwert im Arsenal?
> Greif milde drein und freundlich Glück
> Fliesst, Gottheit, von Dir aus,
> Fass an zum Siege, Macht, das Schwert
> Und über Nachbarn Ruhm.

we take it, in accordance with Humboldt's injunction, not as an erg [quantity of work] but as energy—then the problem immediately assumes a different form. Language then is no longer a given, rigid structure; rather it becomes a form-creating power, which at the same time has to be really a form-breaking, form-destroying one. Even the world of grammatical and syntactical forms is not merely a kind of firm dike and dam, against which the formative, the truly creative forces of language continually break. Rather is it the original, creative power of language which floods through this world as well, and which supplies it with ever new momentum. In this process the hardened forms are also ever and again melted down, so that they cannot "clothe themselves in rigid armor;" but on the other hand, only in this process do even the momentary impulse, the creation of the moment, receive their continuity and stability. This creation would, like a bubble, have to dissolve before every breath of air if it did not, in the midst of its originating and becoming, encounter earlier structures—forms already originated and in existence—to which it may cling and hold fast. Thus even this which has already come into being is for language not merely material, against which foreign and ever stranger material is ever pressing; but it is the product and attestation of the same formative powers to which even language itself owes its existence. Every single act of speech flows again back into the great river-bed of language itself, yet without being entirely lost and perishing therein. Instead, the stronger was its own individuality, borrowed from the originality of its creator, the more it maintains itself and the more strongly it transmits itself—in such a way that, by means of the new momentary impulse, the current as a whole may be altered in its direction and intensity, in its dynamics and rhythm. To be sure, it is evident that all these turns of expression can be nothing other and nothing more than metaphors; but, if at all, it is only in dynamic metaphors like these, and not in any figures whatsoever borrowed from the static world, the world of things and thing-relationships, that the connection between the "particular" and the "general" in language, the relation between "Life" and "Spirit" therein, can properly be described. And the same fundamental relationship exhibited here in the realm of language holds true of every other genuine "symbolic form." The inner contradictoriness, the polarity which necessarily dwells within every such form, does not rend or demolish it; rather it constitutes the condition whereby its unity may again be established out of that contradiction and may thus again present itself to the outside world.

BIBLIOGRAPHY OF THE WRITINGS OF ERNST CASSIRER

To 1946

Compiled by

CARL H. HAMBURG AND WALTER M. SOLMITZ

PREFACE TO THE BIBLIOGRAPHY

THIS list of the published writings by Ernst Cassirer and of their translations contains, as far as we know, all of his publications which have come out, either during his lifetime or posthumously. It also includes a number of books now in preparation.

The material for the publications from 1899 to 1936 could mostly be taken from the *Bibliography of Ernst Cassirer's Writings* by Raymond Klibansky and Walter Solmitz which appeared in the volume *Philosophy and History* (Essays presented to Ernst Cassirer; edited by Raymond Klibansky and H. J. Paton. Oxford, Clarendon Press, 1936). For the period after 1936 we had at our disposal Professor Cassirer's own continuation of this bibliography as well as Mrs. Cassirer's listing of the posthumous publications. To her we are greatly indebted for providing us generously with all the material at her hand; and to the editors and publishers of *Philosophy and History* our thanks are due for allowing us very kindly to use the material from their book. We had the privilege of using the facilities of the Libraries of Bowdoin College and Columbia University, and of the Harvard College Library, and of drawing freely on the collection of Ernst Cassirer's writings which Professor Koelln of Bowdoin College owns, who also kindly helped us with his advice. We also should like to thank Messrs. Max Hamburg from Fordham University, and John E. Smith, Instructor at Barnard College, for their help. We are particularly grateful to Professor Raymond Klibansky of McGill University for reading the proofs and making some valuable suggestions.

As in all the *Bibliographies* of the *Library of Living Philosophers*, the writings have been arranged in the *chronological* order of the dates of publication. The *Bibliography* of 1936 had grouped the items according to subject matter, from a "systematic" point of view. In this respect the earlier list should still prove useful as an initial guide to Ernst Cassirer's philosophy. It represents graphically the universal scope of his work, marking, as it were, on the *globus intellectualis* its widely spread topics, and suggesting their multiple systematic and historical interrelation.—A story of the development of Ernst Cassirer's thought may be read, on the other hand, from the chronological list that follows here. In Cassirer's work as a whole, as is the case in each of his individual writings, this development was as full of surprises as it was methodical. Step by step was taken until, on a higher level each time, a new and wider vista opened up. The basic points of orientation remained the same throughout his life's work. But the same themes, taken up again and again, were carried on by means of ever new variations to ever new phases of interpretation. One of Cassirer's favorite quotations was Goethe's, *"Die Quelle muss fliessend gedacht werden."* The present chronological record of his writings may perhaps be used, in this manner, as a source for the study and the realization of Ernst Cassirer's thought.

CARL H. HAMBURG
WALTER M. SOLMITZ

Summer 1948
COLUMBIA UNIVERSITY
NEW YORK, N.Y.

BOWDOIN COLLEGE
BRUNSWICK, MAINE

WRITINGS OF ERNST CASSIRER

To August 1946

1899

1. DESCARTES' KRITIK DER MATHEMATISCHEN UND NATURWISSEN-
SCHAFTLICHEN ERKENNTNIS. Inaugural Dissertation, Marburg,
1899.

Reprinted: as *Einleitung* in *Leibniz' System*, 1902, pp. 3-102.

1902

1. LEIBNIZ' SYSTEM IN SEINEN WISSENSCHAFTLICHEN GRUND-
LAGEN. Marburg, N. G. Elwert, 1902. xiv, 548 pp.

Contents: Vorrede—EINLEITUNG: DESCARTES' KRITIK DER MATHEMATISCHEN
UND NATURWISSENSCHAFTLICHEN ERKENNTNIS.—I. Die erkenntniskritische
Begründung der Mathematik—II. Die erkenntniskritische Begründung der
Naturwissenschaft—III. Der Begriff der Substanz und die Substanzialisierung
des Raumes—IV. Substanz and Veränderung—V. Der Begriff der Erfahrung
—VI. Das Problem des Unendlichen—VII. Der Begriff der Zeit.—LEIBNIZ'
SYSTEM IN SEINEN WISSENSCHAFTLICHEN GRUNDLAGEN—*PART ONE: DIE
GRUNDBEGRIFFE DER MATHEMATIK.*—Ch. I. Verhältnis von Mathe-
matik und Logik—Ch. II. Die Grundbegriffe der Mathematik—Ch. III. Das
geometrische Raumproblem und die Analysis der Lage—Ch. IV. Das Pro-
blem der Kontinuität—*PART TWO: DIE GRUNDBEGRIFFE DER ME-
CHANIK*—Ch. V. Raum und Zeit—Ch. VI. Der Begriff der Kraft—*PART
THREE: DIE METAPHYSIK*—Ch. VII. Das Problem des Bewusstseins—
Ch. VIII. Das Problem des Individuums—Ch. IX. Das Problem des Indi-
viduums im System der Geisteswissenschaften—*PART FOUR: DIE ENT-
STEHUNG DES LEIBNIZISCHEN SYSTEMS*—I. Die Jugendwerke bis zur
Zeit des Pariser Aufenthaltes. (1633-1673)—II. Der Pariser Aufenthalt.
(1673-1676)—III. Von der Rückkehr nach Deutschland bis zur Abfassung
des metaphysischen Diskurses. (1676-86)—*KRITISCHER NACHTRAG*—
(I. Bertrand Russell, *A critical exposition of the philosophy of Leibniz.*
Cambridge, 1900.—II. Louis Couturat, *La logique de Leibniz d'après des
documents inédits.* Paris, 1901)

1904

1. G. W. LEIBNIZ. PHILOSOPHISCHE WERKE.

HAUPTSCHRIFTEN ZUR GRUNDLEGUNG DER PHILOSOPHIE.

Übersetzt v. *A. Buchenau.* Durchgesehen und mit Einleitungen und Erläuterungen hrsg. von *E. Cassirer.* Vol. I. (Philosophische Bibliothek. Vol. 107). Leipzig, Dürrsche Buchhandlung, 1904. vi, 374 pp.

Second edition: Leipzig, F. Meiner, 1924.

Cassirer's Introductions: Vorrede (pp. iii-vi)—Zur Logik und Mathematik: Einleitung (pp. 1-12)—Schriften zur Phoronomie und Dynamik: Einleitung (pp. 107-119)

1906

1. G. W. Leibniz. Philosophische Werke.

Hauptschriften zur Grundlegung der Philosophie.

Übersetzt von *A. Buchenau.* Durchgesehen und mit Einleitungen und Erläuterungen hrsg. von *E. Cassirer.* Vol. II. (Philosophische Bibliothek. Vol. 108). Leipzig, Dürrsche Buchhandlung, 1906.

Second edition: Leipzig, F. Meiner, 1924. 582 pp.

Cassirer's Introductions: Zur Biologie und Entwicklungslehre: Einleitung (pp. 3-34).—Zur Monadenlehre: Einleitung (pp. 81-122).—Sach- und Namenregister (pp. 561-579).

2. Der kritische Idealismus und die Philosophie des gesunden Menschenverstandes. (*Philosophische Arbeiten,* hrsg. von Cohen und Natorp. Vol. I, No. 1.) Giessen, A. Töpelmann, 1906. 35 pp.

A criticism of Leonhard Nelson's *Die kritische Methode und das Verhältnis der Psychologie zur Philosophie* and *Friedrich Fries und seine jüngsten Kritiker.*

3. Das Erkenntnisproblem in der Philosophie und Wissenschaft der neueren Zeit. Vol. I. Berlin, Bruno Cassirer, 1906. xv, 608 pp.

Second, revised Edition (with some corrections and additions, but omitting an introduction about Greek philosophy, contained in the First Edition), 1911. xviii, 601 pp. Third Edition, 1922.

Contents: Vorreden—Einleitung: Das Erkennen und sein Gegenstand— Bk. I. Die Renaissance des Erkenntnisproblems—*CH. I. NIKOLAUS CUSANUS—Carolus Bovillus—CH. II. DER HUMANISMUS UND DER KAMPF DER PLATONISCHEN UND ARISTOTELISCHEN PHILOSO- PHIE—Einleitung—I.* Die Erneuerung der Platonischen Philosophie—*Georgius Gemistos Plethon—Marsilius Ficinus—II.* Die Reform der Aristotelischen Psychologie—Einleitung—*Pietro Pomponazzi—Giacomo Zarbarella—Francesco Pico della Mirandola—Marius Nizolius—IV.* Die Erneuerung der Natur- und Geschichtsansicht—*CH. III. DER SKEPTIZISMUS—Montaigne —Charron—Sanchez* und *La Mothe le Vayer—*Bk. II. Die Entdeckung

1907

1. DAS ERKENNTNISPROBLEM IN DER PHILOSOPHIE UND WISSENSCHAFT DER NEUEREN ZEIT. Vol. II. Berlin, Bruno Cassirer, 1907. xiv, 732 pp.

Second Edition, 1911. xv, 832 pp. Third Edition, 1922.

Contents: BK. IV. DIE ANFÄNGE DES EMPIRISMUS—*CH. I. BACON*—I. Die Kritik des Verstandes—II. Die Formenlehre—*CH. II. GASSENDI*—*CH. III. HOBBES*—BK. V. FORTBILDUNG UND VOLLENDUNG DES RATIONALISMUS—*CH. I. SPINOZA*—I. Die Erkenntnislehre des "Kurzen Traktats"—II. Der "Tractatus de Intellectus Emendatione"—III. Der Begriff der Substanz—*CH. II. LEIBNIZ*—*CH. III. TSCHIRNHAUS*—*CH. IV. DER RATIONALISMUS IN DER ENGLISCHEN PHILOSOPHIE*—I. *Herbert von Cherbury*—*Kenelm Digby*—II. Die Schule von Cambridge—*Cudworth*—*John Norris*—BK. VI. DAS ERKENNTNISPROBLEM IM SYSTEM DES EMPIRISMUS—*CH. I. LOCKE*—Die Grenzbestimmung des Verstandes. Der Kampf gegen das "Angeborene"—I. Sensation und Reflexion—II. Der Begriff der Wahrheit—III. Der Begriff des Seins—*CH. II. BERKELEY*—I. Die Theorie der Wahrnehmung—II. Die Begründung des Idealismus—III. Kritik der Berkeleyschen Begriffstheorie—IV. Der Begriff der Substanz—V. Die Umgestaltung der Berkeleyschen Erkenntnislehre—*CH. III. HUME*—Die "Gleichförmigkeit der Natur"—Die Kritik der abstrakten Begriffe—I. Die Kritik der mathematischen Erkenntnis—II. Die Kritik des Kausalbegriffs—III. Der Begriff der Existenz—BK. VII. VON NEWTON ZU KANT: Wissenschaft und Philosophie im achtzehnten Jahrhundert—*CH. I. DAS PROBLEM DER METHODE*—I. Die Aufgabe der Induktion—*Joseph Glanvill*—*Newtons* Grundlegung der Induktion—Die Schule *Newtons: Keill* und *Freind*—*d'Alembert*—II. Vernunft und Sprache—*Condillac*—*Lambert, Ploucquet, Sulzer*—III. Der Begriff der Kraft—*Maupertuis*—IV. Das Problem der Materie—Die Chemie—*CH. II. RAUM UND ZEIT.*—1. Das Raum- und Zeitproblem in der Metaphysik und spekulativen Theologie—I. Raumbegriff und Gottesbegriff—*Henry Moore*—*Newton* und seine Schule—*Samuel Clarke*—*Joseph Raphson*—II.

Isaac Watts' Enquiry concerning Space—*Edmund Law*—2. Das Raum- und
Zeitproblem in der Naturwissenschaft—a) *Newton* und seine Kritiker—b) Die
Fortbildung der Newtonischen Lehre—*Leonhard Euler*—*Euler* und *Maclaurin*
3. Die Idealität des Raumes und der Zeit—Die Antinomieen des Unendlichen
—*Maupertuis*—*Maupertuis* und *Kant; Schopenhauers* Urteil—Die Entwick-
lung des *Leibnizischen* Phaenomenalismus: *Joh. Aug. Eberhard* und *Kasimir
von Creuz*—*Maupertuis'* Theorie der Existentialurteile—*Gottfried Ploucquet*
—*Ploucquet* und *Malebranche*—*Grandi* und *Sturm*—Das Unendlichkleine bei
Leibniz und *Maclaurin*—*Fontenelles* "Elements de la Géométrie de l'Infini"
—*Eulers* Kritik des Unendlichkeitsbegriffs—4. Das Raum- und Zeitproblem
in der Naturphilosophie—*Boscowich*—CH. III. DIE ONTOLOGIE—DER
SATZ DES WIDERSPRUCHS UND DER SATZ VOM ZUREICHENDEN
GRUNDE—I. Der Wahrheitsbegriff bei *Leibniz* und *Wolff*—Die Kritik der
Wolffschen Lehre: Andreas Rüdiger—Die neue "Methode" von *Crusius'*
Philosophie und ihre geschichtliche Wirkung: *Lambert* und *Mendelssohn*—
Joh. Heinr. Lambert—II. Der Satz des Widerspruchs und der Satz vom zu-
reichenden Grunde—*Wolff* und seine Schule, der syllogistische Beweis des
Satzes vom Grunde (*Darjes, Carpow, Meier*)—*Crusius'* Kritik des Satzes
vom Grunde—*Crusius* und *Schopenhauer*—Die Kritik des Causalbegriffs:
Nik. Béguelin—*Béguelin* und *Hume*—*Thümmig* und *Crusius*—CH. IV.
DAS PROBLEM DES BEWUSSTSEINS. —SUBJEKTIVE UND OBJEK-
TIVE BEGRÜNDUNG DER ERKENNTNIS—I. Fortbildung und Kritik
von *Lockes* Psychologie—*Peter Browne*—*Hartley* und *Priestley*—*Condillac*
—Psychologie und Aesthetik im 18. Jahrhundert—*Tetens*—II. Das psy-
chologische und das logische Wahrheitskriterium. Die physiologische Be-
dingtheit der Erkenntnis—*Diderots* Lettre sur les aveugles—*Lossius'* "Phy-
sische Ursachen des Wahren"—*Tetens'* Kritik der Common-Sense-Philosophie
—Psychologische und logische Deutung der Grundprinzipien—BK. VIII. DIE
KRITISCHE PHILOSOPHIE—CH. I. DIE ENTSTEHUNG DER KRITISCHEN
PHILOSOPHIE—I. Die Schriften des Jahres 1763—II. Die "Träume eines
Geistersehers" (1765)—Verhältnis zu *Rousseau*—*Kant* und *Hume*—III. Von
den "Träumen eines Geistersehers" bis zur "Dissertation" (1765-69)—IV.
Vorbereitung und Abschluss der Dissertation (1769-70)—*Kant* und *Euler*—
V. Der Fortschritt zur Vernunftkritik (1772-1781)—CH. II. DIE VER-
NUNFTKRITIK—I. Der metaphysische Gegensatz von Subjekt und Objekt
und seine geschichtliche Entwicklung—II. Das Problem der Objektivität.
—Analytisch und synthetisch.—III. Raum und Zeit—IV. Der Begriff des
Selbstbewusstseins—V. Das "Ding an sich"—NAMEN- UND SACHREGISTER.

2. KANT UND DIE MODERNE MATHEMATIK.

MIT BEZIEHUNG AUF BERTRAND RUSSELLS UND LOUIS COUTURATS WERKE
ÜBER DIE PRINCIPIEN DER MATHEMATIK.

Kant-Studien, Vol. XII, 1907, pp. 1-40.

3. ZUR FRAGE DER METHODE DER ERKENNTNISKRITIK.

EINE ENTGEGNUNG.

Vierteljahrsschrift für wissenschaftliche Philosophie und Soziologie.
Vol. XXXI, No. 4. 1907.

1909

1. REVIEW OF: RICHARD HÖNIGSWALD, *BEITRÄGE ZUR ER-KENNTNISTHEORIE UND METHODENLEHRE. Kant-Studien,* Vol. XIV, 1909. No. 1, pp. 91-98.

1910

1. SUBSTANZBEGRIFF UND FUNKTIONSBEGRIFF.

UNTERSUCHUNGEN ÜBER DIE GRUNDFRAGEN DER ERKENNTNISKRITIK.

Berlin, Bruno Cassirer, 1910. vii, 459 pp.

Second Edition: 1923.
Russian Translation: 1912.
English Translation in: SUBSTANCE AND FUNCTION, AND EINSTEIN'S THEORY OF RELATIVITY. Translated by *William Curtis Swabey* and *Mary Collins Swabey.* Chicago and London, The Open Court Publishing Company, 1923. pp. i-xi, 1-346.

Contents: Preface—PART ONE. THE CONCEPT OF THING AND THE CONCEPT OF RELATION—Ch. I. On the Theory of the Formation of Concepts—Ch. II. The Concept of Number—Ch. III. The Concept of Space and Geometry—Ch. IV. The Concepts of Natural Science—PART TWO. THE SYSTEM OF RELATIONAL CONCEPTS AND THE PROBLEM OF REALITY—Ch. V. On the Problem of Induction—Ch. VI. The Concept of Reality—Ch. VII. Subjectivity and Objectivity of the Relational Concepts—Ch. VIII. On the Psychology of Relations.

2. REVIEW OF: JONAS COHN, *VORAUSSETZUNGEN UND ZIELE DES ERKENNENS. Deutsche Literaturzeitung,* Vol. XXXI, 1910, No. 39.

1911

1. LEIBNIZ. Article in the *Encyclopaedia of the Social Sciences,* New York, 1911.

2. ARISTOTELES UND KANT.

ZU GÖRLANDS BUCH: *ARISTOTELES UND KANT.*

Kant-Studien, Vol. XVI, 1911, pp. 431-447.

1912

1. IMMANUEL KANTS WERKE.

GESAMTAUSGABE IN 10 BÄNDEN UND EINEM ERGÄNZUNGSBAND.

In Gemeinschaft mit Hermann Cohen, Arthur Buchenau, Otto
Buek, Albert Görland, B. Kellermann, Otto Schöndörfer, hrsg.
von Ernst Cassirer. Berlin, Bruno Cassirer, 1912.

Volumes edited by *Ernst Cassirer:* Vol. IV. Schriften von 1783-1788.
Hrsg. von *A. Buchenau* und *Ernst Cassirer.*—Vol. VI. Schriften von 1790-
1796. Hrsg. von *Ernst Cassirer* und *Artur Buchenau.*—Vols. IX and X.
Briefe von und an Kant. Hrsg. von *Ernst Cassirer.*—Erläuterungsbände:
1. KANTS LEBEN UND LEHRE. Von *Ernst Cassirer* (see 1918, 1).

2. HERMANN COHEN UND DIE ERNEUERUNG DER KANTISCHEN
   PHILOSOPHIE. *Kant-Studien,* Vol. XVII, 1912. No. 3, pp. 252-
   273.

3. DAS PROBLEM DES UNENDLICHEN UND RENOUVIERS "GESETZ
   DER ZAHL." In: *Philosophische Abhandlungen, Hermann Cohen
   zum 70. Geburtstag dargebracht.* Berlin, Bruno Cassirer, 1912,
   pp. 85-98.

1913

1. ERKENNTNISTHEORIE NEBST DEN GRENZFRAGEN DER LOGIK.
   Jahrbücher der Philosophie, Vol. I. Berlin, E. S. Mittler, 1913, pp.
   1-59.

1914

1. DIE GRUNDPROBLEME DER KANTISCHEN METHODIK UND IHR
   VERHÄLTNIS ZUR NACHKANTISCHEN SPEKULATION. *Die Geisteswissenschaften,* Vol. I. Leipzig, Veit, 1914. Pp. 784-787 and 812-
   815.

1915

1. G. W. LEIBNIZ. PHILOSOPHISCHE WERKE. VOL. III. NEUE
   ABHANDLUNGEN ÜBER DEN MENSCHLICHEN VERSTAND. In 3.
   Auflage mit Benutzung der Schaarschmidtschen Übertragung neu
   übersetzt, eingeleitet und erläutert von *E. Cassirer. Philosophische
   Bibliothek,* Vol. 69. Leipzig, F. Meiner, 1915.

New Edition, with an author and subject index, 1926.

Einleitung, by *Ernst Cassirer:* pp. i-xxv.

1916

1. FREIHEIT UND FORM.

STUDIEN ZUR DEUTSCHEN GEISTESGESCHICHTE.

Berlin, Bruno Cassirer. 1916. xix, 575 pp.

Second Edition: 1918. Third Edition: 1922.

Contents: Vorwort—EINLEITUNG—1. Die Entwicklung des Persönlichkeits-
begriffs bei den modernen Kulturvölkern—2. Das System der mittelalterlichen
Weltanschauung und Lebensordnung—*Luthers* Glaubens- und Freiheitsbegriff
—Die Grundformen des religiösen Individualismus: *Luther* und *Zwingli*—
CH. I. LEIBNIZ—1. Die Anfänge der deutschen Wissenschaft—2. Das Pro-
blem des Bewusstseins und des Individuums—3. Die Monade als Einheit von
Formbegriff und Kraftbegriff—CH. II. DIE ENTDECKUNG DER ÄSTHETISCHEN
FORMWELT—1. Das ästhetische Problem in Leibniz' Metaphysik—2. Die
Anfänge der deutschen Poetik—*Gottsched* und die Schweizer—Der Begriff
der poetischen Wahrheit bei *Bodmer* und *Breitinger*—3. Die Begründung der
philosophischen Ästhetik durch *Baumgarten* und *Meier*—4. Das Problem der
Sinnlichkeit in der *Leibniz*schen Metaphysik—*Leibniz* und *Shaftesbury*—5.
Lessing—6. *Hamann* und *Herder*—*Leibniz* und *Herder*—7. *Winckelmann*—
CH. III. DIE FREIHEITSIDEE IM SYSTEM DES KRITISCHEN IDEALISMUS—
1. Die Stellung des *Kant*ischen Systems in der deutschen Geistesgeschichte—
2. Die Kritik der reinen Vernunft—CH. IV. GOETHE—1. Die neue Stellung
der Subjektivität in Goethes Welt- und Lebensansicht—*Goethe* und *Rousseau*
—2. Weltanschauung und Lebensform des jungen Goethe—3. "Freiheit"
und "Notwendigkeit"—4. Die italienische Reise und die Entwicklung des
"klassischen" Formbegriffs—Die lyrische Symbolik in Goethes Jugend- und
Altersdichtung—5. Naturanschauung und Naturtheorie—Die Überwindung
des naturwissenschaftlichen Klassenbegriffs—Das Problem der "Gestalt" und
die Idee der Metamorphose—Die Urpflanze als Wirklichkeit und als Symbol—
6. Der Begriff der Metamorphose und der Aufbau der geistigen Welt—7. Die
Methodik der Goetheschen Naturbetrachtung und sein Wahrheitsbegriff—8.
Das Faustdrama; Faust und Helena.—CH. V. SCHILLER—FREIHEITSPROBLEM
UND FORMPROBLEM IN DER KLASSISCHEN ÄSTHETIK—1. Die Freiheitsidee
in der Dramatik des jungen Schiller—Die Entwicklungsphasen der Schil-
lerschen Ästhetik—2. Die "Theosophie des Julius"; *Schiller* und *Leibniz*—
Der Briefwechsel mit Körner; die "Autonomie des Organischen"—Der Frei-
heitsgedanke als aesthetisches Prinzip—Verhältnis zu *Kant* und *Goethe*—3.
Schiller und *Fichte*—Klassischer und romantischer Formbegriff—CH. VI.
FREIHEITSIDEE UND STAATSIDEE—1. Der Begriff des Deutschtums bei *Schiller*
und *Fichte*—2. Die Staatstheorie des deutschen Idealismus—*Leibniz* und
Wolff—Der Begriff des Staates und der Staatspersönlichkeit bei *Friedrich
dem Grossen*—3. *Kants* Stellung in der Entwicklung des Staatsproblems—4.
Wilhelm von Humboldt—5. *Fichte*—6. Die Staatslehre *Schellings*—Die ro-
mantische Staatslehre—*Adam Müllers* "Elemente der Staatskunst"—7. *Hegel*.

1917

1. HÖLDERLIN UND DER DEUTSCHE IDEALISMUS. *Logos,* 1917-1918.
Vol. VII, pp. 262-282. Vol. VIII, pp. 30-49.

Reprinted in: *Idee und Gestalt* (see 1921, 2).

1918

1. KANTS LEBEN UND LEHRE. *Immanuel Kants Werke.* In Gemeinchaft mit Hermann Cohen u. a. herausgegeben von Ernst Cassirer, Vol. XI (Ergänzungsband), Berlin, Bruno Cassirer, 1918. xi, 448 pp. (See 1912, 1.)

Second Edition: 1921. VIII, 448 pp.

Contents: Vorrede—Einleitung—Ch. I. Jugend- und Lehrjahre—Ch. II. Die Magisterjahre und die Anfänge der Kantischen Lehre—1. Das naturwissenschaftliche Weltbild—Kosmologie und Kosmophysik—2. Das Problem der metaphysischen Methode—3. Die Kritik der dogmatischen Metaphysik— Die "Träume eines Geistersehers"—4. Die Scheidung der sinnlichen und intelligiblen Welt—5. Die Entdeckung des kritischen Grundproblems—Ch. III. Der Aufbau und die Grundprobleme der Kritik der reinen Vernunft— Ch. IV. Erste Wirkungen der kritischen Philosophie—Die "Prolegomena"— Herders "Ideen" und die Grundlegung der Geschichtsphilosophie—Ch. V. Der Aufbau der kritischen Ethik—Ch. VI. Die Kritik der Urteilskraft— Ch. VII. Letzte Schriften und Kämpfe—Die "Religion innerhalb der Grenzen der blossen Vernunft" und der Konflikt mit der preussischen Regierung.

Spanish Translation: Mexico, Fondo de Cultura Economica (In preparation).

2. GOETHES PANDORA. *Zeitschrift für Ästhetik und allgemeine Kunstwissenschaft.* 1918. Vol. XIII, pp. 113-134.

Reprinted in: *Idee und Gestalt* (see 1921, 2).

3. HERMANN COHEN. Worte gesprochen an seinem Grabe. *Neue Jüdische Monatshefte.* 1918. No. 15-16.

1919

1. HEINRICH VON KLEIST UND DIE KANTISCHE PHILOSOPHIE. *Philosophische Vorträge der Kant-Gesellschaft.* No. 22 Berlin, Reuther und Reichard, 1919. 56 pp.

Reprinted in: *Idee und Gestalt* (see 1921, 2).

1920

1. DAS ERKENNTNISPROBLEM IN DER PHILOSOPHIE UND WISSENSCHAFT DER NEUEREN ZEIT.

DIE NACHKANTISCHEN SYSTEME.

Vol. III. Berlin, Bruno Cassirer. 1920. xiv, 483 pp.

Second Edition: 1923.

Contents: Vorwort—EINLEITUNG—CH. 1. DER "GEGENSTAND DER ERFAHRUNG" UND DAS "DING AN SICH"—1. *Friedrich Heinrich Jacobi*—2. *Reinhold*—I. Die Methode der Elementarphilosophie und der "Satz des Bewusstseins"—II. Begriff und Problem des "Dinges an sich"—3. *Aenesidem*

—4. *Jakob Sigismund Beck—Salomon Maimon*—Maimons Denkform und Stil—I.Der Begriff des "Gegebenen" und das Humesche Problem—II. Die Idee des "unendlichen Verstandes" und die Theorie der Differentiale—III. Der Satz der Bestimmbarkeit—CH. II. FICHTE—I. Die Begründung der Wissenschaftslehre—II. Der Atheismusstreit und die Grundlegung von Fichtes Religionsphilosophie—III. Das Absolute und das Wissen—IV. Problem und Methode der Fichteschen Philosophie—CH. III. SCHELLING—I. Die Grundlegung der Naturphilosophie und das System des transcendentalen Idealismus —II. Das Erkenntnisprinzip der Schellingschen Philosophie—III. Der Ausgang der Schellingschen Philosophie—CH. IV. HEGEL—I. Der Begriff der Synthesis bei Kant und Hegel—II. Die Kritik der Reflexionsphilosophie— III. Die geschichtliche und systematische Stellung der dialektischen Methode —IV. Die Phaenomenologie des Geistes—V. Der Aufbau der Hegelschen Logik—VI. Kritischer und absoluter Idealismus—CH. V. HERBART—I. Die Methode der Beziehungen—II. Die Lehre von den 'Realen'—CH. VI. SCHOPENHAUER—Die Physiologie als Grundlage der Erkenntnistheorie—I. Die physiologische Erkenntnistheorie und die Welt als Vorstellung—II. Die metaphysische Erkenntnistheorie und die Welt als Wille—III. Die Begründung der Apriritätslehre in Schopenhauers System—IV. Erkenntnisproblem und Wertproblem—CH. VII. FRIES—I. Die Lehre von der unmittelbaren Erkenntnis—II. Die Methode der Friesschen Philosophie.

2. HERMANN COHEN. *Vortrag. Korrespondenzblatt des Vereins zur Gründung und Erhaltung einer Akademie des Judentums.* Frankfurt, Kauffmann, 1920. Vol. I, p. 1 ff.

3. PHILOSOPHISCHE PROBLEME DER RELATIVITÄTSTHEORIE. *Die Neue Rundschau.* Berlin, S. Fischer, 1920. Vol. XXXI. No. 12. pp. 1337-1357.

1921

1. ZUR EINSTEINSCHEN RELATIVITÄTSTHEORIE.

ERKENNTNISTHEORETISCHE BETRACHTUNGEN.

Berlin, Bruno Cassirer, 1921. 134 pp.

Second Edition: 1925

Russian Translation: 1922

Japanese Translation: 1923

English Translation in: *Substance and Function and Einstein's Theory of Relativity.* Translated by W. C. *Swabey* and M. C. *Swabey*, 1923 (see 1910, 1)

Contents: I. Concepts of measure and concepts of things—II. The empirical and conceptual foundations of the theory of relativity—III. The philosophical concept of truth and the theory of relativity—IV. Matter, ether and space— V. The concepts of space and time of critical idealism and the theory of relativity—VI. Euclidean and non-Euclidean geometry—VII. The theory of relativity and the problem of reality—Bibliography.

2. IDEE UND GESTALT. Fünf Aufsätze. Berlin, Bruno Cassirer, 1921. II, 200 pp.

Second Edition: 1924.

"Die folgenden Studien wollen eine Ergänzung zu den Studien zur deutschen Geistesgeschichte bilden, die ich unter dem Titel "Freiheit und Form" (Berlin, 1917, 2. Aufl. 1918) veröffentlicht habe" (see 1916, 1)

Contents: I. GOETHES PANDORA (see 1918, 2)—II. GOETHE UND DIE MATHEMATISCHE PHYSIK. Eine erkenntnistheoretische Betrachtung—III. DIE METHODIK DES IDEALISMUS IN SCHILLERS PHILOSOPHISCHEN SCHRIFTEN—IV. HÖLDERLIN UND DER DEUTSCHE IDEALISMUS (see 1917, 1)—V. HEINRICH VON KLEIST UND DIE KANTISCHE PHILOSOPHIE (see 1919, 1)

1922

1. GOETHE UND PLATON. Vortrag in der Goethe-Gesellschaft Berlin. *Sokrates.* 48th year of issue. No. 1. Berlin, Weidmann., 1922. Reprinted in: *Goethe und die geschichtliche Welt* (see 1932, 3).

2. DIE BEGRIFFSFORM IM MYTHISCHEN DENKEN. Studien der Bibliothek Warburg, I. Leipzig, B. G. Teubner, 1922. i, 62 pp.

3. EINSTEIN'S THEORY OF RELATIVITY FROM THE EPISTEMOLOGICAL POINT OF VIEW. *The Monist,* July 1922, pp. 412-418.

A selection from: *Einstein's Theory of Relativity* (see 1921, 1. Ch. VI)

1923

1. PHILOSOPHIE DER SYMBOLISCHEN FORMEN: PART ONE. DIE SPRACHE. Berlin, Bruno Cassirer, 1923. xii, 293 pp. (see 1925, 1; 1929, 1; 1931, 1)

Contents: Vorwort—EINLEITUNG UND PROBLEMSTELLUNG—I. Der Begriff der symbolischen Form und die Systematik der symbolischen Formen—II. Die allgemeine Funktion des Zeichens—Das Bedeutungsproblem—III. Das Problem der "Repräsentation" und der Aufbau des Bewusstseins—IV. Die ideelle Bedeutung des Zeichens—Die Überwindung der Abbildtheorie.—PART ONE: ZUR PHAENOMENOLOGIE DER SPRACHLICHEN FORM—*CH. I. DAS SPRACHPROBLEM IN DER GESCHICHTE DER PHILOSOPHIE*—I. Das Sprachproblem in der Geschichte des philosophischen Idealismus (*Platon, Descartes, Leibniz*)—II. Die Stellung des Sprachproblems in den Systemen des Empirismus (*Bacon, Hobbes, Locke, Berkeley*)—III. Die Philosophie der französischen Aufklärung (*Condillac, Maupertuis, Diderot*)—IV. Die Sprache als Affektausdruck—Das Problem des "Ursprungs der Sprache" (*Giambattista Vico, Hamann, Herder,* Die Romantik)—V. *Wilhelm von Humboldt*—VI. *August von Schleicher* und der Fortgang zur "naturwissenschaftlichen" Sprachansicht—VII. Die Begründung der modernen Sprachwissenschaft und das Problem der "Lautgesetze"—*CH. II. DIE SPRACHE IN DER PHASE*

DES SINNLICHEN AUSDRUCKS—I. Die Sprache als Ausdrucksbewegung —Gebärdensprache und Wortsprache—II. Mimischer, analogischer und symbolischer Ausdruck—*CH. III. DIE SPRACHE IN DER PHASE DES ANSCHAULICHEN AUSDRUCKS*—I. Der Ausdruck des Raumes und der räumlichen Beziehungen—II. Die Zeitvorstellung—III. Die sprachliche Entwicklung des Zahlbegriffs—IV. Die Sprache und das Gebiet der "inneren Anschauung"—Die Phasen des Ichbegriffs—*CH. IV. DIE SPRACHE ALS AUSDRUCK DES BEGRIFFLICHEN DENKENS—DIE FORM DER SPRACHLICHEN BEGRIFFS- UND KLASSENBILDUNG*—I. Die qualifizierende Begriffsbildung—II. Grundrichtungen der sprachlichen Klassenbildung—*CH. V. DIE SPRACHE ALS AUSDRUCK DER LOGISCHEN BEZIEHUNGSFORMEN—DIE RELATIONSBEGRIFFE.*

2. DER BEGRIFF DER SYMBOLISCHEN FORM IM AUFBAU DER GEISTESWISSENSCHAFTEN. *Vorträge der Bibliothek Warburg.* Leipzig, B. G. Teubner, 1923. I. Vorträge 1921-1922, pp. 11-39.

3. DIE KANTISCHEN ELEMENTE IN WILHELM VON HUMBOLDTS SPRACHPHILOSOPHIE. *Festschrift für Paul Hensel.* Greiz i.V., Ohag, 1923, pp. 105-127.

1924

1. ZUR "PHILOSOPHIE DER MYTHOLOGIE." *Festschrift für Paul Natorp, zum 70. Geburtstage.* Berlin, W. de Gruyter, 1924, pp. 23-54. From: *Philosophie der symbolischen Formen*, II. (Einleitung) (see 1925, 1)

2. EIDOS UND EIDOLON.
DAS PROBLEM DES SCHÖNEN UND DER KUNST IN PLATONS DIALOGEN *Vorträge der Bibliothek Warburg.* Leipzig, B. G. Teubner, 1924. II. Vorträge 1922-1923, Pt. 1, pp. 1-27.

1925

1. PHILOSOPHIE DER SYMBOLISCHEN FORMEN: BOOK TWO. DAS MYTHISCHE DENKEN. Berlin, Bruno Cassirer, 1925. xvi, 320 pp. (see 1923, 1; 1929, 1; 1931, 1.)

Contents: EINLEITUNG. Das Problem einer "Philosophie der Mythologie." —PART ONE. DER MYTHOS ALS DENKFORM.—*CH. I. CHARACTER UND GRUNDRICHTUNG DES MYTHISCHEN GEGENSTANDSBEWUSST-SEINS.—CH. II. EINZELKATEGORIEN DES MYTHISCHEN DEN-KENS.*—PART TWO. DER MYTHOS ALS ANSCHAUUNGSFORM. AUFBAU UND GLIEDERUNG DER RÄUMLICH-ZEITLICHEN WELT IM MYTHISCHEN BEWUSST-SEIN. *CH. I. DER GRUNDGEGENSATZ.—CH. II. GRUNDZÜGE EINER FORMENLEHRE DES MYTHOS.—RAUM, ZEIT UND ZAHL.*—I. Die Gliederung des Raumes im mythischen Bewusstsein.—II. Raum und Licht.— Das Problem der "Orientierung."—III. Der mythische Zeitbegriff.—IV. Die

Gestaltung der Zeit im mythischen und religiösen Bewusstsein.—V. Die mythische Zahl und das System der "heiligen Zahlen."—PART THREE. DER MYTHOS ALS LEBENSFORM. ENTDECKUNG UND BESTIMMUNG DER SUBJEKTIVEN WIRKLICHKEIT IM MYTHISCHEN BEWUSSTSEIN.—*CH. I. DAS ICH UND DIE SEELE.—CH. II. DIE HERAUSBILDUNG DES SELBSTGEFÜHLS AUS DEM MYTHISCHEN EINHEITS- UND LEBENSGEFÜHL.* —I. Die Gemeinschaft des Lebendigen und die mythische Klassenbildung. —Der Totemismus.—II. Der Persönlichkeitsbegriff und die persönlichen Götter.—Die Phasen des mythischen Ichbegriffs.—*CH. III. KULTUS UND OPFER.*—PART FOUR. DIE DIALEKTIK DES MYTHISCHEN BEWUSSTSEINS.

2. SPRACHE UND MYTHOS.

EIN BEITRAG ZUM PROBLEM DER GÖTTERNAMEN.

Studien der Bibliothek Warburg, VI, Leipzig, B. G. Teubner, 1925. 87 pp.

English translation: LANGUAGE AND MYTH. Translated by *Susanne K. Langer.* New York, Harper & Brothers. 1946. x, 103 pp.

Contents: I. The Place of Language and Myth in the Pattern of Human Culture. II. The Evolution of Religious Ideas. III. Language and Conception. IV. Word Magic. V. The Successive Phases of Religious Thought. VI. The Power of Metaphor.

3. DIE PHILOSOPHIE DER GRIECHEN VON DEN ANFÄNGEN BIS PLATON. Lehrbuch der Philosophie, hrsg. von M. Dessoir. Vol. I. Die Geschichte der Philosophie. Berlin, Ullstein, 1925. 139 pp.

Contents: Einleitung.—Die Geschichte der Griechischen Philosophie als Geschichte des Sich-selbst-Findens des "Logos."—PART ONE. *DIE VORATTISCHE PHILOSOPHIE.*—I. Die Jonische Naturphilosophie.—II. *Heraklit* und die *Pythagoreer.*—III. *Die Eleaten.*—IV. Die Jüngere Naturphilosophie. —PART TWO. *DIE ATTISCHE PHILOSOPHIE.*—I. Die Sophistik.—II. *Sokrates.*—III. *Platon.*

4. PAUL NATORP. *Kant-Studien.* Vol. XXX, 1925, pp. 273-298.

1927

1. INDIVIDUUM UND KOSMOS IN DER PHILOSOPHIE DER RENAISSANCE. Studien der Bibliothek Warburg, X. Leipzig, B. G. Teubner, 1927. ix, 458 pp.

Italian translation: INDIVIDUO E COSMO NELLA FILOSOFIA DEL RINASCIMENTO. Translated by *F. Federici.* Firenze, "La Nuova Italia," 1935.

Spanish Translation: (In preparation).

Contents: Einleitung.—I. *Nikolaus Cusanus.*—II. *Cusanus* und *Italien.*—III. Freiheit und Notwendigkeit in der Philosophie der Renaissance. IV. Das Subjekt-Objekt Problem in der Philosophie der Renaissance.

2. ERKENNTNISTHEORIE NEBST DEN GRENZFRAGEN DER LOGIK UND DENKPSYCHOLOGIE. Jahrbücher der Philosophie. Vol. III, Berlin, E. S. Mittler, 1927, pp. 31-92.

3. DAS SYMBOLPROBLEM UND SEINE STELLUNG IM SYSTEM DER PHILOSOPHIE. *Zeitschrift für Ästhetik und allgemeine Kunstwissenschaft.* Vol. XXI, Stuttgart, Enke, 1927, pp. 191-208.

4. DIE BEDEUTUNG DES SPRACHPROBLEMS FÜR DIE ENTSTEHUNG DER NEUREN PHILOSOPHIE. *Festschrift für Carl Meinhof,* 1927, pp. 507-14.

1928

1. DIE IDEE DER REPUBLIKANISCHEN VERFASSUNG: Rede zur Verfassungsfeier am 11. August 1928. Hamburg, Friederichsen, 1929. 33 pp.

2. HERMANN COHEN's SCHRIFTEN ZUR PHILOSOPHIE UND ZEITGESCHICHTE. Edited by *Albert Görland* and *Ernst Cassirer.* 2 vols. *Veröffentlichungen der Hermann Cohen-Stiftung bei der Akademie für die Wissenschaft des Judentums.* Berlin, Akademie-Verlag, 1928.

3. ZUR THEORIE DES BEGRIFFS.

BEMERKUNGEN ZU DEM AUFSATZ VON G. HEYMANS.

Kant-Studien. Vol. XXXIII. Berlin, Reuther & Reichard, 1928, pp. 129-36.

4. NEOKANTIANISM. — RATIONALISM. — SUBSTANCE. — TRANSCENDENTALISM. — TRUTH. — Articles in the *Encyclopaedia Britannica,* 14th ed. 1928.

1929

1. PHILOSOPHIE DER SYMBOLISCHEN FORMEN: BOOK THREE. PHÄNOMENOLOGIE DER ERKENNTNIS. Berlin, Bruno Cassirer, 1929. xii, 559 pp. (see 1923, 1; 1925, 1; 1931, 1)

Contents: EINLEITUNG. I. Materie und Form der Erkenntnis.—II. Die Symbolische Erkenntnis und ihre Bedeutung für den Aufbau der Gegenstandswelt.—III. Das "Unmittelbare" der inneren Erfahrung.—Der Gegenstand der Psychologie.—IV. Intuitive und symbolische Erkenntnis in der modernen Metaphysik.—PART ONE: AUSDRUCKSFUNKTION UND AUSDRUCKSWELT.—*CH. I. SUBJEKTIVE UND OBJEKTIVE ANALYSE.—CH. II. DAS AUSDRUCKSPHÄNOMEN ALS GRUNDMOMENT DES WAHRNEHMUNGSBEWUSSTSEINS.—CH. III. DIE AUSDRUCKSFUNKTION UND DAS LEIB-SEELEN-PROBLEM.*—PART TWO: DAS PROBLEM

DER REPRÄSENTATION UND DER AUFBAU DER ANSCHAULICHEN WELT.—*CH. I. DER BEGRIFF UND DAS PROBLEM DER REPRÄSENTATION.—CH. II. DING UND EIGENSCHAFT.—CH. III. DER RAUM.—CH. IV. DIE ZEITANSCHAUUNG.—CH. V. SYMBOLISCHE PRÄGNANZ.—CH. VI. ZUR PATHOLOGIE DES SYMBOLBEWUSSTSEINS.*—I. Das Symbolproblem in der Geschichte der Aphasielehre.—II. Die Veränderung der Wahrnehmungswelt im Krankheitsbild der Aphasie.—III. Zur Pathologie der Dingwahrnehmung.—IV. Raum, Zeit und Zahl.—V. Die pathologischen Störungen des Handelns.—PART THREE: DIE BEDEUTUNGSFUNKTION UND DER AUFBAU DER WISSENSCHAFTLICHEN ERKENNTNIS.—*CH. I. ZUR THEORIE DES BEGRIFFS.*—I. Die Grenzen des "natürlichen Weltbegriffs."—II. Begriff und Gesetz.—Die Stellung des Begriffs in der mathematischen Logik.—Klassenbegriff und Relationsbegriff.—Der Begriff als Satzfunktion.—Begriff und Vorstellung.—*CH. II. BEGRIFF UND GEGENSTAND.—CH. III. SPRACHE UND WISSENSCHAFT.—DINGZEICHEN UND ORDNUNGSZEICHEN. CH. IV. DER GEGENSTAND DER MATHEMATIK.*—I. Formalistische und intuitionistische Begründung der Mathematik.—II. Der Aufbau der Mengenlehre und die "Grundlagenkrise" der Mathematik.—III. Die Stellung des Zeichens in der Theorie der Mathematik.—IV. Die "idealen Elemente" und ihre Bedeutung für den Aufbau der Mathematik.—*CH. V. DIE GRUNDLAGEN DER NATURWISSENSCHAFTLICHEN ERKENNTNIS.*—I. Empirische und konstruktive Mannigfaltigkeiten.—II. Prinzip und Methode der physikalischen Reihenbildung. —III. "Symbol" und "Schema" im System der modernen Physik.

2. FORMEN UND VERWANDLUNGEN DES PHILOSOPHISCHEN WAHRHEITSBEGRIFFS, In: *Hamburger Universitäts-Reden* gehalten beim Rektoratswechsel 1929. Hamburg, 1931, pp. 17-36.
Translated into *Japanese* in 1930 by *Dr. T. Yura.*

3. ETUDES SUR LA PATHOLOGIE DE LA CONSCIENCE SYMBOLIQUE. Traduit par *A. Koyré. Journal de Psychologie Normale et Pathologique.* Vol. XXV, No. 5-8. Paris, Alcan, pp. 289-336; 523-566.

4. LEIBNIZ UND JUNGIUS. *Beiträge zur Jungiusforschung. Festschrift der Hamburgischen Universität,* 1929, pp. 21-26.

5. DIE IDEE DER RELIGION BEI LESSING UND MENDELSSOHN. *Festgabe zum 10 jährigen Bestehen der Akademie für die Wissenschaft des Judentums.* Berlin, Akademie-Verlag, 1929, pp. 22-41.

6. DIE PHILOSOPHIE MOSES MENDELSSOHNS. In: "*Moses Mendelssohn.*" *Zur 200 jährigen Wiederkehr seines Geburtstages.* Published by the "Encyclopedia Judaica," Berlin, Schneider, 1929, pp. 40-60.

7. REDE BEIM BEGRÄBNIS VON ABY WARBURG. *Aby Warburg zum Gedächtnis.* Printed for private circulation. 1929.

8. NACHRUF AUF ABY WARBURG. In: *Hamburger Universitäts-Reden gehalten beim Rektoratswechsel 1929.* Hamburg, 1931, pp. 48-56.

1930

1. "GEIST" UND "LEBEN" IN DER PHILOSOPHIE DER GEGENWART. *Die Neue Rundschau.* Vol. XLI, No. 1. Berlin, S. Fischer, 1930, pp. 244-264.

Translated into *English* in 1947 by *Robert Walter Bretall* and *Paul Arthur Schilpp* and reprinted in the present volume as Part III (pp. 855-880) under the title: " 'Spirit' and 'Life' in Contemporary Philosophy."

2. FORM UND TECHNIK. In: *Kunst und Technik.* Aufsätze hrsg. von *Leo Kestenberg.* Berlin, Wegweiser Verlag, 1930, pp. 15-61.

3. KEPLERS STELLUNG IN DER EUROPÄISCHEN GEISTESGESCHICHTE. *Verhandlungen des naturwissenschaftlichen Vereins, Hamburg,* Vol. IV, 1930, No. 3-4.

1931

1. PHILOSOPHIE DER SYMBOLISCHEN FORMEN: INDEX. Bearbeitet von *Dr. Hermann Noack.* Berlin, Bruno Cassirer Verlag, 1931. 92 pp.

Contents: Subject- and Author-Index; Bibliography.

2. MYTHISCHER, ÄSTHETISCHER UND THEORETISCHER RAUM. *Vierter Congress für Ästhetik und allgemeine Kunstwissenschaft.* Bericht hrsg. von *H. Noack.* Stuttgart, 1931, pp. 21-36.

3. ENLIGHTENMENT. Article in the *"Encyclopedia of the Social Sciences,"* New York, 1931.

4. DEUTSCHLAND UND WESTEUROPA IM SPIEGEL DER GEISTES-GESCHICHTE. In: *Inter-Nationes; Zeitschrift für die kulturellen Beziehungen Deutschlands zum Ausland.* Vol. I, No. 3 and 4. Berlin, deGruyter, 1931.

5. KANT UND DAS PROBLEM DER METAPHYSIK. BEMERKUNGEN ZU MARTIN HEIDEGGER'S KANTINTERPRETATION. *Kant-Studien,* Vol. XXXVI, 1931, pp. 1-26.

1932

1. DIE PLATONISCHE RENAISSANCE IN ENGLAND UND DIE SCHULE VON CAMBRIDGE. Studien der Bibliothek Warburg, XXIV. Leipzig, B. G. Teubner, 1932. 143 pp.

Contents: Einleitung. Die geschichtliche Stellung und die geschichtliche

Mission der Schule von Cambridge.—I. Die Platonische Akademie in Florenz und ihre Wirkung auf den Englischen Humanismus.—II. Die Idee der Religion in der Schule von Cambridge.—III. Die Stellung der Schule von Cambridge in der Englischen Geistesgeschichte.—IV. Die Bedeutung der Schule von Cambridge für die allgemeine Religionsgeschichte.—V. Die Naturphilosophie der Schule von Cambridge.—VI. Ausgang und Fortwirkung der Schule von Cambridge.—Shaftesbury.—Index.

2. DIE PHILOSOPHIE DER AUFKLÄRUNG. Tübingen, Mohr, 1932. xviii, 491 pp.

Italian translation: LA FILOSOFIA DELL'ILLUMINISMO. Translated by *E. Pocar*, Firenze, "La Nuova Italia," 1935.

Spanish translation: FILOSOFIA DE LA ILLUSTRACION. Mexico, Fondo de Cultura Economica, 1943. Translated by *Eugenio Imaz*.

English translation: THE PHILOSOPHY OF THE ENLIGHTENMENT. Translated by *F. C. A. Koelln*. Princeton University Press. (In preparation.)

Contents: *CH. I. DIE DENKFORM DES ZEITALTERS DER AUF-KLÄRUNG.—CH. II. NATUR- UND NATURERKENNTNIS IM DEN-KEN DER AUFKLÄRUNGSPHILOSOPHIE.—CH. III. PSYCHOLOGIE UND ERKENNTNISLEHRE.—CH. IV. DIE IDEE DER RELIGION.—* I. Das Dogma der Erbsünde und das Problem der Theodizee.—II. Die Idee der Toleranz und die Grundlegung der natürlichen Religion.—III. Religion und Geschichte.—*CH. V. DIE EROBERUNG DER GESCHICHTLICHEN WELT.—CH. VI. RECHT, STAAT UND GESELLSCHAFT.—*I. Die Idee des Rechts und das Prinzip der unveräusserlichen Rechte.—II. Der Vertragsgedanke und die Methodik der Sozialwissenschaften.—*CH. VII. DIE GRUNDPROBLEME DER ÄSTHETIK.—*I. Das "Zeitalter der Kritik."—II. Die klassizistische Ästhetik und das Problem der Objektivität des Schönen.—III. Das Geschmacksproblem und die Wendung zum Subjektivismus.—IV. Die Ästhetik der Intuition und das Genieproblem.—V. Verstand und Einbildungskraft.—*Gottsched* und die Schweizer.—VI. Die Grundlegung der systematischen Ästhetik.—*Baumgarten*.—Index.

3. GOETHE UND DIE GESCHICHTLICHE WELT.
DREI AUFSÄTZE.
Berlin, Bruno Cassirer, 1932. 148 pp.

Content: I. *Goethe* und die geschichtliche Welt. II. *Goethe* und das 18. Jahrhundert. III. *Goethe* und *Platon*. (see 1922, 1)

4. GOETHE UND DAS 18. JAHRHUNDERT. *Zeitschrift für Ästhetik und allgemeine Kunstwissenschaft.* Vol. XXVI, 1932, pp. 113-48 (see 1932, 3: II)

5. GOETHES IDEE DER BILDUNG UND ERZIEHUNG. *Pädagogisches Zentralblatt.* Vol. XII, 1932, pp. 340-58.

6. DER NATURFORSCHER GOETHE. *Hamburger Fremdenblatt,* March 19, 1932.

7. DIE SPRACHE UND DER AUFBAU DER GEGENSTANDSWELT. *Bericht über den XII. Kongress der deutschen Gesellschaft für Psychologie. Hamburg.* Jena, G. Fischer, 1932.

French translation: LE LANGUAGE ET LA CONSTRUCTION DU MONDE DES OBJETS. By *P. Guillaume. Journal de Psychologie Normale et Pathologique,* Vol. XXX, pp. 18-44.

Reprint in: PSYCHOLOGIE DU LANGUAGE, par *H. Delacroix, E. Cassirer,* etc. Bibliothèque de Philosophie contemporaine. Paris, Alcan, 1933, pp. 18-44.

8. VOM WESEN UND WERDEN DES NATURRECHTS. *Zeitschrift für Rechtsphilosophie.* Vol. VI, No. I. Leipzig, Meiner, 1932.

9. DIE ANTIKE UND DIE ENTSTEHUNG DER EXAKTEN WISSENSCHAFT. *Die Antike,* Vol. VIII. Berlin, deGruyter, 1932, pp. 276-300.

10. SPINOZA'S STELLUNG IN DER ALLGEMEINEN GEISTESGESCHICHTE. *Der Morgen.* Vol. VIII, No. 5. Berlin, Philo-Verlag, 1932, pp. 325-348.

11. SHAFTESBURY UND DIE RENAISSANCE DES PLATONISMUS IN ENGLAND. *Vorträge der Bibliothek Warburg,* Vol. IX, 1930-31, pp. 136-55.

12. DAS PROBLEM J. J. ROUSSEAU. *Archiv für Geschichte der Philosophie.* Vol. XLI, 1932, pp. 177-213; 479-513.

Italian translation: IL PROBLEMA GIAN GIACOMO ROUSSEAU. Translated by *Maria Albanese,* Firenze, "La Nuova Italia", 1938.

13. KANT. Article in the *"Encyclopedia of the Social Sciences,"* New York, 1932.

1933

1. L'UNITÉ DANS L'OEUVRE DE J. J. ROUSSEAU. (*X. Léon, E. Cassirer,* etc.) *Bulletin de la Société Française de Philosophie.* Vol. XXXII, 1933, pp. 45-85.

2. HENRI BERGSON'S ETHIK UND RELIGIONSPHILOSOPHIE. *Der Morgen,* Vol. IX, No. I. Berlin, Philo-Verlag, 1933.

Swedish translation: *Judisk Tidskrift.* Vol. XIV, June 1941, pp. 13-18.

1935

1. SCHILLER UND SHAFTESBURY. *The Publications of the English Goethe Society.* New Series, Vol. XI, Cambridge, The University Press, 1935, pp. 37-59.

1936

1. DETERMINISMUS UND INDETERMINISMUS IN DER MODERNEN PHYSIK.

HISTORISCHE UND SYSTEMATISCHE STUDIEN ZUM KAUSALPROBLEM.

Göteborgs Högskolas Arsskrift XLII, 1936: 3. ix, 265 pp.

Contents: PART ONE. *HISTORISCHE VORBETRACHTUNGEN.*—I. Der *"Laplacesche* Geist."—II. Metaphysischer und kritischer Determinismus.— PART TWO. *DAS KAUSALPRINZIP DER KLASSISCHEN PHYSIK.*— I. Die Grundtypen physikalischer Aussagen.—Die Massaussagen.—II. Die Gesetzes-Aussagen.—III. Die Prinzipien-Aussagen.—IV. Der allgemeine Kausalsatz.—PART THREE. *KAUSALITÄT UND WAHRSCHEINLICH-KEIT.*—I. Dynamische und statistische Gesetzmässigkeit.—II. Der logische Charakter statistischer Aussagen.—PART FOUR. *DAS KAUSALPROBLEM DER QUANTENTHEORIE.*—I. Die Grundlagen der Quantentheorie und die Unbestimmtheits-Relationen.—II. Zur Geschichte und Erkenntnistheorie des Atombegriffs.—PART FIVE. *KAUSALITÄT UND KONTINUITÄT.*— I. Das Kontinuitätsprinzip in der klassischen Physik.—II. Zum Problem des "materiellen Punktes."—*SCHLUSSBETRACHTUNGEN UND ETHISCHE SCHLUSSFOLGERUNGEN.*

2. INHALT UND UMFANG DES BEGRIFFS.

BEMERKUNGEN ZU KONRAD MARC-WOGAU'S GLEICHNAMIGER SCHRIFT.

Theoria, Göteborg, Vol. II. 1936, pp. 207-232.

1937

1. DESCARTES ET L'IDÉE DE L'UNITÉ DE LA SCIENCE. *Revue de Synthèse.* Vol. XIV, No. 1. Paris, 1937, pp. 7-28. (see 1939, 1, Part One, Ch. II)

2. DESCARTES' WAHRHEITSBEGRIFF. *Theoria,* Göteborg, Vol. III, 1937, pp. 161-87. (see 1939, 1, Part One, Ch. II)

3. WAHRHEITSBEGRIFF UND WAHRHEITSPROBLEM BEI GALILEI. *Scientia,* Milano, Sept.-Oct. 1937, pp. 121-130; 185-193.

1938

1. ZUR LOGIK DES SYMBOLBEGRIFFS. *Theoria,* Göteborg, Vol. IV, 1938, pp. 145-75.

2. LE CONCEPT DE GROUPE ET LA THÉORIE DE LA PERCEPTION. *Journal de Psychologie,* Juillet-Decembre 1938, pp. 368-414.

English translation: THE CONCEPT OF GROUP AND THE THEORY OF PERCEPTION. *Philosophy and Phaenomenological Research,* Vol. V. 1944, pp. 1-35.

3. REVIEW OF A. C. BENJAMIN'S AN INTRODUCTION TO THE PHILOSOPHY OF SCIENCE. (New York, 1937.) *Lychnos,* Upsala, 1938, pp. 456-461.

4. ÜBER BEDEUTUNG UND ABFASSUNGSZEIT VON DESCARTES' "RECHERCHE DE LA VÉRITÉ PAR LA LUMIÈRE NATURELLE." *Theoria,* Göteborg, Vol. IV, 1938, pp. 193-234.

5. DESCARTES' DIALOG "RECHERCHE DE LA VÉRITÉ PAR LA LUMIÈRE NATURELLE" UND SEINE STELLUNG IM GANZEN DER CARTESISCHEN PHILOSOPHIE.

EIN INTERPRETATIONSVERSUCH.

Lärdomshistoriska Samfundets Arsbok, Lychnos, Upsala, 1938, pp. 139-179.

French translation: LA PLACE DE LA "RECHERCHE DE LA VÉRITÉ PAR LA LUMIÈRE NATURELLE" DANS L'OEUVRE DE DESCARTES. *Revue Philosophique,* 1939, pp. 261-300.

Reprinted in: DESCARTES. Lehre-Persönlichkeit-Wirkung. 1939, 1; Part Two, Ch. II.

6. REVIEW OF OEUVRES COMPLÈTES DE MALEBRANCHE, publ. par *D. Roustan* et *Paul Schrecker.* (Vol. I, 1939.) *Theoria,* Göteborg Vol. IV, 1938, pp. 287-300.

1939

1. DESCARTES.
Lehre—Persönlichkeit—Wirkung.
Stockholm, Bermann-Fischer Verlag, 1939. 308 pp.

Swedish translation (Ch. III only): DROTTNING CHRISTINA OCH DESCARTES, Stockholm, Bonniers, 1940; 140 pp.

French translation: DESCARTES, CORNEILLE, CHRISTINE DE SUÈDE. Translated by *Madeleine Frances et Paul Schrecker.* Paris, Vrin, 1942.

Contents: PART ONE. GRUNDPROBLEME DES CARTESIANISMUS.—*CH. I. DES-CARTES' WAHRHEITSBEGRIFF.—CH. II. DIE IDEE DER "EINHEIT DER WISSENSCHAFT" IN DER PHILOSOPHIE DESCARTES'.*—PART TWO. DESCARTES UND SEIN JAHRHUNDERT.—*CH. I. DESCARTES UND CORNEILLE.—CH. II. DESCARTES' "RECHERCHE DE LA VÉRITÉ PAR LA LUMIÈRE NATURELLE."—CH. III. DESCARTES UND DIE KÖNIGIN VON SCHWEDEN. EINE STUDIE ZUR GEISTESGE-SCHICHTE DES 17. JAHRHUNDERTS.*—I. Das Verhältnis von Descartes und Königin Christina als geistesgeschichtliches Problem.—II. Der "universale Theismus" und das Problem der natürlichen Religion im 17. Jahrhundert.—III. Die Renaissance des Stoizismus in der Ethik des 16. und 17. Jahrhunderts.—IV. Descartes' Affektenlehre und ihre geistesgeschichtliche Bedeutung.—V. Königin Christina und das heroische Ideal des 17. Jahrhunderts.

2. AXEL HÄGERSTRÖM.

EINE STUDIE ZUR SCHWEDISCHEN PHILOSOPHIE DER GEGENWART.

Göteborgs Högskolas Arsskrift, XLV, 1939: 1. 119 pp.

Contents: I. Der Kampf gegen die Metaphysik.—II. Die Kritik des Subjektivismus.—III. Die Moralphilosophie.—IV. Recht und Mythos.—V. Zur Logik der Geisteswissenschaften.

3. NATURALISTISCHE UND HUMANISTISCHE BEGRÜNDUNG DER KULTUR-PHILOSOPHIE. *Göteborg Kungl. Vetenskaps och Vitterhets-Samhälles Handlingar.* 5ᵉ földjer, Ser. A, Bil. 7, No. 3. 1939, pp. 1-28.

Reprinted in: *Der Bogen*, Scholz Verlag, Wiesbaden, Germany, Vol. 2, No. 4, April 1947.

4. DIE PHILOSOPHIE IM 17. UND 18. JAHRHUNDERT. Paris, Hermann & Cie, 1939, 94 pp. Published in *Chronique Annuelle*, publ. par l'Institut International de Collaboration Philosophique.

5. WAS IST "SUBJEKTIVISMUS"? *Theoria*, Göteborg, Vol. V, 1939, pp. 111-140.

6. LA PLACE DE LA "RECHERCHE DE LA VÉRITÉ PAR LA LUMIÈRE NATURELLE" DANS L'OEUVRE DE DESCARTES. *Revue Philosophique*, 1939, pp. 261-300. (see 1938, 5)

1940

1. MATHEMATISCHE MYSTIK UND MATHEMATISCHE NATURWISSEN-SCHAFT.

BETRACHTUNGEN ZUR ENTSTEHUNGSGESCHICHTE DER EXAKTEN WISSEN-SCHAFT.

Lychnos, Upsala, 1940, pp. 248-265.

2. NEUERE KANT-LITTERATUR. *Theoria,* Göteborg, Vol. VI. 1940, pp. 87-100.

3. WILLIAM STERN.

ZUR WIEDERKEHR SEINES TODESTAGES.

Acta Psychologica, Vol. V, pp. 1-15.

1941

1. LOGOS, DIKE, KOSMOS IN DER ENTWICKLUNG DER GRIECHISCHEN PHILOSOPHIE. *Göteborgs Högskolas Arsskrift,* Vol. XLVII, 1941: 6. 31 pp.

2. THORILDS STELLUNG IN DER GEISTESGESCHICHTE DES 18. JAHRHUNDERTS. *Svenska Historie—Vitterhetens-och Antikvitet-Akademiens Handlingar,* 1941.

3. THORILD UND HERDER. *Theoria,* Göteborg, Vol. VII. 1941, pp. 75-92.

1942

1. ZUR LOGIK DER KULTURWISSENSCHAFTEN.
Fünf Studien.
Göteborgs Högskolas Arsskrift, Vol. XLVII. 1942: 1. Göteborg, Wettergren & Kerbers Forlag. 139 pp.

Contents: I. Der Gegenstand der Kulturwissenschaft.—II. Dingwahrnehmung und Ausdruckswahrnehmung.—III. Naturbegriffe und Kulturbegriffe.—IV. Formproblem und Kausalproblem.—V. Die "Tragödie der Kultur."

2. THE INFLUENCE OF LANGUAGE UPON THE DEVELOPMENT OF SCIENTIFIC THOUGHT. *The Journal of Philosophy,* Vol. XXXIX, No. 12. June 4, 1942, pp. 309-327.
French translation in *Journal de Psychologie Normale et Pathologique* Vol. XXXIX, 1946, pp. 129-152.

3. GIOVANNI PICO DELLA MIRANDOLA.
A STUDY IN THE HISTORY OF RENAISSANCE IDEAS.
Journal of the History of Ideas. Vol. III, No. 2, April 1942, pp. 123-144 and 319-346.

4. GALILEO.
A NEW SCIENCE AND A NEW SPIRIT.
American Scholar, Vol. XII, 1942, pp. 5-19.

1943

1. SOME REMARKS ON THE QUESTION OF THE ORIGINALITY OF THE RENAISSANCE. *Journal of the History of Ideas.* Vol. IV. 1943, pp. 49-56.

2. THE PLACE OF VESALIUS IN THE CULTURE OF THE RENAISSANCE. *The Yale Journal of Biology and Medicine.* Vol. XVI, No. 2, December 1942, pp. 109-119.

3. NEWTON AND LEIBNIZ. *Philosophical Review,* Vol. LII, 1943, pp. 366-391.

4. HERMANN COHEN, 1842-1918. *Social Research,* Vol. X, No. 2, May 1943, pp. 219-232.

1944

1. AN ESSAY ON MAN.

AN INTRODUCTION TO A PHILOSOPHY OF HUMAN CULTURE.

New Haven. Yale University Press. London, H. Milford, Oxford University Press, 1944, IX. 237 pp.

Second and Third Printing: 1945. Fourth Printing: 1947.

Translated into *Spanish* as: ANTHROPOLOGIA FILOSOFICA. *Introduccion a una filosofia de la cultura.* Version Española de *Eugenio Imaz.* Mexico, Fondo de Cultura Economica, 1945. IX, 419 pp.

German translation: in preparation.

Contents: Preface. PART ONE. *WHAT IS MAN?*—I. The Crisis in Man's Knowledge of Himself.—II. A Clue to the Nature of Man: The Symbol.—III. From Animal Reactions to Human Responses.—IV. The Human World of Space and Time.—V. Facts and Ideals.—PART TWO. *MAN AND CULTURE.*—VI. The Definition of Man in Terms of Human Culture.—VII. Myth and Religion.—VIII. Language.—IX. Art.—X. History.—XI. Science. —XII. Summary and Conclusion.—Index.

2. FORCE AND FREEDOM.

REMARKS ON THE ENGLISH EDITION OF JACOB BURCKHARDT'S "REFLECTION ON HISTORY."

American Scholar, Vol. XIII, Autumn 1944, pp. 407-417.

3. THE MYTH OF THE STATE. *Fortune,* Vol. XXIX, No. 6, June 1944, pp. 165-167, 198, 201, 202, 204, 206.

4. JUDAISM AND THE MODERN POLITICAL MYTHS. *Contemporary Jewish Record,* Vol. VII, 1944, pp. 115-126.

Swedish translation: JUDENDOMEN OCH DE MODERNA POLITISKA MYTERNA. *Judisk Tidskrift*, No. 9, Sept. 1946, pp. 266-274.

POSTHUMOUS PUBLICATIONS

1. ROUSSEAU KANT GOETHE. Translated from the German by *James Gutmann, Paul Oscar Kristeller* and *John Herman Randall, Jr.* History of Ideas Series No. 1. Princeton University Press, 1945, 98 pp.

TWO ESSAYS.

Contents: *KANT AND ROUSSEAU.*—I. Personal influences.—II. *Rousseau* and the doctrine of human nature.—III. Law and the state.—IV. The problem of optimism.—V. "Religion within the limits of mere reason."—VI. Conclusion. *GOETHE AND THE KANTIAN PHILOSOPHY.*—Sources and literature.

2. THOMAS MANNS GOETHEBILD.

EINE STUDIE ÜBER LOTTE IN WEIMAR.

Germanic Review, Vol. XX, No. 3, October 1945, pp. 166-194.

1946

1. THE MYTH OF THE STATE. New Haven, Yale University Press. London, G. Cumberledge, Oxford University Press, 1946. xii, 303 pp. Foreword by Charles W. Hendel.

Spanish translation: EL MITO DEL ESTADO. Translated by *E. Nicol*, Mexico, Fondo de Cultura Economica, 1947, 362 pp.

Partial German translation (Ch. XVIII): "DER MYTHOS ALS POLITISCHE WAFFE" in: *Die Amerikanische Rundschau*, 1943, No. 11, pp. 30-41.

Complete German translation: in preparation.

Swedish translation: in preparation.

Contents: PART ONE. *WHAT IS MYTH?*—I. The Structure of Mythical Thought.—II. Myth and Language.—III. Myth and the Psychology of Emotions.—IV. The Function of Myth in Man's Social Life.—PART TWO. *THE STRUGGLE AGAINST MYTH IN THE HISTORY OF POLITI- CAL THEORY.*—V. "Logos" and "Mythos" in Early Greek Philosophy.— VI. *Plato's* Republic.—VII. The Religious and Metaphysical Background of the Medieval Theory of the State.—VIII. The Theory of the Legal State in Medieval Philosophy.—IX. Nature and Grace in Medieval Philosophy.—X. *Machiavelli's* New Science of Politics.—XI. The Triumph of *Machiavellism* and its Consequences.—XII. Implications of the New Theory of State.— XIII. The Renaissance of Stoicism and "Natural Right" Theories of State.— XIV. The Philosophy of the Enlightenment and its Romantic Critics.— PART THREE. *THE MYTH OF THE TWENTIETH CENTURY.*—XV. The preparation: *Carlyle.*—XVI. From Hero Worship to Race Worship.—

XVII. *Hegel.*—XVIII. The Technique of the Modern Political Myths. Conclusion. Index.

2. GALILEO'S PLATONISM. In: *Studies and Essays in the History of Science.* Offered in homage to *George Sarton.* Edited by *M. F. Ashley Montagu.* New York, H. Schumann, 1946, pp. 276-297.

3. ALBERT SCHWEITZER AS CRITIC OF NINETEENTH-CENTURY ETHICS. *The Albert Schweitzer Jubilee Book.* Edited by *A. A. Roback,* Sci-Art Publishers, Cambridge, Mass., March 1946, pp. 239-258.

4. STRUCTURALISM IN MODERN LINGUISTICS. *Word.* Journal of the Linguistic Circle of New York, Vol. I, No. 11, August 1946, pp. 99-120.

IN PREPARATION

IN GERMAN: *Kleinere Schriften.* (A collection of previously published essays.) Artemis Verlag, Zürich, Switzerland

Das Erkenntnisproblem in der Philosophie und Wissenschaft der neueren Zeit

Vol. IV. Artemis Verlag, Zürich, Switzerland.

(Cf. 1906, 3; 1907, 1; 1920, 1.)

Contents: Einleitung und Problemstellung—*Book One: Die Exakte Wissenschaft*—Ch. I. Das Raumproblem und die Entwicklung der nicht-Euklidischen Geometrie—II. Erfahrung und Denken im Aufbau der Geometrie—III. Ordnungsbegriff und Massbegriff in der Geometrie—IV. Der Zahlbegriff und seine logische Begründung—V. Ziel und Methode der theoretischen Physik—*Book Two: Das Erkenntnisideal der Biologie und seine Wandlungen*—Ch. I. Das Problem der Klassifikation und die Systematik der Naturformen—II. Die Idee der Metamorphose und die "idealistische Morphologie"—III. Die Entwicklungsgeschichte als Problem und als Maxime—IV. Der Darwinismus als Dogma und als Erkenntnisprinzip—V. Die Entwicklungs-Mechanik und das Kausalproblem der Biologie—VI. Der Vitalismus-Streit und die "Autonomie des Organischen"—*Book Three: Grundformen und Grundrichtungen der historischen Erkenntnis*—Ch. I. Der Durchbruch des Historismus.—Herder—II. Die Romantik und die Anfänge der kritischen Geschichtswissenschaft.—Die "historische Ideenlehre"—Niebuhr—Ranke—W. v. Humboldt—III. Der Positivismus und sein historisches Erkenntnisideal—Hippolyte Taine—IV. Staatslehre und Verfassungslehre als

Grundlagen der Geschichtsschreibung—Theodor Mommsen—V. Politische Geschichtsschreibung und Kulturgeschichte—Jacob Burckhardt—VI. Die psychologische Typisierung der Geschichte —Kurt Lamprecht—VII. Der Einfluss der Religionsgeschichte auf das historische Erkenntnisideal—David Friedr. Strauss, Renan, Fustel de Coulanges

Der Mythos vom Staate, Translated from the English. Artemis Verlag, Zürich, Switzerland. (See: 1946, 1)

Philosophische Anthropologie. (Tentative title.) Translated from the English. Artemis Verlag, Zürich, Switzerland. See: 1944, 1

In English: *Das Erkenntnisproblem.* Vol. IV. (English title not yet established.) Translated from the German by Paul Schrecker, Yale University Press

The Philosophy of the Enlightenment. Translated from the German by F. C. A. Koelln, Princeton University Press. See: 1932, 2

Determinism and Indeterminism in Modern Physics (place of publication not yet determined). See: 1936, 1

In Italian: *Essay on Man.* (Italian title not yet established.) Translated from the English. Longanesi, Turino, Italy. See: 1944, 1

In Spanish: *Kants Leben und Lehre.* (Spanish title not yet established.) Translated from the German. Fondo de Cultura Economica, Mexico. See: 1918, 1

Das Erkenntnisproblem. Vol. IV. (Spanish title not yet established.) Translated from the German. Fondo de Cultura Economica, Mexico.

Individuum und Kosmos in der Philosophie der Renaissance. (Spanish title not yet established.) Translated from the German. Fondo de Cultura Economica, Mexico. See: 1927, 1

In Swedish: *The Myth of the State.* (Swedish title not yet established.) Translated from the English. Natur och Kultur, Stockholm, Sweden. See: 1946, 1

CHRONOLOGICAL LIST OF PRINCIPAL WORKS

1902—Leibniz' System in seinen wissenschaftlichen Grundlagen.

1906—Das Erkenntnisproblem in der Philosophie und Wissenschaft der neueren Zeit. Vol. I. (Cusanus to Bayle)

1907—Das Erkenntnisproblem, etc. Vol. II. (Bacon to Kant)

1910—Substanzbegriff und Funktionsbegriff. Untersuchungen über die Grundfragen der Erkenntniskritik.

1916—Freiheit und Form. Studien zur deutschen Geistesgeschichte.

1918—Kants Leben und Lehre.

1920—Das Erkenntnisproblem in der Philosophie und Wissenschaft der neueren Zeit. Vol. III. (Die Nachkantischen Systeme)

1921—Zur Einstein'schen Relativitätstheorie. Erkenntnistheoretische Betrachtungen.

1921—Idee und Gestalt. Fünf Aufsätze. Goethe, Schiller, Hölderlin, Kleist. (Ergänzungsstudien zu "Freiheit und Form")

1922—Die Begriffsform im mythischen Denken.

1923—Die Philosophie der symbolischen Formen. Vol. I. Die Sprache.

1925—Die Philosophie der symbolischen Formen. Vol. II. Das mythische Denken.

1925—Sprache und Mythos.

1925—Die Philosophie der Griechen von den Anfängen bis Platon.

1927—Individuum und Kosmos in der Philosophie der Renaissance.

1929—Die Philosophie der symbolischen Formen. Vol. III. Phänomenologie der Erkenntnis.

1932—Die Platonische Renaissance in England und die Schule von Cambridge.

1932—Die Philosophie der Aufklärung.

1932—Goethe und die geschichtliche Welt.

1936—Determinismus und Indeterminismus in der modernen Physik.

1939—Descartes. Lehre-Persönlichkeit-Wirkung.

1942—Zur Logik der Kulturwissenschaften.

1944—An Essay on Man.

1945—Rousseau Kant Goethe.

1946—The Myth of the State.

INDEX

Arranged by

ROBERT S. HARTMAN AND ROBERT W. BROWNING

INDEX

Abbott, Thomas K., 481, 485, 578
Absolute, 93
Absolute being, 293
Absolute ideal, 674
Absolute mind, 598
Abstraction, 394
Act of creation, subconscious, 320
Activity, 375
Actus purus of Aristotle, 866
Aesthetic, 328
Aesthetic and ethical judgment, 368
Aesthetic attitude, 340
Aesthetic experience, 734; as absorption in living form, 613
Aesthetic fancy, 373
Aesthetic form, 44, 349
Aesthetic logic, 318
Aesthetic theory, 329, 339, 645ff, 871; of the Renaissance, 735
Affinities 341
Affinitive geometry, 203
Alberti, use of perspective, 626
Alchemy, 601
Alhambra of Granada, 301
(Das) Allgemeine im Aufbau der geisteswissenschaftlichen Erkenntnis, 355
Allegorical, 371
Altdorfer, experiments with oblique space, 627
Amor intellectualis, 823
Amphiboly of the concept of reflection, 321
Analogic level of concept, 299; level of language, 298
Analogue, art as, servant of reason, 610, 615-616
Analogues of experience, 195
Analogy, 254, 260
Analysis, 307; infinitesimal, 285; of culture, 118; of experience, 197, 371; of myth, 371; *situs,* 203
Analytical *a priori,* 192
Analytical or tautological propositions, 255
Anaxagoras, 281
Anderson, F. H., 474
Animal rationale, 201

Animal symbolicum, man as, 201, 448, 461, 493, 505, 536
Animals, 363, 869; and environment, 861
Animism, 509, 517
Anthropocentrism, 484
Anthropological philosophy, 446, 449, 451, 457, 458, 461, 463, 464
Anthropology, cultural, 494; Kant's, 484-486; phenomenological, 492; philosophical, 278, 399, 446, 449, 457, 459, 461, 463, 464, 817, 821, 824, 829, 842, 843, 846; spiritual, 491, 500, 541
Anthropomorphism of the child, 366
Anthropomorphism, objective, 663
Antinomies of the culture-concept, 92
Antinomy of all cultural life, 320
Antithesis of nature and spirit, 858
Antithesis between real powers of Being, 872
Anxiety, 67f
Aphasia, 369
A priori, 135, 152ff, 158, 191, 210, 737ff; "basic mental function," 161; development of symbolic forms, 165; diversity, 163; "formal structure of the mind," 173; invariant element of form, 155; Kant's *vs.* Leibniz', 249; pragmatic criticism of, 175ff; result of mental attitude, 179; rule, 161
Archimedes, 282
Architecture, 348
Ariosto, 350
Aristotle, 85, 110, 190, 210, 281, 306, 321, 548, 551f, 555, 569, 573, 625f, 839, 840, 844, 865f; *actus purus* of, 866; on causes, 753; on definition of man, 493; on slavery, 478; on supreme Form, 866; teleology of, 866
Art, 48, 84, 115, 161, 298, 308, 309, 315, 341, 345, 375, 387, 393, 395, 398, 446, 461, 463, 464, 480, 558, 565, 566, 569, 571, 633, 642ff, 832, 850, 851; an analogue, 610, 615-616; autonomy of, 610, 616, 621, 625, 627, 629; forms of, 506, 513, 542; as imaginative penetration